To Mary for a fabulous decade, plus six.

Special thanks to:
My immensely talented and *still* patient editor, Nancy Davis, who like me moved in the middle of producing this book; David Van Ness for being a true Quark master and blooper catcher; Mimi Heft for spotting stuff even spy satellites miss; Emily Glossbrenner for the very best indexing; Marjorie Baer for encouraging email at key moments; Nancy Aldrich-Ruenzel for giving me the chance to do this work; my brother Neil for the world's geekiest jokes and for loaning me a computer "for just a couple of months" that became seven; and Laika, aka Lou the Wonder Dog.

VISUAL QUICKSTART GUIDE

FRONTPAGE 2000

FOR WINDOWS

Nolan Hester

Peachpit Press

Visual QuickStart Guide
FrontPage 2000 for Windows
Nolan Hester

Peachpit Press
1249 Eighth Street
Berkeley, CA 94710
(510) 524-2178
(510) 524-2221

Find us on the World Wide Web at: www.peachpit.com

Peachpit Press is a division of Addison Wesley Longman

Editor: Nancy Davis
Production Coordinator: Mimi Heft
Compositor: David Van Ness
Cover Design: The Visual Group
Indexer: Emily Glossbrenner

ISBN: 0-201-35457-8

0 9 8 7 6 5 4 3

Printed and bound in the United States of America

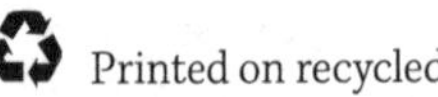
Printed on recycled paper

TABLE OF CONTENTS

PART I

GETTING STARTED

1 Using FrontPage 2000

Welcome to FrontPage 2000. Whether you bought it as a stand-alone program or as part of Microsoft Office 2000 Premium Edition, FrontPage has the tools to make your Web site building quick and easy. FrontPage lets you skip the tedium of creating your Web pages directly in HTML (HyperText Markup Language), the Web's underlying language. Instead you use menus and commands similar to those you already know from Microsoft's other programs, such as Word, Excel, and PowerPoint.

Using FrontPage, you'll find it easy to design your Web site's overall structure, create the necessary pages to flesh out the structure, add multimedia and interactive features to enliven those pages, and, finally, publish the whole thing on the Web by uploading the files to a Web server. Because Office 2000 now recognizes HTML as easily as its own formats, FrontPage can insert many Office documents directly into your new Web pages.

Whether you're working for a one-person business or an international firm, FrontPage includes all the tools and functions you need to build Web sites to post on the Internet or on private intranets.

What's New

FrontPage 2000 boasts so many changes and improvements over FrontPage 98 that it's practically a new program. Here's a quick rundown of the highlights:

- The Editor and Explorer portions of FrontPage 98, which operated as two separate programs, have been integrated into a single application. That makes FrontPage 2000 easier to use because you don't have to jump from one module to another.
- From its menus to its dialog boxes, FrontPage 2000 has been redesigned to mirror the look and functions of Office 2000. Menus, shortcuts, and tools like spell checking now work similarly across the entire suite of programs (**Figure 1.1**). Office 2000 now recognizes HTML as easily as it does its own proprietary formats, so it's easy to insert Word documents, Excel tables, and Access databases into your FrontPage Web pages.
- Building a complex Web site often requires a team of people. FrontPage 2000's enhanced collaboration features make it easier to assign Web tasks to different people and still control the site's workflow to avoid conflicting versions of the same page (**Figure 1.2**).

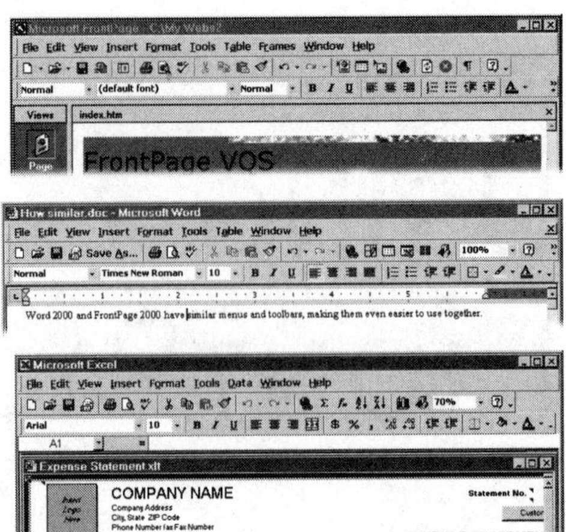

Figure 1.1 The menus, shortcuts, and tools in FrontPage 2000 and Office 2000 now work similarly.

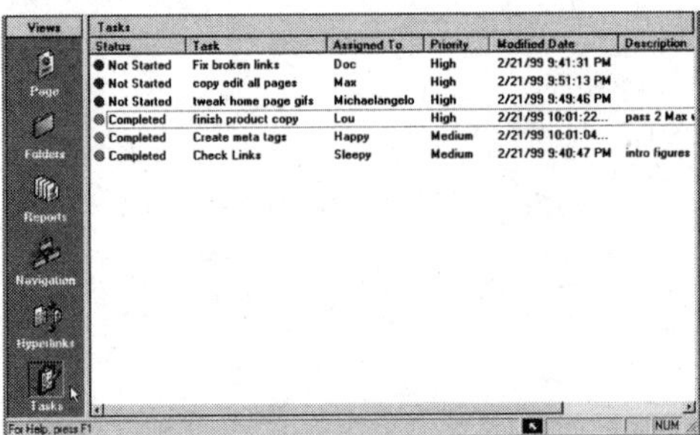

Figure 1.2 FrontPage's tasks view lets you keep track of what work is being done on a Web site—even when multiple people are involved.

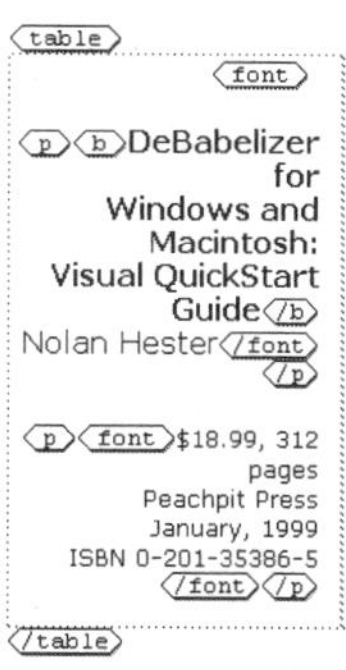

Figure 1.3 The reveal tag command gives you a quick peek at the HTML codes used in a page—without having to switch out of the Normal view.

- FrontPage offers a toggle command to let you quickly see a page's HTML tags while staying in your regular page view (**Figure 1.3**). Now you can check a tag and keep right on working.
- FrontPage now imports HTML code created in other programs without changing the code's order, comments, or spacing. Finally, you have all the control you need. This change alone will reduce many of the frustrations encountered in using FrontPage 98.
- You now also have complete control over which Web pages are uploaded to the Web server, which helps you avoid accidentally publishing not-yet-ready pages.
- Dynamic HTML effects, such as animations, now can be easily added to pages for viewing in any version 4 or later browser.
- Cascading Style Sheets (CSS), which let you set such page-wide factors as typeface, font size, background and foreground colors, and alignments, now can be *easily* applied to a group of pages or an entire Web site. While it was possible to use CSS in FrontPage 98, it was far from easy. The CSS features also enable you to precisely position and layer various page elements.
- FrontPage's expanded library of built-in themes, which offer pre-built graphics and font stylings for your pages, now can be customized.

How to use this book

The key to this book, like all of Peachpit's Visual QuickStart Guides, is that word visual. As much as possible, I've used illustrations with succinct captions to explain how FrontPage works. Ideally, you should be able to quickly find what you need by scanning the table of contents, page tabs, illustrations, or captions. Once you find a relevant topic, the text provides the essential details and tips.

This book's written with the assumption that you're familiar with Windows' basic operation and understand the general concept of how the World Wide Web works. If you're looking for under-the-hood Web server details, this isn't your book. Instead, we take things step by step and whenever a potentially confusing step or concept arises, I'll try to steer you through any rough spots and wrong turns.

Over time, FrontPage has evolved from a basic Web page editor to part of a suite of relatively sophisticated Web site tools. To explain everything about FrontPage would take three books this size, so as the cover says, I focus on getting you "up and running in no time."

Whether you plunge in or skip around the book, the choice is yours. Just avoid the temptation to try and learn everything about FrontPage at once. You'll remember more and learn faster by focusing on one task and learning it well.

Updates and feedback

For FrontPage updates and patches, make a point of checking Microsoft's web site from time to time: www.microsoft.com

This book also has a companion site—built using FrontPage, of course—where you'll find examples from the book, page designs using different FrontPage themes, plus tips and tricks based on real-world tasks. So drop by www.peachpit.com/vqs/frontpage2000 when you can.

Finally, I and Peachpit's editors have done everything possible to make this book error free and clear as glass. Please write me at frontpage@waywest.net if you spot a mistake. Better still, send me your FrontPage tips and suggestions for how I can make the next edition even better. Like a Web site, a book's never really done.

Web Planning Tips

Despite all the hoopla about the Web being an entirely new medium, it revolves around a pretty old phenomenon: our eyeballs. Yep, we *look* at Web sites. We don't taste or smell them. And we don't test drive them. That means we depend on *visual* cues for how to use a site. By following the basic visual principles explained in the next few pages, you'll be more than halfway toward making your Web site a pleasure to use.

By the way, there are plenty of great books out there devoted solely to designing Web sites. If you want to dive deeper, here are three of the best:

The Non-Designer's Web Book: An Easy Guide to Creating, Designing, and Posting Your Own Web Site by Robin Williams and John Tollett (Peachpit Press)

Hot Wired Style: Principles for Building Smart Web Sites by Jeffrey Veen (Wired Books)

Creating Killer Web Sites: The Art of Third-Generation Site Design by David Siegel (Hayden Books)

Keep it clean

Clutter kills. Sites that go a thousand directions at once leave visitors confused or, worse, irritated. Imagine if parking garages were laid out like some Web sites: We'd all still be trying to find the entrance. Make it simple, make it obvious. A rule of thumb: If you have to explain how a site works, it's not working.

Clutter comes in many guises. Everyone, for example, has encountered Web sites with what I call fake front doors. Instead of offering a home page with links to products and staff, the site's first page serves up an absolutely gorgeous graphic or layered animation. It swirls and whirls—as your hard drive churns and churns—until finally there appears the equivalent of the old "Click Here" link: "Discover the power of XYZ Widgets" or "Want to find out more?" So you click one more time and finally come to the company's *real* front door—a home page where you can start looking for the information you need.

Don't make your visitors knock twice to get in the door. And for gosh sakes, don't make them beg. If you want to orient visitors with a series of images, make them small and make them snappy to download. Most importantly, strip away every bit of clutter for the cleanest possible site.

Keep it lean

The Web's too slow. It was too slow last year; it'll still be too slow next year. Wish as we might for connections speedy enough to handle full-motion video, CD-quality sound, and Java applets galore, most folks are still using telephone modems to reach the Web. As palm-sized organizers and email-capable cell phones proliferate, more and more people will be using the Web with less rather than more bandwidth.

Even a state-of-the-art inhouse intranet with fast computers and fast pipes can't entirely escape the bandwidth bogeyman. Most likely the on-the-road sales force will be tapping into that intranet via a dial-up connection for sales data or product listings. See what I mean—the Web's too slow and the speed limit will remain a problem for some years to come. Don't fight—and never ignore—such limits. Instead use them to guide you in building your site. As architect and multimedia trailblazer Charles Eames put it four decades ago: "Design largely depends on constraints."

Make it easy

Nobody has to tell you how to read a newspaper or a magazine for two reasons: You already know the "rules" and even if you didn't they're pretty obvious. Big headlines mean a story's more important than one with a small headline. Items grouped together suggest that they're related. Front page stories carry more urgency than those inside the section. Size, proximity, and placement are hallmarks of the print medium's centuries-old "interface." Because the Web's so new, there's a temptation to think that means it has no rules. But trust your eyeballs; the visual touchstones of size, proximity, and placement are fairly constant even when the medium's new.

Just as the red light is the first on a traffic signal, give visual weight to the most important item on each Web page. That, of course, means you have to decide what's most—and least—important on each page and the site overall. So before you start working on that amazing animated graphic for your home page, make sure you're clear about your site's intended message and about who will be using the site.

Just as you wouldn't put sports stories in a newspaper's food section, you shouldn't build a Web site with your tech-support advice buried in the marketing section. Obvious, you say, but lots of Web sites fail to put related items together. Save your Web visitor some work by grouping similar items.

In planning a Web site, deciding what to put where (placement) is perhaps the hardest guideline for which to find the right balance. If a site's too "deep," visitors will have to click down layer after layer to find the information they need (**Figure 1.4**). The risk is that they'll never find what they're looking for. On the other hand, you can create a site that's too "shallow" with a home page that has so many links that it becomes a confusing mess (**Figure 1.5**).

Ideally, a visitor to your site should be able to find what they're seeking in two or three mouse clicks (**Figure 1.6**). That's easy to say, but hard to achieve. Fortunately, FrontPage's navigation view makes it easy to shuffle your pages around until you strike a happy medium where almost all the site's information can be reached in no more than four mouse clicks.

As you learn how to use FrontPage's various tools in the chapters ahead, remember: keep it clean, keep it lean, and make it easy.

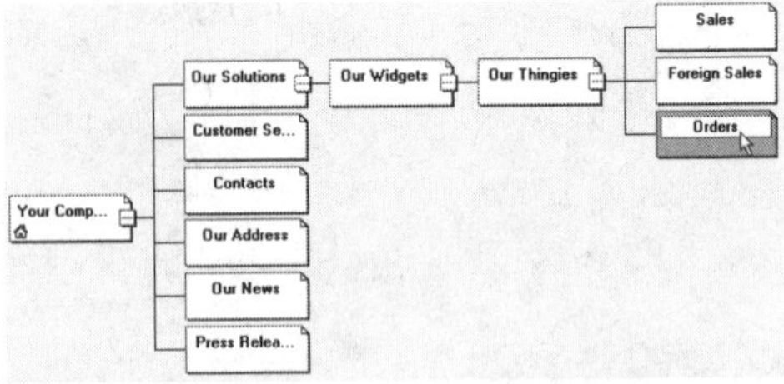

Figure 1.4 In this Web site structure, a key function—ordering products—is buried too "deep" for visitors to easily find it.

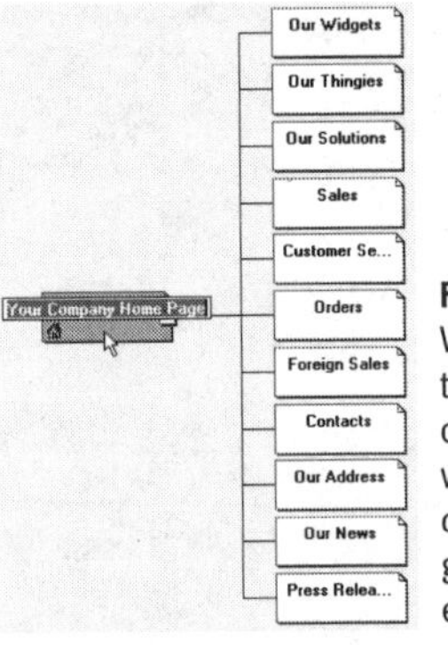

Figure 1.5 If you create a Web site structure that's too "shallow," you risk overwhelming visitors with a home page crammed with links that give equal emphasis to everything.

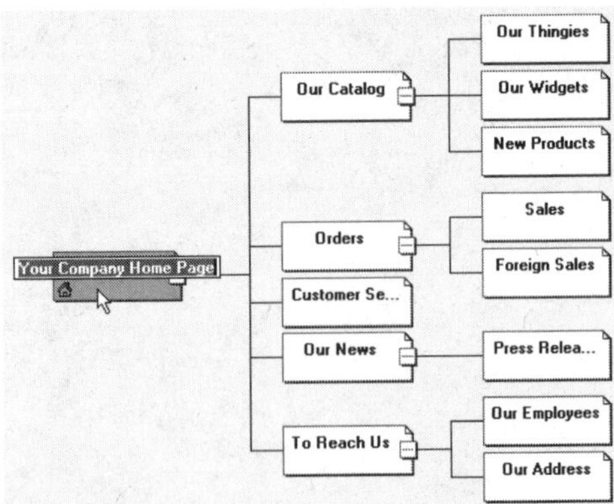

Figure 1.6 With a balanced Web site structure, the home page features only the most important links, items are grouped in logical categories, and everything can be reached in two or three clicks.

2

FrontPage Basics

This chapter gives you a quick overview of FrontPage's main features and the basic tasks of opening, closing, and saving Web pages and sites. Each of the items covered, whether it's FrontPage's views, menus, or toolbars, is explained in more detail later in the book. Starting here gives you an overall feel for the program's organization and functions, letting you dive in deeper when you're ready.

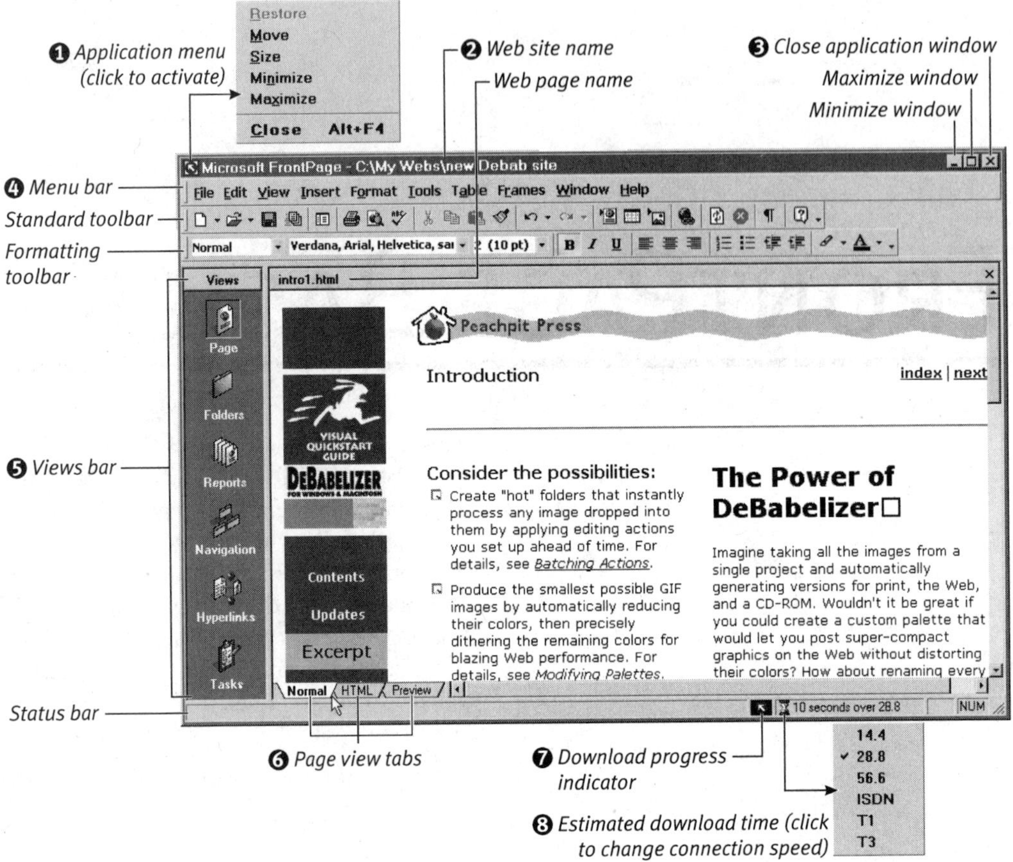

Figure 2.1 The Editor and Explorer screens of FrontPage 98 have been combined into a single window for FrontPage 2000. To change the *page* view, click the *HTML* or *Preview* tabs.

The FrontPage Main Window

The old Editor and Explorer screens of FrontPage 98 have been combined into a single main window for FrontPage 2000. By default, FrontPage's main window now opens in the *Normal* page view setting (**Figure 2.1**).

❶ **Application menu box:** Clicking the FrontPage icon triggers a pop-up box of choices for sizing the FrontPage window: Restore, Move, Size, Minimize, Maximize, and Close.

❷ **Web site and Web page names:** The Web site name is set when a new Web is created (see page 38). You set the Web page name when you first create it.

❸ **Window control buttons:** Clicking the three buttons will (left to right): collapse the window into the taskbar (minimize), expand the window to full screen (maximize), or close the application.

❹ **Menu bar and toolbars:** By default, FrontPage displays the Menu bar, Standard toolbar, and Formatting toolbar. To change which bars appear, choose View > Toolbars and toggle on/off your choices.

❺ **Views bar:** By default, FrontPage opens to the *Page* view. Click any of the other five icons to toggle to another view: *Folders* to arrange files and folders; *Reports* to assess the files, links, and pictures of an open Web site; *Navigation* to see and edit a Web site's structure; *Hyperlinks* to see the links to and from each page in a Web site; and *Tasks* to see, create, or edit a To-do list for the Web site.

❻ **Page view tabs:** By default, FrontPage opens in the *Normal* view, which lets you edit the open Web page. Click *HTML* view to see or edit a page's coding; click *Preview* to see how the page will look in a Web browser. *Preview* will not appear if you don't have Microsoft's Web browser, Internet Explorer, installed on your machine. (Internet Explorer doesn't need to be running, just installed.)

❼ **Download progress:** The icon spins while FrontPage is opening a Web page; it stops once all the page's related files have opened.

❽ **Estimated download time:** By default, FrontPage is set to show how many seconds the current page will take to download over a 28.8 bps modem connection. You can click to change the connection speed, though 28.8 probably reflects the average dial-up user's modem rate.

Starting and Quitting FrontPage

To launch FrontPage

1. Click the *Start* button in the Windows taskbar. Point your cursor to *Programs* and then click the *Microsoft FrontPage* icon (**Figure 2.2**).

2. Once FrontPage launches, you'll be presented with a blank Web page (**Figure 2.3**). You're ready to begin editing that page or creating other pages.

To quit FrontPage

◆ After saving your work (Ctrl S), choose File > Exit (Alt F4) (**Figure 2.4**).

Figure 2.2 To launch Front Page, click the *Start* button, point your cursor to *Programs*, and click the *Microsoft FrontPage* icon.

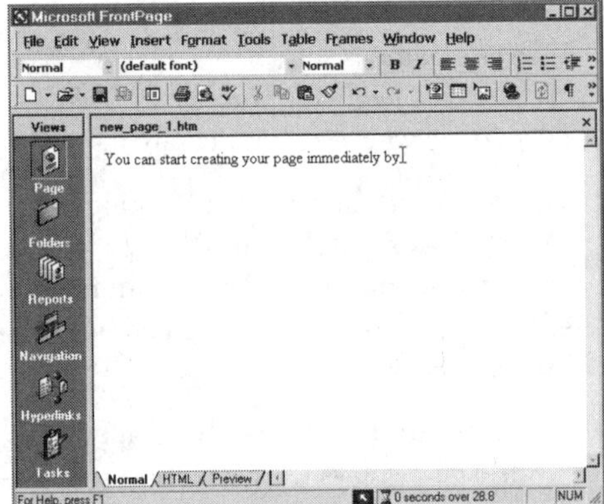

Figure 2.3 When FrontPage launches, it displays a blank Web page, which you can begin editing immediately.

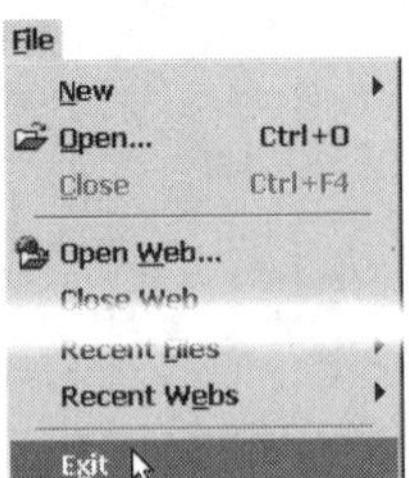

Figure 2.4 To quit FrontPage, choose File > Exit (Alt F4).

intro1.html

```
<td><!-- left margin --></td>
<td colspan="2">
  <hr>
</td>
<td><!-- right margin --></td>
</tr>
<!-- page body -->
<tr>
  <td height="629"><!-- left margin --></td>
  <!-- Figure COLUMN -->
  <td bgcolor="#FFFFFF" align="LEFT" valign="TOP" width="250"
  height="629"><font
    face="Verdana, Arial, Helvetica, sans serif"><b>Consider
    the possibilities:</b></font><font
    face="Verdana, Arial, Helvetica, sans serif" size="-1"> </font><font
    face="Verdana, Arial, Helvetica, sans serif" size="-1">
    <table cellspacing="0" cellpadding="4">
      <tr>
        <td valign="top"><img src="../figures/K2redbox.GIF"
          vspace="2" width="8" height="8"></td>
        <td valign="top"><font
          face="Verdana, Arial, Helvetica, sans serif"
          size="-1">Create &quot;hot&quot; folders that
          instantly process any image dropped into them by
          applying editing actions you set up ahead of time.
          For details, see <i><a href="../toc.html#chap11">Batching
          Actions</a>.</i></font></td>
```

Normal HTML Preview

10 seconds over 28.8 NUM

Figure 2.5 Clicking the *HTML* tab lets you inspect or edit the current page's HTML coding.

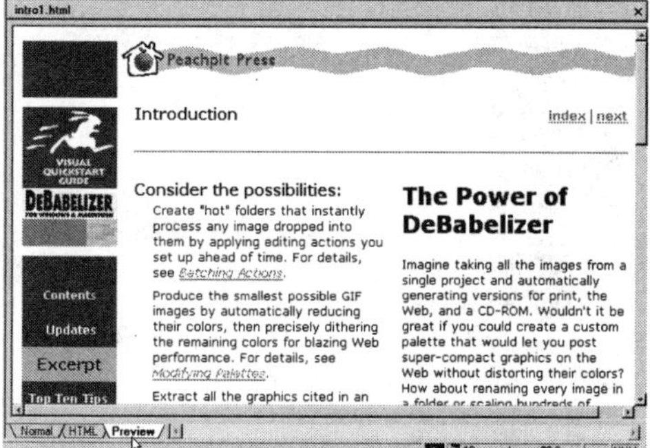

Figure 2.6 Clicking the *Preview* tab lets you see how the current page will appear within a Web browser.

Using Normal, HTML, and Preview Views

When in Page view, you can choose from three different views by clicking the tabs: Normal (the default), HTML, or Preview. The Normal page view lets you directly edit the current Web page—without seeing any of the underlying HTML code (**Figure 2.1**). The HTML view, naturally, shows all the coding and allows you to change the code directly (**Figure 2.5**). Preview view lets you see how the page will look within a Web browser (**Figure 2.6**).

✔ Tip

- Instead of clicking the tabs to change your page view, you also can press Ctrl Pg Up or Ctrl Pg Dn to cycle forward or backward from *Normal* to *HTML* to *Preview*.

Using the Views icons

FrontPage offers six different ways to see and edit your Web pages or sites, depending on which icon you click in the Views bar (**Figure 2.7**). By default, FrontPage displays the Page view (**Figure 2.8**). The other choices let you quickly see the folders, reports, navigation structure, hyperlinks, or tasks related to the current Web page or site. Each view displays a different set of information about your site and pages (**Figures 2.9–2.13**).

Figure 2.7 Click any of the six icons to quickly change your view of the current Web page or site.

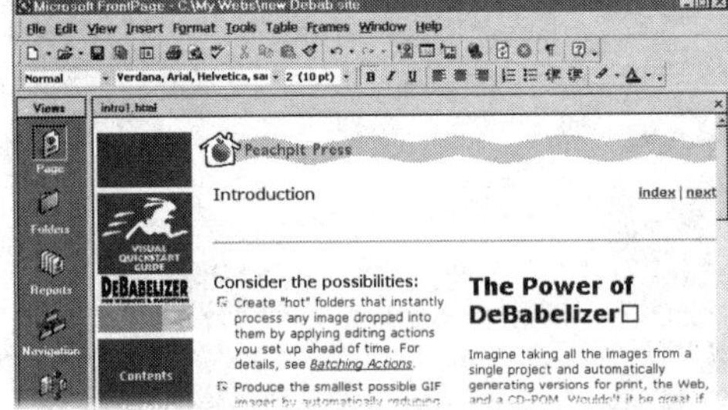

Figure 2.8 By default, FrontPage displays the Page view when you first open a Web site.

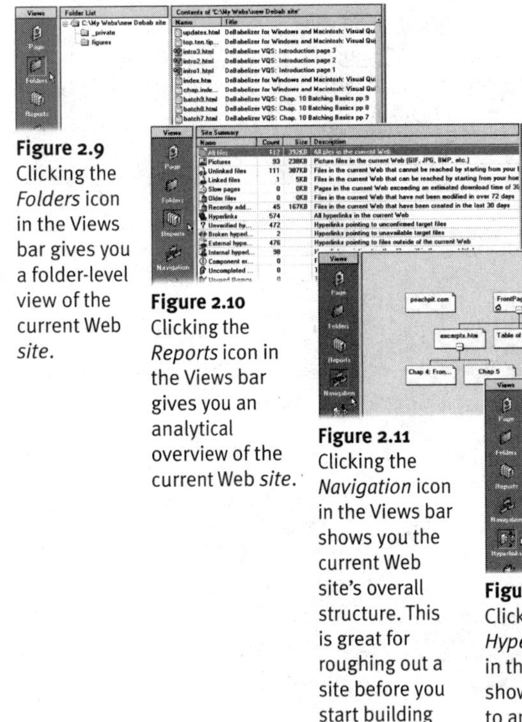

Figure 2.9 Clicking the *Folders* icon in the Views bar gives you a folder-level view of the current Web *site*.

Figure 2.10 Clicking the *Reports* icon in the Views bar gives you an analytical overview of the current Web *site*.

Figure 2.11 Clicking the *Navigation* icon in the Views bar shows you the current Web site's overall structure. This is great for roughing out a site before you start building individual Web pages.

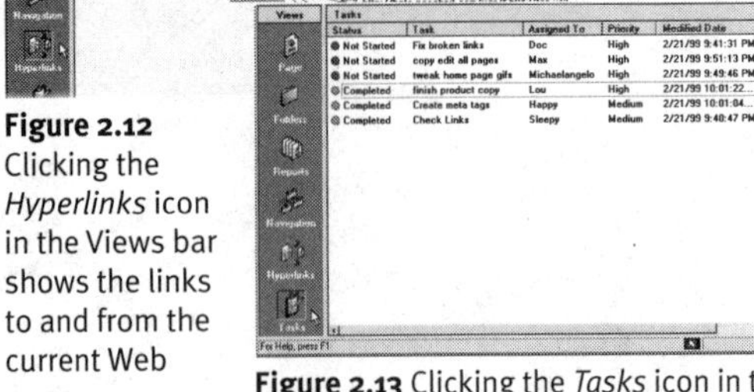

Figure 2.12 Clicking the *Hyperlinks* icon in the Views bar shows the links to and from the current Web *page*.

Figure 2.13 Clicking the *Tasks* icon in the Views bar lets you create a To-do list for the Web *site* and track the status of those tasks. Whether you're a team of 20—or just one—it helps reduce mistakes and mix-ups.

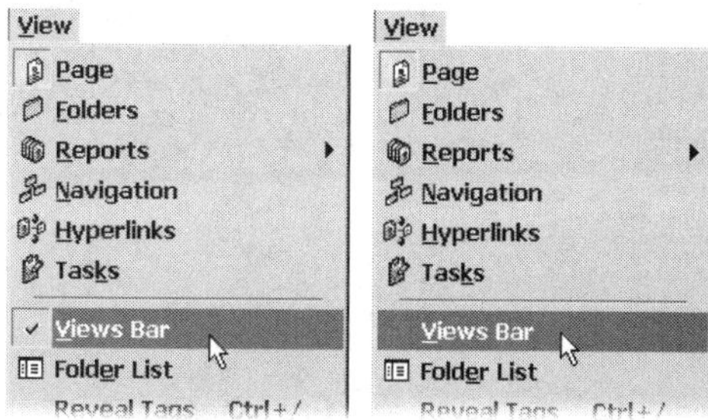

Figure 2.14 The Views Bar can be toggled on or off by choosing View > Views Bar.

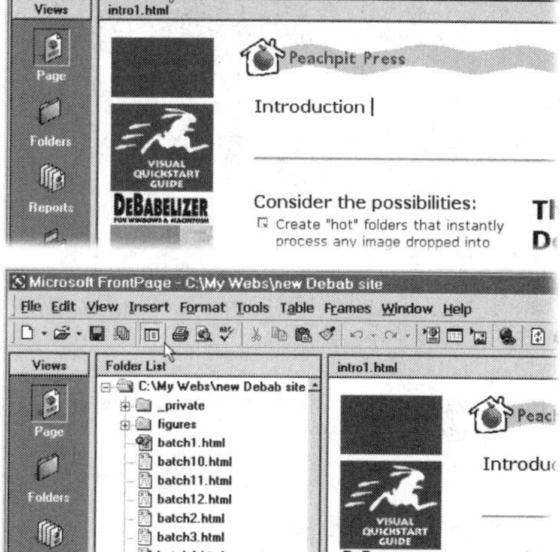

Figure 2.15 To quickly see your Web site's folder structure—no matter which view you're in—click the Folder List icon in the Standard toolbar. To hide the folders, click the icon again.

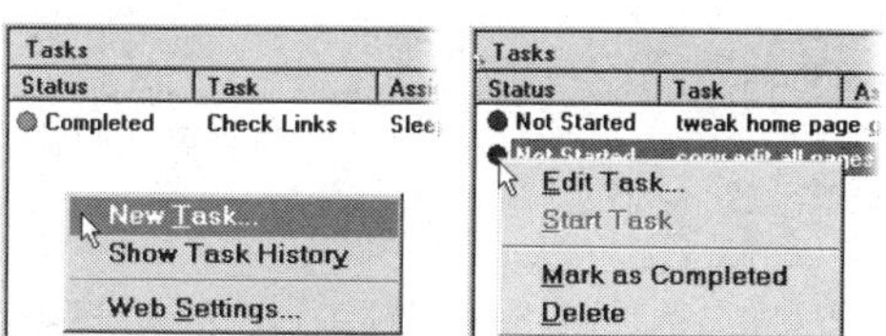

Figure 2.16 To quickly *add* a task, right-click on any blank spot within the Tasks list (left). To *change* an existing task, right-click on any item in the Tasks list (right).

To switch views

1. Make sure the Views bar is visible in FrontPage's left pane. If it is not, choose View > Views Bar (**Figure 2.14**).
2. Click any of the six Views icons in the left pane.
3. FrontPage's right pane will switch to reflect your choice.

✔ Tips

- No matter which view you're using, you can quickly see your site's folder structure by clicking the Folder List icon in the Standard toolbar (**Figure 2.15**). Click the icon again to hide the folders. Or choose View > Folder List to toggle the folders on and off.
- If you want maximum work space for your pages, you can hide the Views bar by choosing View > Views Bar, and clicking your cursor to uncheck the Views Bar. To toggle the Views Bar back on, repeat the steps (**Figure 2.14**).
- While in Tasks view, you can quickly add a *new* task by right-clicking within the Tasks pane. To change an *existing* task, right-click on any item in the Tasks list (**Figure 2.16**).

Using the Toolbars

By default, the Standard and Formatting toolbars (**Figures 2.17** and **2.18**) appear at the top of FrontPage's main window. But depending on which Web tasks you're doing at the moment, displaying one or more of FrontPage's seven other toolbars can be particularly handy (**Figures 2.19–2.25**). Like all of FrontPage's toolbars, they can be customized to your heart's desire. For details, see *To customize an existing toolbar* and *To create a new toolbar* on pages 25 and 26.

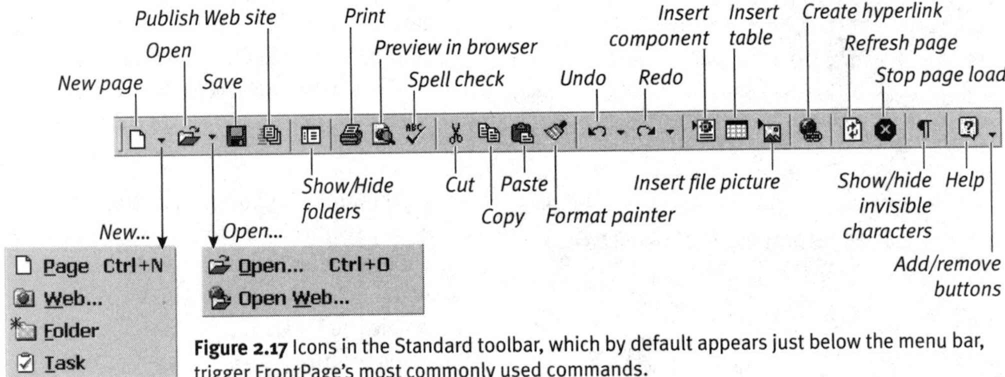

Figure 2.17 Icons in the Standard toolbar, which by default appears just below the menu bar, trigger FrontPage's most commonly used commands.

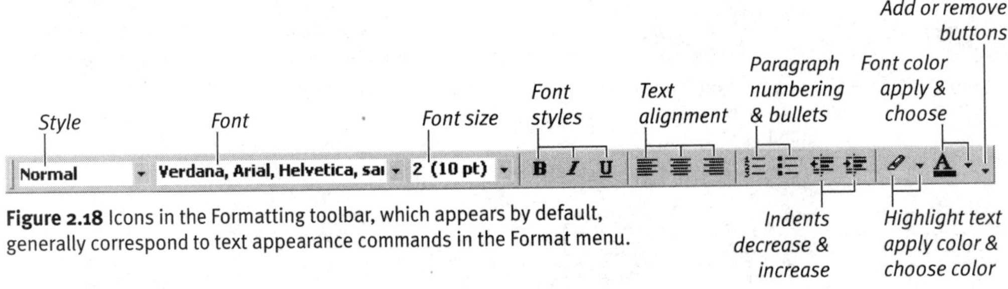

Figure 2.18 Icons in the Formatting toolbar, which appears by default, generally correspond to text appearance commands in the Format menu.

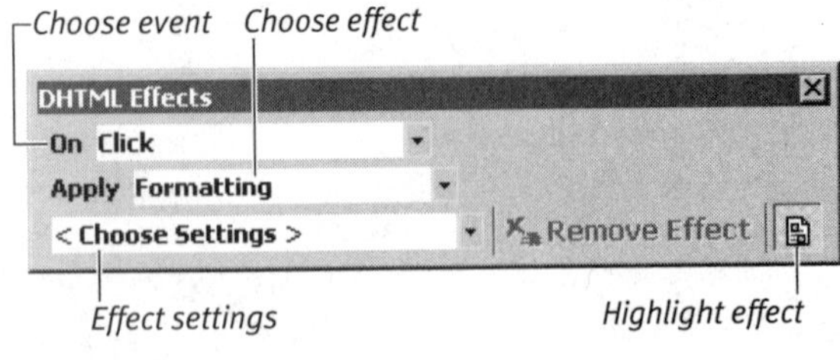

Figure 2.19 The drop-down menus in the DHTML Effects (Dynamic HTML) toolbar let you set up formatting effects that are triggered by the Web user's actions. For details, see page 287.

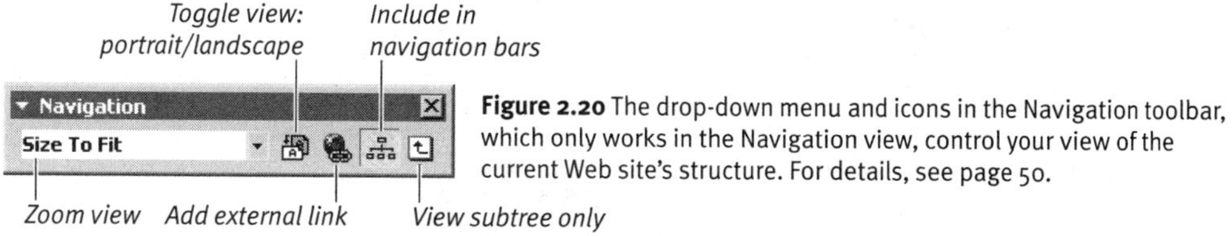

Figure 2.20 The drop-down menu and icons in the Navigation toolbar, which only works in the Navigation view, control your view of the current Web site's structure. For details, see page 50.

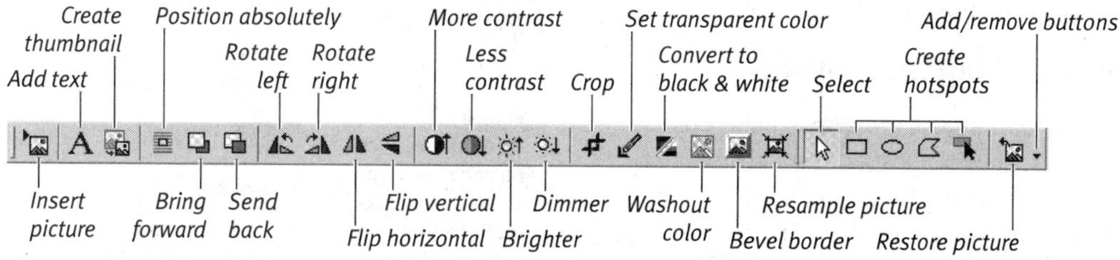

Figure 2.21 The Pictures toolbar's icons help you edit aspects of any selected graphic. For details, see page 143.

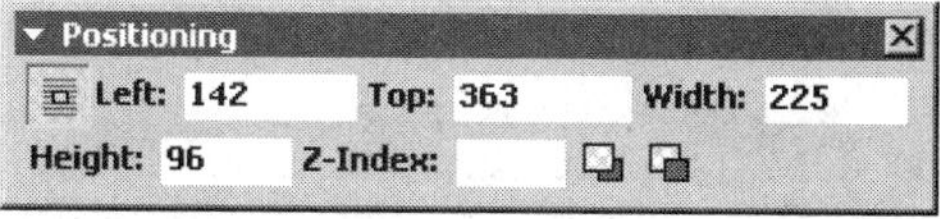

Figure 2.22 The icons and text boxes in the Positioning toolbar help you control the absolute and relative positioning of the selected page element. For details, see page 168.

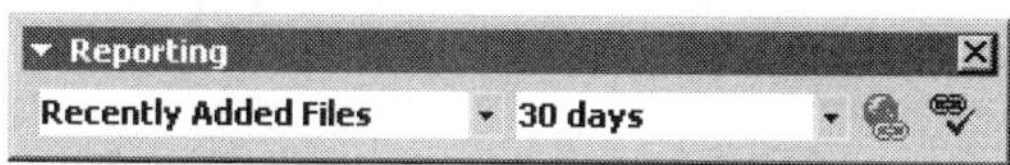

Figure 2.23 The drop-down menus and icons in the Reports toolbar, used only in the Reports view, help you check the current Web site's files, functions, and hyperlinks. For details, see page 293.

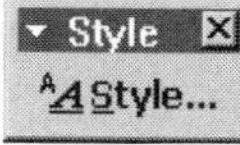

Figure 2.24 The Style toolbar has no buttons and opens the Style dialog box. For details, see page 273.

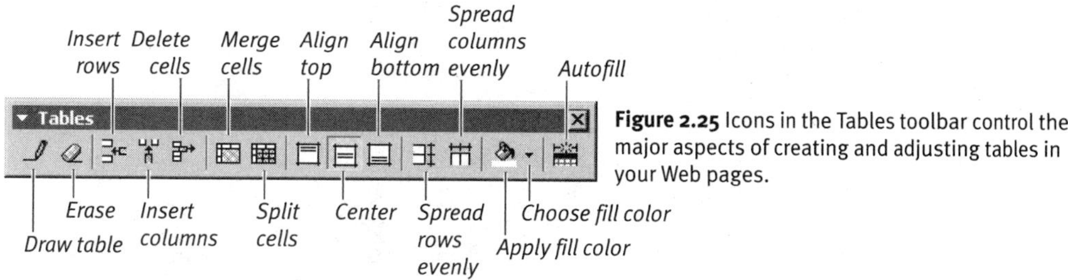

Figure 2.25 Icons in the Tables toolbar control the major aspects of creating and adjusting tables in your Web pages.

To turn on/off toolbars

1. Choose View > Toolbars and select a toolbar from the drop-down menu to turn on or off (**Figure 2.26**). Checked toolbars are already on; unchecked ones are off.
2. Release your cursor on the selected toolbar and it will appear immediately above or below FrontPage's main window.

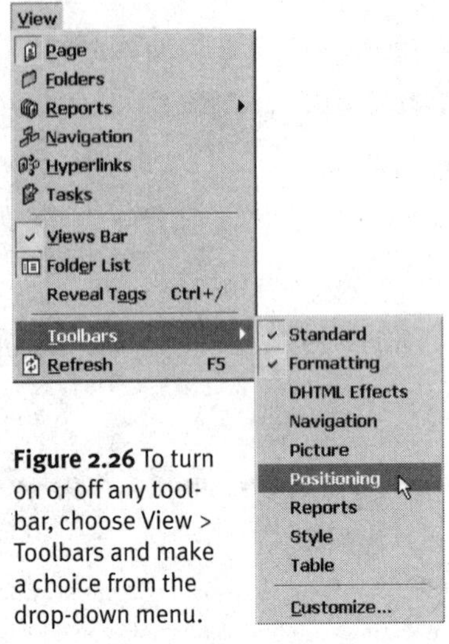

Figure 2.26 To turn on or off any toolbar, choose View > Toolbars and make a choice from the drop-down menu.

Rearranging the toolbars

FrontPage lets you move any of its toolbars to where they're most convenient for your work. Sometimes it's easiest to have your activated toolbars "docked," that is, running horizontally across the top of FrontPage's main window. For some tasks, however, you may prefer to have a toolbar sitting out on the desktop itself. FrontPage also lets you resize the toolbars to fit your workspace.

To move toolbars to the desktop

- To move a docked toolbar (those running across FrontPage's main window), click your cursor on the toolbar, continue pressing the cursor, and drag the toolbar to a new spot on the desktop, where it will then appear with its own title (**Figure 2.27**).

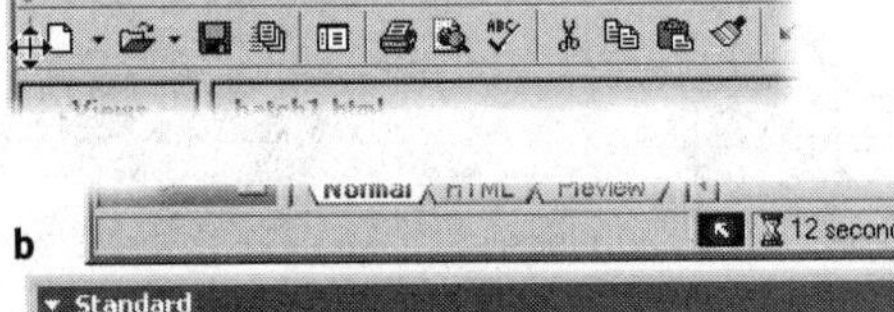

Figure 2.27 To move a docked toolbar, click anywhere in the bar and (a) drag it onto the desktop (b).

To dock toolbars in the main window

- To move a freestanding toolbar into a docked position, click on the toolbar and drag it to the zone just above FrontPage's main window. As your cursor approaches the docking area, the freestanding toolbar will snap into place (**Figure 2.28**).

To resize freestanding toolbars

- To shrink a *freestanding* toolbar, click its outer edge and drag the cursor toward the toolbar's center. To expand the toolbar, drag the cursor away from the toolbar's center (**Figure 2.29**).

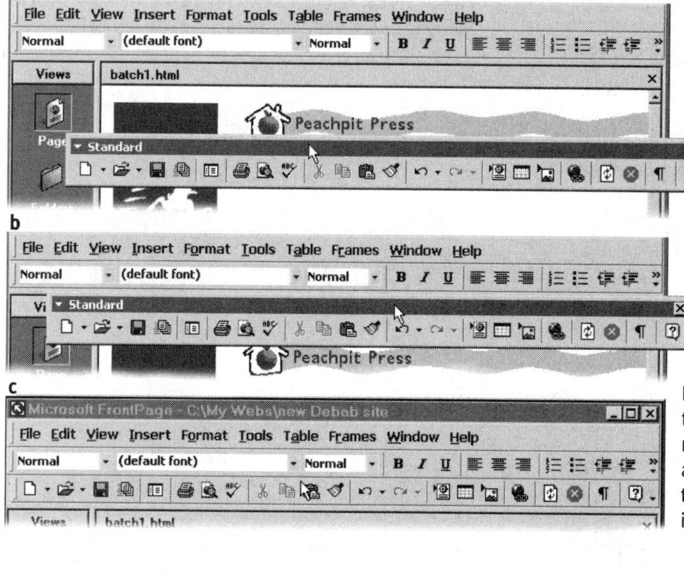

Figure 2.28 To dock a freestanding toolbar, click and drag it to FrontPage's main window (a). As your cursor approaches the docking area (b), the freestanding toolbar will "snap" into place (c).

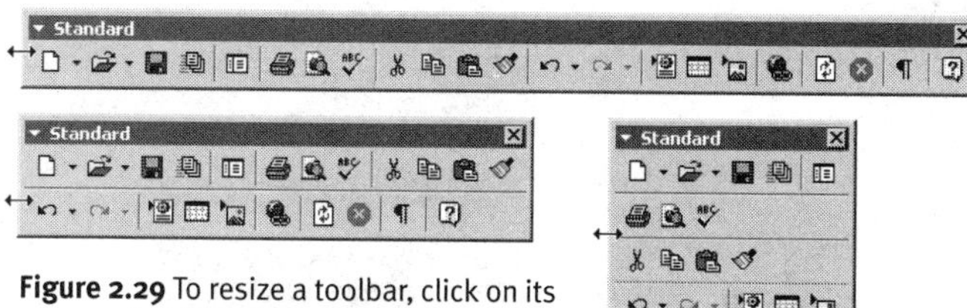

Figure 2.29 To resize a toolbar, click on its edge and while holding down the cursor, drag it horizontally or vertically.

Customizing the toolbars

FrontPage lets you add or remove toolbar buttons. You also can customize toolbars by adding extra buttons to existing toolbars or by creating brand new toolbars.

To add or remove toolbar buttons

1. Click the triangle at the end of the toolbar you want to customize and the *Add or Remove Buttons* drop-down menu will appear (**Figure 2.30**).
2. Move the cursor over the *Add or Remove Buttons* drop-down menu and another drop-down menu will appear showing all the toolbar's current buttons, marked by checks (**Figure 2.31**).
3. Click the item you want to remove and the check will disappear (**Figure 2.32**).
4. Continue unchecking (removing) or checking (adding) items until you're satisfied. Then click anywhere outside the drop-down menu and the toolbar will reflect your changes.

✔ Tip

- It's all too easy to accidentally remove an entire menu. To quickly undo your button changes, you can reset a toolbar to its original condition. Just click the triangle at the end of the toolbar, move to the *Add or Remove Buttons* drop-down menu, and click *Reset Toolbar* (**Figure 2.33**). The toolbar's original buttons will reappear.

Figure 2.30 To add or remove toolbar buttons, click the triangle at the end of the toolbar and the *Add or Remove Buttons* drop-down menu will appear.

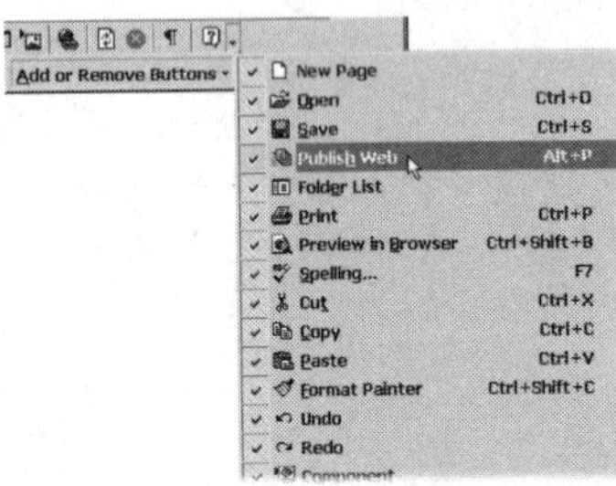

Figure 2.31 When you move the cursor over the *Add or Remove Buttons* menu, a drop-down menu will appear showing all the toolbar's available buttons.

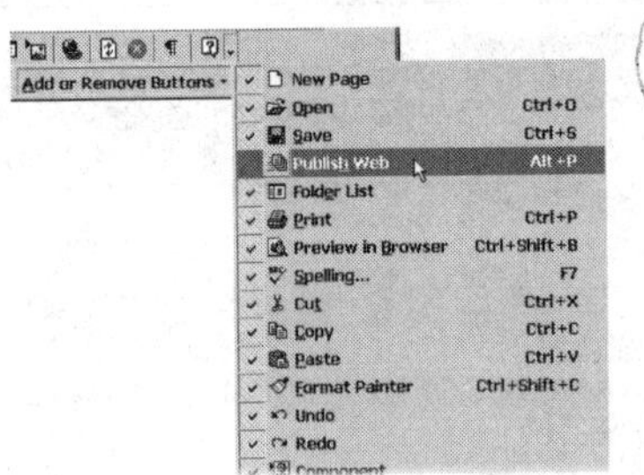

Figure 2.32 Click the item you want to remove or add. When you're done, click anywhere outside the drop-down menu to trigger the change.

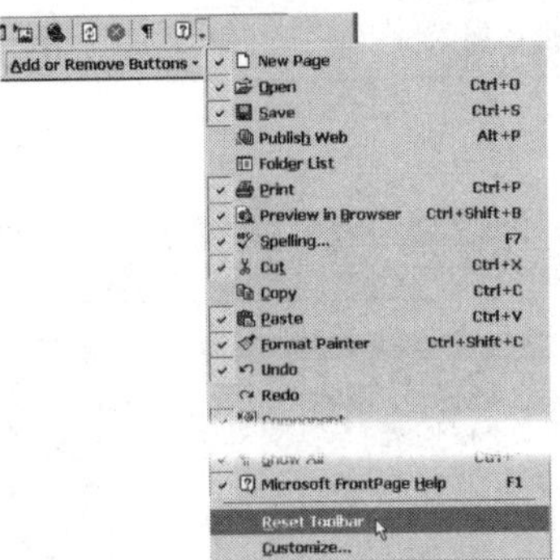

Figure 2.33 To reset the toolbar to its original condition, click the triangle at the end of the toolbar, move to the *Add or Remove Buttons* drop-down menu, and click *Reset Toolbar*.

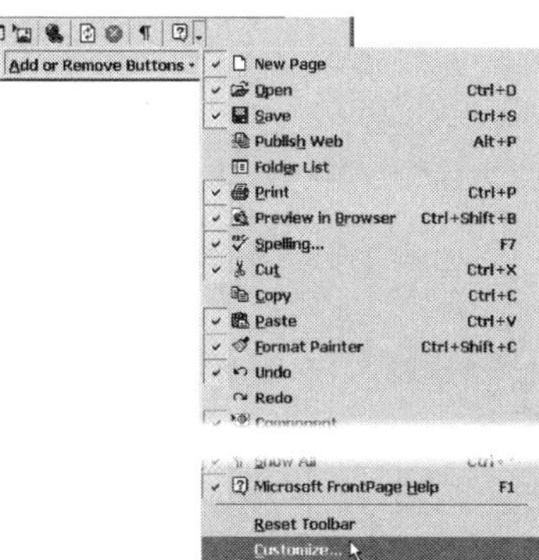

Figure 2.34 To add buttons not already available in a toolbar's add/remove drop-down menu, select Customize.

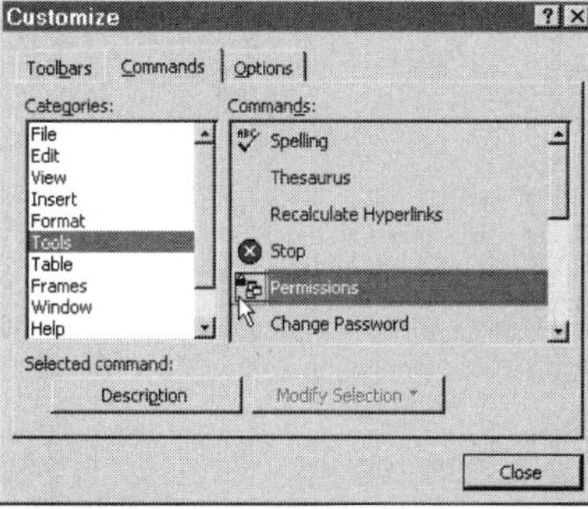

Figure 2.35 Click a category in the left pane, then, in the right pane, click the command you want to add to your toolbar.

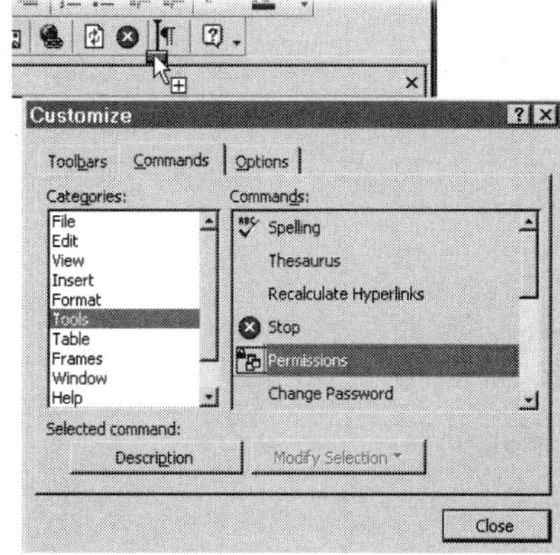

Figure 2.36 Once you choose a command, drag it to the toolbar you're customizing.

To customize an existing toolbar

1. If you want to add buttons not immediately available in a toolbar's add/remove drop-down menu, select Customize at the very bottom of the menu (**Figure 2.34**).
2. When the Customize dialog box appears, make sure the *Commands* tab is selected.
3. Click one of the menu categories in the left pane, then click the command in the right pane that you want to add to your toolbar (**Figure 2.35**).
4. With the command still highlighted, drag your cursor to the spot in the toolbar where you want the button to appear (**Figure 2.36**).
5. Release the cursor and the command button will be inserted into the toolbar.

To create a new toolbar

1. Choose Tools > Customize (**Figure 2.37**).
2. When the Customize dialog box appears, click the *Toolbars* tab, and then click *New* (**Figure 2.38**).
3. When the New Toolbar dialog box appears, type in a descriptive name for your new toolbar, and click *OK* (**Figure 2.39**).
4. The new toolbar will appear in the Customize dialog box's list of available toolbars. The toolbar itself also will appear on the desktop, but since it doesn't have any icons yet, it'll be tiny.
5. To add icons to your new toolbar, click the Customize dialog box's *Commands* tab.
6. Choose the command category in the left pane, then click on a command in the right pane, drag it to your new toolbar and release your cursor. The command will be placed in your new toolbar.
7. As you continue selecting and adding commands, your new toolbar will become large enough to resize. When you've finished adding commands, click *Close* (**Figure 2.40**). Your new toolbar will appear as a freestanding toolbar, but remember that you can always dock it in the main window. For details, see *To dock toolbars in the main window* on page 23.

✔ Tip

- By now you may realize there are three ways to get to the Customize dialog box: 1) View > Toolbars > Customize, 2) Tools > Customize, and 3) the *Add or Remove Buttons* drop-down menu that appears when you click the triangle at the right end of any toolbar. They all work identically, so it's your choice.

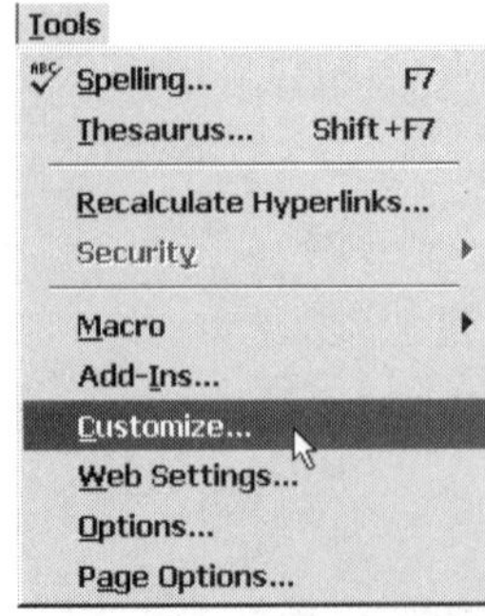

Figure 2.37 To create a new toolbar, choose Tools > Customize.

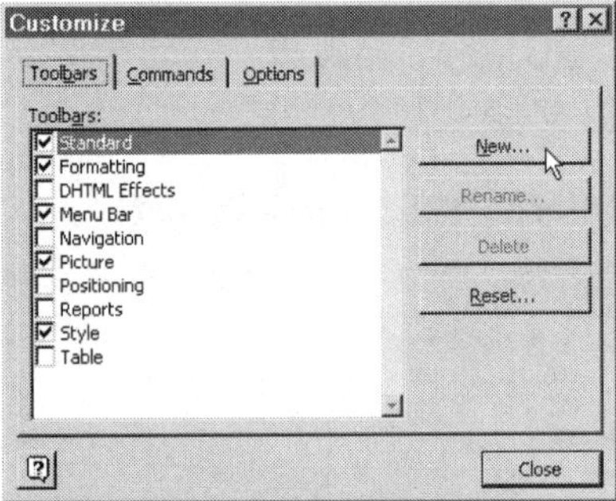

Figure 2.38 In the Customize dialog box, click the *Toolbars* tab, and then click *New*.

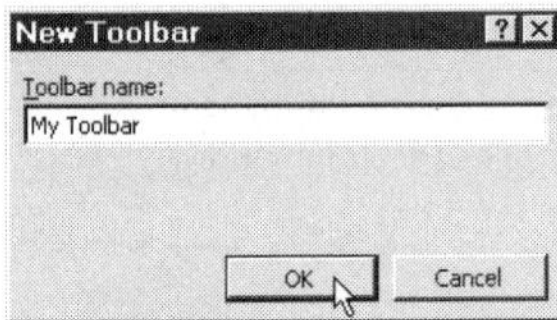

Figure 2.39 Give your new toolbar a descriptive name and click *OK*.

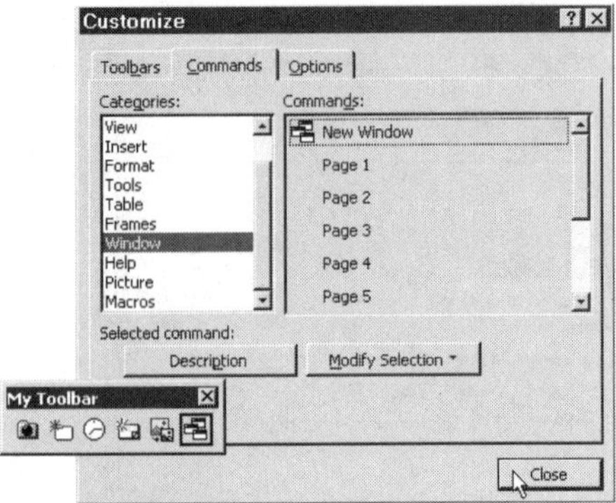

Figure 2.40 Click and drag commands from the right pane onto your new toolbar. When you've finished, click *Close*.

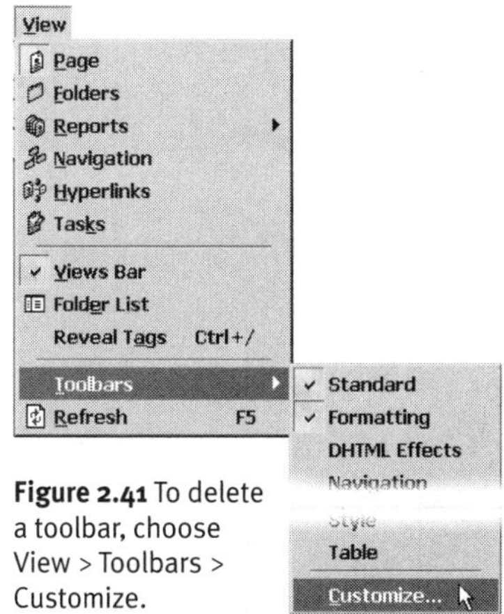

Figure 2.41 To delete a toolbar, choose View > Toolbars > Customize.

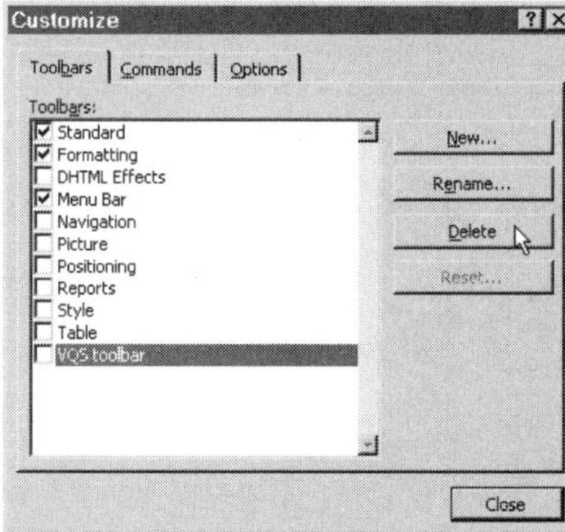

Figure 2.42 When the Customize dialog box appears, click the toolbar you want removed, and click *Delete.*

To delete a toolbar

1. If you want to get rid of a toolbar (instead of just hiding it from view), choose View > Toolbars > Customize (**Figure 2.41**).
2. When the Customize dialog box appears, click on the toolbar you want removed, and click *Delete* (**Figure 2.42**).
3. When the alert dialog box appears, click *OK.* The toolbar will be removed from the list in the Customize dialog box.

The Menus

The menus that appear across the top of FrontPage's main window remain the same no matter what you're doing. However, some of the menus, such as Frames, can be used only while viewing or editing Web pages containing frames.

The File menu

Commands found in the File menu involve application-wide actions: creating, opening, closing, saving, publishing, and importing Web pages or sites (**Figure 2.43**). The File menu also lets you set up print settings, change FrontPage's general properties, and quit the program.

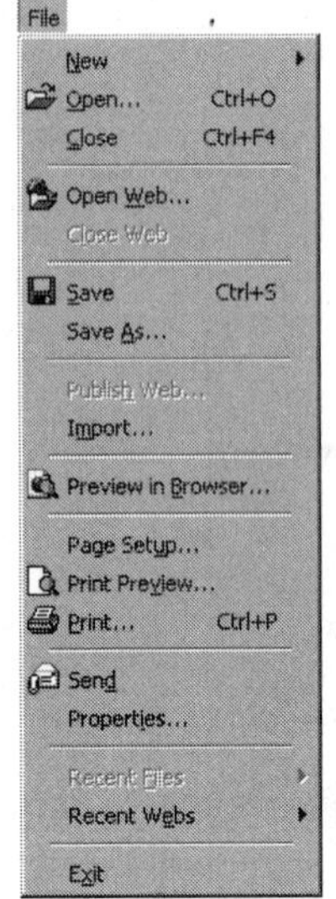

Figure 2.43 The File menu controls application-wide actions such as creating, opening, closing, saving, publishing, and importing Web pages or sites.

The Edit menu

Most of the Edit menu's commands operate just as they do in other programs—except the fifth section of the menu (**Figure 2.44**). That section lets you set up a Check In/Check Out system to avoid file version conflicts when more than one person is working on a Web site. For details, see *Managing Web Site Workflow* on page 293.

Figure 2.44 Most of the Edit menu's commands are common to all programs. The fifth section lets you control file access when more than one person is working on a Web site.

The View menu

Most of the commands found in the View menu duplicate those triggered by clicking the icons in the Views bar (**Figure 2.45**). The menu's Toolbars choice lets you turn on or off any of FrontPage's nine toolbars.

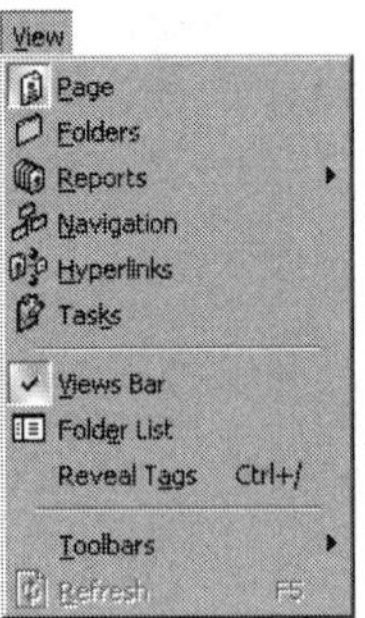

Figure 2.45 The View menu lets you show or hide all six of FrontPage's views, plus the toolbars.

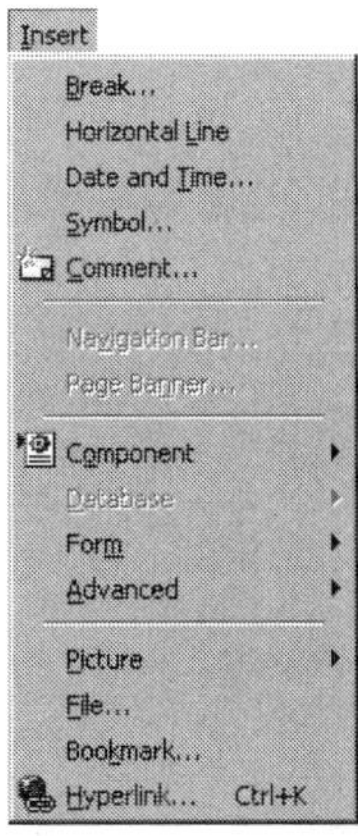

Figure 2.46 The Insert menu lets you place into your Web pages everything from line breaks, dates, and hyperlinks to Java applets and Office 2000 components.

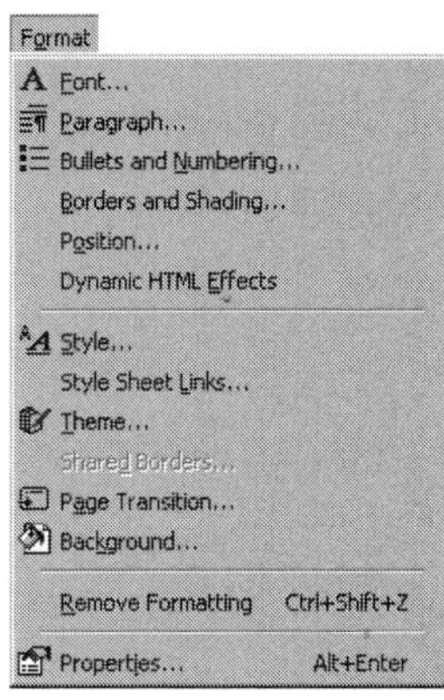

Figure 2.47 The Format menu controls text appearance and generally corresponds to the Formatting toolbar icons.

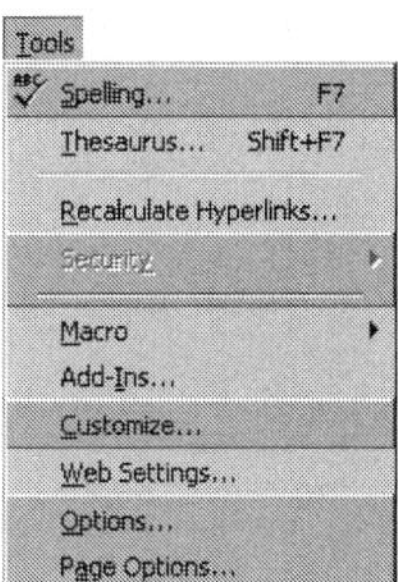

Figure 2.48 The Tools menu controls many of FrontPage's overall settings, plus the dictionary and thesaurus.

The Insert menu

As the name suggests, this enables you to insert into Web pages everything from line breaks, dates, and hyperlinks to Java applets and Office 2000 components, such as charts and spreadsheets (**Figure 2.46**).

The Format menu

Commands found in the Format menu control the appearance of your text, HTML tags, and what FrontPage calls themes, which establish your Web site's overall graphic look (**Figure 2.47**).

The Tools menu

The Tools menu gives you control over many of FrontPage's overall settings (**Figure 2.48**). It also leads to FrontPage's dictionary and thesaurus.

The Table menu

Whether it's adding tables to a page or tweaking the arrangement of individual rows and columns, you'll find the most commonly used commands in the Table menu (**Figure 2.49**).

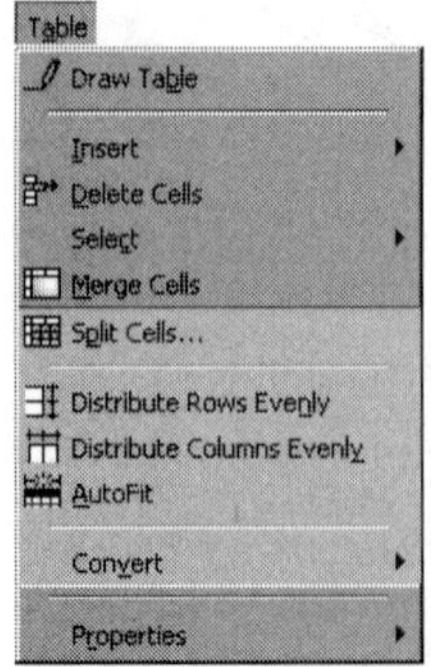

Figure 2.49 The Table menu controls major aspects of creating and adjusting tables in your Web pages and generally corresponds to the Table toolbar icons.

The Frames menu

Commands found in the Frames menu are accessible only when you're viewing a page containing HTML frames (**Figure 2.50**). Frame-based pages are created with the New Page command (Ctrl N). For details, see page 212.

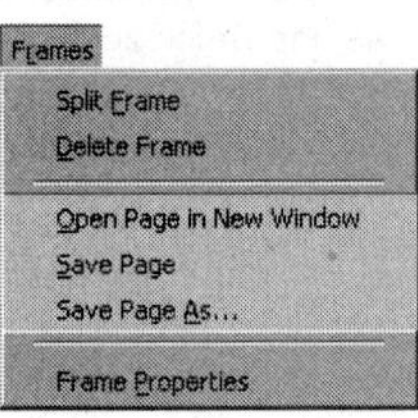

Figure 2.50 The Frames menu controls the formatting of frame-based pages and is not accessible when viewing a non-frame page.

The Window menu

FrontPage lets you open multiple Web pages and sites simultaneously. The Window menu lets you quickly switch from one window to another (**Figure 2.51**).

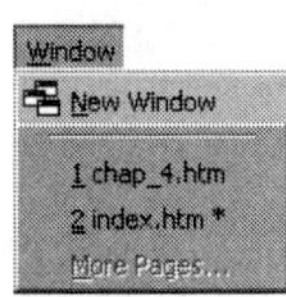

Figure 2.51 Use the Window menu to jump to any open FrontPage window.

The Help menu

Common to any Windows program, the Help menu gives you direct access to FrontPage's help system (**Figure 2.52**).

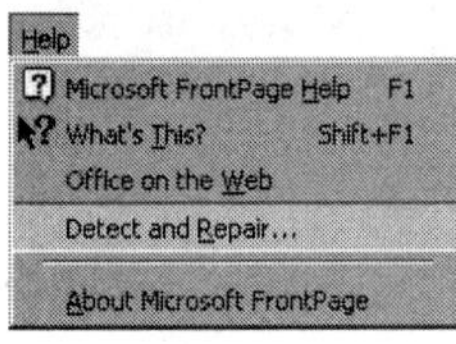

Figure 2.52 Use the Help menu to reach the FrontPage help system.

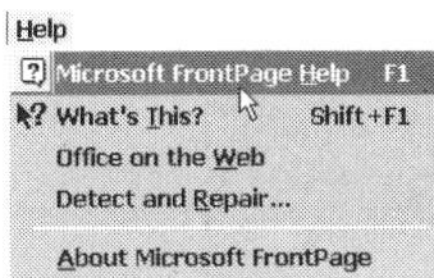

Figure 2.53 To start FrontPage's Help feature, choose Help > Microsoft FrontPage Help.

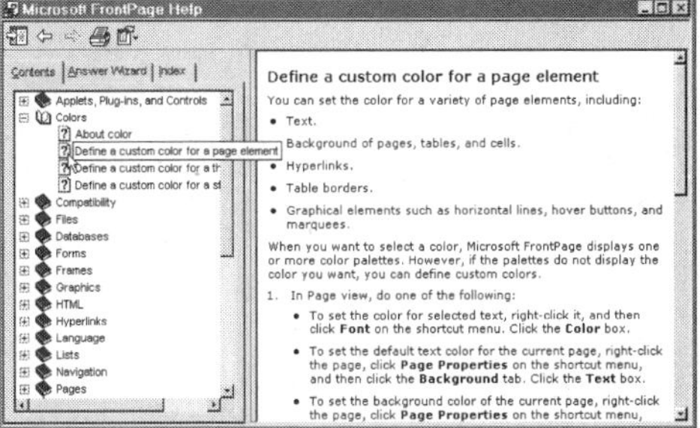

Figure 2.54 The *Contents* tab presents a topical overview of FrontPage—great for broad conceptual questions. Click the left pane's icons to have the information displayed in the right pane.

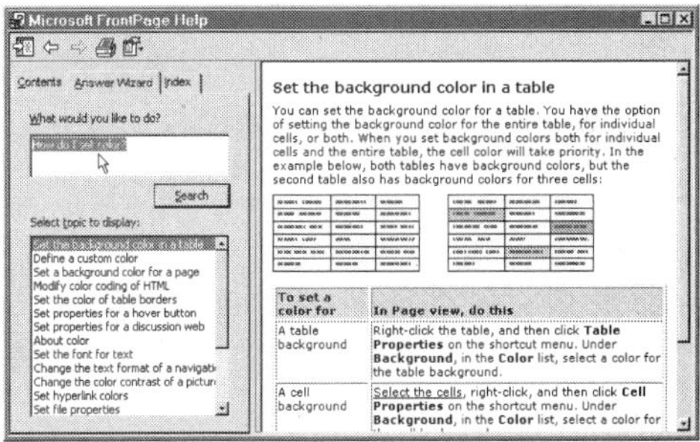

Figure 2.55 The *Answer Wizard* tab lets you type in a sentence-style question, which is sometimes the best approach if you're not sure exactly what to ask.

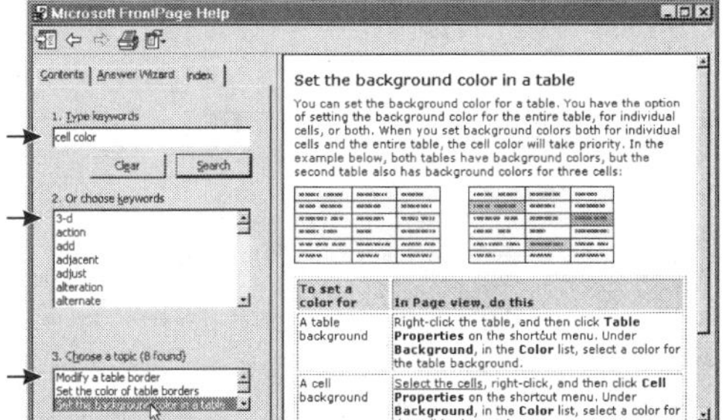

Figure 2.56 Use the *Index* tab to find a specific term or phrase. First enter the phrase in text box 1, then click *Search*. Fine-tune your request based on the initial results in box 2 (keywords) or box 3 (topics). Double-clicking either will display the full text in the right pane. Click *Clear* to start a new search.

To use FrontPage's Help

1. Choose Help > Microsoft FrontPage Help (F1) (**Figure 2.53**).
2. When the FrontPage Help dialog box appears, click one of the three tabs—*Contents*, *Answer Wizard*, or *Index*—depending on your question (**Figures 2.54–2.56**). Whether you click the icons in the *Contents* tab or click *Search* in the *Answer Wizard* or *Index* tabs, the results will appear in the right pane.

✔ Tip

- Which part of FrontPage's Help System you use depends on your question: *Contents* presents a topical overview of the program, which is handy for broad conceptual questions. If you're not sure even what to ask, *Answer Wizard* lets you type in a sentence-style question. *Index* shows every help entry—great for when you have a precise question about a particular problem or feature.

Creating, Opening, Saving, and Closing Web Pages

In building Web pages, you can take two routes: Create new pages from scratch and save them. Or you can open existing pages, alter them, and then save them using the Save As command to give them new names.

To create a new Web page

1. Choose File > New > Page (Ctrl N) (**Figure 2.57**).
2. When the New dialog box appears, you can choose *Normal Page*, which will create a new *blank* Web page, or choose one of the template-based pages, which offer a variety of layouts (**Figure 2.58**). Clicking each template gives you a thumbnail picture of its style within the Preview area of the New dialog box. Once you've made a choice, click *OK*.
3. Depending on your choice in Step 2, either a blank page with a generic title or a fully formatted template-based page will appear (**Figures 2.59** and **2.60**). If you chose a template page, you're now ready to substitute your own text and pictures in the page. For details, see page 61.

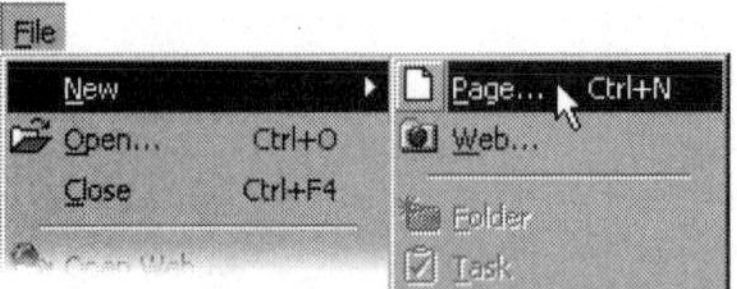

Figure 2.57 To open a new Web page, Choose File > New > Page (Ctrl N).

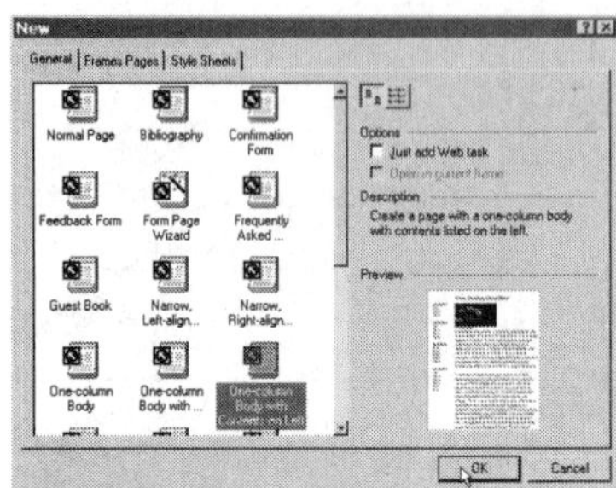

Figure 2.58 When you're creating a new Web page, FrontPage's New dialog box offers a variety of templates. Once you've made a choice, click *OK*.

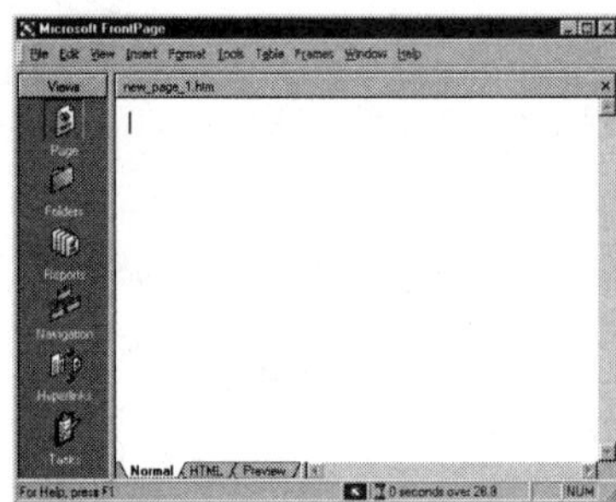

Figure 2.59 If you choose *Normal Page* in the New dialog box, FrontPage will open a blank page with a generic title.

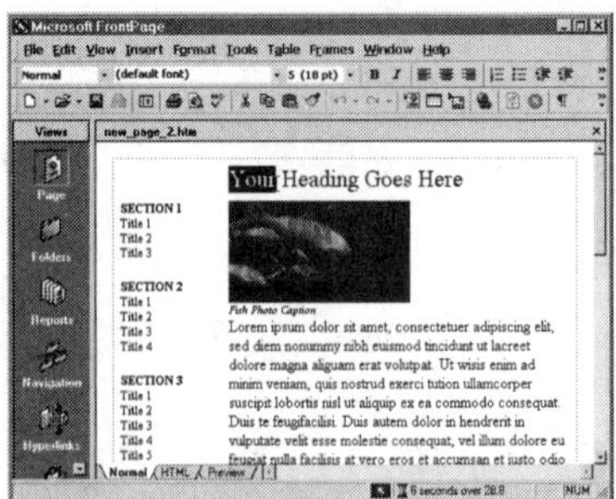

Figure 2.60 If you use a template, FrontPage will open a formatted page into which you then can substitute your own text and pictures.

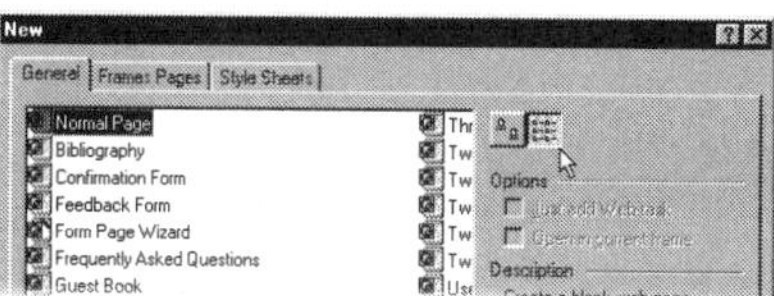

Figure 2.61 Click the New dialog box's List icon to see more styles at once.

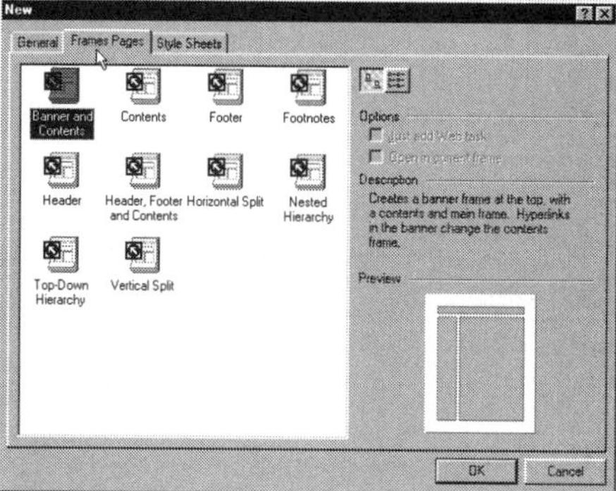

Figure 2.62 Click the New dialog box's *Frames Pages* tab to create frame-based Web pages. For details, see page 211.

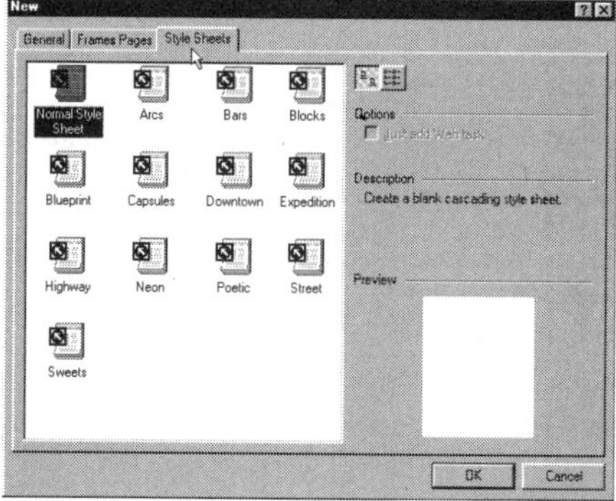

Figure 2.63 Click the New dialog box's *Styles Sheets* tab to create site-wide style sheets. For details, see page 269.

✔ Tips

- If you find the New dialog box's Icon view too cramped (**Figure 2.58**), click the List button to see more page styles simultaneously (**Figure 2.61**).
- The New dialog box also lets you create frame-based Web pages or even new style sheets. Just click their respective tabs, make a choice, and click *OK* (**Figures 2.62** and **2.63**). For details on frames, see page 211; for more on style sheets, see page 269.

To open an existing Web page

1. Choose File > Open (Ctrl O) (**Figure 2.64**).
2. When the Open File dialog box appears, navigate to the file you want to open and either double-click it, or type its name into the File name box and click *Open* (**Figure 2.65**).
3. The Web page appears in FrontPage's main window (**Figure 2.66**).

✔ Tip

- To narrow or widen your search for a Web page in the Open File dialog box, use the *Files of type* drop-down menu.

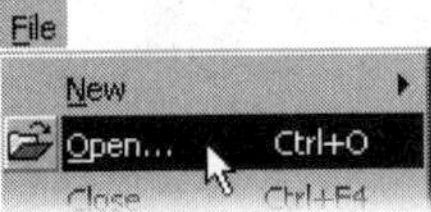

Figure 2.64 To open an existing Web page, choose File > Open (Ctrl O).

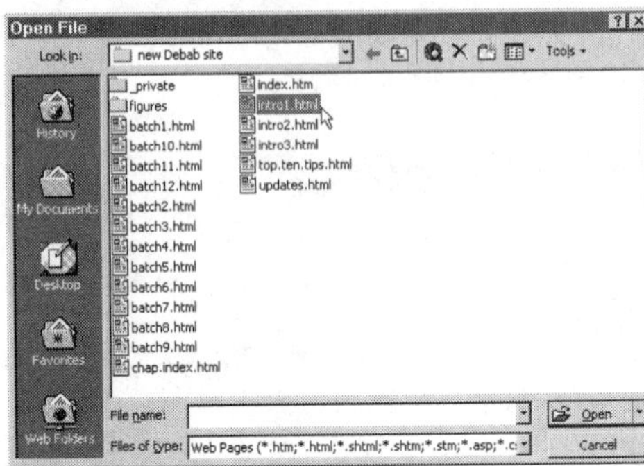

Figure 2.65 When the Open File dialog box appears, navigate to the file you want, and double-click it.

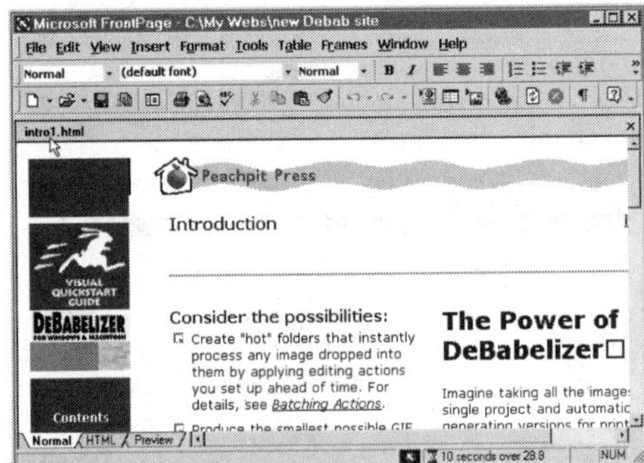

Figure 2.66 Once opened, the existing Web page appears in FrontPage's main window.

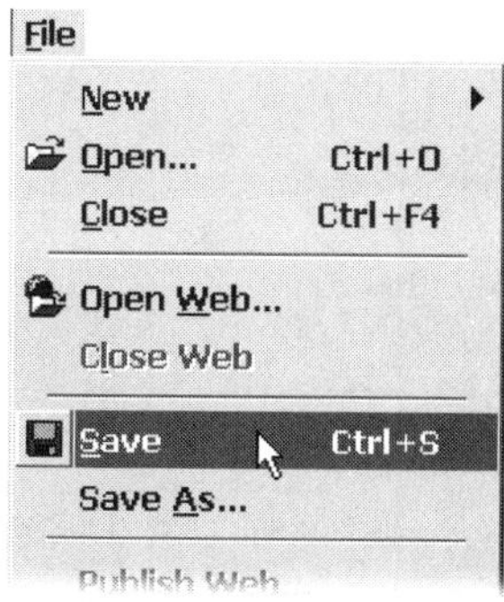

Figure 2.67 Choose File > Save (Ctrl S) to save a Web page.

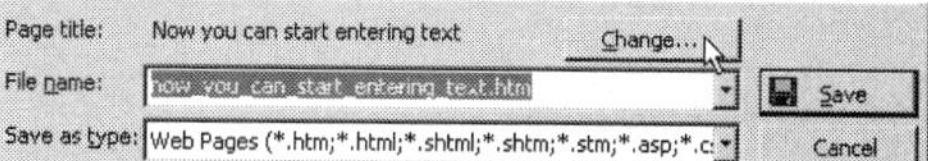

Figure 2.68 To set a title for your Web page, click the *Change* button within the Save dialog box.

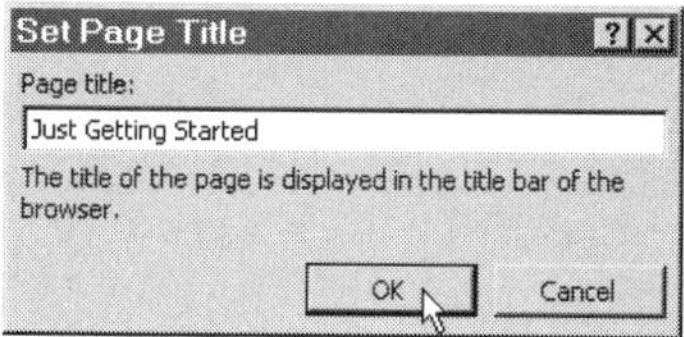

Figure 2.69 In the Set Page Title dialog box, enter the name you want Web browsers to display as the Web page's title, then click *OK*.

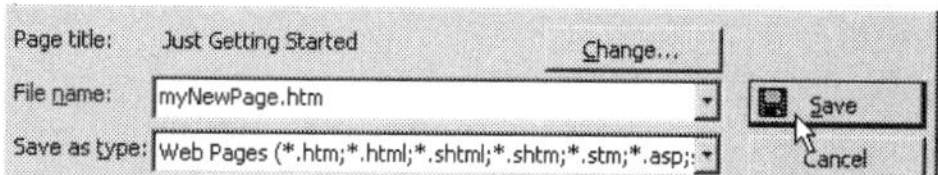

Figure 2.70 Give the page a distinctive file name with an .htm suffix and click *Save*.

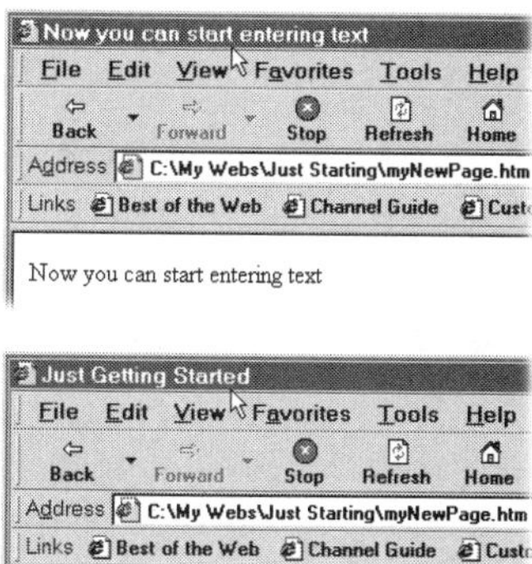

Figure 2.71 Change your page's title when you save it or Web browsers will use the file's first bit of text as the title (top), when you really want a more descriptive title (bottom).

To save a Web page

1. Choose File > Save (Ctrl S) (**Figure 2.67**).
2. When the Save dialog box appears, use the folder-level icon to navigate to where you want to save the page.
3. While still in the Save dialog box, click the *Change* button to choose a title for your page (**Figure 2.68**). When the Set Page Title dialog box appears, type the name you want Web browsers to display as the Web page's title and click *OK* (**Figure 2.69**). For details, see the Tip below.
4. By default, the file name also will be based on the page's first line of text. If that's not what you want it called, type into the *File name* text box a distinctive name. Be sure to end it with the .htm suffix, then click *Save* (**Figure 2.70**). The file will be saved with the name you gave it.

✔ Tip

- If you don't choose a title for your Web page when saving the page, FrontPage will generate one based on the page's first line of text—which will get picked up by Web browsers (**Figure 2.71**).

To save a Web page under another name

1. Choose File > Save As (**Figure 2.72**).
2. When the Save As dialog box opens, navigate to where you want the file saved, then click the *Change* button to give the page a new title (**Figure 2.68**). When the Set Page Title dialog box appears, type the name you want Web browsers to display as the Web page's title and click *OK* (**Figure 2.69**).
3. Enter a distinctive name into the File name field and click *Save*. The file will be saved with the new name.

To close a Web page

- Assuming you've already saved the page, choose File > Close (Ctrl F4) (**Figure 2.73**). FrontPage remains running, leaving you free to open another Web page or move on to other tasks.

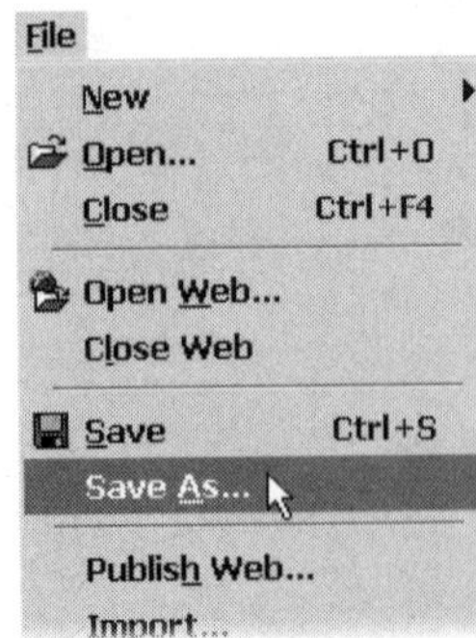

Figure 2.72 To save a Web page under another name, choose File > Save As.

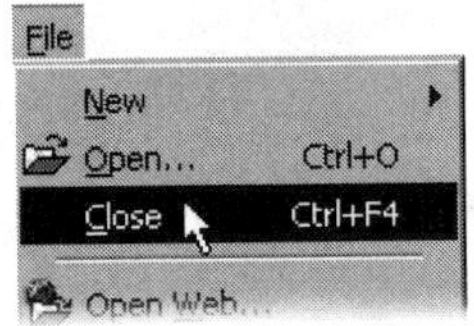

Figure 2.73 To close a Web page, choose File > Close.

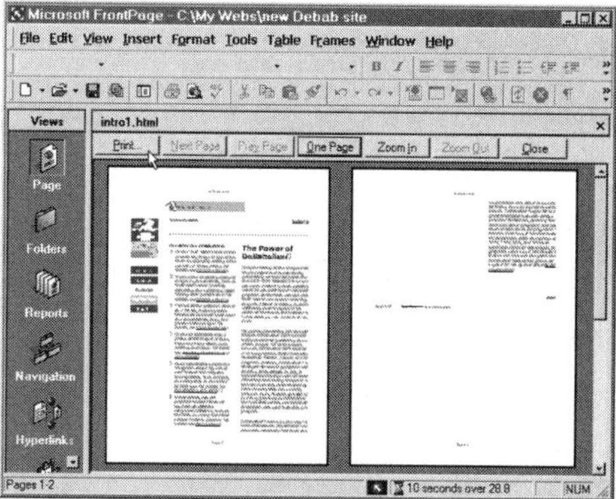

Figure 2.74 FrontPage's print preview window lets you see two pages at a time or zoom in for a closer look.

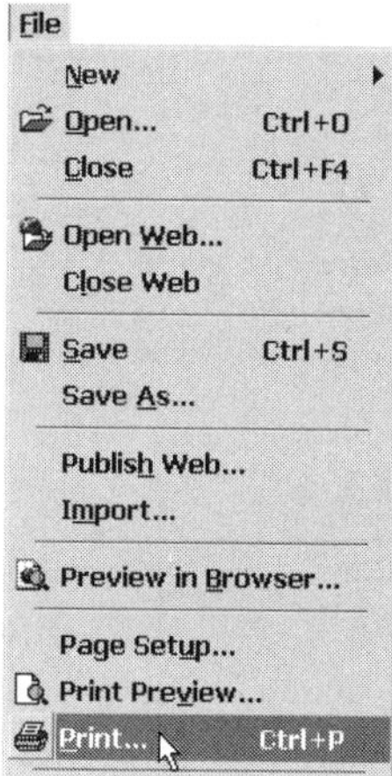

Figure 2.75 To print the current Web page, choose File > Print.

Printing Web Pages

While FrontPage doesn't let you print out an entire Web site at once, you can easily print out individual Web pages.

To print a Web page

1. If you have not already done so, check your printer's settings by choosing File > Page Setup and make any adjustments.
2. If you want to see a preview of the current Web page, choose File > Print Preview.
3. FrontPage's right pane displays the preview and includes buttons to inspect each page, see two pages at a time, or zoom in and out on the pages (**Figure 2.74**). If you're satisfied with the preview, click the *Print* button. Or click *Close* and then choose File > Print (**Figure 2.75**).

Creating, Opening, and Closing Web Sites

Any collection of related, linked Web pages—whether it's just two pages or a thousand—is called a Web *site*. FrontPage, however, calls it a "Web," which includes all the documents and graphics associated with the Web site. By default, FrontPage's Webs are stored in a specially created *My Webs* folder on your C drive.

Figure 2.76 Choose File > New > Web to create a new Web site.

To create a new Web site

1. Choose File > New > Web (**Figure 2.76**).
2. When the New dialog box appears, click on a template or wizard to use in creating your new Web site, then press Tab (**Figure 2.77**). By default, the *Specify the location of the new web* field will create a path name to the My Webs folder, so just type in a name for the site. If you want to store the Web site in another folder, use the drop-down menu to reach the new location.
3. Click *OK* and the Create New Web dialog box will appear briefly (**Figure 2.78**).
4. Depending on your choice in Step 2, a blank single-page Web site or the home page of a multiple-page template-based Web site will appear (**Figures 2.79** and **2.80**). You're ready to begin adding pages to the Web site's structure or to add content within individual pages. For details on structuring your Web site, see page 42.

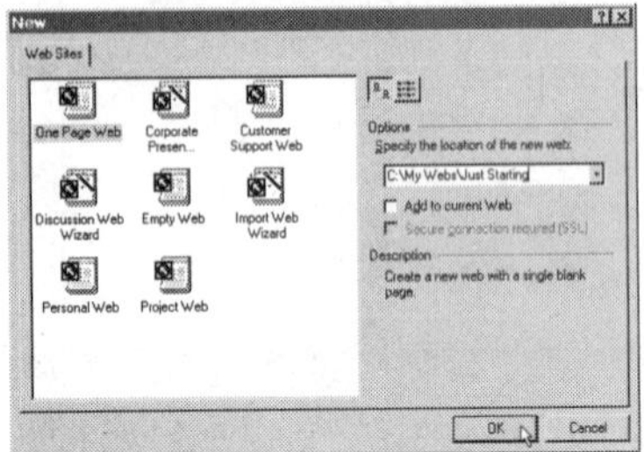

Figure 2.77 The New dialog box includes a variety of Web site templates and wizards. Once you've picked one and given it a name, click *OK*.

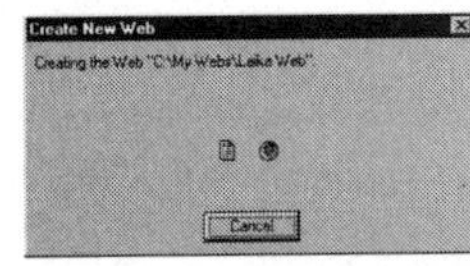

Figure 2.78 The Create New Web dialog box appears while FrontPage generates the Web site.

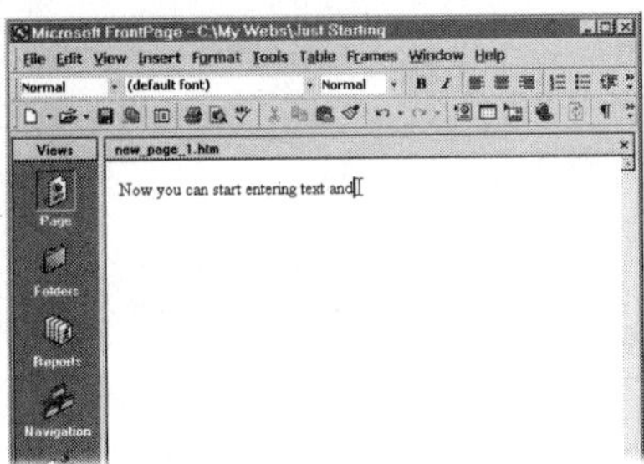

Figure 2.79 In page view, FrontPage displays the One Page Web template as a blank page.

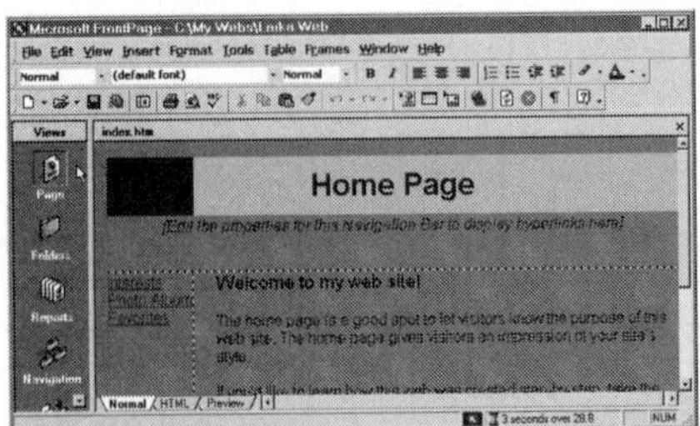

Figure 2.80 If you use one of FrontPage's multiple-page Web site templates, the page view includes instructions on how to add your own content and graphics.

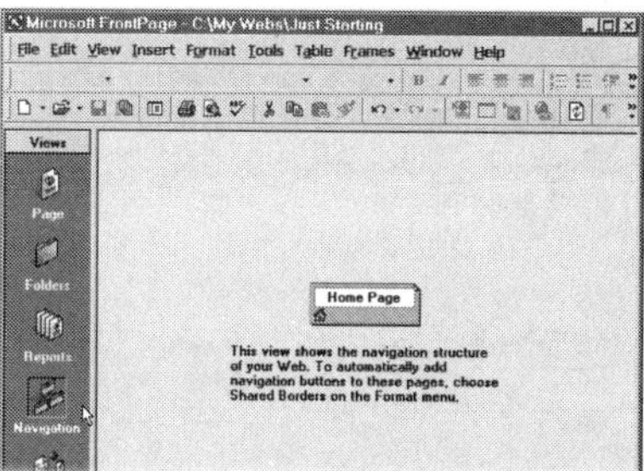

Figure 2.81 If you click the Navigation icon in the Views bar, the One Page Web includes a little house icon—a sign that FrontPage has automatically made it the Home Page.

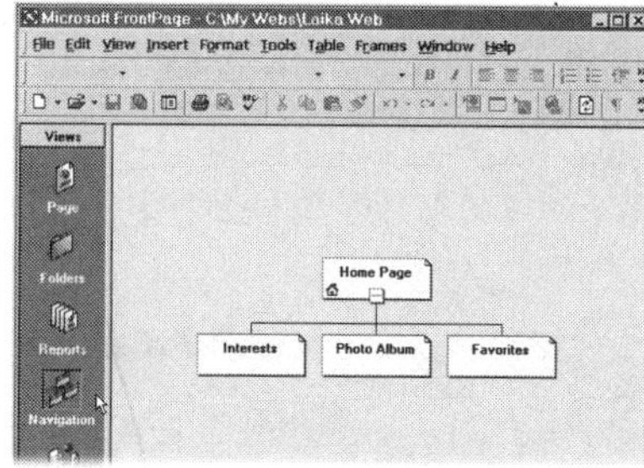

Figure 2.82 To see the *structure* of a new multiple-page Web site, click the Navigation icon in the Views bar.

✔ Tips

- To see the *structure* of your new Web site, click the Navigation icon in the Views bar (**Figures 2.81** and **2.82**).
- If you choose the One Page Web as your Web site template, FrontPage automatically makes it the Home Page—marked by a little house icon (**Figure 2.81**).

To open an existing Web site

1. Choose File > Open Web (**Figure 2.83**).
2. When the Open Web dialog box appears, use the *Look in* drop-down menu, the *Up One Level* icon, or any of the left pane's icons to find a Web site you've stored on your local hard drive or internal network (**Figure 2.84**). Click *Open*.
3. When the Web opens, click the *Folders* icon to see all the Web site's files or click the *Navigation* icon to see its structure (**Figures 2.85** and **2.86**). You're ready to begin adding pages to the site's structure or content to individual pages.

✔ Tip

- You also can open and download a Web site posted on the Internet.

To close a Web site

- Choose File > Close Web (**Figure 2.87**). The current Web site closes.

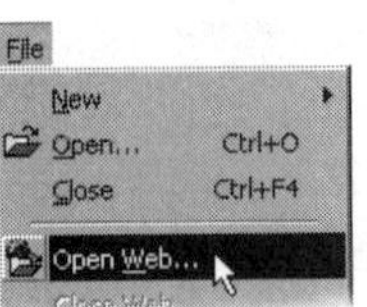

Figure 2.83 Choose File > Open Web to open an existing Web site.

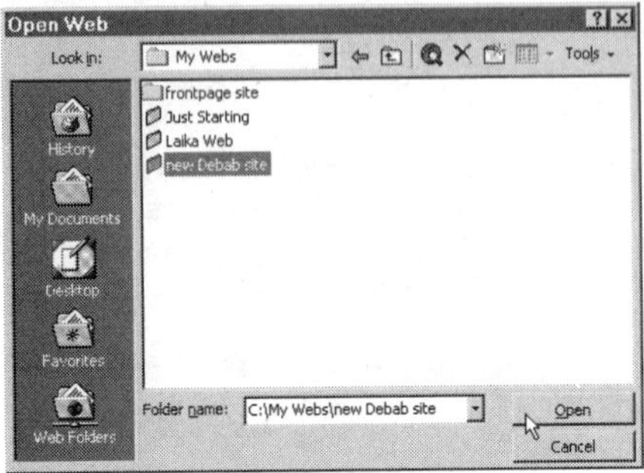

Figure 2.84 When the Open Web dialog box appears, navigate to an existing Web site and click *Open*.

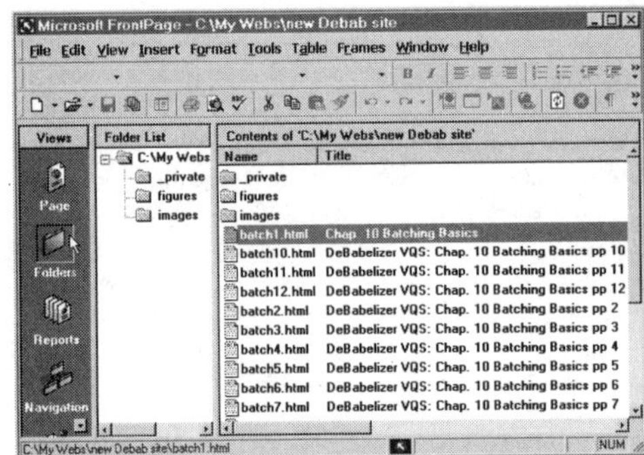

Figure 2.85 Click the *Folders* icon to see all of a Web site's files.

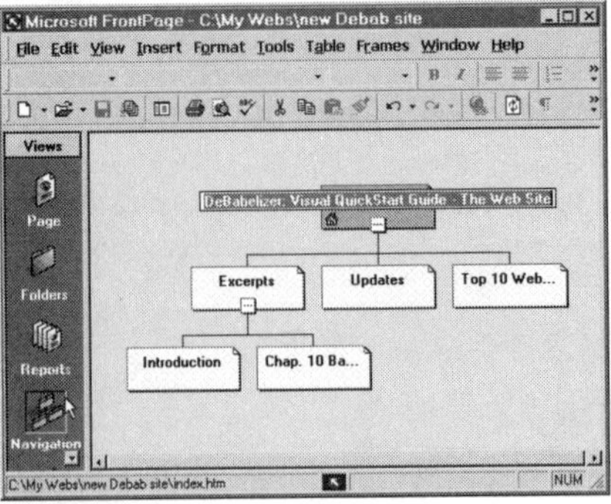

Figure 2.86 Click the *Navigation* icon to see a Web site's structure.

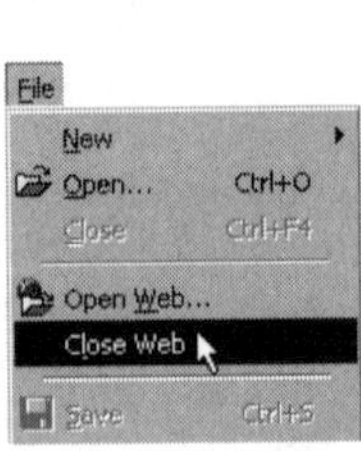

Figure 2.87 Choose File > Close Web to close a Web site.

3

Creating a Web Site

As explained in Chapter 1, some upfront thought about your Web site's purpose and audience will save you a lot of time and headaches once you actually begin creating your site. Assuming you've done your planning, this chapter walks you through the actual creation of your site.

FrontPage's navigation view offers some great tools to help you quickly create a site—and restructure it if you change your mind midway through. Because FrontPage preserves the links among pages even as you restructure the site, it's easy to experiment with various options until you're satisfied.

To add pages to a Web site structure

1. Once you open a Web site (see page 38), switch to navigation view by clicking the Navigation icon in the Views pane (**Figure 3.1**).
2. Within the navigation pane, click on the page to which you want to add a page (**Figure 3.2**). The selected page will change from yellow to blue.
3. Right-click and choose *New Page* from the shortcut menu (**Figure 3.2**). You also can add a new page by pressing Ctrl N. The new page will appear with a generic name (**Figure 3.3**).
4. Continue adding pages until you've roughed out as much of the Web site as you want (**Figure 3.4**). You're now ready to title, rename, and rearrange your Web site's new pages.

✔ Tip

- To give yourself more screen space to work with, you may want to hide the Folder List pane by choosing View > Folder List or by clicking the Folders icon (**Figure 3.5**).

Figure 3.1 Click the Navigation icon in the Views pane to switch to navigation view.

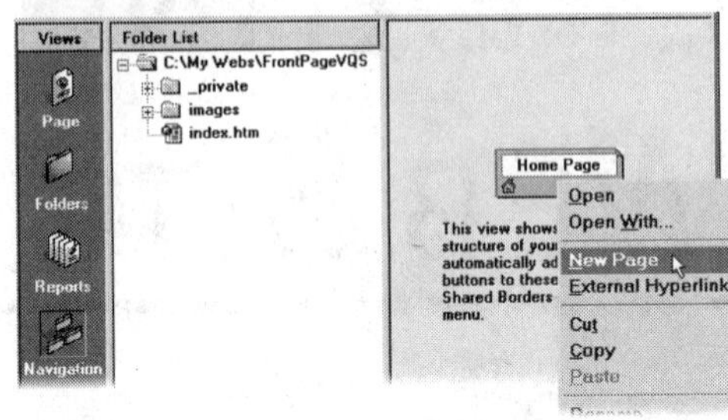

Figure 3.2 To add a new page to your Web structure, right-click and choose *New Page* from the shortcut menu (or press Ctrl N).

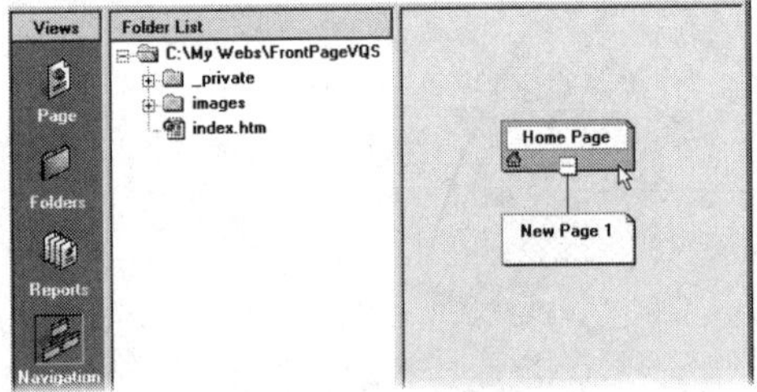

Figure 3.3 The new page, with a generic name, will appear attached to the selected page.

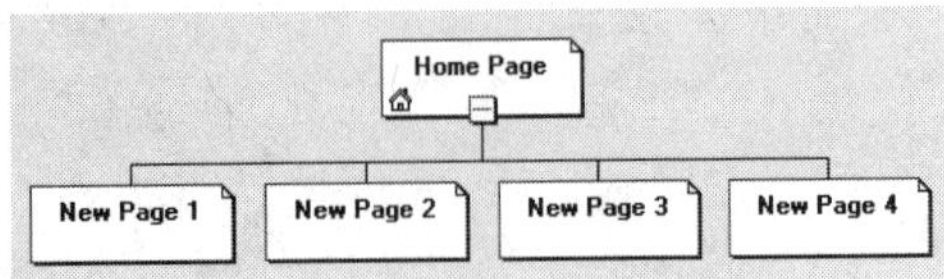

Figure 3.4 By using the New Page command repeatedly, you can quickly rough out a Web site structure.

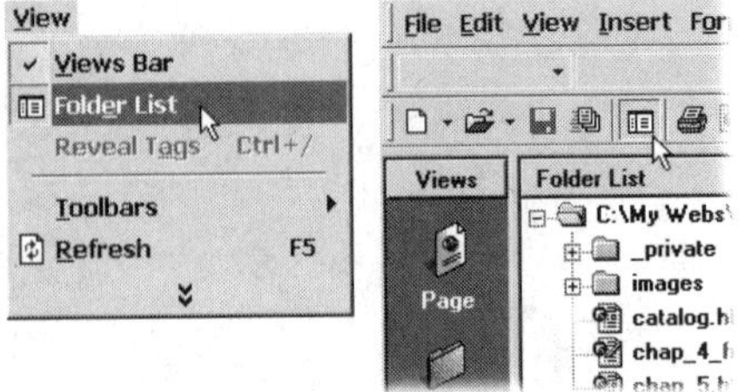

Figure 3.5 Hide site folders and files by choosing View > Folder List (left) or by clicking the Folders icon (right).

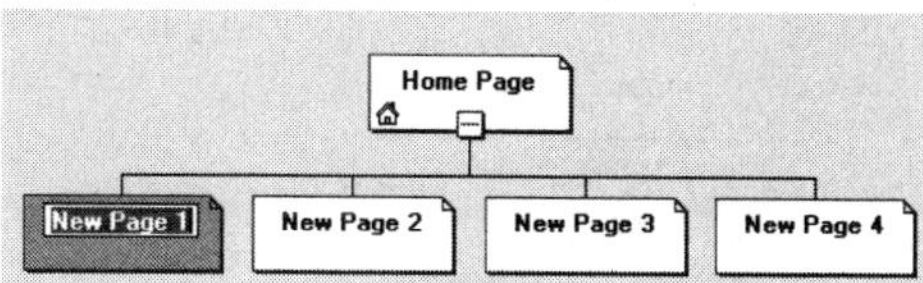

Figure 3.6 To give each new page a distinctive title, press Tab to move to the desired page. When the name becomes highlighted, type in a new title, then press Enter.

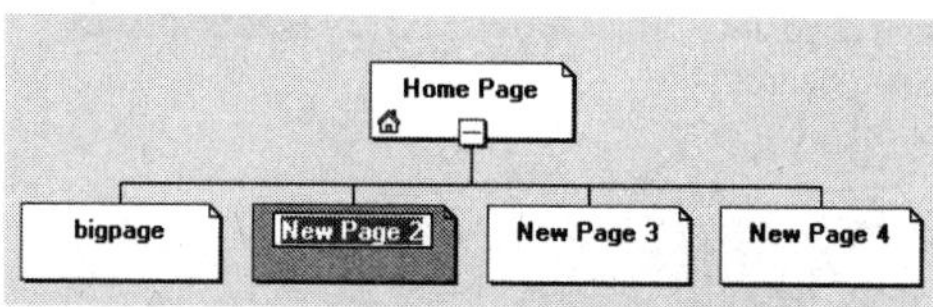

Figure 3.7 Press Tab or Enter to move from page to page and continue giving each a distinct title.

To give a new page a title

1. To give each new page a distinctive title (see *Tips* on next page), press Tab to move to the desired page. The name of the page will become highlighted (**Figure 3.6**).
2. Type in a new name and press Enter or press Tab to move to the next page you want to retitle (**Figure 3.7**).

✔ Tips

- You also can retitle any page by right-clicking it and choosing *Rename* from the shortcut menu (**Figure 3.8**).
- Contrary to what you might expect, changing the name of a page within the right-hand navigation pane doesn't actually rename the page file. It simply changes the page's *title* or what FrontPage also calls the *navigation label.* As long as you remain in the navigation pane, even selecting *Rename* in the short cut menu only changes the page's title—not its file name. Confusing? You bet. To really change the page's file name, see *To rename a Web page*, on the next page.
- If you're ever unsure what a Web page's *title* has become versus its *file name*, switch to page view. Then right-click within the page and choose *Page Properties* from the shortcut menu (**Figure 3.9**). When the Page Properties dialog box opens, compare the file name in the *Location* text box with the name in the *Title* text box (**Figure 3.10**). If the title's not what you intended it to be called, type a new one into the *Title* window. If the file name's not correct, see *To rename a Web page* on the next page.

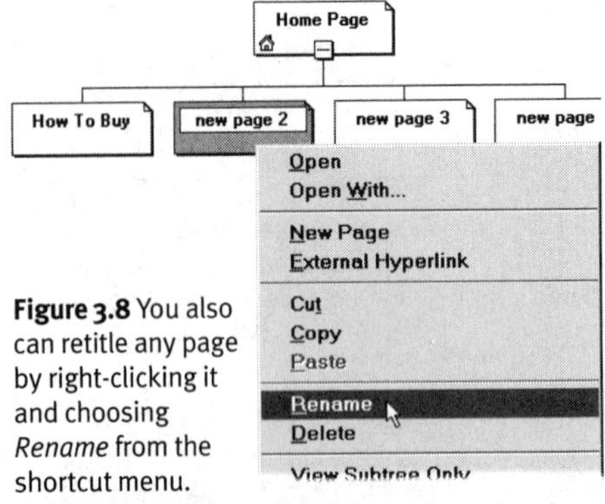

Figure 3.8 You also can retitle any page by right-clicking it and choosing *Rename* from the shortcut menu.

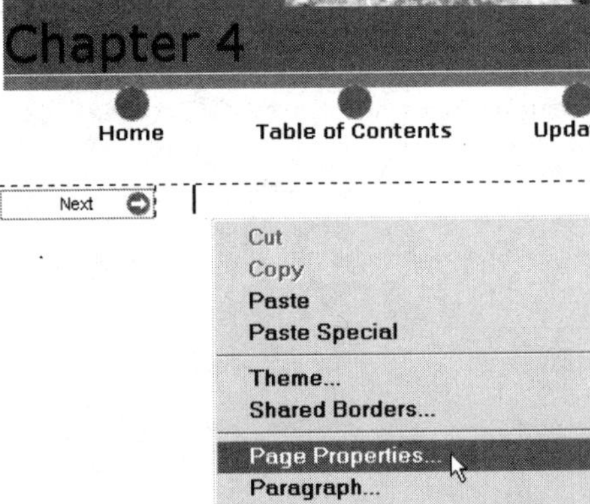

Figure 3.9 To check what a file's really named, right-click within the page and choose *Page Properties* from the shortcut menu.

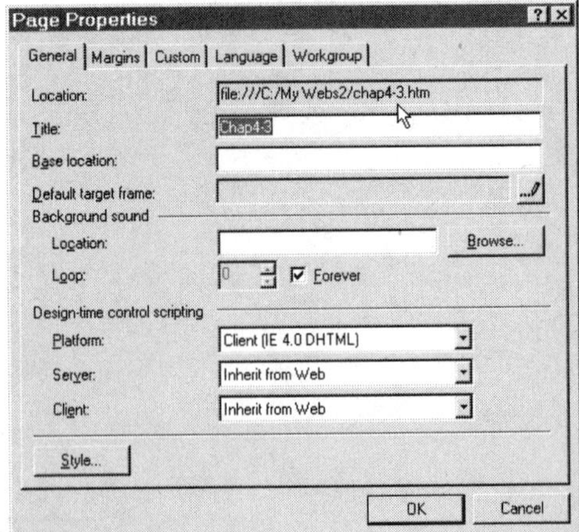

Figure 3.10 The Page Properties dialog box lets you compare the file name (in the *Location* box) with the title (in the *Title* box).

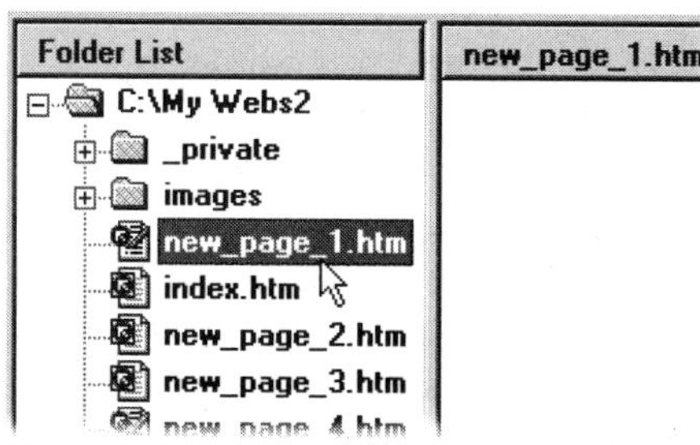

Figure 3.11 To rename a Web page, click *inside* the Folder List pane on the file you want to rename.

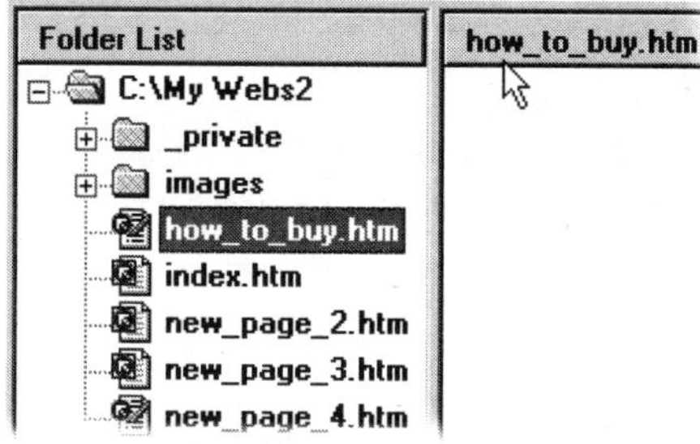

Figure 3.12 Once you rename a file, the new name appears in the Folder List pane and atop the right pane.

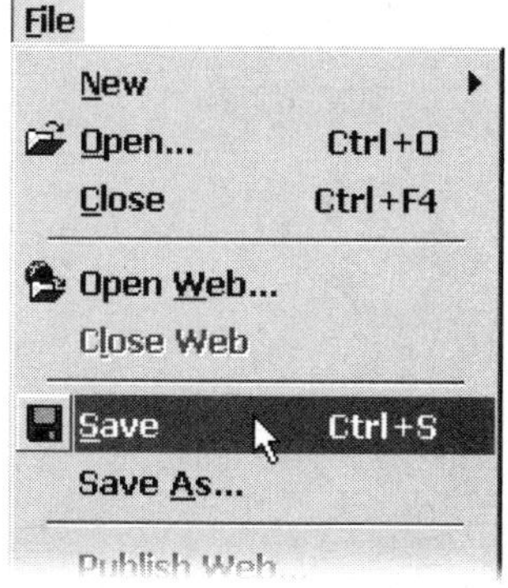

Figure 3.13 To save the name, choose File > Save (Ctrl S).

To rename a Web page

1. Make sure the Folder List is visible by choosing View > Folder List or by clicking the Folder icon (**Figure 3.5**).
2. Click *inside* the Folder List pane on the file you want to rename (**Figure 3.11**).
3. With the file highlighted, type in a new name. Make sure to end it with `.htm` and press Enter. The file's name changes in the Folder List pane and also appears atop the right pane (**Figure 3.12**).
4. Choose File > Save (Ctrl S) (**Figure 3.13**).

Rearranging a Web Site's Structure

The ability to let you quickly restructure your Web site while preserving links between pages is one of FrontPage's best features. Such rearranging is done in the navigation view, where FrontPage presents an easy to understand set of linked boxes, much like an organization chart. This is very handy when you're roughing out a new site and want to experiment with different structures. Move a page—or a whole group of pages— and see if you like it. If not, you can easily move it again.

To rearrange a single page

1. If you're not already in navigation view, click the Navigation icon in the Views pane (**Figure 3.1**).
2. Click inside the right-hand pane on the page you want to move. The page will turn from yellow to blue (**Figure 3.14**).
3. As you drag the page, FrontPage will draw a gray line to possible new destinations for the page (**Figure 3.15**). Continue dragging the page until the line connects to your intended destination (**Figure 3.16**).
4. Release the cursor and the page will move from its original position to its new place in the Web site's structure (**Figure 3.17**).

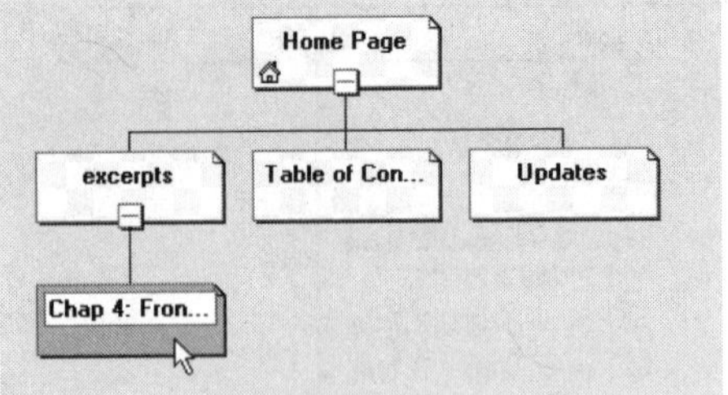

Figure 3.14 To move a page, first click inside the Navigation pane and the page will change color.

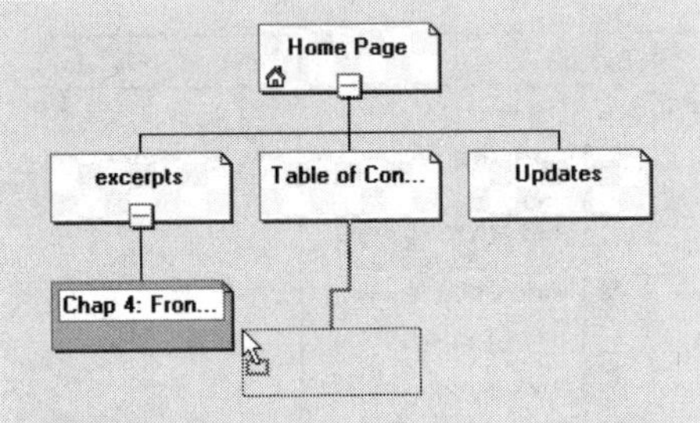

Figure 3.15 As you drag the selected page, a gray line will indicate possible new page destinations.

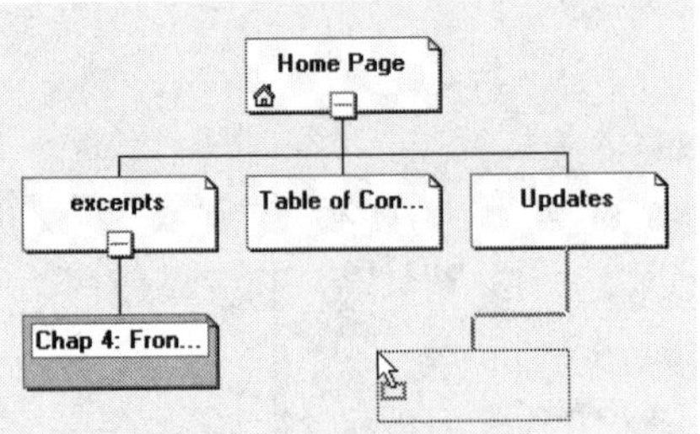

Figure 3.16 Continue dragging the page until the line connects to your intended destination.

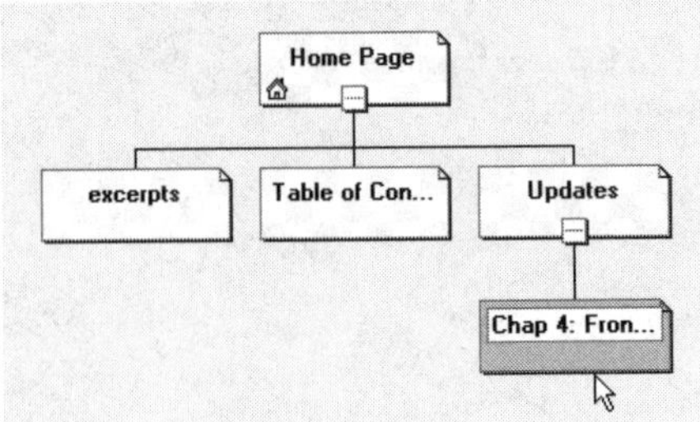

Figure 3.17 Release the cursor and the page will move from its original position to its new place in the Web site's structure.

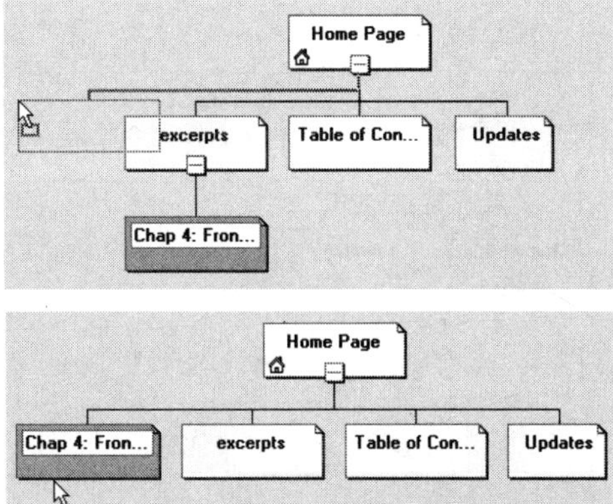

Figure 3.18 To move a page up a level, click and drag the page until a gray line connects it to the same level as its parent page (top). Release the cursor and the page will move to the new spot (bottom).

✔ Tips

- To move a page up a level, click and drag the page until a gray line connects it to the same level as its parent page. Release the cursor and the page will move up a level (**Figure 3.18**).
- To move a page to a site's *top* level, click and drag the page until a gray line connects it to the uppermost page. Release the cursor and the selected page will move to the top level.

To rearrange groups of pages

1. If you're not already in navigation view, click the Navigation icon in the Views pane (**Figure 3.1**).
2. Click inside the right-hand pane on the top page of the subtree of pages you want to move. The page will turn from yellow to blue.
3. Drag the top page of the subtree to a new destination. As you drag the page, FrontPage will draw a gray line to possible new destinations for the page and its subtree (**Figure 3.19**).
4. Release the cursor and the page, along with its entire subtree, will move from its original position to its new place in the Web site's structure (**Figure 3.20**).

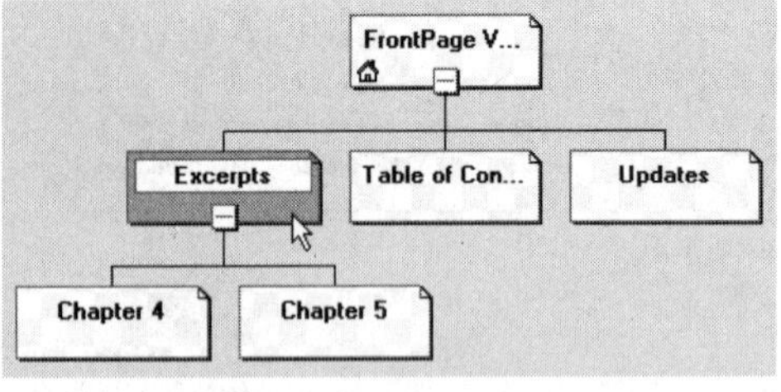

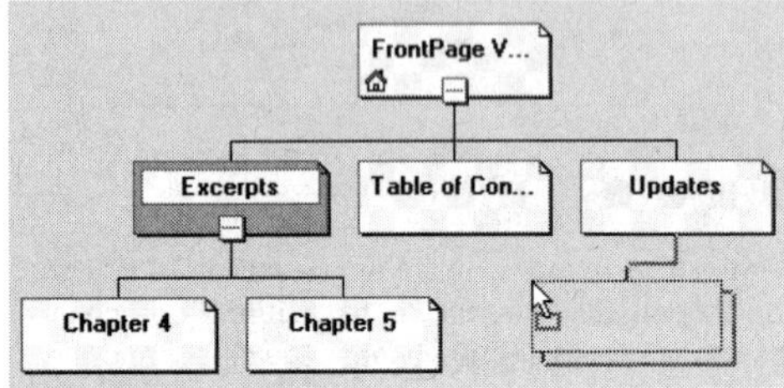

Figure 3.19 To rearrange a group of pages, click the top page of the subtree you want to move and drag it to a new destination.

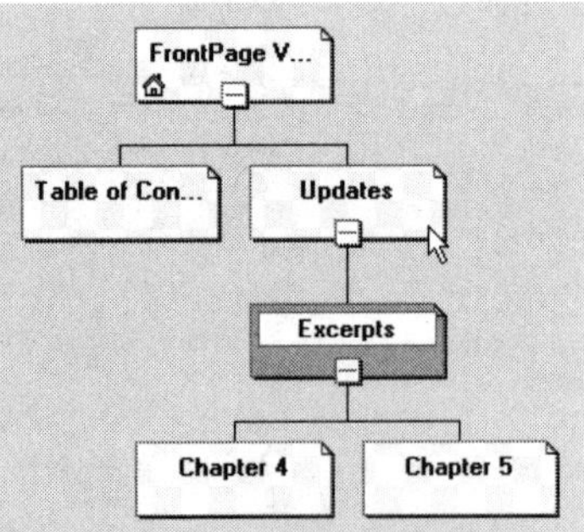

Figure 3.20 Once you release the cursor, the page and its entire subtree will move to its new place in the Web site's structure.

Figure 3.21 Even when a subtree is collapsed (indicated by a ⊞ icon), you can move it by clicking and dragging the visible page.

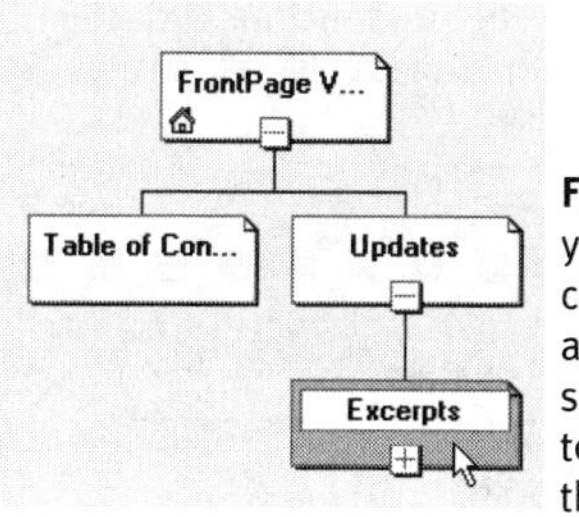

Figure 3.22 When you release the cursor, the page and its hidden subtree will move to the new spot in the site structure.

✔ Tip

- You can move a subtree even when it's collapsed (indicated by a ⊞ icon on the visible page) by dragging the visible page to the desired place in the site structure (**Figures 3.21** and **3.22**). For details on collapsing and expanding site subtrees, see *Controlling Your View of the Site Structure* on the next page.

Controlling Your View of the Site Structure

When you're first setting up a Web site, you'll spend a lot of time in navigation view. For that very reason, FrontPage gives you lots of choices for viewing your Web site's structure. You can look at the entire structure or just a portion. You can zoom in or out in viewing the site, or flip the view from vertical to horizontal. Whether you view the site vertically or horizontally simply depends on which makes more sense for you—there's no right or wrong.

To collapse the site structure

- While in navigation view, click a page's ⊟ icon to *hide* every page below it (**Figure 3.23**). All pages below the icon will disappear from view (**Figure 3.24**).

To expand the site structure

- While in navigation view, click a page's ⊞ icon to *show* every page below it (**Figure 3.24**). Any pages hidden below the page will reappear (**Figure 3.23**).

✔ Tip

- If the Navigation toolbar is active, you can expand or collapse the structure by clicking the toolbar's subtree icon (**Figure 3.25**).

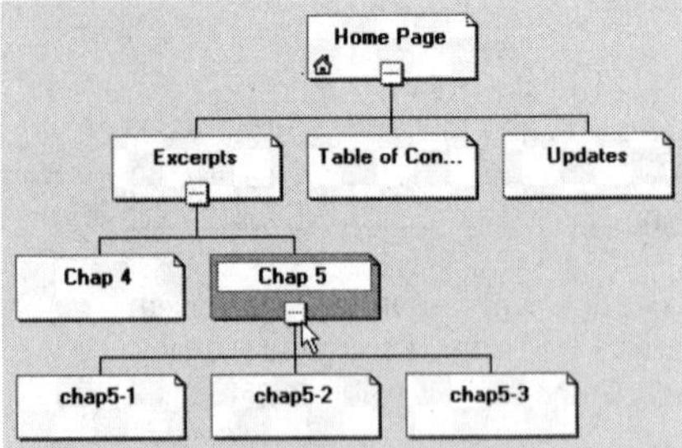

Figure 3.23 To collapse the site structure, click a page's ⊟ icon to hide the pages below it.

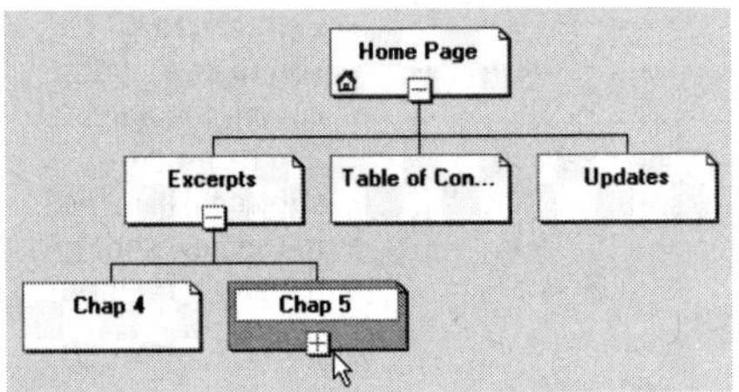

Figure 3.24 Pages with a ⊞ icon indicate that there are more pages hidden from view.

Figure 3.25 To quickly expand or collapse the site structure, click the Navigation toolbar's subtree icon.

Controlling Views of Structure

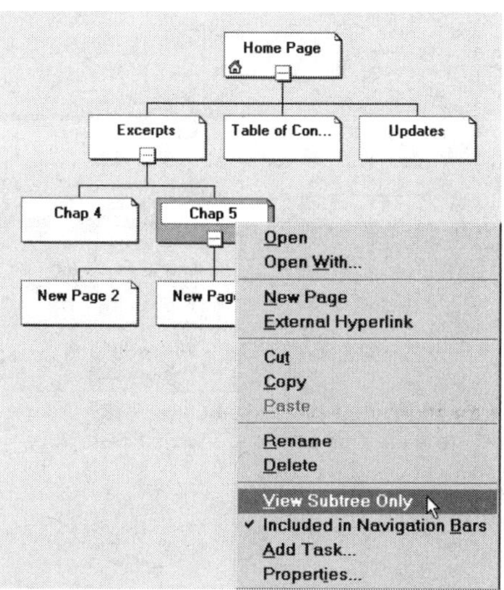

Figure 3.26 To view only the subtree of a selected page, right-click and choose *View Subtree Only* from the shortcut menu.

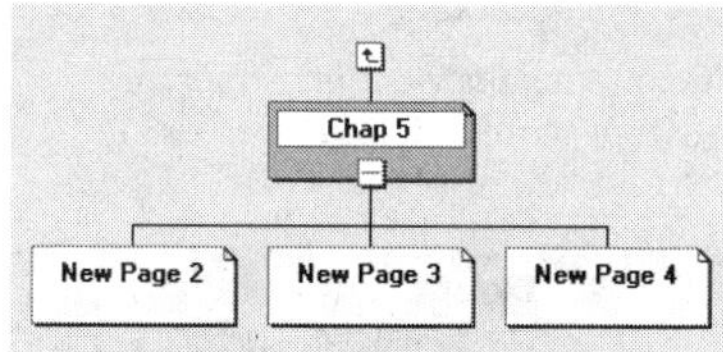

Figure 3.27 When you choose *View Subtree Only*, all the pages above the selected page will be hidden.

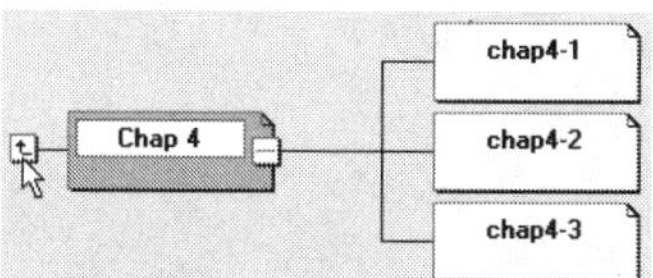

Figure 3.28 To expand a subtree, click the arrow extending from the subtree's top-level page.

To view only a subtree

1. While in navigation view, click the page on which you want to focus.
2. With the page still selected, right-click and choose *View Subtree Only* from the shortcut menu (**Figure 3.26**). All the pages *above* the selected page's level will be hidden (**Figure 3.27**).

To expand a subtree

- While in navigation view, click the arrow extending from the subtree's top-level page (**Figure 3.28**). The entire site's structure will appear (**Figure 3.29**).

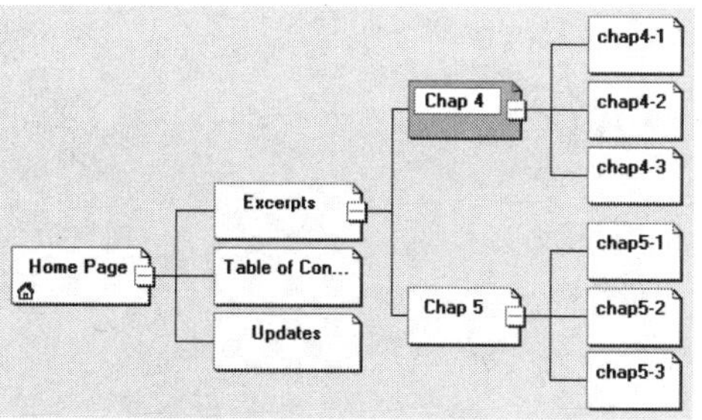

Figure 3.29 After clicking the subtree icon, the entire site's structure will appear.

To rotate the site structure view

◆ While in navigation view, right-click anywhere in the right pane and choose *Rotate* from the shortcut menu (**Figure 3.30**). Depending on your current view, the site's structure will switch from vertical to horizontal or vice versa (**Figure 3.31**). To return the orientation to its original position, choose *Rotate* again.

✔ Tip

■ If the Navigation toolbar is active, you can toggle your view of the structure by clicking the Portrait/Landscape icon (**Figure 3.32**).

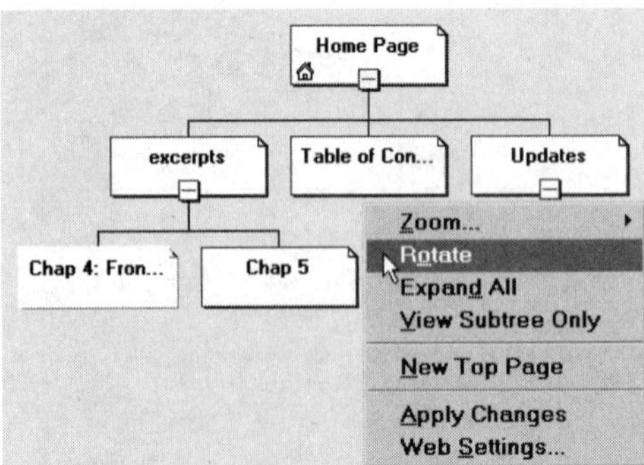

Figure 3.30 To rotate the navigation view, right-click anywhere in the right pane and choose *Rotate* from the shortcut menu.

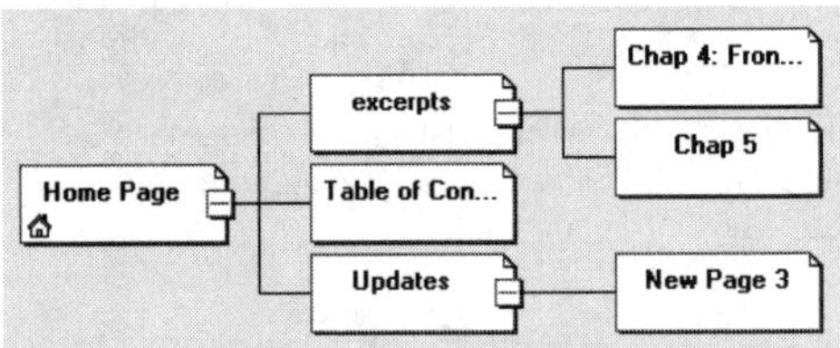

Figure 3.31 After rotating the view, the structure appears in landscape mode.

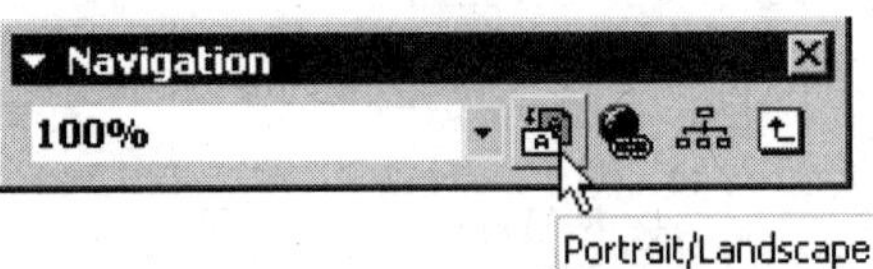

Figure 3.32 To quickly toggle your view of the site's structure, click the Navigation toolbar's Portrait/Landscape icon.

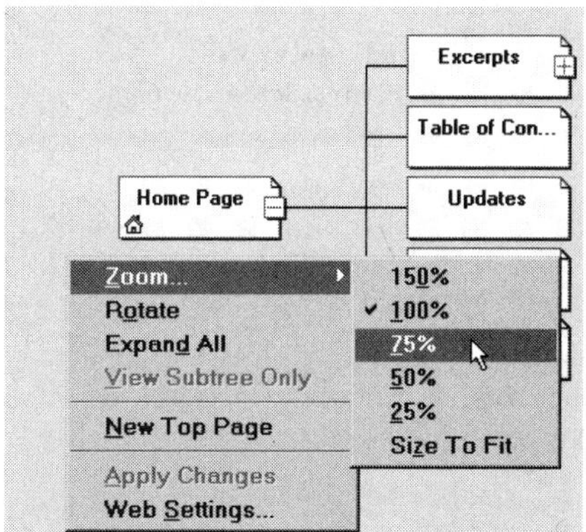

Figure 3.33 To zoom the navigation view in or out, right-click in the navigation pane, point to *Zoom*, and choose a percentage or *Size To Fit* in the shortcut menu.

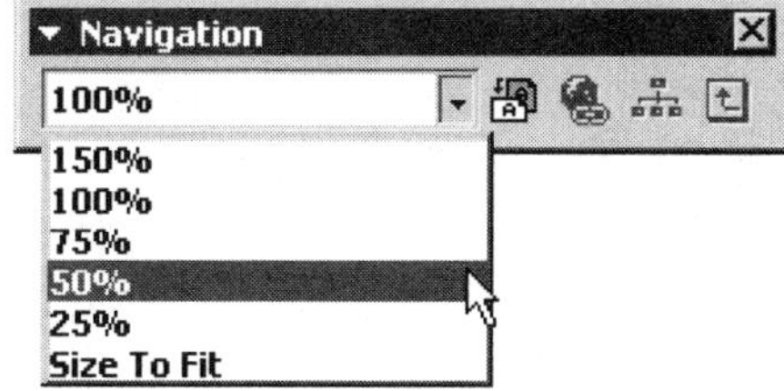

Figure 3.34 To quickly zoom in or out on the site's structure, click the Navigation toolbar's drop-down menu.

To zoom in or out on the site structure

◆ Right-click on a blank spot in the navigation pane, point to *Zoom*, and choose a percentage or *Size To Fit* your monitor view in the shortcut menu (**Figure 3.33**). The view will change to reflect your choice.

✔ Tip

- If the Navigation toolbar is active, you can zoom in or out using the preset percentages on the toolbar's drop-down menu (**Figure 3.34**).

Creating Shared Navigation Bars

FrontPage includes two powerful features—shared borders and navigation bars—that let you quickly create "live" hyperlinks among your Web site's main pages. The links are live in the sense that they're automatically updated even when you completely rearrange your site's structure.

Setting up shared borders and navigation bars can be fairly confusing the first time through. It's essentially a two-step process: First you set up your site's shared borders, which are areas on each page in a Web site set aside for common, or shared, information. In the second step, you add navigation bars to the shared borders and define what links the bars will display.

Whenever you change the site's structure, the links within the navigation bar are updated automatically. Best of all, FrontPage gives you precise control over which pages are linked, based on their *structural* relationship to each other. For example, you can ask FrontPage to generate hyperlinks to any page *above* the selected page (known as a *parent* page), to all pages on the same level as the selected page, or to any page *below* its level (a *child* page) (**Figure 3.35**).

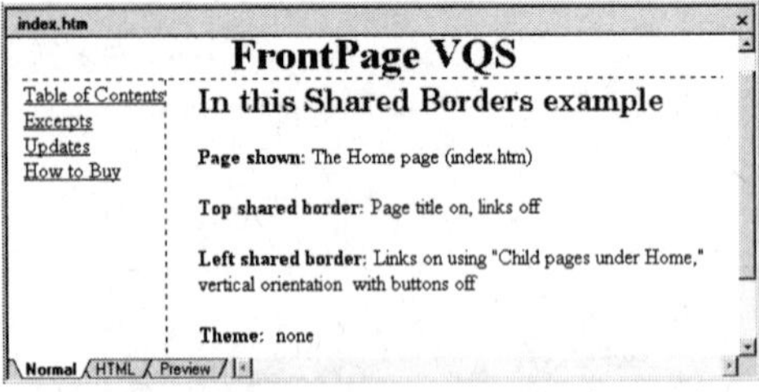

Figure 3.35 Using FrontPage's shared borders and navigation bars, you quickly can generate hyperlinks among your site's main pages.

While you could set up your navigation bars and then create your Web site's structure, it's far easier to create most of your site structure first and then set up the navigation bars. So if you haven't already roughed out your site's structure, see *Creating a Web Site* on page 41.

While this section focuses on combining navigation bars with shared borders to create *site-wide* links, FrontPage also can create navigation bars for single pages. For details, see *Using Single-Page Navigation Bars* on page 141. One last thing: Shared borders can only be used for a Web *site*, not single pages. However, you can turn *off* the shared borders for individual pages. For details, see *To turn off shared borders for single pages* on page 59.

Besides using them with navigation bars, shared borders also are a great place to put any site-wide information that may need regular updating. Obvious candidates include contact numbers, copyright notices, or company logos. With shared borders, you can change the information in one place and it's automatically updated on every page.

To add shared borders

1. Make sure you've already opened the Web site for which you want to set navigation borders, then choose Format > Shared Borders (**Figure 3.36**).
2. When the Shared Borders dialog box appears, choose the *All pages* radio button. To set where on the page the bar will appear, check *Top* or *Left* and the related *Include navigation buttons* box (**Figure 3.43**). (You also can check both *Top* and *Left*.) A dashed line will appear within the dialog box showing where the navigation bar (or bars) will appear. For details on the *Right* and *Bottom* choices, see the *Tips* below.
3. Once you've made your choices, click *OK*. The shared borders will be set, though you still need to set which hyperlinks will appear in the navigation bars. For details see *To set links for site-wide navigation bars* on the next page.

✔ Tips

- Only the *Top* and *Left* choices in the Shared Borders dialog box let you show hyperlinks to other pages—and only if you also check *Include navigation buttons*, even if you only want text links (**Figure 3.37**). The *Right* and *Bottom* choices are used to insert comments or graphics on your pages. For details, see *Adding Hyperlinks* on page 117.
- If you want your navigation bar hyperlinks to be graphical buttons, instead of just text, you'll need to either create your own buttons or use one of FrontPage's built-in graphic themes (**Figure 3.38**). For details, see *Adding and Editing Images* on page 143 or *To apply themes* on page 64.

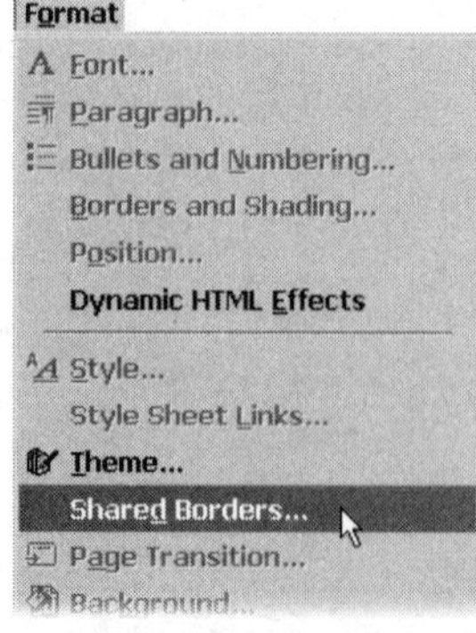

Figure 3.36 To create site-wide navigation bars, first define the areas common to every page by choosing Format > Shared Borders.

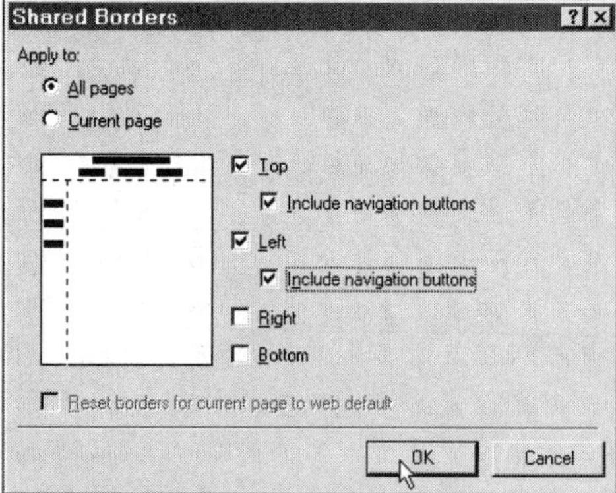

Figure 3.37 When the Shared Borders dialog box appears, choose the *All pages* radio button, then check *Top* or *Left* (or both) and the related *Include navigation buttons* check boxes. Dashed lines show where the shared areas will appear.

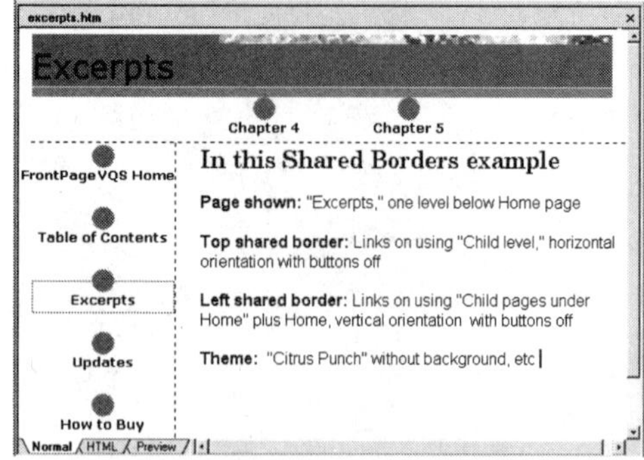

Figure 3.38 By using FrontPage's built-in themes, you can quickly give your site-wide navigation bars a consistent graphical appearance.

CREATING NAVIGATION BARS

Figure 3.39 Click the Page icon in the Views bar to switch to the page view.

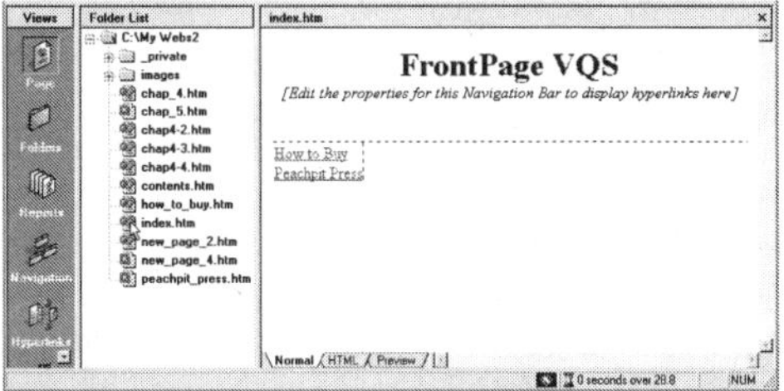

Figure 3.40 Double-click your home page to see your site's preliminary navigation labels.

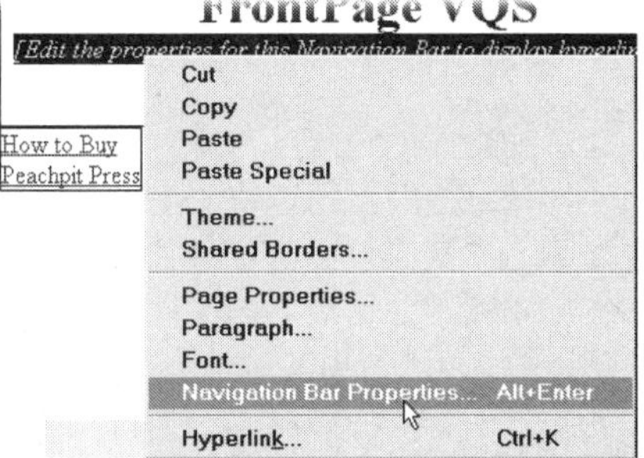

Figure 3.41 To edit a navigation bar's appearance, right-click in the dashed-line area and choose Navigation Bar Properties.

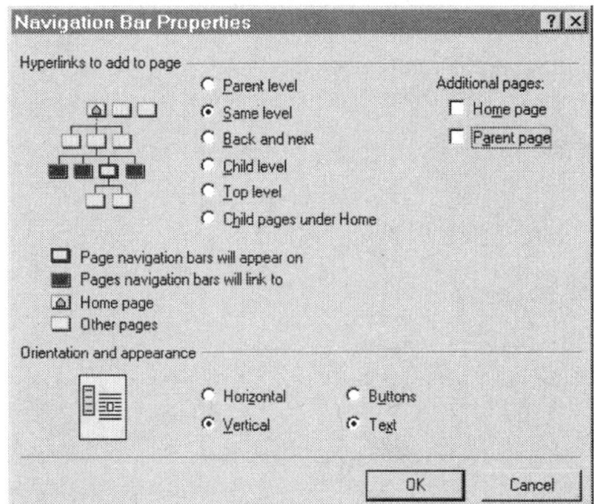

Figure 3.42 Use the Navigation Bar Properties dialog box to choose which hyperlinks you want to appear in the navigation bar.

To set links for site-wide navigation bars

1. To make it easier to keep an eye on your site's overall structure, choose View > Folder List or click the Folder icon (**Figure 3.5**).
2. Click the Page icon in the Views bar to switch to the page view (**Figure 3.39**).
3. Within the Folder List pane, double click `index.htm` (or whatever your site's home page is called). The home page, with its preliminary navigation labels based on your page titles, will appear in the right pane (**Figure 3.40**).
4. To edit the navigation bar's appearance, right-click inside the page's shared border area (marked by a dashed line), and choose Navigation Bar Properties (**Figure 3.41**). Or use your keyboard: Alt Enter.
5. When the Navigation Bar Properties dialog box appears, choose which hyperlinks you want to appear in the navigation bar (**Figure 3.42**). Based on your choices, the squares in the left-hand site tree will change to show which pages relative to the current page will be linked. For details, see *Navigation Bar options* on the next page.
6. When you've finished setting the hyperlink, save your work by choosing File > Save (Ctrl S).

Navigation Bar options

The Navigation Bar Properties dialog box gives you precise control over which pages will be automatically hyperlinked by your site's navigation bars (**Figure 3.42**). It also lets you control the appearance of those links.

- **Hyperlinks to add to a page:** This section gives you six choices for which pages will be linked. The pages highlighted in the dialog box's site tree diagram change to reflect your choice (**Figure 3.43**). The tree doesn't actually show your particular site but simply displays which links will be activated relative to your current page. You can add two other links by clicking the *Additional pages* choices (**Figure 3.44**). In the legend below the tree, the *Page navigation bars will appear on* symbol refers to your current page.
- **Orientation and appearance:** Use this section to further refine your navigation bar links (**Figure 3.45**). While it gives you the choice of displaying the links as buttons, you'll still need to either create your own button graphics or use some of FrontPage's pre-built buttons by applying a page theme. For details, see *Adding and Editing Images* on page 143 or *To apply a theme to a page or Web site* on page 64.

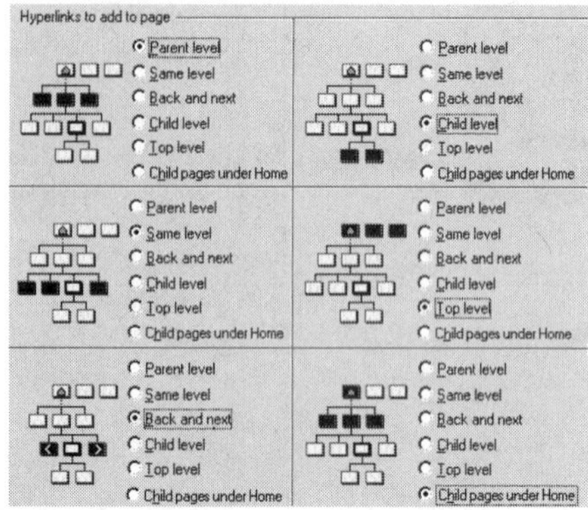

Figure 3.43 Based on your choice, the Navigation Bar Properties dialog box's site tree shows which pages will be hyperlinked to the current page.

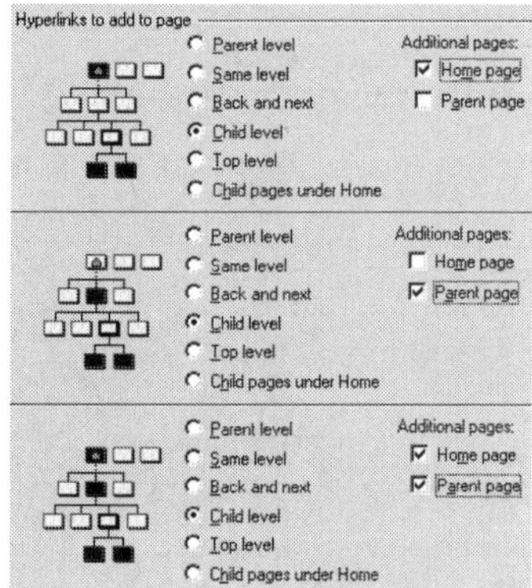

Figure 3.44 Besides the six main hyperlink choices, the Navigation Bar Properties dialog box also lets you include links to the site's *Home page*, your page's *Parent page*, or to both.

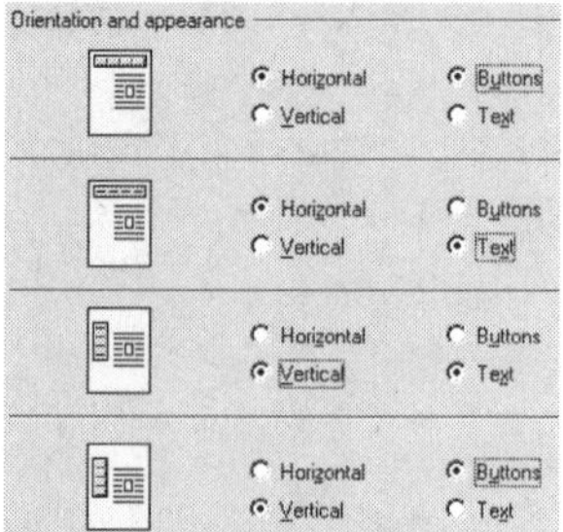

Figure 3.45 In addition to controlling which pages are linked, the Navigation Bar Properties dialog box lets you dictate how the links look.

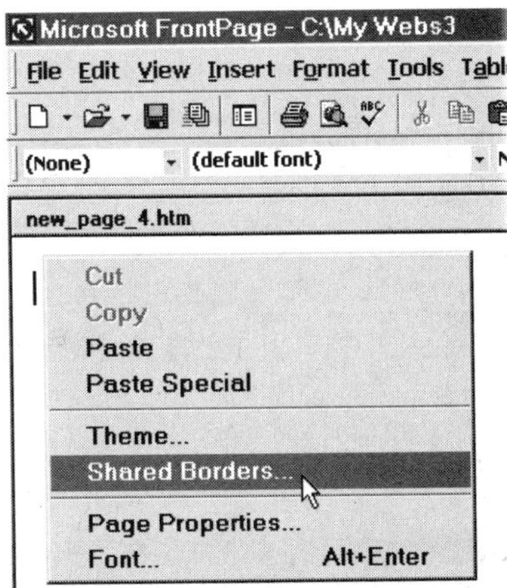

Figure 3.46 To turn off the Shared Borders feature, right-click anywhere in the page and choose *Shared Borders* from the shortcut menu.

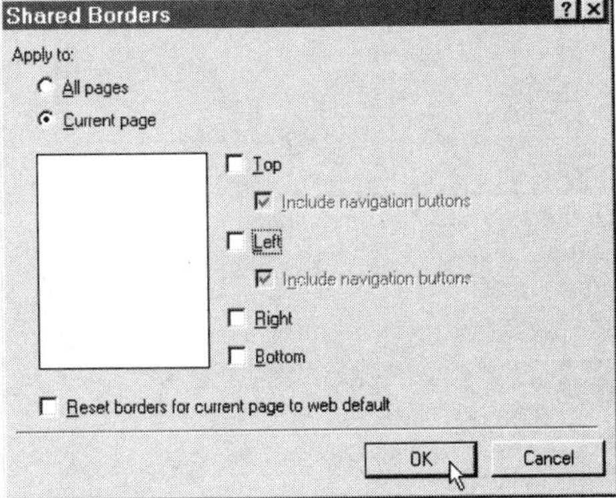

Figure 3.47 To turn off a page's shared border, choose the *Current page* button, uncheck all other boxes, and click *OK*.

To turn off shared borders for single pages

1. Double-click the page in the Folder List pane or the Navigation pane.
2. Right-click anywhere in the page and choose *Shared Borders* from the shortcut menu (**Figure 3.46**).
3. When the Shared Borders dialog box appears, click the *Current page* radio button and uncheck any other boxes (**Figure 3.47**). Click *OK* and the selected page appears without any shared borders.

Changing the default navigation labels

If in the Navigation Bar Properties dialog box you chose *Home page, Parent page, Parent level*, or *Back and next*, FrontPage by default will apply the labels *Home, Up, Back*, and *Next* to any hyperlinks pointing to those pages. Most times, those labels will suit your purposes. However, if you occasionally want more specific labels—*Customer Service* instead of *Home* or *Return to last page* instead of *Back*—FrontPage lets you customize to your heart's content.

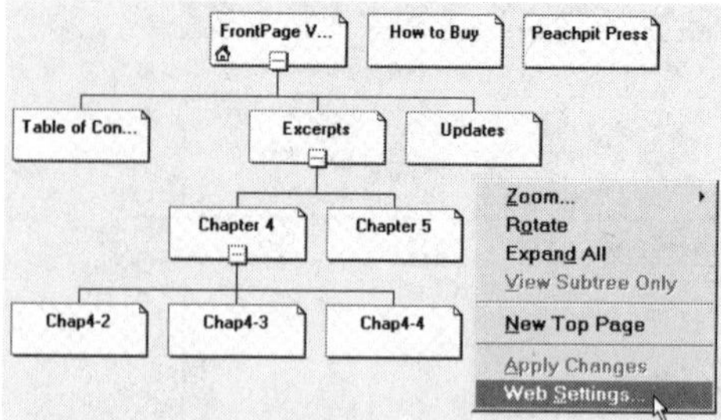

Figure 3.48 To change the default navigation labels, right-click in the right pane and choose *Web Settings* from the shortcut menu.

To change the navigation labels

1. Click the Navigation icon in the Views bar to switch to the navigation view.
2. Right-click on any blank spot in the right pane and choose *Web Settings* (**Figure 3.48**).
3. When the Web Settings dialog box appears, click the *Navigation* tab (**Figure 3.49**).
4. Change any or all of the default navigation labels (*Home, Up, Back*, and *Next*) by typing your own labels into each text box (**Figure 3.50**). Click *OK* and these labels will be used when you add site-wide navigation bars.

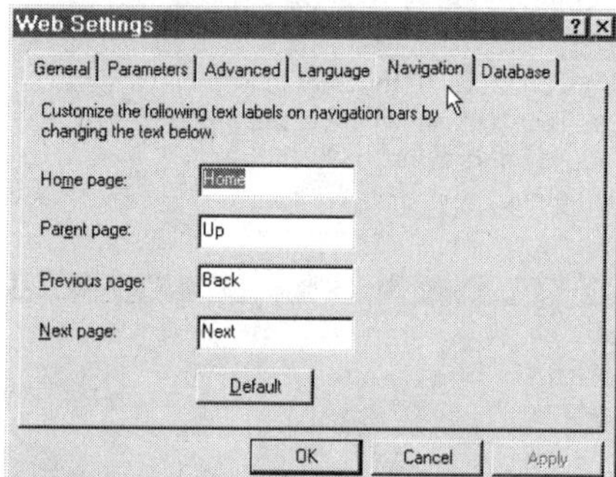

Figure 3.49 Click the *Navigation* tab in the Web Settings dialog box to reach the default navigation labels.

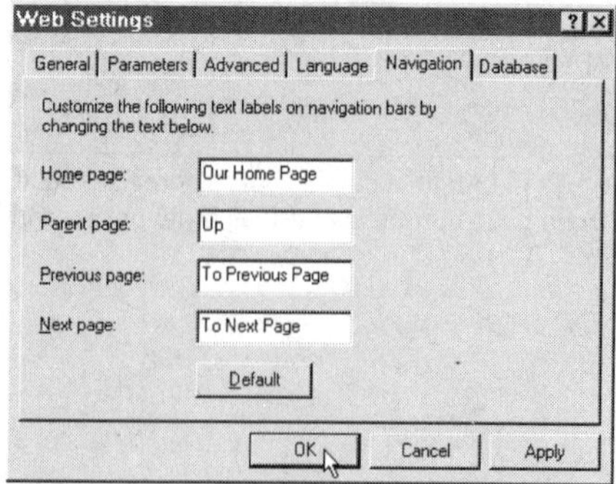

Figure 3.50 Change any of the default labels by typing your own labels into each text box and clicking *OK*. The new labels will be applied to the current Web site only.

✔ Tips

- Your custom navigation labels will be used only in the current Web site, so they won't mess up custom or default labels in your other Web sites.
- If you change your mind about using custom navigation labels, return to the *Navigation* tab in the Web Settings dialog box, click *Default*, and then *OK*. The original *Home, Up, Back*, and *Next* labels will replace the custom labels.

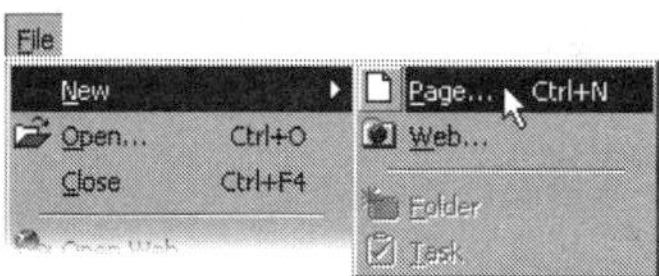

Figure 3.51 To create a Web site from a template, first choose File > New > Page (Ctrl N).

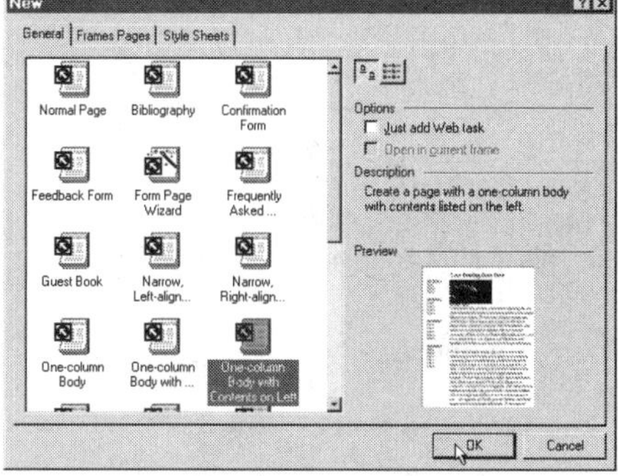

Figure 3.52 The New dialog box's *General* tab offers a variety of page templates. Choose one and click *OK*.

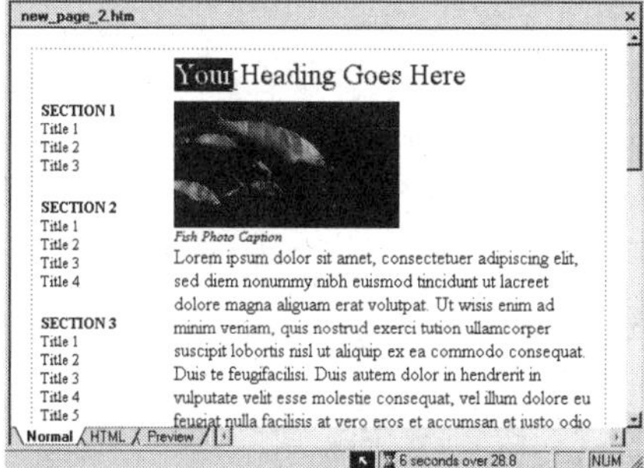

Figure 3.53 Once a template opens, you can begin replacing headings, text, and graphics with your own.

Figure 3.54 To replace a template's picture, right-click on the picture and choose *Picture Properties* from the shortcut menu.

Using Templates and Themes

FrontPage's built-in templates and themes can save you tons of time in producing great-looking pages. Use the templates for building pages and sites, then use the themes to apply graphic touches to a single page or a whole site. To make creation of some of the more complicated templates easier, FrontPage has included several program "wizards" to guide you step-by-step through the process.

To create a page from a template

1. Choose File > New > Page (Ctrl N) (**Figure 3.51**).
2. When the New dialog box appears, click the *General* tab, choose a template for your page, and click the *OK* button (**Figure 3.52**). For help creating form pages, open the *Form Page Wizard* and follow its instructions. For more information on forms, see page 227. (For details on the *Frame Pages* and *Style Sheets* tabs, see pages 212 and 269.)
3. Once the template opens, you can select headings and text, replacing them with your own text (**Figure 3.53**). For details on creating and formatting text, see page 73.
4. To replace a picture, right-click on it and choose *Picture Properties* from the shortcut menu (Alt Enter) (**Figure 3.54**).

(continued)

5. When the Picture Properties dialog box appears (the *General* tab is the default), click *Browse* to navigate to the graphic you want to use instead (**Figure 3.55**). To insert the new graphic, click *OK*. For more on using graphics, see *Adding and Editing Images* on page 143.

6. The new graphic will appear in the template (**Figure 3.56**). To save the page, choose File > Save (Ctrl S), navigate to the folder where you want to save it, then click *Save* (**Figure 3.57**).

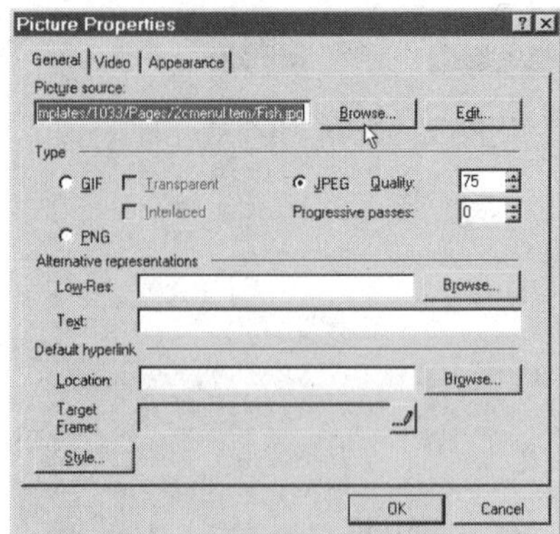

Figure 3.55 When the Picture Properties dialog box appears, click *Browse* to navigate to your replacement graphic.

Figure 3.56 Once you've replaced a template's heads, text, and graphics with your own, choose File > Save (Ctrl S).

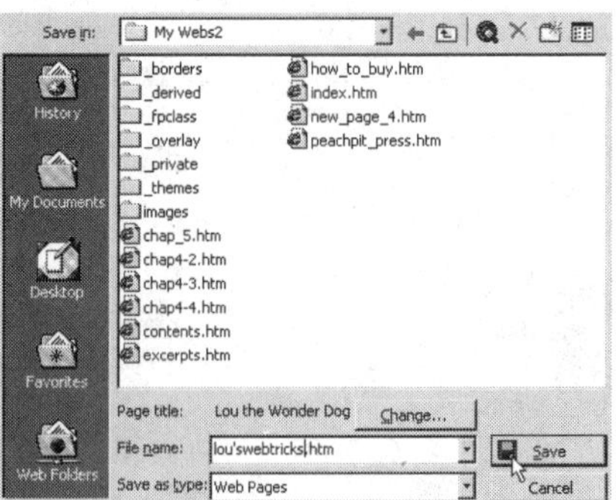

Figure 3.57 Navigate to the folder where you want to save the modified template, then click *Save*.

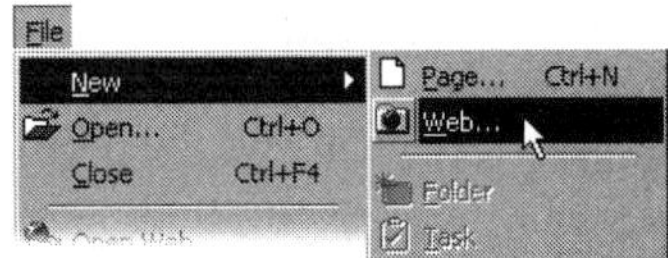

Figure 3.58 To create a Web site from a template, choose File > New > Web (Ctrl N).

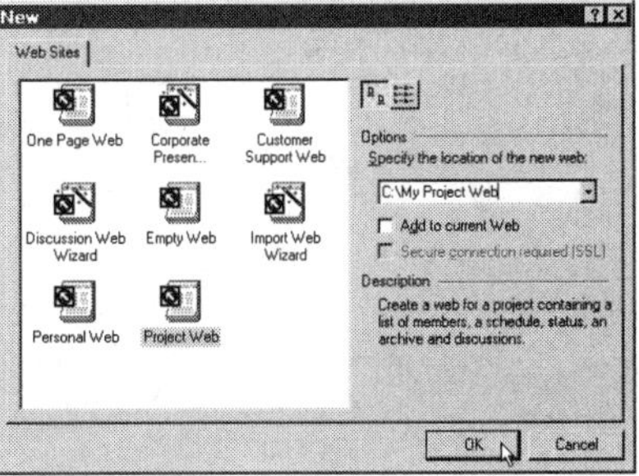

Figure 3.59 Choose a Web site template in the New dialog box, specify where you want it saved, and click *OK*.

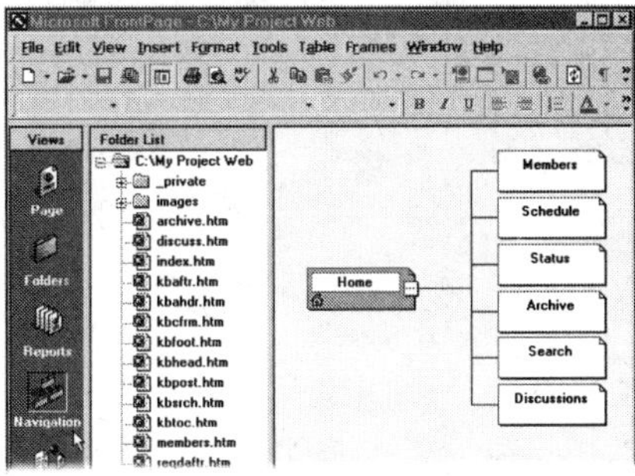

Figure 3.60 Use the Navigation and Folder List icons to see the overall structure and all the pages of your new template-based Web site.

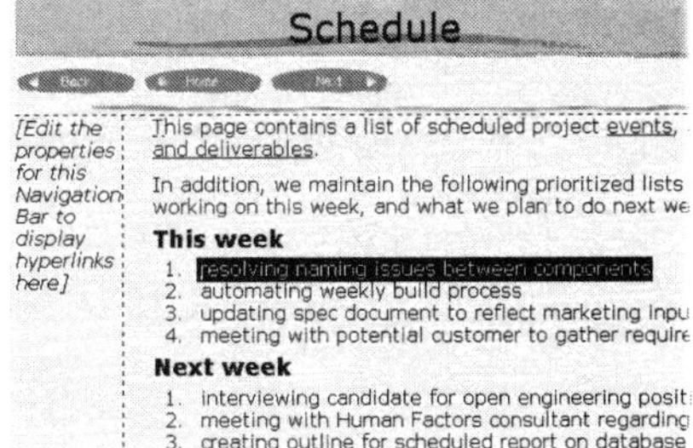

Figure 3.61 Open a page in the template-based Web site and begin substituting your own copy, heads, properties, and graphics. Be sure to save your work with File > Save (Ctrl S).

To create a Web site from a template

1. Choose File > New > Web (Ctrl N) (**Figure 3.58**).
2. When the New dialog box appears, click on one of the Web site templates (**Figure 3.59**). Be sure to specify in the pathname text box where you want it saved, then click *OK*.
3. If the Folder List isn't already visible, click the icon or choose View > Folder. Now click the Navigation icon to see the Web site's overall structure and all its pages (**Figure 3.60**).
4. Double-click on any page in the site to open it and begin substituting your own copy, heads, properties, and graphics (**Figure 3.61**).
5. Save the page by choosing File > Save (Ctrl S). Continue editing other pages in your new template-based Web site until you're done, saving each in turn.

✔ Tip

- You can add a multi-page template to an existing Web site. In the New dialog box (**Figure 3.59**), just be sure to choose the *Add to current Web* checkbox. This enables you, for example, to add a customer support or discussion area to an existing corporate Web site.

To apply a theme to a page or Web site

1. Open a page or Web site to which you want to apply a theme (**Figure 3.62**).
2. Make sure you're in page view, then right-click anywhere in the page, and choose *Theme* from the shortcut menu (**Figure 3.63**).
3. If the page or site does not already have a theme, the sample area will be blank when the Themes dialog box opens (**Figure 3.64**).
4. In the dialog box's upper left, choose one of the two radio buttons to apply a theme to *All pages* or to *Selected page(s)*. By default, it's set to *All pages*, which makes sense since themes mainly are used to give your site a uniform look.

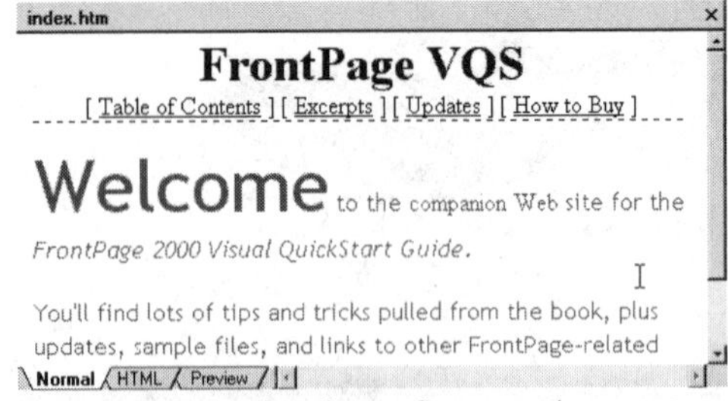

Figure 3.62 To apply a theme, first open the page to which you want it applied.

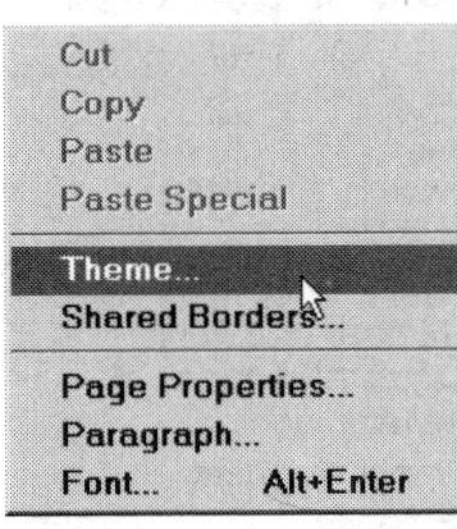

Figure 3.63 To reach the themes, switch to page view, right-click anywhere in the page, and choose *Theme* from the shortcut menu.

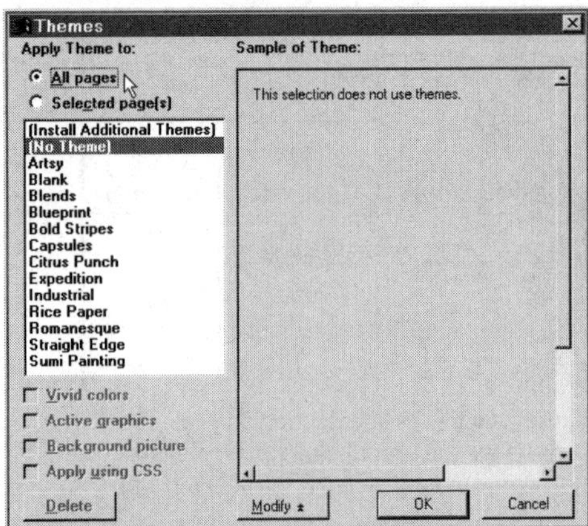

Figure 3.64 If a page or site doesn't already have a theme, the Themes dialog box's sample window will be blank. Choose either *All pages* or *Selected page(s)* in the upper left to control how widely a theme is applied.

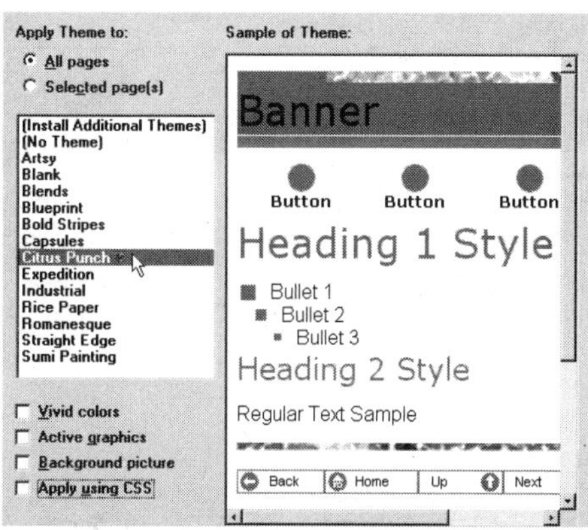

Figure 3.65 Choose a theme in the left-hand list and you'll see a sample of it in the right-hand window.

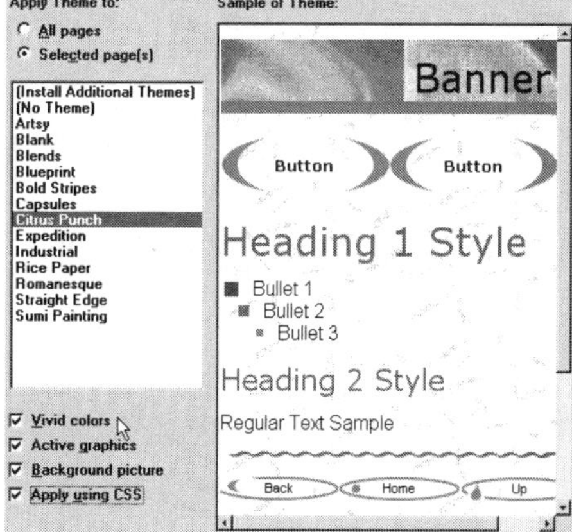

Figure 3.66 The Themes dialog box contains four checkboxes in the lower left—*Vivid colors*, *Active graphics*, *Background picture*, or *Apply using CSS*—that will punch up your pages even more.

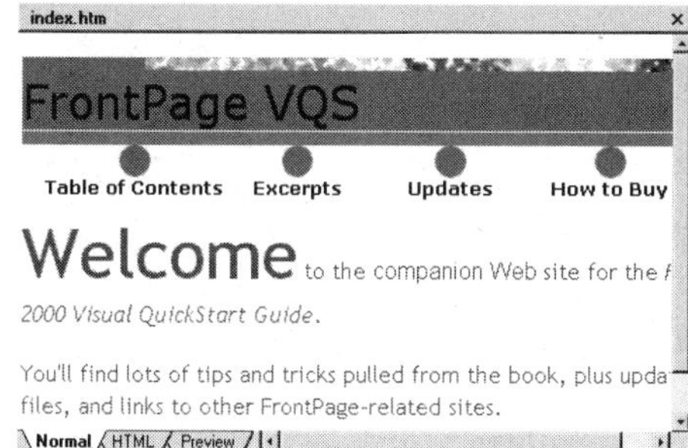

Figure 3.67 A formerly drab page (**Figure 3.62**) after applying FrontPage's Citrus Punch theme.

5. Choose a theme by clicking on it in the left-hand list and you'll see a sample of it in the right-hand window (**Figure 3.65**).
6. You can tweak the theme by choosing any of the four checkboxes in the lower left: *Vivid colors, Active graphics, Background picture*, or *Apply using CSS* (if you're using Cascading Style Sheets). Each effect (except CSS) can be previewed in the right-hand sample window (**Figure 3.66**).
7. Once you've selected a theme and tweaked it to your satisfaction, click *OK* in the Themes dialog box (**Figure 3.64**) and it will be applied to your page or site (**Figure 3.67**). If you want to change the theme even more, see *To modify a theme* on the next page.

✔ Tip

- Even though the Themes dialog box seems to suggest that you can apply a theme to several pages at a time (**Figure 3.64**), you really only have two choices: apply a theme to the single page you have open or to the entire Web site. If you want to apply a theme to just, say, four of your site's pages, you'll have to open each page, one at a time, and then apply the theme to each in turn.

To modify a theme

1. Open a page or Web site whose theme you want to change.
2. Make sure you're in page view, then right-click anywhere in the page, and choose *Theme* from the shortcut menu (**Figure 3.63**).
3. When the Themes dialog box appears, the current theme will automatically appear in the right-hand sample window. If you want to use and modify another theme, click on it in the left-hand column.
4. Click *Modify* at the bottom center of the dialog box (**Figure 3.68**).
5. Just above the Modify button, three buttons will appear: *Colors*, *Graphics*, and *Text* (**Figure 3.69**). Click one of the three (you can come back and modify the other two later if you want).

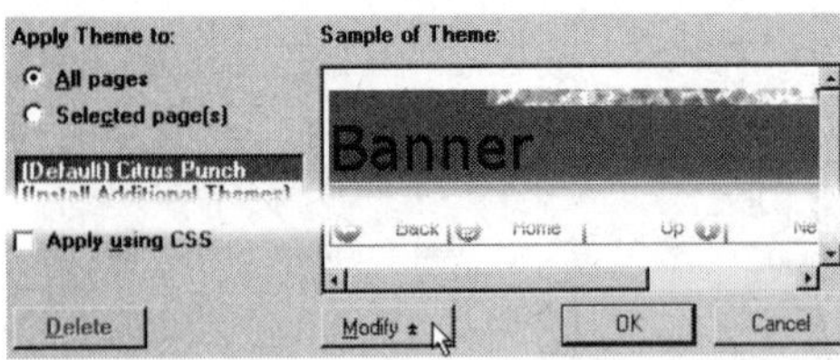

Figure 3.68 Click the *Modify* button at the bottom of the Themes dialog box to customize any theme.

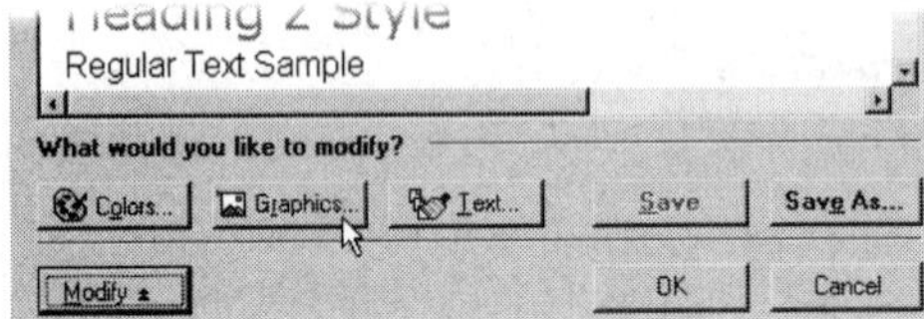

Figure 3.69 FrontPage lets you modify three aspects of a theme: its *Colors*, *Graphics*, or *Text*.

USING TEMPLATES AND THEMES

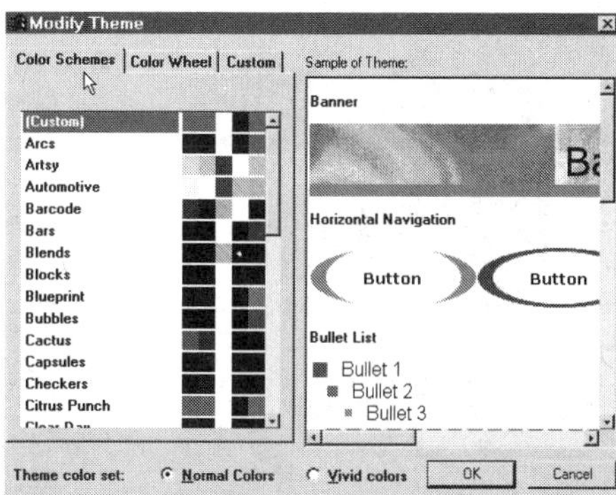

Figure 3.70 The *Color Schemes* tab in the Modify Theme dialog box lets you pick overall combinations and whether you want those colors *Normal* or *Vivid*. The other two tabs set colors for individual items.

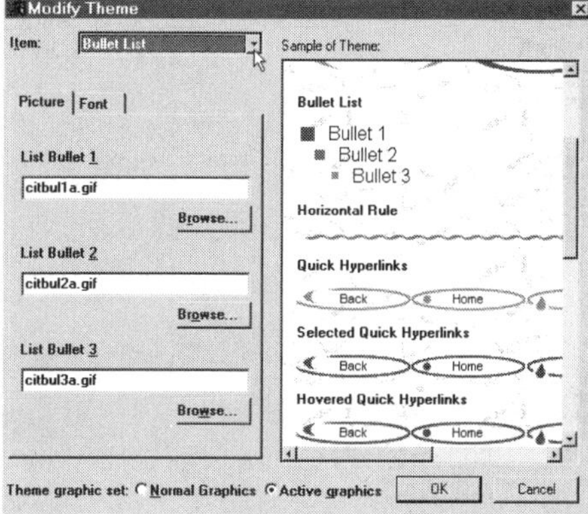

Figure 3.71 The graphics version of the Modify Theme dialog box lets you replace the graphic items used in existing themes.

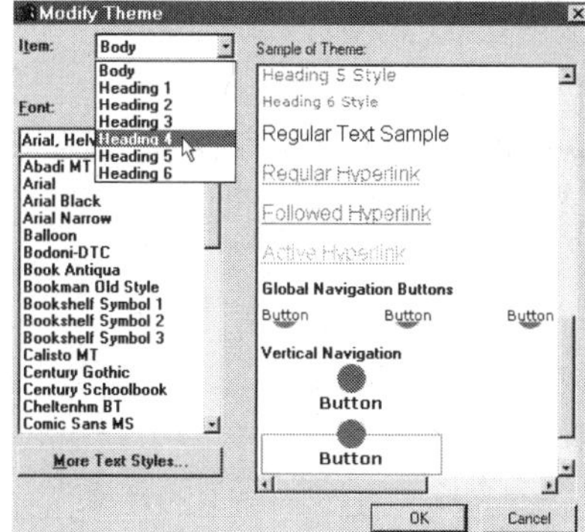

Figure 3.72 The text version of the Modify Theme dialog box lets you change the fonts associated with each HTML item.

6. Depending on your choice, the Modify Theme dialog box that appears will display options for changing your theme colors, graphics, or text (**Figures 3.70–3.72**). For details on the options, see *Theme options*. Make your changes and click *OK*.

7. When the Themes dialog box reappears, you can apply your changes to the existing theme or save them as a new theme. Click *Save* to change the existing theme; *Save As* for a new theme.

8. Finally, click *OK* and the theme modifications will be applied to the selected Web page or site.

Theme options

FrontPage give you a tremendous amount of control in customizing its built-in themes. Follow the steps in *To modify a theme* to reach the Modify Theme dialog box and its various options (**Figures 3.70–3.72**).

- **Colors:** Click any of the three tabs to change aspects of a theme's color. The *Color Schemes* tab lets you apply the color combinations of *another* theme to the current theme (**Figure 3.70**). The *Color Wheel* tab lets you change the hue and brightness of the current color scheme (**Figure 3.73**). The *Custom* tab lets you change the color of individual HTML items, such as all your Level 1 headings or your active hyperlinks (**Figure 3.74**). Choose the *Vivid colors* radio button at the bottom of the dialog box if you want to give the color combinations a bit more punch.
- **Graphics:** The graphics version of the Modify Theme dialog box lets you replace various graphics in existing themes with your own graphics or other clip art (**Figure 3.71**). Use the dialog box's pop-up menu to pick an item or category of items that you want to change, such as all the bullets used in a theme (**Figure 3.75**). Then click *Browse* to navigate to the new graphic you want to use. Choose the *Active graphics* radio button at the bottom of the Modify Theme dialog box if you want to animate buttons when, for example, a user mouses over them. Preview the before, during, and after versions of the animations in the sample window. Just remember to use this option with restraint.

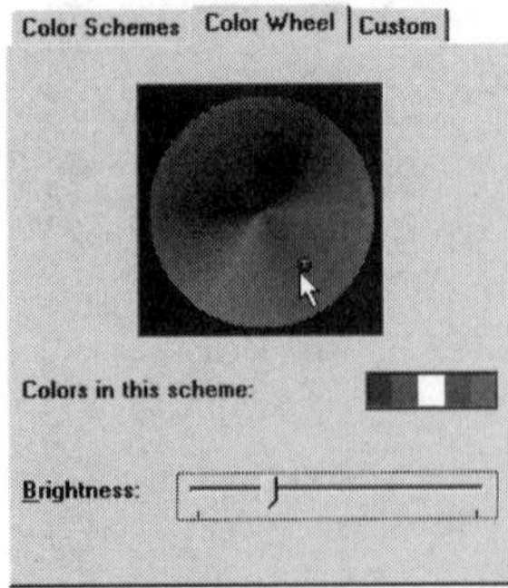

Figure 3.73 The *Color Wheel* tab in the Modify Theme dialog box lets you change the hue and brightness of a selected color combination.

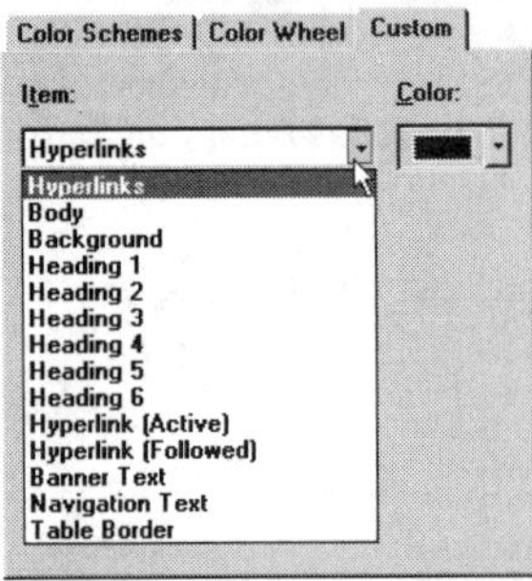

Figure 3.74 The *Custom* tab in the Modify Theme dialog box lets you change the color of individual HTML items within a theme.

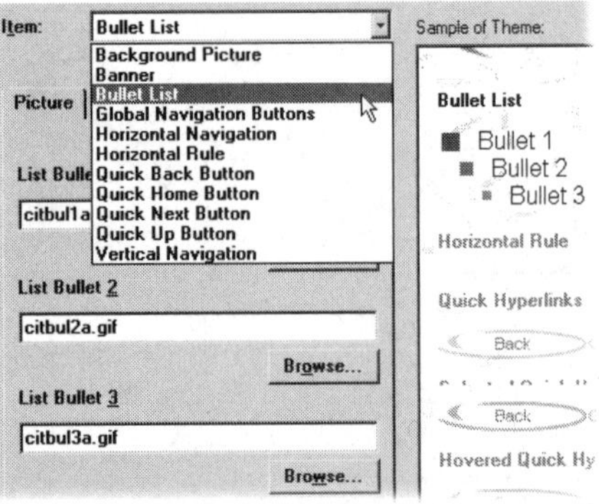

Figure 3.75 Use the pop-up list in the graphics version of the Modify Theme dialog box to change an item or category of items.

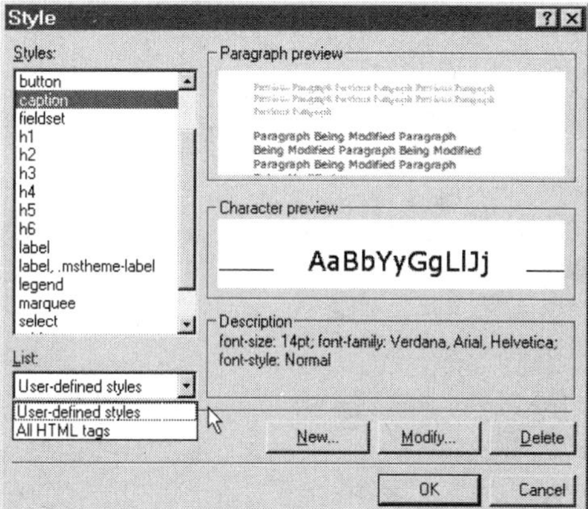

Figure 3.76 The Style dialog box—reached from the Modify Theme dialog box—lets you change the fonts used in any HTML tag.

- **Text:** As you might guess, the text version of the Modify Theme dialog box lets you change the fonts associated with each HTML item, including the text used within such graphics as buttons (**Figure 3.72**). Use the dialog box's pop-up menu to pick your body text or one of your headings. Click the *More Text Styles* button to change even more HTML items (**Figure 3.76**). The *List* pop-up menu will actually let you see all the HTML tags but think first whether you really want to start changing fonts that widely.

✔ Tip

- The choices available to you in the various Modify Theme dialog boxes are affected by which boxes you checked in the Themes dialog box (see Step 6 in *To apply a theme to a page or Web site*). If you find yourself unable to turn on an option in one of the Modify Theme dialog boxes, go back to the Themes dialog box and change your checkbox choices.

PART II

CREATING BASIC WEB PAGES

4 Creating and Formatting Text

The whole point of a program like FrontPage is to spare you the tedium of coding in HTML. For that reason, creating and formatting text with FrontPage is very much like using any word processing program: You type away and the formatting is handled behind the scene. Likewise, most of the standard techniques you use in word processing programs—selecting, moving, cutting, and copying text—work similarly in FrontPage.

Entering and Editing Text

Entering text in FrontPage works almost identically as typing in a word processing program. When your typing reaches the right edge of the document window, the text automatically wraps to the next line. Similarly, you use the cursor to select text, which then can be moved or copied or pasted elsewhere.

To enter text on a Web page

1. If you're not already in page view, click the Page icon in the Views pane (**Figure 4.1**). Also make sure the *Normal* tab at the bottom of the page is active (**Figure 4.2**).
2. Make sure the Folder List is visible by choosing View > Folder List or by clicking the Folder icon (**Figure 4.3**).
3. Select the page on which you want to enter text by double-clicking its listing in the Folder List pane.
4. Within the right pane, click your cursor where you want to enter text on the page. A blinking vertical bar will mark the text insertion spot (**Figure 4.4**).
5. Start typing and the text will appear on the page at the insertion spot (**Figure 4.5**).

Figure 4.1 Before working with text, switch to page view by clicking the Page icon in the Views pane.

Figure 4.2 Whenever you're working with text, make sure the *Normal* tab is active.

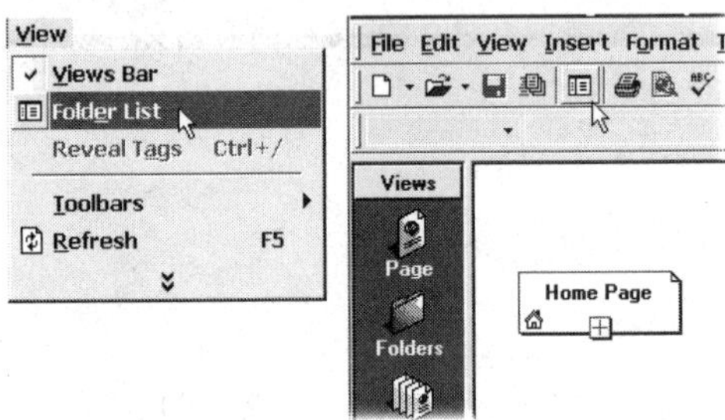

Figure 4.3 It's easier to jump from file to file with the Folder List visible. Choose View > Folder List or click the Folder icon.

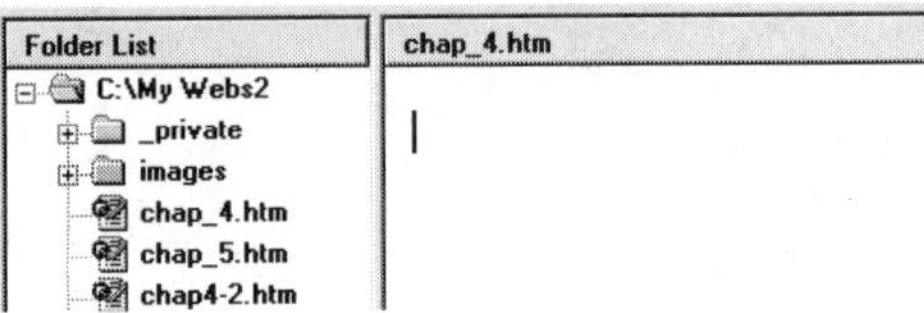

Figure 4.4 Click inside the right pane to begin adding text to a Web page.

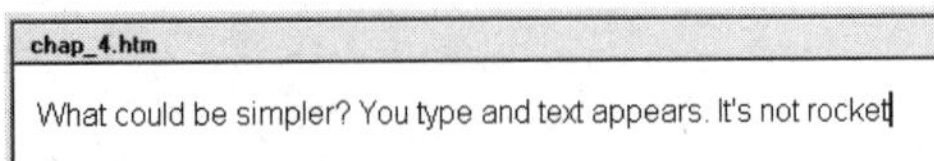

Figure 4.5 Because the HTML code is hidden, entering text in FrontPage is quite similar to using a standard word processor.

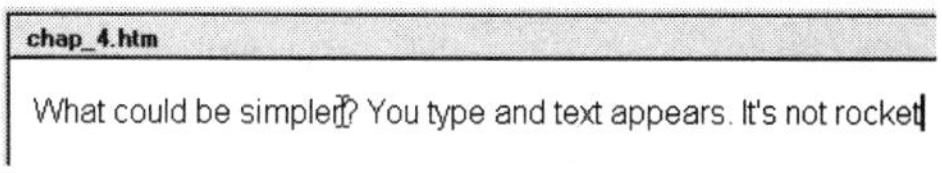

chap_4.htm

What could be simpler? You type and text appears. It's not rocket

Figure 4.6 Click where you want to insert text and a blinking vertical bar will appear.

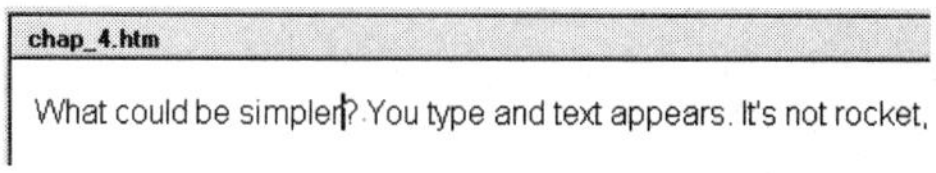

chap_4.htm

What could be simpler? You type and text appears. It's not rocket,

Figure 4.7 Begin typing at the vertical bar and the text will be inserted.

To move the text cursor

1. Use your mouse or the arrow keys to move the cursor to where you want to insert text. An I-beam will mark the cursor's screen location (**Figure 4.6**).
2. Click at the insertion point and the blinking vertical bar will move to that spot (**Figure 4.7**). You're ready to begin typing at the new spot.

✔ Tips

- To jump from word to word, press Ctrl → or Ctrl ←.
- To jump from paragraph to paragraph, press Ctrl ↓ or Ctrl ↑.

To select text

1. Position your cursor at the beginning or end of the text you want to select.
2. Click and drag your cursor to select the text, which will become highlighted (**Figure 4.8**).
3. You now can copy the selected text ((Ctrl)(C)) or cut it to the clipboard ((Ctrl)(X)) for pasting elsewhere ((Ctrl)(V)).

To delete text

1. Position your cursor at the beginning or end of the text you want to select.
2. Click and drag your cursor to select the text, which will become highlighted (**Figure 4.8**).
3. Press (←Backspace) or (Delete) and the text will be deleted (**Figure 4.9**).

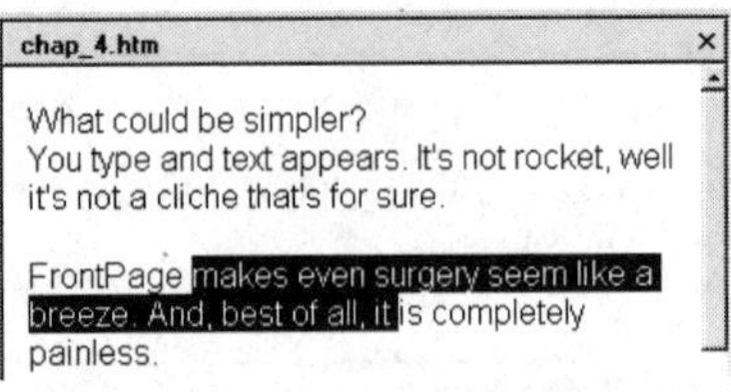
chap_4.htm
What could be simpler?
You type and text appears. It's not rocket, well it's not a cliche that's for sure.
FrontPage makes even surgery seem like a breeze. And, best of all, it is completely painless.

Figure 4.8 Click and drag the cursor to highlight and select text for editing.

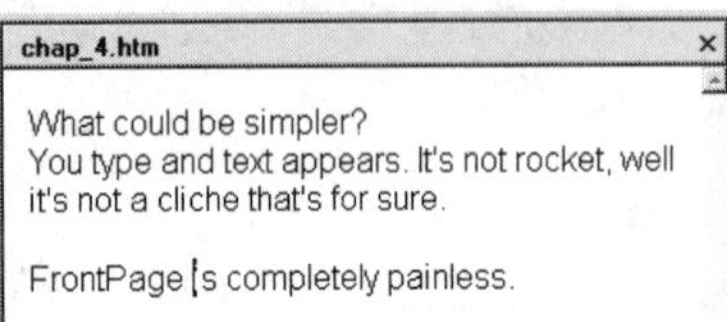
chap_4.htm
What could be simpler?
You type and text appears. It's not rocket, well it's not a cliche that's for sure.
FrontPage is completely painless.

Figure 4.9 Press (←Backspace) or (Delete) and any highlighted text will be deleted.

Table 4.1

Shortcuts for selecting text

TO SELECT	PRESS
Character to right of cursor	(Delete)
Character to left of cursor	(←Backspace)
Single word	Double-click
Word to right of cursor	(Shift)(Ctrl)(→)
Word to left of cursor	(Shift)(Ctrl)(←)
From cursor to end of line	(Shift)(End)
From cursor to beginning of line	(Shift)(Home)
From cursor to line down	(Shift)(↓)
From cursor to line up	(Shift)(↑)
Entire paragraph	(Alt) click
To end of paragraph	(Ctrl)(Shift)(↓)
To beginning of paragraph	(Ctrl)(Shift)(↑)
Paragraph below cursor	(Shift)(Ctrl)(↓)
Paragraph above cursor	(Shift)(Ctrl)(↑)
To end of next screen	(Shift)(Page Down)
To beginning of previous screen	(Shift)(Page Up)

Table 4.2

Shortcuts for deleting text

TO DELETE	PRESS
Character to right of cursor	(Delete)
Character to left of cursor	(←Backspace)
Word to right of cursor	(Ctrl)(Delete)
Word to left of cursor	(Ctrl)(←Backspace)

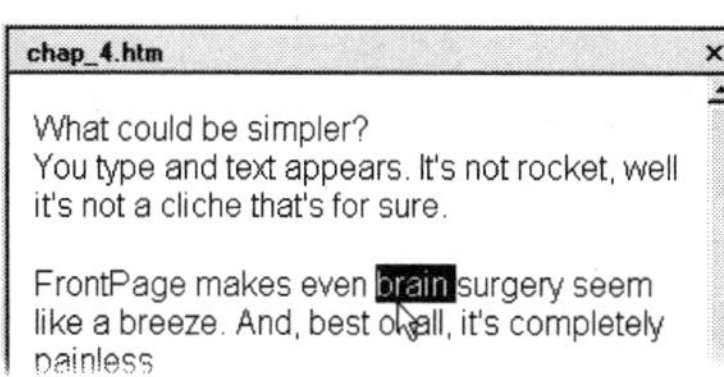

Figure 4.10 To move text, first select with your cursor.

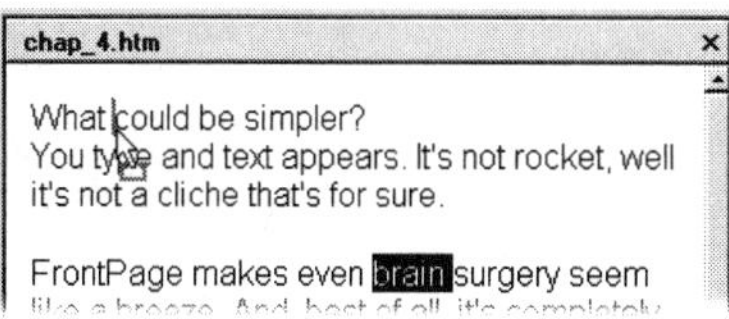

Figure 4.11 Once you've highlighted the text, drag your cursor to the text's new location.

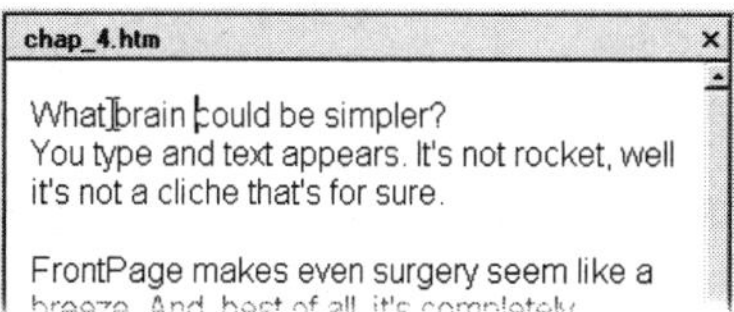

Figure 4.12 Release your cursor where you want the text inserted and it will move from its previous spot.

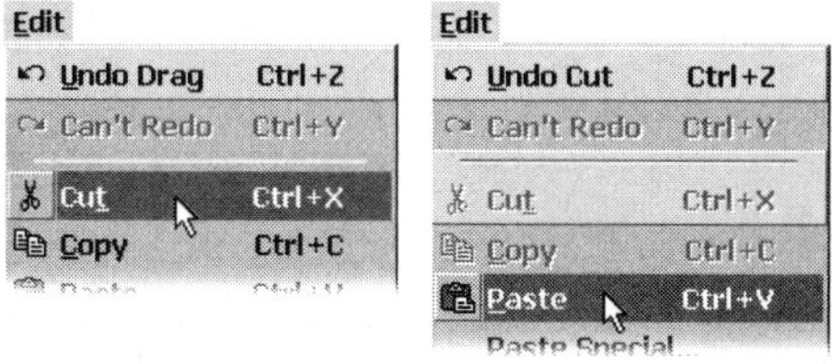

Figure 4.13 To cut text, choose Edit > Cut (Ctrl X). To paste text, choose Edit > Paste (Ctrl V).

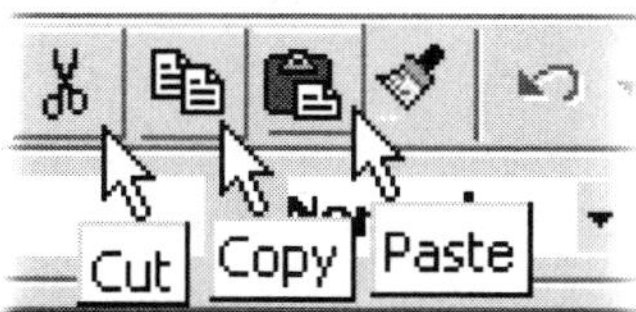

Figure 4.14 FrontPage's Standard toolbar includes icons for cutting, copying, or pasting any text you select.

To move text

1. Select the text you want to move (**Figure 4.10**).
2. Click and drag the highlighted text to its new location (**Figure 4.11**).
3. Release the cursor and the text will be moved to the new spot (**Figure 4.12**).

✔ Tips

- You also can select the text, cut it to the clipboard (Ctrl X), click where you want to move it, and paste it in place (Ctrl V) (**Figure 4.13**).
- If the Standard toolbar is active, you also can click the Cut, Copy, or Paste icons (**Figure 4.14**).

To undo an action

- Choose Edit > Undo or press Ctrl Z. The previous action will be undone.

To redo an action

- Choose Edit > Redo or press Ctrl Y. The previous action will be reapplied.

✔ Tips

- Both the *Undo* and *Redo* choices under the Edit menu change, depending on the previous action (**Figure 4.15**).
- If the Standard toolbar is active, you also can click the Undo or Redo icons, which include drop-down menus listing the most recent actions (**Figure 4.16**).

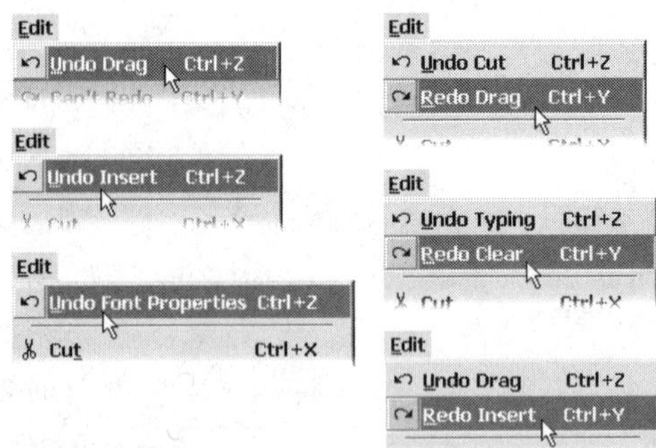

Figure 4.15 The *Undo* (left) and *Redo* (right) choices under the Edit menu change, based on the previous action.

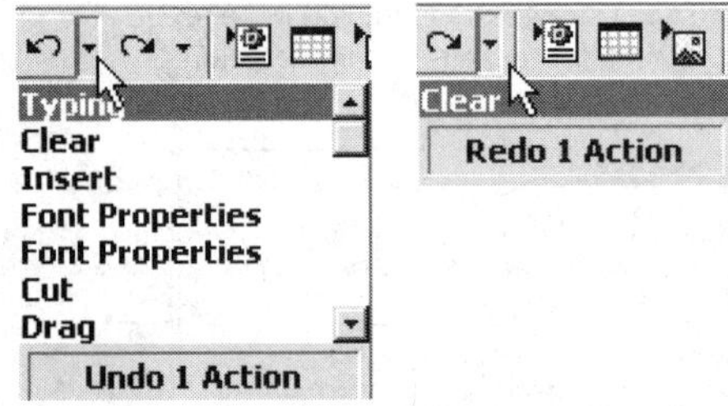

Figure 4.16 The Standard toolbar contains Undo and Redo icons, which include drop-down menus showing the most recent actions.

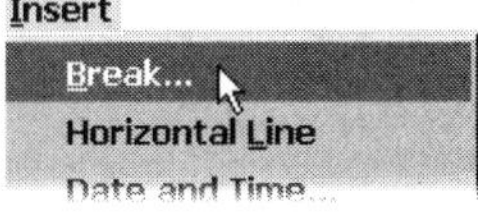

Figure 4.17 To add a line break to text, choose Insert > Break.

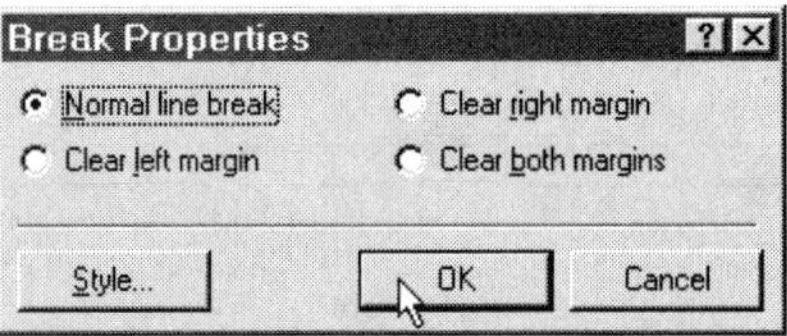

Figure 4.18 In the Break Properties dialog box, *Normal line break* will be selected by default. Click *OK* and the break will be inserted.

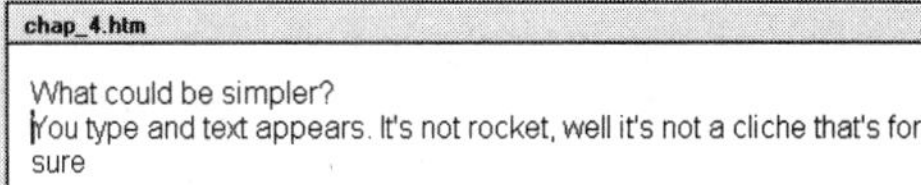

Figure 4.19 Once a line break is inserted, the text will break to the next line—without you having to enter the HTML code.

To add a line break to text

1. Within the right pane, click your cursor where you want the text to break to a new line.
2. Choose Insert > Break (**Figure 4.17**).
3. When the Break Properties dialog box appears, *Normal line break* will be selected by default (**Figure 4.18**). Click *OK* (or press Enter) and a line break will be inserted (**Figure 4.19**). For details on the box's margin-related choices, see *Formatting Paragraphs, Lists, and Headings* on page 101.

✔ Tips

- You also can insert a line break by typing Shift Enter.
- To remove a line break, place the cursor on the beginning of the line before the break and press ←Backspace. The break will be removed.

To add a paragraph

1. Within the right pane, click your cursor where you want the paragraph to appear in the text (**Figure 4.20**).
2. Press Enter and a paragraph will be inserted into the text (**Figure 4.21**).

Showing line break and paragraph marks

Just as with word processing programs, you have the option of displaying normally hidden symbols that mark the location of line breaks and paragraph within the text.

To show/hide break and paragraph marks

◆ Click the Show All icon in the Standard toolbar (**Figure 4.22**). The text will display all line break and paragraph return marks (**Figure 4.23**). To hide the marks, click the Show All icon again.

chap_4.htm
What could be simpler?
You type and text appears. It's not rocket, well it's not a cliche that's for sure. FrontPage makes even brain surgery seem like a breeze. And, best of all, it's completely painless.

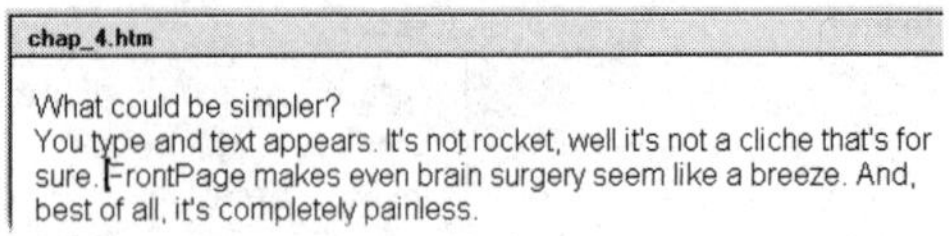

Figure 4.20 Click your cursor where you want a paragraph to appear.

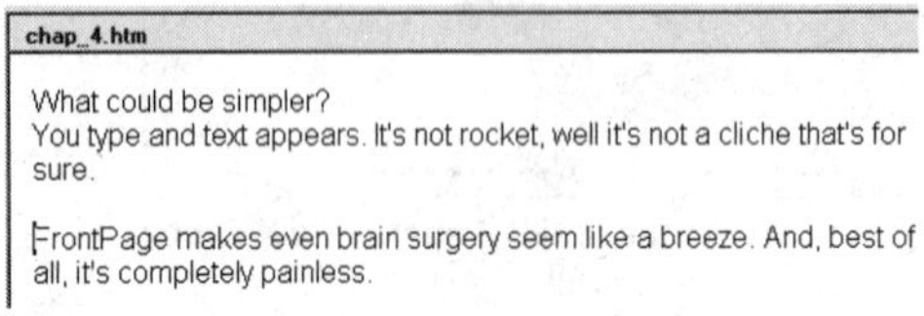

chap_4.htm
What could be simpler?
You type and text appears. It's not rocket, well it's not a cliche that's for sure.
FrontPage makes even brain surgery seem like a breeze. And, best of all, it's completely painless.

Figure 4.21 Press Enter and a paragraph will be inserted into the text.

Show All

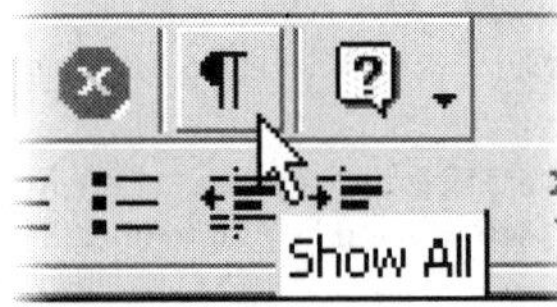

Figure 4.22 To show/hide break and paragraph marks, click the Show All icon in the Standard toolbar.

chap_4.htm
What brain brain be simpler?
You type and text appears. It's not rocket, well it's not a cliche that's for sure. ¶
FrontPage makes even surgery seem like a breeze. And, best of all, it's completely painless.¶

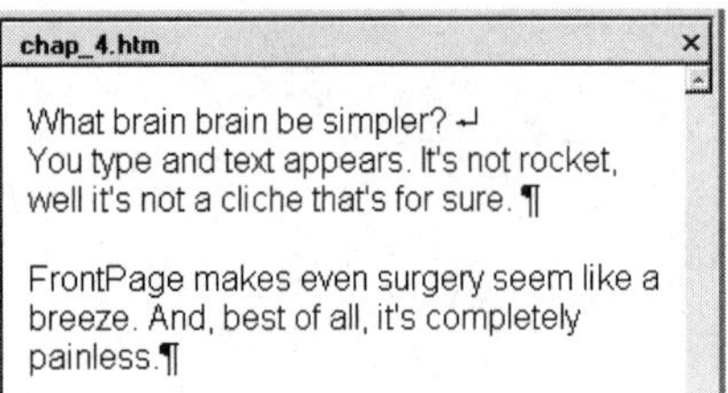

Figure 4.23 The Show All icon lets you see normally hidden symbols that mark line breaks and paragraphs.

Figure 4.24 To find text on a single page or across an entire Web site, choose Edit > Find.

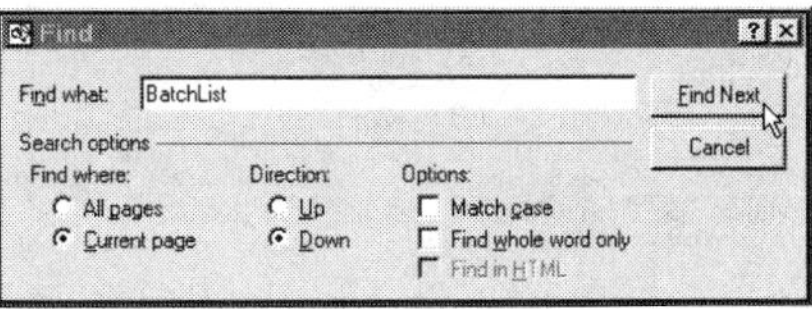

Figure 4.25 In the Find dialog box, type in the word or phrase you're seeking and choose *Current page*. Check any other search criteria and click *Find Next*.

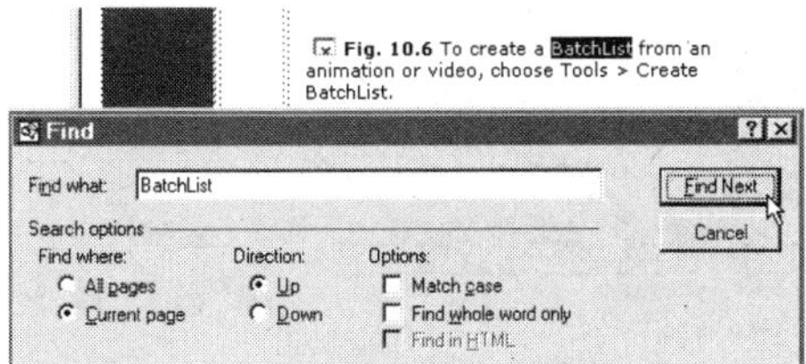

Figure 4.26 The Find dialog box remains visible even after the first instance of the word or phrase is found. Click *Find Next* again to continue searching.

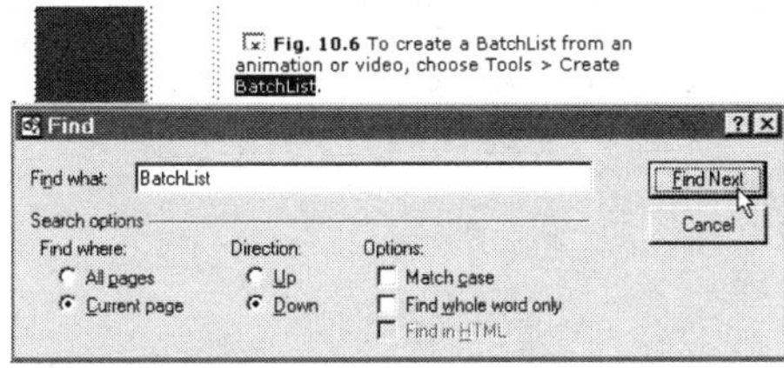

Figure 4.27 The second instance of the search phrase is highlighted. Again, the Find dialog box remains visible, enabling you to keep searching for other instances. When you're done, click *Cancel* or close the window.

Finding and Replacing Text

Besides the standard find and replace functions you'd expect, FrontPage also lets you search the HTML, which means you can find words, phrases, or even bits of code that may not be visible in the Normal view.

To find text on a single page

1. If you're not already in page view, click the Page icon in the Views pane and make sure the *Normal* tab is selected.
2. Make the Folder List visible by choosing View > Folder List or clicking the Folder icon.
3. Choose Edit > Find (Ctrl F) (**Figure 4.24**).
4. When the Find dialog box appears, type in the word or phrase you're seeking and choose *Current page* (**Figure 4.25**).
5. Set whether you want FrontPage to search *Up* or *Down* and whether the search should match the case and whole words used in the text box. Click *Find Next* and the first instance of the word or phrase will be found (**Figure 4.26**).
6. The Find dialog box will remain visible, allowing you to continue clicking *Find Next* until you find the instance you're looking for (**Figure 4.27**).
7. When you're done searching, click *Cancel* or the Close button in the dialog box's upper-right corner.

To find text across a Web site

1. If you're not already in page view, click the Page icon in the Views pane and make sure the *Normal* tab is selected.
2. Make the Folder List visible by choosing View > Folder List or clicking the Folder icon.
3. Choose Edit > Find (Ctrl F) (**Figure 4.24**).
4. When the Find dialog box appears, type in the word or phrase you're seeking and choose *All pages* (**Figure 4.28**).
5. Set whether you want FrontPage to search *Up* or *Down* and whether the search should match the case and whole words used in the text box. Click *Find In Web.*
6. FrontPage will search through all the pages of the current Web site and list the pages containing the search phrase and how many times it appears on those pages (**Figure 4.29**).
7. Double-click on the page listing you'd like to search in detail and you'll be taken to the first instance of the search phrase on that page. A basic Find dialog box also will appear in which you can click *Find Next* to continue searching the page (**Figure 4.30**).

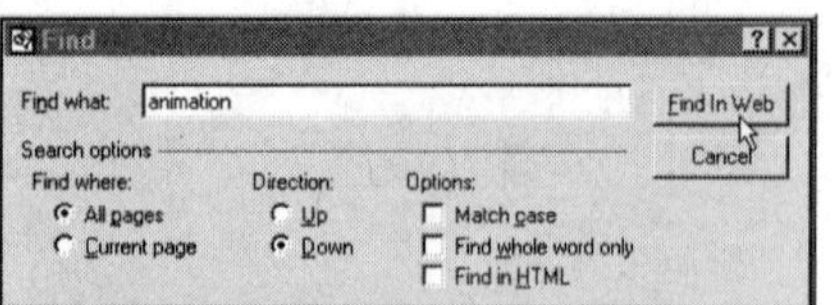

Figure 4.28 To search the entire Web site, choose *All pages*, set your other criteria, and click *Find In Web*.

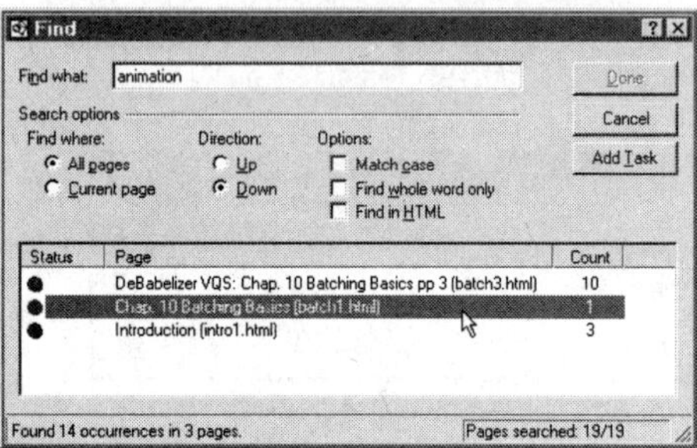

Figure 4.29 After searching the Web site, FrontPage will list every page with the phrase and how many times it appears. Double-click a page listing to search it.

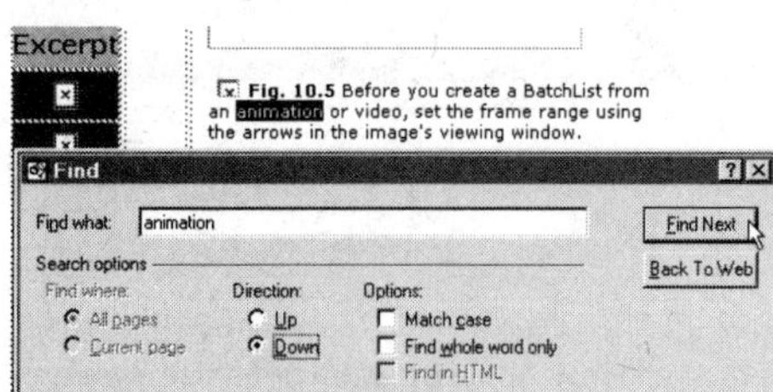

Figure 4.30 A standard Find dialog box will appear. Click *Find Next* to continue searching the individual page.

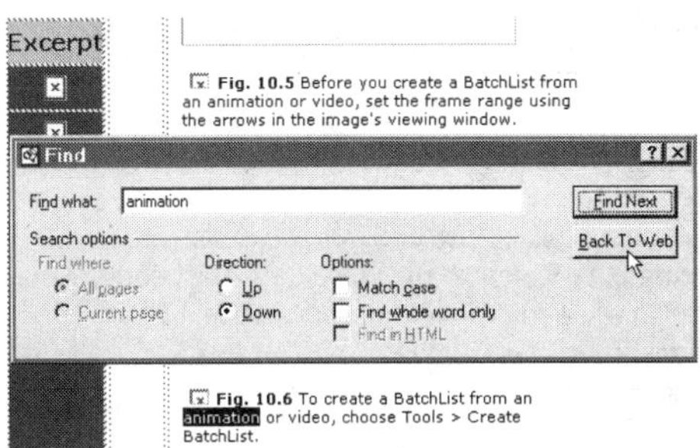

Figure 4.31 To keep searching, continue clicking *Find Next*. To search another Web page, click the *Back To Web* button and you'll be returned to the list of pages containing the search phrase.

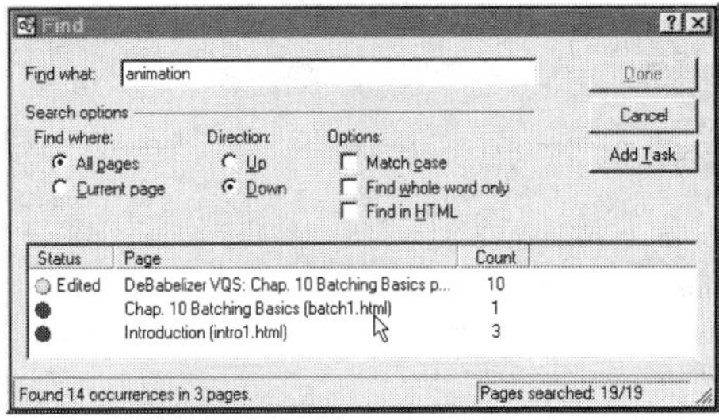

Figure 4.32 To see other pages, click the Find dialog box's *Back To Web* button (**Figure 4.31**) and you'll be returned to the original search results dialog box.

8. The next instance of the search phrase on that page will appear. To keep searching, click *Find Next* again and the next instance will appear (**Figure 4.31**).
9. If you want to see instances of the search phrase on one of the other pages initially listed, click the Find dialog box's *Back To Web* button and you'll be returned to the original search results dialog box (**Figure 4.32**).
10. Double-click any other page in the list and instances of the search phrase on that page will appear.
11. When you're done, click *Cancel* or the Close button in the dialog box's upper-right corner.

To search the site's HTML code

1. If you're not already in page view, click the Page icon in the Views pane and make sure the *Normal* tab is selected.
2. Make the Folder List visible by choosing View > Folder List or clicking the Folder icon.
3. Choose Edit > Find (Ctrl F) (**Figure 4.24**).
4. When the Find dialog box appears, type in the word or phrase you're seeking and choose *All pages*, and set your other search criteria. Then check the *Find in HTML* box and click *Find in Web* (**Figure 4.33**). FrontPage will list every page where the search phrase appears (**Figure 4.34**).
5. Double-click an individual page listing and you'll be taken to the first instance of the search phrase—even if it's in normally invisible HTML coding (**Figure 4.35**).
6. Continue to search that page by clicking *Find Next* or return to other page listings by clicking *Back To Web*. When you're done, click *Cancel* or the Close button in the Find dialog box's upper-right corner.

✔ Tip

- If you know the basics of HTML coding, this option offers a quick way to fix or replace coding across an entire Web site. If you don't understand HTML, this option can get you into deep trouble—fast.

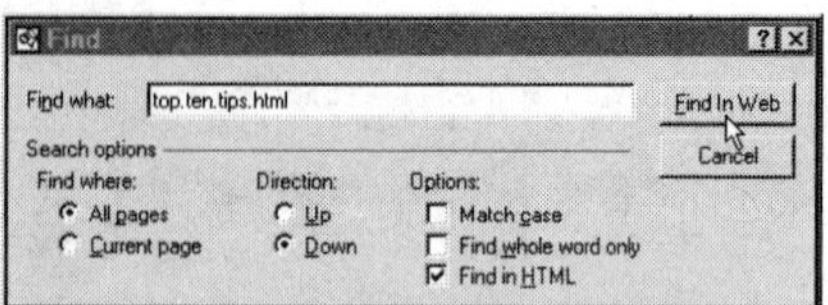

Figure 4.33 To search the Web site's HTML code, type in what you're seeking and choose *All pages*. Then check the *Find in HTML* box and click *Find in Web*.

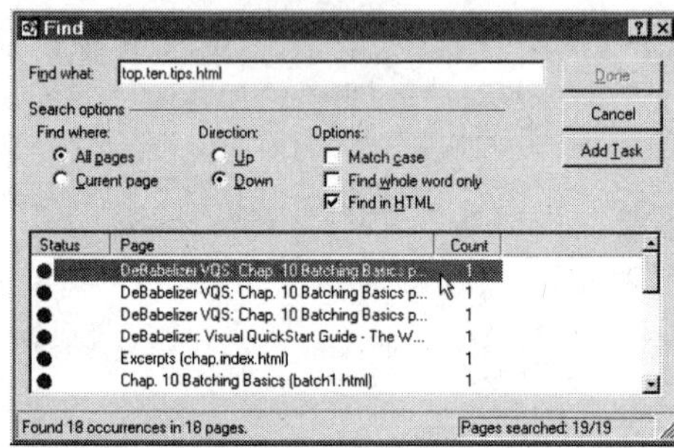

Figure 4.34 FrontPage will list every page where the search phrase appears—even if it's in normally invisible HTML coding.

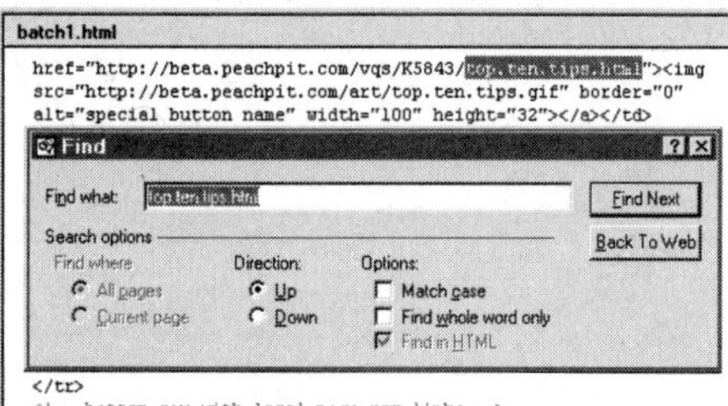

Figure 4.35 Here's an example where FrontPage has found the search phrase in an HTML hyperlink.

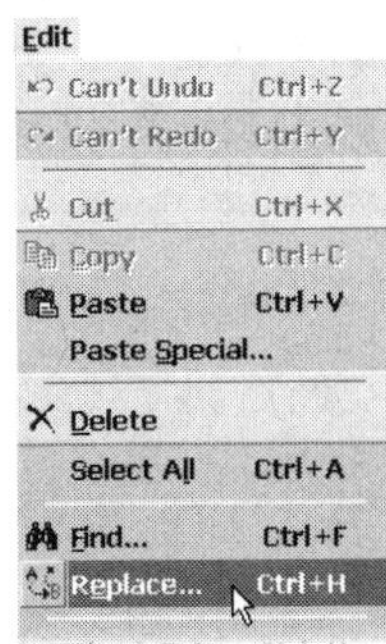

Figure 4.36 To replace text on a single page or the entire site, choose Edit > Replace (Ctrl H).

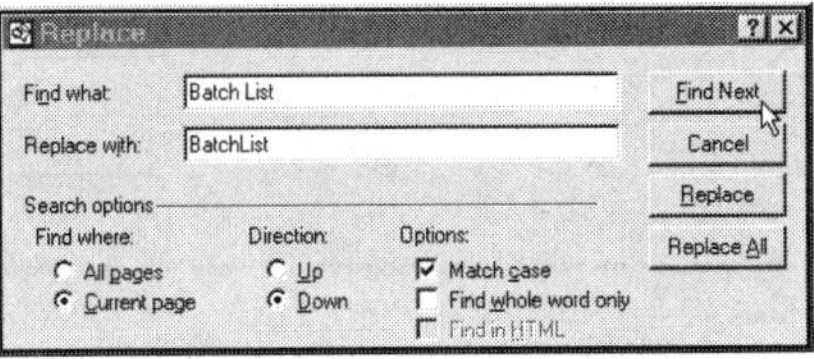

Figure 4.37 To replace text on a single page, type in the word or phrase you're seeking, choose *Current page* and click *Find Next*.

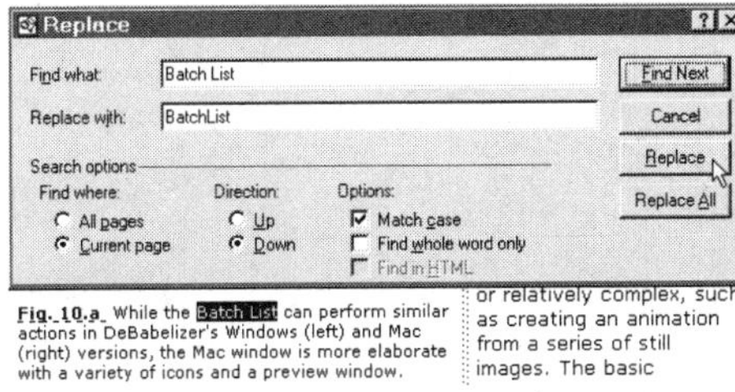

Figure 4.38 Once you begin the search, FrontPage will display the first instance of the word or phrase. Click *Replace*.

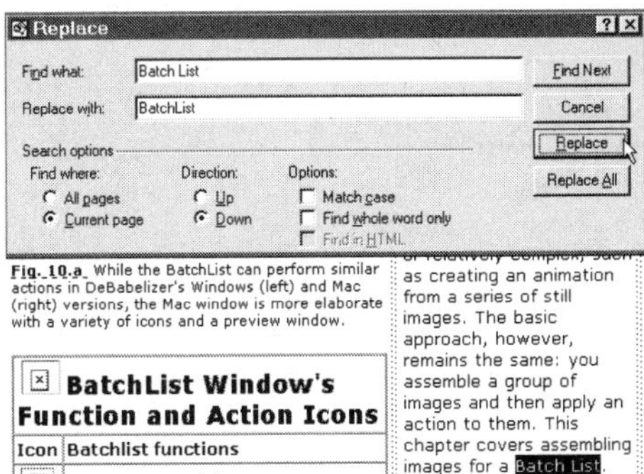

Figure 4.39 After each replace, FrontPage will fix the search phrase and immediately move to the next instance of the phrase.

To replace text on a single page

1. If you're not already in page view, click the Page icon in the Views pane and make sure the *Normal* tab is selected.
2. Make the Folder List visible by choosing View > Folder List or clicking the Folder icon.
3. Choose Edit > Replace (Ctrl H) (**Figure 4.36**).
4. When the Replace dialog box appears, type in the word or phrase you're seeking in the *Find what* window, the word or phrase you want to replace it with in the *Replace with* window, choose *Current page*, and set your other search criteria. (**Figure 4.37**).
5. Click *Find Next* and the first instance of the word or phrase will be found (**Figure 4.38**).
6. Click *Replace* and FrontPage will fix the search phrase and immediately move to the next instance of the phrase (**Figure 4.39**).

(continued)

7. Continue clicking the *Find Next* and *Replace* buttons until an alert dialog box tells you that FrontPage has finished searching the page. Click *OK* (**Figure 4.40**).

8. When the Replace dialog box reappears, click *Cancel* or the Close button in its upper-right corner.

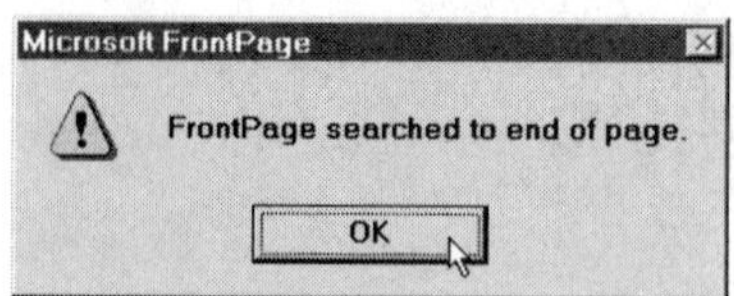

Figure 4.40 An alert dialog box appears once FrontPage has finished searching the page. Click *OK* to see the list of other pages containing the search phrase.

✔ Tip

- If you're absolutely sure you want to replace every instance of a search phrase, click *Replace All* in the Replace dialog box and the search-and-replace process for the entire page will occur automatically (**Figure 4.41**).

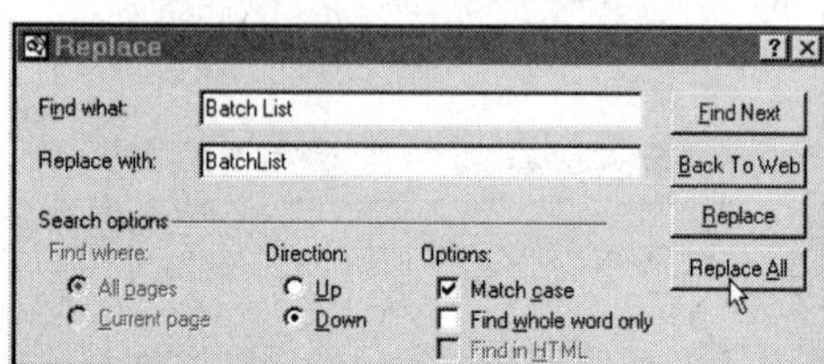

Figure 4.41 To automatically replace every instance of the search phrase, click *Replace All* in the Replace dialog box.

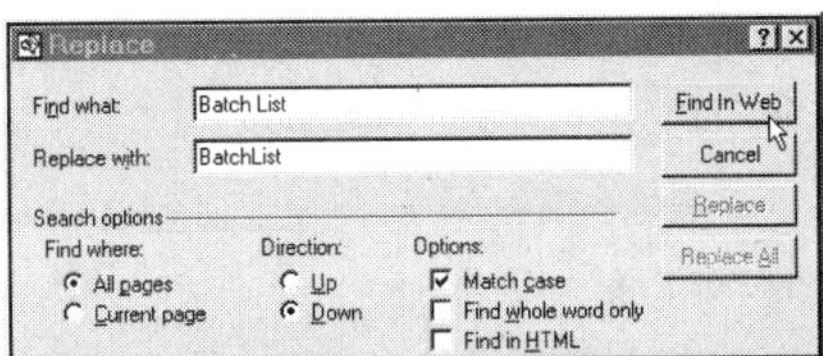

Figure 4.42 To search and replace across an entire Web site, type in the word or phrase you're seeking, choose *All pages,* and click *Find In Web*.

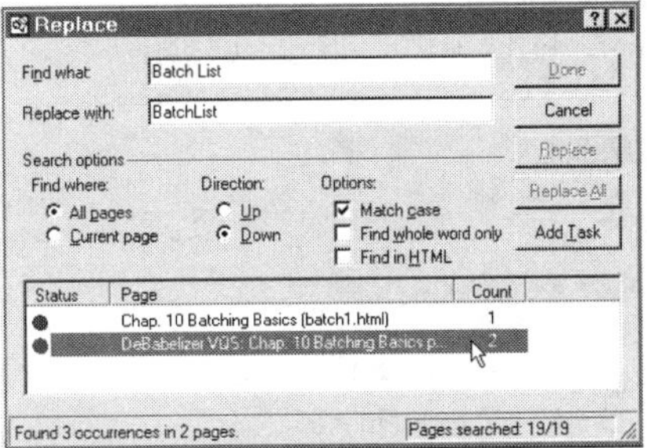

Figure 4.43 FrontPage will list all the pages in the Web site containing the search phrase and how many times it appears in each page. To see any page, double-click its listing.

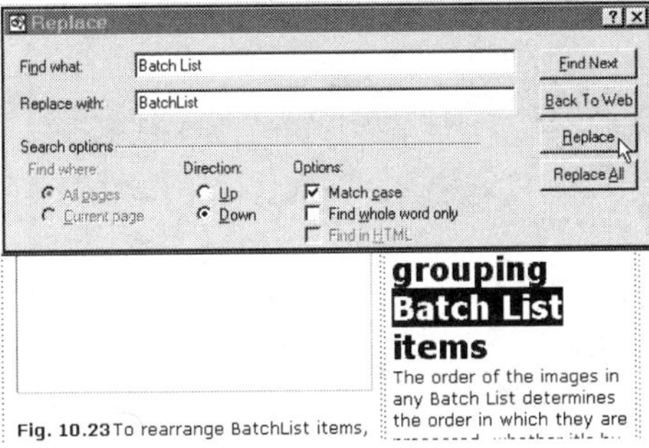

Figure 4.44 Once you double-click a page listing, FrontPage jumps to the page and displays the first instance of the search phrase. To fix it, click *Replace*.

To replace text across a Web site

1. If you're not already in page view, click the Page icon in the Views pane and make sure the *Normal* tab is selected.
2. Make the Folder List visible by choosing View > Folder List or clicking the Folder icon.
3. Choose Edit > Replace (Ctrl H) (**Figure 4.36**).
4. When the Replace dialog box appears, type in the word or phrase you're seeking in the *Find what* window, the word or phrase you want to replace it with in the *Replace with* window, choose *All pages* and set your other search criteria. Click *Find In Web* (**Figure 4.42**).
5. FrontPage will search through all the pages of the current Web site and list the pages containing the search phrase and how many times it appears in those pages (**Figure 4.43**).
6. Double-click any of the pages listed and you'll be taken to that page's first instance of the phrase you'd like to replace (**Figure 4.44**).

(continued)

7. Click *Replace* and FrontPage will fix the search phrase and immediately move to the next instance of the phrase (**Figure 4.45**).

8. When FrontPage has searched and replaced every instance of the phrase on the page, a dialog box will appear asking whether you want to save your changes and close the page (**Figure 4.46**). Click *OK* to save and close the page and you'll be returned to the original search results dialog box. The Replace dialog box marks the page you just searched and replaced as *Edited* (**Figure 4.47**).

9. Double-click any other page in the list and that page's instances of the search phrase will appear. Repeat Steps 7–9.

10. When you're done, click *Cancel* or the Close button in the dialog box's upper-right.

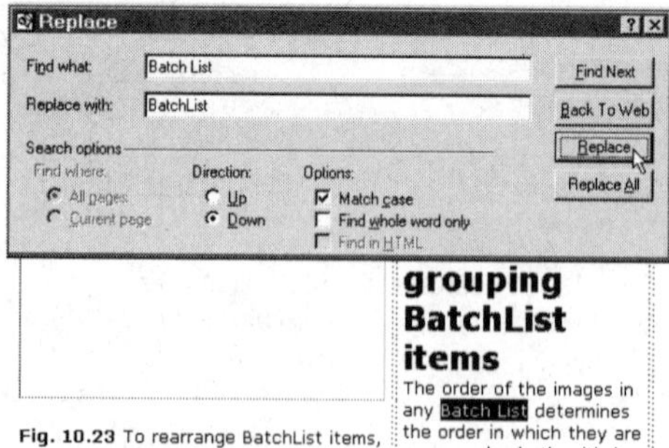

Figure 4.45 After each replace, FrontPage immediately moves to the next instance of the phrase.

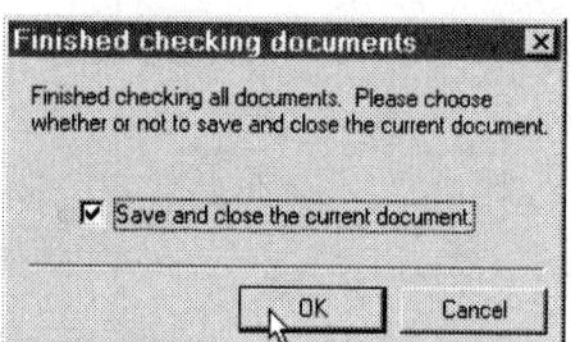

Figure 4.46 After it has replaced every instance of the phrase on a page, FrontPage asks whether you want to save your changes and close the page. Click *OK*.

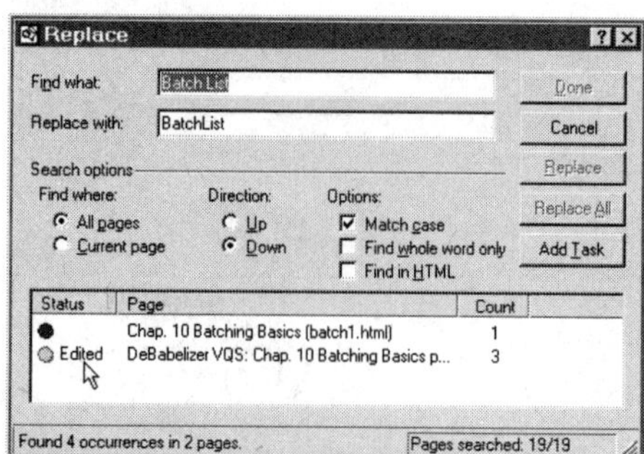

Figure 4.47 Once the fixes on a page have been saved, the Replace dialog box will mark the page as *Edited*. Double-click any other listing to search that page.

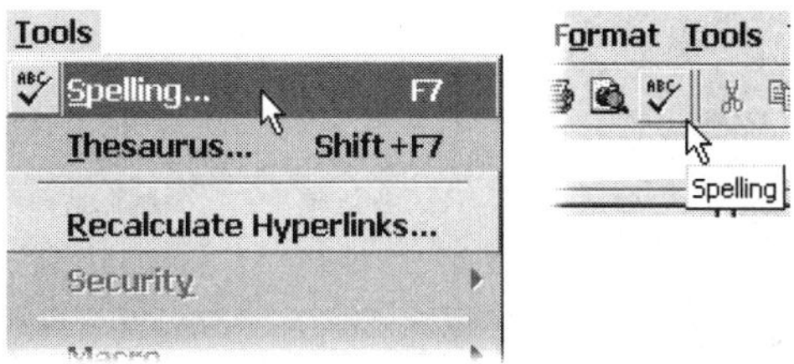

Figure 4.48 To begin spell checking, choose Tools > Spelling (F7) or, if the Standard toolbar is active, click the Spelling icon.

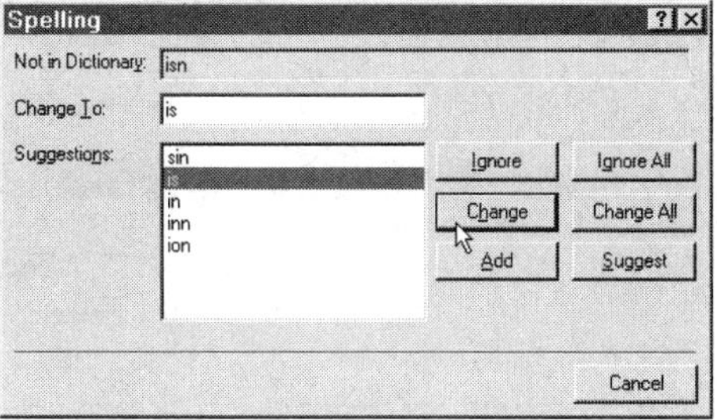

Figure 4.49 When FrontPage finds a suspected error, the Spelling dialog box will display the word and offer suggested spellings.

Figure 4.50 When FrontPage finishes checking the page, it displays an alert dialog box. Click *OK*.

Checking Spelling

FrontPage lets you check the spelling on a single page or across an entire Web site. It even lets you check spelling as you type, though that particular option drives a lot of people crazy. I prefer running the spell check after I've built a page. By the way, FrontPage lets you change the dictionary language from the default U.S. English to more than two dozen other languages.

To check spelling on a single page

1. If you're not already in page view, click the Page icon in the Views pane and make sure the *Normal* tab is selected.
2. Choose Tools > Spelling (F7) or if the Standard toolbar is active, click the Spelling icon (**Figure 4.48**).
3. FrontPage will begin checking the current page. When it finds a suspected error, the Spelling dialog box will display the word and offer a suggested spelling (**Figure 4.49**).
4. If you want to use the suggested word, click *Change* or *Change All* if you want every instance on the page fixed. If you know the word's spelled correctly—perhaps it's a trademark that FrontPage doesn't recognize—check *Ignore* or *Ignore All*. You also can add terms like trademarks to FrontPage's dictionary by clicking *Add*. If the suggested word isn't correct, you can type in your own spelling and click *Change* or *Change All*.
5. FrontPage will continue checking the page and display an alert dialog box when it's done. Click *OK* and you're done (**Figure 4.50**).

To check spelling across a Web site

1. Switch to folder view by clicking the Folders icon in the Views pane (**Figure 4.51**).
2. Choose Tools > Spelling (F7) or if the Standard toolbar is active, click the Spelling icon (**Figure 4.48**).
3. When the Spelling dialog box appears, make sure that the *Entire web* radio button is selected (**Figure 4.52**). Click *Start* and FrontPage will begin checking the entire Web site. FrontPage will search the current Web site and list pages containing suspected misspellings and how many misspellings appear on each page (**Figure 4.53**).
4. Double-click any of the pages listed and you'll be taken to that page's first instance of the suspected misspelling. FrontPage also will show suggested spellings for the word.
5. Just as in spell checking a single page, you may click *Change* or *Change* All, *Ignore* or *Ignore All*, or you can type in your own spelling and click *Change* or *Change All*.
6. When FrontPage has fixed all the misspellings on the site, a dialog box will appear asking whether you want to save your changes and close the page (**Figure 4.54**). Click *OK* to save and close the page and you'll be returned to the list of pages with suspected misspellings. The page you just spell checked will be marked as *Edited*.
7. Double-click any other page in the list and that page's suspected misspellings will appear. Repeat Steps 6-7.
8. When you're done, click *Cancel* or the Close button in the dialog box's upper-right.

Figure 4.51 To check spelling across a Web site, first switch to folder view by clicking the Folders icon in the Views pane.

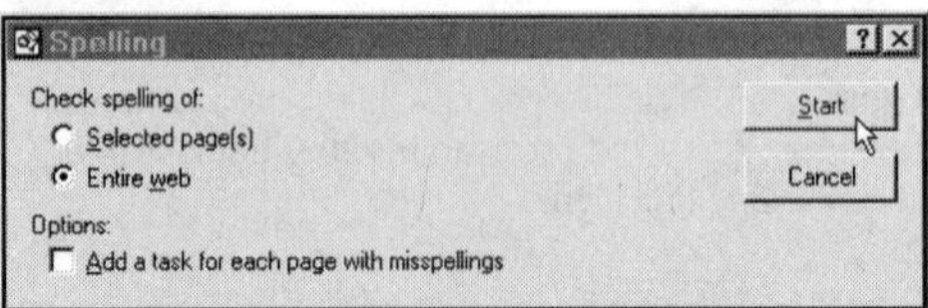

Figure 4.52 Check *Entire web* in the Spelling dialog box and click *Start* to spell check every page.

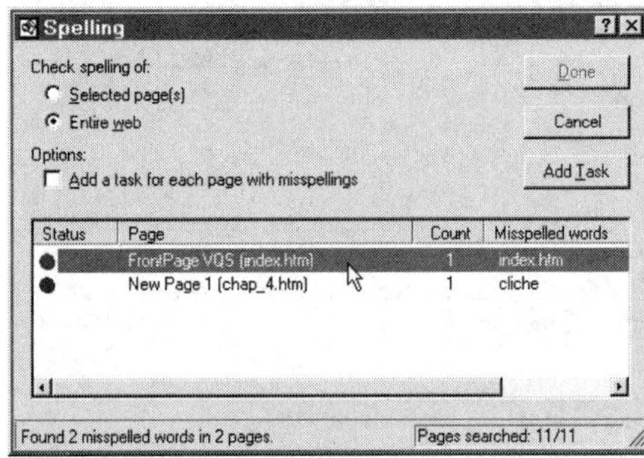

Figure 4.53 FrontPage will search the current Web site and list pages containing suspected misspellings. To see a page, double-click its listing.

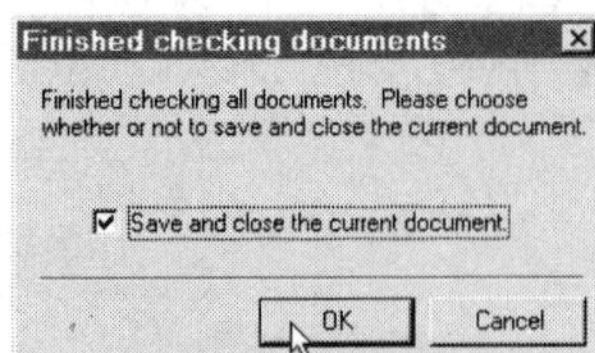

Figure 4.54 When FrontPage has fixed all the misspellings on the site, a dialog box will appear asking whether you want to save your changes and close the page. Click *OK*.

Checking Spelling

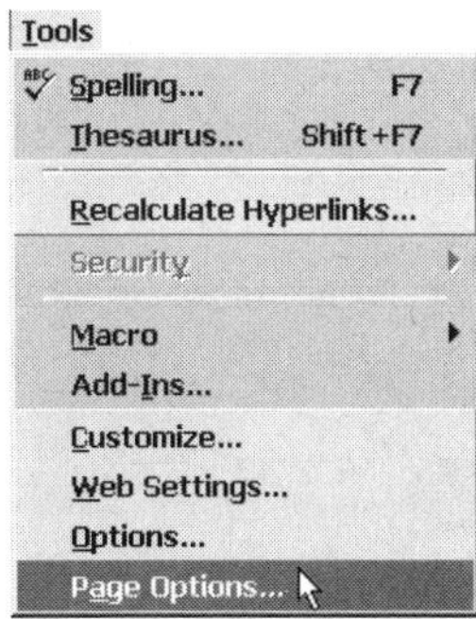

Figure 4.55 To check spelling as you type, choose Tools > Page Options.

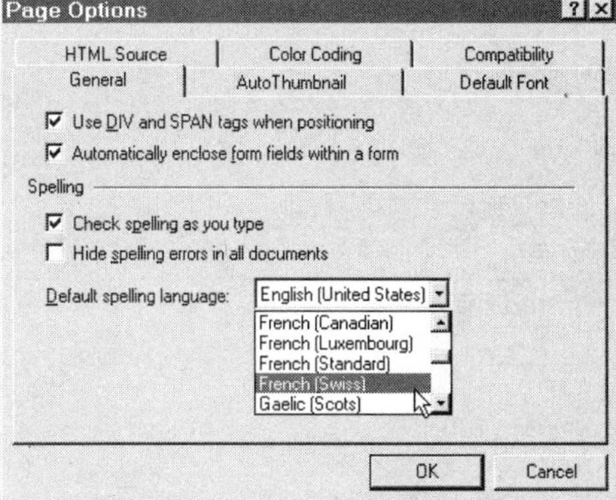

Figure 4.56 The Page Options dialog box lets you control whether FrontPage checks and shows spelling errors as you type. It also lets you set your dictionary's language.

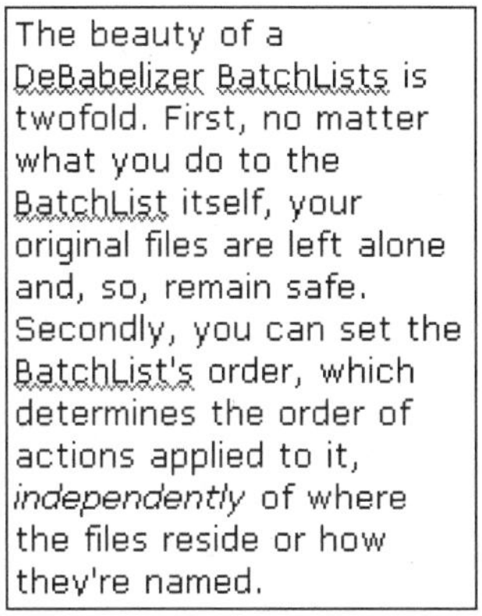

The beauty of a DeBabelizer BatchLists is twofold. First, no matter what you do to the BatchList itself, your original files are left alone and, so, remain safe. Secondly, you can set the BatchList's order, which determines the order of actions applied to it, *independently* of where the files reside or how they're named.

Figure 4.57 The drawback of showing spelling errors as you type: Any word FrontPage doesn't recognize gets underlined, which makes for a messy page.

To check spelling as you type

1. Choose Tools > Page Options (**Figure 4.55**).
2. When the Page Options dialog box appears, click the *General* tab and check the box marked *Check spelling as you type* (**Figure 4.56**).
3. Click *OK* and FrontPage will automatically check your spelling.

✔ Tip

- If you're going to have FrontPage check your spelling as you type, it's probably best to check *Hide spelling errors in all documents* in the Page Options dialog box. Otherwise, FrontPage will underline any word it doesn't recognize—which can make for an awful lot of red underlines. (**Figure 4.57**).

To change the dictionary language

1. Choose Tools > Page Options (**Figure 4.55**).
2. When the Page Options dialog box appears, use the *Default spelling language* drop-down menu to pick a language other than U.S. English (**Figure 4.56**). When you're done, click *OK*.

Formatting Text

If you're hand coding in HTML, making a word appear in bold face involves a surprising amount of rigmarole. In FrontPage, applying character styles works similarly to how it's done in word-processing programs: make a selection, click an icon, and you're done. The Formatting toolbar, which is on by default, includes everything you'll need for the most common text changes (**Figure 4.58**). Still more text formatting choices are available in the Font dialog box, whose details are explained on page 98.

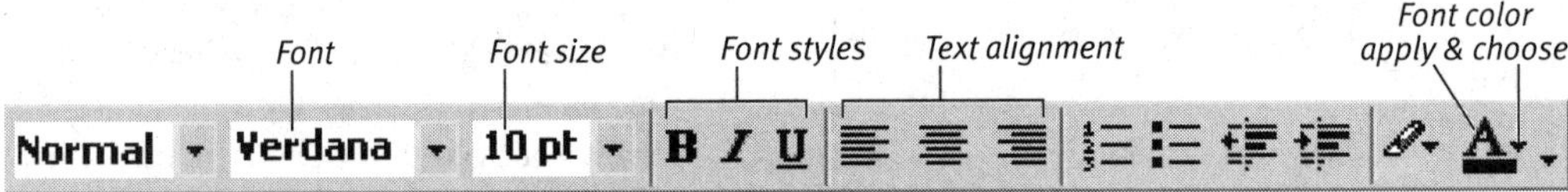

Figure 4.58 The Formatting toolbar includes icons for applying most text changes.

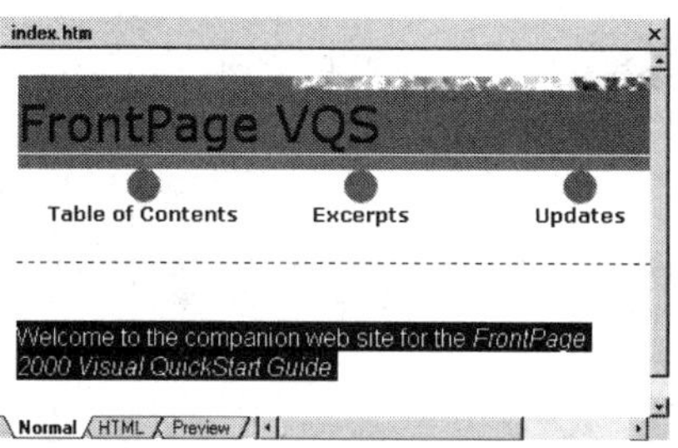

Figure 4.59 Select the text whose font you want to change.

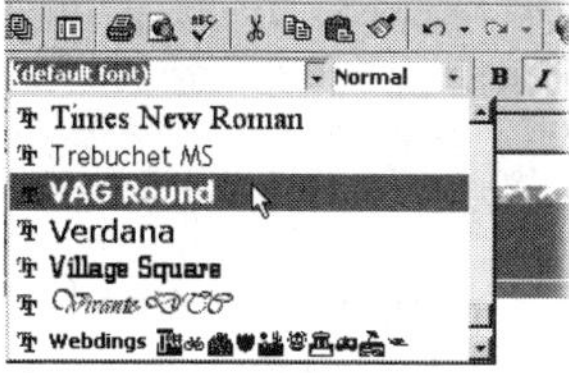

Figure 4.60 To change the font face, click the arrow for the Formatting toolbar's font window and scroll through the drop-down menu for the font you want.

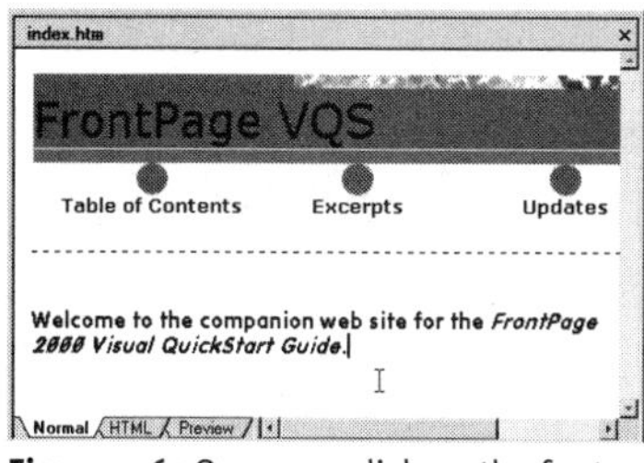

Figure 4.61 Once you click on the font, the change is applied to the selected text.

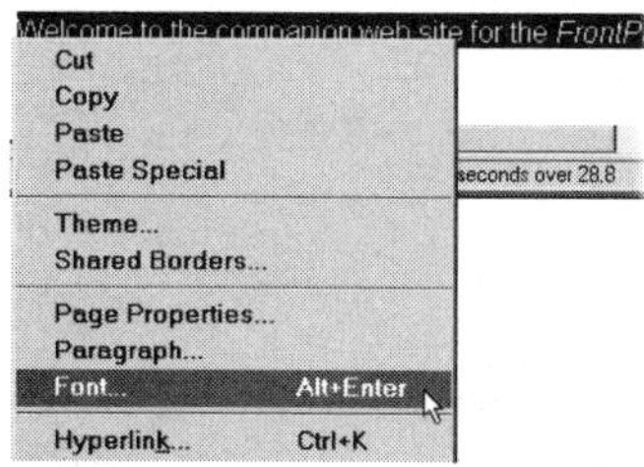

Figure 4.62 You can reach the Font dialog box any time, by selecting text, right-clicking in the page, and choosing *Font* (Alt Enter) from the shortcut menu.

To change the font face

1. Make sure you're in page view by clicking the Page icon in the Views pane.
2. Select the text you want to change (**Figure 4.59**).
3. Click the arrow just to the right of the Formatting toolbar's font window and scroll through the drop-down menu until you find a font you want (**Figure 4.60**).
4. Click on the font you want and it will be applied to the selected text (**Figure 4.61**).

✔ Tip

- You also can change highlighted text by right-clicking in the page and choosing *Font* (Alt Enter) from the shortcut menu. (**Figure 4.62**). When the Font dialog box appears, choose the font from the scrolling Font window, then click *OK* (**Figure 4.63**). For details on the Font dialog box, see *Font options* on page 98.

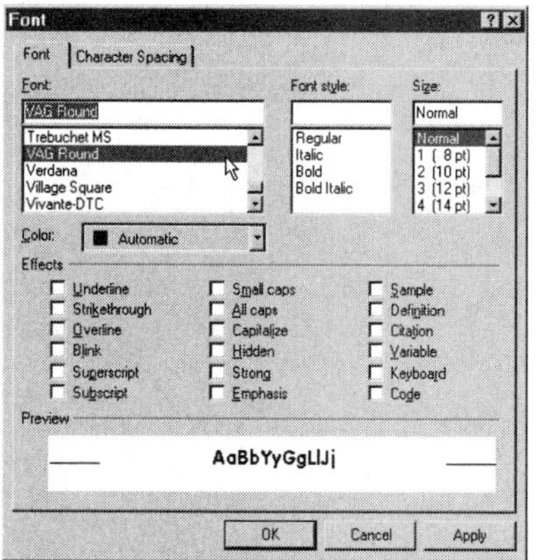

Figure 4.63 The Font dialog box offers extensive control over the appearance and formatting of any highlighted text.

To change the font size

1. Make sure you're in page view by clicking the Page icon in the Views pane.
2. Select the text you want to change (**Figure 4.64**).
3. In the Formatting toolbar, click the arrow just to the right of the Font Size window and choose a size from the drop-down menu (**Figure 4.65**).
4. Release the cursor and the new size will be applied to the selected text (**Figure 4.66**).

✔ Tip

- You also can change the text's font size by right-clicking the page and choosing *Font* (Alt Enter) from the shortcut menu. (**Figure 4.62**). Within the Font dialog box, click the *Size* drop-down menu, make your choice, and click *OK* (**Figure 4.63**). For details see *Font options* on page 98.

Welcome to the companion Web site
QuickStart Guide. You'll lots of tips a
with updates, sample files, and links

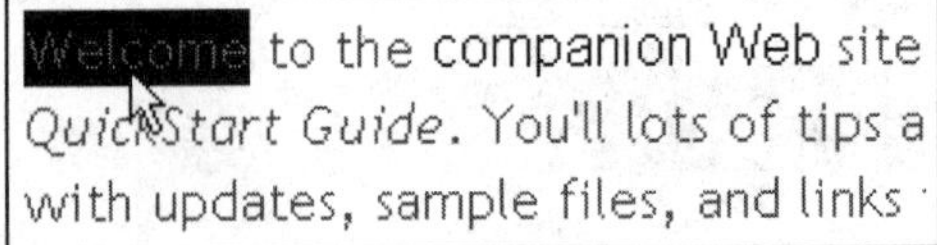

Figure 4.64 Select the text whose size you want to change.

Normal
1 (8 pt)
2 (10 pt)
3 (12 pt)
4 (14 pt)
5 (18 pt)
6 (24 pt)
7 (36 pt)

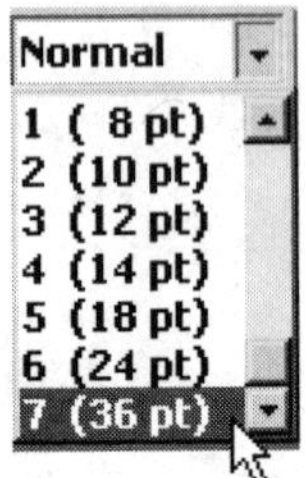

Figure 4.65 To change the text size, click the arrow for the Formatting toolbar's Font Size window and scroll through the drop-down menu for the size you want.

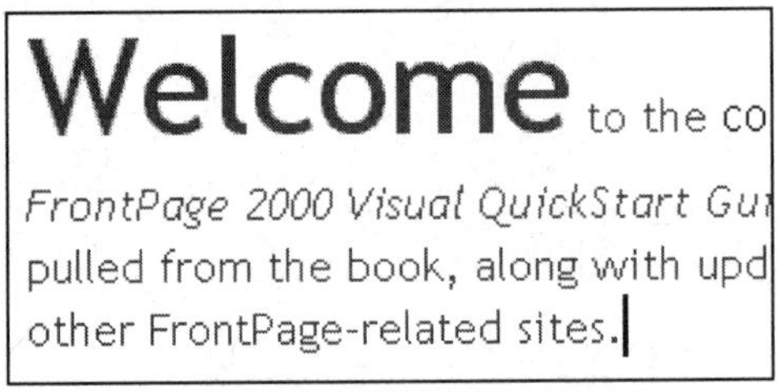

Welcome to the co
FrontPage 2000 Visual QuickStart Gu
pulled from the book, along with upd
other FrontPage-related sites.

Figure 4.66 Once you click on the size, the change is applied to the selected text.

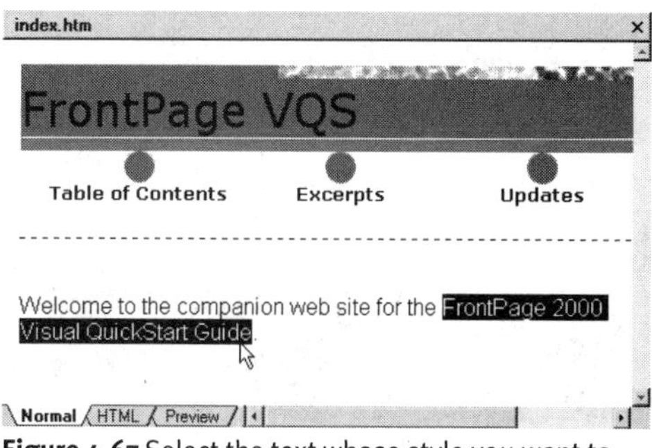

Figure 4.67 Select the text whose style you want to change.

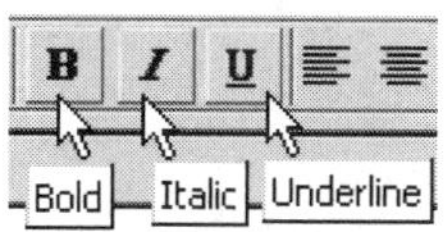

Figure 4.68 Click one of the three style icons in the Formatting toolbar.

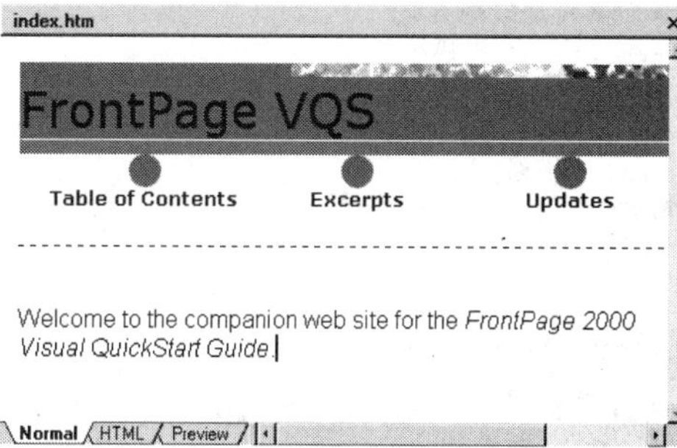

Figure 4.69 Once you click one of the style icons, the change is applied to the selected text.

To change the font style

1. If you're not already in page view, click the Page icon in the Views pane and make sure the *Normal* tab is selected.
2. Select the text you want to change (**Figure 4.67**).
3. Click one of the three style icons (*Bold, Italic*, or *Underline*) in the Formatting toolbar (**Figure 4.68**).
4. The style is applied to the selection (**Figure 4.69**).

To change the font color

1. Make sure you're in page view by clicking the Page icon in the Views pane.
2. Select the text you want to change (**Figure 4.70**).
3. Click the arrow just to the right of the Font Color icon and choose a color from the drop-down menu (**Figure 4.71**).
4. Release the cursor and the color will be applied to the selected text (**Figure 4.72**).

✔ Tip

- You also can change the text's color by right-clicking the page and choosing *Font* (Alt Enter) from the shortcut menu. (**Figure 4.62**). Within the Font dialog box, click the *Color* drop-down menu, make your choice, and click *OK* (**Figure 4.63**). For details see *Font options* on page 98.

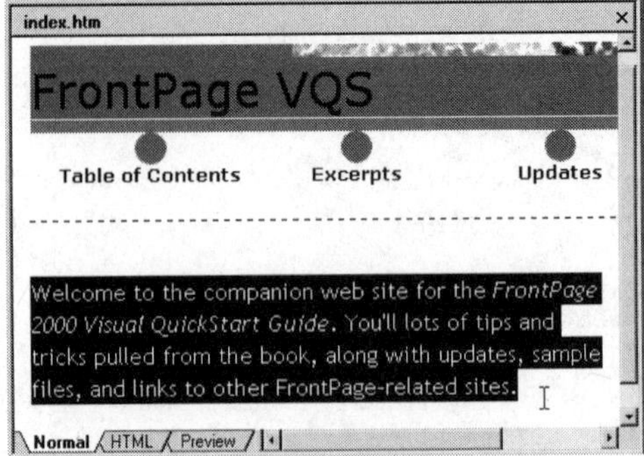

Figure 4.70 Select the text whose color you want to change.

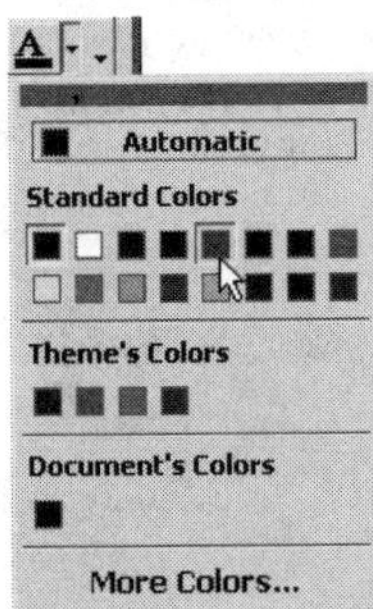

Figure 4.71 Click the arrow next to the Font Color icon and choose a color from the drop-down menu.

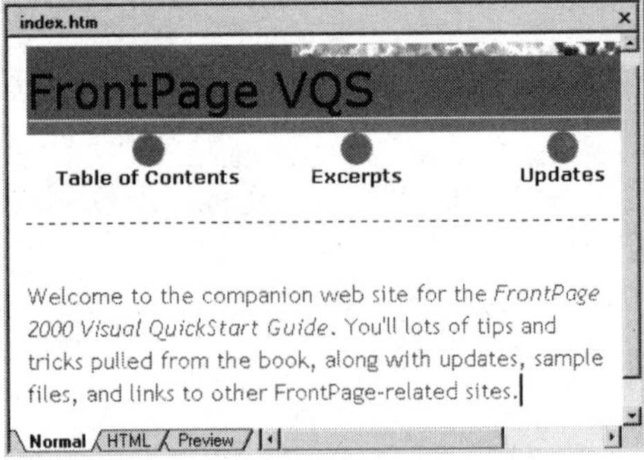

Figure 4.72 Once you release the cursor, the color change is applied to the selected text.

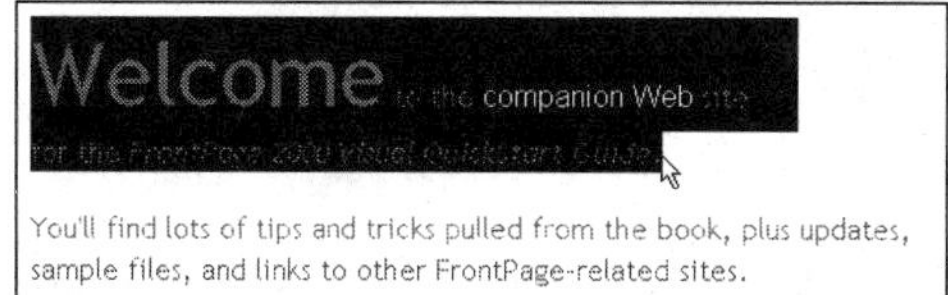
Welcome
companion Web
You'll find lots of tips and tricks pulled from the book, plus updates, sample files, and links to other FrontPage-related sites.

Figure 4.73 Select the text whose alignment you want to change.

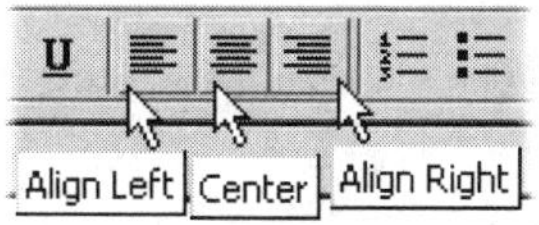
U
Align Left
Center
Align Right

Figure 4.74 Click one of the three alignment icons in the Formatting toolbar.

Figure 4.75 Once you click one of the alignment icons, the change is applied to the selected text.

To change text alignment

1. Make sure you're in page view by clicking the Page icon in the Views pane.
2. Select the text you want to change (**Figure 4.73**).
3. In the Formatting toolbar, click one of the three alignment icons (**Figure 4.74**).
4. Release the cursor and the text will be aligned based on which icon you clicked (**Figure 4.75**).

Font options

The Font dialog box is reached by selecting some text, then right-clicking and choosing *Font* from the shortcut menu (**Figures 4.76** and **4.77**). The dialog box's *Font* tab ❶ is active by default and lets you change the font, font style, size ❷, plus the text color ❸. It also lets you apply text effects ❹ not available within the Formatting toolbar. Check a box and you can see its effect within the *Preview* window ❺.

Clicking the Font dialog box's *Character Spacing* tab ❻ displays the *Spacing* ❼ and *Position* ❽ drop-down menus, which let you adjust the horizontal spacing and vertical positioning of the text you've selected (**Figure 4.78**). The *Preview* window ❾ lets you see the effects of various spacing and positioning combinations. For details on spacing and positions, see the next page.

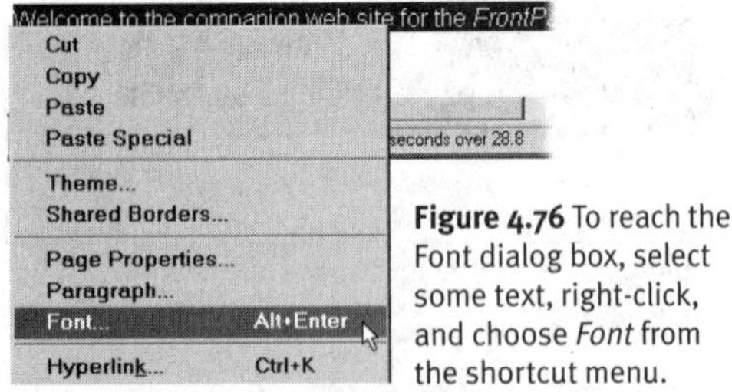

Figure 4.76 To reach the Font dialog box, select some text, right-click, and choose *Font* from the shortcut menu.

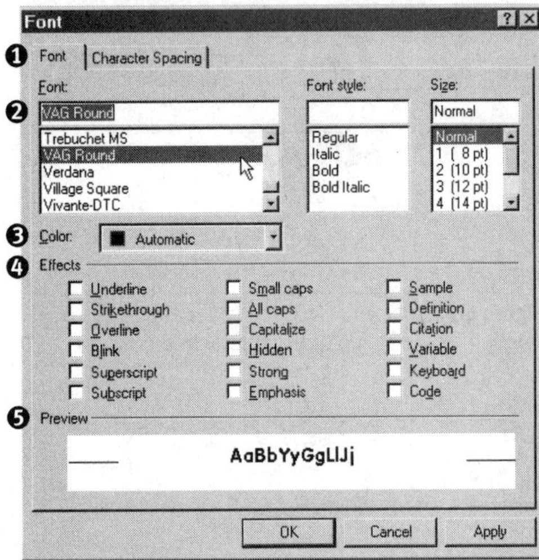

Figure 4.77 The Font dialog box's *Font* tab lets you change the selected text's font, font style, size, and text color.

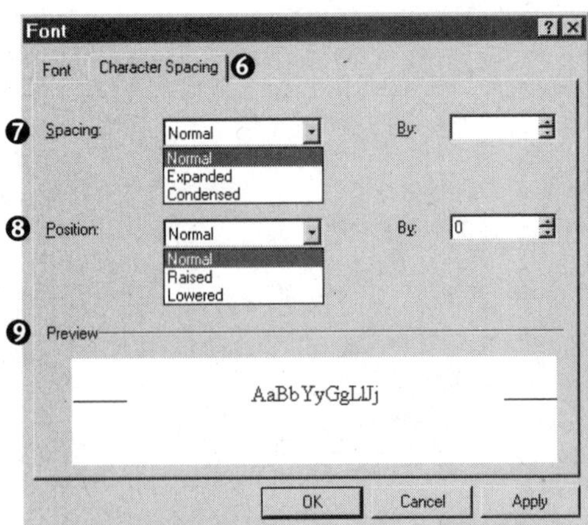

Figure 4.78 The *Character Spacing* tab lets you change the selected text's horizontal spacing and vertical positioning.

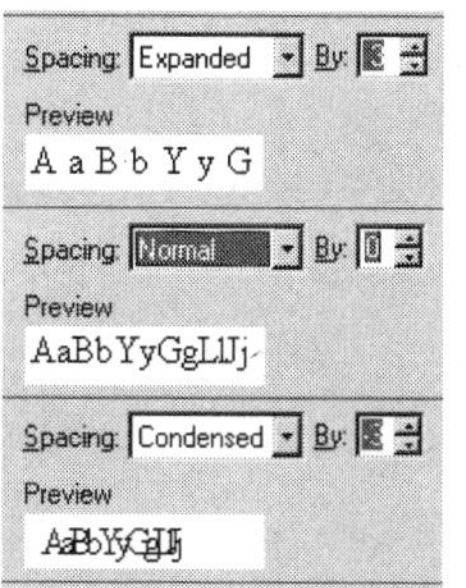

Figure 4.79 Within the Font dialog box, use the *Spacing* drop-down menu to control whether the text is *Expanded*, *Normal*, or *Condensed*. The adjacent *By* window lets you fine tune the spacing.

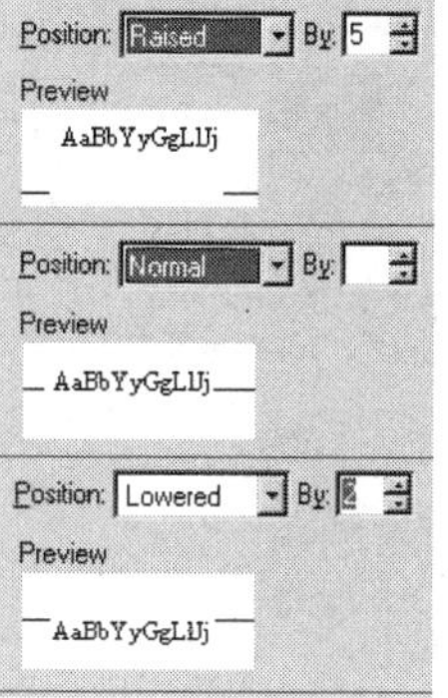

Figure 4.80 Within the Font dialog box, use the *Position* drop-down menu to control whether the text is *Raised*, *Normal*, or *Lowered*. The adjacent *By* window lets you fine tune the positioning.

To change character spacing

1. Make sure you're in page view by clicking the Page icon in the Views pane.
2. Select the text you want to change.
3. Right-click and choose *Font* from the shortcut menu (**Figure 4.76**).
4. When the Font dialog box appears (**Figure 4.78**), click the *Character Spacing* tab ❻.
5. Use the *Spacing* drop-down menu ❼ to quickly choose whether you want the text's horizontal spacing to be *Expanded, Normal,* or *Condensed.* The results will be displayed in the *Preview* window ❾. To fine tune the horizontal spacing, use the arrows of the adjacent *By* window to adjust the spacing in either direction (**Figure 4.79**).
6. When you're done, click *OK* and the spacing will be applied to the selected text.

To change character positioning

1. Make sure you're in page view by clicking the Page icon in the Views pane.
2. Select the text you want to change.
3. Right-click and choose *Font* from the shortcut menu (**Figure 4.76**).
4. When the Font dialog box appears (**Figure 4.78**), click the *Character Spacing* tab ❻.
5. Use the *Position* drop-down menu ❽ to quickly choose whether you want the text's vertical positions to be *Raised, Normal,* or *Lowered.* The results will be displayed in the *Preview* window ❾. To fine tune the horizontal spacing, use the arrows of the adjacent *By* window to adjust the spacing in either direction (**Figure 4.80**).
6. When you're done, click *OK* and the spacing will be applied to the selected text.

To remove text formatting

1. Make sure you're in page view by clicking the Page icon in the Views pane.
2. Select the text whose formatting you want to remove.
3. Choose Format > Remove Formatting (Ctrl Shift Z) (**Figure 4.81**).
4. All of the text's formatting will be removed, reverting back to its default settings.

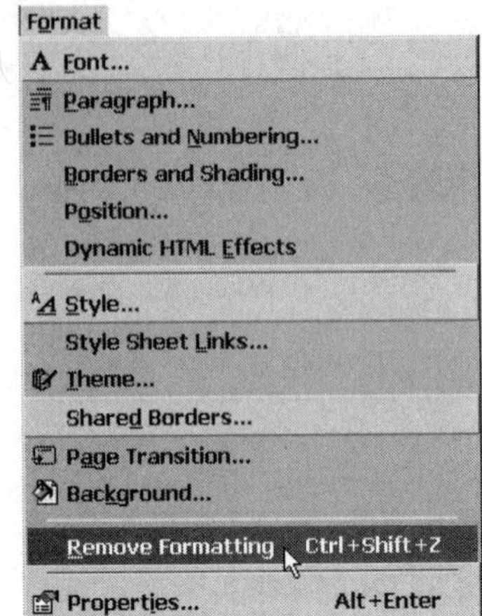

Figure 4.81 To remove all text formatting, select the text and choose Format > Remove Formatting (Ctrl Shift Z).

5 Formatting Paragraphs, Lists, and Headings

While graphics give your Web pages pizzazz, it's the paragraphs, lists, and headings that handle the real workload of setting your pages' visual hierarchy. FrontPage lets you easily set and control all three, primarily with the Formatting toolbar (**Figure 5.1**). If those controls, however, don't provide exactly what you need—or you want to create a custom style and use it repeatedly—consider using style sheets. See *Building Style Sheets and Dynamic Effects* on page 269.

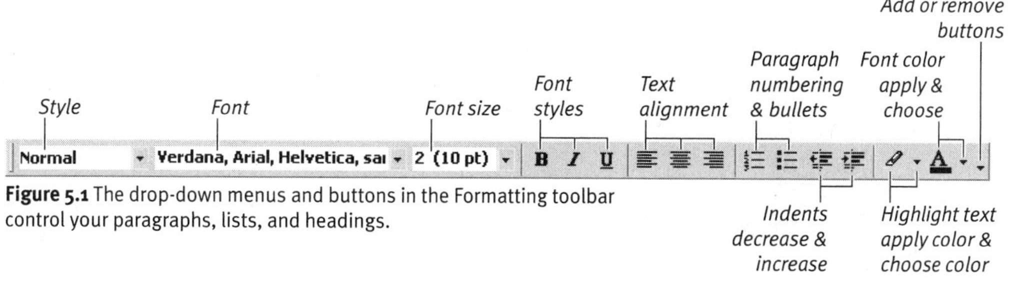

Figure 5.1 The drop-down menus and buttons in the Formatting toolbar control your paragraphs, lists, and headings.

Using Paragraphs

FrontPage lets you change the appearance of your paragraphs by adjusting their alignment, indentation, the spacing above and below the paragraph, and line spacing (leading).

To align a paragraph

1. Make sure you're in page view by clicking the Page icon in the Views pane (**Figure 5.2**).
2. Click anywhere in the paragraph you want to realign and choose one of the three alignment buttons in the Formatting toolbar (**Figure 5.3**). (By default, paragraphs are aligned to the left.) The new alignment will be applied (**Figure 5.4**).

Page

Figure 5.2 Whenever you're formatting, make sure you're in page view by clicking the Page icon in the Views pane.

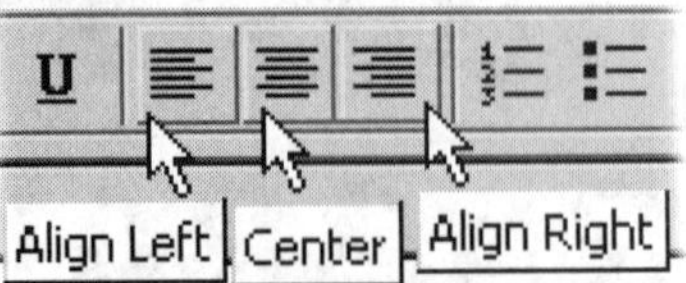
U
Align Left
Center
Align Right

Figure 5.3 To align a paragraph, click one of the three alignment buttons in the Formatting toolbar.

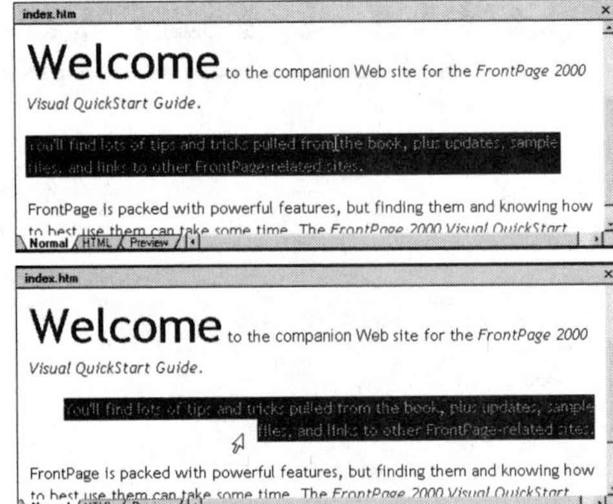
index.htm
Welcome to the companion Web site for the FrontPage 2000
Visual QuickStart Guide.
You'll find lots of tips and tricks pulled from the book, plus updates, sample files, and links to other FrontPage-related sites.
FrontPage is packed with powerful features, but finding them and knowing how
Normal
HTML
Preview
index.htm
Welcome to the companion Web site for the FrontPage 2000
Visual QuickStart Guide.
You'll find lots of tips and tricks pulled from the book, plus updates, sample files, and links to other FrontPage-related sites.
FrontPage is packed with powerful features, but finding them and knowing how
Normal
HTML
Preview

Figure 5.4 The paragraph was aligned to the left (top) until being reformatted to align on the right (bottom).

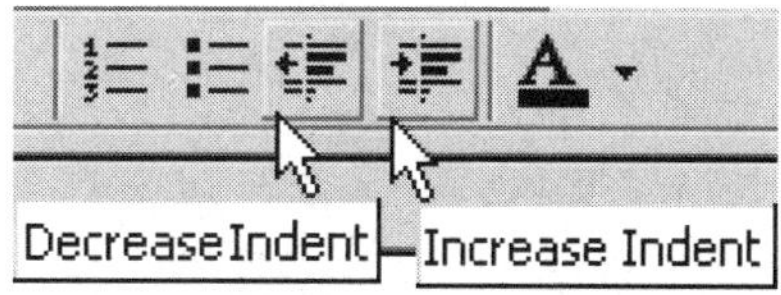
Decrease Indent
Increase Indent

Figure 5.5 To change a paragraph's indentation, click the Increase Indent or the Decrease Indent button.

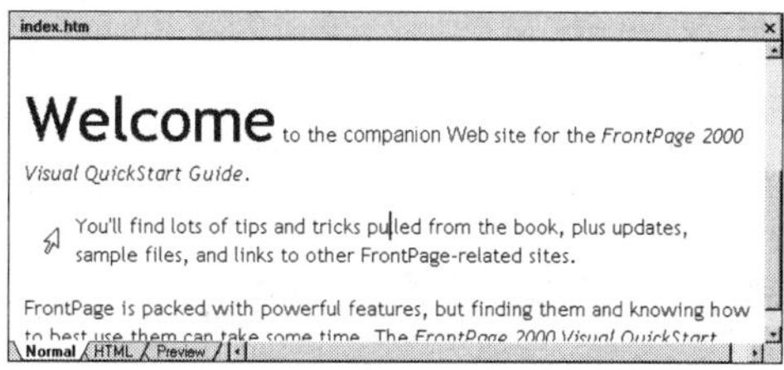
index.htm
Welcome to the companion Web site for the FrontPage 2000 Visual QuickStart Guide.
You'll find lots of tips and tricks pulled from the book, plus updates, sample files, and links to other FrontPage-related sites.
FrontPage is packed with powerful features, but finding them and knowing how
Normal
HTML
Preview

Figure 5.6 After applying the indent, the paragraph will shift to reflect your choice.

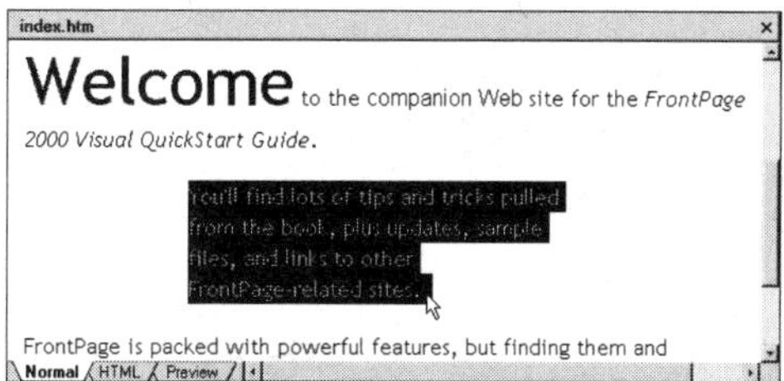
index.htm
Welcome to the companion Web site for the FrontPage 2000 Visual QuickStart Guide.
FrontPage is packed with powerful features, but finding them and
Normal
HTML
Preview

Figure 5.7 To indent a paragraph even more, keep clicking the Increase Indent button.

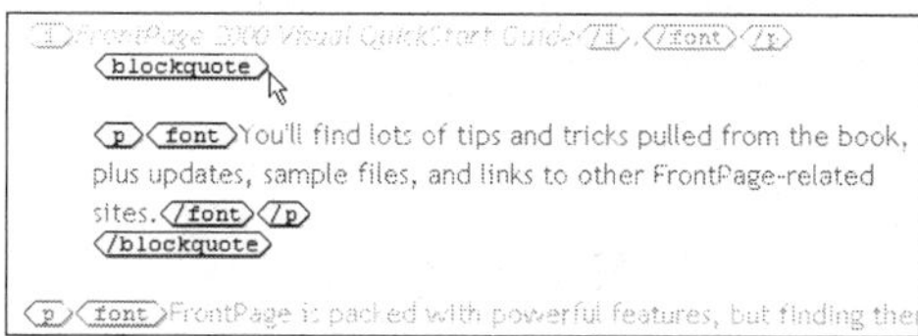
blockquote
p font You'll find lots of tips and tricks pulled from the book, plus updates, sample files, and links to other FrontPage-related sites. /font /p
/blockquote

Figure 5.8 To see any of the normally hidden HTML tag as you work, choose View > Reveal Tags. Repeat to hide them again.

Indenting paragraphs

FrontPage gives you several ways to indent paragraphs. The quickest way involves using the buttons in the Formatting toolbar; the more precise method requires setting custom indentations within the Paragraph dialog box.

To indent paragraphs

1. Be sure you're in page view, then click anywhere in the paragraph you want to indent.
2. Click the Increase Indent button or the Decrease Indent button in the Formatting toolbar (**Figure 5.5**). The indenting will be applied (**Figure 5.6**).
3. If you want to indent the paragraph even more, continue clicking the Increase Indent button until you're satisfied with the result (**Figure 5.7**).

✔ Tips

- The indent buttons affect both margins of the selected text *equally* (**Figure 5.7**). To set *different* indents for each margin, see *To customize paragraph indents* on the next page.
- As with all Web editors, FrontPage uses HTML tags to format your text. But to keep the document from getting cluttered, FrontPage ordinarily hides the coding from sight. To see the tags at any point, choose View > Reveal Tags (Control /) (**Figure 5.8**). Repeat the command to hide the tags again.

To customize paragraph indents

1. Be sure you're in page view, then right-click anywhere in the paragraph whose style you want to change and choose *Paragraph* from the shortcut menu (**Figure 5.9**).
2. When the Paragraph dialog box appears, use the *Indentation* section's arrows to set the indentation in points *Before text* and *After text* (**Figure 5.10**).
3. Click *OK* and your custom indentation will be applied (**Figure 5.11**).

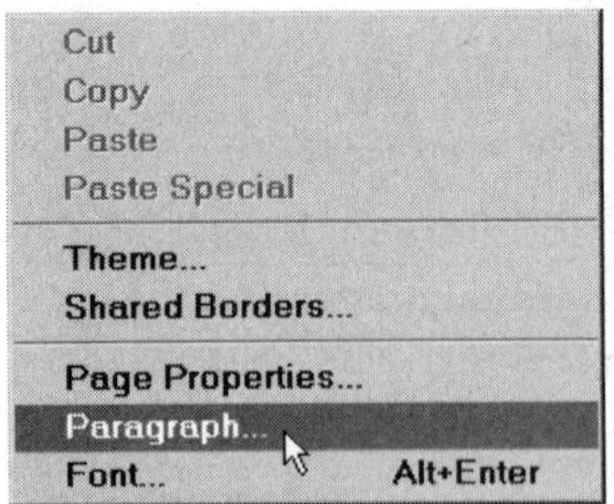

Figure 5.9 To modify the Normal paragraph style, right-click anywhere in the paragraph and choose *Paragraph* from the shortcut menu.

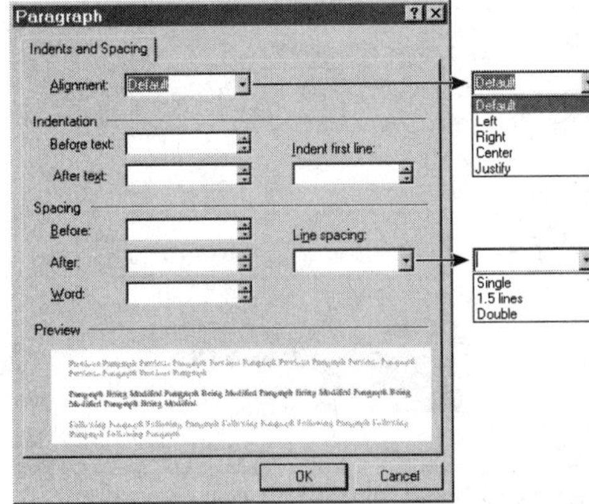

Figure 5.10 Use the Paragraph dialog box's pop-up menus and arrows to simultaneously change multiple aspects of a paragraph. The *Preview* area at the bottom shows how the changes will look.

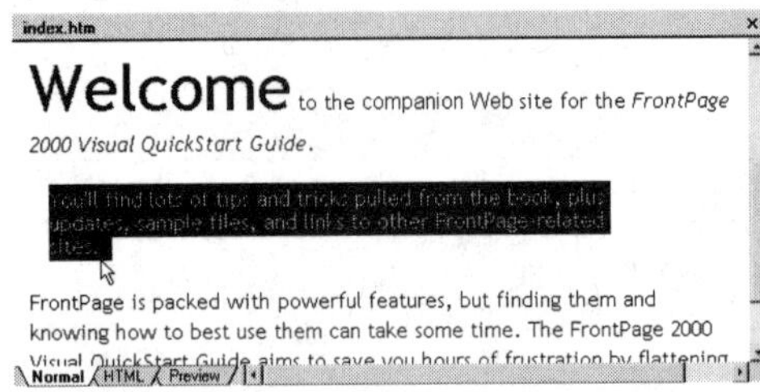

Figure 5.11 Custom indentation of 15 points on the left, 60 points on the right applied to the highlighted paragraph.

Paragraph styling

To change several aspects of a paragraph at once, the easiest way is to modify FrontPage's *Normal* style, which by default uses the Times New Roman font with single line spacing that's left-aligned with no indentations. Or you can use the built-in *Formatted* style, which uses Courier monospaced in a type-writer-like style that requires you to manually enter any line returns. It looks clunky but before fancy HTML came along, it was often the only way to make text wrap exactly.

To modify the Normal paragraph style

1. Be sure you're in page view. Right-click anywhere in the paragraph whose style you want to change and choose *Paragraph* from the shortcut menu (**Figure 5.9**).
2. When the Paragraph dialog box appears, use the pop-up menus and arrows to set your paragraph's alignment, indentation, indentation for the paragraph's first line only, the amount of blank space you want before and after the paragraph, and the line spacing within the paragraph (**Figure 5.10**). The *Preview* area at the bottom of the dialog box lets you see how the indents and spacing will be applied.
3. Once you're satisfied with the changes, click *OK* and the styling will be applied to the selected paragraph.

✔ Tip

- The Paragraph dialog box includes the option of changing the spacing between words (**Figure 5.10**). Unfortunately, FrontPage can't show how the word spacing will appear. You'll have to switch to your Web browser to see the effect—and most browsers don't support the feature. You're better off skipping the word spacing feature entirely.

To apply the Formatted paragraph style

1. Be sure you're in page view and click where you want the Formatted style to begin.
2. Use the Style drop-down list in the Formatting toolbar to choose Formatted (**Figure 5.12**).
3. Begin typing, using the spacebar to align and wrap the text (**Figure 5.13**).
4. When you're ready to switch back to the Normal format, use the Style drop-down list in the Formatting toolbar to choose Normal (**Figure 5.14**).

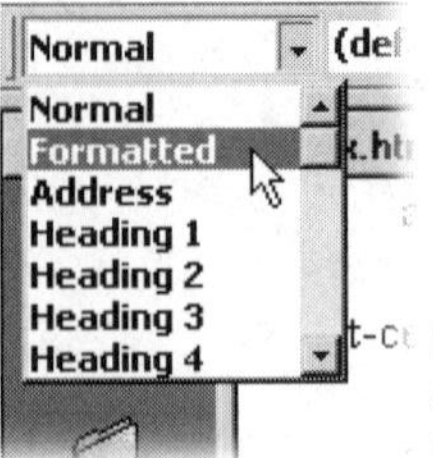

Figure 5.12 To apply the *Formatted* paragraph style, use the Style drop-down list.

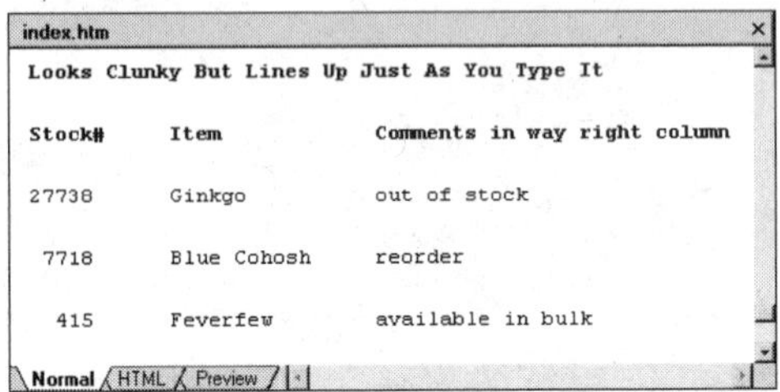

Figure 5.13 The Formatted style looks terrible, but lets you align these inventory numbers.

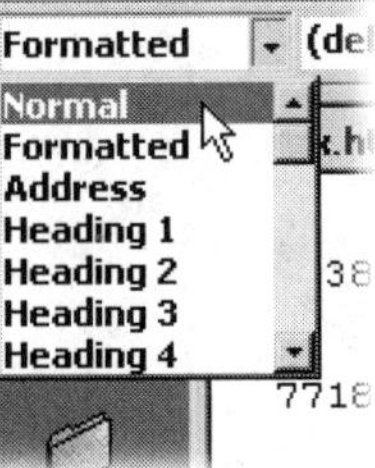

Figure 5.14 Use the Style drop-down list to switch back to the Normal format.

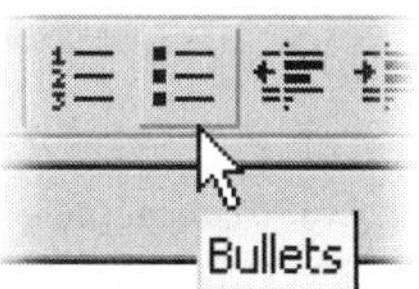

Figure 5.15 To quickly create a bulleted list, click the Bullets button in the Formatting toolbar.

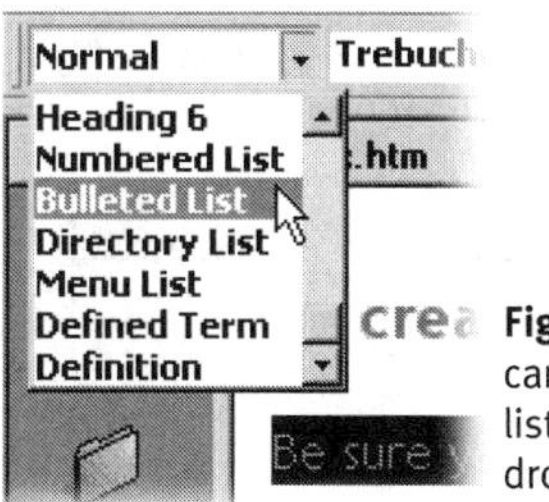

Figure 5.16 You also can create a bulleted list using the Style drop-down menu.

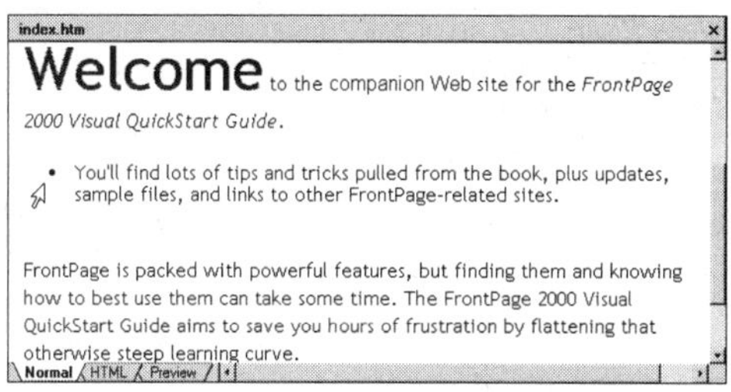

Figure 5.17 Nothing fancy: The default bullet style.

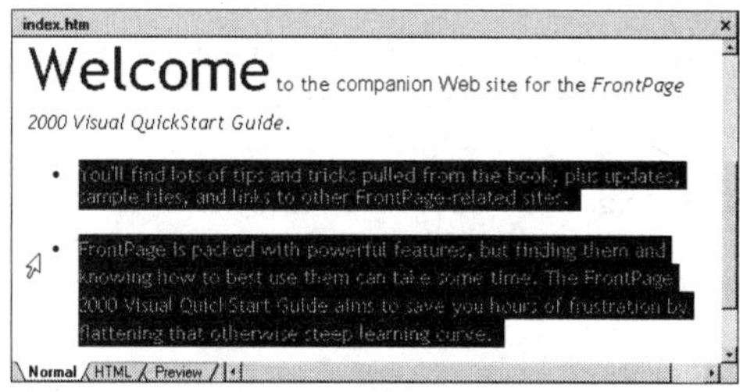

Figure 5.18 To apply bullets to several paragraphs at once, just select them and click the Bullets button.

Using Lists

FrontPage lets you create a variety of list styles, which can be broken into two general groups: unordered lists and ordered lists. Unordered, also known as unnumbered or bulleted, lists are great for presenting a series of items that have no particular order, such as a list of supplies. Use ordered or numbered lists whenever you want to present a list of items in sequence. While FrontPage will create directory and menu lists, they're not supported by most browsers, so it's best to avoid using them.

Creating unordered lists

By default, FrontPage uses solid, round bullets. However, you can use any of the bullets within FrontPage's built-in themes—or create custom bullets. For details, see *Customizing lists* on page 110.

To create a bulleted list

1. Be sure you're in page view. Click anywhere in the line or paragraph that you want bulleted.
2. Click the Bullets button in the Formatting toolbar (**Figure 5.15**). Or use the Style drop-down list in the Formatting toolbar to choose *Bulleted List* (**Figure 5.16**). A bullet will be added to the line or paragraph (**Figure 5.17**).
3. To continue adding bullets to the list, press Enter. Once you're done building the list, press Enter twice and FrontPage will switch to regular body type.

✔ Tips

- To apply bullets to several paragraphs at once, just select them and click the Bullets button (**Figure 5.18**).
- To remove bullets, click anywhere in the bulleted line or paragraph and click the Bullets button once more.

Creating definition lists

Definition lists are handy for glossaries and other dictionary-style information because the format puts a word or term on a single line with the definition indented immediately below it. Though you can type in all the terms and definitions and then format them, it's generally easier to switch to the Defined Term format and begin typing since all the formatting will be handled automatically.

To create a definition list

1. Place your cursor where you want the first definition to appear.
2. Use the Style drop-down list in the Formatting toolbar to choose *Defined Term* (**Figure 5.19**).
3. Release the cursor and type in your first term. Then press Enter and the cursor will jump to the next line, automatically add an indent, and switch to the Definition format (**Figure 5.20**)
4. Type in your definition. If you want to add more terms, press Enter again and FrontPage will jump to a new line and switch back to the Defined Term format.
5. Once you're done adding terms, press Enter *twice* and FrontPage will switch back to the normal body text (**Figure 5.21**).

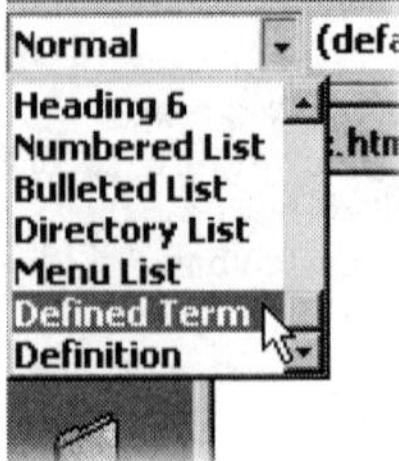

Figure 5.19 To create a definition list, place your cursor where the first definition should appear and choose *Defined Term* from the Style drop-down list.

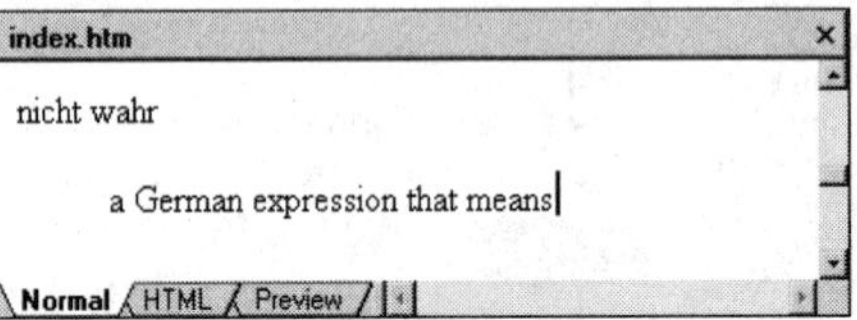

Figure 5.20 After you type in your first term and press Enter, the cursor will jump to the next line, automatically add an indent, and switch to the Definition format.

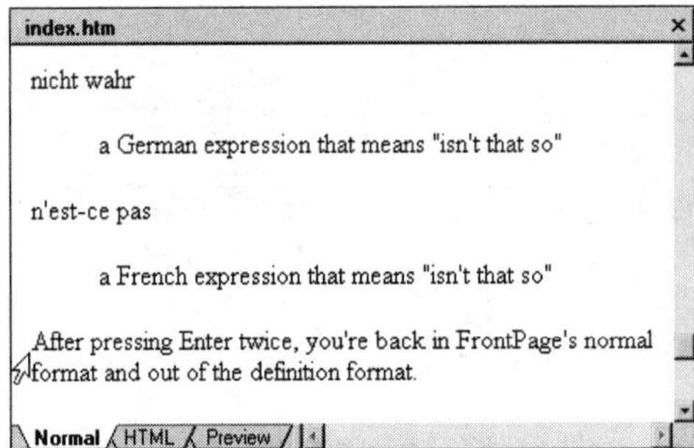

Figure 5.21 Once you're done adding terms, press Enter *twice* and FrontPage will switch back to the normal body text.

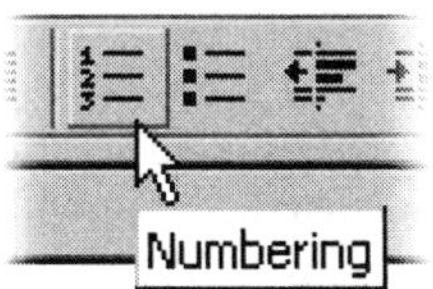

Figure 5.22 To create a numbered list, select your text and click the Numbering button in the Formatting toolbar.

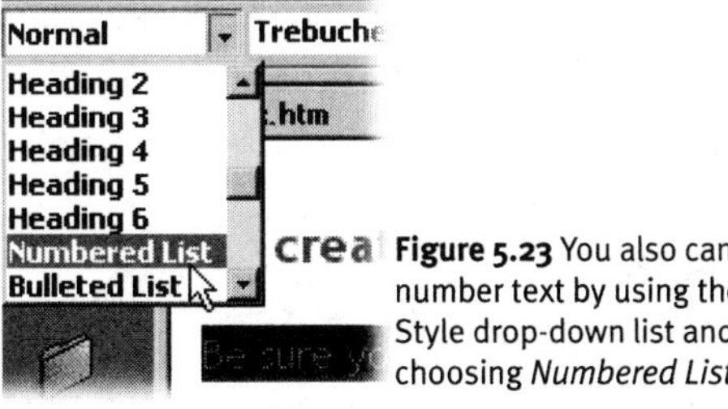

Figure 5.23 You also can number text by using the Style drop-down list and choosing *Numbered List*.

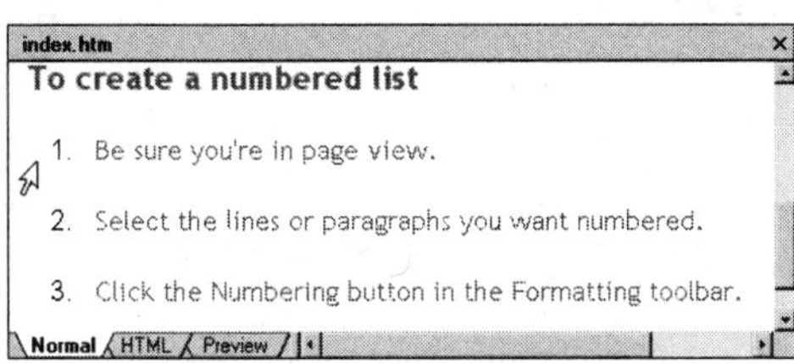

Figure 5.24 Once numbering is applied, press Enter to continue adding items to the list.

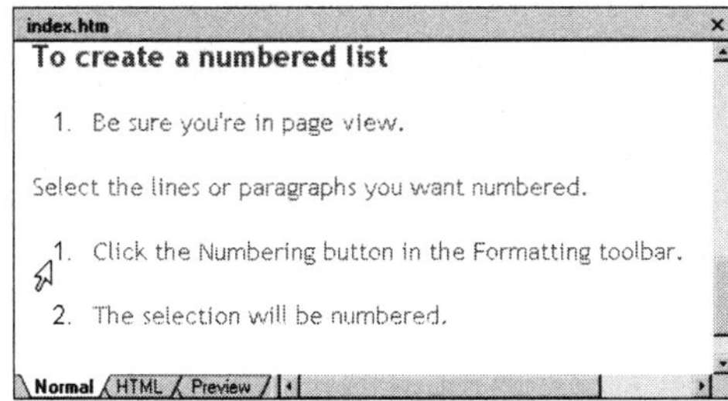

Figure 5.25 If you reformat a previously numbered item to regular text, FrontPage automatically renumbers the remaining text into *two* sequences.

Creating ordered lists

Use ordered lists whenever you want to present a list of items in sequence. Though ordered lists usually are numbered, FrontPage also lets you use letters (A, B, C,...) as well. For details, see *Customizing lists* on the next page.

To create a numbered list

1. Be sure you're in page view. Select the lines or paragraphs you want numbered.
2. Click the Numbering button in the Formatting toolbar (**Figure 5.22**). Or use the Style drop-down list in the Formatting toolbar to choose *Numbered List* (**Figure 5.23**). In either case, the selected lines or paragraphs will be numbered in sequence (**Figure 5.24**).
3. To continue adding numbered items to the list, press Enter. Once you're done building the list, press Enter twice and FrontPage will switch to regular body type.

✔ Tips

- To remove numbers, click anywhere in the numbered line or paragraph and click the Numbering button once more. The remaining items will be renumbered and even broken into two sequences if necessary (**Figure 5.25**).
- Instead of numbering items after you've written them, you can number them as you type. Just place your cursor where you want the first item in the list to appear, click the Numbering button, and the number 1 will appear. Begin typing, pressing Enter whenever you want the next number to begin.

Customizing lists

As usual, FrontPage offers you several choices for customizing your lists. Your sources of bullets for unordered lists are particularly wide: FrontPage's built-in themes, the clip art that comes with FrontPage, or any graphic of your own. To use the bullets built into FrontPage's themes, see *To apply a theme to a page or Web site* on page 64.

To customize lists

1. Click anywhere in the page and choose Format > Bullets and Numbering (**Figure 5.26**). If you are changing an existing list, just right-click in the list and choose *List Properties* from the shortcut menu (**Figure 5.27**).
2. Depending on what you clicked on in step 1, either the Bullets and Numbering or List Properties dialog box will appear (**Figures 5.28** and **5.29**). Choose one of the tabs, which can include: *Picture Bullets, Plain Bullets, Numbers,* or *Other.*
3. Make your choices and click *OK* to apply the change to your page. For details, see *List options* on the next page.

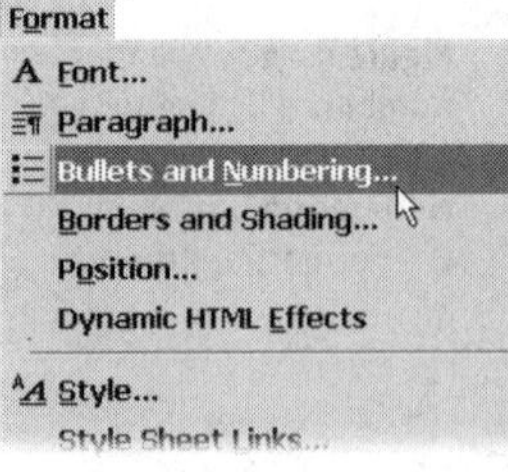

Figure 5.26 To customize your bullets or numbers, click anywhere in the page and choose Format > Bullets and Numbering.

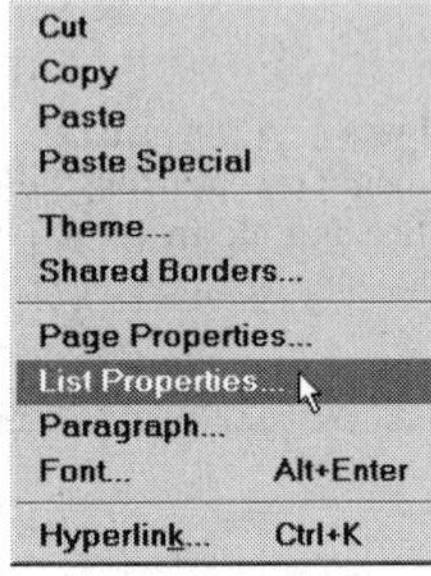

Figure 5.27 To customize an existing list, right-click in the list and choose *List Properties* from the shortcut menu.

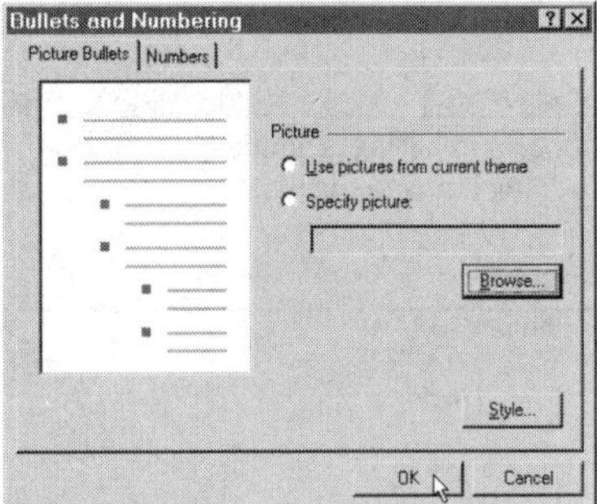

Figure 5.28 The Bullets and Numbering dialog box lets you insert your own pictures as graphical bullets.

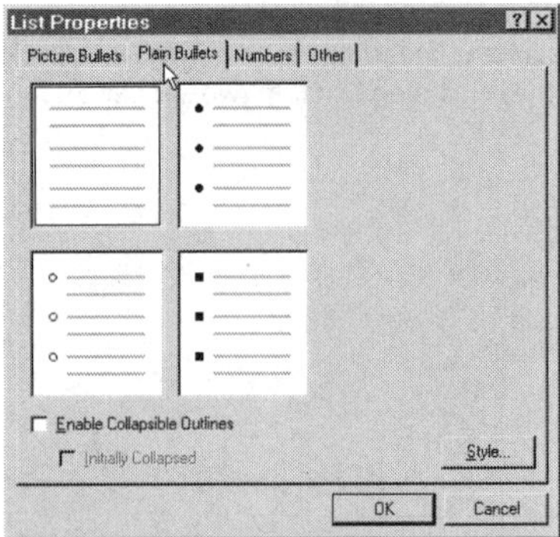

Figure 5.29 The List Properties dialog box gives you complete control over customizing bullets, numbers, and lists.

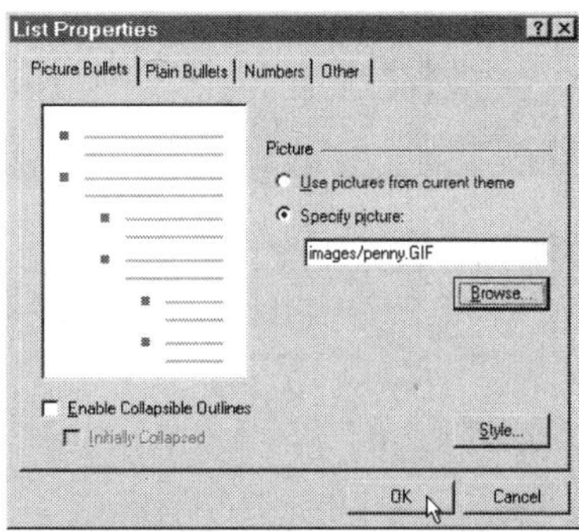

Figure 5.30 To use your own graphic as a bullet, navigate to the file and then click *OK*.

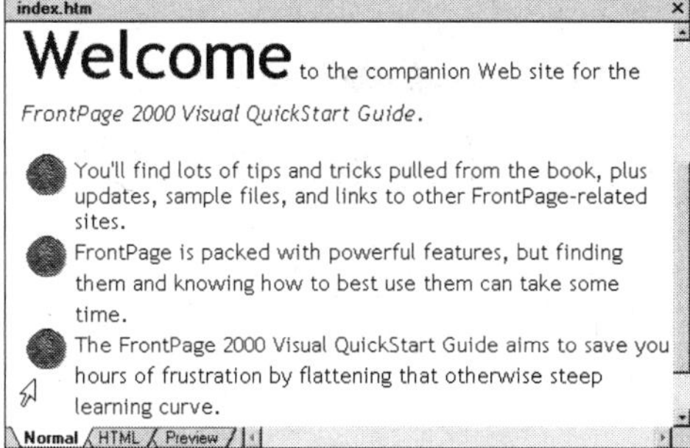

Figure 5.31 Once you've picked a graphic, FrontPage uses it instead of the plain bullets.

List options

Follow the steps in *To customize lists* to reach the Bullets and Numbering or List Properties dialog box (**Figures 5.28** and **5.29**). Both boxes offer the Picture Bullets and Numbers tabs; the other two tabs appear only in the List Properties box:

- **Picture Bullets:** This tab lets you use your own graphics as bullets—even if you're also using one of FrontPage's built-in themes. To turn off the theme's bullets, click *Specify picture*, then click *Browse* and navigate to the graphic file you want to use (**Figure 5.30**). Click *OK* and the selected graphic will be used for your bullets (**Figure 5.31**).
- **Plain Bullets:** This tab lets you choose one of three plain bullet styles (**Figure 5.29**). The fourth, upper-left choice offers a somewhat roundabout option for canceling the bullets entirely. Once you've made your choice, click *OK* to apply the plain bullet style.

(continued)

- **Numbers:** This tab lets you choose five numbering/lettering styles (**Figure 5.32**). Again, the upper-left choice lets you cancel numbering. Use the *Start at* arrows if you want to start the numbering at, say, 4 or the fifth letter, E. Once you've made your choice, click *OK* to apply.
- **Other:** This tab lets you quickly switch the style of an entire list to any of the other styles in the text window (**Figure 5.33**). Once you've made your choice, click *OK* to apply.

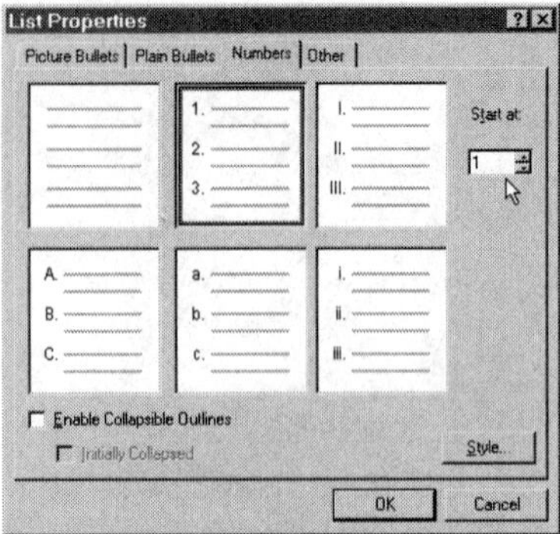

Figure 5.32 The *Numbers* tab of the List Properties dialog box gives you five numbering/lettering styles plus a blank option.

✔ Tip

- Every tab of the List Properties dialog box includes checkboxes for *Enable Collapsible Outlines* and *Initially Collapsed.* These features are available only if you're using Dynamic HTML (DHTML) and are recognized only by version 4 or later browsers. For details, see *Building Style Sheets and Dynamic Effects* on page 269.

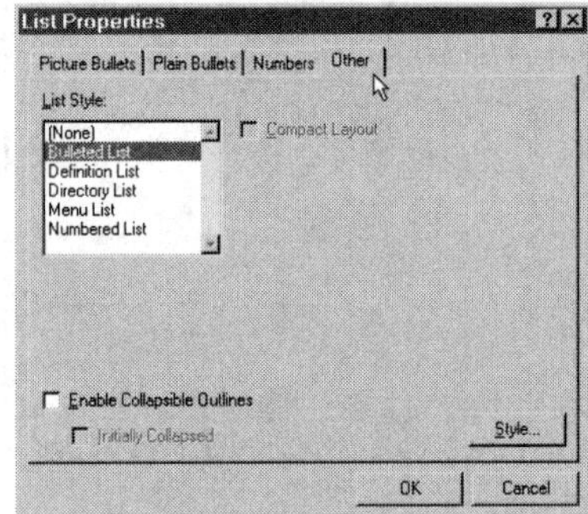

Figure 5.33 The *Other* tab of the List Properties dialog box lets you change an entire list to another style.

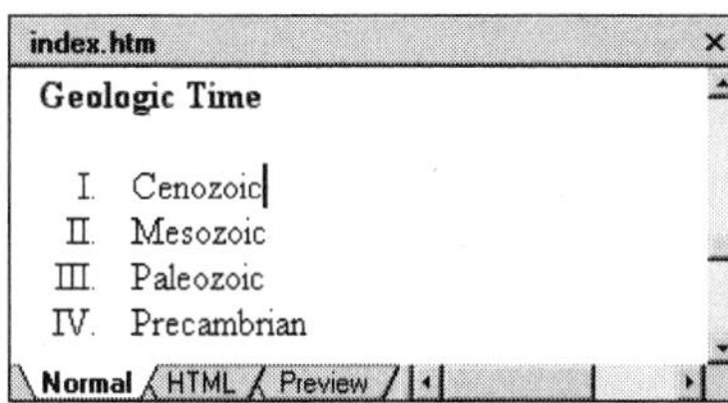

Figure 5.34 To create a nested list, click in a bulleted or numbered list right where you want the subdivision to start.

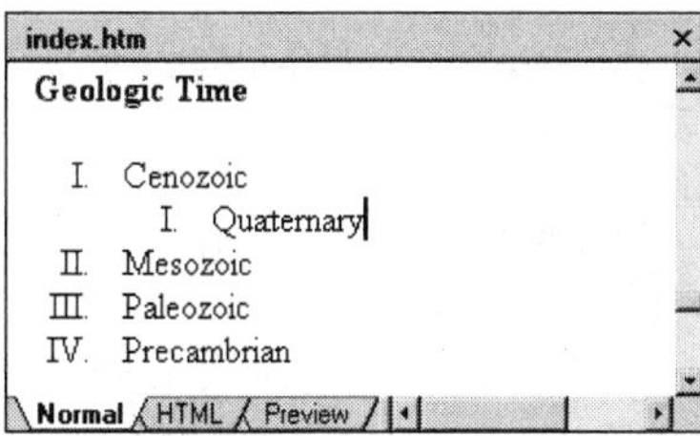

Figure 5.35 By default, the nested subdivision's numbering or lettering matches the level above it.

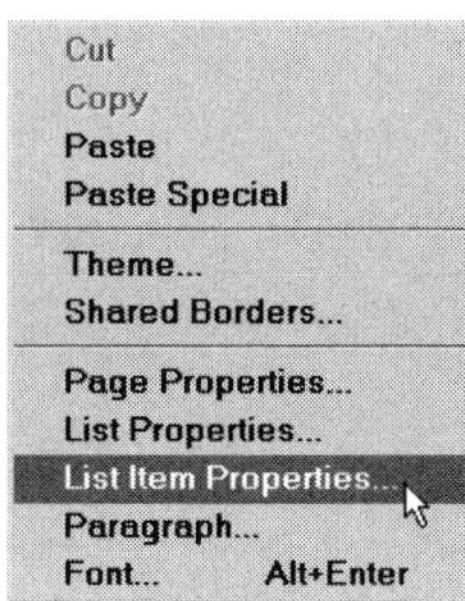

Figure 5.36 To change a *subdivision's* numbering or lettering scheme, right-click and choose *List Item Properties*.

Nested lists

Nested lists, sometimes called multilevel lists, enable you to create subdivisions within an overall list. They also lend themselves to customizing, such as using numbers at one level and letters at another.

To create a nested list

1. First create a bulleted or numbered list, then click in that list just before where you want to insert a nested subdivision (**Figure 5.34**).
2. Press Enter and click the Increase Indent button *twice* (**Figure 5.5**).
3. When a new, blank line is inserted into the list, begin typing your first nested item. By default, it will be numbered or lettered just like the level above it (**Figure 5.35**).
4. If you want to change the *subdivision's* numbering or lettering scheme, right-click and choose *List Item Properties* from the shortcut menu (**Figure 5.36**).

(continued)

5. When the List Item Properties dialog box appears, choose a numbering or lettering style, click *OK*, and the style will be applied to the nested item only (**Figure 5.37**).

6. To add another item at this same nested level, press Enter and it will be numbered or lettered in the same style you chose in step 5. Continue adding items at that level until you're done.

7. If you want to nest still another level in the list, repeat steps 1–6 (**Figure 5.38**).

8. When you're done building the nested list, press Enter twice to switch back to regular body type.

✔ Tip

- In step 4, be sure to choose *List Item Properties* not *List Properties* (**Figure 5.36**). *List Item Properties* controls the nested list items; *List Properties* controls the overall list in which the item nests.

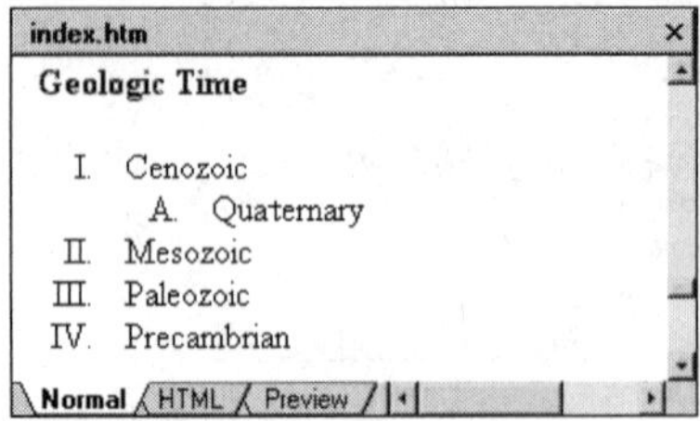

Figure 5.37 The nested item, Quaternary, now has a letter instead of a number.

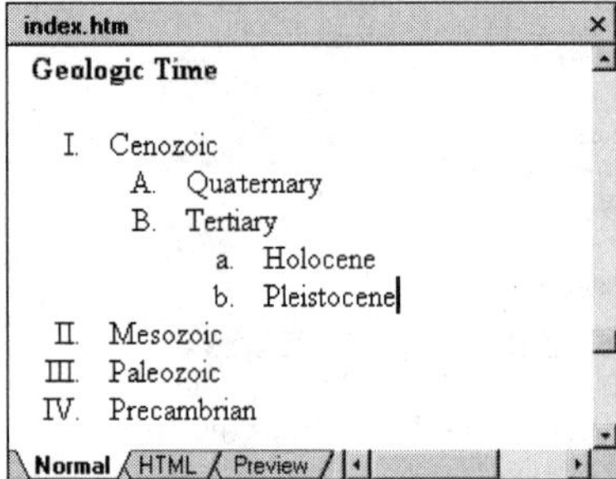

Figure 5.38 FrontPage lets you nest items within already nested items, changing the numbering or lettering style at each level.

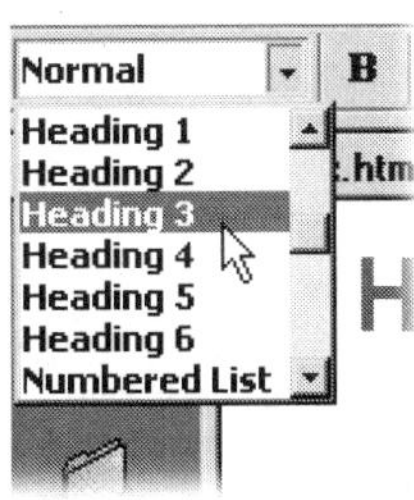

Figure 5.39 To convert text to a heading, use the Style drop-down menu to select the heading size you want.

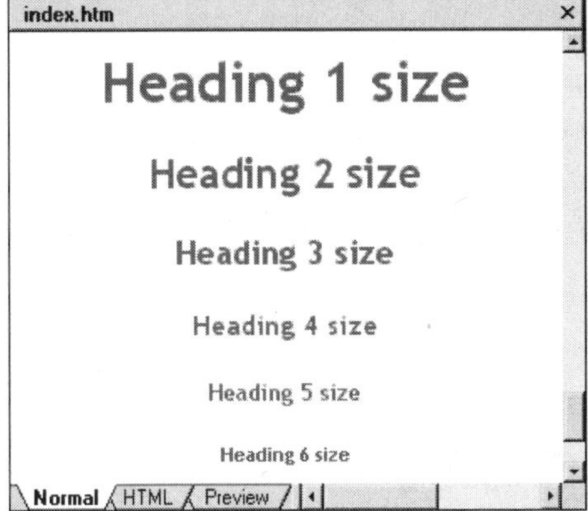

Figure 5.40 Sizes range from Heading 1, the largest, to Heading 6, the smallest.

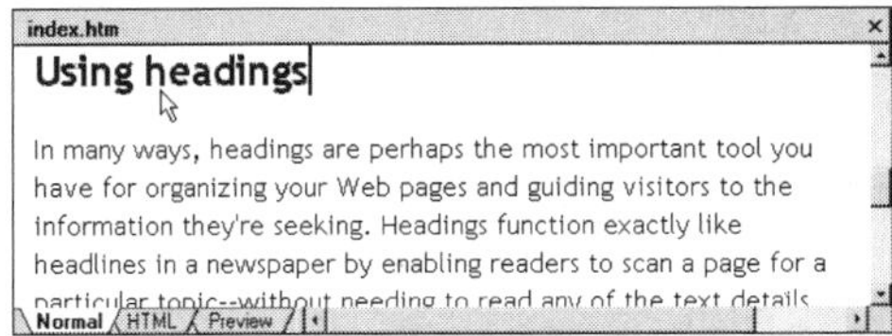

Figure 5.41 Once you release the cursor, the heading will be applied to the selected text.

Using Headings

In some ways, headings are your most important tool for guiding visitors through your Web pages to the information they're seeking. Headings function exactly like headlines in a newspaper by enabling readers to scan a page for a particular topic—without needing to read any of the text details. As with a newspaper, big headings should be used for your most important topics and smaller headings for less important items. It's simple—but vital—in bringing visual order to your pages. While this section just deals with heading sizes, remember you also can change heading font, color, and style. For details, see *Formatting Text* on page 92.

To add headings

1. Click anywhere in the line of text you want to make into a heading.
2. Click on the Style drop-down menu in the Formatting toolbar and select the heading size you want to apply (**Figure 5.39**). Heading 1 is the largest; Heading 6 the smallest (**Figure 5.40**).
3. Release your cursor and the heading will be applied (**Figure 5.41**).

✔ Tip

- While you can apply a heading to as much as a full paragraph of text, generally it's easier to read a heading if you use no more than two short lines of text. In fact, the fewer words the better.

To change a heading size

1. Click anywhere in the heading whose size you want to change.
2. Click on the Style drop-down menu in the Formatting toolbar and select a new heading size.
3. Release your cursor and the new heading size will be applied.

ADDING HYPERLINKS

The Web's essential beauty springs from the user's ability to jump from file to file anywhere in the world. Hyperlinks make that possible. Hyperlinks, or simply links, come in several varieties: links to other files around the globe, links to other spots within the document already on your screen, links to send email, links embedded in pictures. FrontPage makes it easy to create them all.

Text links are explained on the next page; image links are covered separately on page 132. It's also worth remembering that *Creating a Web Site* on page 41 discusses how to automatically link entire pages as you build or reorganize your site.

Absolute and Relative Links

Fundamental to using links is understanding the difference between what are called absolute and relative hyperlinks. Confusion about which to use when is common, but it's pretty simple.

An absolute link shows a file's full Web address (`http://www.peachpit.com/books/catalog/K5914.htm`) while a relative link just includes the file name and the folder it's stored in (`/My Webs2/formatting.htm`). You *must* use an absolute link any time you create a link to a Web page or file *not* on your own Web site, sometimes called an external link. Relative links *should* be used to link to files within your own Web site.

The advantage of relative links is that you can rearrange your Web site and files without breaking any links, which stymies Web browsers. Precisely because your home page has an absolute address, a Web browser can bounce from relative link to relative link within your Web site even if you move `expensivepart.htm` from `www.yoursite.com/parts/` to `www.yoursite.com/supplies/`. Rearranging your site is inevitable. You'll outgrow the original structure, find a better way to do it, or whatever. Use relative links to avoid *manually* updating all those links. Ugh!

Figure 6.1 Switch to page view by clicking the Page icon in the Views pane.

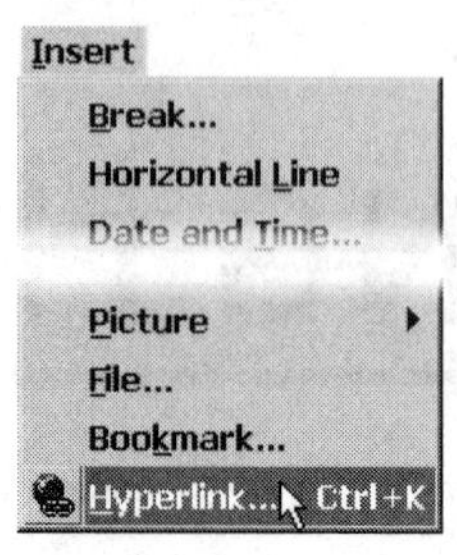

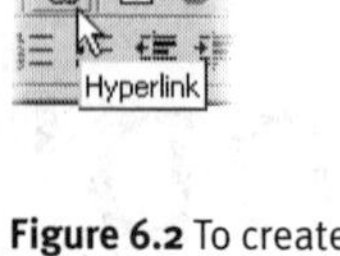

Figure 6.2 To create a link, choose Insert > Hyperlink (left) or click the Hyperlink button in the Standard toolbar (right).

Figure 6.3 To quickly create a link, right-click your selection and choose *Hyperlink* from the shortcut menu.

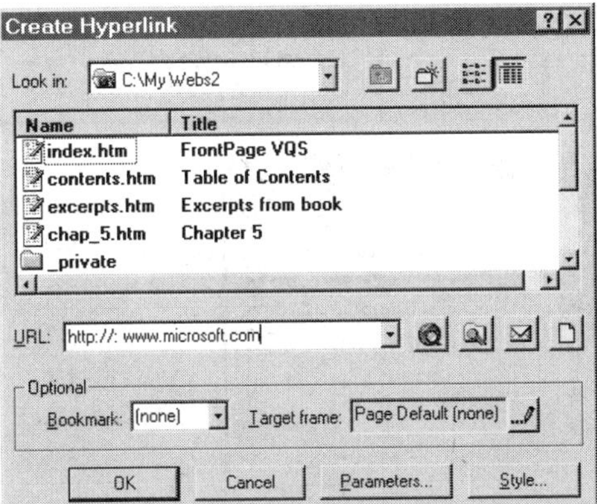

Figure 6.4 You can type a site's URL directly into the text window of the Create Hyperlink dialog box.

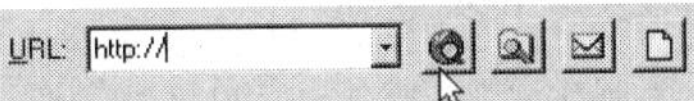

Figure 6.5 If you don't know a site's URL, find it by clicking the Web browser button in the Create Hyperlink dialog box.

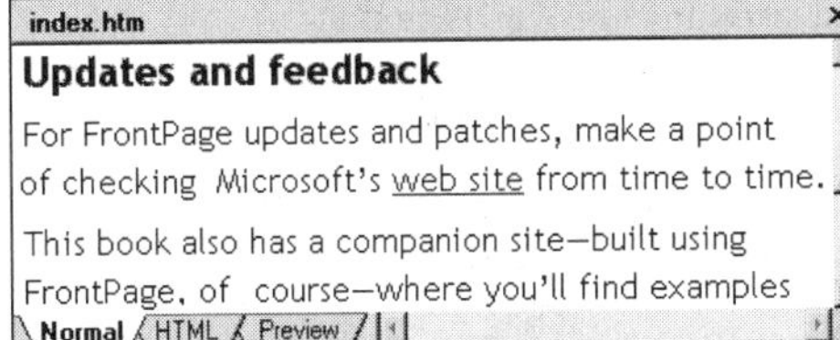

Figure 6.6 FrontPage marks linked text with an underline.

To link to an external Web page

1. Make sure you're in page view by clicking the Page icon in the Views pane (**Figure 6.1**).
2. Select the text you want to link.
3. Choose Insert > Hyperlink or click the Hyperlink button in the Standard toolbar (**Figure 6.2**). You also can right-click and choose *Hyperlink* from the shortcut menu ((Ctrl)(K)) (**Figure 6.3**).
4. When the Create Hyperlink dialog box appears, if you know the site's URL type it directly into the URL text window and skip to step 7 (**Figure 6.4**). If you don't know the URL, click the Web browser button (**Figure 6.5**). For details on the dialog box, see *Create Hyperlink options* on page 121.
5. When your default Web browser launches, use it to hunt down the external Web page to which you want to link.
6. Once you reach the external Web page you're seeking, switch back to the Create Hyperlink dialog box and the URL will be automatically pasted into the text window.
7. Click *OK* and your selection will be linked—indicated by the underline (**Figure 6.6**).

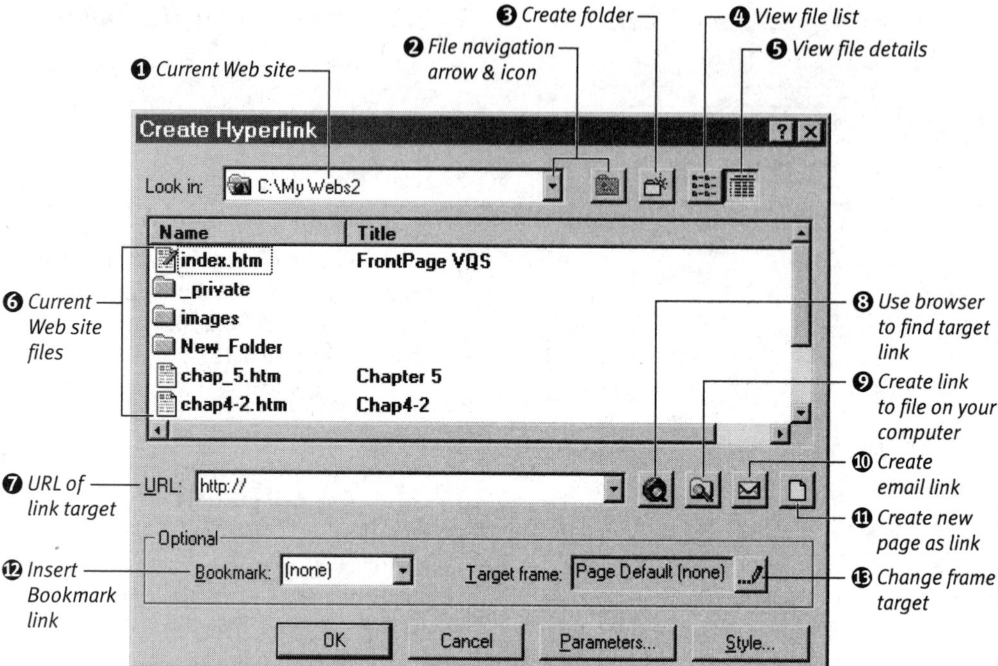

Figure 6.7 The Create Hyperlink dialog box offers total control over FrontPage's hyperlinks.

Create Hyperlink options

The Create Hyperlinks dialog box offers total control over FrontPage's hyperlinks (**Figure 6.7**). To reach the dialog box, choose Insert > Hyperlink (Ctrl K).

❶ **Current Web site:** By default, the dialog box opens to the Web site you're working on.

❷ **File navigation arrow and folder icon:** If you want to switch from your current site, use the arrow's drop-down menu to open your other FrontPage Web sites. Use the folder icon to navigate around your computer.

❸ **Create folder:** Click to add a new folder to your Web site.

❹ **View file list:** Click to see just the names of the files.

❺ **View file details:** Click to see the site's names and *titles* (what appears at the top of a visitor's browser).

❻ **Current Web site's files:** Use the far-right scroll bar to see all the files and folders in your site.

❼ **URL of link target:** This is the Web address, the Uniform Resource Locator destination, of your link. FrontPage automatically begins the URL with an http:// but just type ftp:// to replace it if you're creating a File Transfer Protocol link for visitors to download a file.

❽ **Use browser to find target link:** Click to create an *absolute* link (see page 119). Your Web browser will launch so you can hunt down an external page out on the Web. Once you reach the page, switch back to FrontPage and the address is pasted automatically into the URL window.

❾ **Create link to file on your computer:** Click to create a *relative* link (see page 122). FrontPage will let you navigate to any file on your hard drive and paste the address into the URL window.

❿ **Create email link:** Click to link your selected text or image to an email address (see page 122).

⓫ **Create new page as link target:** Click if you want to create a link to a page on your Web site that you've not yet created (see page 123). The New dialog box will open, allowing you to create a normal page or one based on FrontPage's templates.

⓬ **Insert a Bookmark:** Use the drop-down menu to select and insert an existing bookmark (FrontPage's term for anchor links), which are links *within* the page you're working on. For details, see page 127. To create a bookmark from scratch, see page 126.

⓭ **Change Target frame link:** Click only if your Web site contains frames (see *Creating and Formatting Frames* on page 211).

To link to a page in your Web site

1. Make sure you're in page view by clicking the Page icon in the Views pane (**Figure 6.1**).
2. Select the text you want to link, right-click, and choose *Hyperlink* from the shortcut menu (Ctrl K) (**Figure 6.3**).
3. The Create Hyperlink dialog box offers several ways to link to a file on your computer. If the file's already part of your Web site, use the dialog box's scroll bar to find the file, click it, and the name will be pasted into the URL text box (**Figure 6.8**). If the file's elsewhere on your computer, click the find local file button and use the Select File dialog box to navigate to the file (**Figures 6.9** and **6.10**).
4. Click *OK* in either the Create Hyperlink or Select File dialog box, depending on your choice in step 3. Your selected text will be linked to the file—as indicated by an underline.

To create an email link

1. Select the text you want linked to an email address, right-click, and choose *Hyperlink* from the shortcut menu (Ctrl K) (**Figure 6.3**).
2. When the Create Hyperlink dialog box appears, click the email button (**Figure 6.11**).
3. When the Create E-mail Hyperlink dialog box appears, type in the email address and click *OK* (**Figure 6.12**). The address will be pasted into the Create Hyperlink's text window. Click *OK* again and your selected text will be linked.

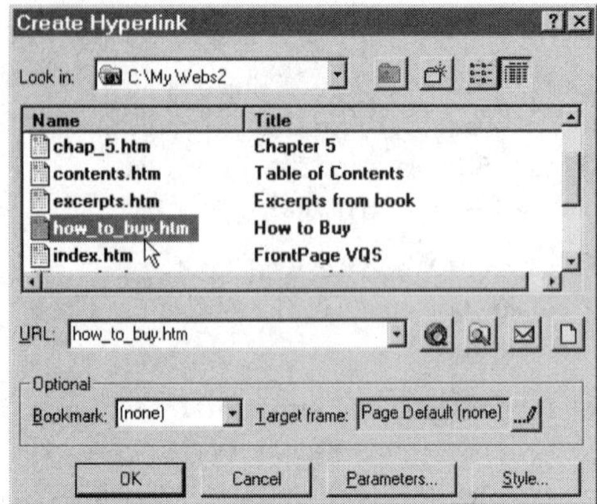

Figure 6.8 If a file's already part of your Web site, click on it and its name will be pasted into the URL text box.

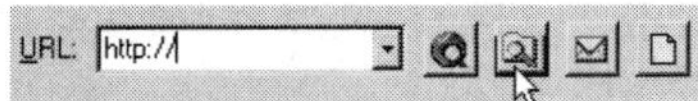

Figure 6.9 To link to a file on your computer, click the local file button in the Create Hyperlink dialog box.

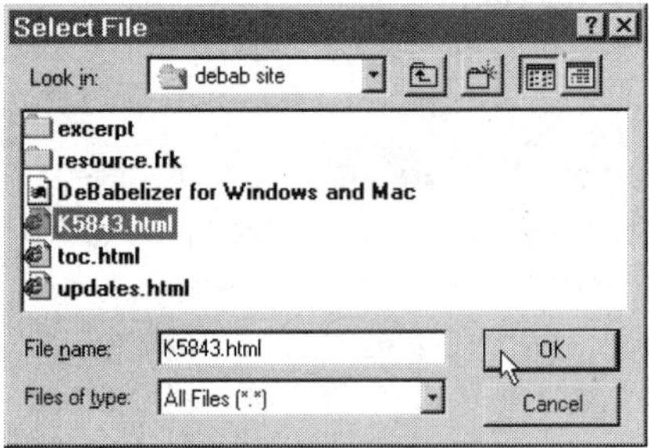

Figure 6.10 Once you track down a local file, click *OK* in the Select File dialog box.

Figure 6.11 To add an email link, click the envelope button in the Create Hyperlink dialog box.

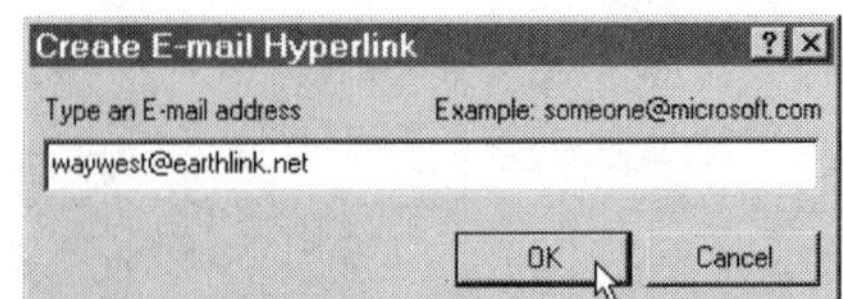

Figure 6.12 Type the email address into the text window and click *OK*.

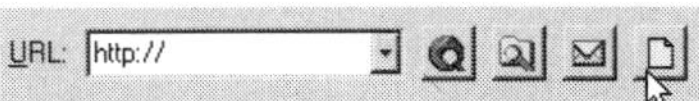

Figure 6.13 To link to a not-yet-created page, click the new page icon in the Create Hyperlink dialog box.

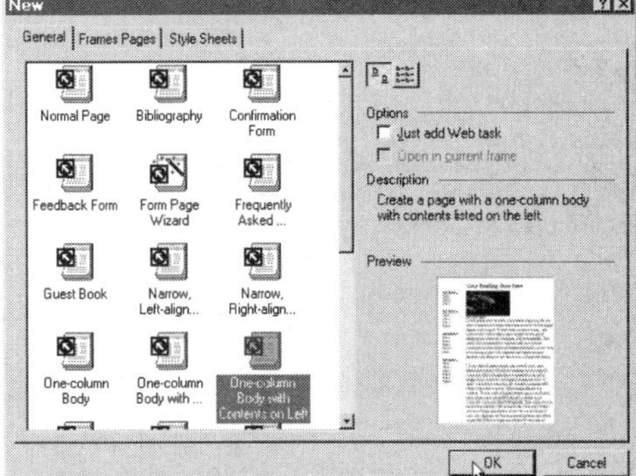

Figure 6.14 The New dialog box lets you create a normal page or one based on a template.

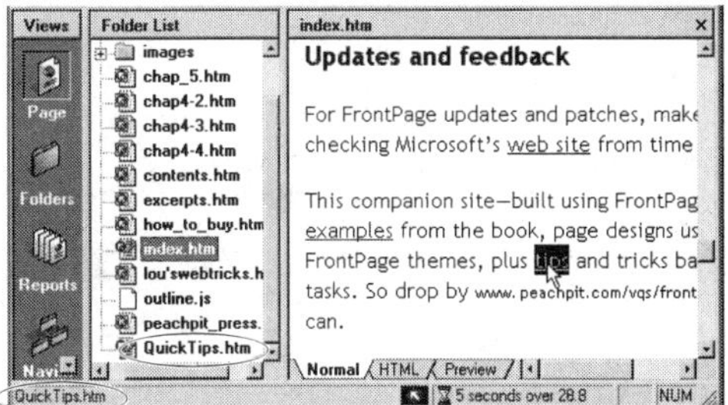

Figure 6.15 After the new page (QuickTips.htm) is created, its address appears in the bottom status bar. The new page also appears in the Folder List.

Linking to pages not yet created

On the face of it, this sounds weird: Why would you link to a non-existent page? In truth, it's common as you're creating links to realize you've forgotten to create a necessary page. This option lets you quickly make the new page and link to it from the page you're already working on.

To create a new page and link to it

1. Select the text you want linked to a not-yet-created page, right-click, and choose *Hyperlink* from the shortcut menu (Ctrl K) (**Figure 6.3**).
2. When the Create Hyperlink dialog box appears, click the create new page button (**Figure 6.13**).
3. The New dialog box will appear where you can choose to create a *Normal Page* or a page based on any of the templates (**Figure 6.14**). Make your choice, click *OK* and quickly name and title the new page. For details, see *To open a new Web page* on page 32 and *To rename a page* on page 45.
4. Using either the Navigation icon or the Folder List, click on the page you were originally working in, and you'll see that the selected text now links to the newly created page (**Figure 6.15**).

Changing links

FrontPage automatically updates links as you move pages around on your Web site. But if you want to completely change a link address, or delete a link, it's easy. If you've deleted entire pages—especially without using FrontPage in the first place—running an update will guard against broken links (see *To update links* on the next page.).

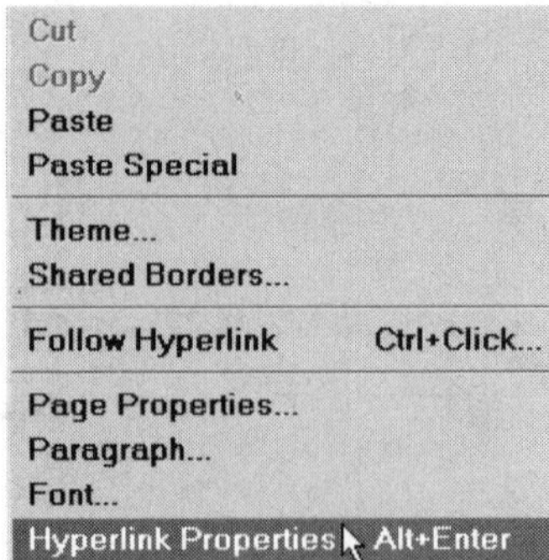

Figure 6.16 To change a link, right-click it and choose *Hyperlink Properties* from the shortcut menu.

To edit a link

1. Right-click on any link you want to change and choose *Hyperlink Properties* from the shortcut menu (**Figure 6.16**). Or type Alt Enter.
2. When the Edit Hyperlink dialog box opens, the link's *present* URL will be highlighted (**Figure 6.17**). You can:

   ❶ type a *new* URL directly into the text window,

   ❷ click the URL text window's right-side arrow to choose from a drop-down menu of recent URLs, or

   ❸ click any of the dialog box's four far-right buttons to navigate to a new URL or file.
3. When you've changed the URL, click *OK* and the link will be updated to reflect the new address.

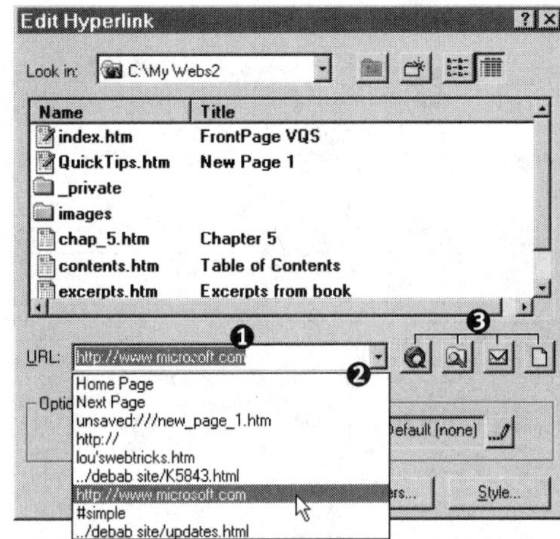

Figure 6.17 Use the Edit Hyperlink dialog box to change a link's URL.

CHANGING LINKS

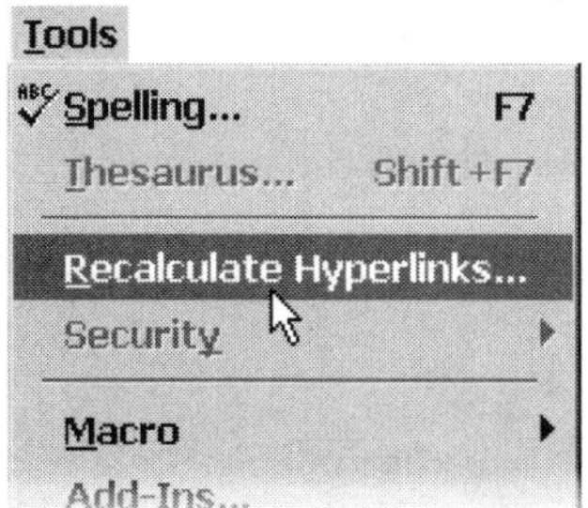

Figure 6.18 If you delete pages without using FrontPage, update their links by choosing Tools > Recalculate Hyperlinks.

To delete a link

1. Right-click on any link you want to change and choose *Hyperlink Properties* from the shortcut menu (**Figure 6.16**). Or type Alt Enter.
2. When the Edit Hyperlink dialog box opens, the link's URL is highlighted (**Figure 6.17**). Press ←Backspace or Delete and the URL will be deleted from the text window.
3. Click *OK* and the selected text will no longer be linked.

To update links

1. Choose Tools > Recalculate Hyperlinks (**Figure 6.18**).
2. FrontPage will warn you that this might take a few minutes, depending on the size of your Web site. If you've got the time, click *Yes*. FrontPage will repair any links broken when site pages were rearranged but it can't fix a link if you entered the wrong URL in the first place.

Using Bookmarks

Bookmarks, often called anchor links, let visitors jump to specific spots, such as section headings, within a long Web page. Creating anchors is a two-step process: first you create the bookmark itself (the anchor), then you create hyperlinks (the anchor links) that point to the bookmark.

Insert anchor links into your Web pages to let readers jump ahead or back without scrolling through the whole document. Anchors aren't limited to headings. Feel free to link to a citation, a word or image, or a single character.

If you ever want to update or remove some bookmarks in a lengthy Web page and don't want to scroll through searching for them one by one, FrontPage makes it easy to find them.

To create a bookmark

1. Select the text you want the reader to jump to, that is, the target or destination.
2. Choose Insert > Bookmark (**Figure 6.19**).
3. When the Bookmark dialog box opens, it automatically uses the selected text as the name of the bookmark (**Figure 6.20**). However, you can type in another name if that suits your purposes.
4. When you're done naming the bookmark, click *OK* and the selected text will be bookmarked, as indicated by a dashed underline (**Figure 6.21**). See *To link to a bookmark* to complete the process.

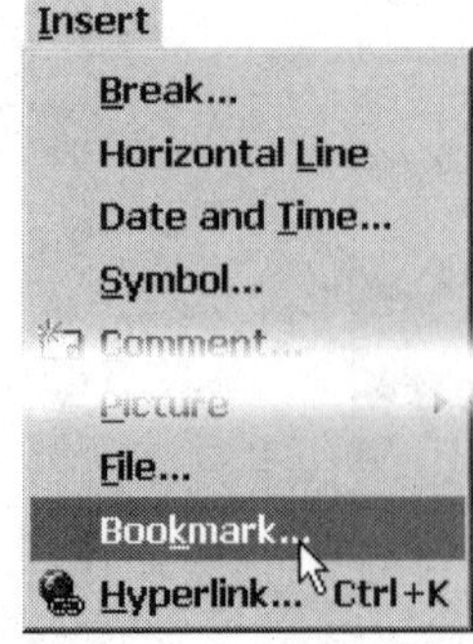

Figure 6.19 To create a bookmark, select the target text, then choose Insert > Bookmark.

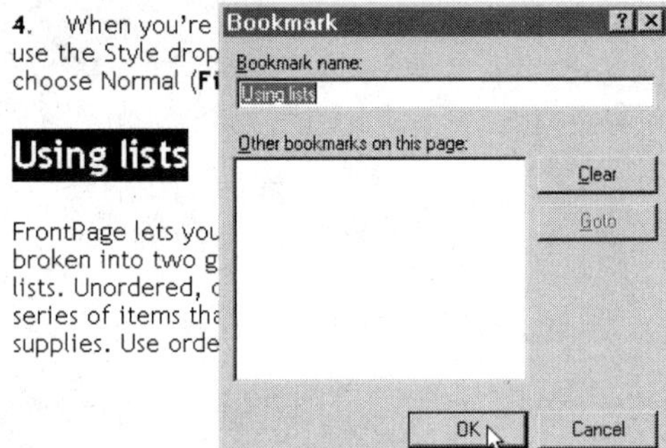

Figure 6.20 By default, the bookmark (right) assumes the name of the selected text (left). Type in another name if you prefer.

Figure 6.21 FrontPage places a *dashed* line beneath bookmarked text.

URL: formatting.htm
Optional
Bookmark: (none)
Target frame: Page Default (none)
(none)
Using headings
Using lists
Using paragraphs
Cancel
Parameters...
Style...

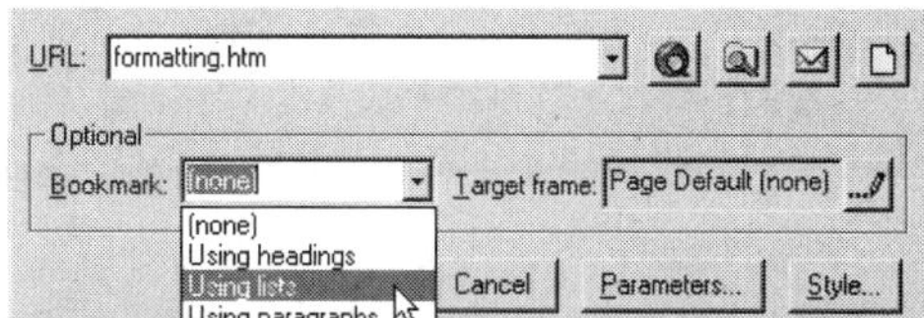

Figure 6.22 To link to a bookmark, use the Bookmark drop-down menu in the Create Hyperlink dialog box.

FORMATTING PARAGRAPHS, LISTS, AND HEADINGS
While graphics give your Web pages pizazz, its the paragraphs, lists, and headings that handle the real workload of setting your pages' visual hierarchy. FrontPage lets you easily set and control all three, primarily with
Normal
HTML
Preview

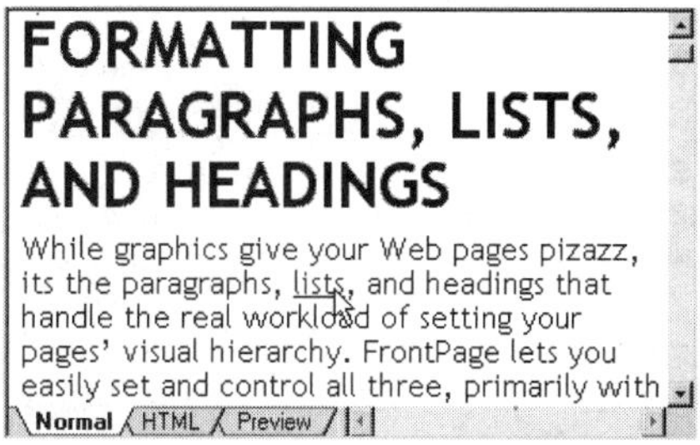

Figure 6.23 The selected text, now underlined, links directly to the bookmark.

To link to a bookmark

1. Select the text you want linked to a bookmark, right-click, and choose *Hyperlink* from the shortcut menu (Ctrl K) (**Figure 6.3**).
2. When the Create Hyperlink dialog box appears, use the *Bookmark* drop-down menu to choose the bookmark you've already created (**Figure 6.22**).
3. Click *OK* and your selected text will be linked to the bookmark (**Figure 6.23**).

✔ Tips

- As you create more bookmarks, they'll be added to the drop-down menu. However, the menu will display only the bookmarks for the page you're working on, not the entire site.
- Revising the link to a bookmark follows the same steps, except that in step 2, the Edit Hyperlink dialog box will appear. For details, see *To edit a link* on page 124.

To find bookmarks

1. Start by finding any bookmark in a page (marked by a dashed underline). Right-click it and choose *Bookmark Properties* from the shortcut menu ((Alt)(Enter)) (**Figure 6.24**).
2. The Bookmark dialog box will appear with the selected bookmark highlighted in the top text window. Highlight any other bookmark by clicking it within the list, then click *Goto* (**Figure 6.25**).
3. The Bookmark dialog box will remain open, but your Web page will jump to the chosen bookmark (**Figure 6.26**). Once you find the bookmark, click *OK* and you'll be returned to the Web page. To clear the bookmark, see the next page.

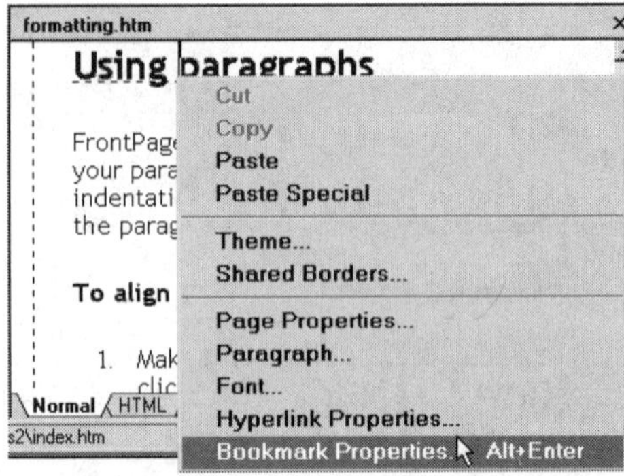

Figure 6.24 To find any other bookmarks in a page, right-click any bookmark and choose *Bookmark Properties* from the shortcut menu.

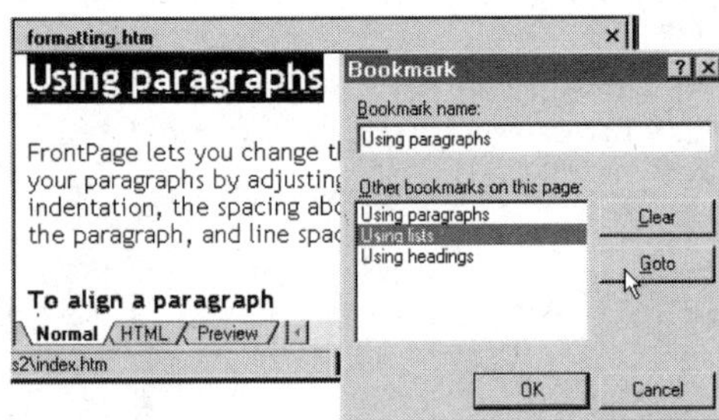

Figure 6.25 Choose the bookmark you're looking for with the drop-down menu, then click *Goto*.

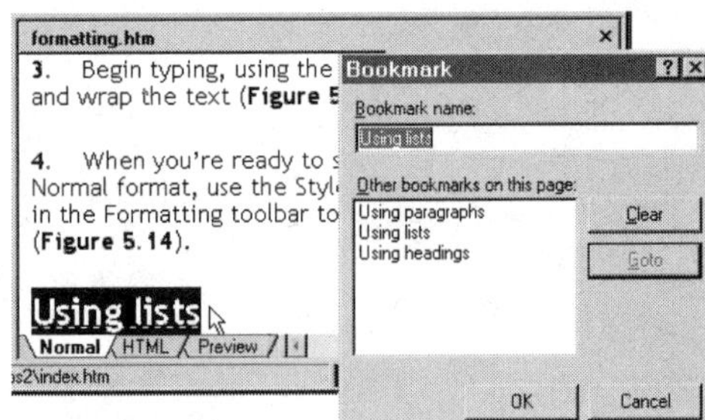

Figure 6.26 After clicking *Goto*, the Bookmark dialog box remains open but your Web page jumps to the chosen bookmark.

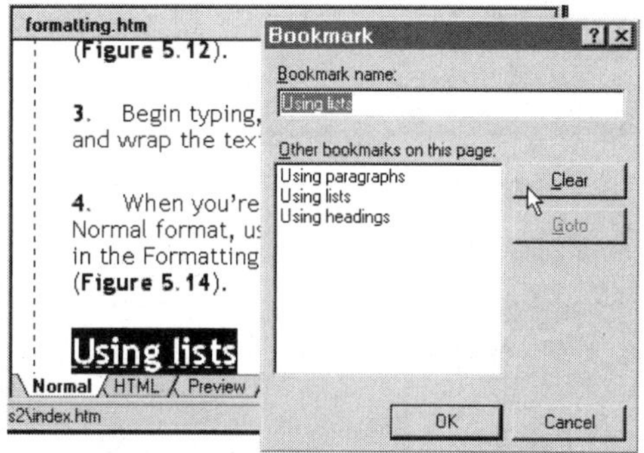

Figure 6.27 To clear a bookmark after you've found it, click *Clear*.

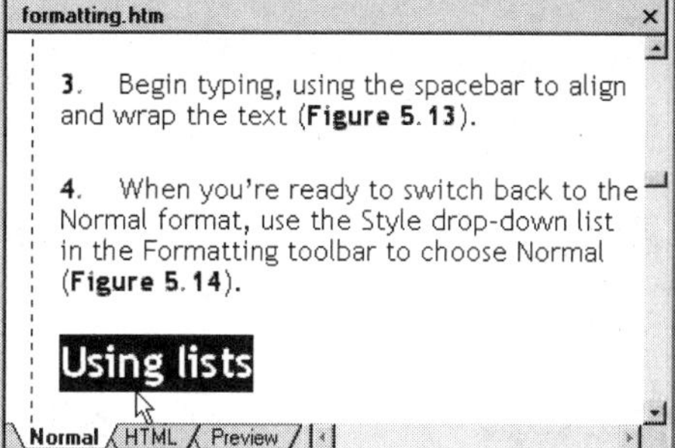

Figure 6.28 Once you've cleared a bookmark, the text remains highlighted but without a dashed underline.

To clear a bookmark

1. To find a bookmark you want to clear, first follow the steps in *To find bookmarks* on the previous page.
2. Once you find the bookmark, click *Clear* in the Bookmark dialog box (**Figure 6.27**). The Bookmark dialog box will close, returning you to the Web page, where the text remains highlighted but without the dashed underline of a bookmark (**Figure 6.28**).

Setting Link Colors

By default, FrontPage follows the Web convention of showing unvisited links as blue and visited ones as dark purple. However, you can assign any Web-safe color you want to your hyperlinks. FrontPage also lets you set colors for active links (the instant you click them) and rollover links (when your cursor moves over them).

To change a link's color

1. Make sure you're in page view by clicking the Page icon in the Views pane.
2. Right-click anywhere in the page and choose *Page Properties* from the shortcut menu (**Figure 6.29**).
3. When the Page Properties dialog box opens, click the *Background* tab (**Figure 6.30**).
4. To change the color for any of a link's three states, click the far-right arrows and pick a new color from the pop-up box (**Figure 6.31**). If you want to create a custom color, choose *More Colors* in the pop-up box, click the *Select* button, then pick a color and click *OK* (**Figure 6.32**).
5. If you've already changed the link colors on another page, check *Get background information from another page*, then click the *Browse* button to find that page and automatically apply its colors to the current page's links (**Figure 6.33**).
6. When you've finished making your color choices for the hyperlinks, click *OK* and the links *for that page only* will be changed.

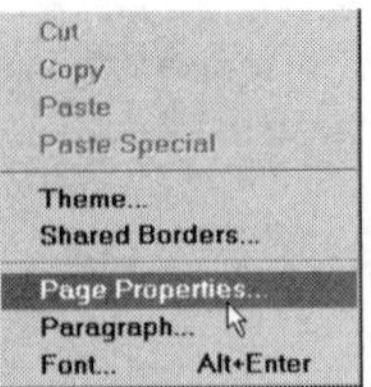

Figure 6.29 To change a link's color, right-click in the page and choose *Page Properties* from the shortcut menu.

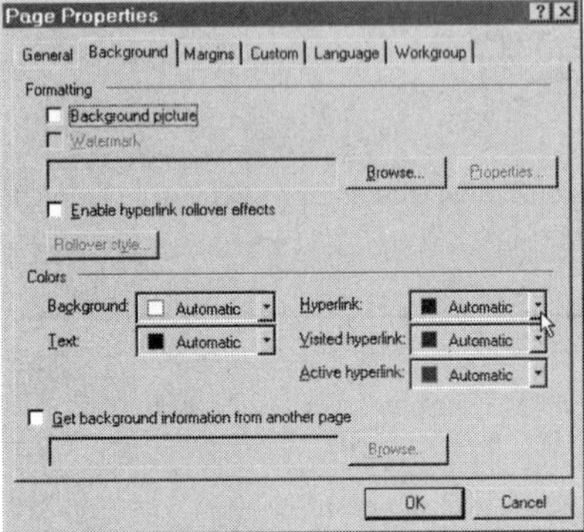

Figure 6.30 To reach the color section, click the *Background* tab in the Page Properties dialog box.

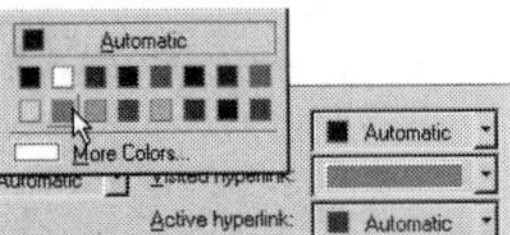

Figure 6.31 Use the pop-up box to change the color of your hyperlinks. To pick a custom color, click *More Colors*.

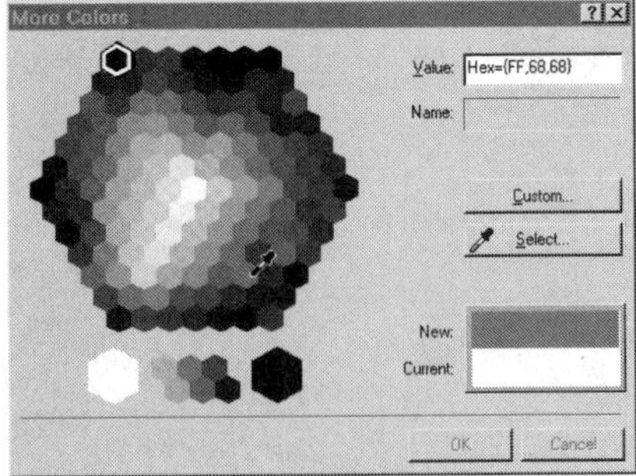

Figure 6.32 The More Colors dialog box lets you use any Web-safe color for your links.

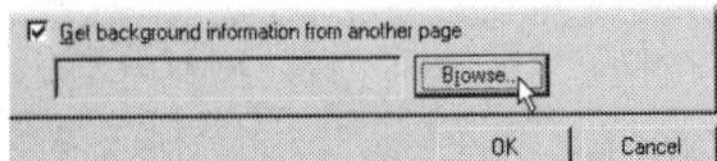

Figure 6.33 To apply link colors from another page, click the *Background* tab's *Get background information from another page* checkbox. Click the *Browse* button to locate the other page.

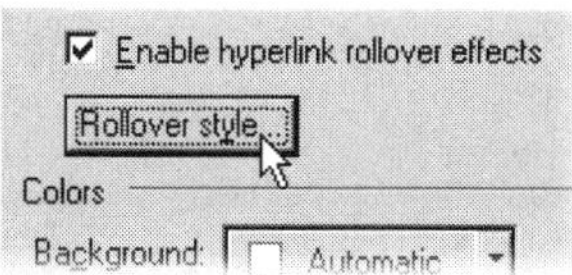

Figure 6.34 To trigger a color change when a cursor moves over a link, choose the *Background* tab's *Enable hyperlink rollover effects* checkbox and click *Rollover style*.

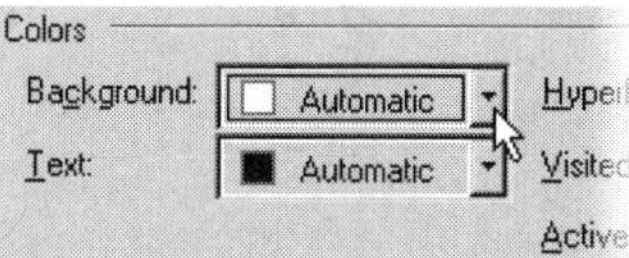

Figure 6.35 The *Background* tab also lets you change the page's background color and the text color.

Figure 6.36 Check *Background picture*, then click *Browse* to add a tiled background graphic to a page.

✔ Tips

- Blue and dark purple, the most common default colors, have become so pervasive that you may risk confusing some visitors by using custom colors. At the very least, make sure your custom color stands out against the background and that unvisited and visited link colors are not so similar that it's unclear which is which.
- If you ever change your mind and want to use the default link colors, just choose *Automatic* within each link's pop-up box in step 4.
- The *Background* tab includes an option to have your links change color whenever a visitor's cursor moves over the link. Just check *Enable hyperlink rollover effects,* then click the *Rollover style* button (**Figure 6.34**). When the Font dialog box opens, use the *Color* pop-up menu to make your choice.
- The *Background* tab also lets you change the page's background color and the text color (**Figure 6.35**). Click the arrows to make your choices, then click *OK* to apply them to the current page.
- If you absolutely must add a background (tiled) picture to the page, the *Background* tab includes a checkbox to do just that (**Figure 6.36**). Check the *Background picture* box, click *Browse* to find your image, then click *OK* to apply the picture to the current page. Tile images plagued the Web early on—with headache inducing results. It's best to use a simple, light-toned image that doesn't obliterate your text.
- To change the link colors in a *theme,* see *To modify a theme* on page 66.

Creating Image Links

Obviously the Web isn't limited to text-only links and FrontPage makes it easy to insert links into any image. You can link an entire image to a file or you can create what's called a hotspot, which links a defined area of the image to another file. By putting multiple hotspots in an image, you can create links to multiple files.

To link an entire image to a file

1. Make sure the Pictures toolbar is visible by choosing View > Toolbars > Pictures (**Figures 6.37** and **6.38**).
2. Open the page containing the image you want linked and click the image to select it (**Figure 6.39**). Square black handles will appear on the image's corners, indicating it's selected.
3. With the image still selected, right-click and choose *Hyperlink* from the shortcut menu (Ctrl K) (**Figure 6.40**).
4. When the Create Hyperlink dialog box opens, you've got all the choices already explained in *Create Hyperlink options* on page 121. To link the image to another page in your current Web site, choose a file in the center window and click *OK*. The image will be linked to the selected page—as indicated by the status bar and the cursor pop-up (**Figure 6.41**).

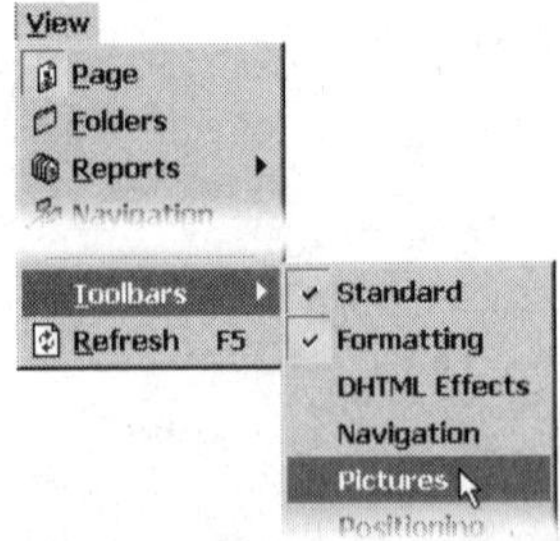

Figure 6.37 Before working with images, choose View > Toolbars > Pictures.

Figure 6.38 The Pictures toolbar includes tools for adding links and hotspots to images.

Figure 6.39 Once an image is selected, square black handles will appear on the image's corners.

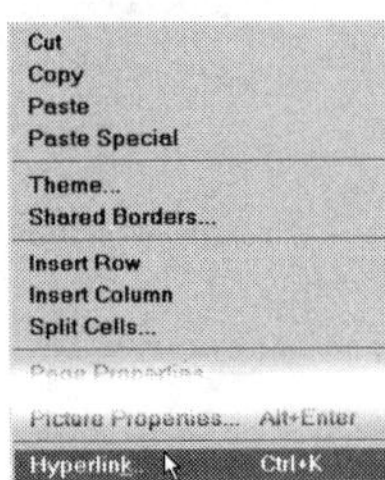

Figure 6.40 To link a selected image, right-click it and choose *Hyperlink* from the shortcut menu.

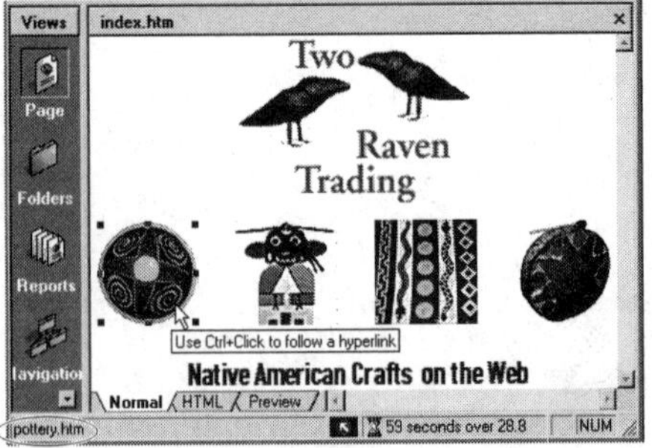

Figure 6.41 Once linked, an image displays pop-up instructions whenever FrontPage's cursor moves over it. The link address appears in the bottom status bar.

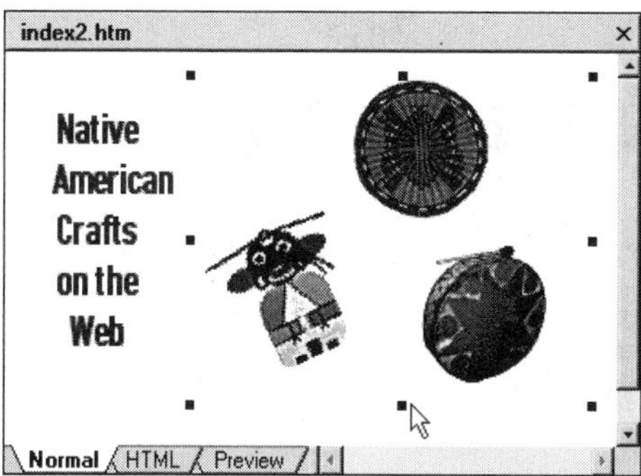

Figure 6.42 To create a hotspot, first select the entire image.

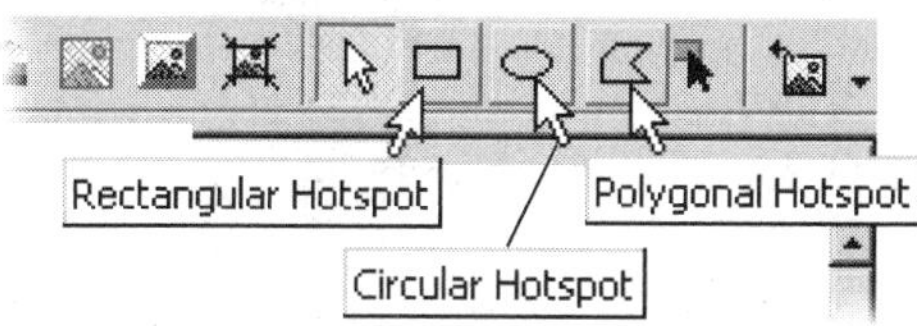

Figure 6.43 Click a shape for your hotspot—rectangle, circle, or polygon—in the Pictures toolbar.

Figure 6.44 Once you choose a shape tool, the cursor becomes a pencil, allowing you to draw a hotspot boundary around the image. Don't worry if it's not exact—you can adjust it later.

To create an image hotspot

1. Make sure the Pictures toolbar is visible by choosing View > Toolbars > Pictures (**Figure 6.38**).
2. Open the page containing the image you want linked and click the image to select it (**Figure 6.42**).
3. Decide what shape your hotspot will be—rectangle, circle, or freeform polygon—and click the appropriate symbol in the Pictures toolbar (**Figure 6.43**).
4. Once you choose a shape tool, the cursor will turn into a pencil, allowing you to draw the hotspot's boundary in the image (**Figure 6.44**). Don't worry about getting the boundary exactly right—you can fix it in a moment.
5. The Create Hyperlink dialog box will open, allowing you to choose which file to link to the hotspot. Choose the file, click *OK*, and you'll be returned to the image.

(continued)

6. Now you can click *inside* the hotspot and move it to exactly where you want it (left, **Figure 6.45**).
7. If you need to resize the hotspot—and you'll want it big enough for visitors to click on it easily—use your cursor to grab the hotspot's black rectangular "handles" to enlarge or shrink the hotspot (right, **Figure 6.45**). If you need to reposition the hotspot, repeat step 6.
8. Repeat steps 3–7 if you want to add more hotspots to the image and link them to separate files. When you're done, the image will contain multiple hotspots, each with its own link (**Figure 6.46**).

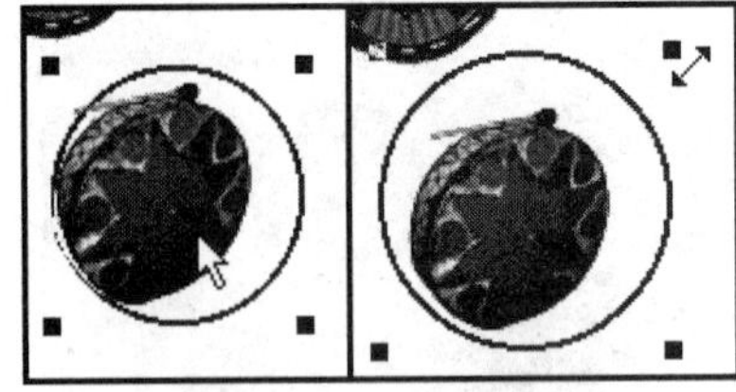

Figure 6.45 Once you've linked the image, click *inside* the hotspot and move it to exactly where you want (left). To resize the hotspot, drag any image handle (right).

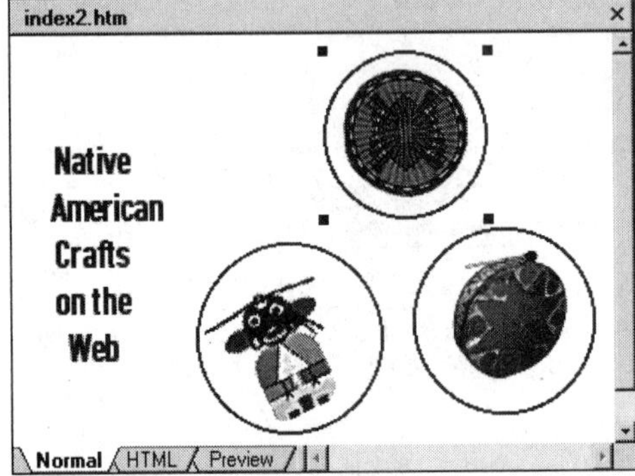

Figure 6.46 By adding several hotspots, a single image can link to multiple files.

✔ Tips

- Your hotspots cannot overlap, nor extend beyond the edge of the selected image. For both reasons, you may realize the image itself needs to be enlarged. Just grab one of the *image's* handles and drag it to give your hotspots more room, then reposition and resize the hotspots as needed. If you wind up enlarging the image more than about 10 percent, however, go back and create a larger original. Otherwise the image will wind up looking fuzzy.
- Hotspots don't have to link to *another* file. You also can use them with anchors to link to text somewhere else in the *same* file.

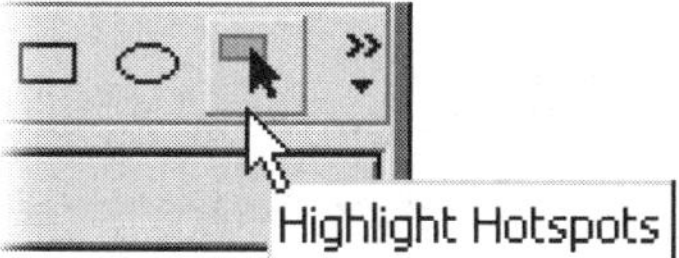

Figure 6.47 If an image obscures your view of its hotspots, click the Pictures toolbar's Highlight Hotspots button.

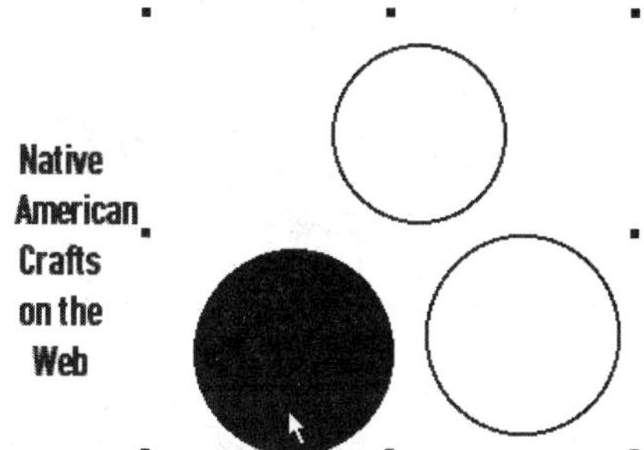

Figure 6.48 With highlighting applied, an image's hotspots are clearly outlined with the active hotspot in black.

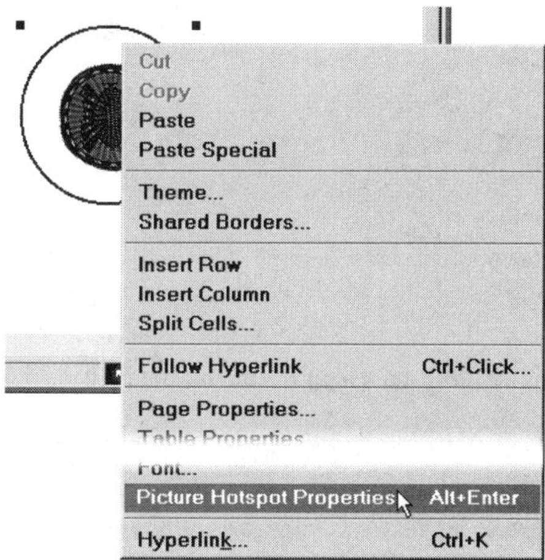

Figure 6.49 To edit a hotspot link, right-click it and choose *Picture Hotspot Properties* from the shortcut menu.

Finding image hotspots

Sometimes your image can keep you from easily seeing your hotspot boundaries. FrontPage includes a feature that lets you see the hotspots—without the images.

To find image hotspots

1. While in page view, select the image you want to inspect by clicking on it.
2. Click the Highlight Hotspots button in the Pictures toolbar (**Figure 6.47**). The image's hotspots will be outlined against a clean background. When a hotspot is selected, it will turn black (**Figure 6.48**).
3. To see the image again, click anywhere outside the image.

To delete a hotspot

◆ Click on the hotspot you want removed and press [←Backspace] or [Delete].

To change a hotspot link

1. Right-click on the hotspot you want to edit and choose *Picture Hotspot Properties* ([Alt][Enter]) from the shortcut menu (**Figure 6.49**).
2. When the Edit Hyperlink dialog box appears, use the buttons and arrows to navigate to the new link. For details, see *To edit a link* on page 124.

Using Hover Buttons

Through the use of what FrontPage calls hover buttons, it's incredibly easy to add cool effects activated by your visitors' mouse actions. You can have a button change appearance or even trigger sounds when the mouse hovers over the button. Essentially hover buttons trigger different kinds of links, which is why they're discussed in this chapter.

To add a hover button

1. Make sure you're in page view by clicking the Page icon in the Views pane. Also be sure the Normal tab is clicked at the bottom of the page window.
2. Click where you want to add a hover button and choose Insert > Component > Hover Button (**Figure 6.50**).
3. When the Hover Button Properties dialog box appears, set your button's text and font, its URL link, color, hover effect, and size (**Figure 6.51**). For details see *Hover Button options* on the next page.
4. Once you've made your choices, click *OK*.
5. Click the *Preview* tab at the bottom of the page window to see how the effect will appear whenever a browser's cursor rolls over the button (**Figure 6.52**).

✔ Tips

- Be sure you've saved all your pages and images, otherwise the hover buttons may not appear in Preview.
- Be careful using the color pop-up menus: Unless you keep a short leash on your cursor, it's all too easy to change a hover color without even realizing it.

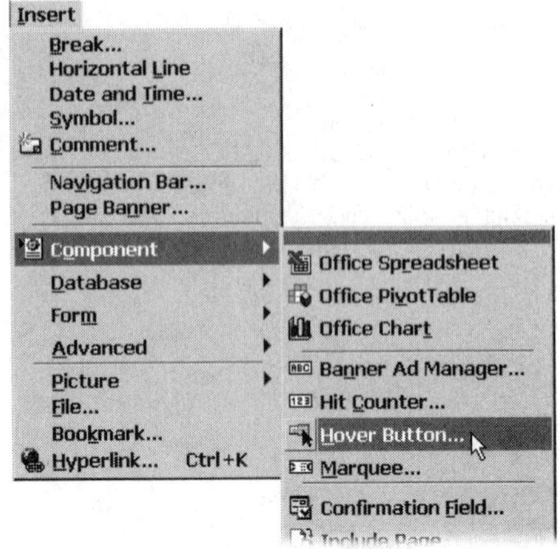

Figure 6.50 To add a hover button, choose Insert > Component > Hover Button.

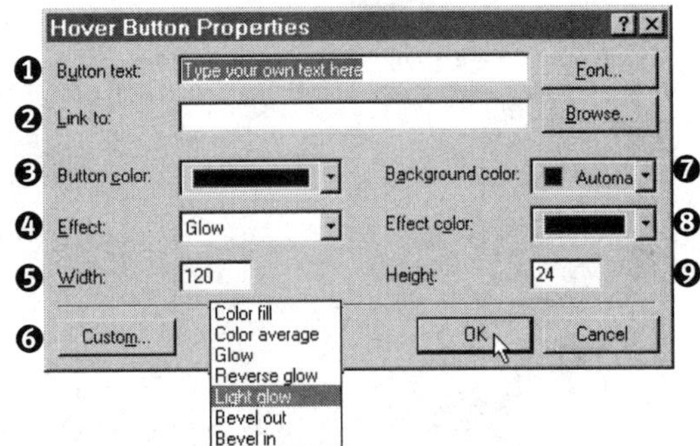

Figure 6.51 The Hover Button Properties dialog box controls the button's appearance and action.

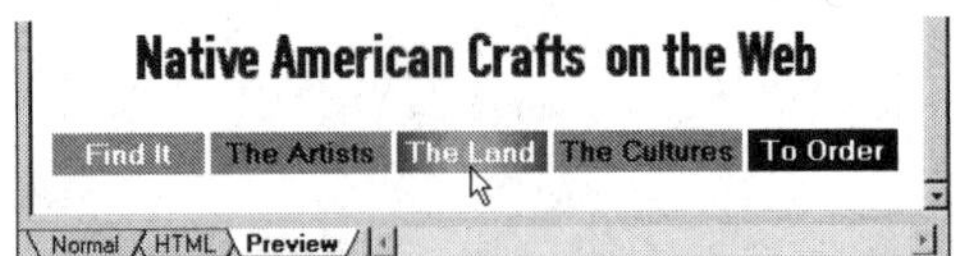

Figure 6.52 After you've applied a button effect, switch to Preview to see the result. "The Land" button glows when the cursor moves over it.

Hover button options

The Hover Button Properties dialog box lets you apply all kinds of mouse-over special effects (**Figure 6.51**). To reach the dialog box, choose Insert > Component > Hover Button or double-click an existing hover button.

❶ **Button text:** Type the button's name or label into the text box, using the *Font* button to change the font face, style, size, and most importantly, the color. Make sure the color contrasts with the Button color and Effect color, explained below.

❷ **Link to:** Either type a URL/file path directly into the text box or click *Browse* to open the Select Hover Button Hyperlink dialog box, which works exactly like the Create Hyperlink dialog box (**Figure 6.7**).

❸ **Button color:** Use the pop-up menu to reach the standard color dialog box, explained earlier in *Setting Link Colors* on page 130.

❹ **Effect:** Use the drop-down menu to pick one of seven effects, which will be triggered when the visitor's cursor passes over the button. For the best look, try different combinations using the *Effect color* pop-up menu and the text's color, reached with the *Font* button.

❺ **Width:** Enter numbers in the text box to set the button's width. You also can adjust the button's size in Normal view by clicking and dragging its corner handles.

❻ **Custom:** Click to reach the Custom dialog box, where you can select sounds or custom graphics that are triggered when a visitor's cursor hovers over or clicks the button.

❼ **Background color:** Use the pop-up menu to reach the standard color dialog box.

❽ **Effect color:** Click the arrow to reach the color pop-up menu. Use with the *Effect* pop-up menu and the *Font* button to give your effect maximum graphic snap.

❾ **Height:** Works just like the *Width* box.

To edit a hover button

1. Make sure the Normal tab is clicked at the bottom of the page window.
2. Right-click the button and choose *Hover Button Properties* from the shortcut menu (Alt Enter) (**Figure 6.53**). Or just double-click the button.
3. When the Hover Button Properties dialog box appears, use it to change your button's characteristics (**Figure 6.51**). Click *OK* when you're done and the changes will be applied.
4. Switch to Preview and move your cursor over the button to see the change in the hover effect.

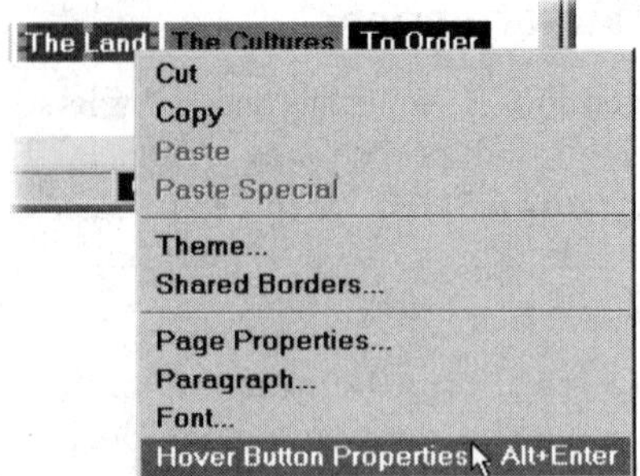

Figure 6.53 To edit a hover button, right-click it and choose *Hover Button Properties* from the shortcut menu.

To customize hover buttons

1. To add a sound or custom graphic to a button, double-click any hover button to reach the Hover Button Properties dialog box (**Figure 6.51**).
2. Click the *Custom* button in the box's lower-left corner.
3. When the Custom dialog box opens, use the *Browse* buttons to navigate to the appropriate file (**Figure 6.54**). Once you've found the file, click *OK* in the Custom dialog box.
4. Switch to Preview and move your cursor over the button to check its custom sound or graphic.

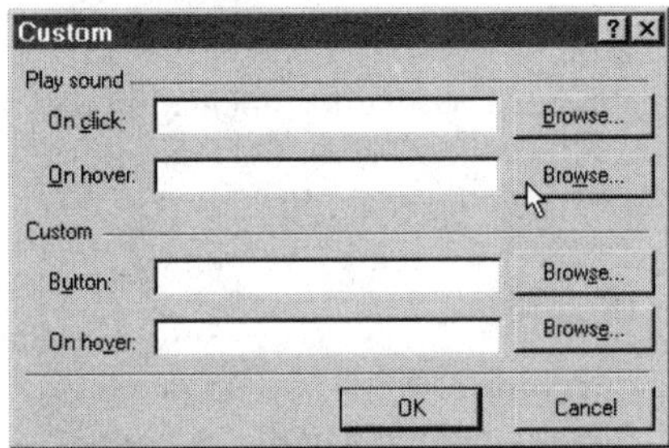

Figure 6.54 When linking a sound or special graphic to a hover button, click *Browse* in the Custom dialog box to reach the appropriate file.

✔ Tip

- When adding custom art, click the Select Picture dialog box's *Clip Art* button to reach FrontPage's collection of clip art (**Figure 6.55**).

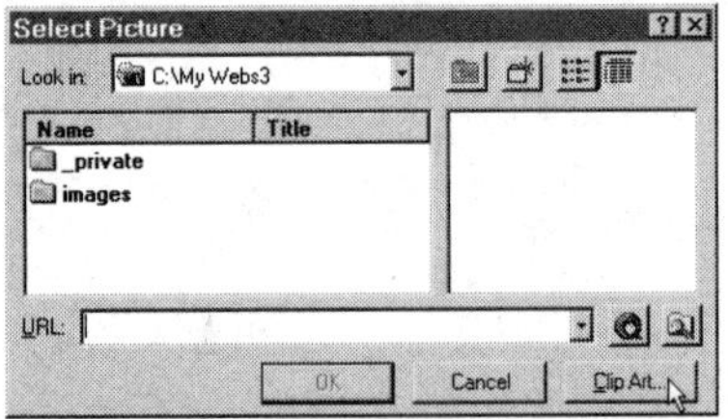

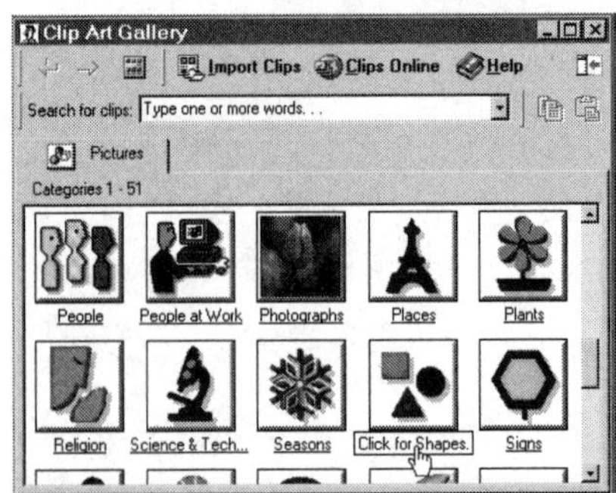

Figure 6.55 To customize hover button graphics, click *Clip Art* (top) to reach FrontPage's clip art collection (bottom).

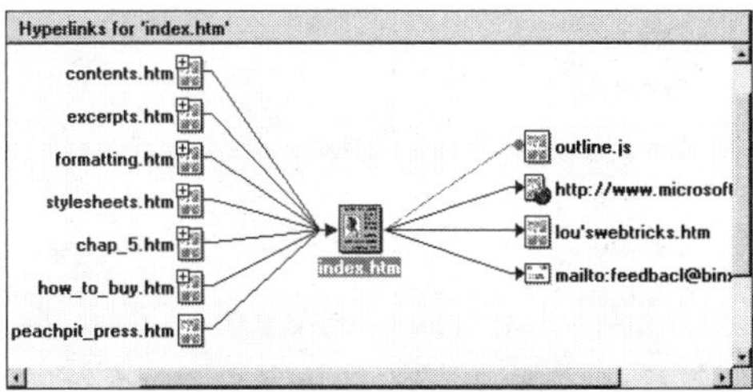

Figure 6.56 The Hyperlinks view shows links *into* your page on the left and links *out from* the page on the right. The [+] marks indicate pages with links of their own.

Figure 6.57 In hyperlinks view, external links are marked by a globe icon (top), internal Web site links by a plain page (middle), and email links by an envelope (bottom).

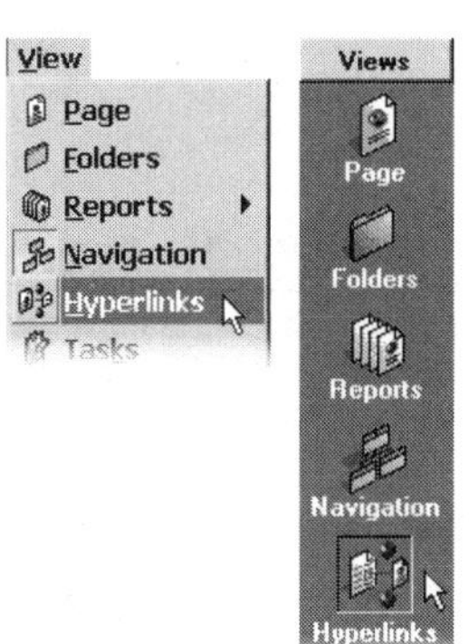

Figure 6.58 To switch to hyperlinks view, choose View > Hyperlinks (left) or click the Hyperlinks icon in the Views bar (right).

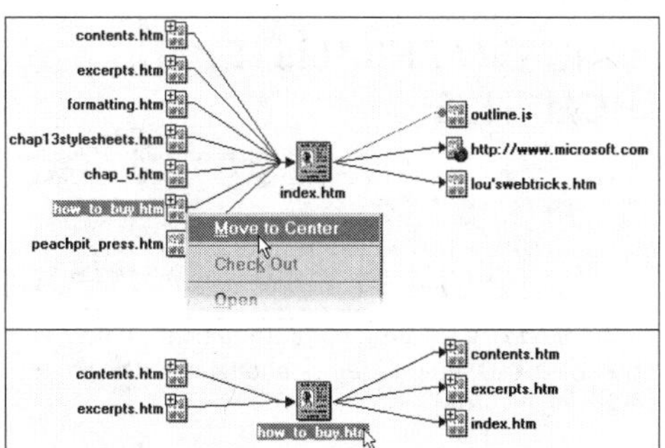

Figure 6.59 In Hyperlinks view, a peripheral page (top) can be inspected by right-clicking it and choosing *Move to Center*. The peripheral page will jump to the center with its links showing (bottom).

Using the Hyperlinks View

Sometimes the easiest way to spot a missing link, or to analyze the links you already have is to use FrontPage's Hyperlinks view (**Figure 6.56**). Each page's link type is marked by a distinct icon, which makes for easy reviewing (**Figure 6.57**). Want to quickly look at links for one of the peripheral pages appearing in the hyperlink view? For details, see *To inspect links on another page* below.

To switch to hyperlinks view

- Choose View > Hyperlinks or click the Hyperlinks icon in the Views bar (**Figure 6.58**). The hyperlinks view will appear in the right pane with the current page in the center (**Figure 6.56**).

To inspect links on another page

- If you want to see the links for a page sitting on the periphery of a hyperlinks view, right-click it and choose *Move to Center* from the shortcut menu. The peripheral page will jump to the center of the view, showing all its links (**Figure 6.59**).

Using Single-page Navigation Bars

Navigation bars are usually shared across an entire Web site. Sometimes, however, it's useful to create a navigation bar for a single page or a limited set of pages. For more on using navigation bars, see *Creating Shared Navigation Bars* on page 54.

To add single-page navigation bars

1. Make sure you're in page view by clicking the Page icon in the Views pane, then click at the top of the page where you want the navigation bar.
2. Choose Insert > Navigation Bar (**Figure 6.60**).
3. When the Navigation Bar Properties dialog box opens, make your choices and click *OK* (**Figure 6.61**). For details on the choices, see *Navigation Bar options* on page 58. The navigation bar will appear in the page (**Figure 6.62**).

✔ Tip

- Make sure you position *single-page* navigation bars in a margin not already being used by a *site-wide* bar. For example, if you've created site-wide navigation bars across the top of all your pages, you'll need to put your single-page bar below that area or on the sides or bottom of the page.

Figure 6.60 To add single-page navigation bars, choose Insert > Navigation Bar.

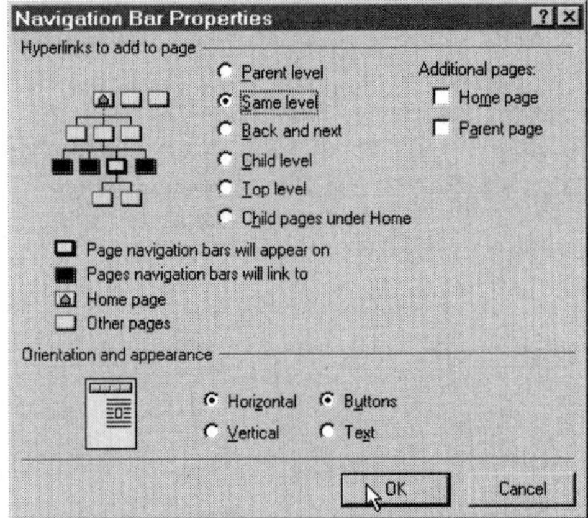

Figure 6.61 The Navigation Bar Properties dialog box sets the placement and relationship for links. For details, see *Navigation Bar options* on page 58.

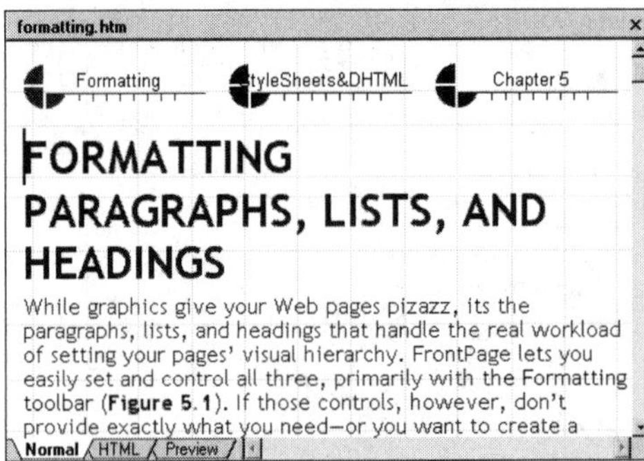

Figure 6.62 A navigation bar automatically links to other pages based on their relationship to the page where it's inserted.

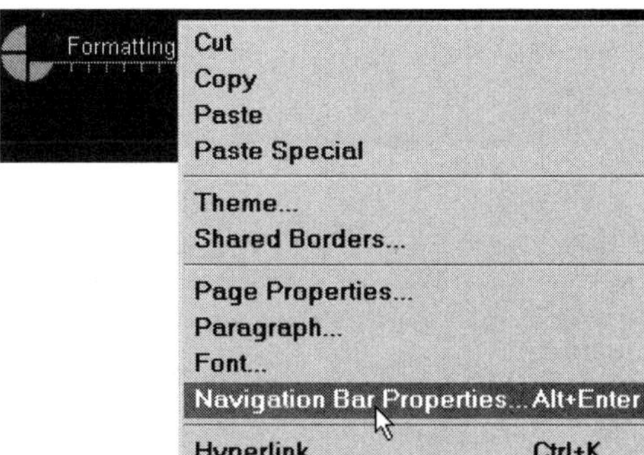

Figure 6.63 To edit a navigation bar, right-click it and choose *Navigation Bar Properties* from the shortcut menu.

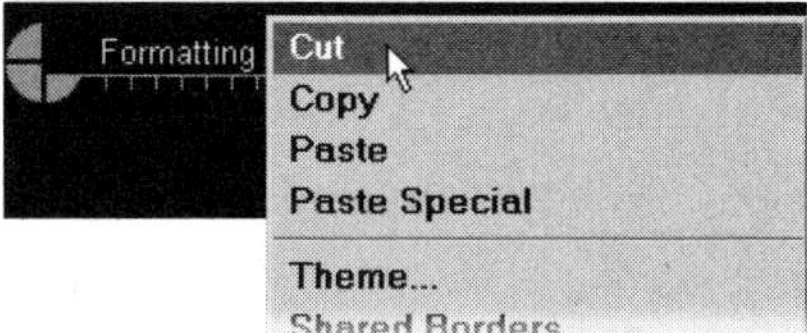

Figure 6.64 To delete a navigation bar, right-click it and choose *Cut* from the shortcut menu.

To edit a single-page navigation bar

1. Right-click on the navigation bar and choose *Navigation Bar Properties* from the shortcut menu (**Figure 6.63**).
2. When the Navigation Bar Properties dialog box opens, make your choices and click *OK* (**Figure 6.61**). The changes will be applied to the current page's navigation bar.

To delete a navigation bar

◆ Right-click on the navigation bar and choose *Cut* from the shortcut menu (**Figure 6.64**). The bar will be removed.

7 Adding and Editing Images

Putting pictures on the Web requires using images in the right formats, which is what's discussed in *Web Image Formats*, this chapter's first section. The second section, *Adding Images*, covers adding images to a Web page and setting such basic aspects of the image as its size, alignment, and whether it should have borders. *Editing Images* covers tricks built right into FrontPage's Pictures toolbar (**Figure 7.1**). The final section, *Positioning Images Absolutely*, explains how images can escape the confines of grid-like layouts. To add images links or hotspots, see *Creating Image Links* on page 132. To use built-in graphic themes, see *Using Templates and Themes* on page 61. To add videos to Web pages, see *Adding and Editing Multimedia* on page 171.

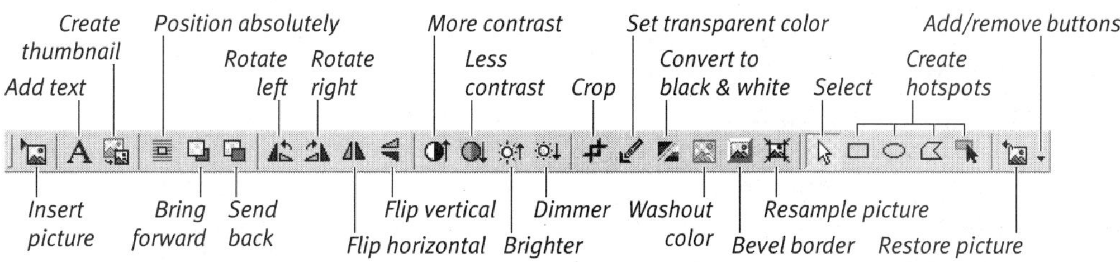

Figure 7.1 The Pictures toolbar contains a variety of image-editing tools.

Web Image Formats

The world's awash with a virtual alphabet soup of image formats: BMPs, TIFFs, TGAs, EPSs, RASs—the list goes on and on. Fortunately when it comes to the World Wide Web, it really boils down to just two formats—GIFs and JPEGs. GIFs (CompuServe's Graphical Interchange Format) are used for everything but medium to large photographs, which are best formatted as JPEGs (developed by the Joint Photographic Experts Group).

Another file format, PNG (Portable Network Graphics) has been touted for several years now because it compresses images nicely without losing as much information as a JPEG and sidesteps an ongoing dispute over GIF rights. While version 4 and later browsers support PNG, the inability of earlier browsers to display the format has hampered its growth and acceptance. For now, GIFs and JPEGs remain your best bets. For details, see *Converting image formats* on page 150.

Let's get small

Before you start adding images to a Web page, make sure the files are as small—no make that as *tiny*—as possible. Bloated images can slow the downloading of your pages so much that visitors simply click on rather than wait. Take the time on your end to shave those files to save the viewer's time.

With the exception of cropping, most of this graphical liposuction should be done in a Web-savvy graphics program, such as Photoshop, DeBabelizer, or Flash. Start by cropping the image's width and height to remove everything but the visual gist of the picture. Who needs that blurry background or that parking lot foreground?

The real key to small files, however, is how well you compress the images. For GIFs, that means reducing the number of colors in the

Table 7.1

GIF vs JPEG: What's best?

WEB PAGE ITEM	BEST FORMAT
buttons, arrows	GIF
illustrations	GIF
animations	GIF
blocks of solid color	GIF
button-size photographs	GIF
all but tiny photographs	JPEG

Table 7.2

Bit depth, number of colors, & file size

NON-INDEXED ORIGINAL IMAGE		
24 bits	17 million colors	1.1 MB (original size)
15 bits	32,768 colors	816K
INDEXED AS A GIF		
8 bits	256 colors	417K
7 bits	128 colors	111K
6 bits	64 colors	94K
5 bits	32 colors	77K
4 bits	16 colors	60K
3 bits	8 colors	43K
2 bits	4 colors	17K
1 bit	2 colors	9K

image. For JPEGs, it's a matter of how much compression you can apply to the photograph while keeping it from looking artificial.

The number of colors in an image, commonly called the bit depth, has a big influence on the file's size (**Table 7.2**). Many Web surfers still use 8-bit monitors, which can only render 256 colors anyway. And since up to 40 of those colors wind up being reserved for the computer's operating system, most GIFs use just 216 colors in what's called a Web- or browser-safe palette. Converting a high-resolution image to one with a palette is sometimes called *indexing* or *mapping* the image. That's because the color information for every pixel in the image is stored as a grid-like index.

While taking a graphic containing millions of colors and indexing it down to a few hundred may seem crazy, the whole point of the Web is that it work no matter which operating system and monitor are used. To find that balance point between a minimum bit depth and decent image quality, experiment in your graphics program at saving images at various bit depths to see just how low you can go.

Photographs don't lend themselves to bit depth reduction—skin tones especially end up looking just terrible in GIFs. That's where JPEGs come in, which use an entirely different compression method. With JPEGs, you can use FrontPage to control the file size by experimenting with the level of compression. For details, see *To convert image formats* on page 150. One limitation to JPEGs is that they don't work well for one-color transparency (they wind up looking termite damaged).

Finally, if you've trimmed and slimmed an image down to a willowy minimum and it's still big, consider using FrontPage's auto thumbnail feature. For details, see *Creating Thumbnails* on page 163.

Adding Images

Once you've done the sometimes tedious work within a graphics program of slimming your image files down to the smallest possible size, adding them to a FrontPage Web page is a breeze.

To insert an image

1. Switch to page view by clicking the Views pane's Page icon, then click where you want the image placed within a page.
2. Choose Insert > Picture, then choose *Clip Art* or *From File* from the submenu (**Figure 7.2**).
3. If you choose *Clip Art*, FrontPage's Clip Art Gallery will appear (**Figure 7.3**). If you choose *From File*, the Picture dialog box will appear (**Figure 7.4**). For details, see *Picture options* on page 148 or *Clip art options* on page 149.
4. Use each dialog box's drop-down menus, folder icons, or buttons to navigate to the desired file, and then click *OK*. The image will be inserted into the Web page.
5. Save the page and its new image (Ctrl S). If the image didn't come from your current Web site, the Save Embedded Files dialog box will appear (**Figure 7.5**).
6. Click *Rename* if you want to change the file name and *Change Folder* if you want to save the file in another location. When you're done, click *OK* and the image will be saved.
7. Once the image is inserted and saved, you can edit it if necessary. See *Editing Images* on page 158.

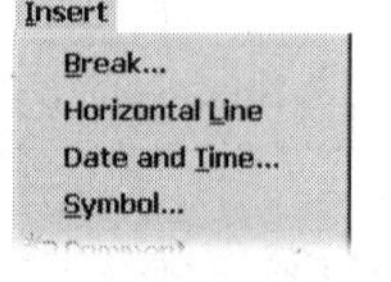

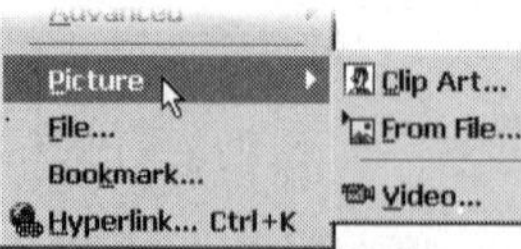

Figure 7.2 To insert an image, choose Insert > Picture, then *Clip Art* or *From File* from the submenu.

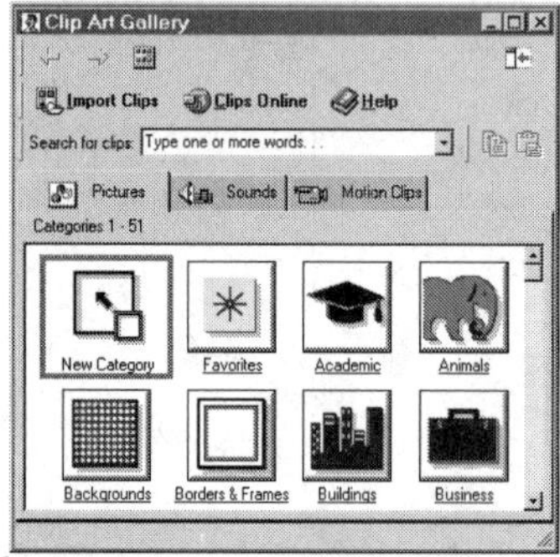

Figure 7.3 The Clip Art Gallery provides a central access point for royalty free art.

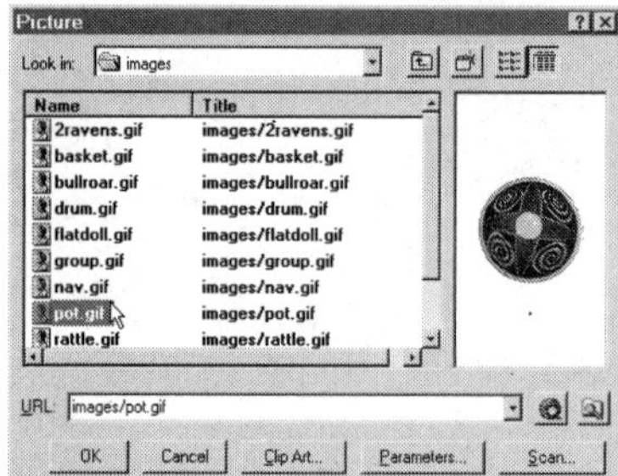

Figure 7.4 The Picture dialog box lets you choose images from your computer or the Web itself.

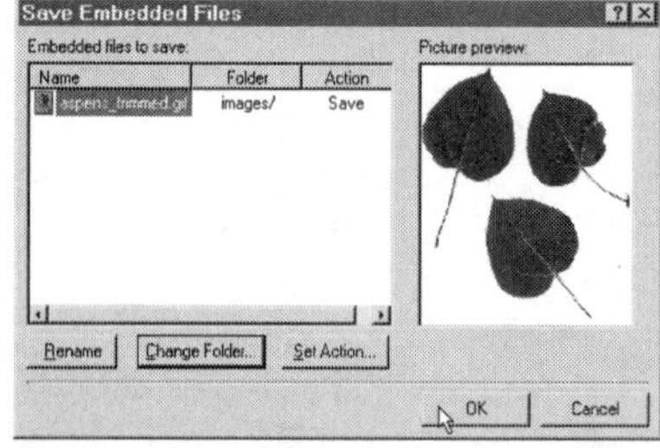

Figure 7.5 The Save Embedded Files dialog box lets you rename images added to your Web site and choose where they're stored.

Figure 7.6 If the Pictures toolbar is active, you can insert an image from your computer's hard drive.

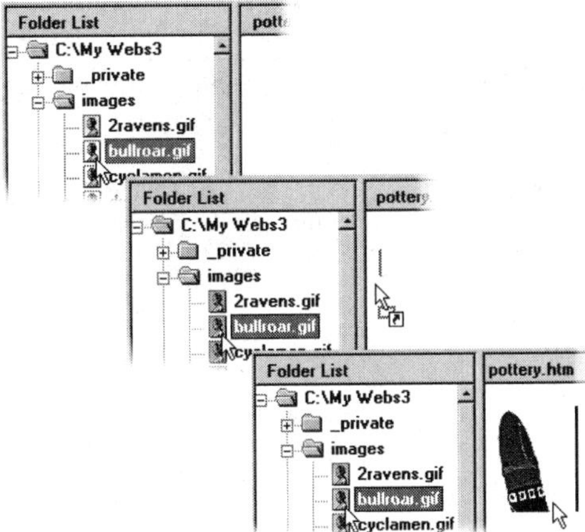

Figure 7.7 If the Folder List is visible, you can click and drag an image into a page from your Web site.

✔ Tips

- If the Pictures toolbar is active, you also can insert a picture by clicking the first icon (**Figure 7.6**).
- If the Folder List is visible and you're inserting an image already in your Web site folder, just click and drag the file into the page pane (**Figure 7.7**).
- Every FrontPage Web site automatically includes an Images folder, but imported images don't always get saved to it. To keep your images together, use the *Change Folder* button to select the folder as you add images to your site (**Figure 7.5**).

Picture options

To reach the Picture dialog box (**Figure 7.8**), choose Insert > Picture > From File.

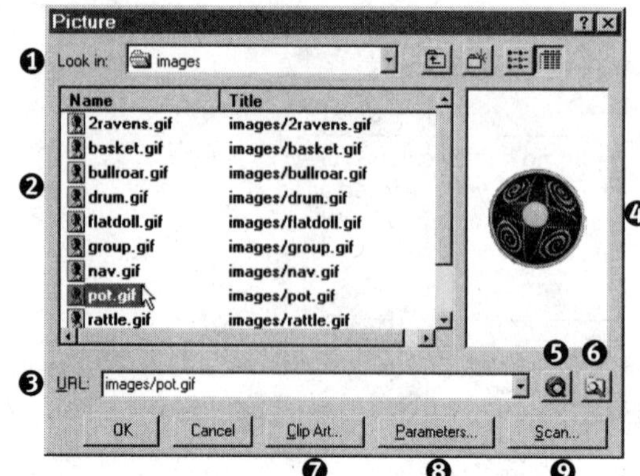

Figure 7.8 The Picture dialog box lets you choose images from your computer or the Web itself.

❶ **Look in:** By default, the dialog box opens to the Web site you're working on. Use the *Look in* drop-down menu to find images in any of your existing FrontPage Web sites.

❷ **Current Web site's images:** Use the vertical-scroll bar to see all the files and folders in your site.

❸ **URL of image:** The text box displays the relative Web address of image files within your Web site or the absolute address of a file found on the Web.

❹ **Preview window:** Once an image file is selected, a preview of it will appear in the window.

❺ **Use browser to insert image:** Click to launch your Web browser so you can hunt down an image out on the Web. Once you reach the page, switch back to FrontPage and the address is pasted automatically into the URL window.

❻ **Insert image from your computer:** Click to use FrontPage to navigate to any file on your hard drive and paste the address into the URL window.

❼ **Clip Art:** Click to use an image in the Clip Art Galley (**Figure 7.9**).

❽ **Parameters:** If you're building a Web site database, click this to add information about the selected image. For details, see *Adding Database Connections* on page 227.

❾ **Scan:** If you've got a scanner hooked up, click this to scan an image directly into FrontPage.

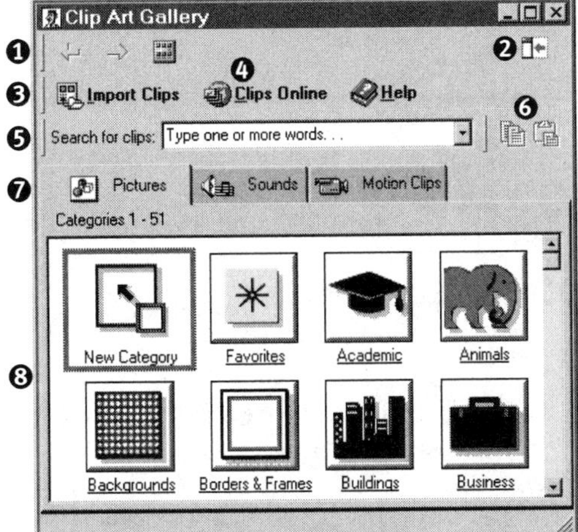

Figure 7.9 The Clip Art Gallery provides a central access point for royalty free art.

Clip Art options

FrontPage 2000 comes with a bunch of clip art. If you've installed Office 2000, FrontPage can use its ample clip art as well. The Clip Art Gallery dialog box provides a central access point for clips, whether they're image, sound, or video files (**Figure 7.9**). To reach the Clip Art Gallery, either choose Insert > Picture > Clip Art or click the *Clip Art* button in the Picture dialog box.

1. **Navigation icons:** Click the arrows to move forward and back in your clip search. Click the book-like icon to see all clip categories.
2. **Resize icon:** Click to toggle the Clip Art Gallery dialog box between a large and small view.
3. **Import Clips:** Click to add images to the gallery itself.
4. **Clips online:** Click to search Microsoft's royalty free online clip gallery.
5. **Search for clips:** Type key words into the text window to quickly find potential clips within the gallery.
6. **Copy/Paste icons:** Click to copy a clip into the clipboard or paste it into your page.
7. **Clip file type:** Click one of the three tabs depending on whether you're seeking an image, sound, or video clip.
8. **Preview window:** By default, the window displays clip categories. Click on any category to see all the images within it.

Converting image formats

By default, FrontPage saves images created in any other format as GIFs or JPEGs. If the image's color depth is 8 bits or less, it's saved as a GIF; anything over 8 bits is saved as a JPEG. FrontPage also makes it easy to convert a GIF to a JPEG, a JPEG to a GIF, or either to a PNG.

To convert image formats

1. Right-click the image you want to convert and choose *Picture Properties* from the shortcut menu (Alt Enter) (**Figure 7.10**).
2. When the Picture Properties dialog box appears, click the *General* tab (**Figure 7.11**).
3. Within the *Type* section, a radio button will indicate the image's current format (**Figure 7.12**). To change it, click another of the three formats: GIF, JPEG, or PNG.
4. If you choose *JPEG*, set the *Quality* and *Progressive passes* levels using the right-side arrows (**Figure 7.13**). For details, see *Tips*, on the next page.
5. Once you've made your choices, click *OK* and the image format will be converted.

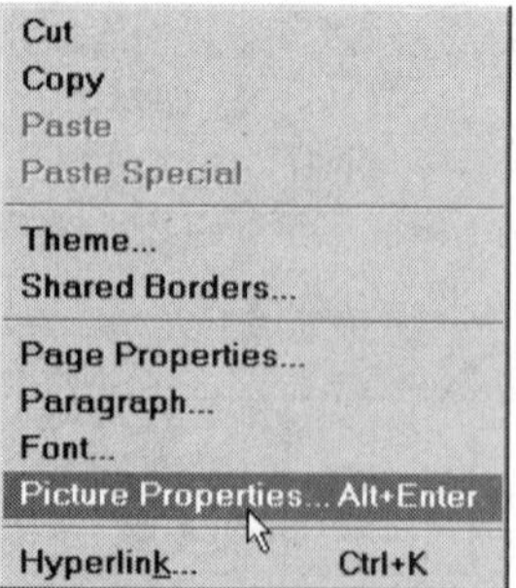

Figure 7.10 To change an image, right-click it and choose *Picture Properties* from the shortcut menu.

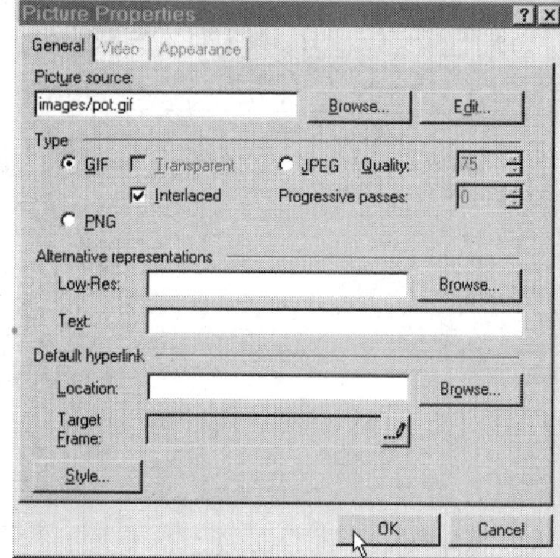

Figure 7.11 To convert an image's format, click the *General* tab in the Picture Properties dialog box.

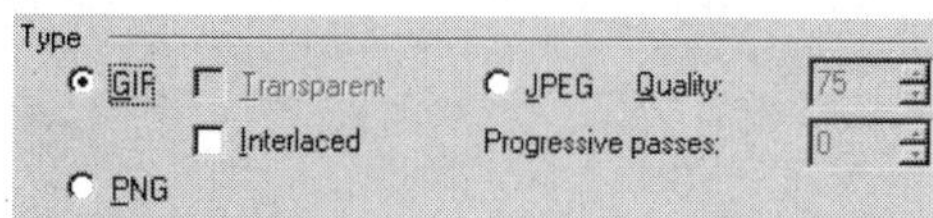

Figure 7.12 Within the *General* tab's *Type* section, choose one of three radio buttons to format an image as a GIF, JPEG, or PNG.

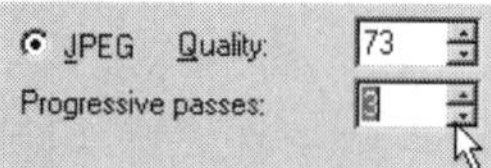

Figure 7.13 If you want an image saved as a *JPEG*, set the compression *Quality* and how many *Progressive passes* a browser will make to download it.

✔ Tips

- In setting the quality of a JPEG, the higher the *Quality* number, the more accurate—but less compressed—the image will be. The default is 75 for moderate compression; 100 is the maximum, which would leave the image uncompressed. The *Progressive passes* number controls how many passes it takes a Web browser to completely download the picture.
- If you choose *GIF* as the file type, you can make the image *Interlaced*, which will cause the image to download in several increasingly detailed passes. The full image downloads no faster this way, but interlacing gives the viewer a quick sense of its content.
- The GIF *Transparent* option will be dimmed unless you've previously made one color transparent. The checkbox can only be used to turn *off* GIF transparency. For details on turning transparency *on*, see *To make a GIF color transparent* on page 166.

Creating alternates for images

It's common for folks using a slow dial-up Web connection to set their browsers to not download images. By creating alternate text for each image on your site, you can give those visitors at least some sense of a page's images (**Figure 7.14**). There's another reason for including alternate text for images: Visually impaired Web users depend on special programs that read aloud what's on the page. With alternate text, those users get dealt in—not left out.

FrontPage also offers another tool for dealing with slow-to-download images: low-resolution images that act as quick-to-appear placeholders. See *To create low-resolution alternate images* on the next page.

To create alternate text

1. Right-click the image and choose *Picture Properties* from the shortcut menu (Alt Enter) (**Figure 7.10**).
2. When the Picture Properties dialog box appears, click the *General* tab (**Figure 7.11**).
3. Within the *Alternative representation* section type a label or brief description in the *Text* window (**Figure 7.15**).
4. When you're done, click *OK* and the alternate text will become part of the image's HTML coding.

✔ Tip

- To check the ordinarily invisible alternate text, click the image and then click the *HTML* tab (**Figure 7.16**).

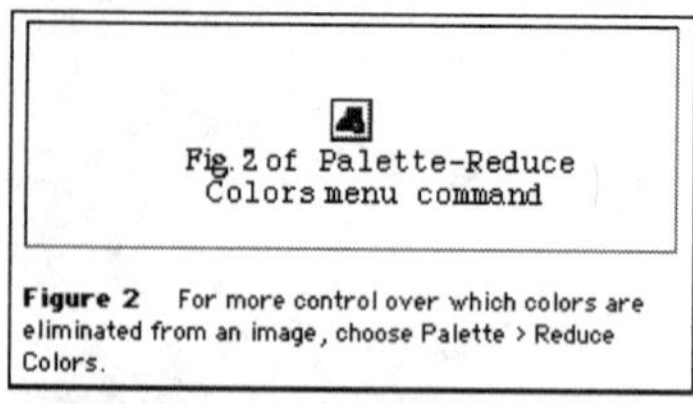

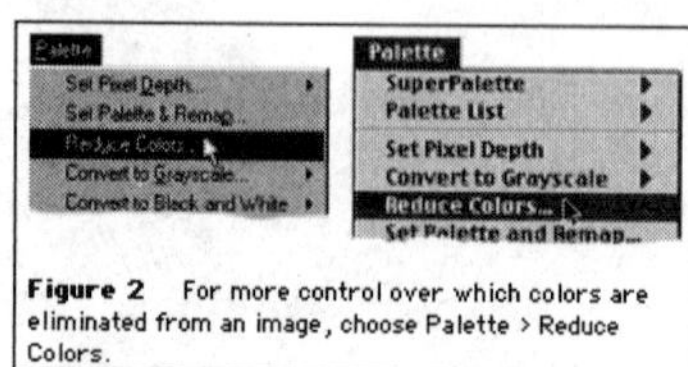

Figure 7.14 By creating alternate text for images (top), visitors can get a sense of an image's content before it completely downloads (bottom).

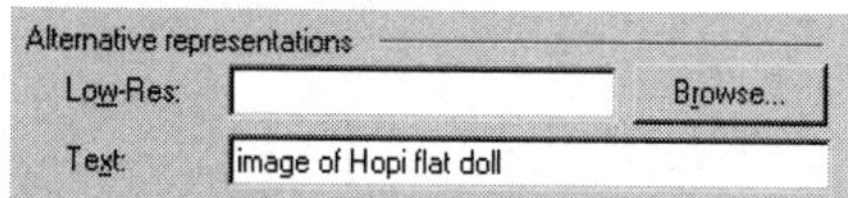

Figure 7.15 Use the *General* tab's *Alternative representations* section to enter a brief description of an image.

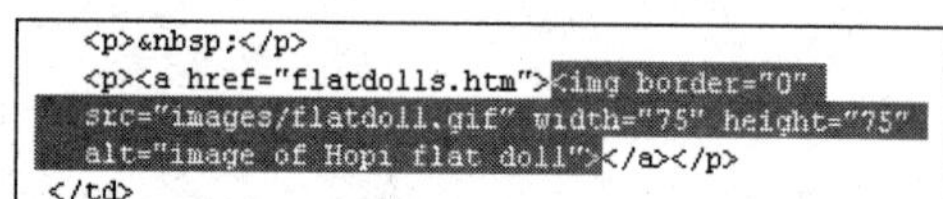

Figure 7.16 To see the usually invisible alternate text, click the image and then click the *HTML* tab.

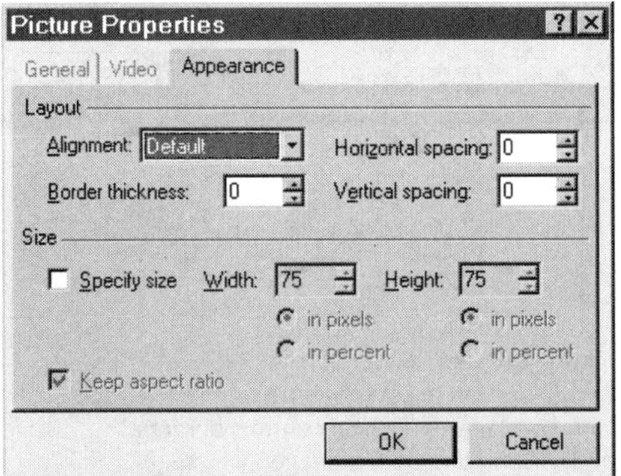

Figure 7.17 To align an image, click the *Appearance* tab within the Picture Properties dialog box.

To create low-resolution alternate images

1. Right-click the regular resolution image within its Web page and choose *Picture Properties* from the shortcut menu ((Alt)(Enter)) (**Figure 7.10**).
2. When the Picture Properties dialog box appears, click the *Appearance* tab. Within the *Size* section, note the image's *Width* and *Height* (**Figure 7.17**). Click *Cancel* to close the dialog box.
3. Now switch to whatever graphics program you use to create images and make a duplicate of your original image. When you save the duplicate, however, save it at 18 dpi instead of the usual 72 dpi. Be sure to give the duplicate the same physical dimensions as the original (75 by 75 pixels in our example)—otherwise at 18 dpi it's going to be a tiny, tiny picture.
4. Switch back to FrontPage, right-click your *regular resolution* image and once more choose *Picture Properties* from the shortcut menu ((Alt)(Enter)) (**Figure 7.10**).
5. When the Picture Properties dialog box appears, click the *General* tab (**Figure 7.11**).
6. Within the dialog box's *Alternative representations* section, click *Browse* to navigate to your *low-resolution* version of the image (**Figure 7.15**).
7. When you return to the Picture Properties dialog box the name of the low-resolution image will appear in the text window. Click *OK*, and the low-resolution version will be paired with the regular resolution image. That way, when Web browsers download the page, the low-resolution version will download almost immediately to hold the page space until the regular resolution image takes its place.

Aligning images

Sometimes the trickiest thing about creating a Web page is getting the text to align and wrap correctly around your images.

To align images

1. Right-click the image within its Web page and choose *Picture Properties* from the shortcut menu (Alt Enter) (**Figure 7.10**).
2. When the Picture Properties dialog box appears, click the *Appearance* tab (**Figure 7.17**).
3. Within the *Layout* section, click the arrow on the Alignment drop-down box and choose how you want the picture aligned (**Figure 7.18**).
4. Click *OK* and the alignment will be applied to the image (**Figure 7.19**). To see the effect, however, you'll have to click the *Preview* tab. For how each alignment choice affects the image, see **Figure 7.20**.

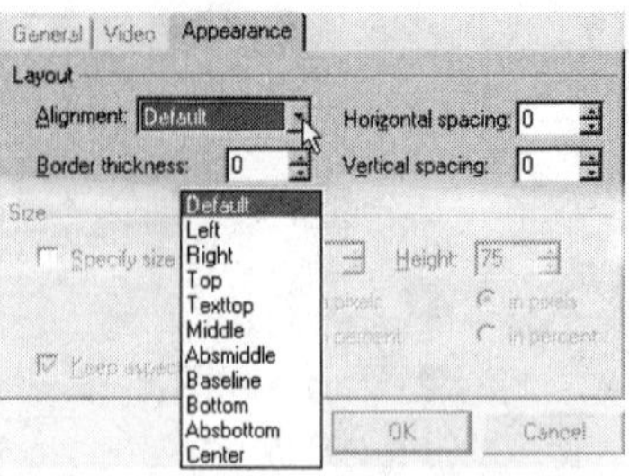

Figure 7.18 Use the *Appearance* tab's *Layout* section to set how an image aligns with adjacent text. It also controls borders and spacing around the image.

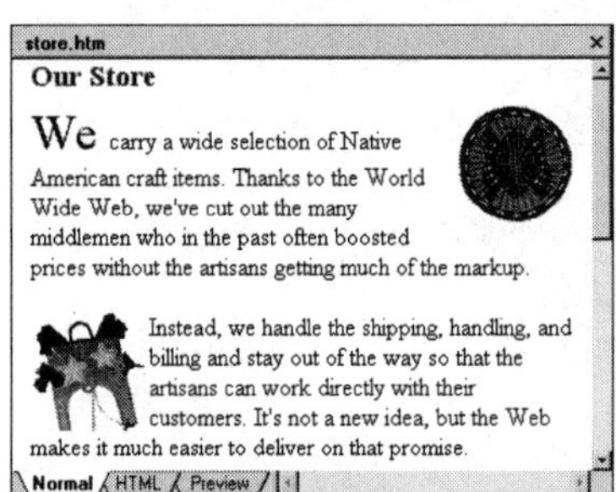

Figure 7.19 The top image is aligned right, the bottom image aligned left.

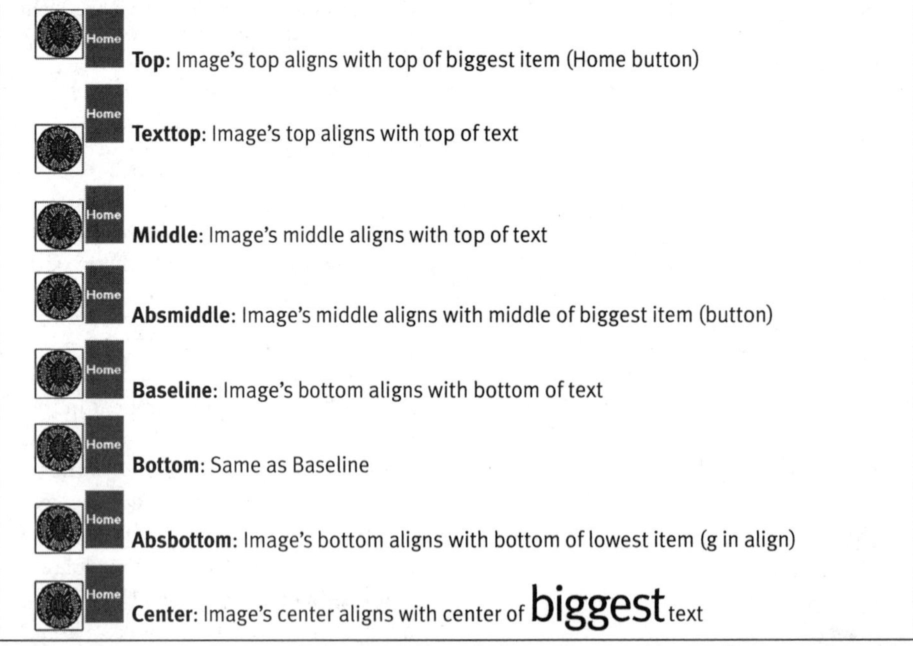

Figure 7.20 FrontPage's alignment choices control how the image lines up with same-line text and graphics.

We carry a wide selection of Native American craft items. Thanks to the World Wide Web, we've cut out the many middlemen who in the past often boosted prices without the artisans getting much of the markup.

Instead, we handle the shipping, handling, and billing and stay out of the way so that the artisans can work directly with their customers. It's not a new idea, but the Web makes it much easier to deliver on that promise.

Figure 7.21 A 6-pixel border has been applied to the top image, a 2-pixel border to the bottom image.

We carry a wide selection of Native American craft items. Thanks to the World Wide Web, we've cut out the many middlemen who in the past often boosted prices without the artisans getting much of the markup.

Instead, we handle the shipping, handling, and billing and stay out of the way so that the artisans can work directly with their customers. It's not a new idea, but the Web makes it much easier to deliver on that promise.

Figure 7.22 A horizontal spacing of 30 has been applied to the top image; a vertical spacing of 15 to the bottom one.

To add an image border

1. Right-click the image within its Web page and choose *Picture Properties* from the shortcut menu (Alt Enter) (**Figure 7.10**).
2. When the Picture Properties dialog box appears, click the *Appearance* tab (**Figure 7.17**).
3. Within the *Layout* section, you can type a number directly into the *Border thickness* text window or use the arrows just to the right to choose a number. (The numbers represent pixels.) Click *OK* and the border will be applied to the image (**Figure 7.21**).

To add space around an image

1. Right-click the image within its Web page and choose *Picture Properties* from the shortcut menu (Alt Enter) (**Figure 7.10**).
2. When the Picture Properties dialog box appears, click the *Appearance* tab (**Figure 7.17**).
3. Within the *Layout* section, you can type a number directly into the *Horizontal spacing* and *Vertical spacing* text windows or use the arrows to set how many pixels of blank space should be placed around the image (**Figure 7.18**). Click *OK* and the space will be added to the page (**Figure 7.22**).

Adding horizontal lines

OK, OK, it's not exactly an image. But a horizontal line is a basic *graphic* element for Web pages. A couple of other graphic-based approaches for dressing up pages—changing the page color and adding a background image—are covered in the tips for *To change a link's color* on page 130.

To insert a horizontal line

1. Make sure you're in page view by clicking the Page icon in the Views pane, then click where you want the rule placed within a page (**Figure 7.23**).
2. Choose Insert > Horizontal Line (**Figure 7.24**). The line will be inserted into the page (**Figure 7.25**).

To edit a horizontal line

1. Right-click on the line and choose *Horizontal Line Properties* from the shortcut menu (Alt Enter) (**Figure 7.26**).
2. When the Horizontal Line Properties dialog box appears, you can adjust the line's size, alignment, and color (**Figure 7.27**). For details see *Horizontal line options* on the next page.
3. When you're done editing the line, click *OK* and the changes will be applied.

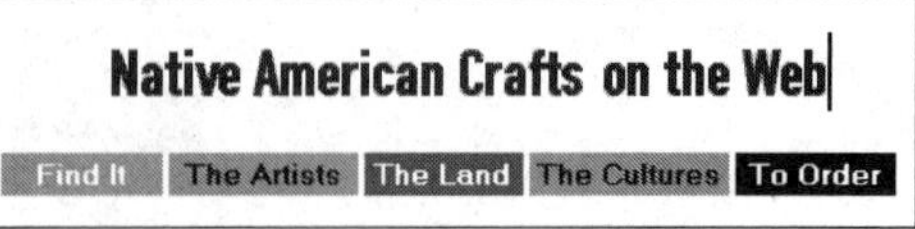

Figure 7.23 Click where you want to insert a horizontal line.

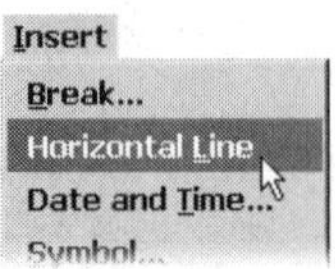

Figure 7.24 To add a line, choose Insert > Horizontal Line.

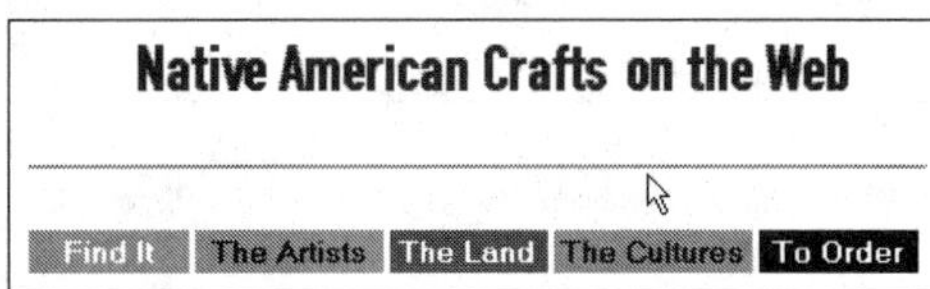

Figure 7.25 The horizontal line inserted into the document.

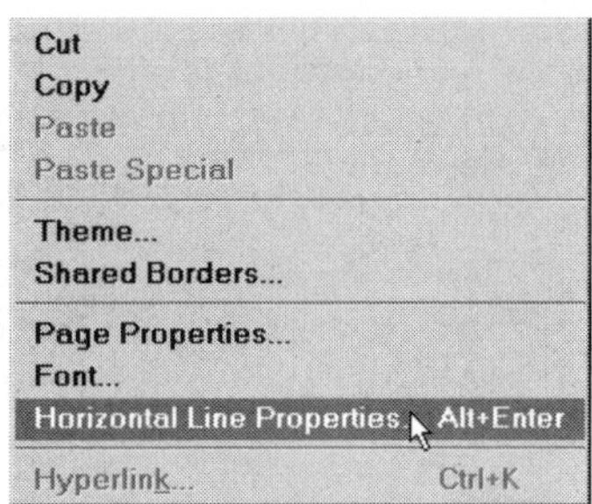

Figure 7.26 To edit a horizontal line, right-click it and choose *Horizontal Line Properties* from the shortcut menu.

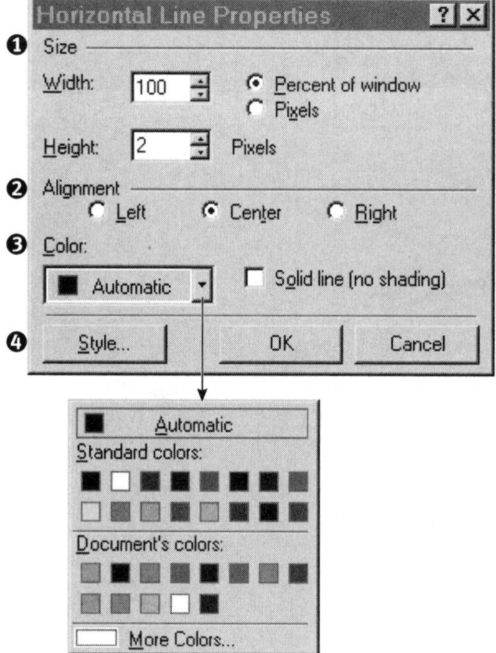

Figure 7.27 Use the Horizontal Line Properties dialog box to adjust a line's size, alignment, and color.

Horizontal line options

Use the Horizontal Line Properties dialog box to adjust a line's size, alignment, and color (**Figure 7.27**).

❶ **Size:** By default, FrontPage sets the line width as a percentage of the browser window's width. Choose *Pixels* if you want to set an absolute width. The *Height* is always set in pixels. Use the arrows to adjust the numbers or enter numbers directly in the text windows.

❷ **Alignment:** By default, FrontPage centers the line. Choose *Left* or *Right* to have the line start from either side.

❸ **Color:** Click the arrow just to the right of *Automatic* (the default color) and a pop-up menu lets you pick from *Standard colors* (HTML's 16 predefined colors), the *Document's colors* (very handy for maintaining the color scheme of a page or site), or *More Colors*, which displays FrontPage's standard color wheel of all 216 Web-safe colors. By default, FrontPage adds a shadowed effect to the line. Check *Solid line (no shading)* to cancel the effect.

❹ **Style:** This button can only be used if you've created style sheets for your Web site. See *Building Style Sheets and Dynamic Effects* on page 269.

Editing Images

For major image editing, it's best to use a dedicated graphics program, but FrontPage's Pictures toolbar can easily handle a lot of basic editing (**Figure 7.1**). Remember that all changes are applied to the actual image. To be safe, always keep a duplicate of the original stored outside your Web site. The Restore button, explained below, also will become one of your best friends.

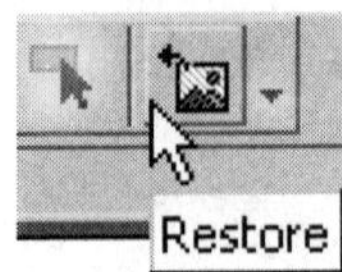

Figure 7.28 To undo an image change, click the Restore button.

To undo image editing

- Select the image, then click the Restore button in the Pictures toolbar (**Figure 7.28**). The image will revert to the last saved version.

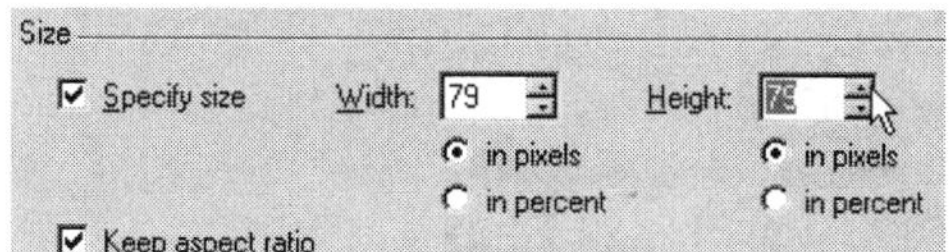

Figure 7.29 Use the *Appearance* tab's *Size* section to set an image's width and height.

Resizing images

The simplest way to resize an image is to just grab one of its square black handles with the cursor and drag it. If you're looking for more precision with *minor* resizing, the following method will do it. Also see *Resampling images* on the next page.

To resize images

1. Right-click the image within its Web page and choose *Picture Properties* from the shortcut menu (Alt Enter) (**Figure 7.10**).
2. When the Picture Properties dialog box appears, click the *Appearance* tab (**Figure 7.17**).
3. Within the *Size* section, check *Specify size* and either type numbers into the *Width* and *Height* text windows or use the arrows just to the right (**Figure 7.29**). By default, the numbers represent pixels, unless you choose *in percent.*
4. Check *Keep aspect ratio* if you want to preserve the image's overall proportions even as you shrink or enlarge it.
5. Click *OK* and the image will be resized.

✔ Tip

- If you're making anything other than minor size adjustments (10 percent or less), you should go back to your image editing program, create a new image, and insert it into your Web page.

Resampling images

If you want to significantly enlarge or shrink an image, you'll get better looking results resizing it with a separate graphics program. But resampling, which involves FrontPage making its best guess at adding or deleting image pixels, is OK for minor size changes. In general, using resampling to shrink an image creates less distortion than enlarging it.

Figure 7.30 To resample an image, first drag any of the image's square black handles to shrink or enlarge it.

To resample an image

1. Be sure to click the Normal tab and the Page icon, then select your image by clicking on it.
2. Drag any of the image's square black handles to shrink or enlarge it (**Figure 7.30**). Use a corner handle if you want to maintain the image's original proportions.
3. Once you've shrunk or enlarged the image, click the Resample button in the Pictures toolbar to apply the resampling (**Figure 7.31**).

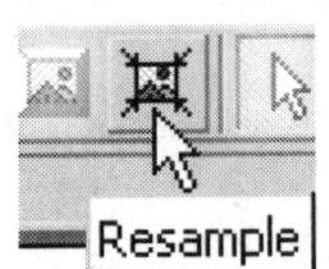

Figure 7.31 Once you've shrunk or enlarged the image, click the Resample button to apply the change.

Figure 7.32 To add text to images, first click the Text button and a text box will appear centered within the image.

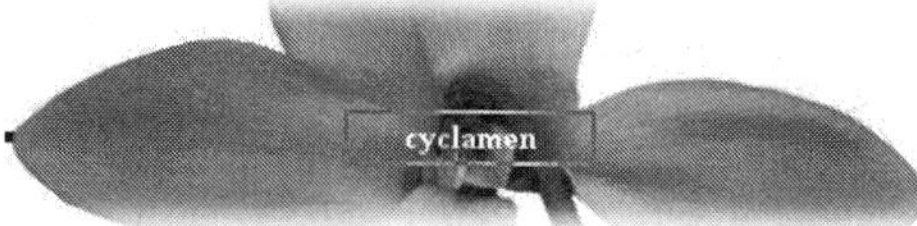

Figure 7.33 Type into the box, resizing if necessary by clicking and dragging its handles.

Figure 7.34 Once you've adjusted the text's position, font and color, the changes are applied.

To add text to images

1. Be sure to click the *Normal* tab and the Page icon, then select your image by clicking on it.
2. Click the Text button (**Figure 7.32**) and a text box will appear centered within the image. Type in your text (**Figure 7.33**). You may need to enlarge the text box by clicking and dragging its handles for all your text to show, though the box cannot extend beyond the image's edges.
3. To move the text box, select it and drag any of its square black handles. To set the text size or color, right-click the text box, choose *Font* from the shortcut menu, make your choices in the dialog box and click *OK*. The changes will be applied to the text (**Figure 7.34**).

✔ Tips

- Make sure the text is readable against the image. Change the text's color or size by right-clicking it and choosing *Font* from the shortcut menu. Or use the Pictures toolbar's Wash Out button. See the next page.
- To delete an image's text, select the text box and press ←Backspace or Delete.
- A great thing about the Text button is that you can go back and change the text or move the box even after you've saved it.

To wash out an image

1. Be sure to click the *Normal* tab and the Page icon, then select your image by clicking on it (**Figure 7.35**).
2. Click the Pictures toolbar's Wash Out button (**Figure 7.36**). The image will be brightened in a single step, making it easier to use the image as a backdrop to text or another image (**Figure 7.37**).

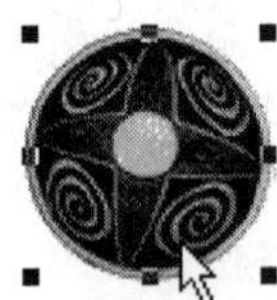

Figure 7.35 Click to select the image you want to wash out.

Figure 7.36 Use the Wash Out button to reduce the image's contrast.

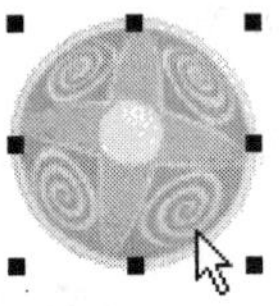

Figure 7.37 Once an image has been washed out, it will be easier to see objects placed atop it.

Figure 7.38 Downloading the large original image would test the patience of uninterested viewers.

Figure 7.39 To create a thumbnail of a large image, click the Auto Thumbnail button.

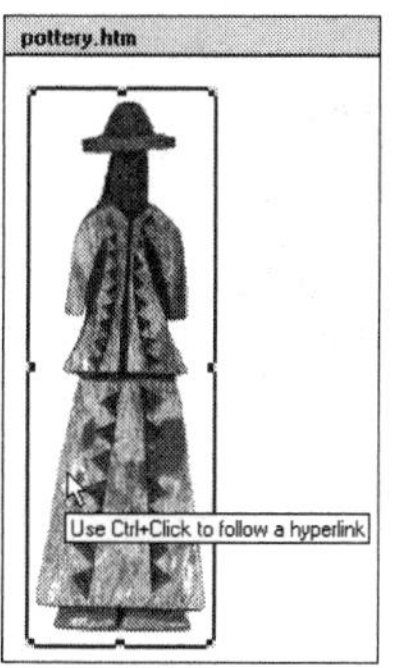

Figure 7.40 The thumbnail image includes a hyperlink to the larger image for viewers wanting a detailed look.

Creating thumbnails

Thumbnails let visitors get the gist of an image without waiting for the detailed, slow-to-download original. If they want to see the larger file version, clicking the thumbnail automatically takes them to it. Thumbnails are particularly useful for quickly presenting a catalog-style page of products.

To create thumbnail images

1. Be sure to click the *Normal* tab and the Page icon, then select your image by clicking on it (**Figure 7.38**).
2. Click the Pictures toolbar's Auto Thumbnail button (**Figure 7.39**). (If the image is already fairly small, the button will be dimmed.) A smaller version of the image will be created and automatically linked to the large original image (**Figure 7.40**).

To rotate or flip images

1. Be sure to click the *Normal* tab and the Page icon, then select your image by clicking on it (**Figure 7.41**).
2. Click one of the four rotate/flip buttons in the Pictures toolbar (**Figure 7.42**). The image will be rotated or flipped, depending on your choice (**Figure 7.43**).

✔ Tip

- To undo any rotate or flip action, click the same button again and the image will be restored to its original position.

Figure 7.41 The original image before being flipped or rotated.

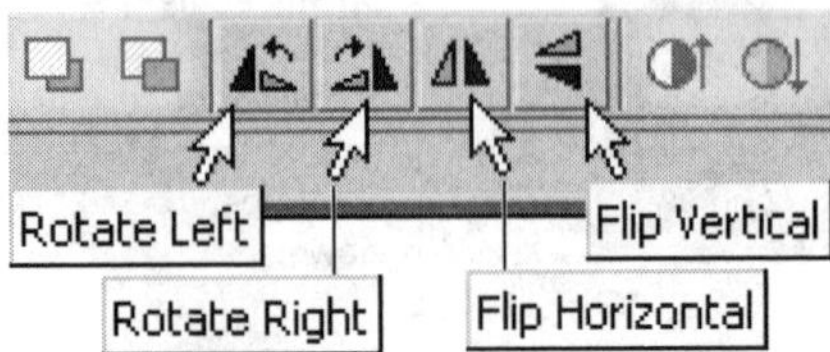

Figure 7.42 The Pictures toolbar includes four rotate/flip buttons.

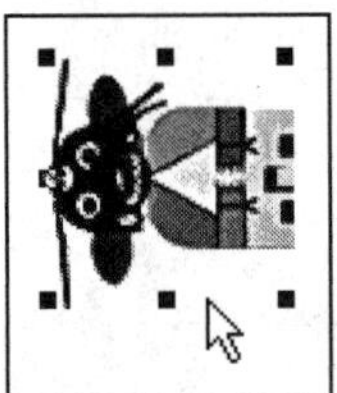
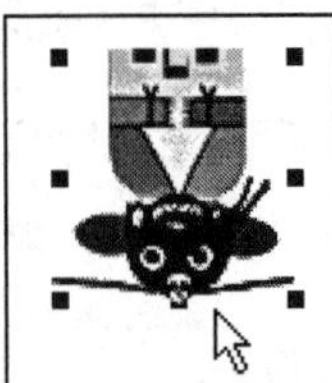

Figure 7.43 Left: The image after being rotated to the left. Right: The image after being flipped vertically.

Figure 7.44 The original image before changing its contrast.

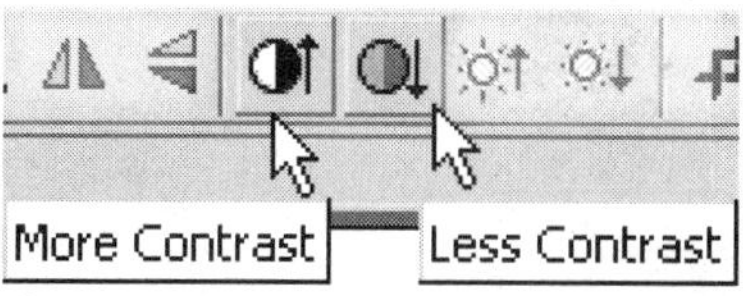

Figure 7.45 Click the More Contrast or Less Contrast buttons to boost or reduce the image's contrast.

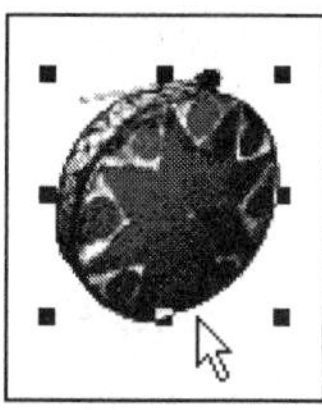

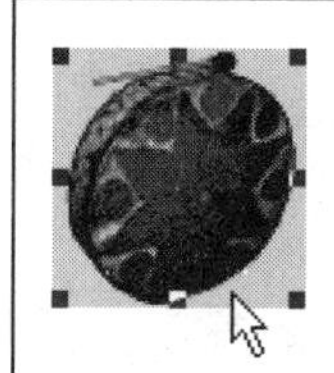

Figure 7.46 Left: Image contrast boosted to maximum. Right: Image contrast reduced to a minimum.

Figure 7.47 The original image before adjusting the brightness.

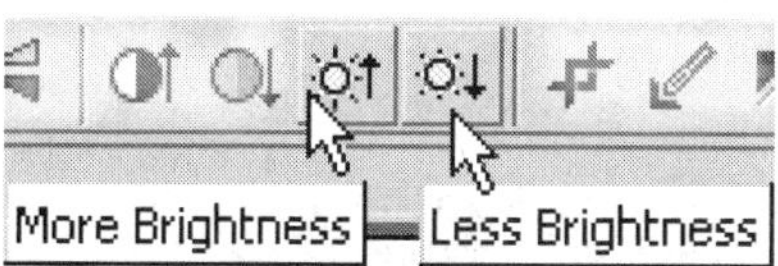

Figure 7.48 Click either the More Brightness or Less Brightness buttons to lighten or darken the image.

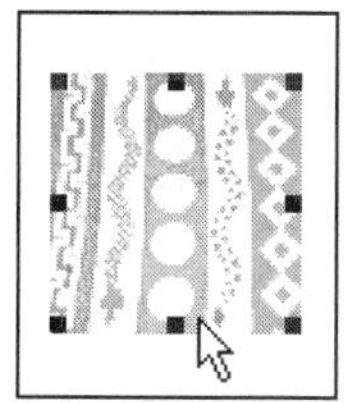

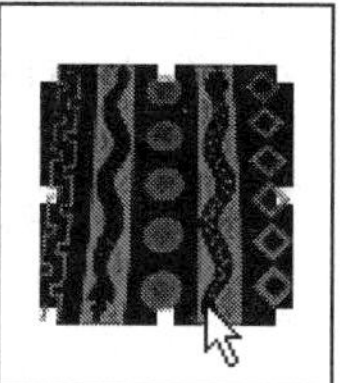

Figure 7.49 Left: Image brightened. Right: Image darkened.

To change image contrast

1. Be sure to click the *Normal* tab and the Page icon, then select your image by clicking on it (**Figure 7.44**).
2. Click the More Contrast or Less Contrast buttons as many times as you need to boost or reduce the image's contrast (**Figures 7.45** and **7.46**). If the image gets too contrasty or too flat, use the other button of the pair to rebalance its appearance. You also can undo each incremental change by pressing Ctrl Z.

To change image brightness

1. Be sure to click the *Normal* tab and the Page icon, then select your image by clicking on it (**Figure 7.47**).
2. Click either the More Brightness or Less Brightness buttons as many times as you need to lighten or darken the image (**Figures 7.48** and **7.49**).

To crop images

1. Be sure to click the *Normal* tab and the Page icon, then select your image by clicking on it.
2. Click the Crop button (**Figure 7.50**).
3. When a dashed line surrounds the image, click and drag any of the black handles to shape the cropping boundary (**Figure 7.51**).
4. Press [Enter] or click the Crop button again and the image will be trimmed (**Figure 7.52**).

To make a GIF color transparent

1. Be sure to click the *Normal* tab and the Page icon, then select your image by clicking on it.
2. Click the Set Transparent Color button in the Pictures toolbar (**Figure 7.53**). Move your cursor back over the selected image and it will turn into an eraser-like icon (**Figure 7.54**).
3. Click the tip of the icon on the color in the image that you want to be transparent. The change will be applied, though you may not detect the change until you drag the image over another image (**Figure 7.55**).

Figure 7.50 To trim an image, select it and click the Crop button.

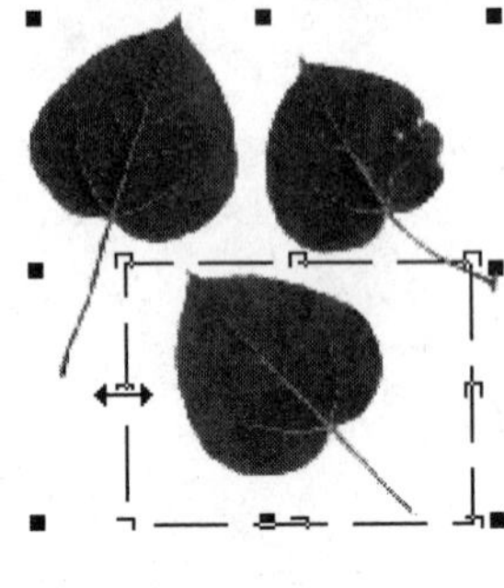

Figure 7.51 Click and drag any of the black handles to shape the cropping boundary.

Figure 7.52 After you press [Enter] or click the Crop button again, the image is trimmed.

Figure 7.53 To make a color transparent in a GIF image, click the Set Transparent Color button.

Figure 7.54 Move your cursor back over the selected image and click the eraser-like icon on the color you want made transparent.

Figure 7.55 After making the image's white background transparent, the underlying image shows through.

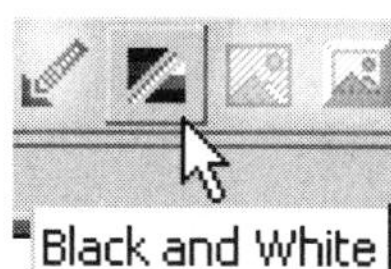

Figure 7.56 To remove color from an image, click the Black and White button.

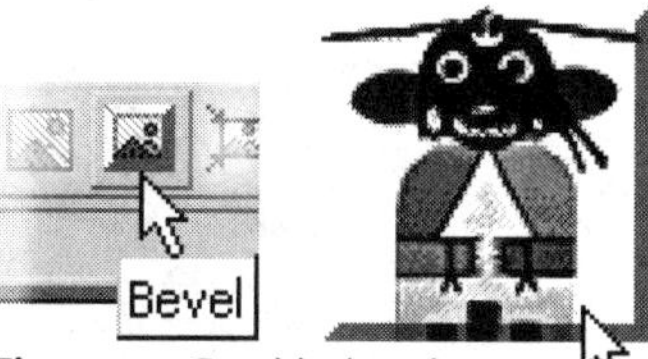

Figure 7.57 To add a bevel to an image, click the Bevel button (left) and the effect is applied (right).

To remove image color

1. Be sure to click the *Normal* tab and the Page icon, then select your image by clicking on it.
2. Click the Black and White button in the Pictures toolbar (**Figure 7.56**) and the previously full-color image will turn to black and white.

To add a bevel to an image

1. Be sure to click the *Normal* tab and the Page icon, then select your image by clicking on it.
2. Click the Bevel button in the Pictures toolbar and a button-like beveled edge will be added to the image (**Figure 7.57**).

Positioning Images Absolutely

FrontPage supports Cascading Style Sheets (CSS) for version 4 or later browsers, which means you can position images in ways not possible before. Without CSS, images and other objects can only be positioned in sequence, that is, one after another across and down the Web page. With CSS, you can position images absolutely, for example, stacking them in front of or behind other images and objects. Two wrinkles to consider: First, visitors without version 4 or later browsers will see the absolutely positioned images aligned to the left, which might not look so good; second, absolute positioning can't be used with Dynamic HTML.

To position images absolutely

1. Be sure to click the *Normal* tab and the Page icon, then select your image by clicking on it (**Figure 7.58**).
2. Click the Position Absolutely button in the Pictures toolbar (**Figure 7.59**).
3. A four-arrowed icon will appear as you grab the image and begin moving it into position (**Figure 7.60**). Once you've positioned the image, click anywhere outside the image to deselect it.

✔ Tip

- The click and drag method may not be precise enough if you're working with a design requiring that images be positioned at predetermined x, y coordinates. For pixel-based precision, choose View > Toolbars > Positioning to activate the Positioning toolbar (**Figure 7.61**). Use the number-entry windows to set the image's pixel coordinates.

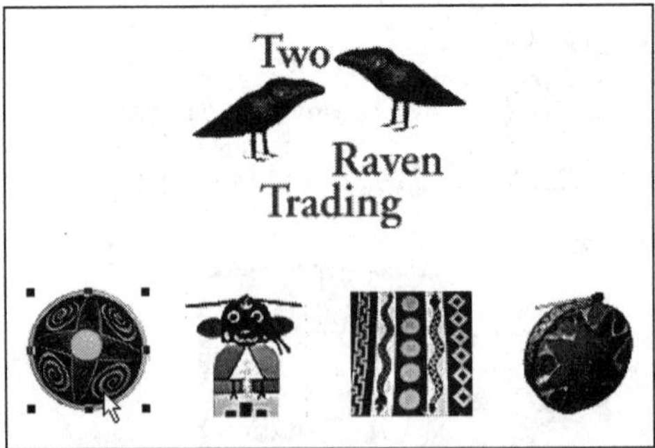

Figure 7.58 To position an image absolutely, first select it.

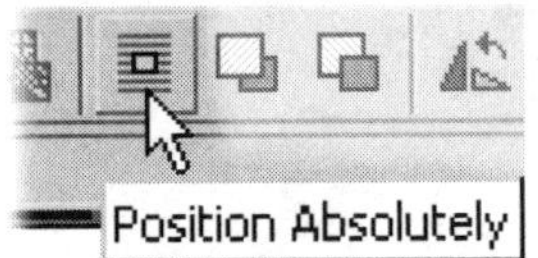

Figure 7.59 After selecting the image, click the Position Absolutely button.

Figure 7.60 A four-arrowed icon will appear as you grab the image and begin moving it into position.

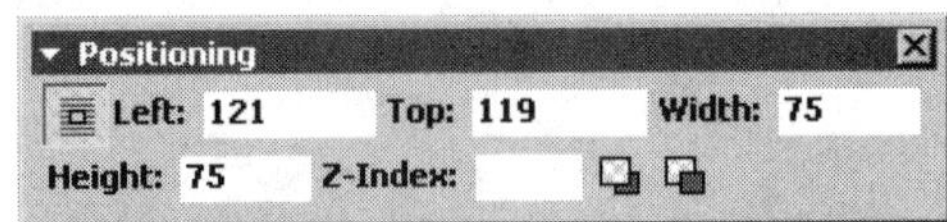

Figure 7.61 For greater precision, use the Positioning toolbar's number-entry windows to set the image's pixel coordinates.

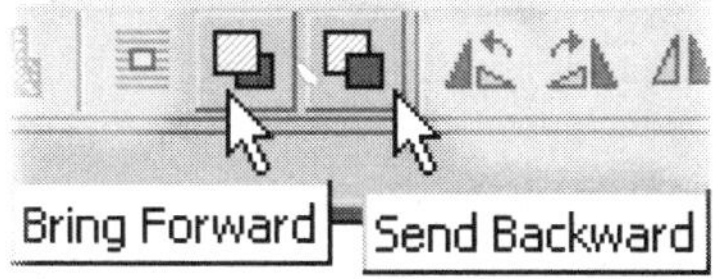

Figure 7.62 Use the Bring Forward or Send Backward buttons to place the selected image in front of or behind other page items.

Figure 7.63 The Mimbres pot has been sent behind the raven.

Figure 7.64 Left: Clicking the pot winds up selecting the raven image because it's in front and larger. Right: After sending the ravens to the back, the pot can be selected.

Figure 7.65 By making the white areas transparent in all three images, the stacking arrangement is more flexible.

To move absolutely positioned images forward and backward

1. Select your image by clicking on it (**Figure 7.58**).
2. Depending on whether you want to place the selected image in front of or behind the other page items, click the Bring Forward or Send Backward buttons in the Pictures toolbar (**Figure 7.62**). The stack order of the selected image will change (**Figure 7.63**).

✔ Tips

- If you have multiple overlapping images, you may need to click the Bring Forward or Send Backward buttons several times to get the stack order right.
- If you position an image completely behind a much larger one, you won't be able to select it by clicking it. To reach the smaller image, first select the larger image, then click the Send Backward button until the smaller image moves forward to where you can click it (**Figure 7.64**).
- For more flexibility when stacking images, remember the option of making the background color transparent. In the GIFs used in these examples, the white background color was made transparent (**Figure 7.65**).
- Bear in mind that many of the layered effects created by absolute positioning also can be simulated using a graphics program—without the browser compatibility problems.

8 Adding and Editing Multimedia

Used judiciously, a little bit of multimedia can juice up your Web pages and grab visitor attention. As always, bear in mind that visitors won't wait around for downloads, so use FrontPage's download progress indicator to gauge how long pages with multimedia elements will take to appear on screen (see page 14).

FrontPage gives you three basic categories for turning your Web pages into a multimedia extravaganza: videos or animations; background page sounds; and Java-based banner ads, ticker-tape marquees, and visitor-driven hit counters. FrontPage also lets you create moving type and layers, but that's covered in *Building Style Sheets and Dynamic Effects* on page 269.

Adding Videos or Animations

Although you technically could add an hour-long training video to your Web site, there are precious few network connections fast enough to handle such a huge file. In practice, Web videos/animations are best kept small—things like logos with moving type or animated arrows. Used judiciously, video/animation can liven up a site. Just remember: a little motion goes a long way.

To insert a video or animation

1. Switch to page view and click where you want the video or animation placed within a page.
2. Choose Insert > Picture > Video (**Figure 8.1**).
3. When the Video dialog box appears, it will show all the files already in your Web site (**Figure 8.2**). If the video/animation you want isn't listed, use the drop-down menus, folder icons, or buttons to navigate to the desired file (**Figure 8.3**). For details, see *Video options* on page 174.

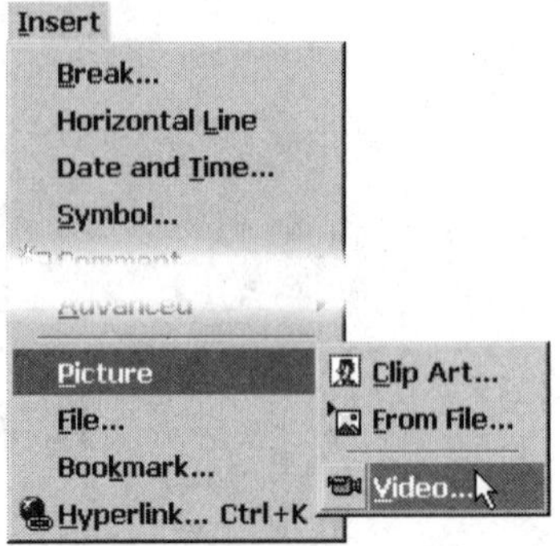

Figure 8.1 To insert a video or animation, choose Insert > Picture > Video.

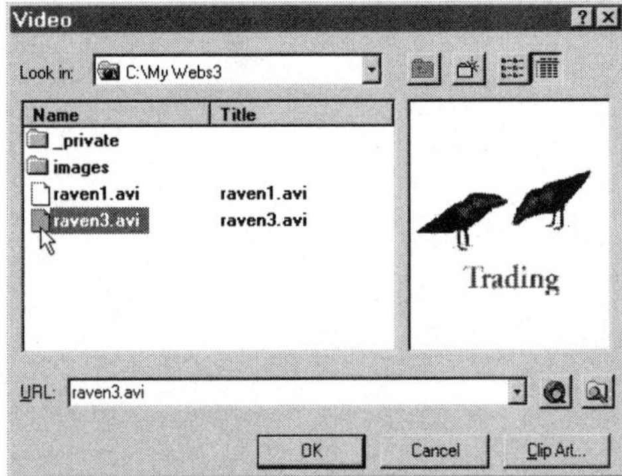

Figure 8.2 The Video dialog box, which lists all of your current Web site's files, also can be used to find a file on your hard drive or the Web itself.

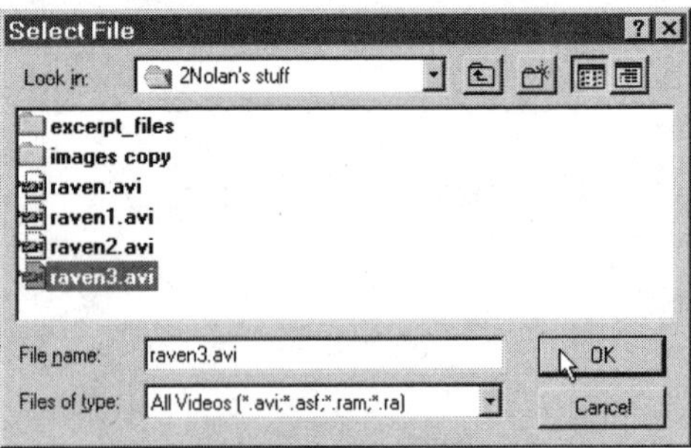

Figure 8.3 Use the Select File dialog box to locate the video or animation you want inserted.

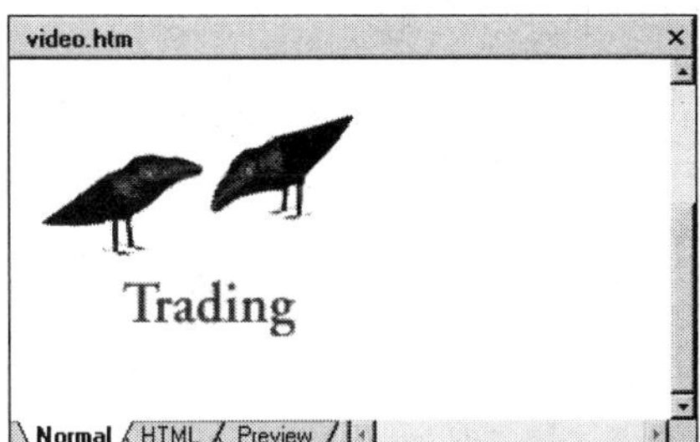

Figure 8.4 Once the video/animation is inserted, FrontPage will display its first frame.

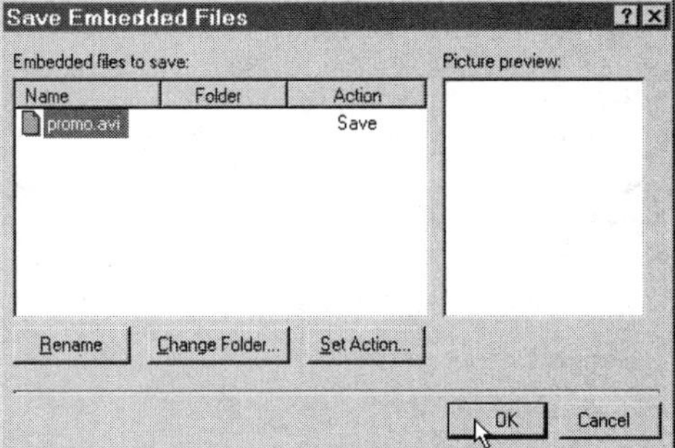

Figure 8.5 If the video/animation didn't come from your current Web site, the Save Embedded Files dialog box will give you a chance to save it.

4. Once you find the file and return to the Video dialog box, click *OK* to insert the video/animation into the Web page (**Figure 8.4**).
5. Save the page and its new video/animation (Ctrl S). If the file didn't come from your current Web site, the Save Embedded Files dialog box will appear (**Figure 8.5**).
6. Click *Rename* if you want to change the file name and *Change Folder* if you want to save the file in another location. When you're done, click *OK* and the video/animation will be saved.
7. Once the video/animation is inserted and saved, you can set how often it repeats and other aspects. See *To set loops for videos/animations* on page 175.

Video options

To reach the Video dialog box (**Figure 8.6**), choose Insert > Picture > Video.

❶ **Look in:** By default, the dialog box opens to the Web site you're working on. Use the *Look in* drop-down menu to find videos or animations in any one of your existing FrontPage Web sites.

❷ **Current Web site's files:** If all the files are not visible in the list, use the vertical scroll bar that appears to see all the files and folders in your site.

❸ **URL of video/animation:** The text box displays the relative Web address of image files within your Web site or the absolute address of a file found on the Web.

❹ **Preview window:** Once a video/animation file is selected, a preview of its first frame will appear in the window.

❺ **Use browser to insert video/animation:** Click to launch your Web browser so you can hunt down a video/animation out on the Web. Once you reach the page, switch back to FrontPage and the address is pasted automatically into the URL window. Remember to use only royalty free images, such as those at Microsoft's online clip gallery, or get permission to use an image. Just because you see it on the Web, that doesn't mean it's yours for the taking.

❻ **Insert video/animation from your computer:** Click to use FrontPage to navigate to any file on your hard drive and paste the address into the URL window.

❼ **Clip Art:** Click to use a video/animation in the Clip Art Galley (**Figure 8.7**).

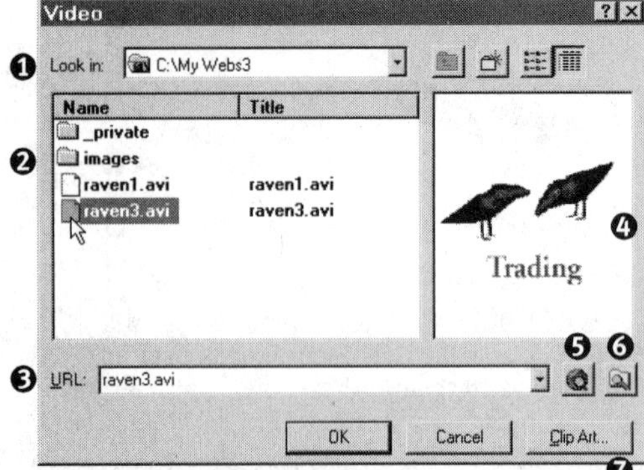

Figure 8.6 The Video dialog box, which lists all of your current Web site's files, also can be used to find a file on your hard drive or the Web itself.

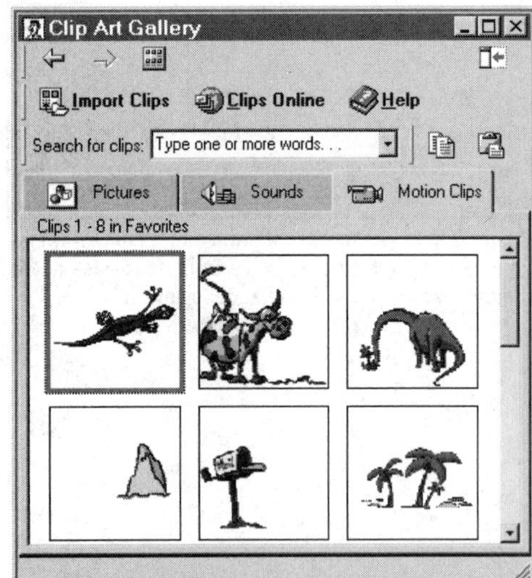

Figure 8.7 FrontPage's Clip Art Galley can be used to find and store royalty free videos and animations.

VIDEO OPTIONS

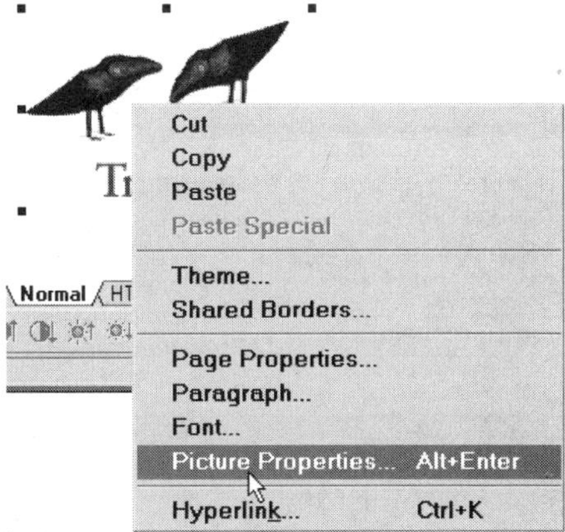

Figure 8.8 To set looping for a video or animation, right-click it and choose *Picture Properties*.

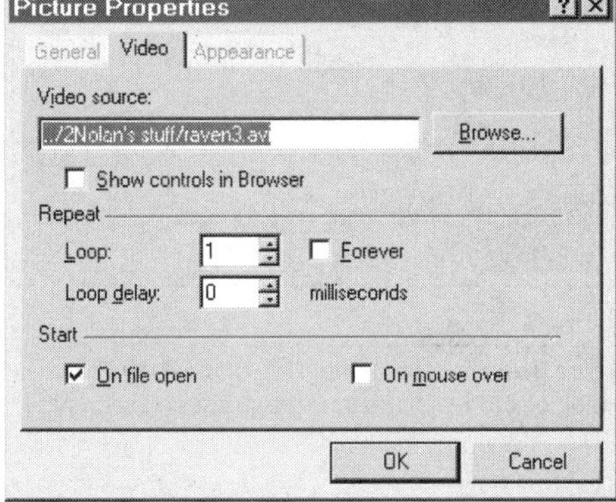

Figure 8.9 The *Video* tab in the Picture Properties dialog box lets you set how the video/animation repeats.

Figure 8.10 By including a playback slider control with the video/animation, you give the user more control.

To set loops for videos/animations

1. Switch to page view, right-click the video/animation and choose *Picture Properties* from the shortcut menu (Alt Enter) (**Figure 8.8**).
2. When the Picture Properties dialog box appears, click the *Video* tab (**Figure 8.9**).
3. If you want to substitute another video/animation for the current one, click *Browse* to find it.
4. If you want the video/animation to include a play button and slider (**Figure 8.10**), click *Show controls in Browser*.
5. Use the arrows and text windows in the *Repeat* section to set how many times the video/animation will play (or choose *Forever*) and how long the delay should be between the loop finishing and starting again.
6. By default, the video/animation is set to start as soon as the file opens, but you can give more control to the user by checking *On mouse over* in the *Start* section.
7. Once you're made your choices, click *OK* and the changes will be applied to the video/animation.

Adding Sounds

Short sound loops can be effective mood setters on the appropriate pages—and maddening on strictly business pages. Pick and choose your sound pages carefully.

To add a page background sound

1. Switch to page view, right-click anywhere in the page and choose *Page Properties* from the shortcut menu (**Figure 8.11**).
2. When the Page Properties dialog box opens, click the *General* tab (**Figure 8.12**).
3. Within the *Background sound* section, click *Browse* to locate a sound file (**Figure 8.13**). By default, *Forever* is checked. If you want the sound to play a short time, uncheck the box and use the text window or arrows to set the number of loops.
4. Click *OK* and the sound will become part of your Web page. Click the *Preview* tab at the bottom of FrontPage's main window to hear the sound or test it with your Web browser.

✔ Tips

- Since background sounds are linked to pages, you can give different pages different sounds.
- To remove a sound from a page, right-click in the page, choose *Page Properties* from the shortcut menu, and delete the file from the *Location* window.

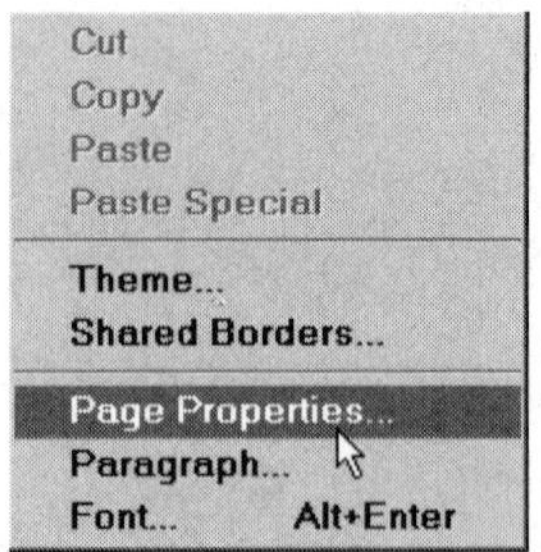

Figure 8.11 To add a page background sound, right-click anywhere in the page and choose *Page Properties*.

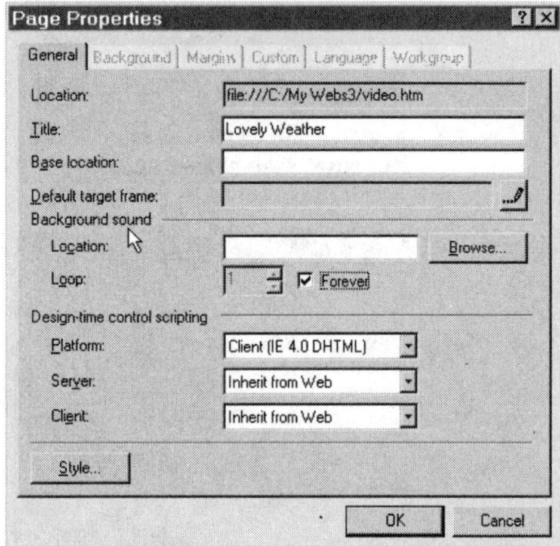

Figure 8.12 Click the *General* tab of the Page Properties dialog box to reach the *Background sound* section.

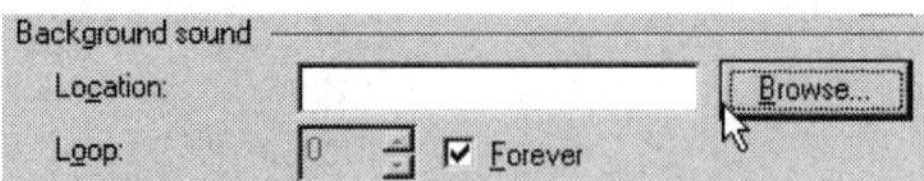

Figure 8.13 Click *Browse* to find a sound file. By default, playing the sound *Forever* is checked. Or use the *Loop* number window to limit the repetitions.

Adding Java Components

FrontPage includes several other multimedia components that can make your pages more interactive. All of these components—rotating banners, page hit counters, and marquees work their magic with Java, a cross-platform programming language. Rest assured: All the Java coding is handled behind the scenes and you don't have to mess with it. Hover buttons, which also use Java, are covered separately in the *Adding Hyperlinks* chapter on page 117.

Using banner ads

With a constantly rotating selection of images, banner ads are powerful attention getters. No wonder they've become a staple of commercial Web sites. Banner ads, however, need not be confined to product advertising. Corporate intranets, for example, can use them to alert users to items of company wide interest, whether it's a new pension policy or the Friday beer bash.

To add a banner ad

1. Switch to page view, click in the page where you want the banner ad, and choose Insert > Component > Banner Ad Manager (**Figure 8.14**).
2. When the Banner Ad Manager Properties dialog box appears (**Figure 8.15**), set the dimensions for the banner images ❶.
3. Using the drop-down menu, select a *Transition effect* for moving from one image to another ❷.
4. Decide how long you want to *Show each picture for* and enter the number of seconds in the text window ❸.
5. Use the *Browse* button to select which Web page users will be linked to if they click the banner ad ❹.
6. Use the *Add* button ❻ to locate the images you want displayed by the banner ad ❺. Use the *Move Up* and *Move Down* buttons to rearrange the display order of the images.
7. Once you've made your choices, click *OK*, then save the page (Ctrl S). The banner ad will be inserted into the Web page.
8. FrontPage can only show the banner ad's first image, so launch your Web browser to see the images actually change (**Figure 8.16**).

✔ Tips

- By default, the Banner Ad Manager is set to show each image for 5 seconds but that's often a tad slow—3 seconds sets a better pace. Experiment to find what's best for your particular images.
- You can freely mix JPEGs and GIFs in your banner ad's rotation of images.
- You cannot link each image to a separate Web page. Every image in a banner ad must link to the same page.

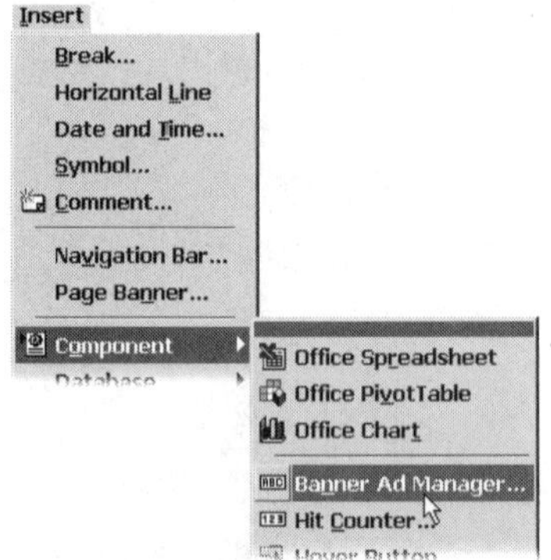

Figure 8.14 To add a banner ad, choose Insert > Component > Banner Ad Manager.

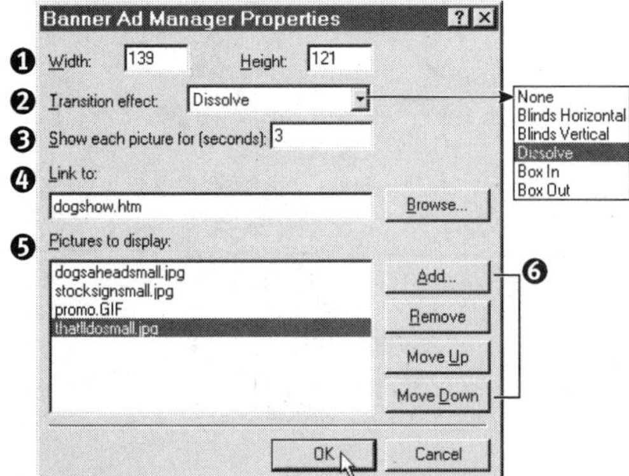

Figure 8.15 Use the Banner Ad Manager Properties dialog box to set the ad's size, the transition from one image to another, and the images used.

Figure 8.16 FrontPage can only display a banner ad's first image (top); switch to your Web browser to see the full image rotation (bottom).

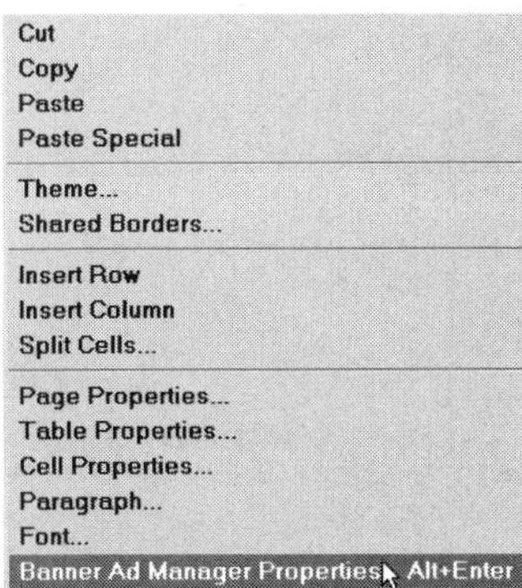

Figure 8.17 To change a banner ad, right-click it and choose *Banner Ad Manager Properties*.

To change a banner ad

1. Right-click the banner and choose *Banner Ad Manager Properties* from the shortcut menu (**Figure 8.17**).
2. When the Banner Ad Manager Properties dialog box appears, choose another transition effect, add or remove images, and rearrange the image order (**Figure 8.15**).
3. When you're satisfied with the changes, click *OK*, and save the page (Ctrl S).
4. To see the banner changes, switch to your Web browser and open the Web page.

To delete a banner ad

◆ Right-click the banner and choose *Cut* from the shortcut menu. The banner will be deleted.

To add a page hit counter

1. Switch to page view, and click in the page where you want the counter to appear.
2. Choose Insert > Component > Hit Counter (**Figure 8.18**).
3. When the Hit Counter Properties dialog box appears, choose a *Counter Style* or pick *Custom Picture* to navigate to your own image (**Figure 8.19**).
4. Check *Reset counter to* and enter a number in the text window if you want the counter to start with a particular number.
5. Check *Fixed number of digits* if you want the counter to roll back to zero when it reaches 10, 100, 1,000, or whatever.
6. Once you've made your choices, click *OK*. A hit counter placeholder will appear on your page, but you will not see the actual counter until you publish the site (**Figure 8.20**).

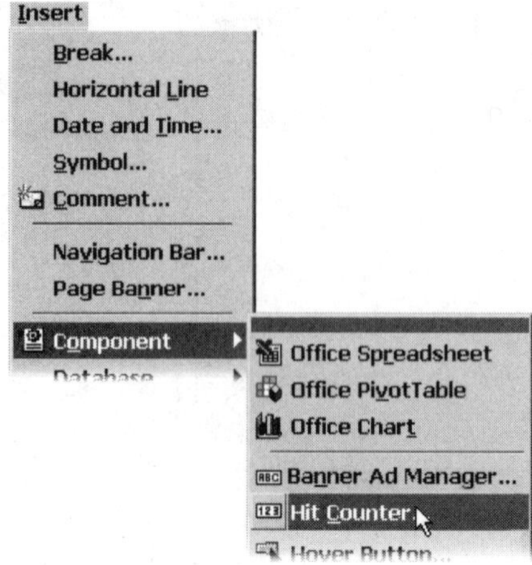

Figure 8.18 To add a page hit counter, choose Insert > Component > Hit Counter.

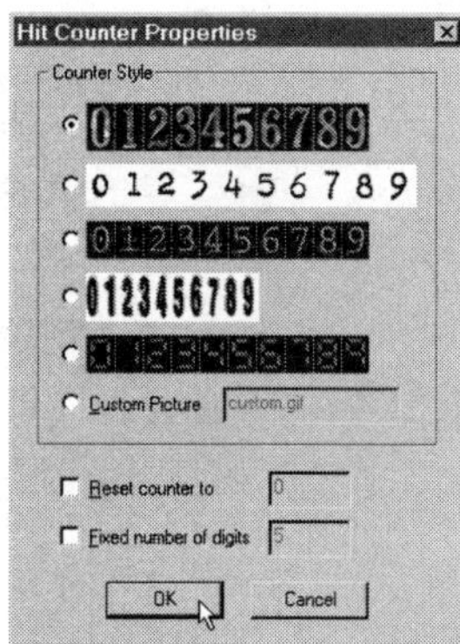

Figure 8.19 Use the Hit Counter Properties dialog box to pick a *Counter Style* or *Custom Picture*.

Figure 8.20 After you add a hit counter, a placeholder will appear on the page. The actual counter won't show until you publish the site.

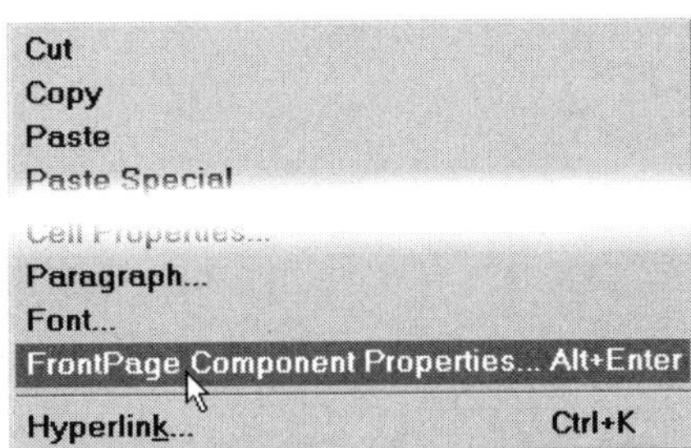

Figure 8.21 To change a hit counter, right-click it and choose *FrontPage Component Properties*.

To change a hit counter

1. Right-click the counter and choose *FrontPage Component Properties* from the shortcut menu (**Figure 8.21**).
2. When the Hit Counter Properties dialog box appears, change the *Counter Style*, reset the counter, or limit the number of digits (**Figure 8.19**).
3. When you're satisfied with the changes, click *OK*, and save the page (Ctrl S).

To delete a hit counter

- Make sure you're in page view, right-click the counter and choose *Cut* from the shortcut menu. The counter will be deleted.

To add a marquee

1. Switch to page view and click in the page where you want the marquee to appear.
2. Choose Insert > Component > Marquee (**Figure 8.22**).
3. When the Marquee Properties dialog box appears, enter the text you want displayed in the marquee; set its direction, speed, behavior, and alignment; its size; how often it should repeat; and the background color (**Figure 8.23**). For details, see *Marquee options* on the next page.
4. Once you've made your choices, click *OK*, then save the page (Ctrl S). The marquee will be inserted into the Web page.
5. To see how the marquee looks and decide if it needs adjustment, click FrontPage's *Preview* tab (**Figure 8.24**). To edit the marquee, see *To change a marquee* on page 184.

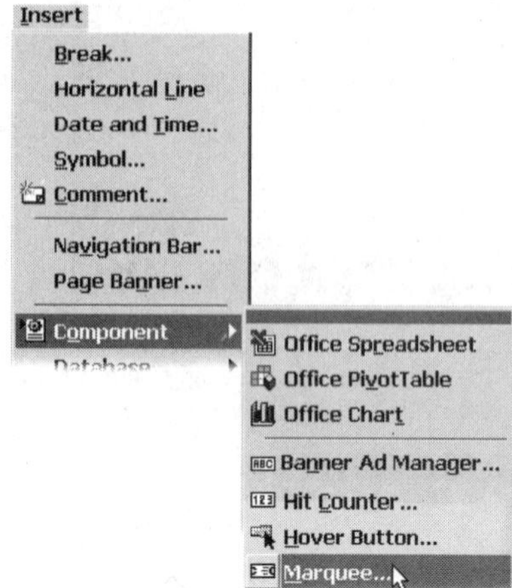

Figure 8.22 To add a marquee, choose Insert > Component > Marquee.

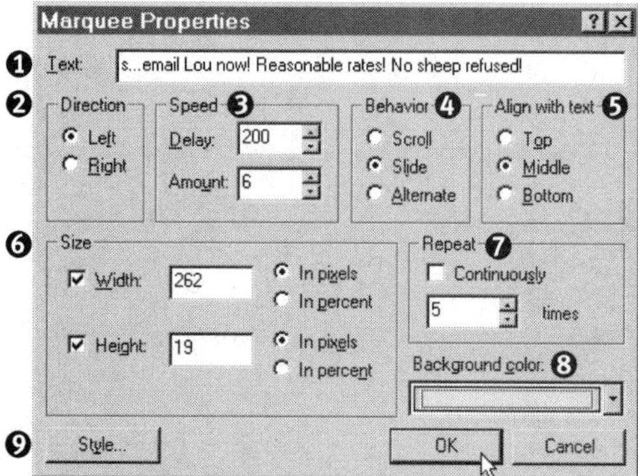

Figure 8.23 Use the Marquee Properties dialog box to enter the display text and control its motion and appearance.

Figure 8.24 Click the *Preview* tab to see if the marquee needs adjusting.

USING MARQUEES

Marquee options

To reach the Marquee Properties dialog box (**Figure 8.23**), choose Insert > Component > Marquee or right-click an existing marquee and choose *Marquee Properties* from the shortcut menu.

❶ **Text:** Type in the message you want the marquee to display.

❷ **Direction:** By default, *Left* will be selected since Western languages are read left to right. Choose *Right* for languages that read right to left.

❸ **Speed:** The marquee's speed is controlled by two factors. *Delay* sets how *often* (in milliseconds) the marquee moves. *Amount* controls the *distance* (in pixels) the marquee moves each time. Experiment with both settings to find the best speed.

❹ **Behavior:** The difference between *Scroll* and *Slide* is subtle and only appears at the end of your text message (**Figure 8.25**). With *Scroll*, the message keeps moving until the marquee is *blank*, then the message repeats. With *Slide*, the marquee is never blank. *Alternate* switches from *Scroll* to *Slide* after each sequence.

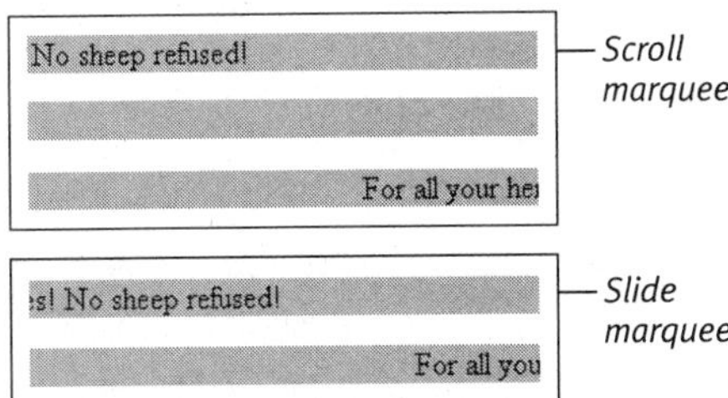

Figure 8.25 A subtle difference: marquee *scroll* (top sequence) leaves the marquee blank before the text begins again; marquee *slide* does not.

❺ **Align with text:** By default, the text will run across the *Middle* of the marquee. Choose *Top* or *Bottom* to change the text's vertical alignment.

❻ **Size:** Set the *Width* and *Height* of the marquee in pixels or as percent of the browser window.

❼ **Repeat:** Set the marquee to run *Continuously* or use the text window or arrows to set a limited number of repetitions.

❽ **Background color:** Use the drop-down menu to choose a marquee color. Since the text is always black, choose a lighter color for good contrast.

❾ **Style:** This button can only be used if you've created style sheets for your Web site. See *Building Style Sheets and Dynamic Effects* on page 269.

To change a marquee

1. Right-click the marquee and choose *Marquee Properties* from the shortcut menu (Alt Enter) (**Figure 8.26**).
2. When the Marquee Properties dialog box appears (**Figure 8.23**), make your changes to the marquee, and click *OK*.
3. Save the page (Ctrl S) and the changes will be applied to the marquee.
4. To see the changes, click the *Preview* tab.

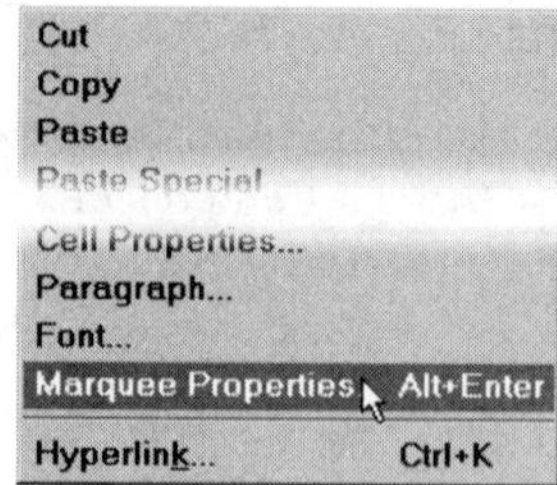

Figure 8.26 To change a marquee, right-click it and choose *Marquee Properties*.

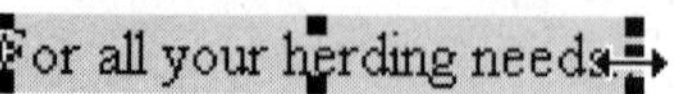

Figure 8.27 To resize a marquee, click and drag any of its handles.

✔ Tip

- If you just need to resize the marquee, don't bother with the Marquee Properties dialog box. Instead, click on the marquee while in page view and drag any of its handles to resize the marquee's text area (**Figure 8.27**).

To delete a marquee

- Make sure you're in page view, right-click the marquee and choose *Cut* from the shortcut menu. The marquee will be deleted.

PART III

CREATING ADVANCED WEB PAGES

9 Creating and Formatting Tables

Tables make it easy to present related text or images in a quick-to-scan form. With their rows and columns composed of individual cells, tables also lend themselves to clean-looking border and color treatments. A major plus of using tables is their consistent appearance no matter which browser Web visitors use. That's why so many commercial Web sites are designed around page-sized tables, similar to the layout grids favored by traditional paper-based designers. By the way, you'll find it much quicker building tables using the Tables toolbar (**Figure 9.1**). Activate it by choosing View > Toolbars > Tables.

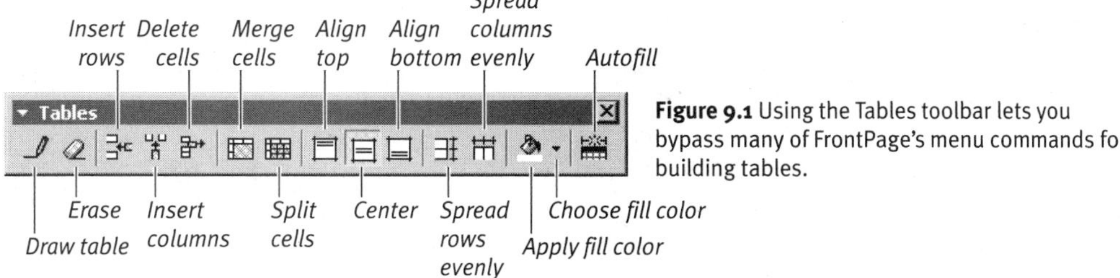

Figure 9.1 Using the Tables toolbar lets you bypass many of FrontPage's menu commands for building tables.

Creating and Formatting Tables

Creating Tables

FrontPage offers two main ways to create tables: one based on freehand drawing and one driven by dialog boxes. With the free-handed approach, you use a pencil-shaped cursor to draw directly in your Web page. It's straightforward and will quickly become your favorite way to handle tables. If you ever need absolute precision, however, the dialog box approach lets you create a table of predetermined dimensions.

To draw a table

1. Switch to page view and click where you want a table placed within the page.
2. Choose Table > Draw Table or, if the Tables toolbar is active, click the Draw Table button in the Tables toolbar (**Figure 9.2**).
3. A pencil icon will appear on the page. Click and drag the pencil until the dashed box is roughly the size of the table you want, release the mouse, and a simple table will appear on the page (**Figure 9.3**).
4. To further divide the table into columns and rows, click and drag the pencil to draw in their boundaries (**Figure 9.4**).
5. To resize any part of the table, move your cursor over the cell border until the cursor becomes a two-headed arrow. Then click and drag the border until you're satisfied, release the cursor, and the table is resized (**Figure 9.5**). Double-click to switch the pencil back to an I-beam cursor.

✔ Tip

- Unfortunately, FrontPage won't let you proportionately resize the table by grabbing one of its corners.

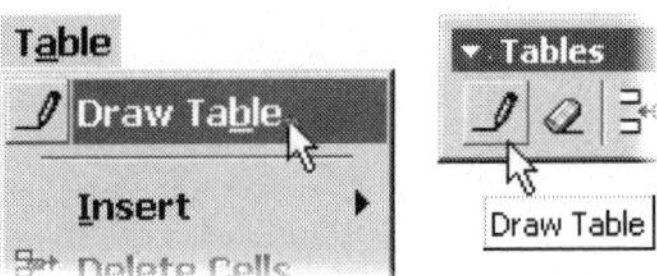

Figure 9.2 To draw a table directly, choose Table > Draw Table from the menu (left) or click the Draw Table button in the Tables toolbar (right).

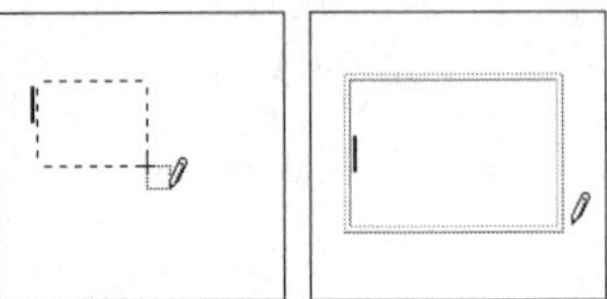

Figure 9.3 Draw a table by dragging the pencil icon across the page (left), then release the cursor (right).

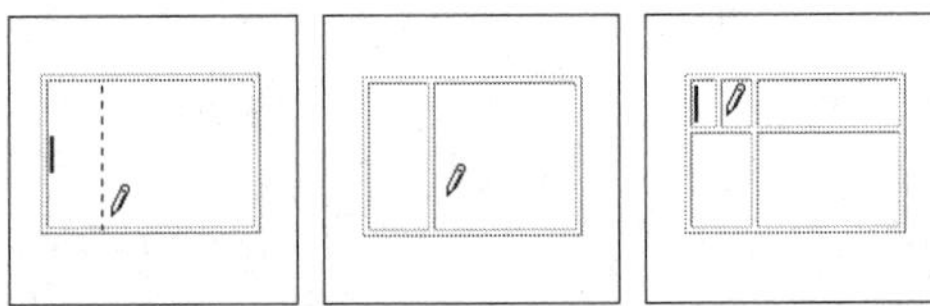

Figure 9.4 To further divide a table into columns and rows, click, drag, and release the pencil cursor.

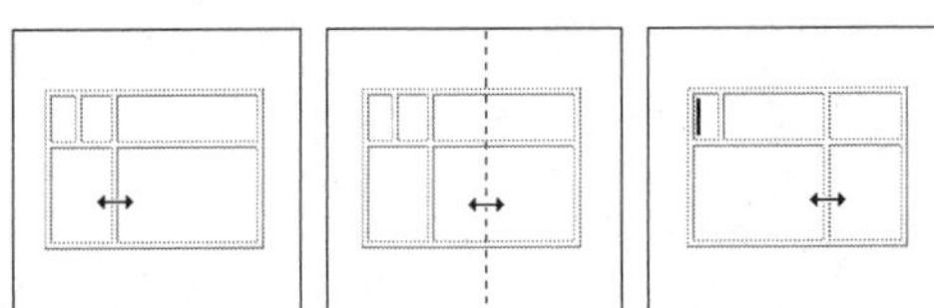

Figure 9.5 To resize any part of a table, move the cursor until it becomes a two-headed arrow. Then click, drag, and release the cursor.

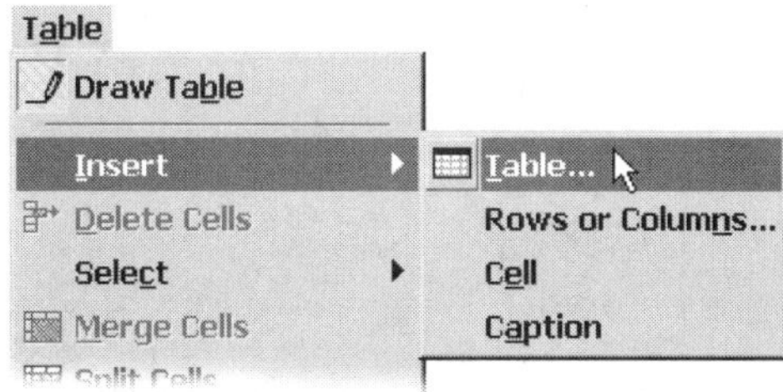

Figure 9.6 To insert a table, choose Table > Insert > Table from the menu.

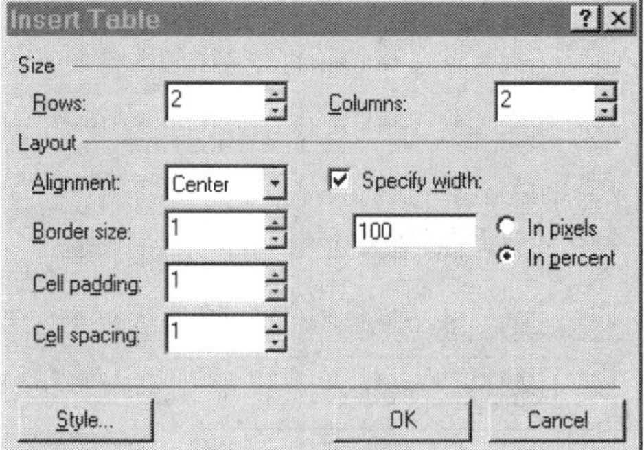

Figure 9.7 Use the Insert Table dialog box to set the table's size and layout.

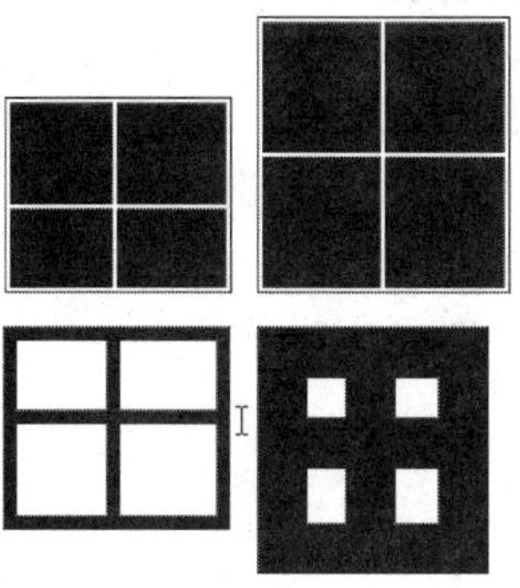

Figure 9.8 Black areas show changes in cell *padding*, which is the area *inside* the cells (top), versus changes in cell *spacing*, which is the area *between* cells (bottom).

Figure 9.9 For quick tables, click the Insert Table button in the Standard toolbar and drag your cursor to choose how many rows and columns you want.

To insert a table

1. Switch to page view and click where you want a table placed in the page.
2. Choose Table > Insert > Table (**Figure 9.6**).
3. When the Insert Table dialog box appears (**Figure 9.7**), use the *Size* section to set how many *Rows* and *Columns* the table should have.
4. Use the dialog box's *Layout* section to set the table's *Alignment* (left, center, or right), the *Border size* (the area around the outside of the entire table), and the *Cell padding* and *Cell spacing* (**Figure 9.8**).
5. Check *Specify width* to control the entire table, and use the radio buttons to choose whether the width should be absolute (*In pixels*) or relative to the width of the visitor's Web page (*In percent*).
6. Once you're done, click *OK* and the table will be inserted into your Web page.

✔ Tips

- Whatever changes you make in the Insert Table dialog box become the *default* settings for the next time you insert a table. That's great if you're churning out copies of that very same customized table but a real pain if you just want a plain vanilla table. To avoid constantly monkeying with the default settings, insert a plain table based on the default settings. Then customize it as explained in *To format tables* on page 204.
- For quick tables using the default settings, click the Insert Table button in the Standard toolbar and drag your cursor into the pop-up table to choose how many rows and columns you want (**Figure 9.9**). Release the cursor and a table of that size will be inserted into the page.
- If you want a borderless table, set *Border size* to 0 in the Insert Table dialog box.

To add table text

1. If your cursor doesn't have the familiar I-beam shape, first click outside the table. Then click inside any table cell (**Figure 9.10**).
2. Start typing and the cell will grow to accommodate your text (**Figure 9.11**).

To add table images

1. If your cursor doesn't have the familiar I-beam shape, first click outside the table. Then click inside any table cell (**Figure 9.10**).
2. Click the Insert Picture From File button in either the Standard or Pictures toolbar (**Figure 9.12**).
3. When the Picture dialog box appears, navigate to the image you want inserted (**Figure 9.13**). For details, see *Picture options* on page 148.
4. Click *OK* and the image will be inserted into the table cell, which will expand to accommodate its size (**Figure 9.14**).

✔ Tip

- FrontPage includes what it calls AutoFit to automatically fit any material inserted into a cell. First, make sure the Tables toolbar is active, then after you've inserted an item, just click the AutoFit button (**Figure 9.15**).

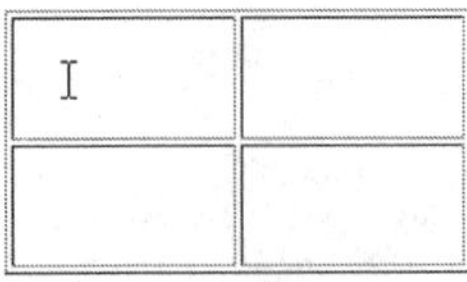

Figure 9.10 To add table text, just click inside a table cell.

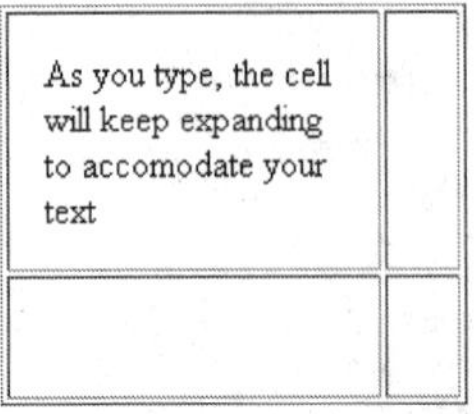

Figure 9.11 As you type, the cell grows to accommodate your text.

Figure 9.12 To add images to a table, click the Insert Picture From File button.

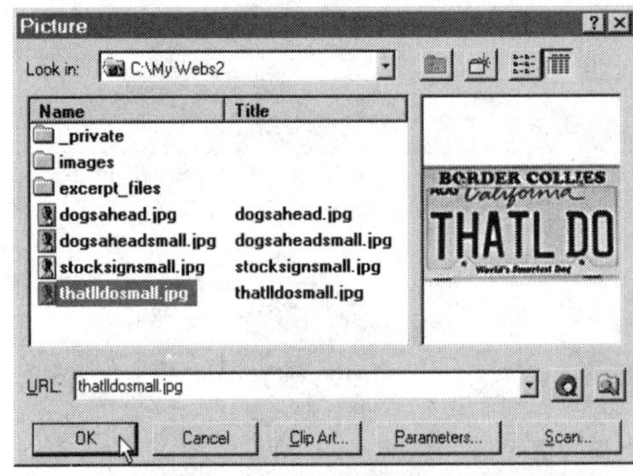

Figure 9.13 Use the Picture dialog box to navigate to the image you want inserted in the table.

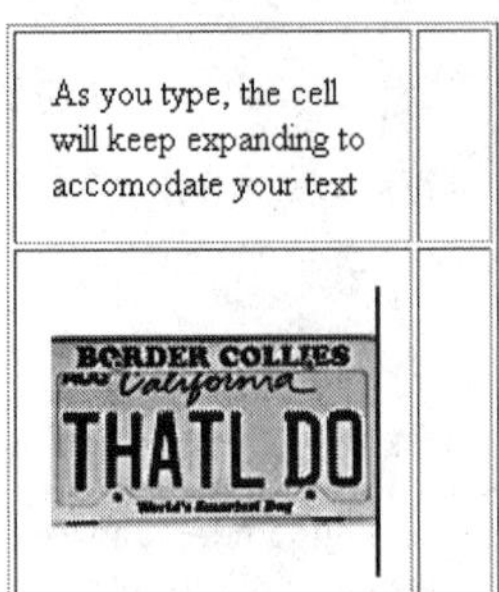

Figure 9.14 When a picture is inserted, the table cell expands to hold it.

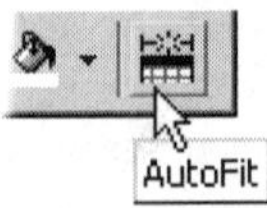

Figure 9.15 If material inserted into a cell doesn't fit, click the AutoFit button in the Tables toolbar.

Adding Table Content

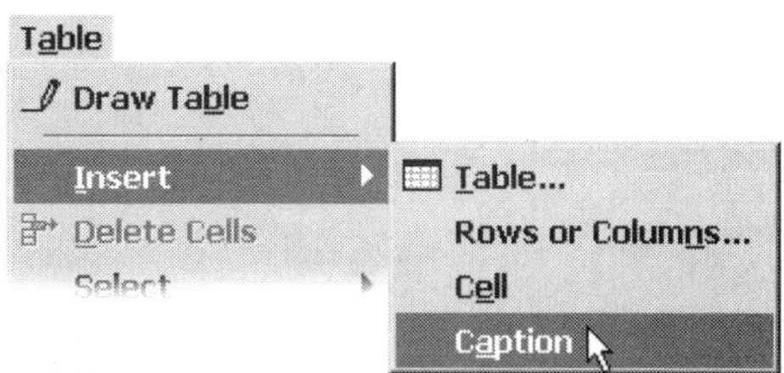

Figure 9.16 To add a caption, click inside the table and choose Table > Insert > Caption from the menu.

Figure 9.17 By default, captions are centered at the top of tables.

Figure 9.18 Use the Caption Properties dialog box to reposition captions beneath tables.

To add table captions

1. Click anywhere inside the table and choose Table > Insert > Caption (**Figure 9.16**).
2. When the cursor appears, it will be centered on the top of the table. Type in your caption (**Figure 9.17**).
3. Once you've entered the caption, you can change the font or size just like any other FrontPage text.

✔ Tip

- You can move the caption beneath the table, by right-clicking it and choosing *Caption Properties* from the shortcut menu. When the Caption Properties dialog box appears, choose *Bottom of table* and click *OK* (**Figure 9.18**). The caption will move to the bottom.

Adding Excel spreadsheets

FrontPage offers several ways to add Excel spreadsheets to your Web pages. The first simply creates a table based on the Excel data *at the time you import it.* In other words, it's static data—not a "live" spreadsheet that's dynamically updated.

The second method actually lets you use Excel inside Web pages for entering dynamic numbers and formulas. There's a catch of course: The page's visitors must have Microsoft Office 2000 installed on their computers, along with Microsoft's Office Web Components. Obviously, that's not much help if you're a solo worker or don't have a network administrator to handle the component installation But if you're working in a networked office across a corporate intranet, those requirements are easily met. And the payoff is being able to share—and dynamically update—Excel spreadsheets over the Web.

To add static Excel data

1. Make sure you're in page view, then click where you want the Excel data inserted into the Web page.
2. Choose Insert > File (**Figure 9.19**).
3. When the Select File dialog box appears, use the *Files of type* drop-down menu to select *Microsoft Excel Worksheet (*.xls,*xlw)* (**Figure 9.20**).
4. Navigate to the spreadsheet you need, click *Open*, and the data will be inserted into the Web page as a borderless table (denoted by the dashed outlines) (**Figure 9.21**).

✔ Tip

- You can easily reformat the borderless Excel-based table into something more "Webby" (**Figure 9.22**). For details, see *To format tables* on page 204.

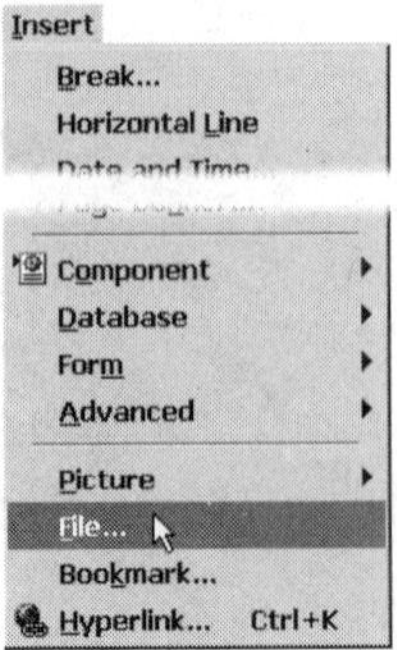

Figure 9.19 To add static Excel data to a table, choose Insert > File.

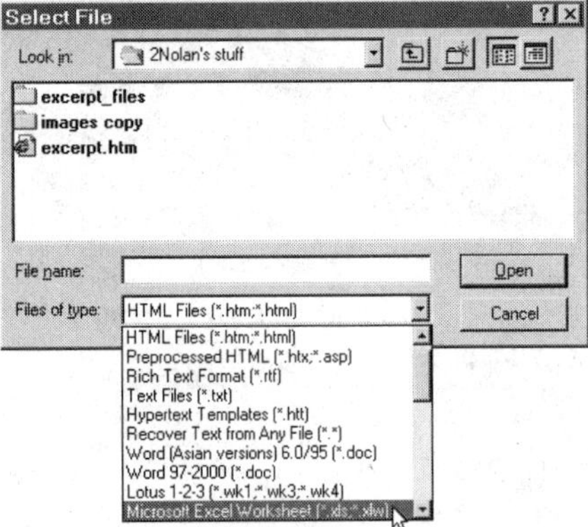

Figure 9.20 To find Excel files, use the Select File dialog box's drop-down menu to select *Microsoft Excel Worksheets*.

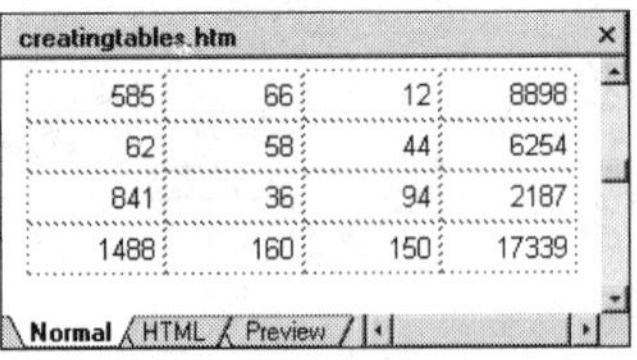

Figure 9.21 Excel files inserted into FrontPage initially appear as borderless tables, denoted by the dashed outlines.

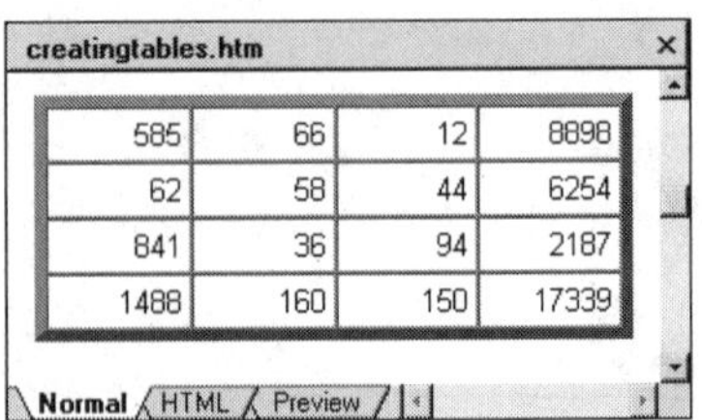

Figure 9.22 It's easy to reformat an Excel-based table into a more traditional Web-styled table.

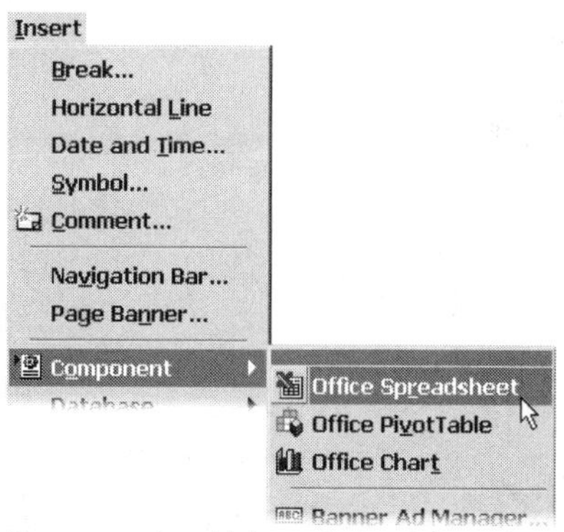

Figure 9.23 To add dynamic Excel data, choose Insert > Component > Office Spreadsheet.

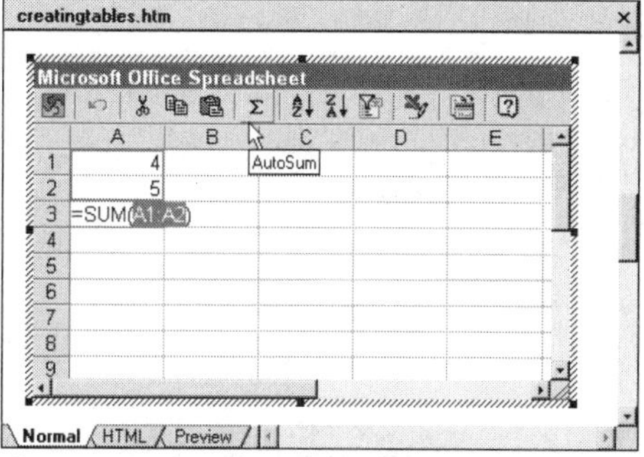

Figure 9.24 A blank Excel spreadsheet inserted into the Web page can be filled in with Excel-based formulas.

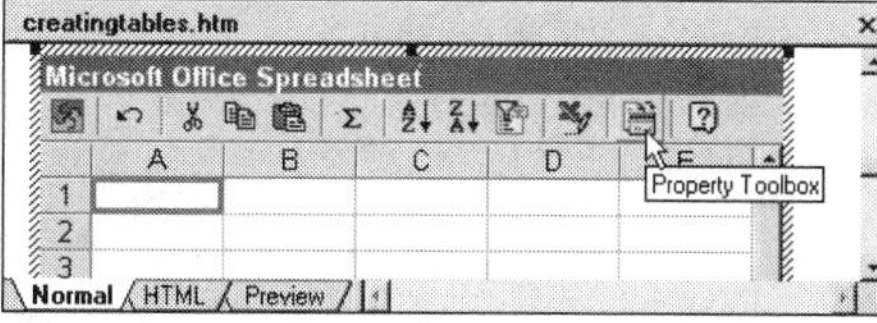

Figure 9.25 To import an *existing* Excel spreadsheet into a Web page, click the *blank* spreadsheet's *Property Toolbox* button.

To add dynamic Excel data

1. Make sure you're in page view, then click where you want the Excel spreadsheet inserted into the Web page.
2. Choose Insert > Component > Office Spreadsheet (**Figure 9.23**). A blank Excel spreadsheet will appear inside the Web page, which can then be filled in with numbers and formulas (**Figure 9.24**).

✔ Tip

- To import an *existing* Excel spreadsheet into the Web page you just created, click the *blank* spreadsheet's *Property Toolbox* button (**Figure 9.25**). That will trigger a drop-down menu within Excel. Use the Excel menu's *Import Data* section, enter the spreadsheet's URL or pathname, check *Refresh from URL at run time*, and click *Import Now*. The latest version of the data will be dumped into your blank spreadsheet.

Selecting Table Elements

Unlike many FrontPage procedures, selecting cells, rows, and columns within tables isn't always a click-and-drag affair.

To select a cell

- Press Alt and click inside any cell. The cell will be selected, denoted by its colors reversing (**Figure 9.26**).

or

- Click anywhere in a cell and choose Table > Select, then choose *Cell* from the submenu (**Figure 9.27**). The cell will be selected, denoted by its colors reversing (**Figure 9.26**).

To select multiple cells

- To select *adjacent* cells, click and hold your cursor in a cell, then drag the cursor to select additional cells (**Figure 9.28**).

or

- To select *non-adjacent* cells, press Alt and click inside any cell, then press Alt Shift and click another cell. Repeat until you've selected all the cells you need (**Figure 9.29**).

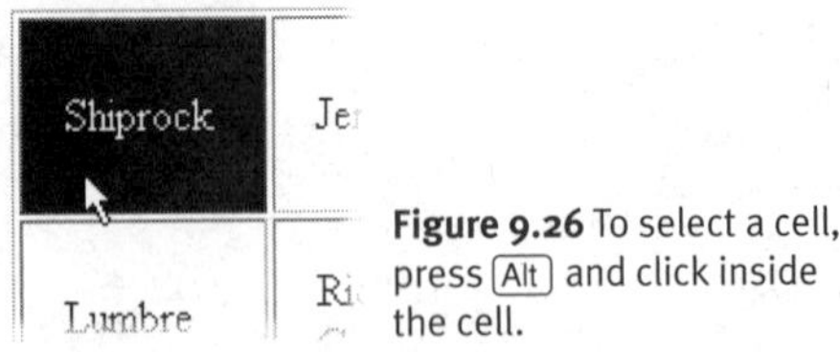

Figure 9.26 To select a cell, press Alt and click inside the cell.

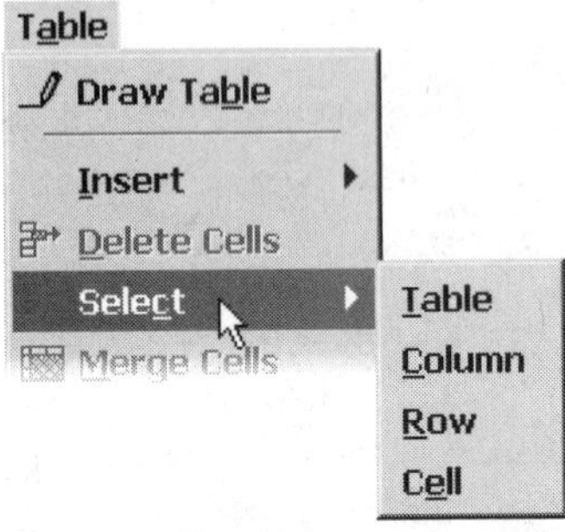

Figure 9.27 To select any element of a table, choose Table > Select and make a choice from the submenu.

Shiprock	Jemez	Tres Piedras
Lumbre	Rio Grande	Tucumcari
Mogollon	Hatch	Kiowa

Figure 9.28 To select *adjacent* cells, click the cursor in a cell, then drag the cursor to select additional cells.

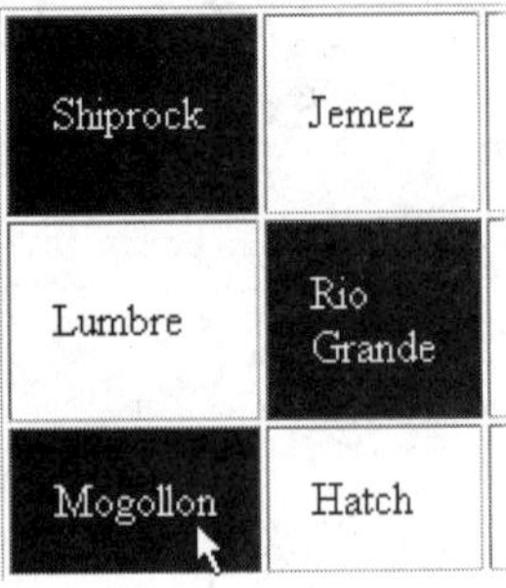

Figure 9.29 To select *non-adjacent* cells, press Alt and click inside any cell, then press Alt Shift as you select other cells.

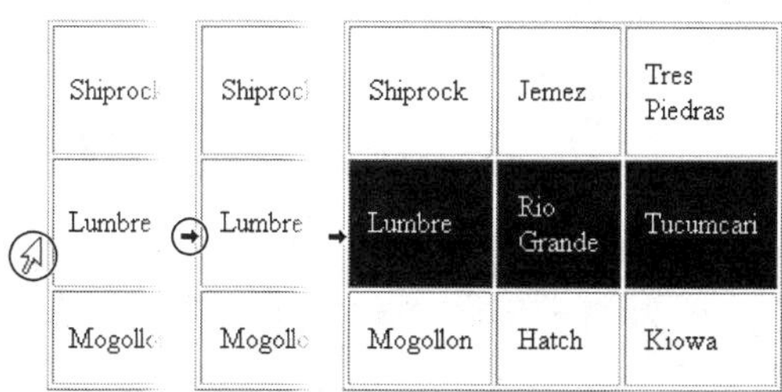

Figure 9.30 To select a row, move the cursor up to the edge of a row (left). When it becomes a black arrow (middle), click once and the row will be selected (right).

To select a row

- Click anywhere in a row and choose Table > Select, then choose *Row* from the submenu (**Figure 9.27**). The row will be selected.

or

- Click and hold your cursor anywhere in a row, then drag the cursor to select the rest of the cells in the row.

or

- Move the cursor slowly up to the left edge of a row until it becomes an arrow, then click once. The row will be selected (**Figure 9.30**).

To select a column

- Click anywhere in a column and choose Table > Select, then choose *Column* from the submenu (**Figure 9.27**). The column will be selected.

or

- Click and hold your cursor anywhere in a column, then drag the cursor to select the rest of the cells in the column.

or

- Move the cursor slowly up to the left edge of a column until it becomes an arrow, then click once. The column will be selected.

To select an entire table

- Click anywhere in a table and choose Table > Select, then choose *Table* from the submenu (**Figure 9.27**). The entire table will be selected.

or

- Click your cursor at the table's upper-left or lower-right corner and, while keeping the mouse pressed, drag the cursor to select the entire table.

Changing Table Structure

With FrontPage you can go back and expand a table at any time, whether it's by adding a single cell, a row or column, or even inserting another table into the table.

To add cells

1. Click in the cell to the right of where you want to add a cell (**Figure 9.31**).
2. Choose Table > Insert, then choose *Cell* from the submenu (**Figure 9.32**).
3. A single cell will be inserted into the table just left of the cell selected in step 1 (**Figure 9.33**).

✔ Tip

- Adding or deleting single cells in a table can produce a strangely shaped table. So what's the point? Well, if you're using tables to design Web *pages*, this ability might give you just what you need. The moral: Experiment!

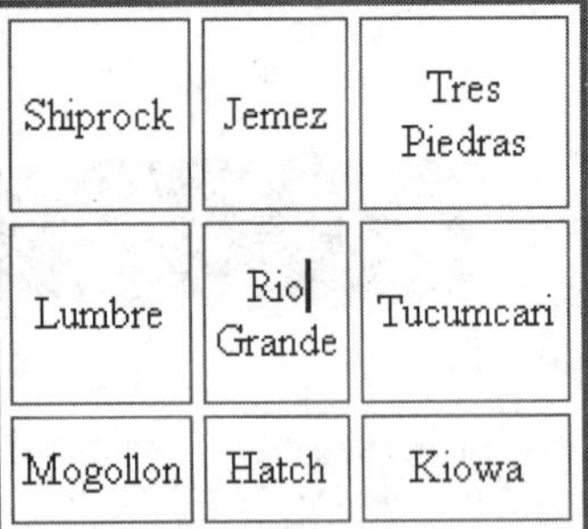

Figure 9.31 Click in the cell to the *right* of where you want to add a cell.

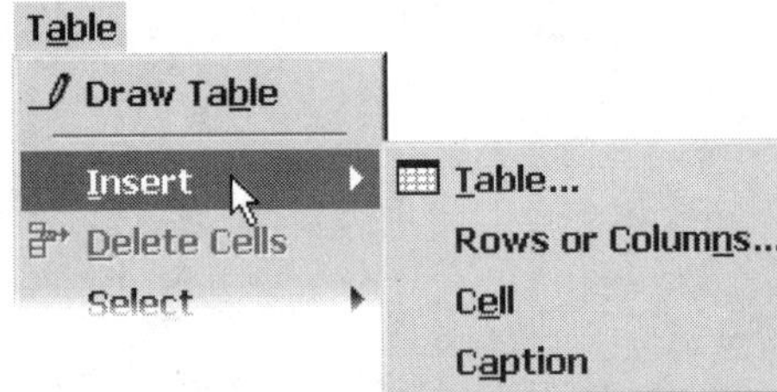

Figure 9.32 To add any element of a table, choose Table > Insert and make a choice from the submenu.

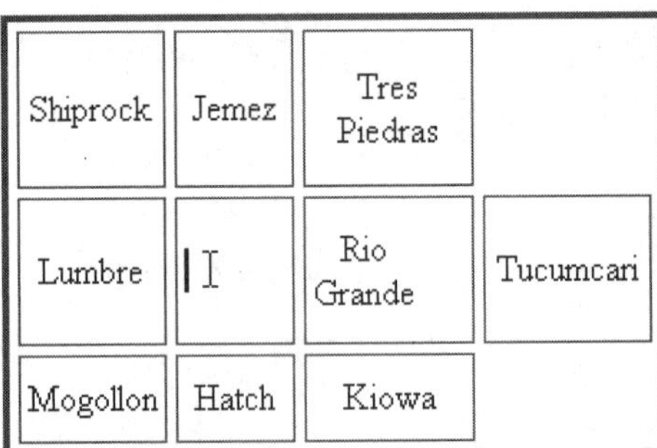

Figure 9.33 A single cell is inserted into the table left of the cell selected in Figure 9.31.

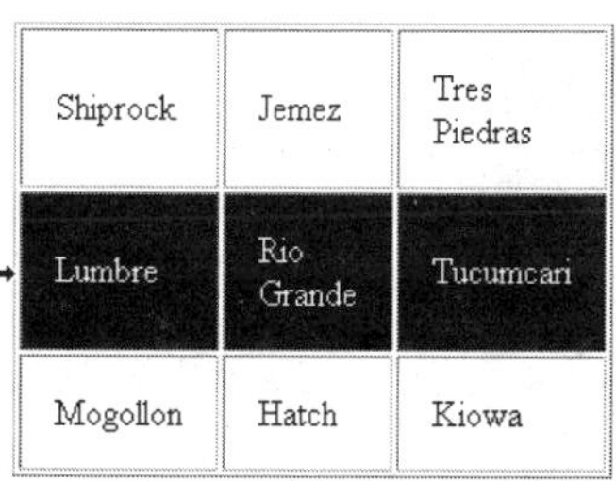

Figure 9.34 Select the row next to where you want to insert a new row.

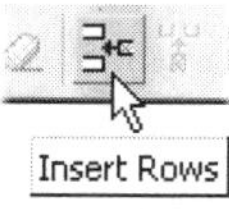

Figure 9.35 If the Tables toolbar is active, you also can add rows by clicking the Insert Rows button.

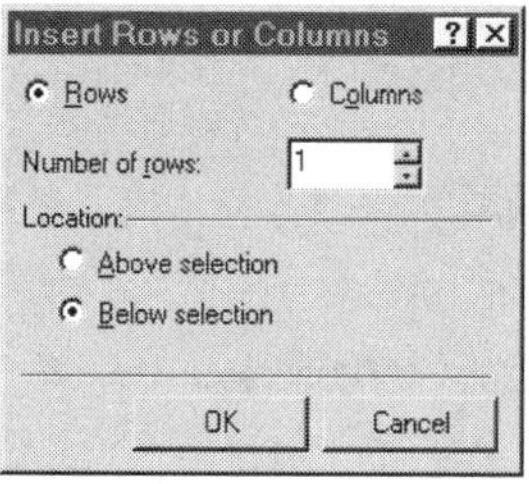

Figure 9.36 Use the Insert Rows or Columns dialog box to set how many rows you want added.

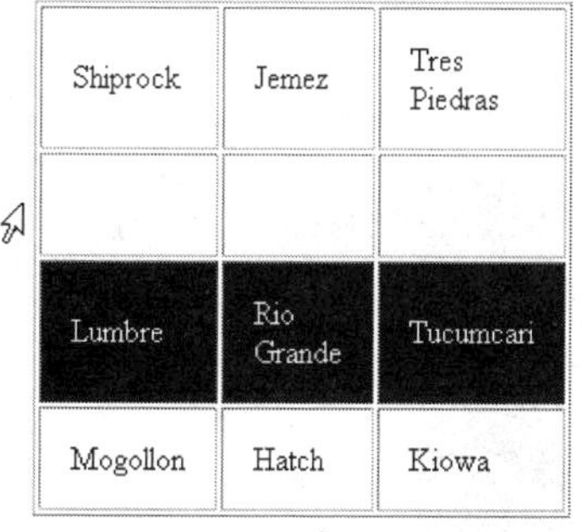

Figure 9.37 A new row inserted into the table will be blank.

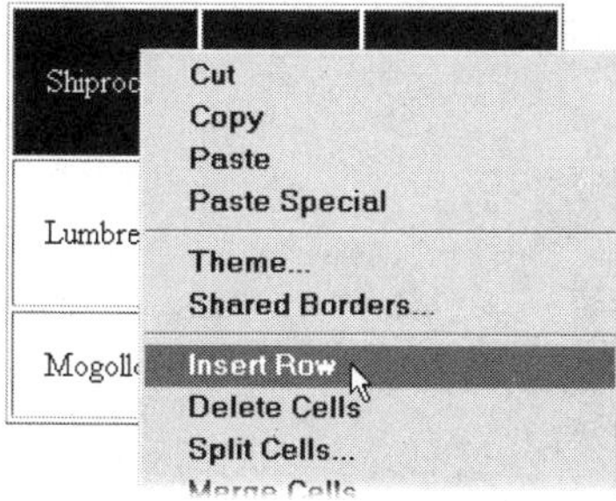

Figure 9.38 To quickly add rows, right-click and choose *Insert Row* from the shortcut menu.

To add rows

1. Select a row next to where you want to insert a new row (**Figure 9.34**).
2. Choose Table > Insert, then choose *Row or Columns* from the submenu (**Figure 9.32**). Or, if the Tables toolbar is active, click the Insert Rows button (**Figure 9.35**).
3. When the Insert Rows or Columns dialog box appears, *Rows* will already be selected (**Figure 9.36**). Use the text window or arrows to choose the *Number of rows* you want to add and decide whether to add the rows above or below the row selected in step 1.
4. Click *OK* and the row(s) will be inserted into the table (**Figure 9.37**).

✔ Tip

■ You also can select a row, right-click, and choose *Insert Row* from the shortcut menu (**Figure 9.38**). When the Insert Rows or Columns dialog box appears, follow steps 3 and 4.

To add columns

1. Select a column next to where you want to insert a new column (**Figure 9.39**).
2. Choose Table > Insert, then choose *Row or Columns* from the submenu (**Figure 9.32**). Or, if the Tables toolbar is active, click the Insert Columns button (**Figure 9.40**).
3. When the Insert Rows or Columns dialog box appears, *Columns* will already be selected (**Figure 9.41**). Use the text window or arrows to choose the *Number of columns* you want to add and decide whether to add the columns to the left or right of the column selected in step 1.
4. Click *OK* and the column(s) will be inserted into the table (**Figure 9.42**).

✔ Tip

- You also can select a column, right-click, and choose *Insert Column* from the shortcut menu (**Figure 9.43**). When the Insert Rows or Columns dialog box appears, follow steps 3 and 4.

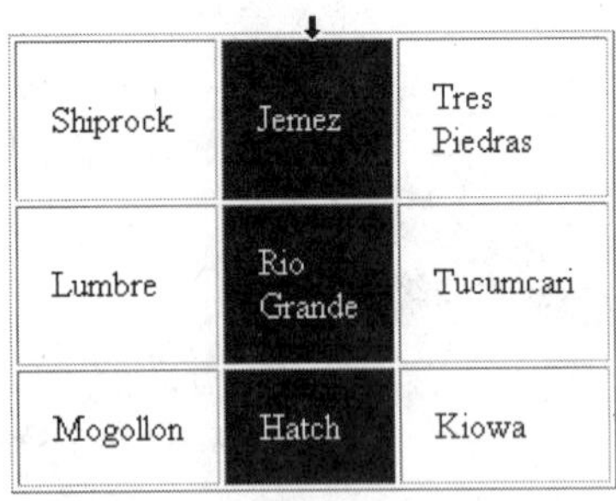

Figure 9.39 Select the column next to where you want to insert a new column.

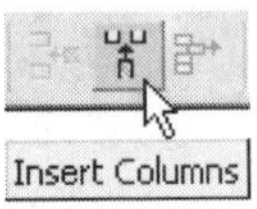

Figure 9.40 If the Tables toolbar is active, you also can add columns by clicking the Insert Columns button.

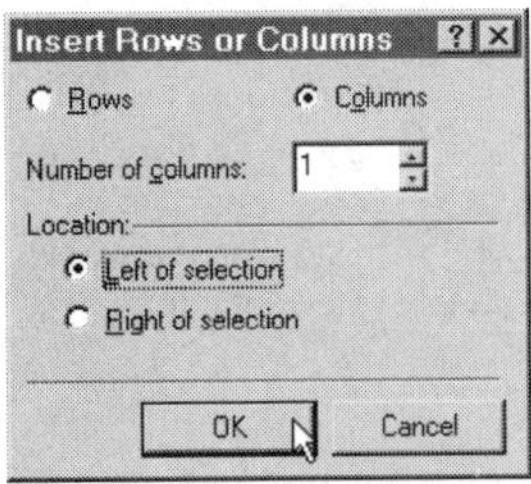

Figure 9.41 Use the Insert Rows or Columns dialog box to set how many columns you want added.

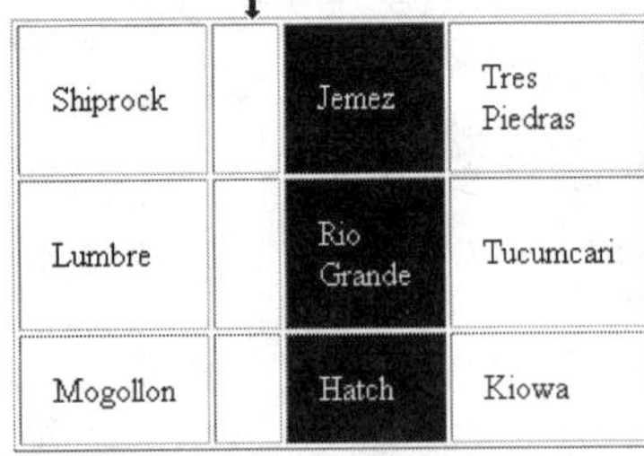

Figure 9.42 A new column inserted into the table will be blank.

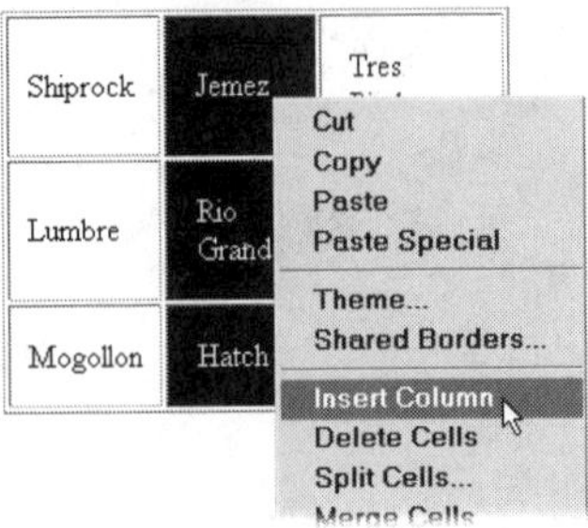

Figure 9.43 To quickly add columns, right-click and choose *Insert Column* from the shortcut menu.

Changing Table Elements

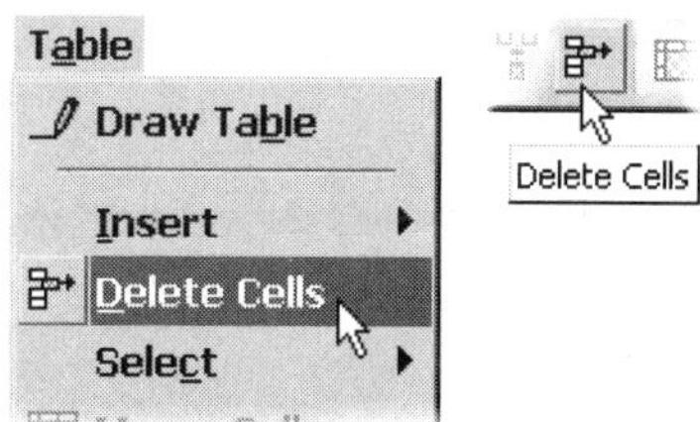

Figure 9.44 To delete any part of a table, select it and choose Table > Delete Cells from the menu (left) or click the Delete Cells button (right).

Figure 9.45 To quickly remove any table element, select it, right-click and choose *Cut*.

To delete any part of a table

1. Select the parts of table you want to delete, whether it's a cell, a single row, or several rows or columns.
2. Choose Table > Delete Cells or if the Tables toolbar is active, click the Delete Cells button (**Figure 9.44**). All the selected cells will be deleted.

✔ Tip

- For even faster deletion, select any part of the table, right-click and choose *Cut* from the shortcut menu (**Figure 9.45**).

Splitting and merging cells

While it's easy to add or delete parts of a table, sometimes you'll want to create or delete an individual cell and not affect the overall dimensions of the rest of the table. That's where the ability to split a cell into two cells, or merge several cells into a single cell, becomes especially handy. You can, for example, create a large cell in the center of a table by merging several adjacent cells and avoid messing up anything else in the table.

To split cells

1. Click inside the cell you want to split.
2. Choose Table > Split Cells (**Figure 9.46**) or if the Tables toolbar is active, click the Split Cells button (right, **Figure 9.47**).
3. When the Split Cells dialog box appears, choose whether you want the selected cell divided horizontally into two rows or vertically into two columns (**Figure 9.48**).
4. Use the arrows or enter numbers directly in the text window to set the *Number of rows* or *Number of columns* you want the cell split into. When you're done, click *OK* and the cell will be split.

✔ Tip

- The fastest way to split a cell is simply to right-click inside it, choose *Split Cells* from the shortcut menu, and follow steps 3 and 4, above.

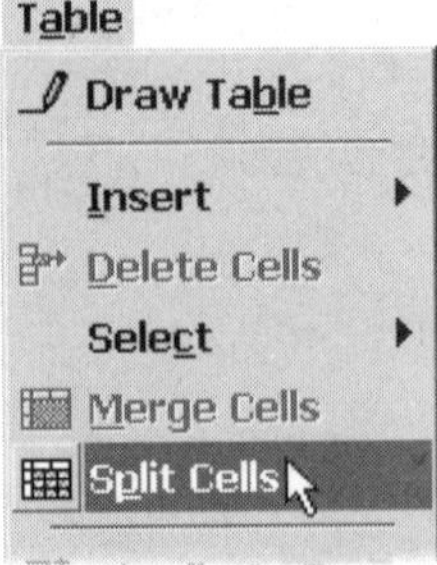

Figure 9.46 To split a cell, click inside it and choose Table > Split Cells.

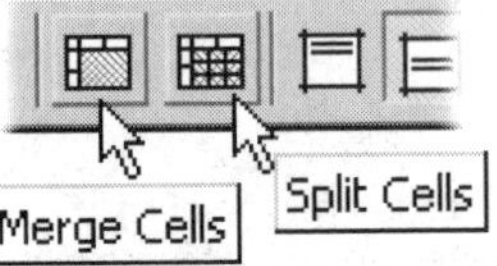

Figure 9.47 If the Tables toolbar is active, you also can combine cells with the Merge Cells button or split them with the Split Cells button.

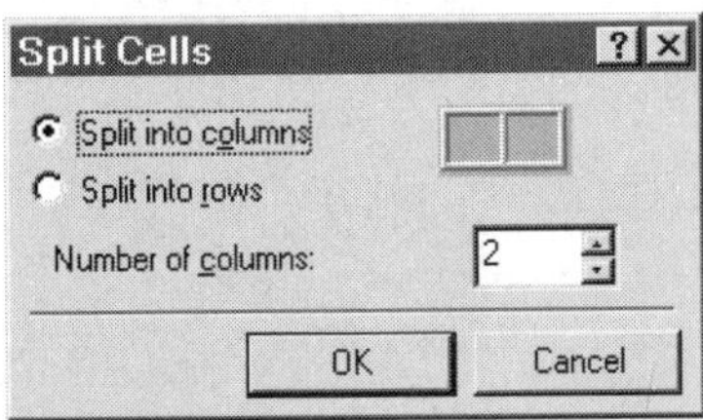

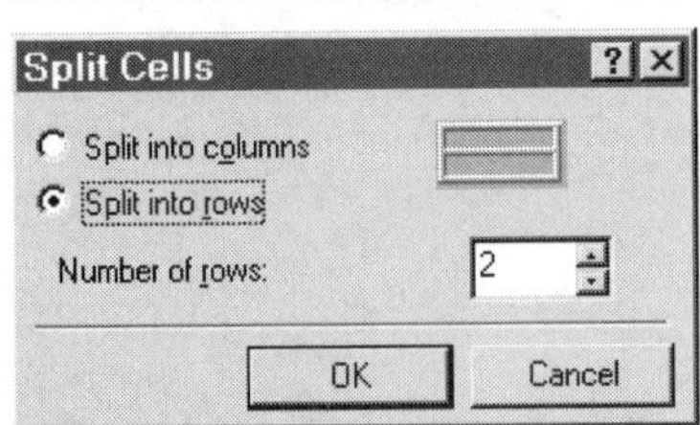

Figure 9.48 Use the Split Cells dialog box to divide a cell horizontally into rows or vertically into columns.

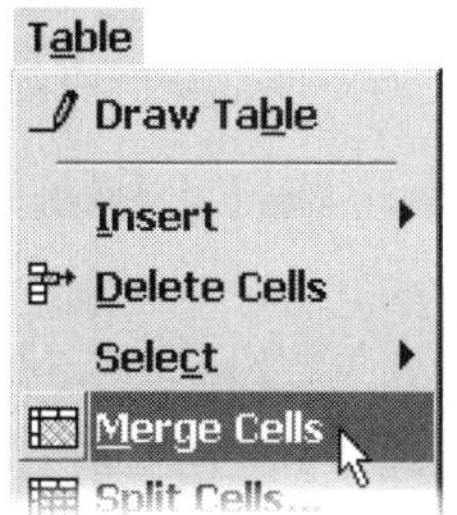

Figure 9.49 To merge cells, select them and choose Table > Merge Cells.

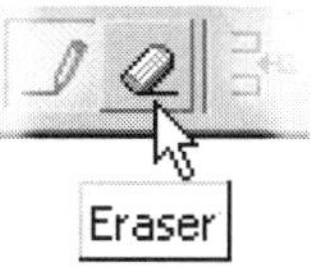

Figure 9.50 The Eraser button in the Tables toolbar offers a quick way to merge cells.

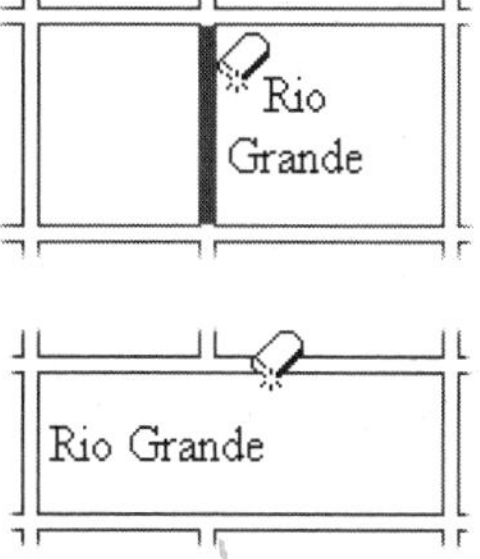

Figure 9.51 Drag the eraser-shaped cursor across a cell border until it's highlighted, release the mouse, and the border disappears.

To merge cells

1. Select the cells you want merged.
2. Choose Table > Merge Cells (**Figure 9.49**) or if the Tables toolbar is active, click the Merge Cells button (left, **Figure 9.47**). The selected cells will be combined into a single cell.

✔ Tips

- Akin to the freehand Pencil button, the Tables toolbar's Eraser button offers a quick way to merge cells (**Figure 9.50**). Click the button, press and drag your now eraser-shaped cursor across a cell border until it's highlighted, and then release the mouse. The border will disappear (**Figure 9.51**). To deactivate the eraser, double-click anywhere outside the table.
- You also can expand a cell by increasing its span, explained in *To format cells* on page 206.

Evening up rows and columns

Inevitably as you work on a table things get messy. Fortunately, FrontPage offers a way to tidy things up by making all your rows the same height or all your columns the same width. The process, by the way, initially seems a bit backward because you select a *column* to even up the *row* height and select a *row* to even up the *column* width.

To make rows the same height

1. Select a *column* containing a cell from each uneven *row* (**Figure 9.52**).
2. Choose Table > Distribute Rows Evenly (left, **Figure 9.53**). If the Tables toolbar is active, you also can click the Distribute Rows Evenly button (left, **Figure 9.54**). The height of the rows will be evened up (**Figure 9.55**).

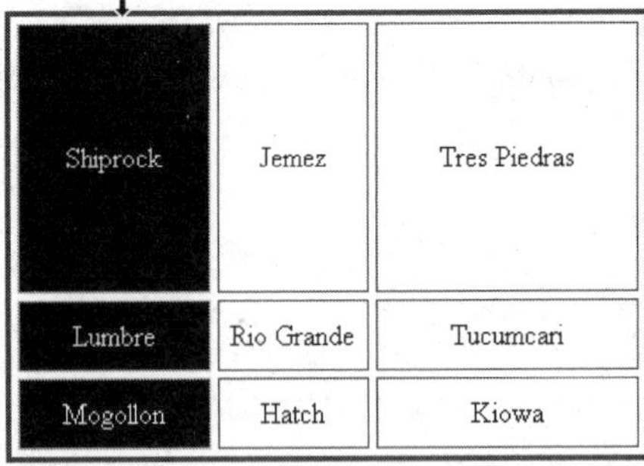

Shiprock	Jemez	Tres Piedras
Lumbre	Rio Grande	Tucumcari
Mogollon	Hatch	Kiowa

Figure 9.52 To make rows the same height, select a *column* containing a cell from each uneven row.

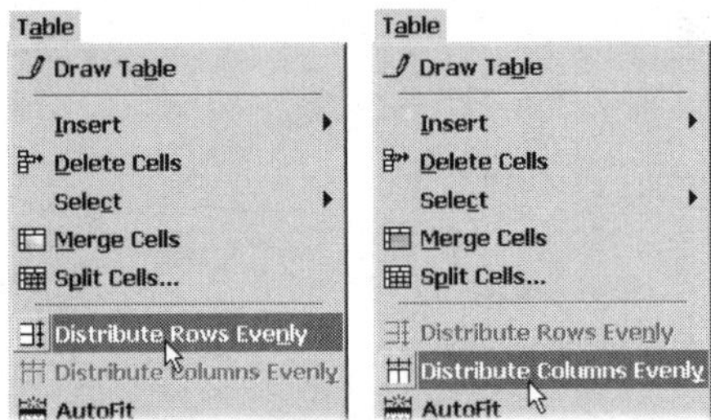

Figure 9.53 To even up a table, choose Table > Distribute Rows Evenly (left) or Table > Distribute Columns Evenly.

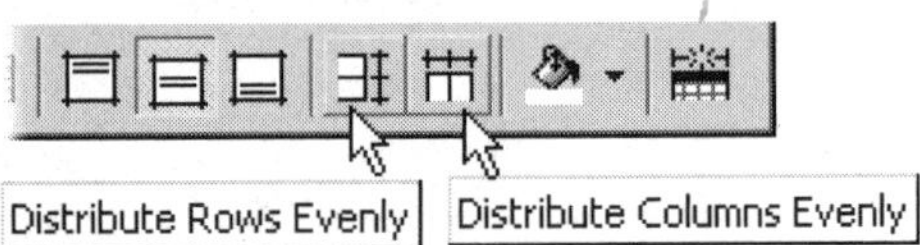

Figure 9.54 If the Tables toolbar is active, you also can even up a table with the Distribute Rows Evenly button (left) or the Distribute Columns Evenly button (right).

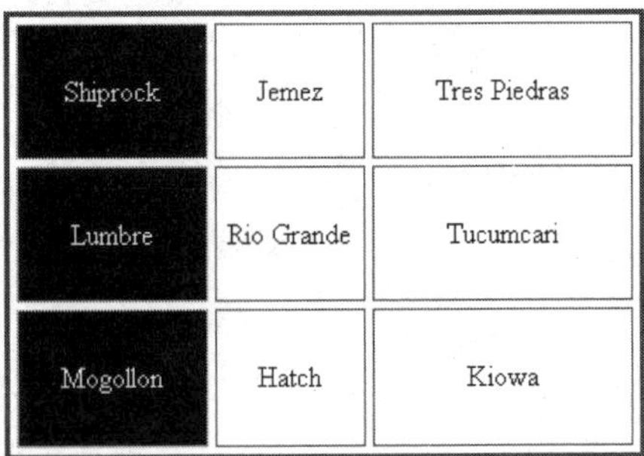

Shiprock	Jemez	Tres Piedras
Lumbre	Rio Grande	Tucumcari
Mogollon	Hatch	Kiowa

Figure 9.55 Once evened up, the rows will have the same height.

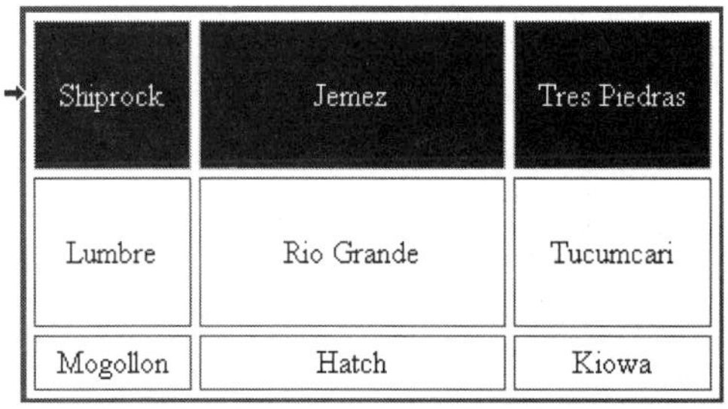

Shiprock	Jemez	Tres Piedras
Lumbre	Rio Grande	Tucumcari
Mogollon	Hatch	Kiowa

Figure 9.56 To make columns the same width , select a *row* containing a cell from each uneven column.

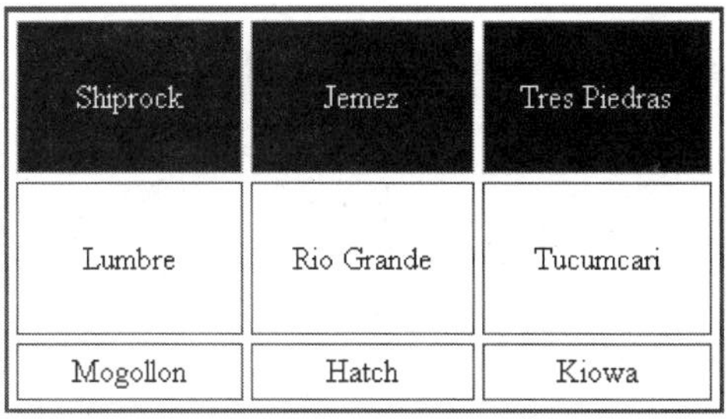

Shiprock	Jemez	Tres Piedras
Lumbre	Rio Grande	Tucumcari
Mogollon	Hatch	Kiowa

Figure 9.57 Once evened up, all the columns will have the same width.

To make columns the same width

1. Select a *row* containing a cell from each uneven *column* (**Figure 9.56**).
2. Choose Table > Distribute Columns Evenly (right, **Figure 9.53**). If the Tables toolbar is active, you also can click the Distribute Columns Evenly button (right, **Figure 9.54**). The width of the columns will be evened up (**Figure 9.57**).

✔ Tip

- If the Tables toolbar is active and you want to tidy up a whole table at once, select all of it. That will activate the Distribute Rows Evenly button *and* the Distribute Columns Evenly button, allowing you to click one button right after the other without bothering to make a second selection.

Formatting Tables and Cells

Once you've added a table to your page, put some text and images into it, and perhaps changed its structure, you're ready for the final step: formatting the full table and individual cells.

To format tables

1. Right-click the table and choose *Table Properties* from the shortcut menu (**Figure 9.58**).
2. When the Table Properties dialog box appears (**Figure 9.59**), use the *Layout* section to set the table's *Alignment*, width, and the *Cell padding* and *Cell spacing* (**Figure 9.8**). The *Float* drop-down menu lets you have the table "float" on the left or right side of text that ordinarily would appear below the table (**Figure 9.60**).
3. Use the dialog box's *Borders* section to set the table's border. For details, see *To format table borders* on the next page.
4. If you want to apply the same color to every cell in the table, use the pop-up box in the Background section to choose your color. For details, see *To color cells* on page 208.
5. Once you're done, click *OK* and the changes will be applied to your table.

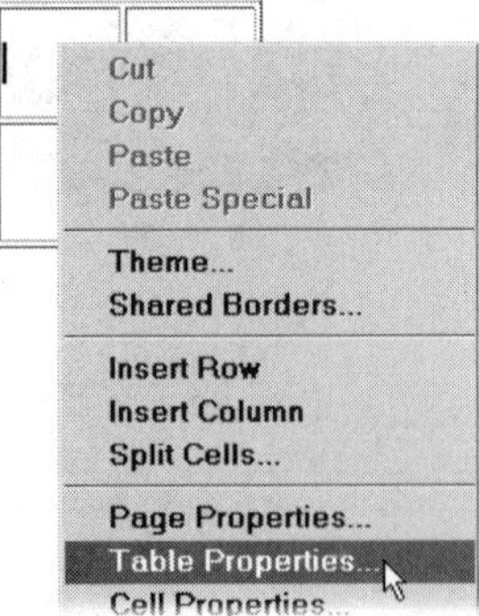

Figure 9.58 To format a table, right-click it and choose *Table Properties*.

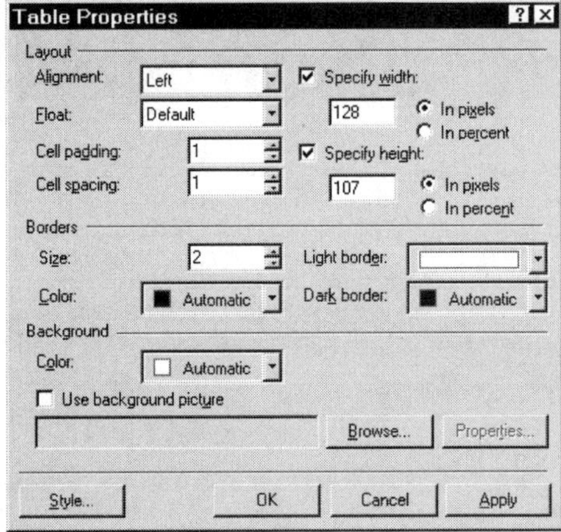

Figure 9.59 Use the *Layout* section of the Table Properties dialog box to set the table's *Alignment*, width, and the *Cell padding* and *Cell spacing*.

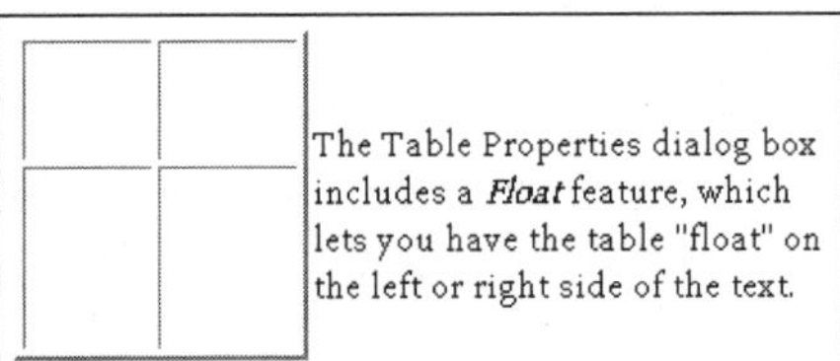

Figure 9.60 The Table Properties dialog box's *Float* checkbox lets you have the table "float" on the left or right side of text.

585	66	12	8898
62	58	44	6254
841	36	94	2187
1488	160	150	17339

Figure 9.61 A plain table with a border width of 1.

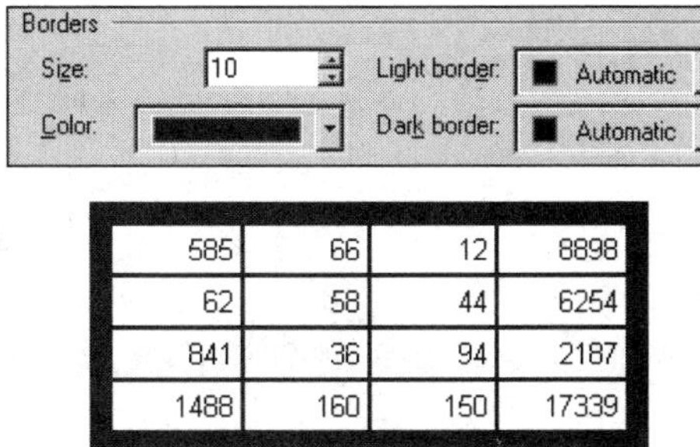

585	66	12	8898
62	58	44	6254
841	36	94	2187
1488	160	150	17339

Figure 9.62 To create a single-color border, use the *Color* pop-up box and leave the *Light border* and *Dark border* pop-up boxes set to *Automatic*.

585	66	12	8898
62	58	44	6254
841	36	94	2187
1488	160	150	17339

Figure 9.63 To create a two-color 3D effect, use the *Light border* and *Dark border* pop-up boxes.

To format table borders

1. Select the table to which you want borders applied (**Figure 9.61**).
2. Right-click and choose *Table Properties* from the shortcut menu (**Figure 9.58**).
3. When the Table Properties dialog box appears (**Figure 9.59**), use the *Borders* section to set the *Size* (width) of your border. The larger the number, the wider the border. For a borderless table, set the number at 0.
4. If you want a single-color border, use the *Color* pop-up box to pick a color and leave the *Light border* and *Dark border* pop-up boxes set to *Automatic* (top, **Figure 9.62**).

   If you want a two-color 3D effect, use the Light border and Dark border pop-up boxes to pick your colors (top, **Figure 9.63**).
5. Once you've set the width and color, click *OK* and the border will be applied (bottom, **Figures 9.62** and **9.63**).

✔ Tips

- In using *Light border* and *Dark border* colors for a 3D effect, it'll look best if the two colors are the same hue, for example, a light red and a dark red.
- If you use the two-color 3D effect, it will automatically appear instead of whatever single color you set.

To format cells

1. Select the cell or cells, then right-click and choose *Cell Properties* from the shortcut menu (**Figure 9.64**).
2. When the Cell Properties dialog box appears (**Figure 9.65**), use the *Layout* section to change the alignment and size of the selected cell.
3. Check *Specify width* and *Specify height* if you want to set the cell's dimensions. Choose *In pixels* to make either dimension absolute or *In percent* to make it relative to the size of the viewer's Web browser window.
4. If you want to have the selected cell span more than one row, enter a number in the *Rows spanned* window. To have the cell span more than one column, enter a number in the *Columns spanned* window.
5. Click *OK* and the changes will be applied to the selected cell(s).

✔ Tips

- While the Cell Properties dialog box offers the option of setting border colors for individual cells, it's more effective visually to adjust borders for an entire table. For details, see *To format table borders* on page 205.
- For details on the dialog box's *Background* section, see *To color cells* on page 208.

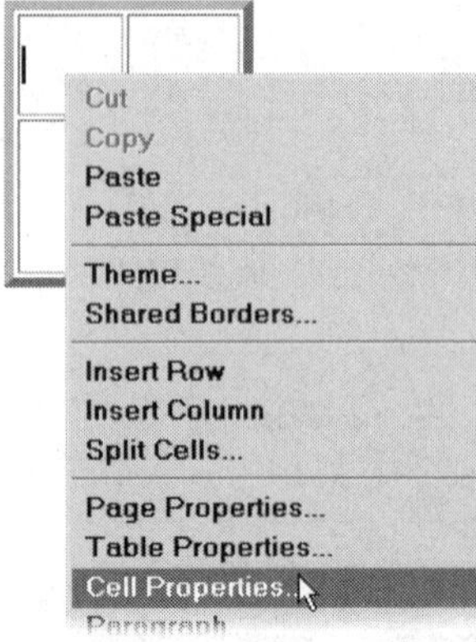

Figure 9.64 To format cells, select them, right-click, and choose *Cell Properties*.

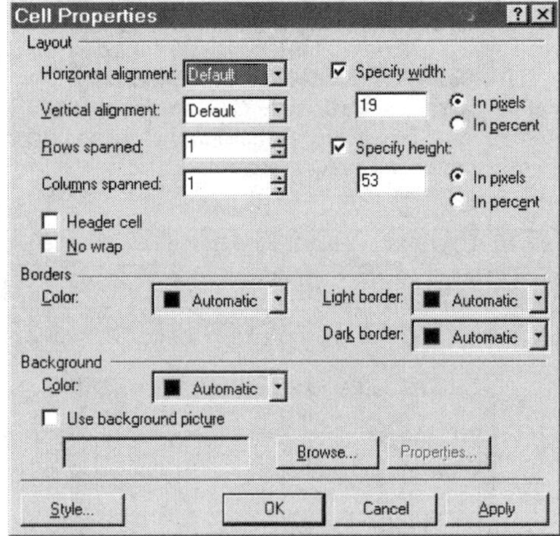

Figure 9.65 Use the Cell Properties dialog box to change a cell's alignment, size, and span.

FORMATTING TABLES AND CELLS

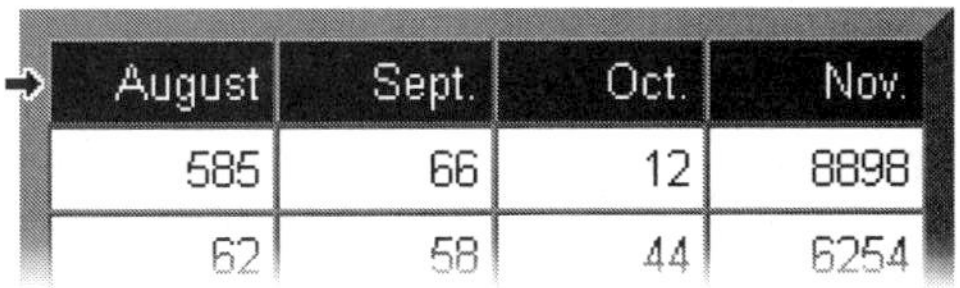

August	Sept.	Oct.	Nov.
585	66	12	8898
62	58	44	6254

Figure 9.66 Select the cell or cells you want to turn into header cells.

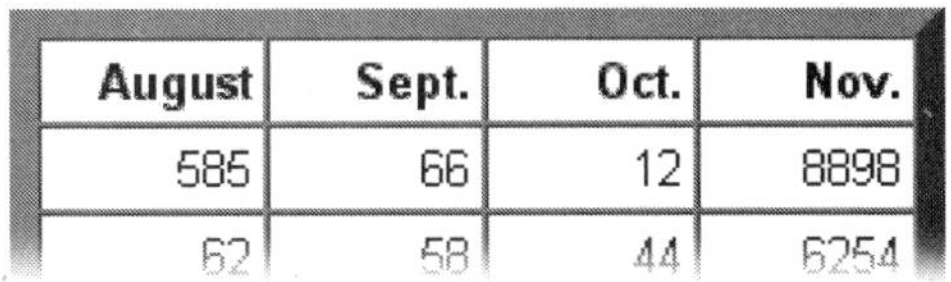

August	**Sept.**	**Oct.**	**Nov.**
585	66	12	8898
62	58	44	6254

Figure 9.67 Once you've made cells into headers, the text in the selected cell(s) will be boldfaced.

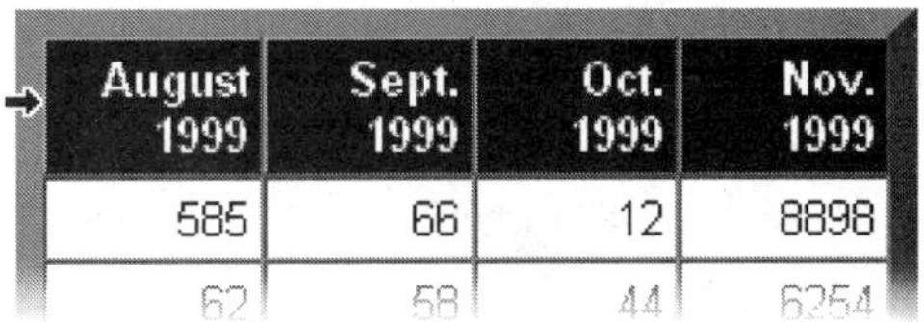

August 1999	**Sept. 1999**	**Oct. 1999**	**Nov. 1999**
585	66	12	8898
62	58	44	6254

Figure 9.68 To keep cell text on one line, select the text that's wrapping to the next line.

August 1999	**Sept. 1999**	**Oct. 1999**	**Nov. 1999**
585	66	12	8898
62	58	44	6254

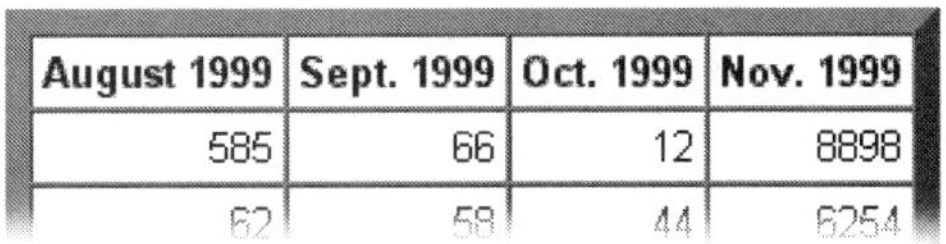

Figure 9.69 After No wrap is applied, the text in the selected cell(s) will rewrap to a single line.

Making cells into headers

Header cells typically act as labels for rows or columns within a table. FrontPage makes the text in header cells boldfaced.

To make cells into headers

1. Make sure you're in page view, then select the cell or cells you want as headers (**Figure 9.66**).
2. Right-click and choose *Cell Properties* from the shortcut menu (Alt Enter) (**Figure 9.64**).
3. When the Cell Properties dialog box appears (**Figure 9.65**), check *Header cell* in the *Layout* section.
4. Click *OK* and the text in the selected cell(s) will become boldfaced (**Figure 9.67**).

To keep cell text on one line

1. Make sure you're in page view, then select the cell or cells with text that's wrapping to the next line (**Figure 9.68**).
2. Right-click and choose *Cell Properties* from the shortcut menu (Alt Enter) (**Figure 9.64**).
3. When the Cell Properties dialog box appears (**Figure 9.65**), check *No wrap* in the *Layout* section. Line wrapping is the default.
4. Click *OK* and the text in the selected cell(s) will rewrap to a single line (**Figure 9.69**).

To color cells

1. Make sure you're in page view and that the Tables toolbar is activated.
2. Select a cell by clicking inside the cell while pressing Alt.
3. Click and hold the cursor on the arrow next to the paint bucket-shaped Fill Color button. When the pop-up box of colors appears, keep pressing your cursor and move to the color of your choice (left, **Figure 9.70**). Release the cursor and the fill color will be applied to the selected cell.

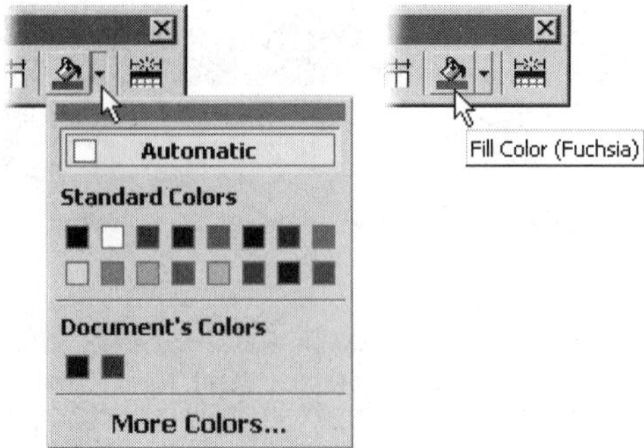

Figure 9.70 Left: To add color to a selected cell, click the arrow next to the paint bucket-shaped button and move the cursor to the color of your choice. Right: To fill with the default color—in this case, fuchsia—just click the Fill Color button.

✔ Tips

- If your fill color is already set to what you want—denoted by the color bar just below the Fill Color button and the pop-up tag (right, **Figure 9.70**), follow steps 1 and 2 above, and then click the button once to fill the cell.
- You also can color a cell by right-clicking it and using the *Background* section of the Cell Properties dialog box (**Figure 9.71**). Click the *Color* arrow to reach a pop-up box of possible colors. Check *Use background picture* and click *Browse* if you want to drop a graphic into the cell. Click *OK* and the changes will be applied to the cell.

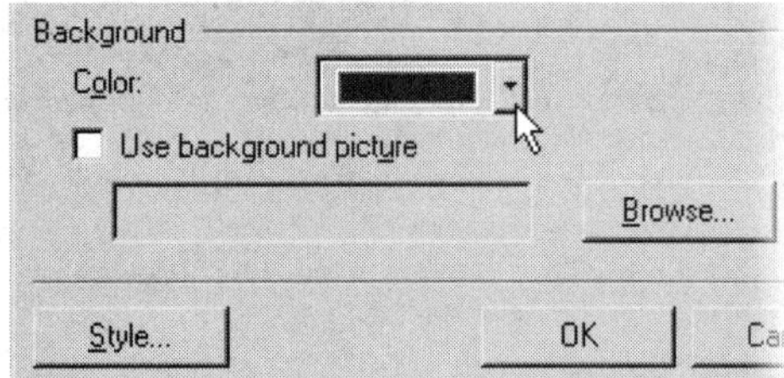

Figure 9.71 You also can color a cell by right-clicking it and using the *Background* section of the Cell Properties dialog box.

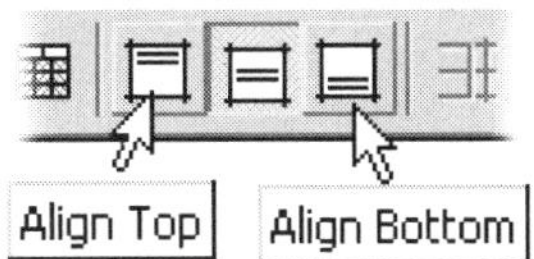

Figure 9.72 To align the contents to the top or bottom of the cell, click the respective button in the Tables toolbar.

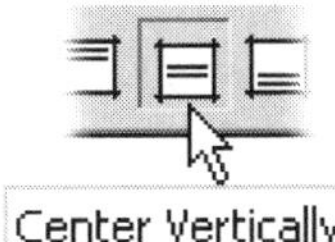

Figure 9.73 To align the contents equidistant from the cell's top and bottom, click the Center Vertically button.

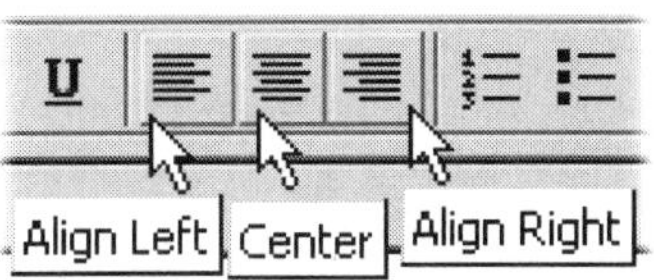

Figure 9.74 To realign the cell contents *horizontally*, click any of the three alignment buttons in the Formatting toolbar.

To realign cell contents

1. Make sure the Tables and Formatting toolbars are active, then click inside the cell you want realigned.
2. If you want to realign the contents *vertically*, click any of the three alignment buttons in the Tables toolbar (**Figures 9.72** and **9.73**). The changes will be applied to the cell.
3. If you want to realign the contents *horizontally*, click any of the three alignment buttons in the Formatting toolbar (**Figure 9.74**). The changes will be applied to the cell.

✔ Tip

- You also can realign a cell's contents using the Cell Properties dialog box as explained in *To format cells* on page 206.

10 Creating and Formatting Frames

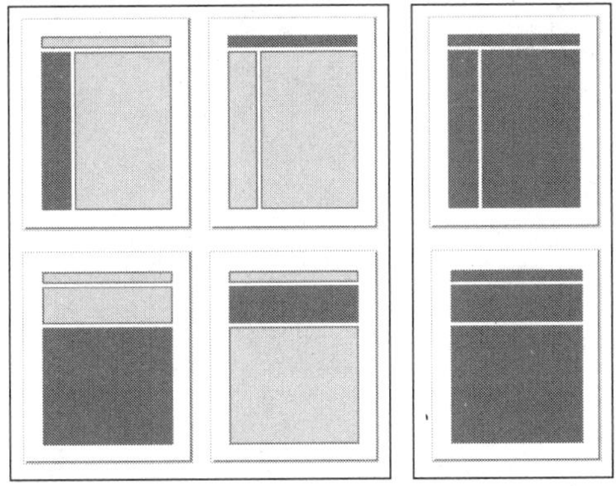

Figure 10.1 Left: Each of the four thumbnails contains one darkened *frame*. Right: Collectively, all the frames make up a *frames page*.

One of the big advantages of creating frame-based pages is that you can have site-wide navigation links or buttons that remain visible in one frame even as visitors scroll around in the main frame. That's a great help in keeping visitors oriented while enabling them to easily jump to other parts of your Web site. Version 3 and later browsers support frames, by the way, so you can create frame-based pages without leaving too many folks in the dark.

A couple of terms need explaining: Individual *frames* are collectively displayed in a special page called a *frames page* (**Figure 10.1**). Frames pages used to be called *framesets*, a term you'll still come across. Finally, FrontPage lets you set a hyperlink's *target frame*, which is the frame where the link's content will be displayed.

Creating Frames

Each frame you create can display a separate Web page. Whether you create those content pages before or after you create the frames themselves is up to you. Generally, however, it's less confusing to at least rough out the content pages first, then create the frames that will contain them. At that point, it's common to tweak the content for the frame. In creating frames and frames pages, sometimes it's helpful to see just the content without any frames. For details, see *To show a frame in a new window* on page 215.

A frames page can contain as many frames as you like. Bear in mind, however, that each page and its content must be downloaded, increasing the potential wait for your visitors. Use FrontPage's download progress indicator to gauge how long pages will take to appear on screen (see page 14).

To create a frames page

1. Make sure you're in page view, then choose File > New > Page (Ctrl N) (**Figure 10.2**).
2. When the New dialog box appears, click the *Frames Pages* tab (**Figure 10.3**). Use the dialog box's *Preview* area to choose a frames page template and click *OK*. A blank frames page, based on the template, will appear with each frame offering two choices: *Set Initial Page* and *New Page*. (**Figure 10.4**).

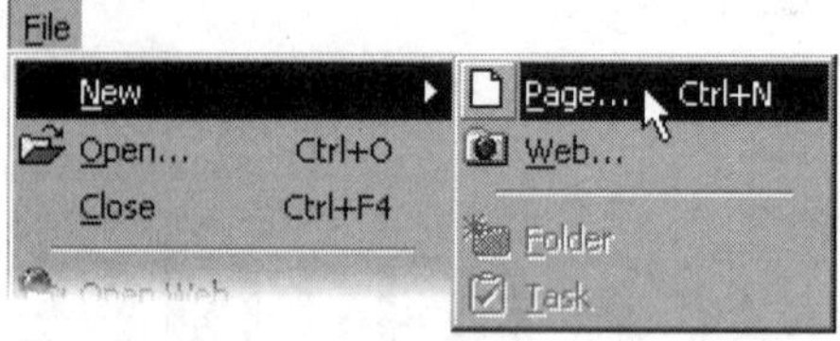

Figure 10.2 To create a frames page, choose File > New > Page.

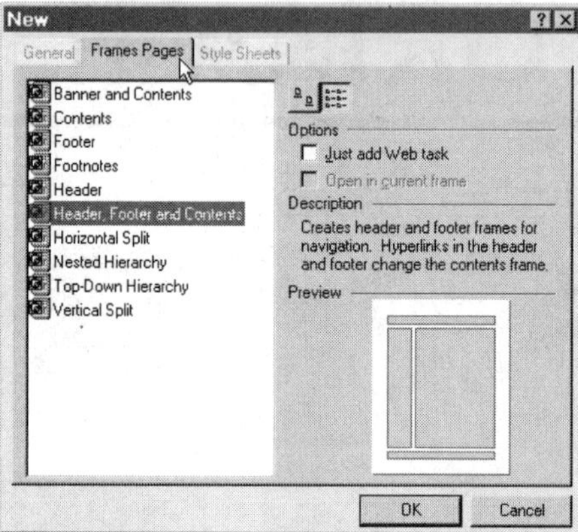

Figure 10.3 Click the *Frames Pages* tab in the New dialog box to reach a collection of frames page templates.

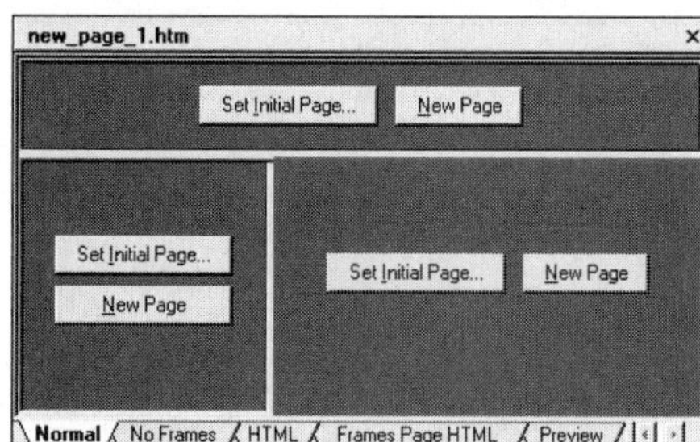

Figure 10.4 A new blank frames page offers two choices in each frame: *Set Initial Page* for linking to an existing page and *New Page* for creating a page from scratch.

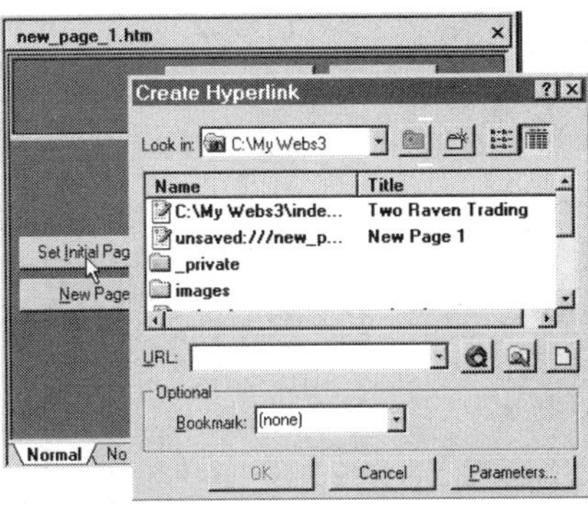

Figure 10.5 To link a frame to an existing page, use the Create Hyperlink dialog box to navigate to the page.

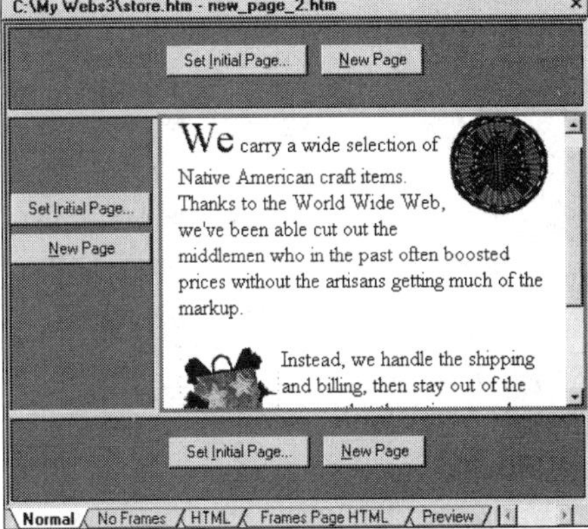

Figure 10.6 Once you link an existing page to a frame, the page will appear in the frame.

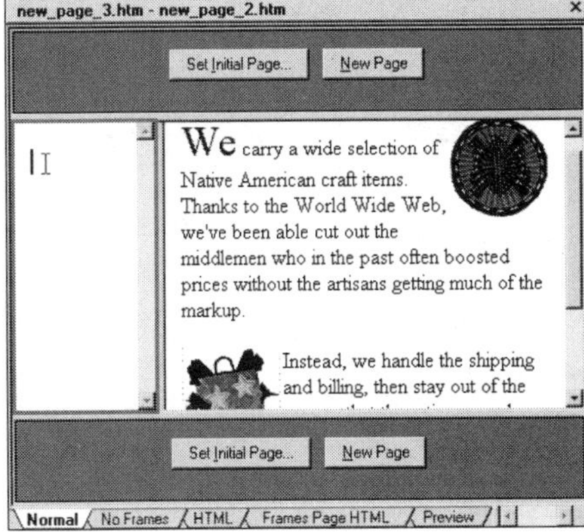

Figure 10.7 If you choose *New Page* in setting up a frame, a blank page will appear—allowing you to start creating content.

3. To link a frame to an *existing* page on your Web site, click *Set Initial Page.* When the Create Hyperlink dialog box appears (**Figure 10.5**), navigate to the page you want to use and click *OK.* The existing page will appear in the frame (**Figure 10.6**). For details on using the Create Hyperlink dialog box, see page 121.

   To create a *new* page from scratch for the frame, click *New Page.* A blank page based on the Normal template will appear within the frame (**Figure 10.7**). You then can begin adding content to the frame.

(continued)

4. Press Ctrl S to save any new frame and the *frames page* itself. If you've created a brand new page for any of your frames, that page will be the first to appear in the Save As dialog box (**Figure 10.8**).

5. Give the new page a distinct name and title, then click *Save*. The new page will be saved and a new Save As dialog box will appear for saving the entire frames page, denoted by a heavy blue border surrounding the full page in the preview window (**Figure 10.9**).

6. Give the frames page a distinct name and title, then click *Save*. The frames page will be saved.

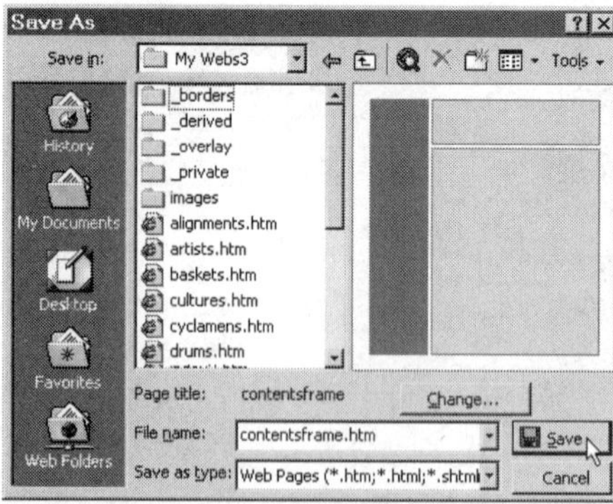

Figure 10.8 If you've created a brand new page for any frame, that page's frame will be highlighted in the Save As dialog box's preview area.

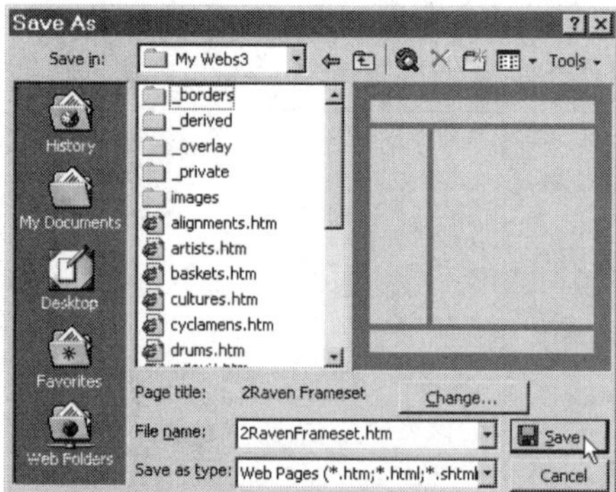

Figure 10.9 When you save a frames page, the entire page is highlighted in the Save As dialog box's preview area.

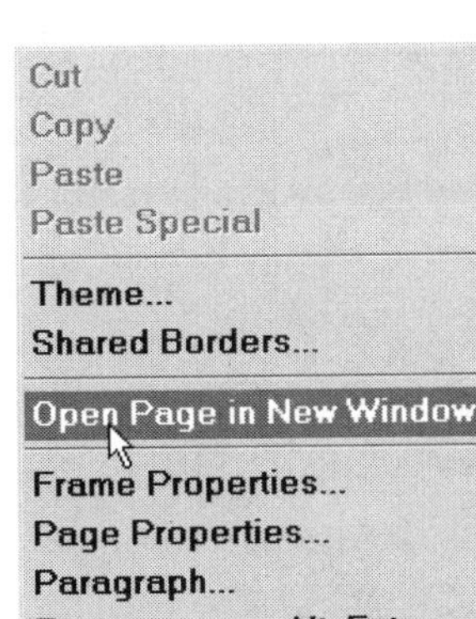

Figure 10.10 To show a frame in a full-sized window, right-click the frame and choose *Open Page in New Window* from the shortcut menu.

To show a frame in a new window

- Right-click in the frame and choose *Open Page in New Window* from the shortcut menu (**Figure 10.10**). The content of the frame will expand to a full-size window, replacing your view of the frames page.

✔ Tip

- If you want to return to the frames page, make sure the Folder List is visible and double-click the frames page file. The frames page will become visible in FrontPage's main window once more.

Setting target frames

In general, FrontPage will automatically set the large, main frame as the target for links clicked in, say, a left-hand table of contents frame. FrontPage, however, gives you a way to directly set any frame as the target of a link.

You won't need to mess with changing the default target frame, because FrontPage usually gets it right based on the context of the rest of the page's frames. But if you need to, see *To change the target frame default* on page 218.

To set a link's target frame

1. Right-click the link for which you want to set a target frame and choose *Hyperlink Properties* from the shortcut menu (Alt Enter) (**Figure 10.11**).
2. When the Edit Hyperlink dialog box appears, make sure the link's *URL* is correct. If not, change it. For details on using the Edit Hyperlink dialog box, which works identically to the Create Hyperlink dialog box, see page 121.
3. If you're happy with the link address, look in the Edit Hyperlink dialog box's *Optional* section and click the Target Frame button (**Figure 10.12**). When the Target Frame dialog box appears, you'll see that the *Target setting* text box says *main*, which is the main frame of the current page (**Figure 10.13**).

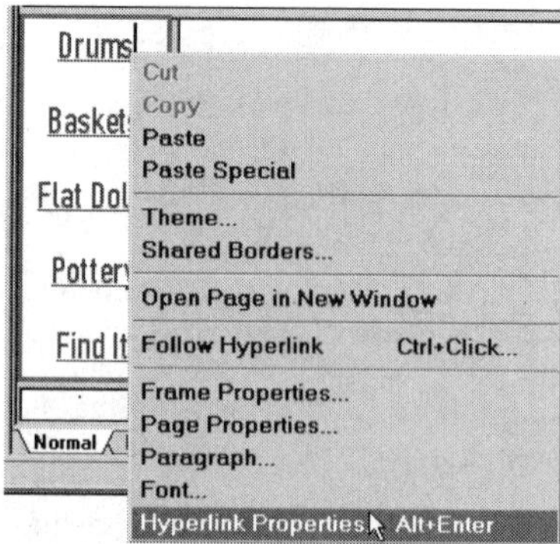

Figure 10.11 To set a target frame for a link, right-click it and choose *Hyperlink Properties* from the shortcut menu.

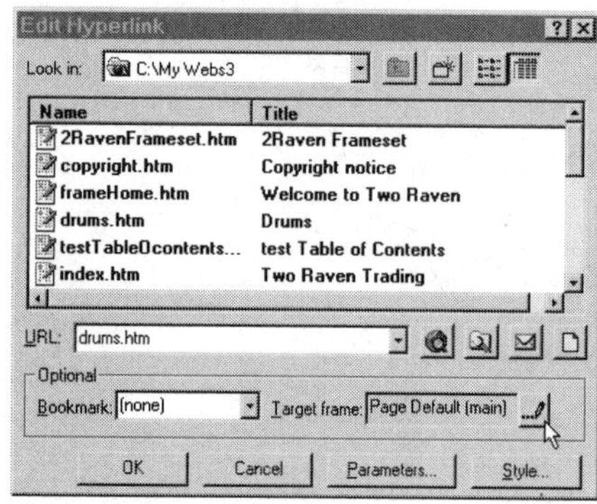

Figure 10.12 Click the Target Frame button within the Edit Hyperlink dialog box to set or change the target frame.

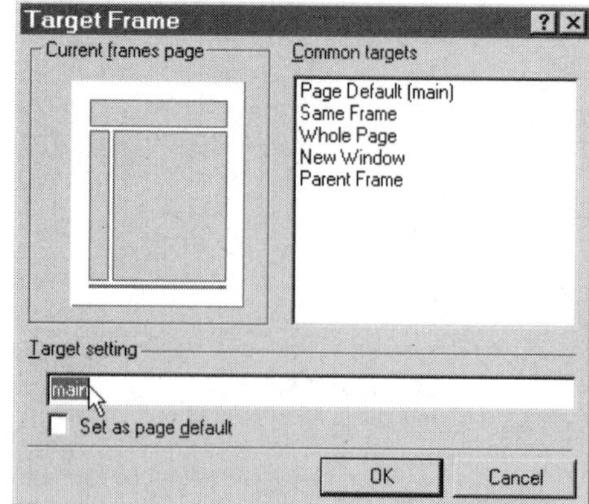

Figure 10.13 Use the Target Frame dialog box to change your link's targeted frame.

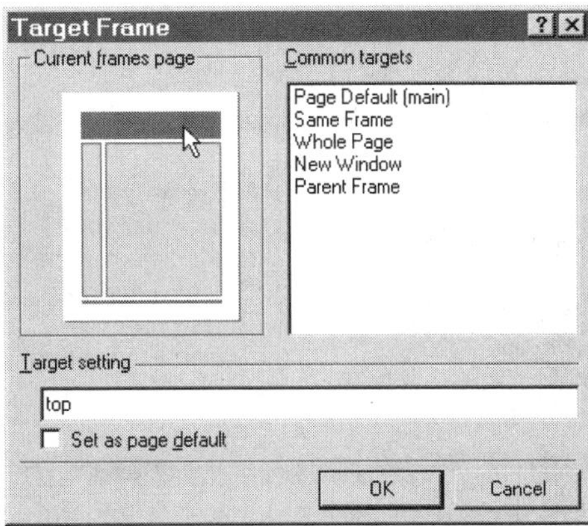

Figure 10.14 Clicking the top frame in the *Current frames page* pastes its name into the *Target setting* text window.

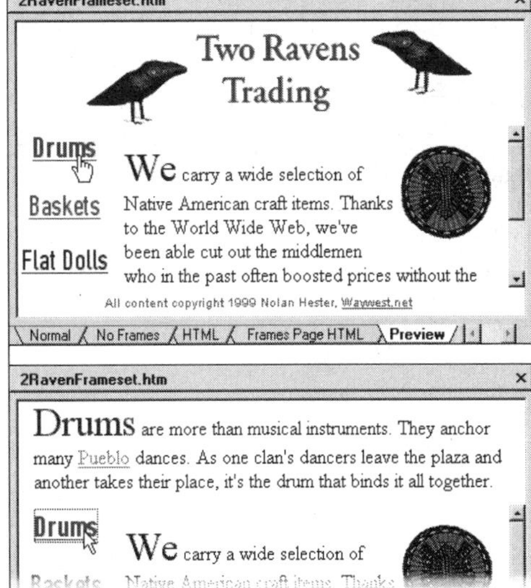

Figure 10.15 When clicked (top), the *Drums* link content replaces the Two Ravens Trading logo in the targeted frame (bottom).

Figure 10.16 You can check the *Target frame* text box to see what's listed as the default target.

4. To change the setting, either click a frame in the *Current frames page* thumbnail or click a listing in the *Common targets* window. The frame's name will be pasted into the *Target setting* text window (**Figure 10.14**). For details, see *Target Frame options* on page 219.
5. Click *OK* and when the Edit Hyperlink dialog box reappears, click *OK* again.
6. To check the link target, click the *Preview* tab in FrontPage's main window (top, **Figure 10.15**). When clicked, the link selected in step 1 will now display its linked page in the selected target (bottom, **Figure 10.15**).

✔ Tip

- Much of the time, FrontPage will automatically assign the correct frame as the target. Just check what the Edit Hyperlink dialog box lists as the Page Default in the Target frame text box (**Figure 10.16**).

To change the target frame default

1. Make sure you're in page view, then right-click anywhere in the page and choose *Page Properties* from the shortcut menu (**Figure 10.17**).
2. When the Page Properties dialog box appears, click the *General* tab, then click the Change Target Frame button (**Figure 10.18**).
3. When the Target Frame dialog box appears (**Figure 10.19**), either click a frame in the *Current frames page* thumbnail or click a listing in the *Common targets* window. The frame's name will be pasted into the *Target setting* text window. For details, see *Target Frame options* on the next page.
4. Click *OK* and when the Page Properties dialog box reappears, the target frame's name will be pasted into the *Default target frame* text box.
5. Click *OK* again and that frame will become the page's default target.

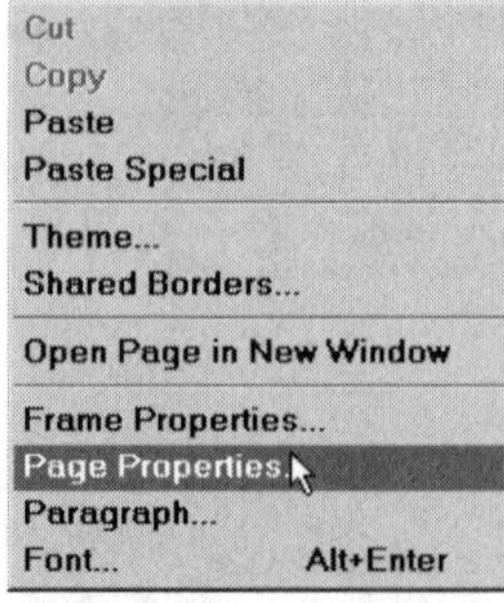

Figure 10.17 To change the target frame default, right-click the page and choose *Page Properties* from the shortcut menu.

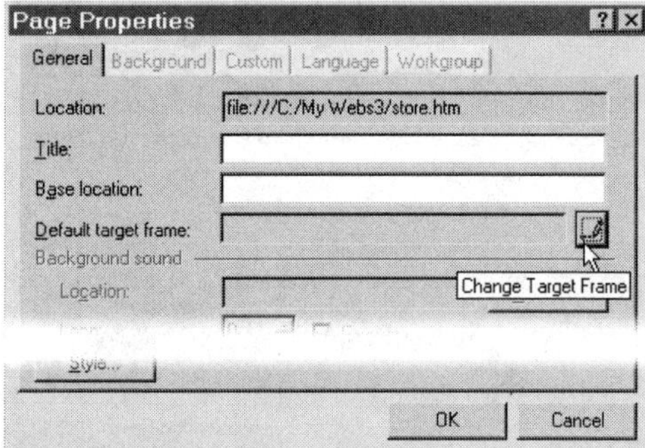

Figure 10.18 When the Page Properties dialog box appears, click the *General* tab, then click the Change Target Frame button.

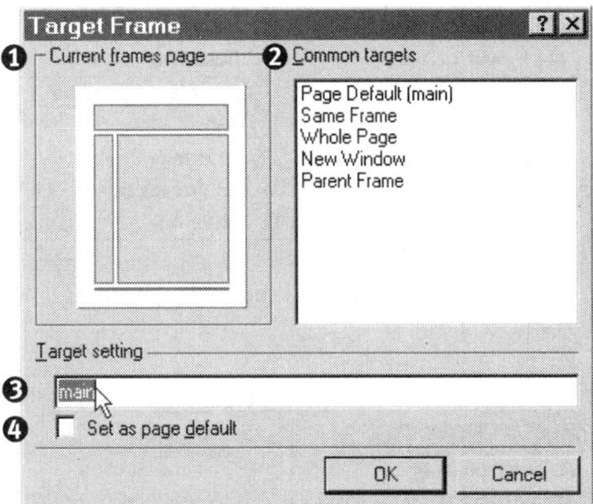

Figure 10.19 Use the Target Frame dialog box to change your link's targeted frame.

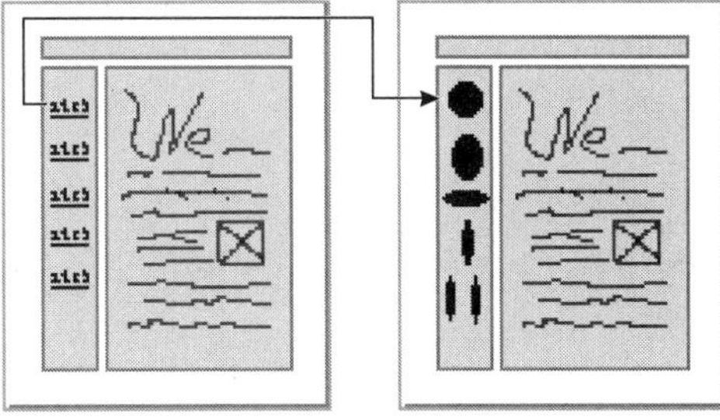

Figure 10.20 If you use *Same Frame* as your target frame, clicking the link will replace its frame with the link's content.

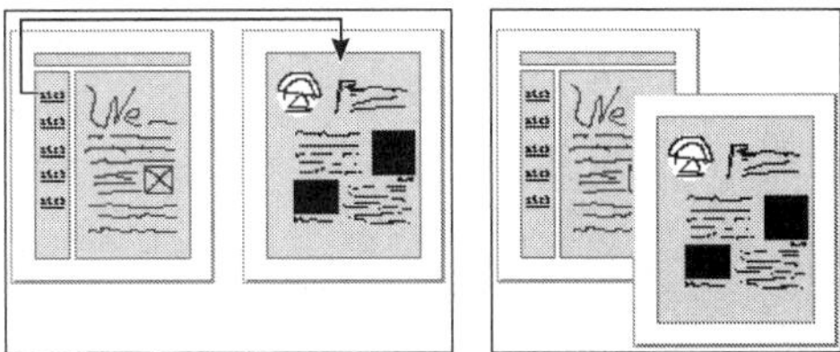

Figure 10.21 Left: If you use *Whole Page* as your target, clicking the link replaces the entire frames page. Right: Using *New Window* instead opens another window, leaving the frames page undisturbed.

Target Frame options

To reach the Target Frame dialog box (**Figure 10.19**), right-click a link in a frame, then click the *Target Frame* button in the Edit Hyperlink dialog box.

❶ **Current frames page:** Click any frame in the thumbnail to make it the frame where the link's content will be displayed.

❷ **Common targets:** Click any of these listings, which supplement those in the *Current frames page*.

Page Default: With this option chosen, clicking a link will display its content in the frame designated as the default page—in this example the main frame of the current frame page.

Same Frame: With this option, clicking a link in a frame will replace *that same frame* with the linked content (**Figure 10.20**).

Whole Page: With this option, clicking a link in a frame will replace the entire frames page with a single page showing the linked content (left, **Figure 10.21**).

New Window: With this option, clicking a link in a frame will open up a new browser window to display the linked content (right, **Figure 10.21**). It's a good choice if you're linking a visitor to a page off your own site because your site will remain visible in the original browser window. That increases the chances the visitor will remain on your site.

Parent Frame: This advanced option is used in creating discussion groups.

❸ **Target setting:** The text box will be filled automatically based on your choice in either the *Current frames page* or the *Common targets* list.

❹ **Set as page default:** Check the box to make *every* link in the selected page default to the selected target frame.

Setting a frames page as the home page

By default, FrontPage names your home page index.htm. If your site already has a frameless home page that you'd like to replace with a frames-based home page, you simply have to replace the old index.htm with a new one containing your frames page. (On some servers, the home page is named default.htm. The steps are the same.)

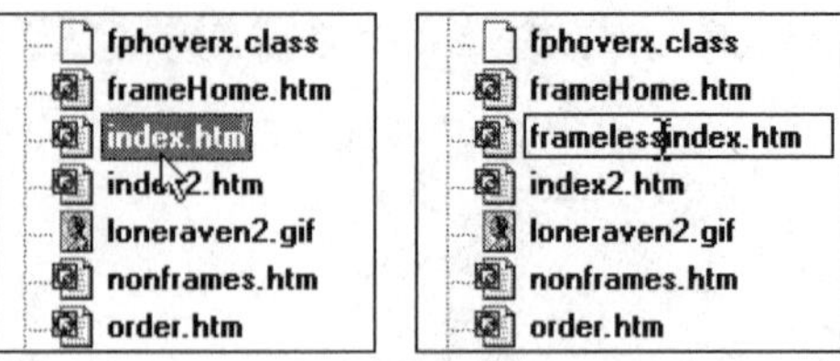

Figure 10.22 To make a frames page your home page, find the original home page in the Folder List (left) and rename it (right).

Figure 10.23 To finish making a frames page your home page, change the frames page's name (left) to index.htm (right).

To make a frames page your home page

1. Make sure the Folder List is visible, find the index.htm file, and click it so that its name becomes highlighted (left, **Figure 10.22**).
2. Type in a new name, such as frame-lessindex.htm, being sure to preserve the .htm suffix (right, **Figure 10.22**).
3. Again looking in the Folder List, find the frame-based file you want to use as your home page, and click it so that its name becomes highlighted (left, **Figure 10.23**).
4. Replace its name by typing in `index.htm` as the file's new name (right, **Figure 10.23**). Now when FrontPage looks for the home page, it will open your frames-based page.

Figure 10.24 Top: To select a *frame*, click anywhere inside it. Bottom: To select an entire *frames page*, it's easiest to click its border in the lower right.

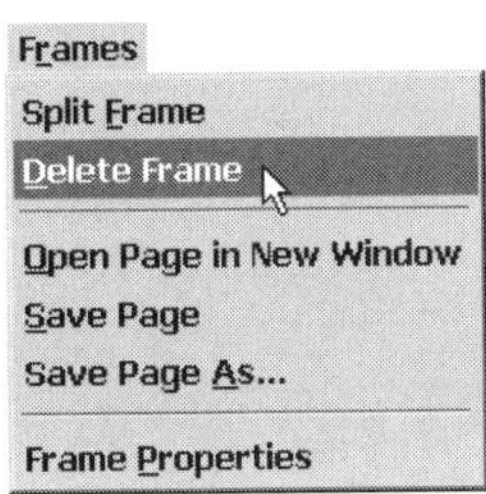

Figure 10.25 To delete a frame, click inside the frame and choose Frames > Delete Frame.

Formatting Frames

Once you've created some frames and set targets for the links inside them, you may find yourself wanting to reformat or modify some frames. FrontPage includes options for resizing, splitting, and changing basic properties of your frames. It also lets you customize a message to help visitors whose Web browsers don't support frames.

To select a frame

- To select a frame, click anywhere *inside* the frame. The selected frame will become highlighted by a dark blue border (top, **Figure 10.24**).

To select a frames page

- To select the whole frames page, click the page's outer border. Because the outer border is so narrow, it's easiest to find it by clicking in the bottom-right corner of the status bar. Once you click the right spot, a dark blue border will surround the frames page (bottom, **Figure 10.24**).

To delete a frame

- Click inside the frame you want to delete and choose Frames > Delete Frame (**Figure 10.25**). The frame will be removed *from the frames page*, although the page that had been displayed in the frame will remain part of your Web site's files.

To resize a frame

1. Make sure you're in page view, then select the frame you want to resize by clicking anywhere inside the frame.
2. Move your cursor over one of the dark blue frame borders where it will become a double-headed arrow (left, **Figure 10.26**). Click and drag the cursor to make the frame smaller or larger (right, **Figure 10.26**). When it reaches the size you want, release the cursor and the frame will be resized.

✔ Tip

- If you need more precision in resizing a frame, right-click it, choose *Frame Properties* from the shortcut menu, and use the dialog box's *Frame size* area to enter numerical values.

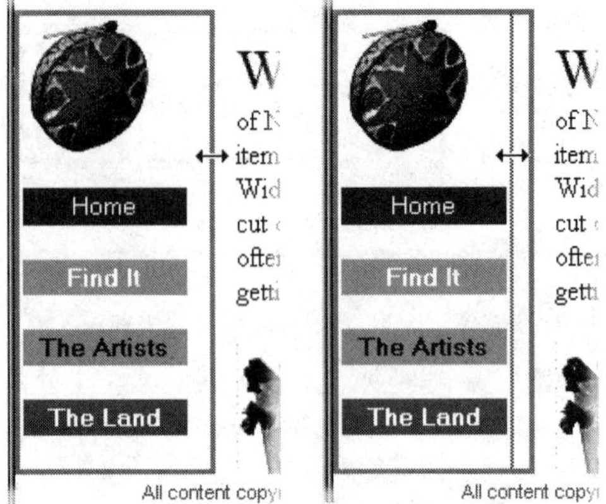

Figure 10.26 To resize a frame, move your cursor over a frame border until it becomes a double-headed arrow (left), then click and drag to make the frame smaller or larger (right).

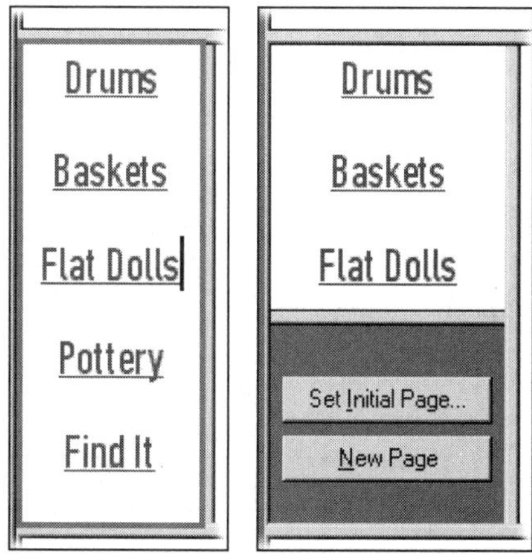

Figure 10.27 Before a frame is split (left) and afterward (right).

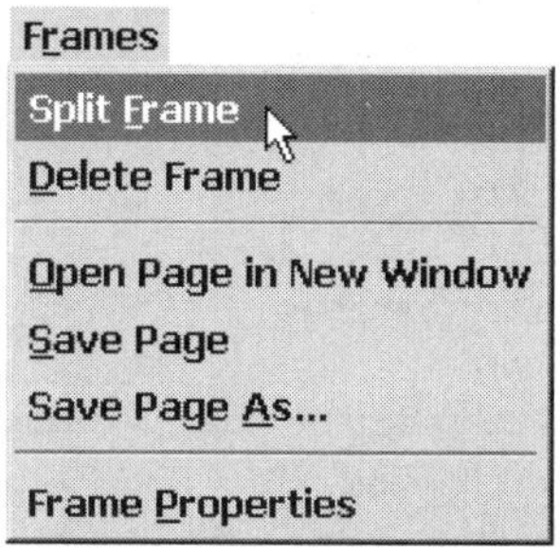

Figure 10.28 To split a frame, choose Frames > Split Frame.

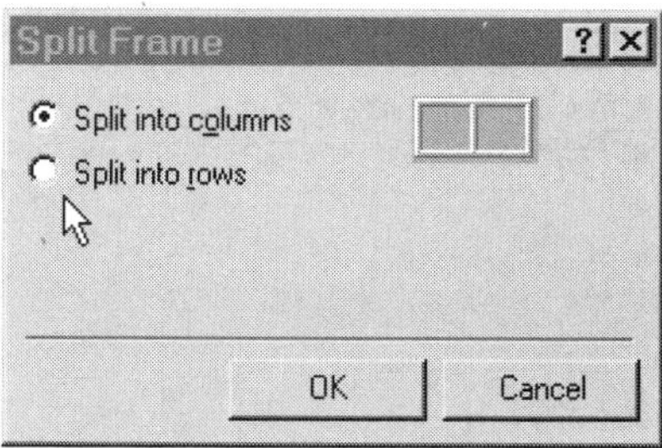

Figure 10.29 The Split Frame dialog box offers the choice of dividing a frame vertically into columns or horizontally into rows.

Splitting frames

You can split frames as a quick way to add another frame to an existing frames page.

To split a frame

1. Click inside the frame you want split (left, **Figure 10.27**).
2. Choose Frames > Split Frame (**Figure 10.28**).
3. When the Split Frame dialog box appears, choose whether you want to divide the frame vertically into columns or horizontally into rows (**Figure 10.29**). Click *OK* and the frame will be split into two equal-sized frames (right, **Figure 10.27**).

✔ Tips

- An even faster way to split a frame is to click and drag its border while pressing Ctrl.
- If the frame you split didn't have a scroll bar initially, you may need to add one to see all its contents. For details, see *Frame Properties options* on page 225.

To change frames

1. Right-click the frame you want to change and choose *Frame Properties* from the shortcut menu (**Figure 10.30**).
2. When the Frame Properties dialog box appears (**Figure 10.31**), set the frames' name, size, and margins.
3. FrontPage will have assigned the frame a name based on its position (e.g., top, left, center). Type in a new *Name* if you like.
4. Use the dialog box's *Options* section to restrict the user's ability to resize the frame. You also can turn on or off scroll-bars for the selected frame.
5. When you're done, click *OK* and the changes will be applied to the selected frame.

To change spacing or borders in frames pages

1. Right-click anywhere in the frames page and choose *Frame Properties* from the shortcut menu (**Figure 10.30**).
2. When the Frame Properties dialog box appears (**Figure 10.31**), click *Frames Page* in the lower right.
3. When the Page Properties dialog box appears, click the *Frames* tab (**Figure 10.32**).
4. Type a number directly into the *Frame Spacing* text window or use the arrows to change the distance *between* the page's frames.
5. To hide the boundaries of the page's frames, uncheck *Show Borders*.
6. Click *OK* to return to the Frame Properties dialog box, then click *OK* again to apply the changes to the frames page.

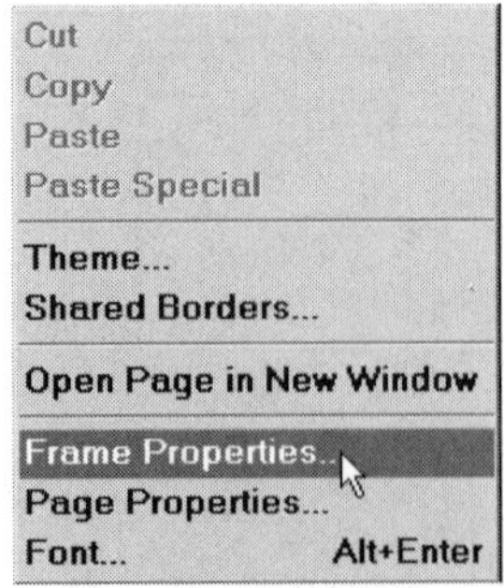

Figure 10.30 To change a frame or frames page, right-click the frame or page and choose *Frame Properties* from the shortcut menu.

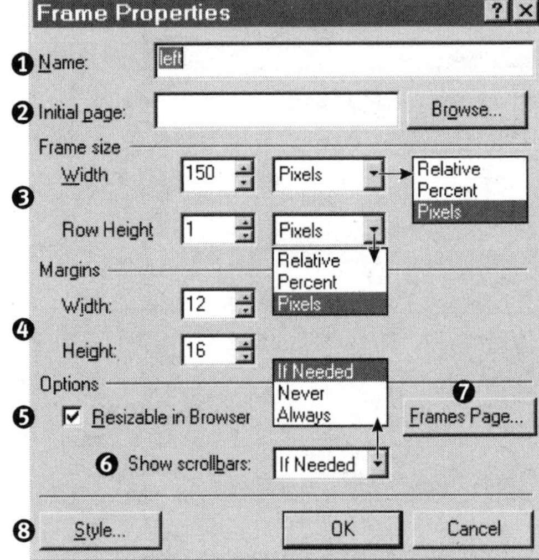

Figure 10.31 Use the Frame Properties dialog box to change a frame's name, size, and margins. Or click *Frames Page* in the lower right to change the frames page.

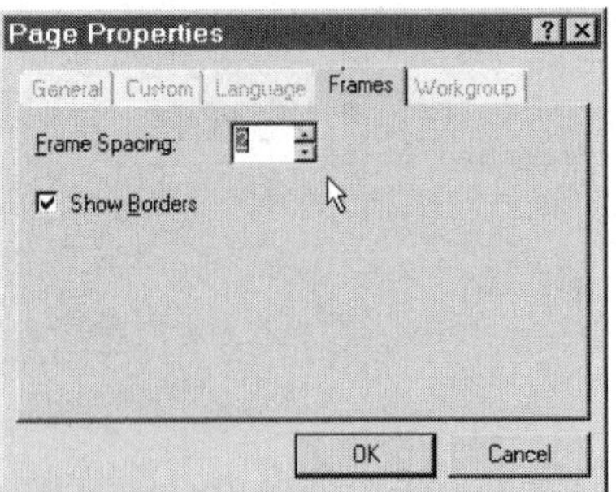

Figure 10.32 Use the Page Properties dialog box's *Frames* tab to set the spacing and borders between a page's frames.

Frame Properties options

To reach the Frame Properties dialog box (**Figure 10.31**), right-click any frame and choose *Frame Properties*.

❶ **Name:** By default, FrontPage assigns a name to the frame based on its position. Type in another name if you prefer.

❷ **Initial page:** Click *Browse* to find a new page to appear in the frame.

❸ **Frame size:** By default, the *Width* is set to *Pixels*. *Row Height* is dimmed unless the current frame is part of a row of frames. Use the drop-down menus of each to change the measures. *Relative* sets the width relative to other frames in the frames page: If you set a value of 1 for one frame and 2 for another, the second frame will be twice as wide. *Percent* sets the frame's width as a percentage of the browser window's width.

❹ **Margins:** The *Width* and *Height* windows set the frame's margin in pixels.

❺ **Resizable in Browser:** By default, this box is checked, allowing the user to resize the frame. Uncheck the box if you want the frame size fixed.

❻ **Show scrollbars:** Use the drop-down menu to choose whether you want the frame to *Always* or *Never* have a scrollbar. *If Needed* will add a scrollbar only if the frame's content extends beyond the visible area.

❼ **Frames Page:** Click the button to change properties for the entire frames page. For details, see *To change spacing or borders in frames pages* on the previous page.

❽ **Style:** This button can only be used if you've created style sheets for your Web site. See *Building Style Sheets and Dynamic Effects* on page 269.

Helping older browsers

No, we're not talking about octogenarian bookstore patrons. We're talking about pre-version 3 Web browsers that can't display frame-based pages. At this point, most folks have switched over to newer browsers. Still, FrontPage offers a way to help out the old-timers by letting you display an explanatory message. More importantly, it makes it easy to link those visitors to a frame-free alternate page.

To set a message for non-frame browsers

1. While displaying your frames page, click the *No Frames* tab at the bottom of FrontPage's main window (**Figure 10.33**).
2. FrontPage's default message somewhat curtly tells visitors using older Web browsers that their browser doesn't support frames (top, **Figure 10.34**). To soften the message—and give visitors an alternate page link—type your own text into the page and create a link to a frame-free page (bottom, **Figure 10.34**).
3. Save the page (Ctrl S) and click the *Normal* tab to return to the frames page.

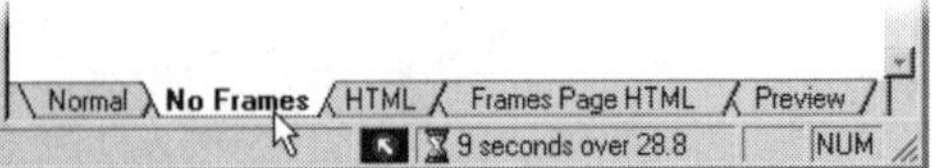

Figure 10.33 Click the *No Frames* tab at the bottom of the main window to set a message for non-frame browsers.

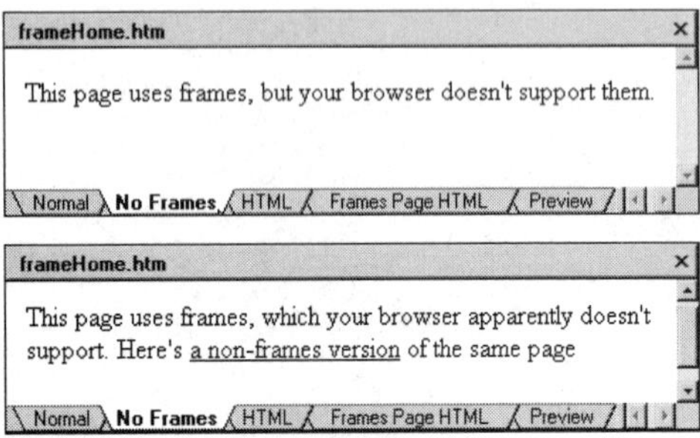

Figure 10.34 To change the default message that non-frame browsers will display (top), enter your own message and a link to a frame-free page (bottom).

11 Creating and Processing Forms

Forms enable you to collect information from your users by presenting them with questions, interactive radio buttons, check boxes, and multiple-choice menus. The first step in setting up forms is creating the forms and adding the fields you need to collect information. As you add and edit fields within the form, you have the option of setting up data entry rules for the users. FrontPage calls this process validating the data. Once that's done, you can create a confirmation page, which provides crucial feedback to the user and cuts down on incorrect form entries. Finally, you set whether you want the form results saved as a file, email, a database entry, or as part of a custom script.

Creating Forms

The fastest way to create a form is use a template and customize it to meet your needs. FrontPage's form templates include a confirmation form and a feedback form, plus a form wizard that walks you through creating a custom form. Of course, you also can build a form from scratch.

To create a form from a template

1. Choose New > Page (**Figure 11.1**).
2. When the New dialog box appears (**Figure 11.2**), choose *Feedback Form* and click *OK*.
3. When the template-based page appears, save it (Ctrl S).
4. When the Save As dialog box appears, give the form page a distinctive name and title, then click *Save* (**Figure 11.3**). You're now ready to change and add form fields to the template-based form page (**Figure 11.4**). For details, see *Adding Form Fields* on page 230.

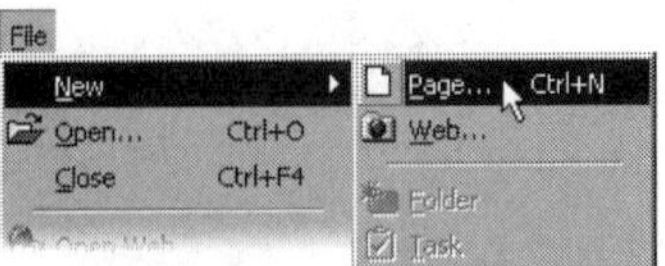

Figure 11.1 To create a new form, choose New > Page.

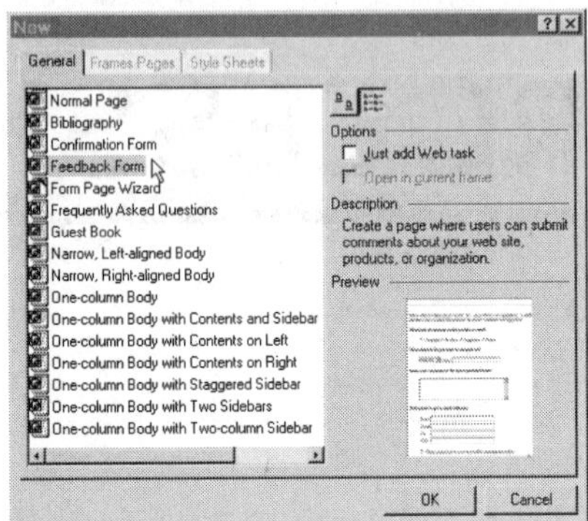

Figure 11.2 When the New dialog box appears, choose *Feedback Form* and click *OK*.

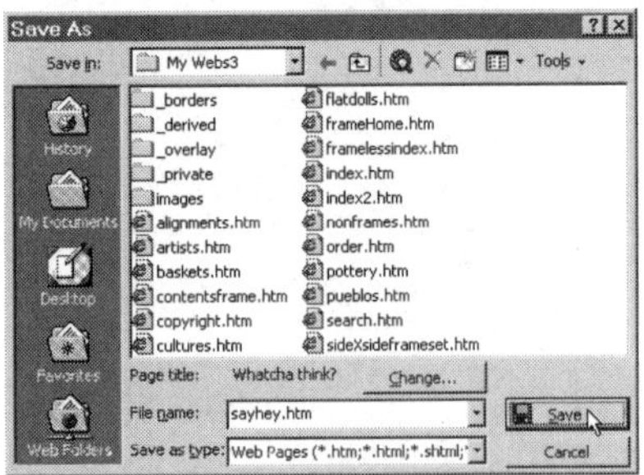

Figure 11.3 Use the Save As dialog box to give the page a distinctive name and title.

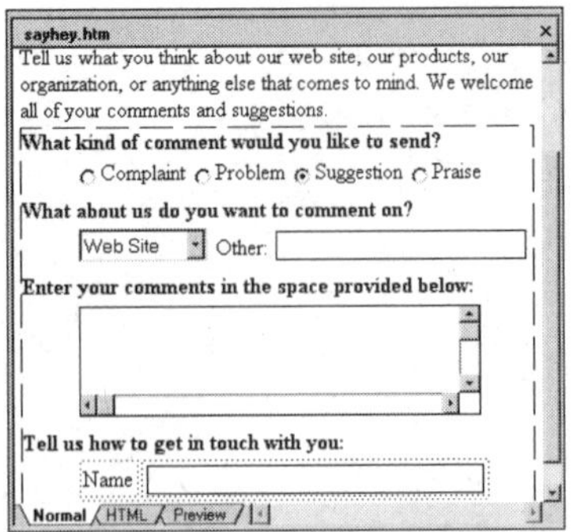

Figure 11.4 By basing your form on a FrontPage template, you can reduce the time needed to add fields.

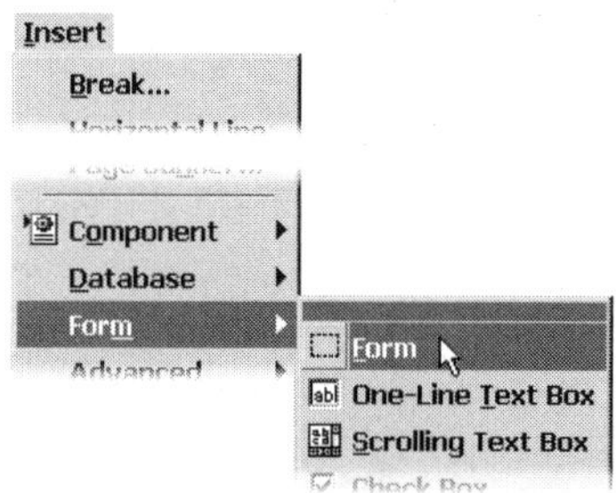

Figure 11.5 To create a form from scratch, choose Insert > Form > Form.

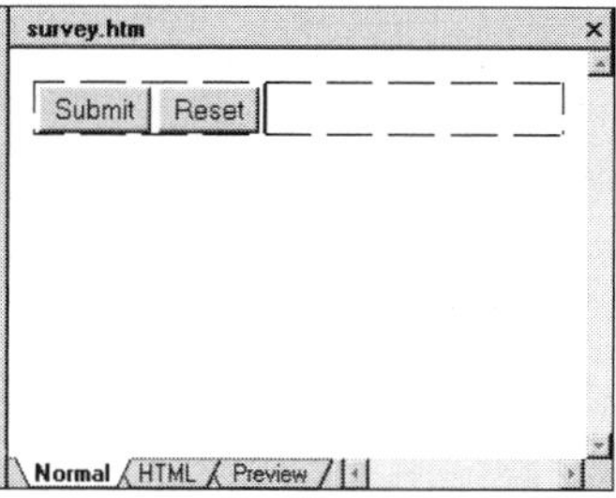

Figure 11.6 A dashed outline denotes a new form, along with a *Submit* button and a *Reset* button.

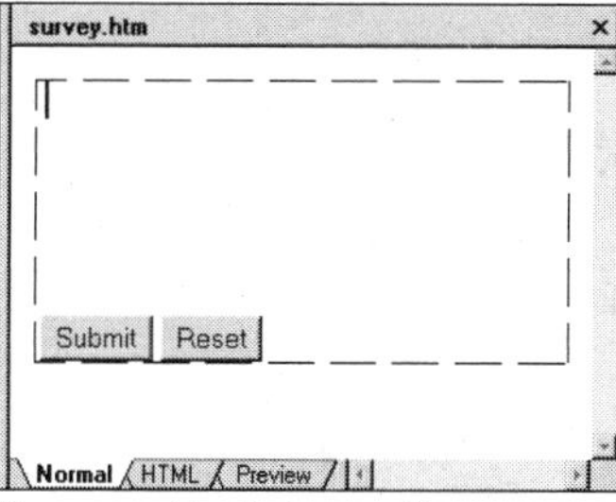

Figure 11.7 To give yourself some working space in a new form, press [Enter] several times.

Figure 11.8 To delete a field, right-click it and choose *Cut* from the shortcut menu.

To create a form from scratch

1. Open an existing Web page or create a new page by choosing File > New > Page ([Ctrl][N]) (**Figure 11.1**). If you're creating a new page, go ahead and save it ([Ctrl][S]) and give it a distinctive name in the Save As dialog box (**Figure 11.3**).
2. Click in the page where you want the form inserted and choose Insert > Form > Form (**Figure 11.5**).
3. The form, bounded by a dashed outline, will be inserted into the page, along with a *Submit* button and a *Reset* button (**Figure 11.6**).
4. Give yourself some working space within the form by pressing [Enter] several times (**Figure 11.7**). You're now ready to add whatever form fields you need. For details, see *Adding Form Fields* on page 230.

To delete a field

- Make sure the *Normal* tab is active, select the field you want to delete, and press [←Backspace] or [Del]. The field will be deleted.

or

- Right-click the field and choose *Cut* from the shortcut menu (**Figure 11.8**). The field will be deleted.

To change a field's properties

1. Make sure you're in page view, then double-click the field.
2. When the field's properties dialog box opens, make your changes, click *OK*, and they will be applied to the field. For details on the dialog boxes for each field type, see *Adding Form Fields* on page 230.

Adding Form Fields

Whether you create a form from scratch or start with one of FrontPage's form templates, it's easy to add a variety of form fields to match your needs.

To add a single-line text field

1. Click in the form page where you want to add the field, typically next to text that identifies the field for users (**Figure 11.9**).
2. Choose Insert > Form > One-Line Text Box (**Figure 11.10**).
3. When the one-line field appears in the page, right-click it and choose *Form Field Properties* from the shortcut menu ((Alt)(Enter)) (**Figure 11.11**).

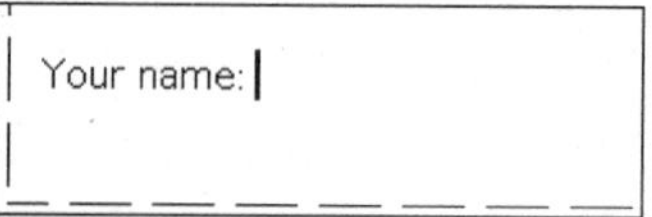

Figure 11.9 First create some text to identify the field for the user, then click in the form page where you want to add the field.

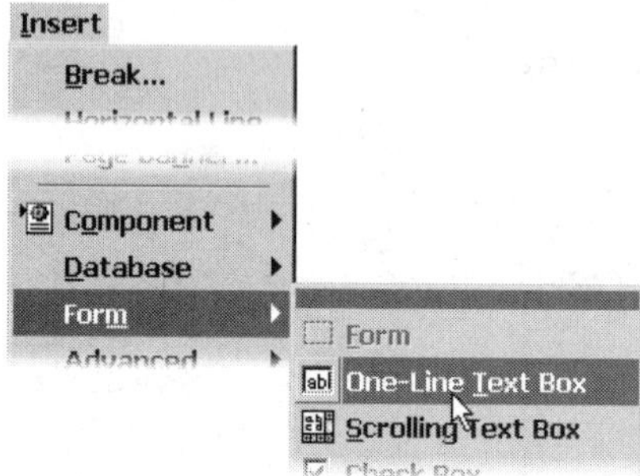

Figure 11.10 To add a single-line text field, choose Insert > Form > One-Line Text Box.

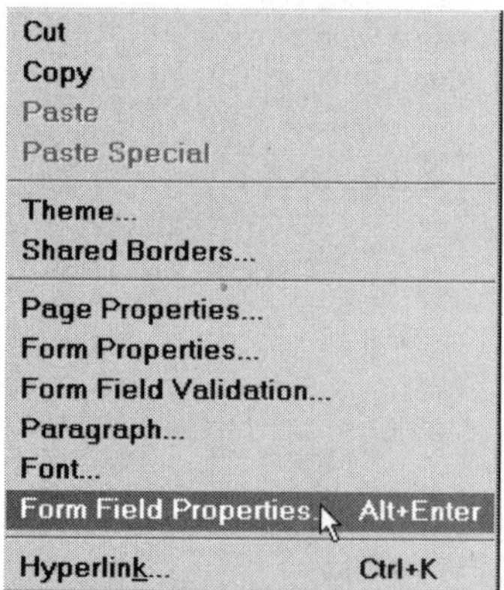

Figure 11.11 To modify any form field, right-click it and choose *Form Field Properties* from the shortcut menu.

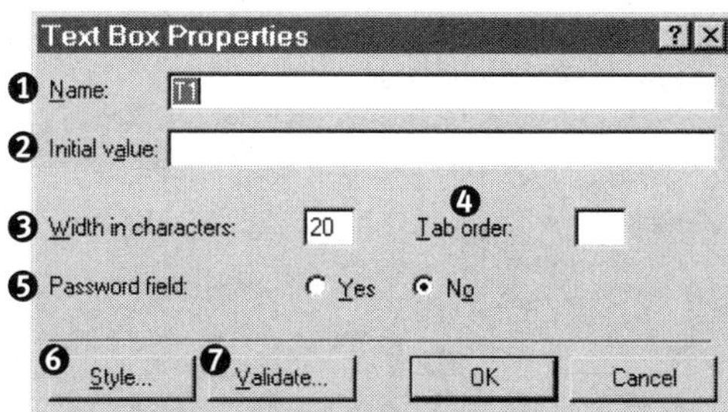

Figure 11.12 Use the Text Box Properties dialog box to give your field a name, initial value, size, and password.

4. When the Text Box Properties dialog box appears, FrontPage will have assigned the field an arbitrary name, such as T1 (**Figure 11.12**). Type in a distinctive name of your own ❶, which won't be visible to site visitors.

5. If you want some text to appear *inside* the one-line box, such as "Enter your name here," type it into the *Initial value* text box ❷.

6. Set how many characters wide you want the line to be ❸ and enter a number for the field's tab order ❹ within the form.

7. If the field will be used for a password ❺, choose *Yes*, otherwise leave it set to the default *No*. By the way, *Style* ❻ is used only if you're building style sheets.

8. If you want to define entry requirements for the field, click *Validate* ❼. For details, see *Text Box Validation options* on page 233.

9. When you're done, click *OK* and the properties will be applied to the one-line text field. To see how the field looks and decide if it needs adjustment, click FrontPage's *Preview* tab.

✔ Tip

- If you need to resize a one-line text box, don't bother using the Text Box Properties dialog box. Just click the box and use one of its square black handles to enlarge or shrink it.

To add a scrolling text box

1. Click in the form page where you want to add the field, typically next to text that identifies the field for users or asks them to enter comments in the field.
2. Choose Insert > Form > Scrolling Text Box (**Figure 11.13**).
3. When the field appears in the page, click it and use the square black handles to enlarge or shrink it (**Figure 11.14**).
4. Right-click the field and choose *Form Field Properties* from the shortcut menu ((Alt)(Enter)) (**Figure 11.11**).
5. When the Scrolling Text Box Properties dialog box appears, FrontPage will have assigned the field an arbitrary name, such as S1 (**Figure 11.15**). Type in a distinctive name of your own, which won't be visible to site visitors.
6. If you want some text to appear *inside* the one-line box, such as "Enter your name here," type it into the *Initial value* text box.
7. If you aren't happy with your initial resizing, set the *Width in characters* and *Number of lines* using the text boxes. Enter a number for the field's tab order within the form.
8. If you want to define entry requirements for the field, click *Validate*. For details, see *Text Box Validation options* on the next page.
9. When you're done, click *OK* and the properties will be applied to the scrolling text field. To see how the field looks and decide if it needs adjustment, click FrontPage's *Preview* tab.

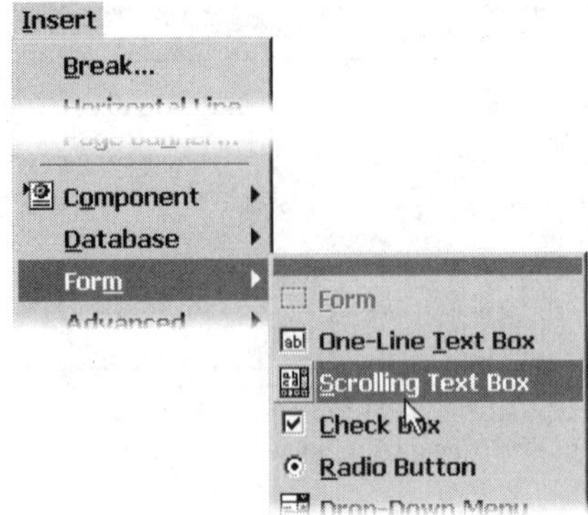

Figure 11.13 To add a scrolling text box, choose Insert > Form > Scrolling Text Box.

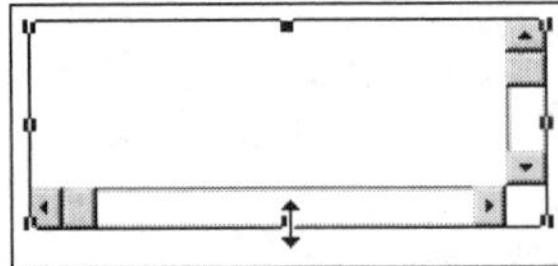

Figure 11.14 To resize a scrolling text box, click and drag the square black handles.

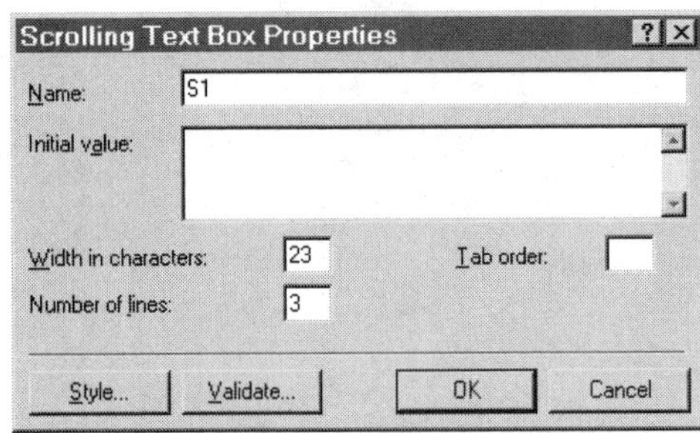

Figure 11.15 Use the Scrolling Text Box Properties dialog box to give the field a name, initial value, and size.

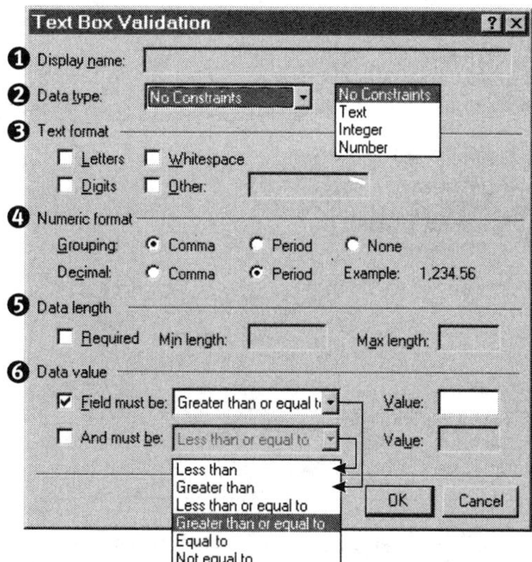

Figure 11.16 Use the Text Box Validation dialog box to set data entry rules for one-line text and scrolling text fields.

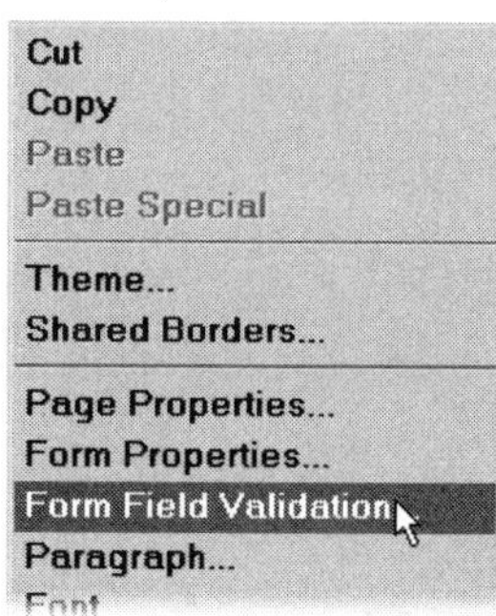

Figure 11.17 To reach the Text Box Validation dialog box, right-click any field and choose *Form Field Validation* from the shortcut menu.

Text Box Validation options

Use the Text Box Validation dialog box to set rules for the kind of data users can enter in one-line text and scrolling text fields (**Figure 11.16**). To reach the dialog box, right-click any single-line or scrolling text box and choose *Form Field Validation* (**Figure 11.17**) or double-click the text box and choose *Validate* from the dialog box that appears.

❶ **Display name:** Though it sits at the top of the dialog box, this text box won't become available until after you've used the other boxes to set the data entry requirements. Once you've filled out your data requirements, you can then enter a distinctive name.

❷ **Data type:** By default, the drop-down menu is set to *No Constraints*. Use the drop-down menu to narrow the valid options for users. If you choose *Text*, use the *Text Format* section to define what text will be allowed. If you choose *Integer* or *Number*, use the *Numeric format* section to define entry requirements.

❸ **Text format:** These options are available only if you choose *Text* as your *Data type*. Check which types of data you will *allow*. Check *Whitespace* to allow spaces, returns, or tabs. Check *Other* to allow such characters as punctuation marks and hyphens. Use the adjacent text box to specify which characters are allowed.

❹ **Numeric format:** These options are available only if you choose *Integer* or *Number* as your *Data type*.

❺ **Data length:** If you don't want the field left blank, check *Required*. Use *Min length* and *Max length* to ensure that users enter a number correctly, for example a 16-digit credit card number.

❻ **Data value:** Use the check boxes, drop-down menus, and text boxes to further define what information users must enter.

Adding check boxes and radio buttons

Unlike text boxes in which users can enter a variety of information, check boxes and radio buttons have only two states: On (checked) or Off (not checked). The main difference between check boxes and radio buttons is that users can choose *several* check boxes, while radio buttons force users to make *one* choice among several in a single group.

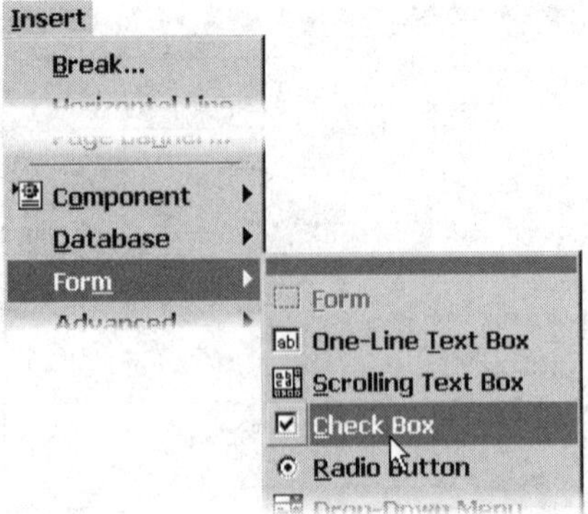

Figure 11.18 To add a check box, choose Insert > Form > Check Box.

To add a check box

1. Click in the form page where you want to add the check box.
2. Choose Insert > Form > Check Box (**Figure 11.18**).
3. When the check box appears in the page, add text that explains the field for users (**Figure 11.19**).
4. Right-click the field and choose *Form Field Properties* from the shortcut menu (Alt Enter) (**Figure 11.11**).

☐ Please send me more information

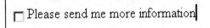

Figure 11.19 Once the check box appears in the page, be sure to add some explanatory text.

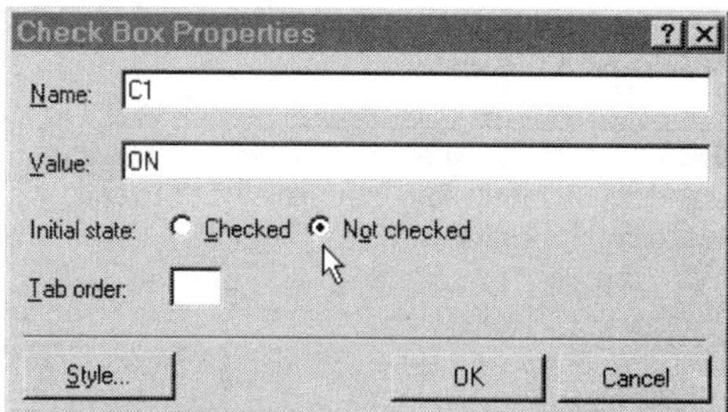

Figure 11.20 Use the Check Box Properties dialog box to set the field's name and whether its default is *Checked* or *Not checked*.

5. When the Check Box Properties dialog box appears, FrontPage will have assigned the field an arbitrary name, such as C1 (**Figure 11.20**). Type in a distinctive name of your own (which, by the way, won't be visible to site visitors).
6. By default, the *Value* will be *ON*. This text is not seen by the user, and you can type in any word that helps you quickly identify the user's response. In **Figure 11.20**, for example, it'd be clearer to use something like *Contact*.
7. By default, the check box's *Initial state* is *Not checked*. Choose *Checked* if you're sure most users will want the box already selected.
8. Enter a number for the field's tab order within the form and click *OK*.
9. If you want to add more check boxes, repeat steps 1–8. Once you're done, you can see how the check boxes look and decide if any need adjustment by clicking FrontPage's *Preview* tab.

To add radio buttons

1. Click in the form page where you want to add the radio button, typically next to text asking users to choose among what will be several radio buttons (**Figure 11.21**).
2. Choose Insert > Form > Radio Button (**Figure 11.22**).
3. When the radio button appears in the form, type in some text identifying that choice (**Figure 11.23**).
4. Click where you want the next radio button inserted and repeat steps 2 and 3. Continue until you've added as many radio buttons as you need.
5. Right-click the first radio button and choose *Form Field Properties* from the shortcut menu (Alt Enter) (**Figure 11.11**).
6. When the Radio Button Properties dialog box appears, FrontPage will have assigned the field an arbitrary *Group name*, such as *R1*, a *Value* of *V1* and set the *Initial state* as *Selected* (**Figure 11.24**).

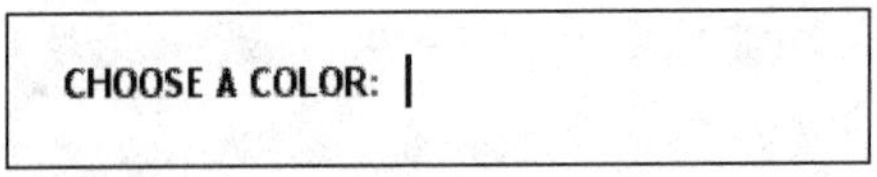

CHOOSE A COLOR: |

Figure 11.21 Click in the form page where you want to add one or more radio buttons. Be sure to add text to prompt users to make a choice.

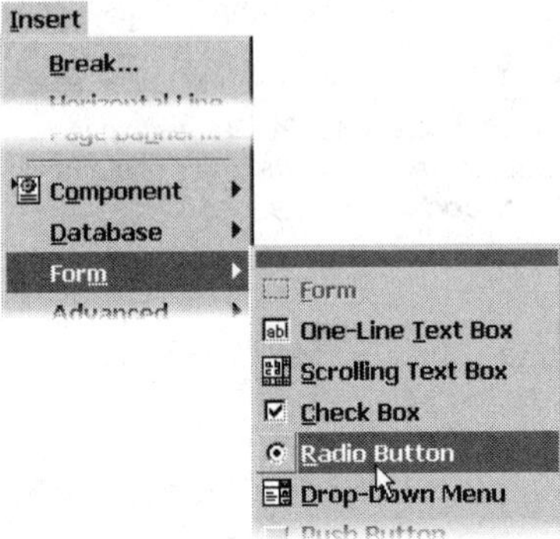

Figure 11.22 To add radio buttons, choose Insert > Form > Radio Button.

CHOOSE A COLOR: GREE

Figure 11.23 Add a label to your first radio button when it appears in the form.

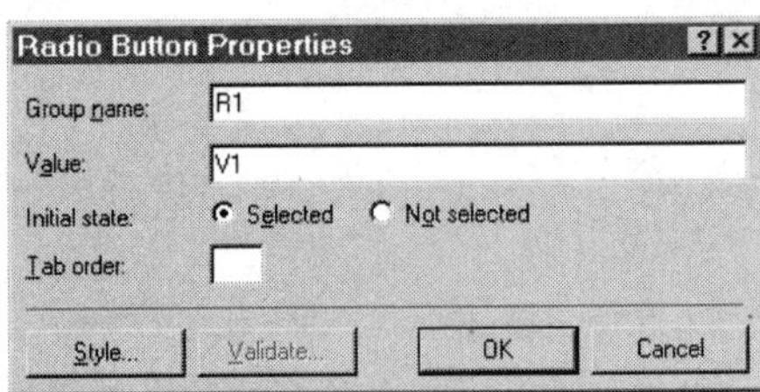

Figure 11.24 When the Radio Button Properties dialog box appears, FrontPage will have assigned the field an arbitrary *Group name*, a *Value*, and set the *Initial state*.

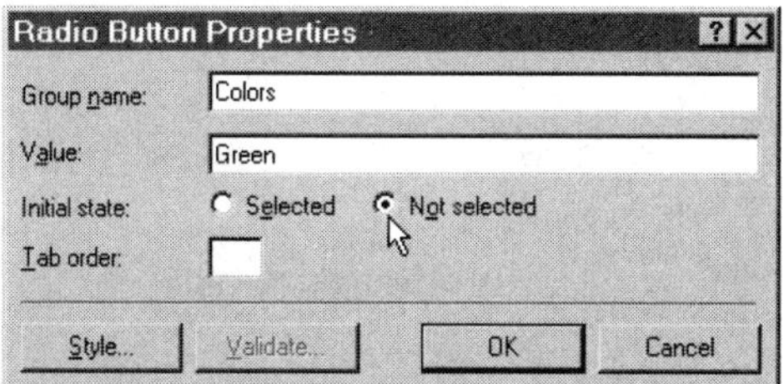

Figure 11.25 Once you've typed in descriptive names for the *Group name* and the *Value*, set the button's *Initial state* and *Tab order*.

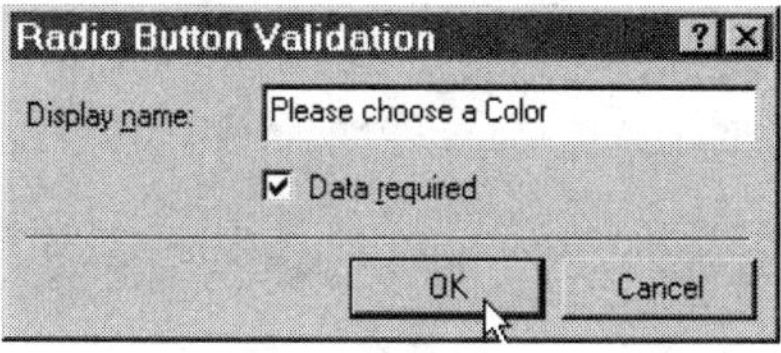

Figure 11.26 Use the Radio Button Validation dialog box to enter a message to prompt users or to require a selection.

Figure 11.27 All three radio buttons belong to the same group.

7. Type in descriptive names of your own for the *Group name* and the *Value*. Since you want the user to pick a color, change the *Initial state* to *Not selected* (**Figure 11.25**). Click *OK* and the changes will be applied to that radio button only.
8. Select each of the other radio buttons you've created and choose *Form Field Properties* from the shortcut menu. In the Radio Button Properties dialog box for each, give them the same *Group name*, a different *Value* to match the choice represented by that individual button, and choose *Not selected* as the *Initial state*. Click *OK* to close each dialog box.
9. If you want to make sure that users actually choose one of the radio buttons and don't ignore them, double-click any of the radio buttons. When the Radio Button Properties dialog box appears, click *Validate* to reach the Radio Button Validation dialog box (**Figure 11.26**). Check *Data required* and type a message in *Display name* to prompt the user. Click *OK* to close the dialog box.
10. Once you're done, you can see how the radio buttons look and decide if any need adjustment by clicking FrontPage's *Preview* tab (**Figure 11.27**).

✔ Tip

- If you create multiple radio buttons and expect that most users will choose one choice over the others, set its *Initial state* to *Selected* in step 7 above.

To add a drop-down menu

1. Click in the form page where you want to add the field, typically next to text that identifies the field for users or asks them to pick from the drop-down choices.
2. Choose Insert > Form > Drop-Down Menu (**Figure 11.28**).
3. When the drop-down menu appears in the page, right-click the field and choose *Form Field Properties* (Alt Enter) (**Figure 11.11**). Or double-click the field.
4. When the Drop-Down Menu Properties dialog box appears, FrontPage will have assigned the field an arbitrary name, such as D1 (**Figure 11.29**). Type in a distinctive name of your own.
5. To add choices to the drop-down menu, click *Add*. When the Add Choice dialog box appears (**Figure 11.30**), enter your first *Choice*.
6. If you want to create another name for the choice, such as a part number or shorter name, check *Specify Value* and enter it in the text box. Choose whether you want the choice's *Initial state* to be *Selected* or *Not selected*. Click *OK* and the choice will be added to the Drop-Down Menu Properties dialog box.
7. Repeat steps 5 and 6 using the *Add* button ❷ until you have added all the choices you want (**Figure 11.31**).
8. To change, delete, or reorder choices, select each in the *Choice* list ❶ and click *Modify* ❸, *Remove* ❹, or *Move Up* or *Move Down* ❺. Set the menu's height ❻, tab order in the form ❼, and whether multiple choices are allowed ❽. For details, see *Drop-Down Menu options* on the next page.
9. Once you adjust the drop-down menu, click *OK* and the changes will be applied.

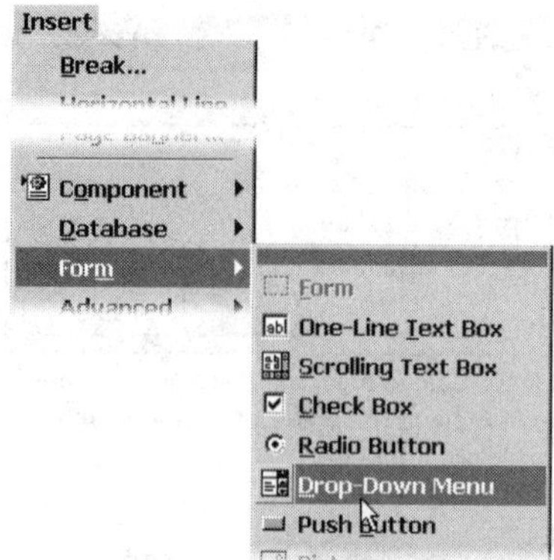

Figure 11.28 To add a drop-down menu, choose Insert > Form > Drop-Down Menu.

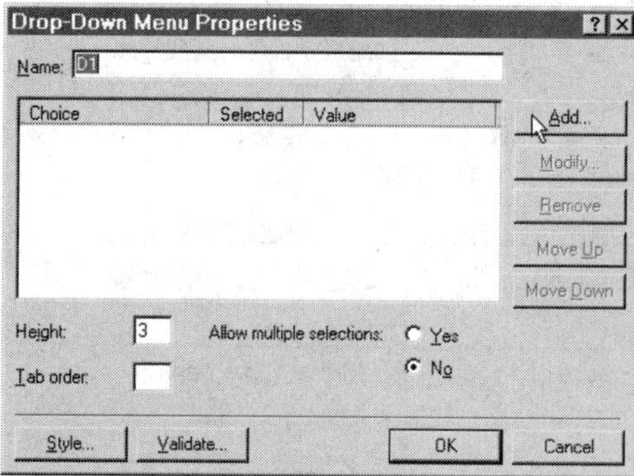

Figure 11.29 When the Drop-Down Menu Properties dialog box appears, click *Add* to create menu choices.

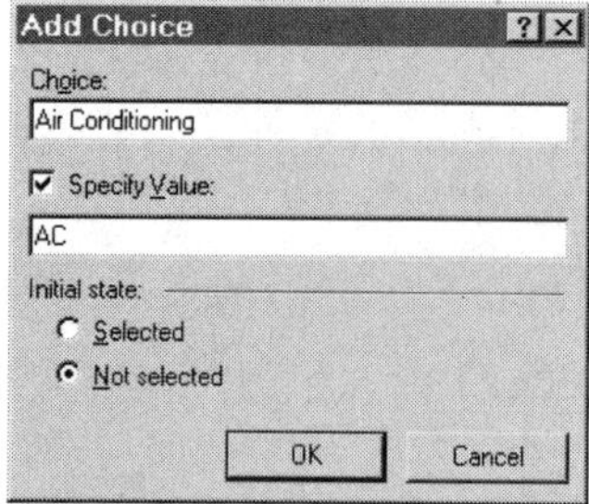

Figure 11.30 Use the Add Choice dialog box to create a menu choice, give it a value, and set an initial state.

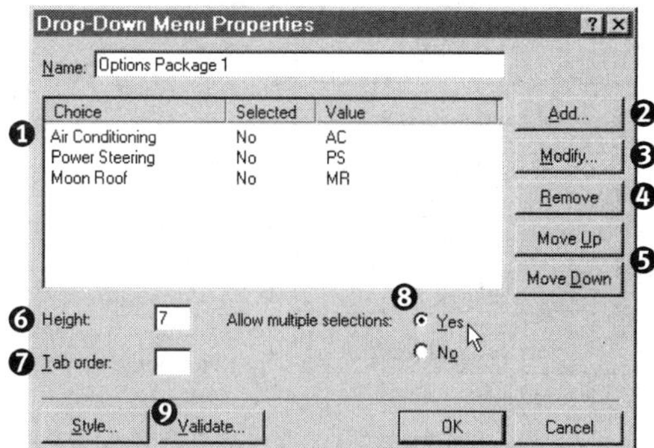

Figure 11.31 Once you've created menu choices, you can rearrange them and allow multiple selections.

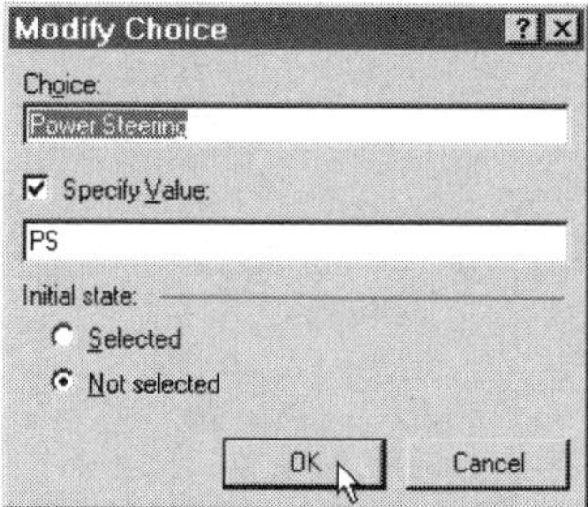

Figure 11.32 The Modify Choice dialog box lets you change an item's description, value, and initial state.

Drop-Down Menu options

To reach the Drop-Down Menu Properties dialog box (**Figure 11.31**), right-click the field and choose *Form Field Properties* from the shortcut menu (Alt Enter) (**Figure 11.11**).

❶ **Choice list:** Click any listing in the window to select it. The window displays all the drop-down menu's choices, whether they will be selected within the menu, and the shorthand value you assigned each choice.

❷ **Add:** Click to add more choices to the drop-down menu.

❸ **Modify:** To change one of your menu choices, select it in the *Choice* list and click *Modify*. The Modify Choice dialog box will appear (**Figure 11.32**), which works identically to the Add Choice dialog box (**Figure 11.30**).

❹ **Remove:** To remove an item, select it in the *Choice* list and click *Remove*. It will be deleted immediately.

❺ **Move Up/Move Down:** To rearrange your choices, select one in the *Choice* list and click *Move Up* or *Move Down*. The item will move up or down by one position.

❻ **Height:** Use the text box to set how many lines of the drop-down menu should appear in the form. If you enter a number and the list has more items than that, a scrollbar will be added to the menu.

❼ **Tab order:** Enter a number in the text box to set the drop-down menu's tab order within the form.

(continued)

❽ **Allow multiple selections:** By default, *No* is chosen. Choose *Yes* if, as in the example, you want users to be able to choose more than one item.

❾ **Validate:** Click to define entry requirements for the drop-down menu. When the Drop-Down Menu Validation dialog box appears (**Figure 11.33**), check *Data Required* if you want users to choose at least one item from the menu. Use the *Minimum Items* and *Maximum Items* text boxes to further refine your requirements. Click *OK* and you'll be returned to the Drop-Down Menu Properties dialog box.

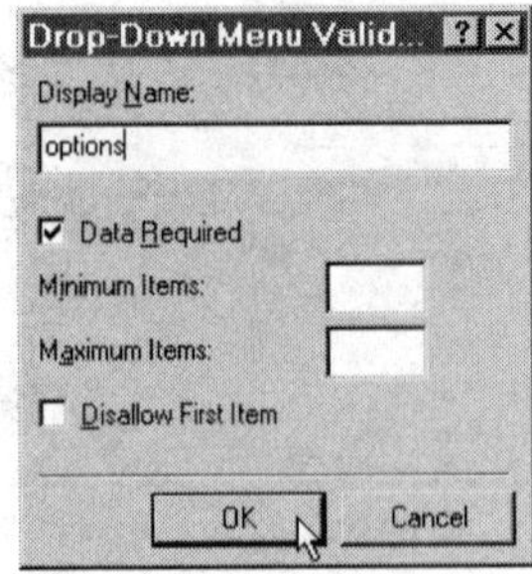

Figure 11.33 Use the Drop-Down Menu Validation dialog box to set data entry rules for the menu.

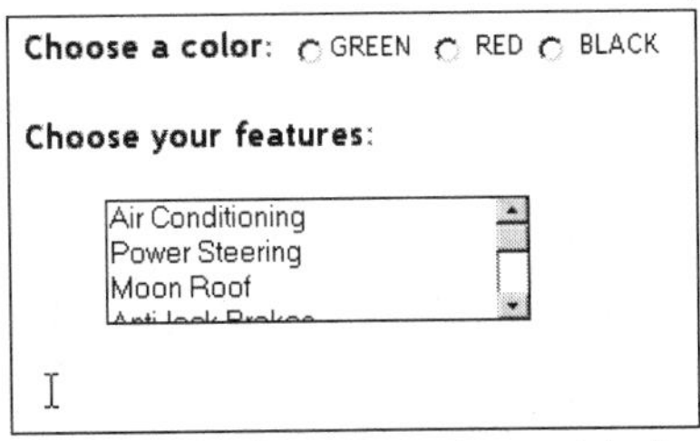

Figure 11.34 Before you create a push button, click in the form where you want it to appear.

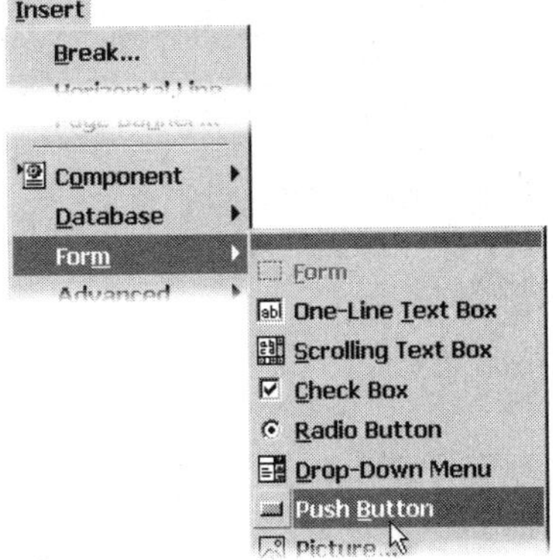

Figure 11.35 To add a push button, choose Insert > Form > Push Button.

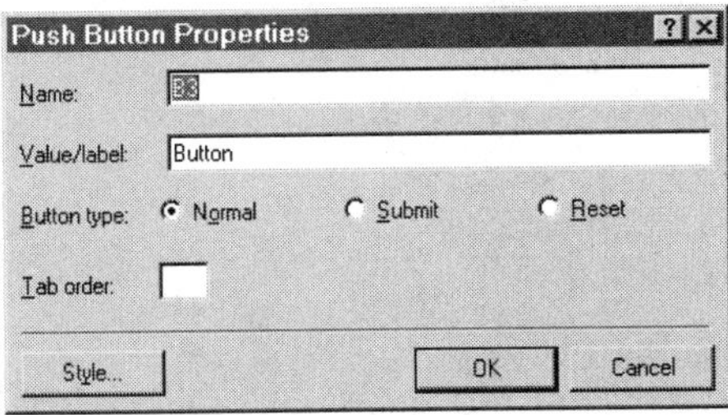

Figure 11.36 Use the Push Button Properties dialog box to name the button, create a label for it, and choose its type.

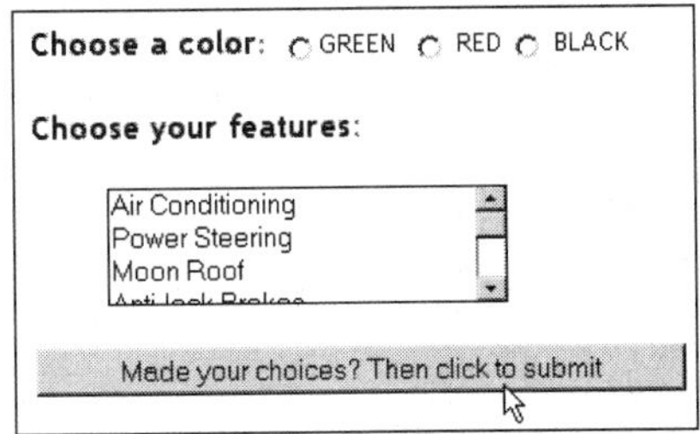

Figure 11.37 After you've created a push button, switch to the *Preview* view to see how it looks.

Using push buttons

Once you've created a form using text boxes, check boxes, radio buttons, or drop-down menus, you'll need to give users some way to submit their information. That's where FrontPage's push buttons, sometimes called command buttons, come in. While you can link push buttons to custom scripts, most of the time you'll be using them to have visitors submit their information or reset the form if they want to start over.

To add a push button

1. Click in the form page where you want to add the push button (**Figure 11.34**).
2. Choose Insert > Form > Push Button (**Figure 11.35**).
3. When the button appears in the page, right-click it and choose *Form Field Properties* from the shortcut menu (Alt Enter) (**Figure 11.11**).
4. When the Push Button Properties dialog box appears, FrontPage will have assigned the button an arbitrary name, such as *B1* and labeled it *Button* (**Figure 11.36**). If you like, type in a distinctive name of your own, which won't be seen by site visitors. Type in a button label, such as "Click to Submit," which will help users know what to do.
5. Choose which *Button type* you want to use. By default, the button is set to *Normal*, which is used if you plan on creating your own script that will be triggered by the button. More typically, users will be using the button to *Submit* form information or to *Reset* the form to its original, blank condition.
6. Enter a number for the field's tab order within the form and click *OK*. Your choices will be applied to the button. To see how the button looks, switch to FrontPage's *Preview* view (**Figure 11.37**).

Creating Confirmation Pages

The idea behind a confirmation page is simple: You take some or all of the information your visitors have entered in form fields and present it back to them so they can confirm that it's correct.

While it's relatively easy to create a custom confirmation letter, FrontPage also includes a template to get you started. No matter which route you take, the confirmation pages use the *names* of your form fields to serve back to the user the values they've entered within those fields. If you get the field name wrong, the confirmation page won't work.

To create a confirmation page

1. Make sure you're in page view, then choose File > New > Page (Ctrl N) (**Figure 11.1**).
2. When the New dialog box appears, select *Confirmation Form* and click *OK*.
3. When the new confirmation page appears, save it (Ctrl S).
4. When the Save As dialog box appears (**Figure 11.3**), give the confirmation page a distinctive name and title, then click *Save*.
5. You're now ready to modify the page's text and existing confirmation fields, which are set off by [brackets] (**Figure 11.38**). You'll also notice that if you move the cursor over a pair of brackets, it turns into a hand holding a page.
6. To change the field name used in an *existing* confirmation field, right-click it and choose *Confirmation Field Properties* from the shortcut menu (Alt Enter) (**Figure 11.39**).

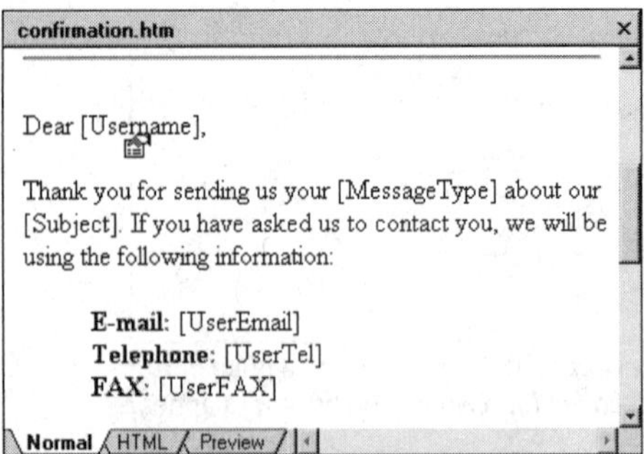

Figure 11.38 Confirmation fields are set off by [brackets] and trigger a hand-and-page icon to appear when the cursor moves over them.

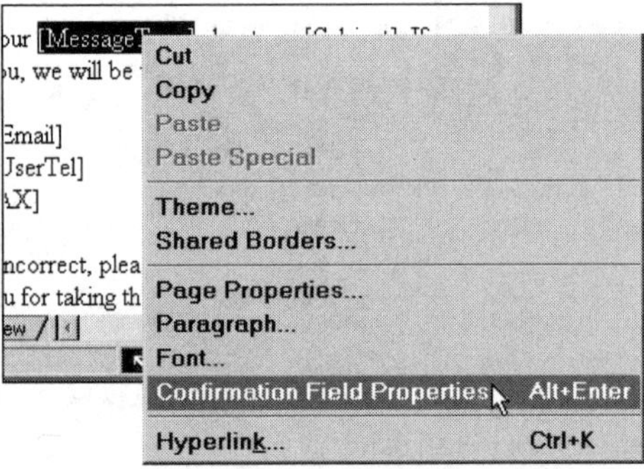

Figure 11.39 To rename an *existing* confirmation field, right-click it and choose *Confirmation Field Properties* from the shortcut menu.

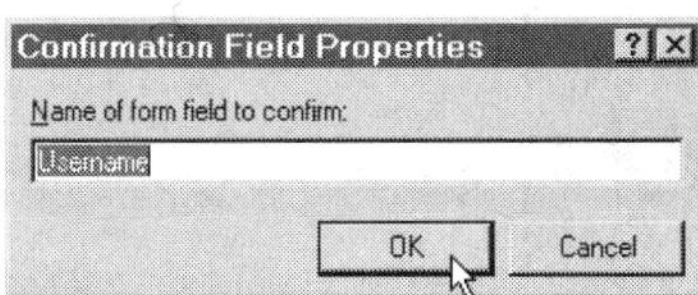

Figure 11.40 Use the Confirmation Field Properties dialog box to enter a field name from your form page.

Thank you for sending us your [StreetAddress] about our [Subject]. If you have asked us to contact you, we will be using the following information:

Figure 11.41 Field names used in confirmation pages must exactly match those used in the form page.

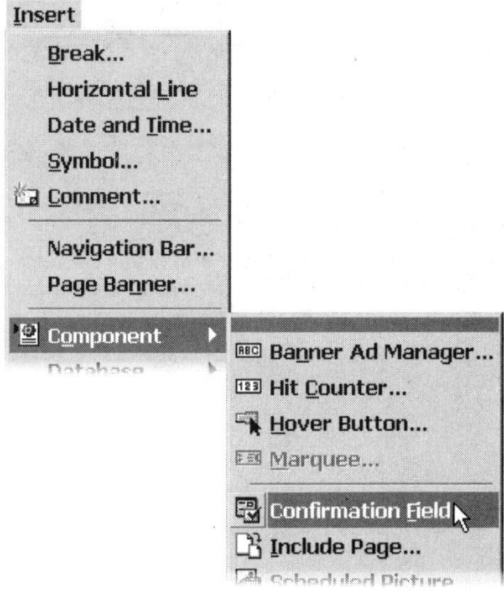

Figure 11.42 To add a *new* confirmation field, choose Insert > Component > Confirmation Field.

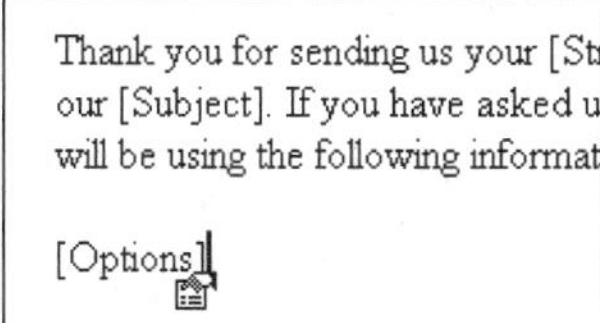

Figure 11.43 Just like existing confirmation fields, new ones will be marked by brackets in the confirmation page.

7. When the Confirmation Field Properties dialog box appears (**Figure 11.40**), type in the name you assigned to a field when creating your form page. Click *OK* and the new name will appear in the brackets (**Figure 11.41**).
8. To add a *new* confirmation field, choose Insert > Component > Confirmation Field (**Figure 11.42**).
9. When the empty Confirmation Field Properties dialog box appears (**Figure 11.40**), type the name of the form field you want to use into the text box and click *OK*. The confirmation field will be added to the page (**Figure 11.43**).
10. Continue adding text and confirmation fields, then save the confirmation page (Ctrl S) when you're done.

✔ Tip

- It'd be helpful if FrontPage presented a drop-down menu of your form field names to jog your memory. If you forget a field's name, double-click it in the form page and check what's in the *Name* field.

Saving Form Results

You can save the results collected in a form as a file, an email, a database record, or as data handled by custom scripts. Depending on your choices, FrontPage will configure what are called form handlers to save the results.

If you save the results of a form as a file, FrontPage gives you eight different formats in which to store the data. If you like, by the way, FrontPage lets you save the results as a file *and* as email, rather than forcing you to choose one or the other.

By default, FrontPage uses the Save Results Component to handle your form results. But it also includes a Discussion Form Handler and a Registration Form Handler. FrontPage also recognizes a variety of custom scripts.

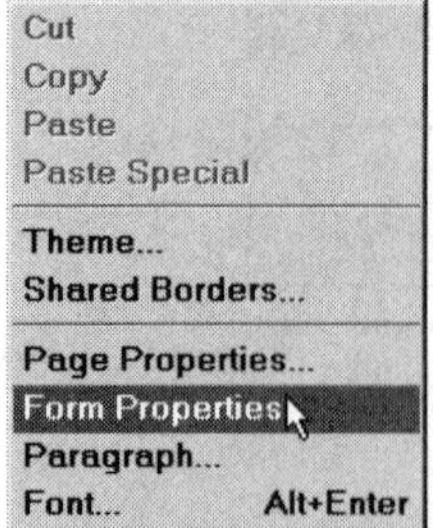

Figure 11.44 To control how form results will be saved, right-click the form and choose *Form Properties* from the shortcut menu.

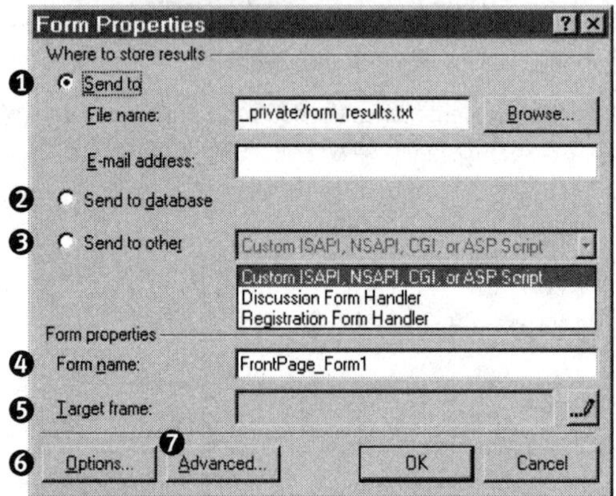

Figure 11.45 Use the Form Properties dialog box to choose whether form results are saved as a file, an email, a database record, or as customized data.

To save form results to a file

1. While in page view, right-click the form and choose *Form Properties* from the shortcut menu (**Figure 11.44**).
2. When the Form Properties dialog box appears (**Figure 11.45**), choose *Send to* ❶ in the *Where to store results* section.
3. By default, FrontPage gives the file a name and places it in your Web site's *private* folder, which can't be found by Web search engines. If you want to change the name or folder location, type a new path and name into the text box or click *Browse* if you want the results stored in an existing file.
4. Use the *Form properties* section if you want to give the form another name ❹ or if you want to set a target frame for the form ❺. For details on target frames, see *Setting target frames* on page 216.
5. Click *Options* ❻, and the *File Results* tab of the Options for Saving Results of Form dialog box (**Figure 11.46**) will appear with the file name already entered.

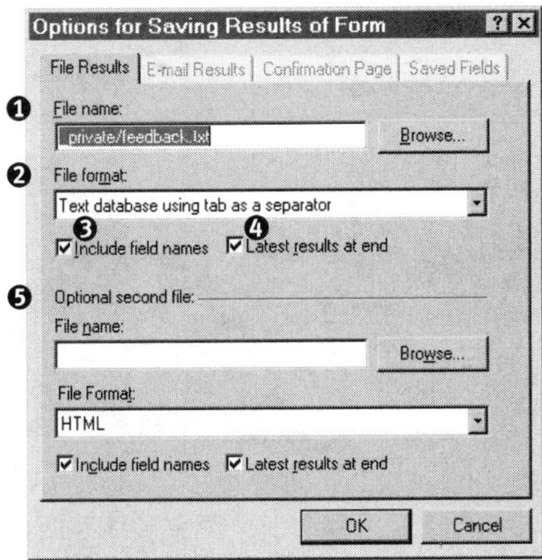

Figure 11.46 The File Results tab lets you set the file's name, format, and other details of saving the data.

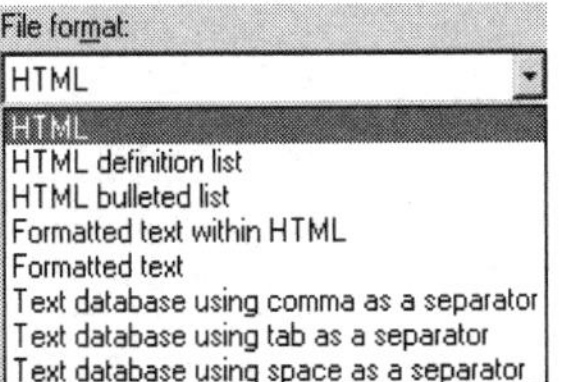

Figure 11.47 The File format drop-down menu offers eight choices for formatting the results data.

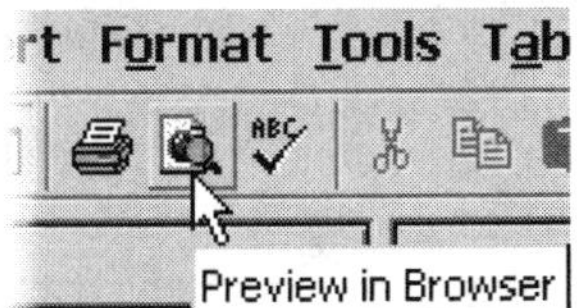

Figure 11.48 To test and inspect a form, click the Preview in Browser button in FrontPage's Standard toolbar.

6. Use the *File format* drop-down menu ❷ to choose one of the eight text choices (**Figure 11.47**).

7. Check *Include field names* ❸ if you want to pair the values from each form field with the field's name. Unless you choose *HTML*, the *Latest results at end* ❹ box will be checked, meaning new results will appear at the bottom of the file.

8. If you want to create another file for the results, perhaps in another of the eight formats, use the *Optional second file* section ❺ to enter a new name or *Browse* to an existing file. The section's other choices work identically to those described in steps 6 and 7.

9. Click *OK* to return to the Form Properties dialog box. Click *OK* again and the settings will be applied to the form. To test the form, click the Preview in Browser button in FrontPage's Standard toolbar (**Figure 11.48**).

Form options

To reach the Form Properties dialog box (**Figure 11.50**), choose Insert > Form > Form Properties (**Figure 11.49**) or right-click the form and choose *Form Properties* from the shortcut menu.

❶ **Send to:** Choose this option and use *File name* to save the form results as a text or HTML file. Use *E-mail address* and enter an address in the text box if you want the results saved in that form.

❷ **Send to database:** Choose this option to save the results to a database.

❸ **Send to other:** Use the drop-down menu to select a handler other than FrontPage's default. Use the *Options* button to configure the custom handler you choose.

❹ **Form name:** By default, FrontPage will assign a name to the form. If you prefer, use the text box to type in a distinctive name for the form.

❺ **Target frame:** Click the pencil icon to set a target frame. For details, see *Setting target frames* on page 216.

❻ **Options:** Click to configure the details of how the form results will be saved.

❼ **Advanced:** Click to set Hidden fields, which are needed only if you're using CGI scripts to handle the form results.

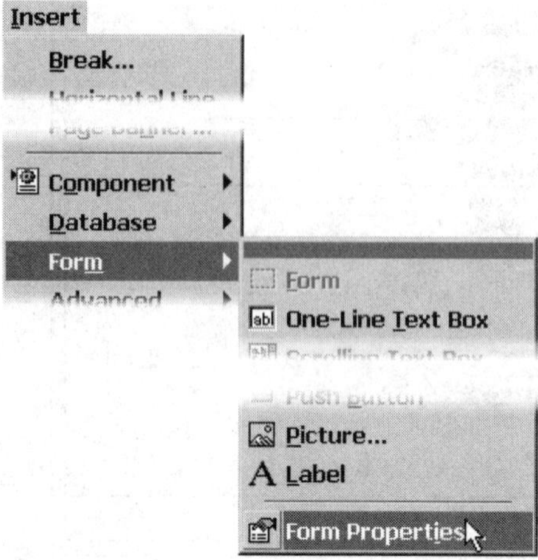

Figure 11.49 To reach the Form Properties dialog box, choose Insert > Form > Form Properties.

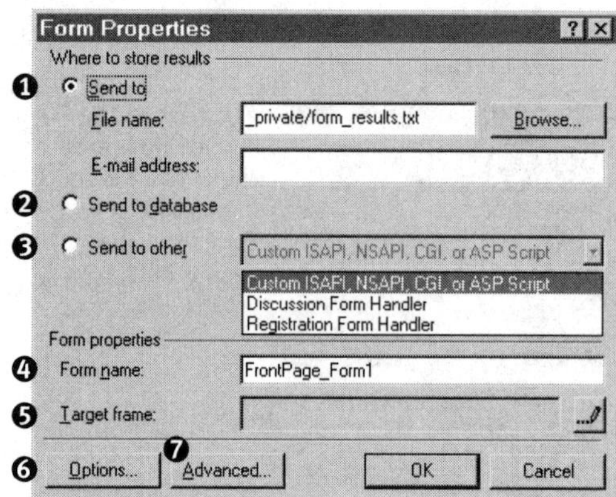

Figure 11.50 Use the Form Properties dialog box to choose whether form results are saved as a file, an email, a database record, or as customized data.

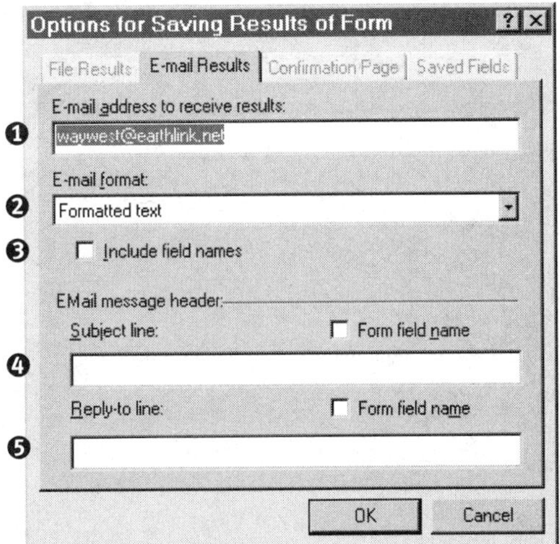

Figure 11.51 The E-mail Results tab lets you set the message's address, format, subject line, and reply address.

To save form results as email

1. While in page view, right-click the form and choose *Form Properties* from the shortcut menu (**Figure 11.44**).
2. When the Form Properties dialog box appears (**Figure 11.50**), choose *Send to* ❶ in the *Where to store results* section.
3. Type into the *E-mail address* text box the address of where you want the results sent.
4. By default, FrontPage fills in the *File name* text box. If you want your results saved *only* as email, delete the name from the text box. If you want the results saved as email *and* as a file, leave the *File name* as it is.
5. Use the *Form properties* section if you want to give the form another name ❹ or if you want to set a target frame for the form ❺. For details on target frames, see *Setting target frames* on page 216.
6. Click *Options* ❻ and when the Options for Saving Results of Form dialog box appears, click the *E-mail Results* tab (**Figure 11.51**). The address you entered in step 3 will already be entered in the *E-mail address to receive results* text box ❶.
7. Use the *E-mail format* drop-down menu ❷ to choose one of the eight text choices (**Figure 11.47**).
8. Check *Include field names* ❸ if you want to pair the values from each form field with the field's name.
9. By default, the email's subject line ❹ would be *Form Results*. If you want something more descriptive, type it into the text box or check *Form field name* to have it appear in the subject line.

(continued)

10. Type into the *Reply-to line* text box ❺ the address you want used as the *sender* of the email. However, if your form includes a field that collects the user's email address, check *Form field name* and enter that field's name in the text box. That way the reply will go directly to the person who filled out the form in the first place.
11. Click *OK* to return to the Form Properties dialog box. Click *OK* again and the settings will be applied to the form. To test the form, click the Preview in Browser button in FrontPage's Standard toolbar (**Figure 11.48**).

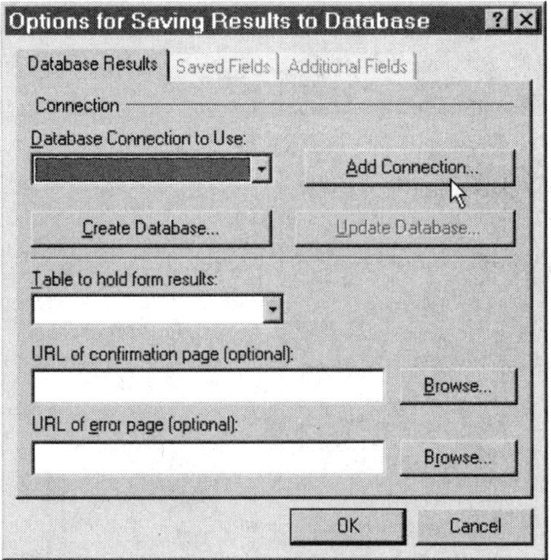

Figure 11.52 The Database Results tab lets you port the form results to an existing or new database.

To save form results to a database

1. While in page view, right-click the form and choose *Form Properties* from the shortcut menu (**Figure 11.44**).
2. When the Form Properties dialog box appears (**Figure 11.50**), choose *Send to database* in the *Where to store results* section.
3. Use the *Form properties* section if you want to give the form another name or if you want to set a target frame for the form. For details on target frames, see *Setting target frames* on page 216.
4. Click *Options* and when the Options for Saving Results to Database dialog box appears, click the *Database Results* tab (**Figure 11.52**).
5. Click *Add Connection* to link to your Web site's database. For details, see *Adding Database Connections* on page 253.
6. Click *OK* to return to the Form Properties dialog box. Click *OK* again and the settings will be applied to the form. To test the form, click the Preview in Browser button in FrontPage's Standard toolbar (**Figure 11.48**).

To save form results with a custom script

1. While in either the folders view or with the Folder List visible, right-click the folder containing your custom script. Choose *Properties* from the shortcut menu (**Figure 11.53**).
2. When the folder's properties dialog box appears, check *Allow scripts or programs to be run* (**Figure 11.54**). Click *OK* to close the dialog box.
3. Switch back to page view, right-click your form, and choose *Form Properties* from the shortcut menu (**Figure 11.44**).
4. When the Form Properties dialog box appears (**Figure 11.50**), choose *Send to other* in the *Where to store results* section and use the drop-down menu to select *Custom ISAPI, NSAPI, CGI, or ASP Script.*
5. Use the *Form properties* section if you want to give the form another name or if you want to set a target frame for the form. For details on target frames, see *Setting target frames* on page 216.
6. Click *Options* and the Options for Custom Form Handler dialog box will appear (**Figure 11.55**).
7. Type the URL for your script into the *Action* text box and use the *Method* drop-down menu to choose which way information will be submitted to the script: *POST* or *GET.*
8. Leave the *Encoding type* text box blank.
9. Click *OK* to return to the Form Properties dialog box. Click *OK* again and the settings will be applied to the form. To test the form, click the Preview in Browser button in FrontPage's Standard toolbar (**Figure 11.48**).

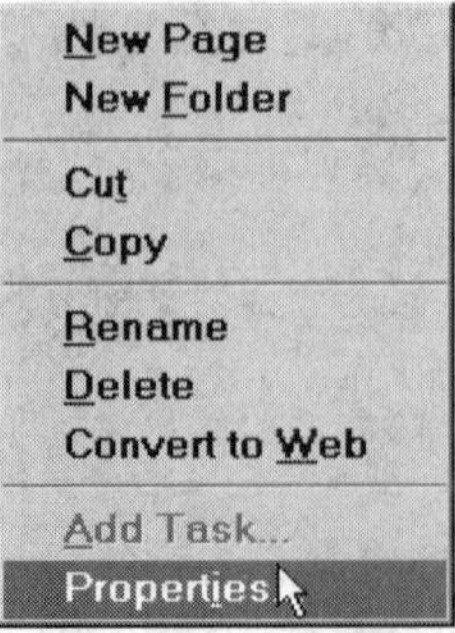

Figure 11.53 Right-click the folder containing your custom script and choose *Properties* from the shortcut menu.

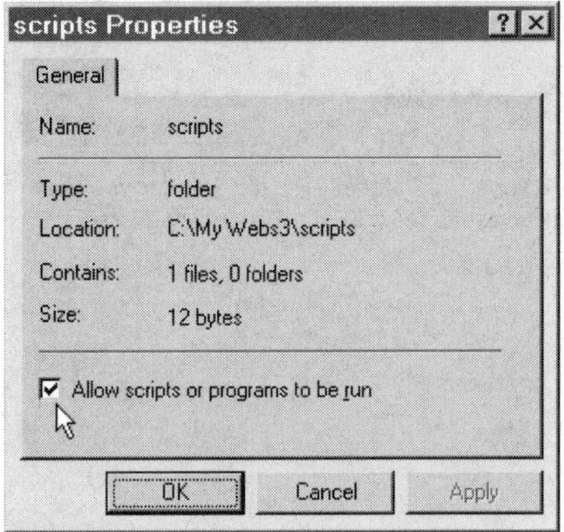

Figure 11.54 When the properties dialog box for the folder containing your custom script appears, check *Allow scripts or programs to be run*.

Figure 11.55 Use the Options for Custom Form Handler dialog box to set the URL for your custom script and the method for submitting the script's data.

SAVING FORM RESULTS

✔ Tips

- In step 7, *POST* passes the field name and its value straight to the script; *GET* encodes the same data and presents it as a QUERY_STRING variable. To learn more about custom scripts, get yourself a copy of *Perl and CGI for the World Wide Web: Visual QuickStart Guide* by Elizabeth Castro (Peachpit Press, 1999).
- You also can use the *Send to other* drop-down menu to select handlers for discussion groups and registering users.

Adding Database Connections

12

Figuring out how to link databases to Web sites can be a tail-chasing mess of missed deadlines and endless nights. Fortunately, FrontPage includes the Database Results Wizard, which walks you step by step through the entire procedure. While a bit lengthy, the process involves five basic steps.

First, you create a connection between FrontPage and the database you want to work with. Once the connection's established, you choose the database records you want to use. The third step involves filtering and sorting out which fields and records will be displayed. At that point, you decide how to format the results. Finally, you have the option of displaying all the results at once or breaking them into smaller groups.

Importing Databases

Whether the database is part of your Web site or resides on a server somewhere else doesn't really matter. However, if you want to place the database on your Web site, you'll need to import it in a format compatible with FrontPage (**Table 12.1**). If the database uses some other file extension, then use your database application to export it or save it in one of the formats FrontPage supports. Once you've done that, you're ready to import the database using FrontPage.

To import databases into your Web site

1. Switch to Windows Explorer to locate the database you want to import.
2. Once you find the database, right-click it and choose *Copy* from the shortcut menu (**Figure 12.1**).
3. Switch back to your Web site in FrontPage and make sure the Folder List is visible. Right-click the Web site in the Folder List and choose *Paste* from the shortcut menu (**Figure 12.2**). The database will be added to the Web site. You're now ready to create a database connection. For details, see *To create a database connection* on the next page.

Table 12.1

Compatible Database Formats for FrontPage

FILE EXTENSION	FORMAT
.MDB	Microsoft Access
.DBF	dBase, Microsoft FoxPro
.XLS	Microsoft Excel
.TXT	Tab-separated text
.CSV	Comma-separated text

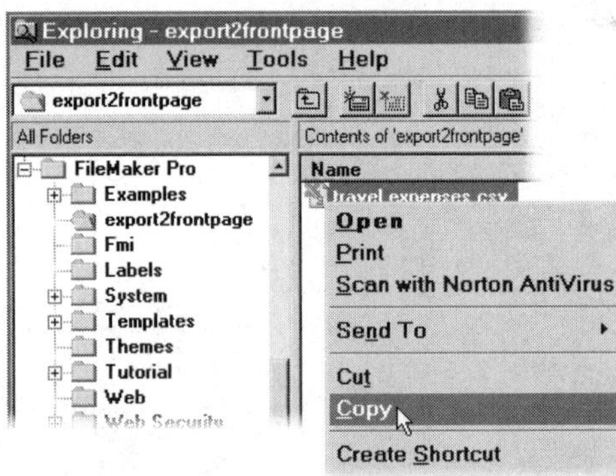

Figure 12.1 To import a database, switch to Windows Explorer, then right-click the database and choose *Copy*.

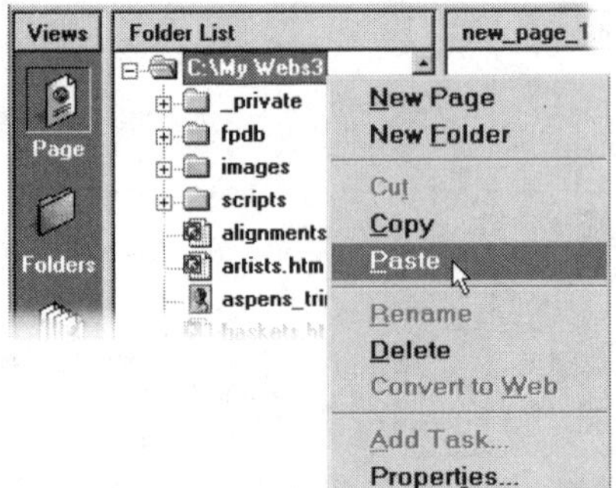

Figure 12.2 Right-click your Web site in the Folder List and choose *Paste* to import a database into FrontPage.

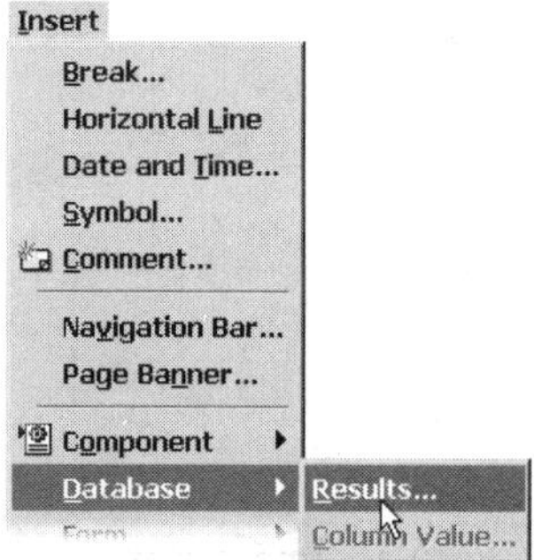

Figure 12.3 To create a database region in your Web page, choose Insert > Database > Results.

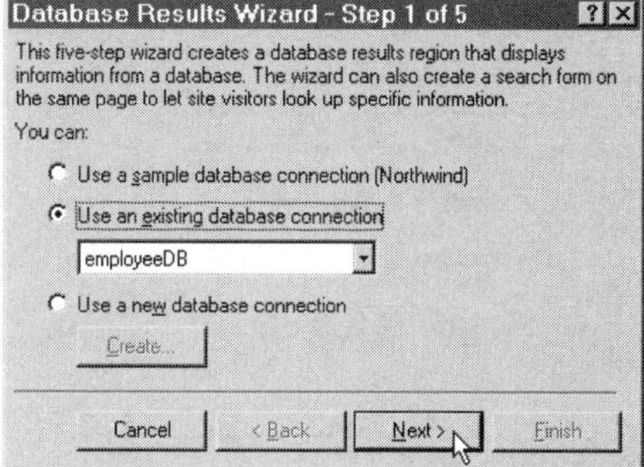

Figure 12.4 Use the first screen of the Database Results Wizard to choose a database connection.

Creating Database Connections

By using FrontPage to create a connection between a Web page and a database, you're giving your Web visitors a selected view of information within the database. With all the steps involved, it's easy to forget that you're making a *connection* with a database, not creating the database itself. In some programs, this process is called creating a view or query.

To create a database connection

1. Make sure you know the pathname or URL for the database you want to use, whether it's already part of your Web site or on a remote server.
2. Open an existing Web page and click where you want the database to appear or create a new page by choosing File > New > Page (Ctrl N).
3. Once the page appears, choose Insert > Database > Results (**Figure 12.3**).
4. When the first screen of the Database Results Wizard appears (**Figure 12.4**), choose the connection you want to use: a *sample* connection with FrontPage's example database (Northwind), an *existing* connection, or a *new* connection. Most likely you'll want to use a new connection, so see *To create a new database connection* on page 259 before going on to step 5.

(continued)

5. Once you've made your choice, click *Next* and, after a moment, the second screen of the Database Results Wizard appears (**Figure 12.5**). Decide whether you want to select a *Record source* using the existing fields listed in the drop-down list or create a *Custom query*. (Custom queries use SQL statement syntax, which falls beyond the scope of this book.)
6. Once you've made your choice, click *Next* and the third screen of the Database Results Wizard appears (**Figure 12.6**). By default, all of the record source's fields will be listed for display. If you want to exclude some fields, click *Edit List*.
7. When the Displayed Fields dialog box appears (**Figure 12.7**), compare the *Available fields* list and *Displayed fields* list, then use the *Add* or *Remove* buttons to expand or narrow the Displayed fields listings. Use the *Move Up* and *Move Down* buttons to rearrange the order in which the fields will be displayed on your Web page. Click *OK* when you're done and you'll return to the wizard's third screen (**Figure 12.6**). If you want to sort or filter the fields more precisely, click *More Options*. For details, see *Filtering and sorting options* on page 262.

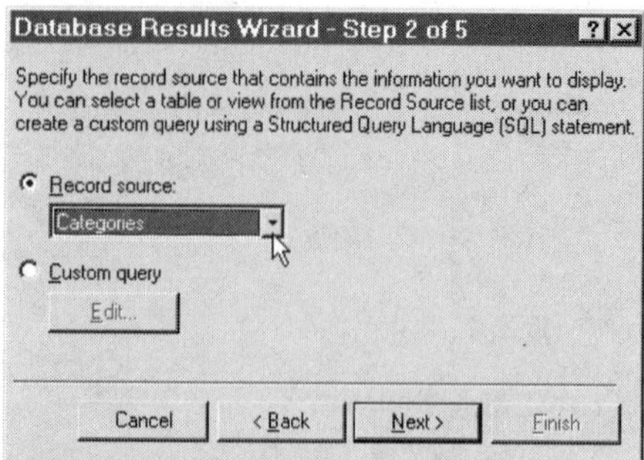

Figure 12.5 Use the second screen of the Database Results Wizard to select a *Record source* using an existing field or to create a *Custom query*.

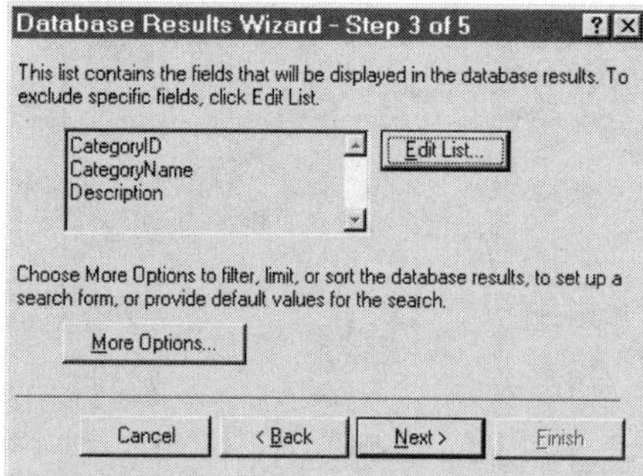

Figure 12.6 Use the third screen of the Database Results Wizard to edit which fields will appear.

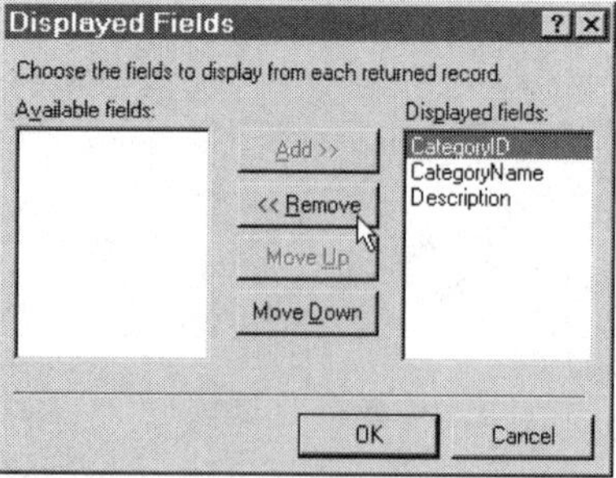

Figure 12.7 The Displayed Fields dialog box lets you add, remove, or rearrange the database fields shown.

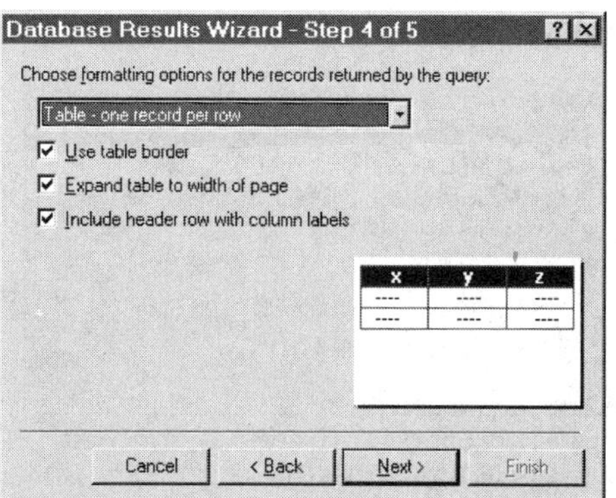

Figure 12.8 Use the drop-down menu in the Database Results Wizard's fourth screen to format the results.

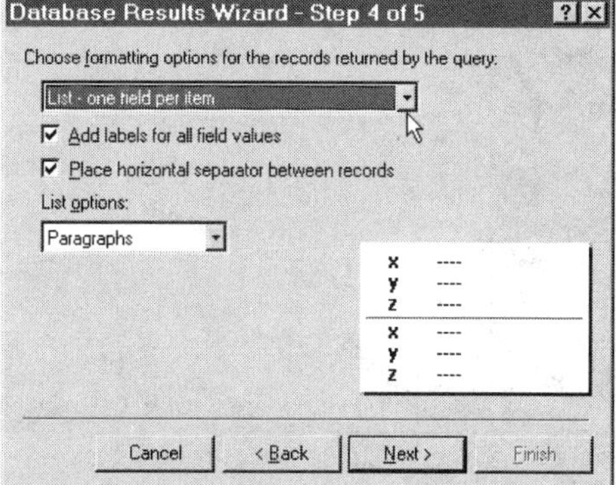

Figure 12.9 If you choose a list format, use the checkboxes and *List options* drop-down menu to fine-tune the results.

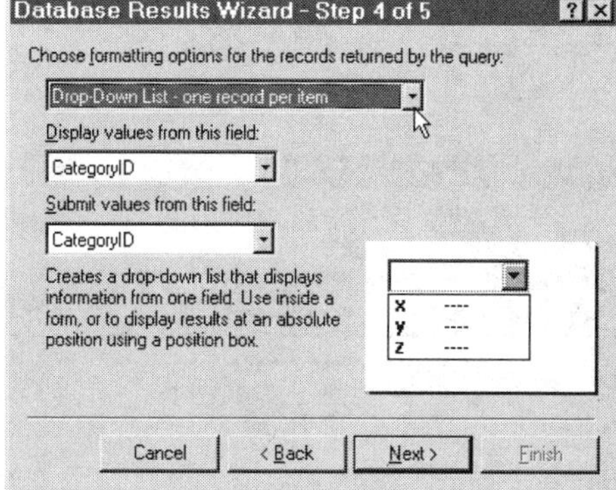

Figure 12.10 If you choose a drop-down menu format, use the dialog box's drop-down menus to fine-tune the results.

8. Once you've made your choices, click *Next* and the fourth screen of the Database Results Wizard appears (**Figure 12.8**). Use the first formatting drop-down list to choose whether to display the results as a table, a list, or a drop-down list. Depending on your choice, the dialog box will offer additional choices for formatting the results (**Figures 12.9** and **12.10**). Use the check boxes and drop-down menus to refine the appearance of the records and click *Next*.

9. When the fifth screen of the Database Results Wizard appears (**Figure 12.11**), choose whether to *Display all records together* or *Split records into groups*. If you decide to split them, enter a number into the *records per group* text box.

(continued)

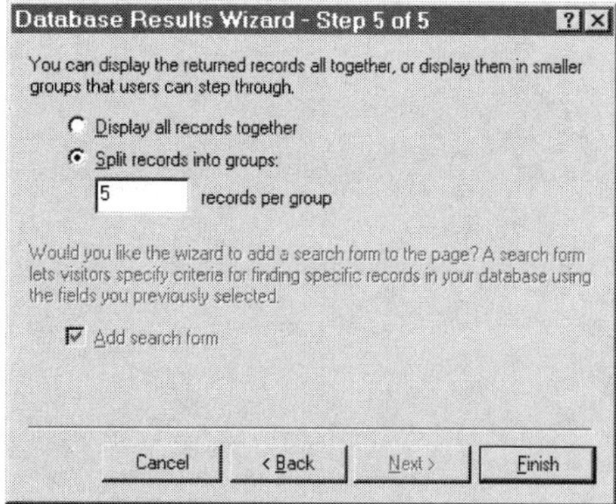

Figure 12.11 Use the fifth screen of the Database Results Wizard to decide whether to split the results into smaller groups.

10. Click *Finish* and you'll be returned to your page where the database results will be displayed (**Figure 12.12**).

11. Save the page (Ctrl S) and when the Save As dialog box appears, FrontPage will have automatically given the file an .asp file suffix (**Figure 12.13**). ASP (Active Server Page) files contain scripts linked to the server where the database resides. Click *OK* and the page will be saved as a database region.

12. Click the Preview in Browser button in FrontPage's Standard toolbar (**Figure 12.14**), to get a more accurate sense of how the results will look to site visitors (**Figure 12.15**). To modify the results, see *To change a database connection* on page 265.

✔ Tip

- If you have only a handful of records to display, the *Split records into groups* choice will be dimmed in the wizard's fifth screen.

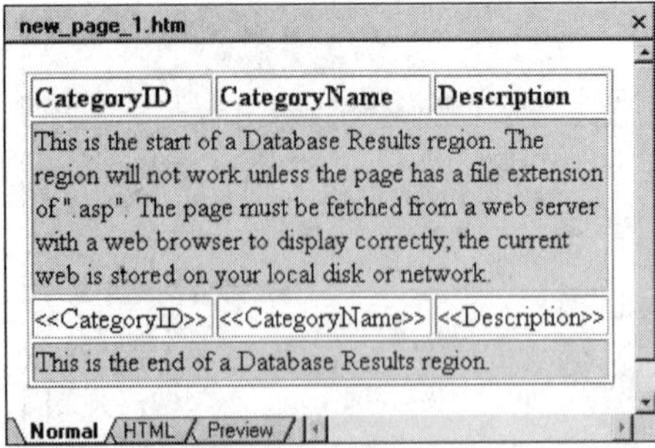

Figure 12.12 Once you've finished using the Database Results Wizard, FrontPage returns you to the now-formatted page.

Figure 12.13 When you save a page containing a database connection, FrontPage automatically assigns it an .asp suffix.

Figure 12.14 To see how the database connection will appear, click the Preview in Browser button in the Standard toolbar.

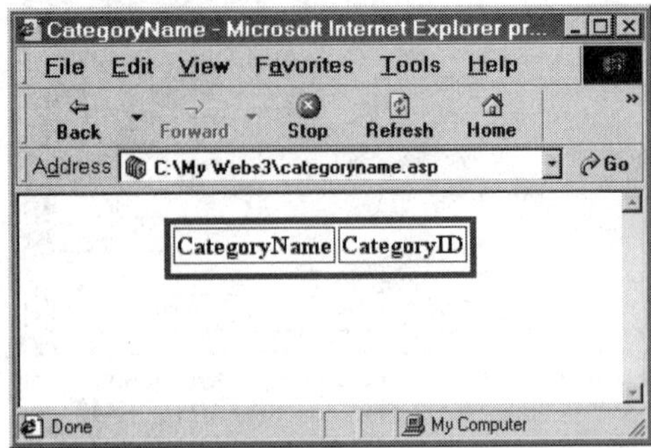

Figure 12.15 The database connection as it appears from within a Web browser.

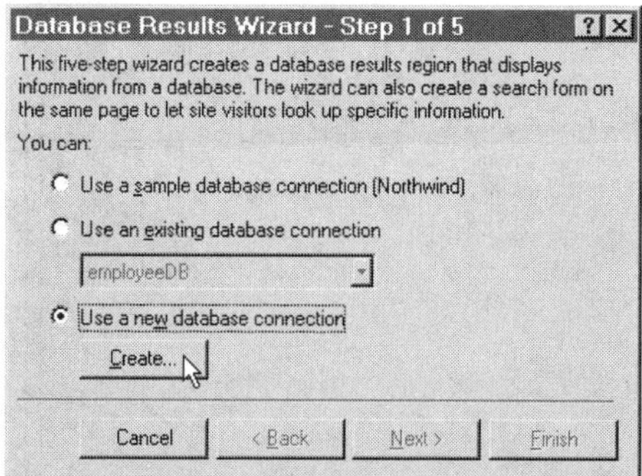

Figure 12.16 To establish a new connection, choose *Use a new database connection* and click *Create*.

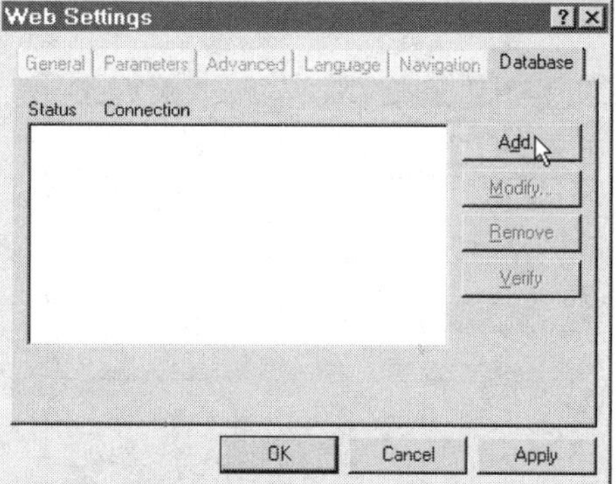

Figure 12.17 When the Web Settings dialog box appears, click the *Database* tab, then click *Add*.

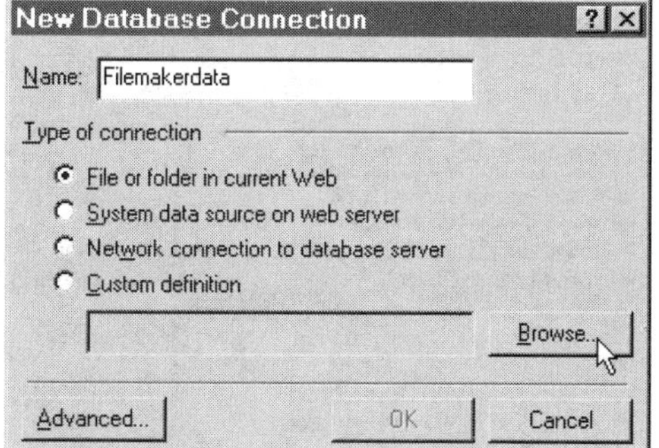

Figure 12.18 When the New Database Connection dialog box appears, name the connection, choose a type, and click *Browse* to find the database.

To create a new database connection

1. Click in the page where you want the database to appear and choose Insert > Database > Results (**Figure 12.3**)
2. When the Database Results Wizard appears (**Figure 12.16**), choose *Use a new database connection* and click *Create*.
3. When the Web Settings dialog box appears, click the *Database* tab, then click *Add* (**Figure 12.17**).
4. When the New Database Connection dialog box appears, type in a distinctive *Name* (**Figure 12.18**).
5. Use the *Type of connection* section to choose the kind of database you'll be using: a file-based database already on your Web site, data on a *Web* server, or data on a *database* server. For details on the choices, see *New Database Connection options* on page 261.
6. Click *Browse* to navigate your way to the database you want to use.
7. Once you find the database you're looking for, click *OK* to return to the New Database Connection dialog box, where the pathname for the database will be pasted into the text box.

(continued)

8. Click *OK* and the database connection will be listed in the Web Settings dialog box's *Database* tab (**Figure 12.19**). Click *OK* one more time, and you'll be returned to the first screen of the Database Results Wizard.

9. Click *Next* and, after a moment, the second screen of the Database Results Wizard will appear (**Figure 12.5**). To continue, see step 5 in *To create a database connection* on page 256.

✔ Tips

- If you choose *File or folder in current Web* in step 5 (**Figure 12.18**), when the Database Files in Current Web dialog box appears (**Figure 12.20**), you may need to use the *Files of type* drop-down menu (**Figure 12.21**) to find databases you've imported to your Web site.
- If you like, you can skip past the Database Results Wizard and create a new connection directly by choosing Tools > Web Settings and jumping to step 3 on page 259.

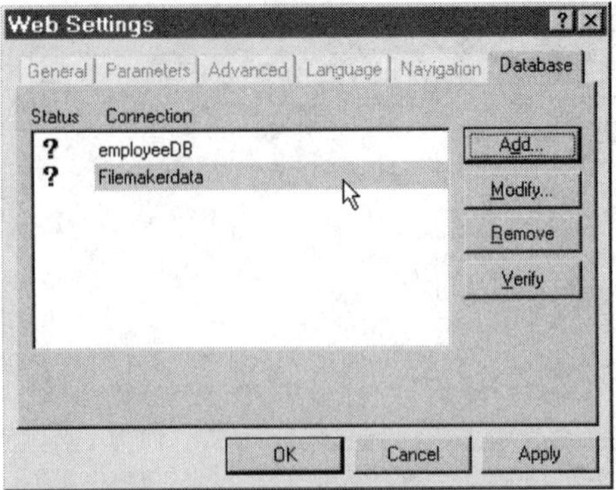

Figure 12.19 Established database connections are listed under the *Database* tab of the Web Settings dialog box.

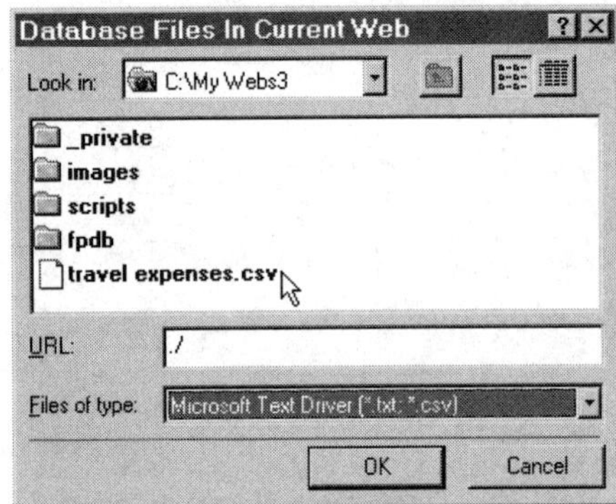

Figure 12.20 When the Database Files in Current Web dialog box appears, use the *Files of type* drop-down menu to find a database you've imported.

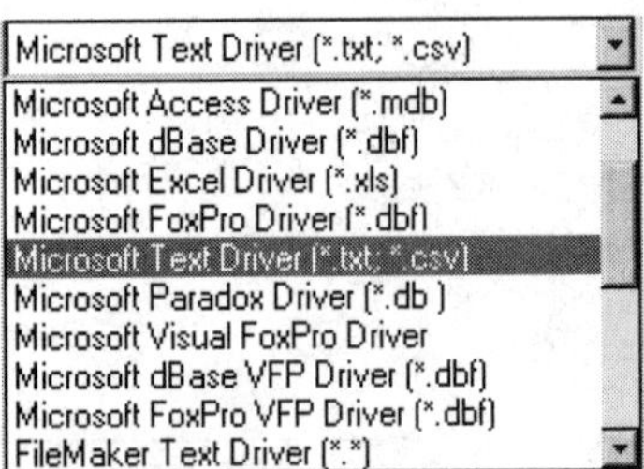

Figure 12.21 The *Files of type* drop-down menu lists the database formats FrontPage supports.

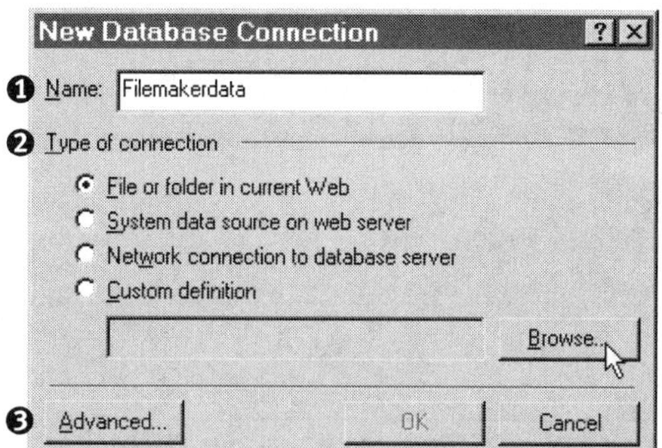

Figure 12.22 When the New Database Connection dialog box appears, name the connection, choose a type, and click *Browse* to find the database.

New Database Connection options

To reach the New Database Connection dialog box (**Figure 12.22**), choose Tools > Web Settings. When the Web Settings dialog box appears, click the *Database* tab, then click *Add* (**Figure 12.17**).

❶ **Name:** By default, FrontPage will have assigned the field a generic name, such as Database1. When you type in a distinctive name, remember that this is the name of the database *connection*, not the database itself.

❷ **Type of connection:** Make your choice based on the kind of database you're connecting to and where it resides.

File or folder in current Web: Use this choice to connect to a database stored within your Web site. FrontPage will automatically create a connection for Microsoft Access databases placed on your site. For other databases, make sure you import it in a format FrontPage supports. For details, see *Importing Databases* on page 254.

System data source on web server: Use this choice to connect to a System Data Source Name on a Web server. The data can be a file-based database or a database management system.

Network connection to database server: Use this choice to connect to a server dedicated to handling a large database, such as a Microsoft SQL Server.

Custom definition: Use this choice to connect to a custom file or query designed to retrieve the necessary data. Use this option to edit the connection string when, for example, you're using a database that requires parameters that FrontPage can't set directly.

❸ **Advanced:** Click to set up user names, and passwords if Web users will be connecting to a password-protected database.

Filtering and sorting options

Use FrontPage's filtering and sorting options if you want to fine-tune—or restrict—the data that Web visitors see.

To filter or sort the database results

1. To filter or sort the database more precisely, click *More Options* in the third screen of the Database Results Wizard appears (**Figure 12.6**).
2. When the *More Options* dialog box appears (**Figure 12.23**), click *Criteria* if you want to filter the database records or *Ordering* to sort the results.
3. When the Criteria dialog box appears (**Figure 12.24**), click *Add* to set up the filtering criteria.
4. When the Add Criteria dialog box appears (**Figure 12.25**), use the drop-down menus to select a *Field Name* and create a *Comparison* with the *Value*, then choose *And/Or*. Once you've set up the relationship, click *OK* and it will be added to the Criteria dialog box. Repeat until you've set up all your filtering criteria, then click *OK* (**Figure 12.26**).

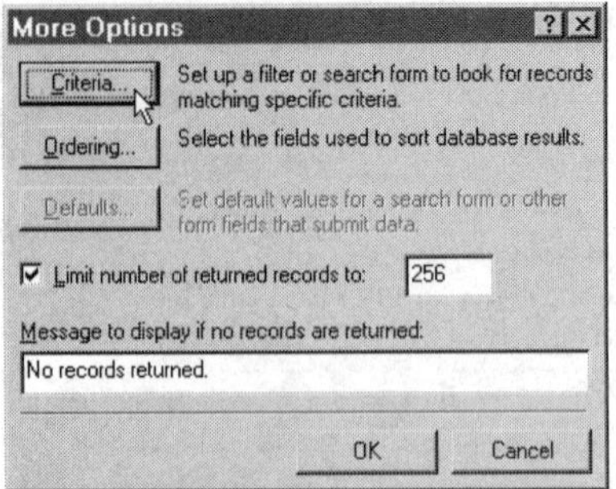

Figure 12.23 To filter records, click *Criteria* in the More Options dialog box. To sort the results, click *Ordering*.

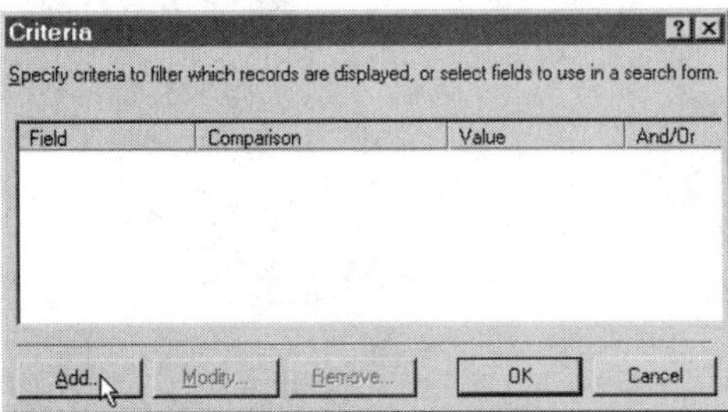

Figure 12.24 When the Criteria dialog box appears, click *Add* to set up the criteria for filtering records.

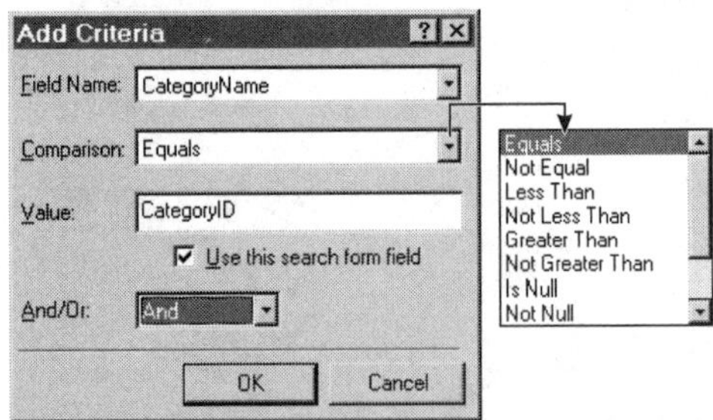

Figure 12.25 Use the drop-down menus to select a *Field Name*, set up a *Comparison* with the *Value*, and choose *And/Or*.

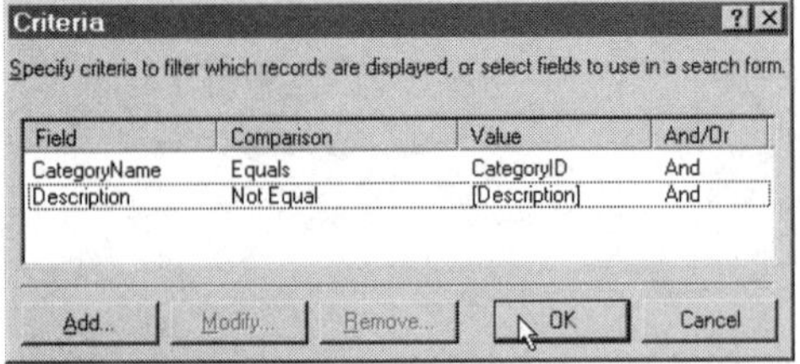

Figure 12.26 Once you've set your criteria using the *Add* button, click *OK*.

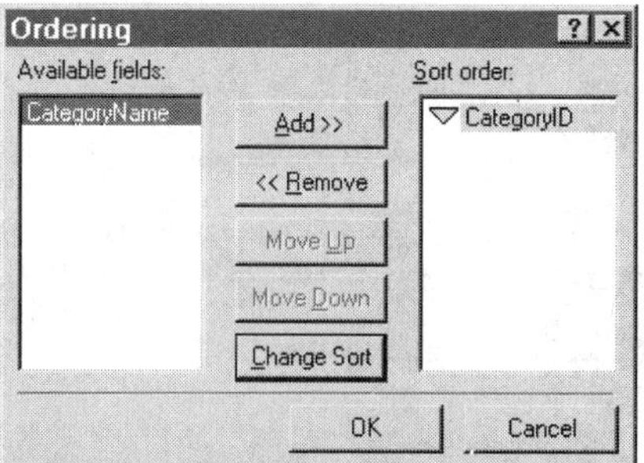

Figure 12.27 Use the Ordering dialog box to set which fields to sort and their sort order.

5. When the More Options dialog box reappears, click *Ordering* if you want to sort the database results.

6. When the Ordering dialog box appears, click listings in *Available fields* that you want to *Add* to the *Sort order* (**Figure 12.27**). To reverse the sort of any field in the *Sort order*, click *Change Sort*. When you're done, click *OK* and you'll be returned to the More Options dialog box.

7. Click *OK* one more time, and you'll be returned to the third screen of the Database Results Wizard (**Figure 12.6**).

8. Click *Next* and, after a moment, the fourth screen of the Database Results Wizard will appear (**Figure 12.8**). To continue, see step 7 in *To create a database connection* on page 256.

Verifying a database connection

Make sure your database connection will work by first verifying it. If FrontPage verifies that the connection is correct, you're all set to publish your Web pages containing database connections. If FrontPage cannot verify the connection, probably because the database has been moved, you'll need to modify the connection. For details, see *To change a database connection* on page 265.

To verify a database connection

1. Choose Tools > Web Settings (**Figure 12.28**).
2. When the Web Settings dialog box appears, click the *Database* tab, choose an unverified connection (marked by a question mark in the *Status* column), and click *Verify*. (**Figure 12.29**).
3. If FrontPage verifies the connection, the question mark will become a checkmark. If there's a problem, the question mark will become a broken chain link (**Figure 12.30**). To fix a broken link, see *To change a database connection* on the next page.

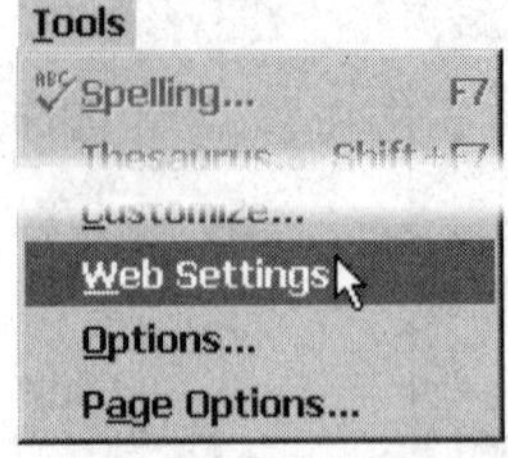

Figure 12.28 To check or change your database settings, choose Tools > Web Settings.

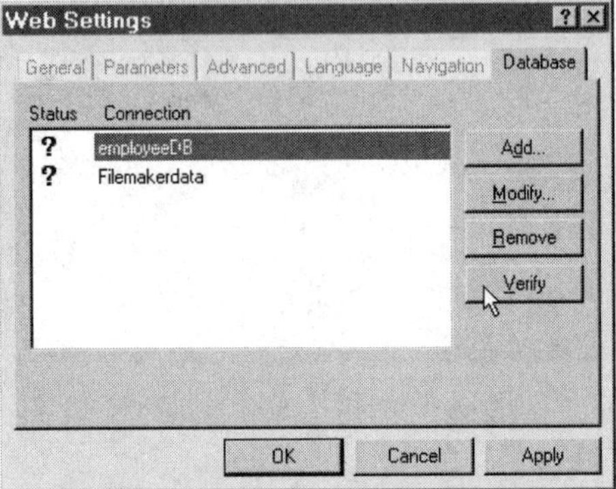

Figure 12.29 To check an unverified connection—marked by a question mark—click *Verify*.

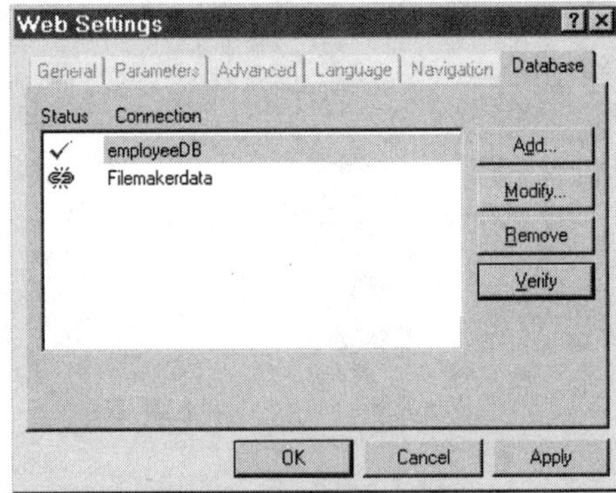

Figure 12.30 Verified connections are marked by a checkmark, connections with problems by a broken chain.

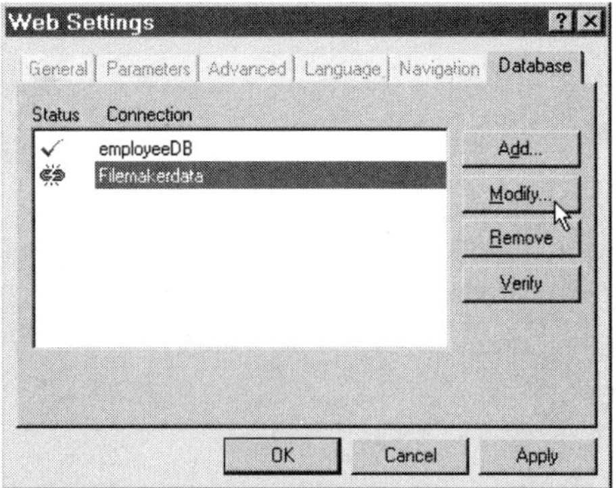

Figure 12.31 To change a database connection, select it in the Web Settings dialog box and click *Modify*.

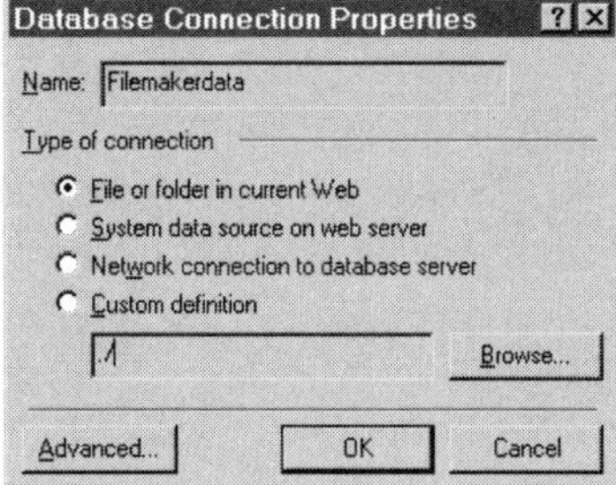

Figure 12.32 Use the Database Connection Properties dialog box to change the connection or to find a database's new location.

Changing a database connection

If you move a database to another location, the connection to it will stop working. Fortunately, FrontPage makes it easy to change any database connection.

To change a database connection

1. Choose Tools > Web Settings (**Figure 12.28**).
2. When the Web Settings dialog box appears, click the *Database* tab, choose one of the database connections listed, and then click *Modify* (**Figure 12.31**).
3. When the Database Connection Properties dialog box appears (**Figure 12.32**), change the *Type of connection* or click *Browse* to find a database's new location.
4. Click *OK* and the changes will be applied to the database connection.

✔ Tip

- The Database Connection Properties dialog box works identically to the New Database Connection dialog box (**Figure 12.22**). For details, see page 261.

To remove a database connection

1. Choose Tools > Web Settings (**Figure 12.28**).
2. When the Web Settings dialog box appears, click the *Database* tab, choose from the database connections listed, and then click *Remove*. The connection will be deleted.
3. Find any Web pages containing regions linked to the previously connected database and either delete the regions or connect them to another database by changing the connection. For details, see *To change a database connection* on the previous page.

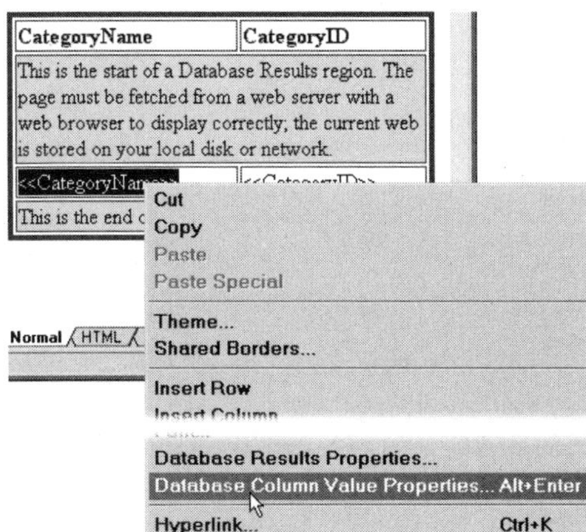

Figure 12.33 To change a database's column values, right-click the database field and choose *Database Column Value Properties*.

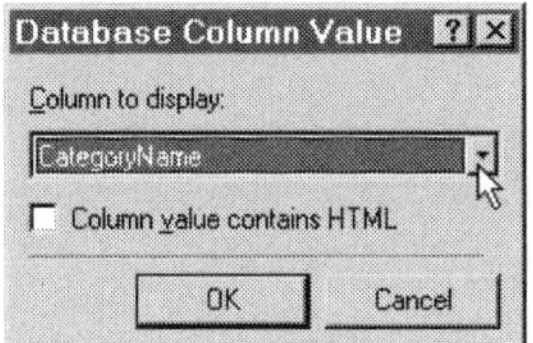

Figure 12.34 Use the *Column to display* drop-down menu to choose another column.

Changing column values

If you want to change the columns displayed in a database connection, FrontPage offers a quick way to do it without running the Database Results Wizard again.

To change column values in a database

1. While in page view, right-click the database field and choose *Database Column Value Properties* from the shortcut menu (Alt Enter) (**Figure 12.33**).
2. When the Database Column Value dialog box appears, use the *Column to display* drop-down menu to choose another column (**Figure 12.34**).
3. Click *OK* and the new column value will be pasted into the Web page.

13 Building Style Sheets and Dynamic Effects

Cascading style sheets, known as CSS, represent a huge leap forward for Web designers. Before CSS came along, you had much less control over the appearance and positioning of text in your Web pages. Now that version 4 and later Web browsers fully support CSS, it's much easier to lay out a Web page without constantly worrying about how it looks on different computer platforms.

CSS lets you apply a set of styles across your entire Web site, which means your pages will look more consistent. It also means a whole lot less work. Want to revise a headline style? Just make the change in your external style sheet. Bam, it's applied to the whole site. It's a tool too cool to be ignored. Take the time to learn how to use external style sheets and you just might be able to retire early—or at least have a weekend.

Using Dynamic HTML, you can make text and graphics fly onto your page. If used judiciously, it can give a page a bit of dramatic snap. Sometimes mistakenly called text "animation," DHTML uses a completely different process than animated graphics, which are explained in *Adding and Editing Multimedia* on page 171.

Since FrontPage is designed to shield you, as much as possible, from coding by hand, this chapter just focuses on what you need to get rolling. Explaining all the ins and outs of style sheets and DHTML would take another whole book. If you want to get down to the nitty-gritty of both, check out Jason Teague's *DHTML for the World Wide Web: Visual QuickStart Guide* (1999, Peachpit Press).

Using Cascading Style Sheets

Style sheets come in three varieties: *external style sheets* control styles across multiple pages or an entire Web site, *embedded style sheets* control styles for individual pages, and *inline styles* control individual page elements. Put them all together and you have Cascading Style Sheets.

With CSS you can define in one place exactly how you want all of your headings to appear on every page, right down to the size and color. At the same time, if you like, you can create a special heading style for a particular page—without disturbing your site-wide styles. That's the *cascading* part of CSS, which contains a set of definitions dictating which style takes precedence. In FrontPage, for example, if a single page contains inline styles, embedded styles, and a link to an external style sheet, the inline style comes first and the external style sheet last.

Inline styles are the least powerful of the three since their effect is confined to a single HTML element. They also are not implemented consistently in FrontPage 2000. For example, inline styles are automatically used whenever you choose Paragraph, Borders and Shading, or Position in the Format menu. But other choices in the Format menu still use traditional HTML. For those reasons, this chapter focuses on embedded and external style sheets.

Compared with embedded style sheets, external style sheets take a bit more work to set up. But because external style sheets can be applied site wide, they will save you hours of work in the long run. External style sheets offer another welcome bonus—faster downloads since each page doesn't have to contain all the HTML formatting data.

To activate cascading style sheets

1. Choose Tools > Page Options (**Figure 13.1**).
2. When the Page Options dialog box appears, click the *Compatibility* tab (**Figure 13.2**).
3. Use the *Browser versions* drop-down menu to select *4.0 browsers and later.*
4. In the *Technologies* section, make sure that *CSS 1.0 (formatting)* and *CSS 2.0 (positioning)* are checked (**Figure 13.3**). Click *OK* to close the dialog box and activate the cascading style sheets feature.

To activate DHTML

1. Choose Tools > Page Options (**Figure 13.1**).
2. When the Page Options dialog box appears, click the *Compatibility* tab (**Figure 13.2**).
3. Use the *Browser versions* drop-down menu to select *4.0 browsers and later.*
4. In the *Technologies* section, make sure that *Dynamic HTML* is checked (**Figure 13.4**). Click *OK* and DHTML will be activated for use in your pages.

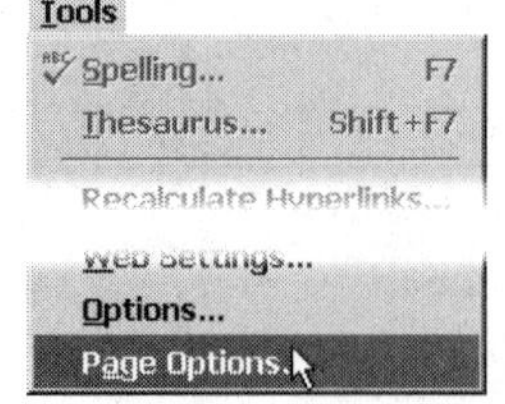

Figure 13.1 To activate CSS or DHTML, choose Tools > Page Options.

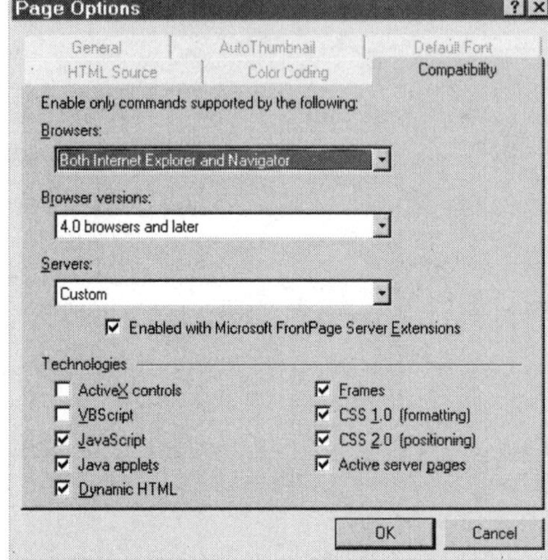

Figure 13.2 Click the Page Options' *Compatibility* tab to set which browser technologies your pages will use.

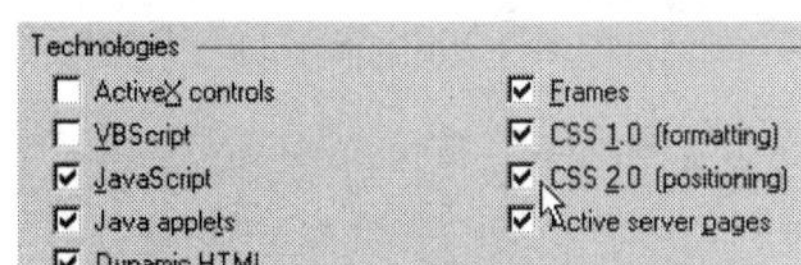

Figure 13.3 To activate CSS, make sure that *CSS 1.0 (formatting)* and *CSS 2.0 (positioning)* are checked in the *Technologies* section.

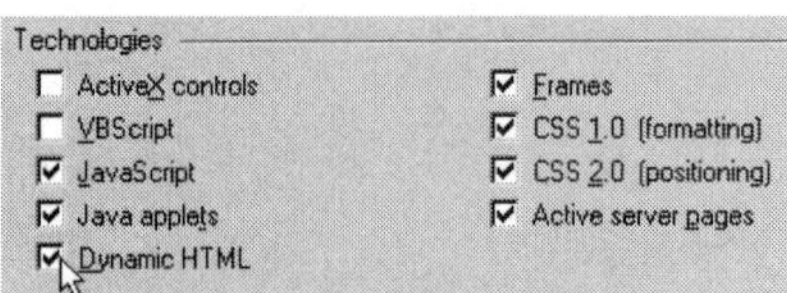

Figure 13.4 To activate DHTML, make sure that *Dynamic HTML* is checked in the *Technologies* section.

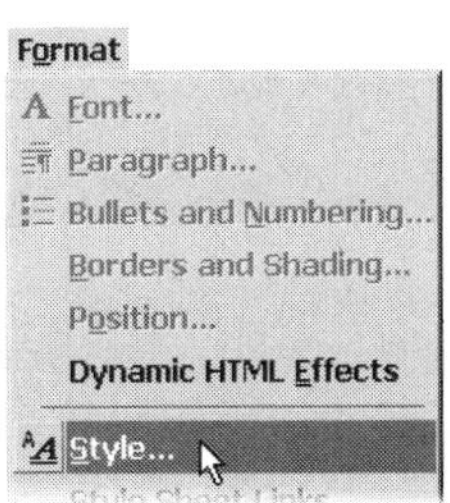

Figure 13.5 To reach the Style dialog box, choose Format > Style (left) or click the Style toolbar (right).

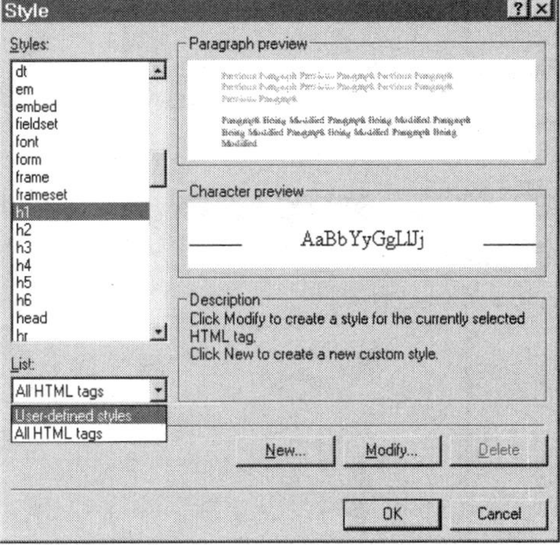

Figure 13.6 To create a new style, click *New* in the Style dialog box.

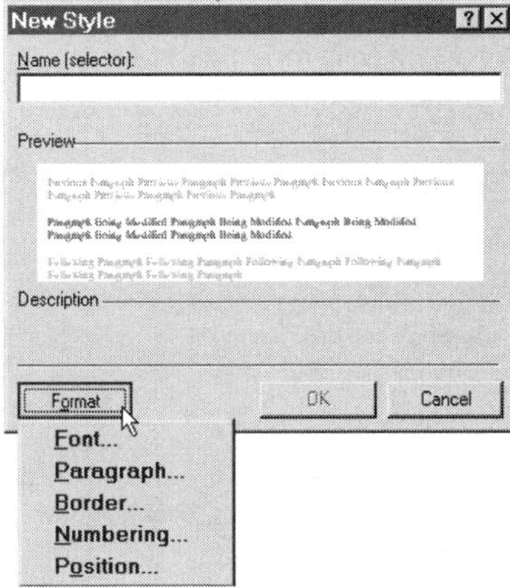

Figure 13.7 When the New Style dialog box appears, type a distinctive name into the *Name (selector)* text box and pick one of the *Format* drop-down menu items—*Font, Paragraph, Border, Numbering*, or *Position*.

Creating and Editing Embedded Style Sheets

An embedded style sheet can only be used for the single page in which it was created. To apply styles across multiple pages or an entire Web site, see *To create an external style sheet* on page 276. By the way, just in case you come across the term, embedded style sheets are sometimes called *internal* style sheets.

To create an embedded style sheet

1. Make sure you're in page view and choose Format > Style or click the Style toolbar if it is active (**Figure 13.5**).
2. When the Style dialog box appears (**Figure 13.6**), click *New*.
3. When the New Style dialog box appears, type a distinctive name into the *Name (selector)* text box and click *Format* (**Figure 13.7**).
4. Pick one of the *Format* drop-down menu items—*Font, Paragraph, Border, Numbering*, or *Position*—and use the dialog box that appears to choose properties for your new style. Once you've made one set of choices for, say, *Font*, you can use the *Format* drop-down menu to add *Border* properties.

(continued)

5. Once you're done, inspect the results in the *Preview* area, and click *OK* (**Figure 13.8**). The new style—and any other HTML styles that you change—will be listed as a *User-defined style* in the Style dialog box (**Figure 13.9**).

6. If you want to create another new style, click *New* again and repeat steps 3-5. When you're done creating styles, click *OK* in the Style dialog box and the style will be embedded within the page's HTML header code (**Figure 13.10**).

✔ Tip

- FrontPage encloses embedded style sheets with pairs of comment tags <!-- and --> to hide the coding from version 3 and earlier Web browsers. Otherwise, all that coding would show up in the browser window—not a pretty sight.

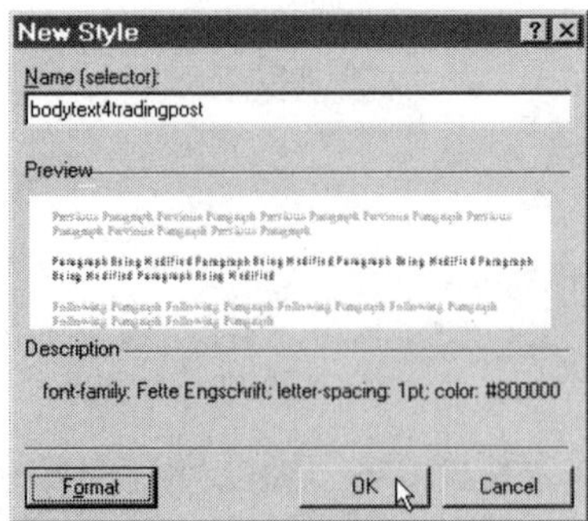

Figure 13.8 Once you've defined your new style, inspect it in the *Preview* area, and then click *OK*.

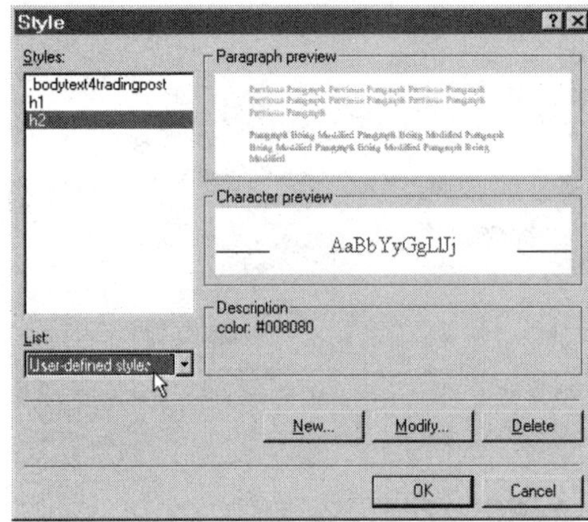

Figure 13.9 A new or modified style will be listed as a *User-defined style* in the Style dialog box.

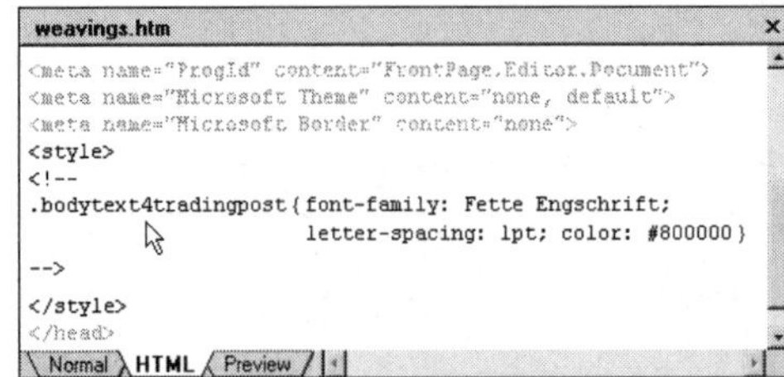

Figure 13.10 The HTML for embedded style sheets is placed in the header code of your Web page, hence the moniker *embedded*.

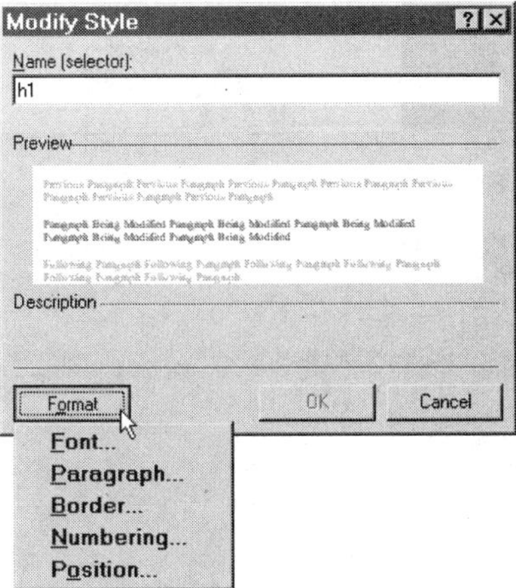

Figure 13.11 The Modify Style dialog box works just like the New Style dialog box.

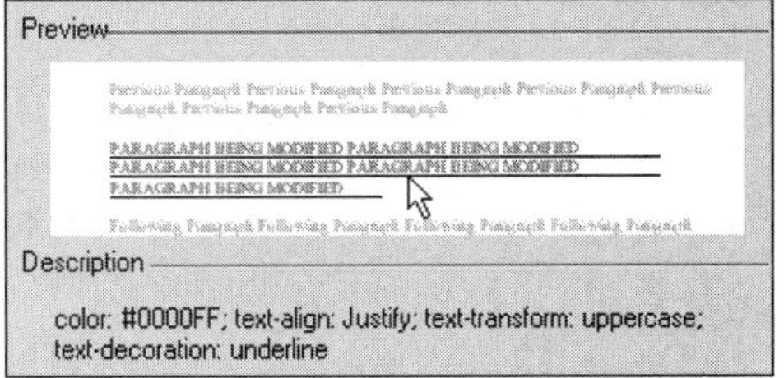

Figure 13.12 Once you modify a style, you can inspect the changes in the Modify Style dialog box's *Preview* and *Description* areas.

To edit an embedded style sheet

1. Make sure you're in page view and choose Format > Style or click the Style toolbar if it is active (**Figure 13.5**).
2. When the Style dialog box appears (**Figure 13.6**), use the *List* drop-down menu to find a style you've already created (*User-defined styles*) or a standard HTML tag (*All HTML tags*). Select in the *Styles* list the style you want to change and click *Modify*.
3. When the Modify Style dialog box appears, the item will be listed in the *Name (selector)* text box (**Figure 13.11**). Click *Format* and choose an option from the drop-down menu.
4. Based on your choice, the related dialog box will appear. Make your changes, click *OK* and they will be displayed in the Modify Style dialog box's *Preview* area and listed in the *Description* area (**Figure 13.12**).
5. If you want to change other aspects of the style as well, use the *Format* drop-down menu to make additional choices. Once you're done, click *OK* in the Modify Style dialog box and you'll be returned to the Style dialog box (**Figure 13.9**).
6. If you want to change another style, select it in the *Styles* list and click *Modify*.
7. When you're done changing styles, click *OK* in the Style dialog box and the changes will be made within the page's HTML code.

Building External Style Sheets

Using external style sheets is a three-step process: First you create the sheet, then you build it or edit it by defining its styles, and finally you link your Web site or individual pages to the sheet.

Parts of the process are similar to working with embedded style sheets, but there are some key differences. For that reason, the entire process of creating, building, editing, and linking external style sheets is laid out here in detail.

To create an external style sheet

1. Choose File > New > Page (**Figure 13.13**).
2. When the New dialog box appears, click the *Style Sheets* tab (**Figure 13.14**).
3. If you want to start from scratch with a blank style sheet, choose the *Normal Style Sheet*. Otherwise, choose one of the style sheet templates listed, which you can easily tweak later to suit your purposes by editing it.

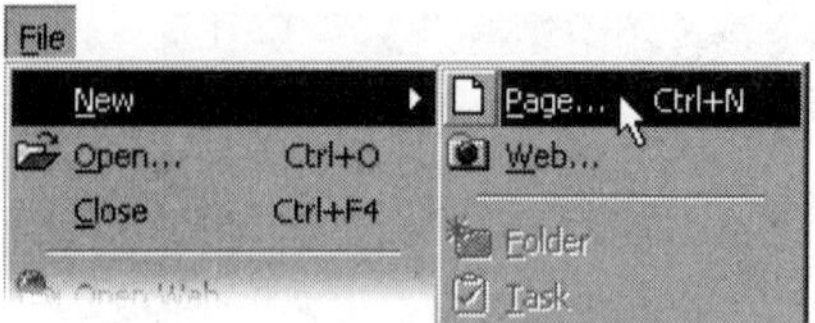

Figure 13.13 To create an external style sheet, choose File > New > Page.

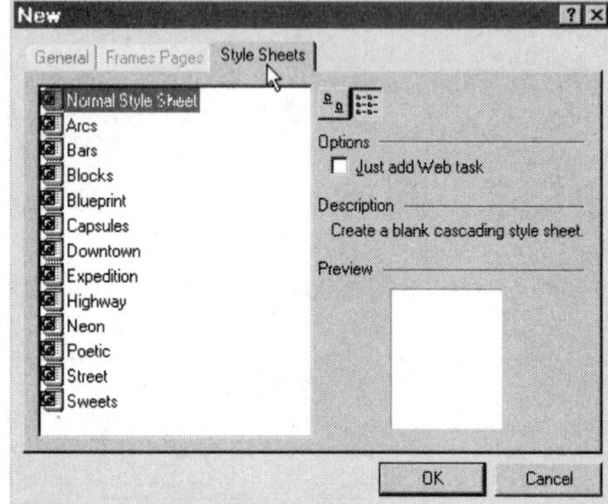

Figure 13.14 When the New dialog box appears, click the *Style Sheets* tab and choose *Normal Style Sheet* or one of the style sheet templates.

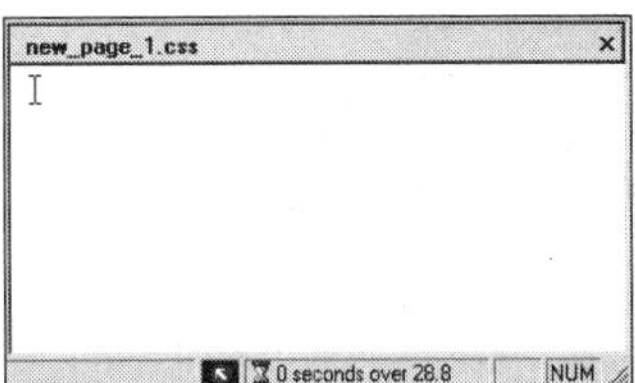

Figure 13.15 Until you add to it by defining styles, there's not much to see in a new external style sheet.

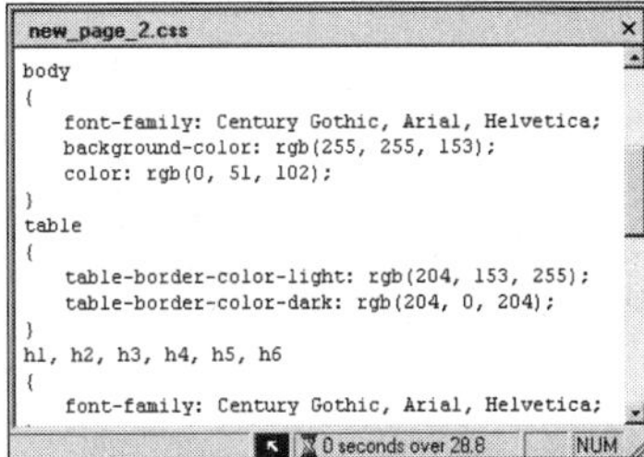

Figure 13.16 A template-based external style sheet gives you a head start by including definitions of a variety of HTML elements.

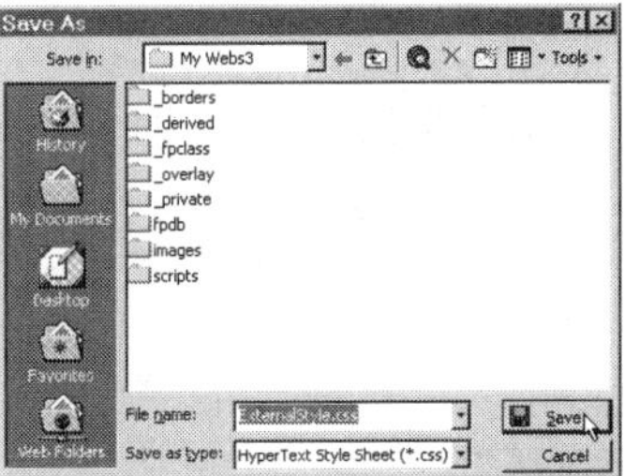

Figure 13.17 When saving and naming an external style sheet, be sure to keep the .css suffix.

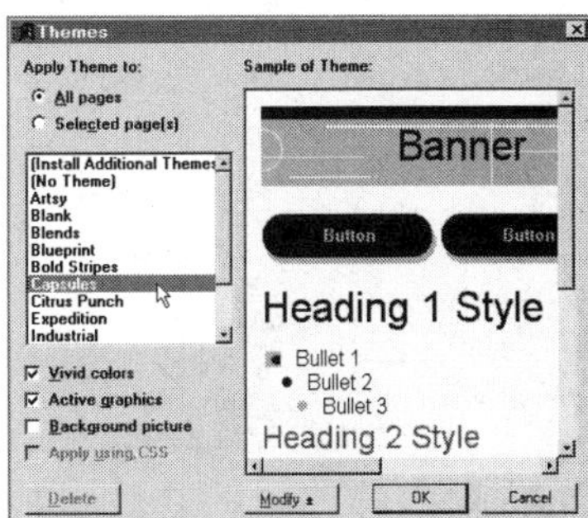

Figure 13.18 You can preview some of the template-based style sheets in the Themes dialog box.

4. Click *OK* and FrontPage will create a page, give it a .css suffix, and display the page in the main window. If it's a new style sheet, there's not much to see (**Figure 13.15**). If it's based on a template, it already will include definitions for a variety of HTML elements (**Figure 13.16**). In either case, save the page (Ctrl S). When the Save As dialog box appears, give the page a distinctive name, making sure to keep the .css suffix (**Figure 13.17**). You're now ready to build your new style sheet by defining styles for it. Or, if you've used a template for your style sheet, you're ready to modify the styles that already exist within it. For details, see *To build an external style sheet* on page 278 or *To edit an external style sheet* on page 280.

✔ Tips

- When creating a new style sheet, do not press Ctrl N or you'll bypass the New dialog box and wind up with a new HTML page, when what you want is a CSS page.
- While the New dialog box includes a text description of the various style sheet templates, the *Preview* area isn't available. Many of the templates, however, are based on FrontPage themes, which you can take a peek at by choosing Format > Theme to reach the Themes dialog box (**Figure 13.18**).
- If this is the first time you've created a style sheet, the Style toolbar will pop up right in the middle of the main window. Get it out of the way by dragging it to the side of your monitor window or drag it into the Standard toolbar where it will become a button.

To build an external style sheet

1. To open the style sheet, double-click its icon in the Folder List (**Figure 13.19**). If you're starting from scratch, the style sheet will be completely blank (**Figure 13.20**).
2. Choose Format > Style or click the Style toolbar if it is active (**Figure 13.5**).
3. When the Style dialog box appears (**Figure 13.21**), select from the *Styles* list an HTML tag for which you want to create a style, and then click *Modify*.
4. When the Modify Style dialog box appears, the HTML tag you selected will be listed in the *Name (selector)* text box (**Figure 13.11**). Click *Format*, then choose *Font, Paragraph, Border, Numbering*, or *Position* and use the related dialog box to modify the HTML tag. Your style changes will appear in the Modify Style dialog box's *Preview* and *Description* areas.
5. If you want to change other aspects of the HTML tag, use the *Format* drop-down menu to make additional choices. Once you're done, click *OK* in the Modify Style dialog box and you'll be returned to the Style dialog box where your new style will be listed in the *User-defined styles* (**Figure 13.22**).
6. To create styles for other HTML tags in your style sheet, use the Style dialog box's *List* drop-down menu to switch back to *All HTML tags*. Repeat steps 3-5 until you've created styles for all the HTML tags you want.

Figure 13.19 To open a style sheet, double-click its icon in the Folder List.

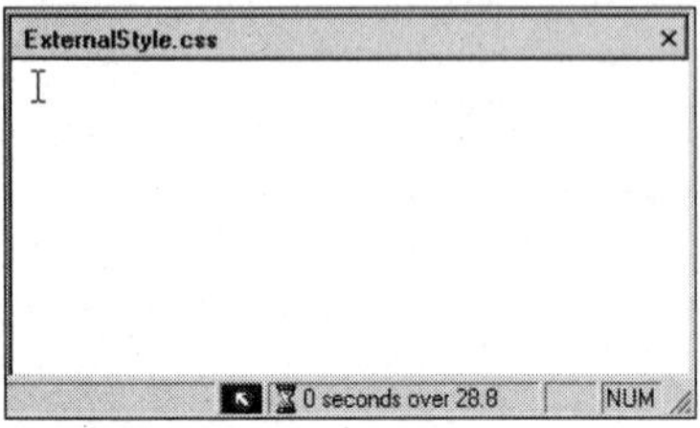

Figure 13.20 If you're starting from scratch, a new external style sheet will be completely blank.

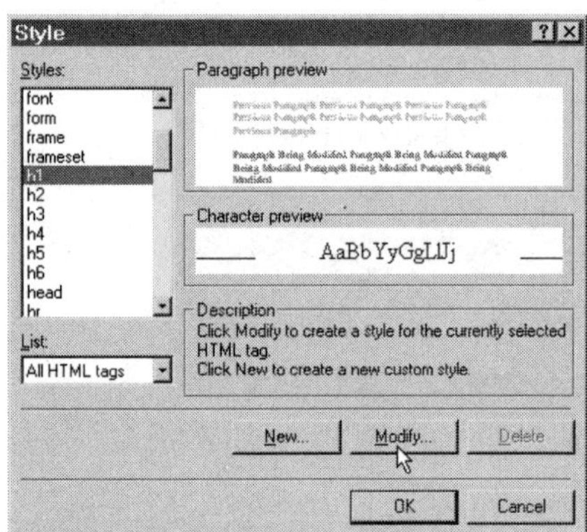

Figure 13.21 Use the *Styles* list in the Style dialog box to select an HTML tag you want to modify.

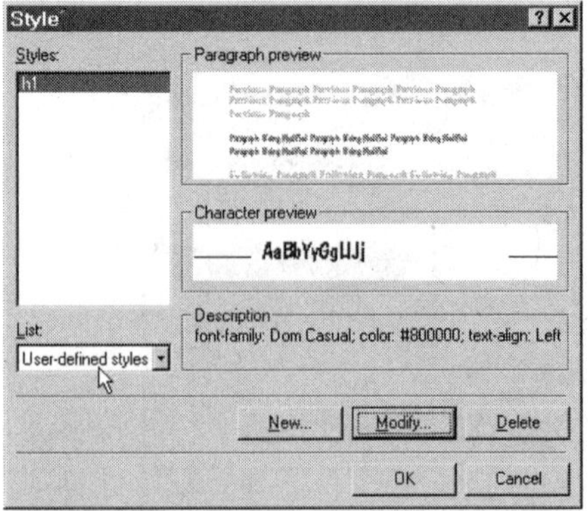

Figure 13.22 After you've defined a style, the Style dialog box will include it in the *User-defined styles* list and offer a preview.

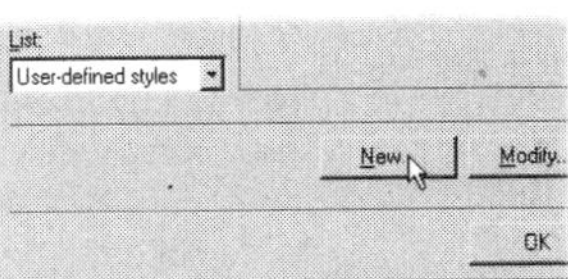

Figure 13.23 To create a custom style in the Style dialog box, switch to *User-defined styles* and click *New*.

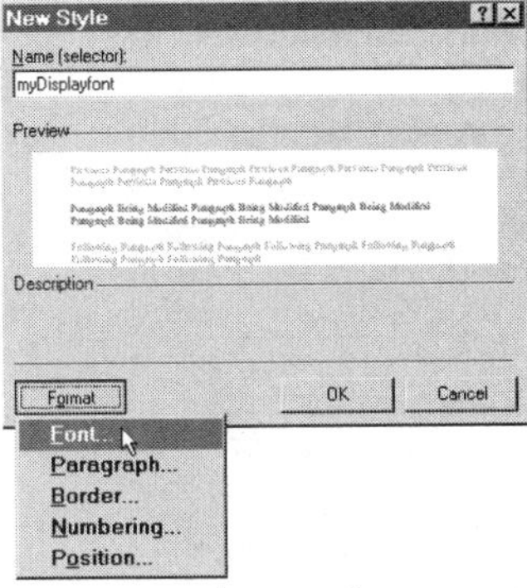

Figure 13.24 When creating a new style, give it a distinctive name and use the *Format* button's choices to define it.

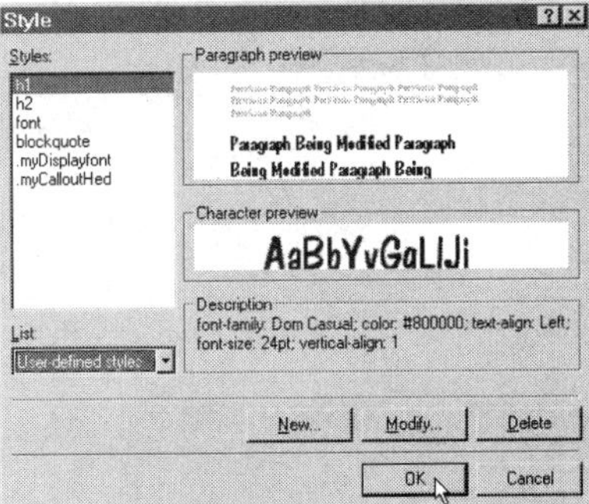

Figure 13.25 The Style dialog box will list all your new styles as you define them in your external style sheet.

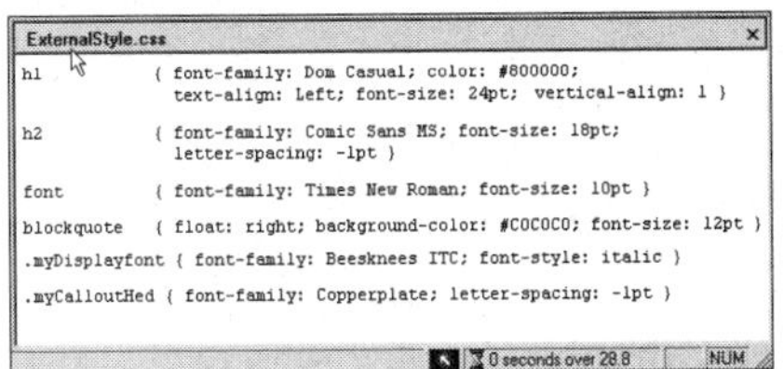

Figure 13.26 After you have defined your styles, the once-blank external style sheet will list all the additions that will be applied.

7. If you want to create some new custom styles, use the Style dialog box's *List* drop-down menu to switch to *User-defined styles* and then click *New* (**Figure 13.23**).
8. When the New Style dialog box appears, type a distinctive name for your custom style into the *Name (selector)* text box and click *Format* (**Figure 13.24**).
9. Choose *Font*, *Paragraph*, *Border*, *Numbering*, or *Position*, and use the related dialog boxes to define your new custom style. As you proceed, the style changes will appear in the New Style dialog box's *Preview* and *Description* areas.
10. Once you're done, click *OK* in the New Style dialog box and you'll be returned to the Style dialog box where your custom styles—along with the HTML tags you customized—will be listed in the *User-defined styles* (**Figure 13.25**).
11. Once you're satisfied with your custom styles, click *OK* and the changes will be added to your external style sheet (**Figure 13.26**). Save the page (Ctrl S) and you're ready to apply it to your Web site's pages. See *To link to external style sheets* on page 283.

To edit an external style sheet

1. To open the style sheet, double-click its icon in the Folder List (**Figure 13.27**).
2. Choose Format > Style or click the Style toolbar if it is active (**Figure 13.5**).
3. When the Style dialog box appears (**Figure 13.28**), select an item in the left-hand *Styles* list that you want to edit, and then click *Modify*.
4. When the Modify Style dialog box appears, the style you selected will be listed in the *Name (selector)* text box (**Figure 13.29**). Click *Format* and choose an option from the drop-down menu.
5. Make your changes in the dialog box that appears, then click *OK*. Continue clicking *Format* and choosing options from the drop-down menu until you've made all your changes.
6. Click *OK* and the changes will be previewed and listed in the Style dialog box (**Figure 13.30**).
7. If you want to change the style of another item, select it in the *Styles* list, click *Modify*, and repeat steps 4–6.
8. Once you've made all the style changes you want, click *OK* in the Style dialog box and the style sheet will list all your style changes.

Figure 13.27 To edit an external style sheet, double-click its icon in the Folder List.

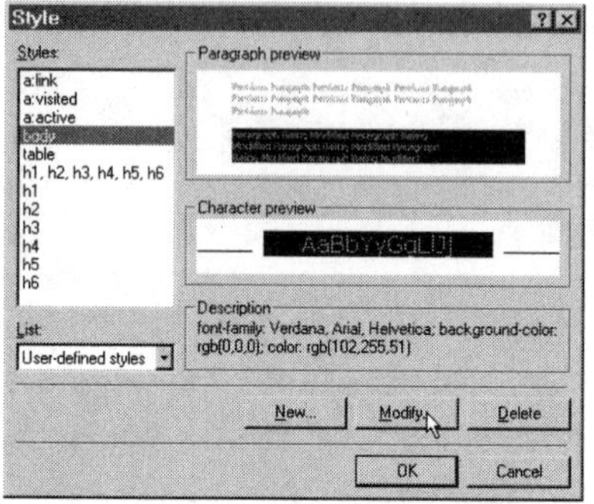

Figure 13.28 When the Style dialog box appears, select an item in the left-hand *Styles* list that you want to edit and click *Modify*.

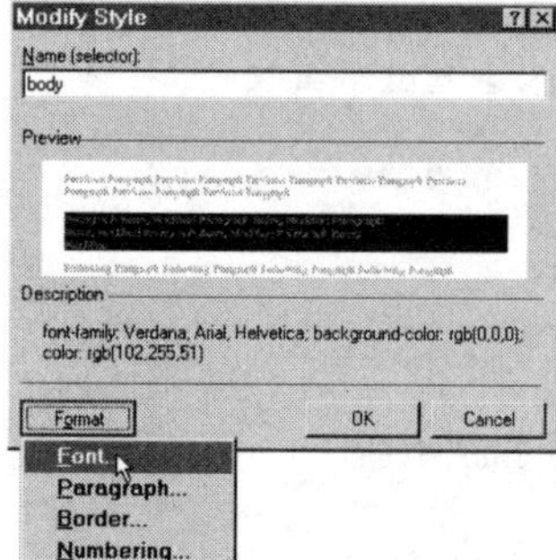

Figure 13.29 Use the *Format* drop-down menu options to change aspects of the selected style.

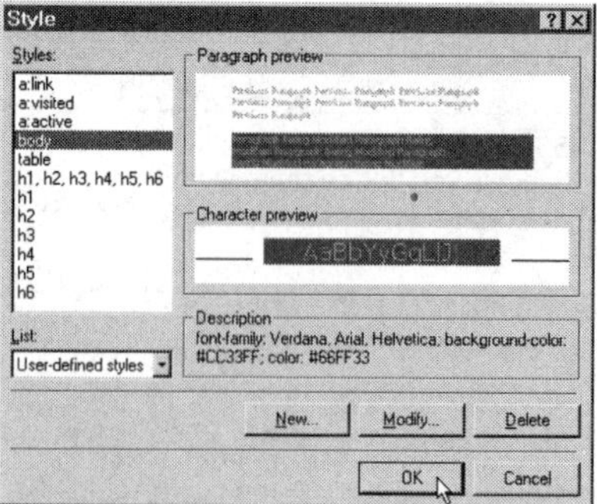

Figure 13.30 Once you've made your changes, the Style dialog box will present a preview of the edited style.

Table 13.1

Most Common Font Families		
SERIF	WINDOWS	MACINTOSH
	Times	Times
	Times New Roman	Palatino
SANS SERIF	WINDOWS	MACINTOSH
	Arial	Geneva
		Helvetica

Table 13.2

CSS Generic Font Values	
CSS VALUE	SOME EXAMPLES
serif	Times, Garamond, Bodoni
sans serif	Arial, Helvetica, Geneva, Futura
monospace	Courier, Monaco, Letter Gothic
cursive (script)	Mistral, Park Avenue
fantasy (decorative)	Copperplate Gothic, VAG Round

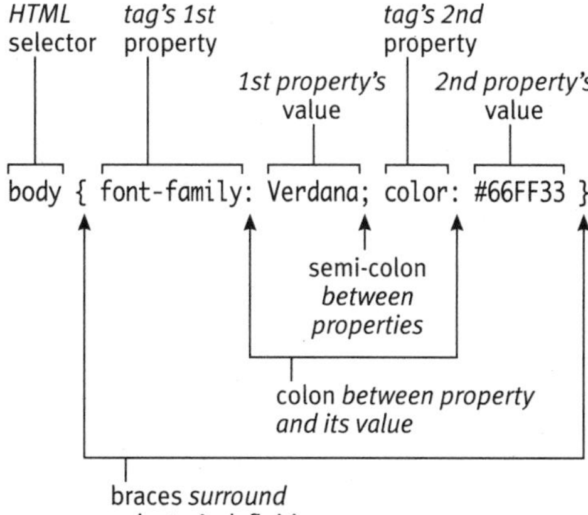

Figure 13.31 Each CSS style contains a *selector*, and at least one *property* and one *value*, which are set off by *braces*, *colons*, or *semi-colons*.

Specifying Multiple Fonts in External Style Sheets

Being able to specify multiple fonts in your styles is one of the best reasons for using external style sheets. In effect, you're telling the visitor's Web browser to use Font A and, if it can't find that on the visitor's computer, then use Font B, and if Font B's not present, then use Font C, and so on. That way if your Web visitor doesn't have the oh-so-cool font you've specified, at least they can see it in something roughly similar.

For example, if your first-choice font family for H1 headings is a classic Oldstyle face, such as Bembo, then you'll want to specify similar looking but perhaps more common serif faces, such as Garamond and Caslon, as the second- and third-choice font families. As a backup plan for site visitors who have very few fonts on their computers, you also can include *generic* font family specifications so that their Web browsers will at least use a serif face. For a list of the most common font families found on computers, see **Table 13.1**. For a list of CSS's generic font specifications, see **Table 13.2**.

Unfortunately, FrontPage includes no way to specify multiple fonts without coding directly in the external style sheet. Fortunately, however, if you've already created an external style sheet it's pretty easy to add the multiple font specs.

Still, it's helpful to understand a little about how CSS styles are constructed (**Figure 13.31**). Each HTML element (known as a *selector* in CSS jargon) has at least one *property* and a *value* for that property. It's also possible for a selector to have several properties, and each property to have several values, such as multiple fonts.

To specify multiple fonts

1. First create a style sheet following *To build an external style sheet* on page 278, then open it by double-clicking its icon in the Folder List (**Figure 13.19**).
2. When the external style sheet opens, find the font definition to which you want to add multiple fonts (**Figure 13.32**).
3. Click your cursor at the end of the first font family listed (**Figure 13.33**), immediately in front of the semi-colon.
4. Type a comma, a space, and the name of a second font family you want included in the definition. Continue adding font families, preceding each with a comma and space until you've added all the font families you want specified (**Figure 13.34**). Be sure to add a generic font specification as well.
5. Save the page (Ctrl S) and you're ready to apply it to your Web site's pages. See *To link to external style sheets* on the next page.

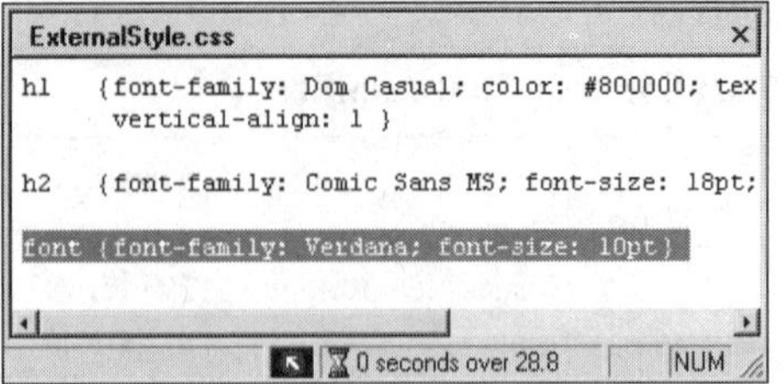

Figure 13.32 Find within the external style sheet the font definition to which you want to add multiple fonts. This example uses the *font* selector, but you also could specify multiple fonts for *h1*, *h2*, or any selector that accepts fonts.

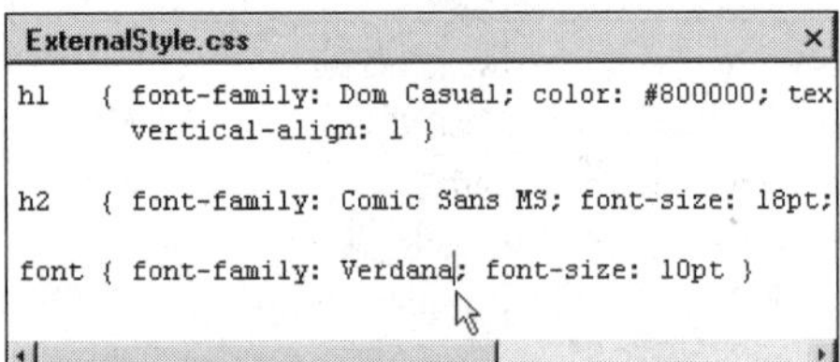

Figure 13.33 To list additional fonts, click between the font name and the semi-colon.

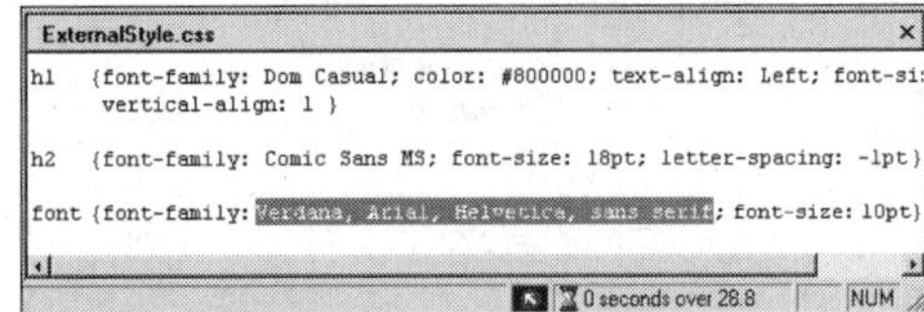

Figure 13.34 Separate each font you add with a comma and a blank space, then save the page (Ctrl S).

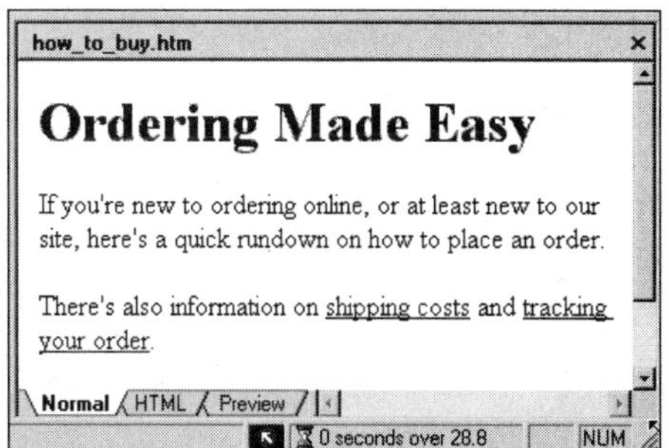

Figure 13.35 Open the page to which you want the external style sheet applied.

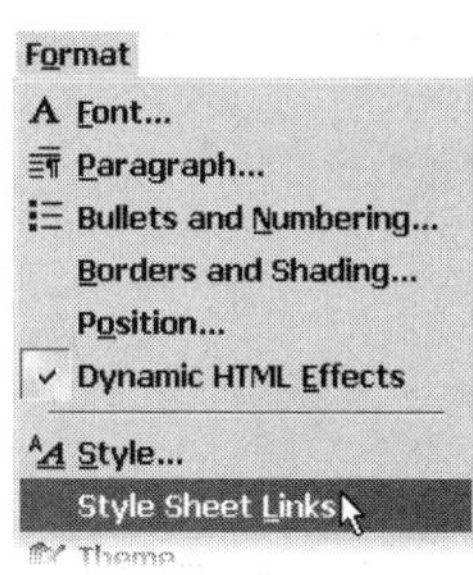

Figure 13.36 To link the page to the external style sheet, choose Format > Style Sheet Links.

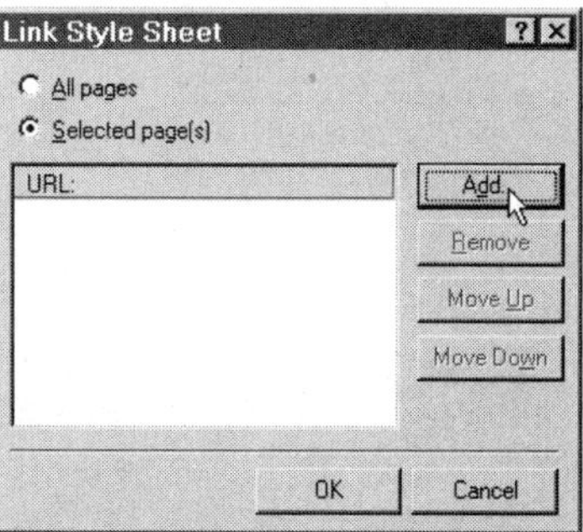

Figure 13.37 When the Link Style Sheet dialog box appears, choose *All pages* to apply the style sheet to your entire Web site or *Selected page(s)* to apply it just to the current page. Click *Add* to find the style sheet.

Linking to External Style Sheets

You can define an external style sheet to your heart's content, but you must link pages to that style sheet for its styles to be applied.

To link to external style sheets

1. Make sure you're in page view and open the page you want linked to the external style sheet (**Figure 13.35**).
2. Choose Format > Style Sheet Links (**Figure 13.36**).
3. When the Link Style Sheet dialog box appears (**Figure 13.37**), choose *All pages* if you want to apply the external style sheet to your entire Web site. If you want to apply the style sheet to only the current page, choose *Selected page(s)*. Click *Add*.

(continued)

4. When the Select Hyperlink dialog box appears, navigate to the style sheet you want to use, select it, and its URL or pathname will be pasted into the *URL* text box (**Figure 13.38**). Click *OK*.

5. The external style sheet will appear in the Link Style Sheet dialog box (**Figure 13.39**). Click *OK* and the style sheet will be applied to the page(s) you selected (**Figure 13.40**).

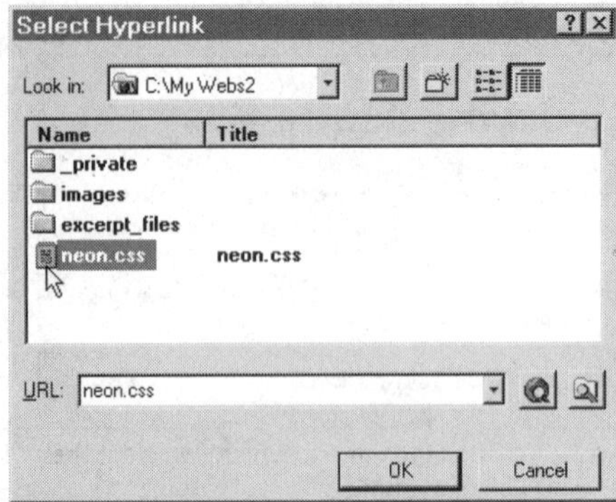

Figure 13.38 Use the Select Hyperlink dialog box to navigate to the style sheet you want to use.

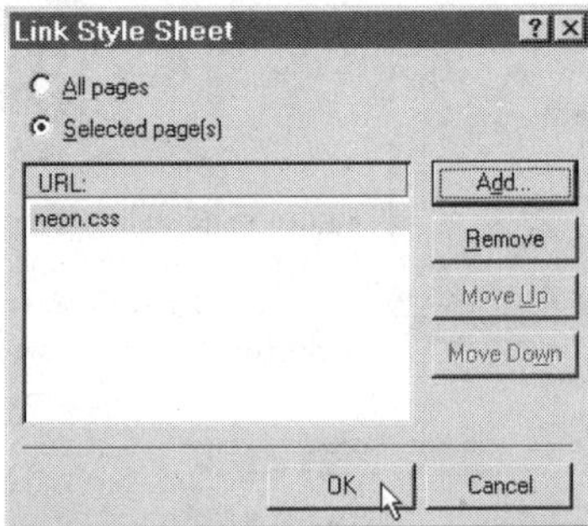

Figure 13.39 Once you've added the style sheet, click *OK* to apply it to the selected pages.

Figure 13.40 After applying the style sheet, the Web page from Figure 13.35 displays the new style.

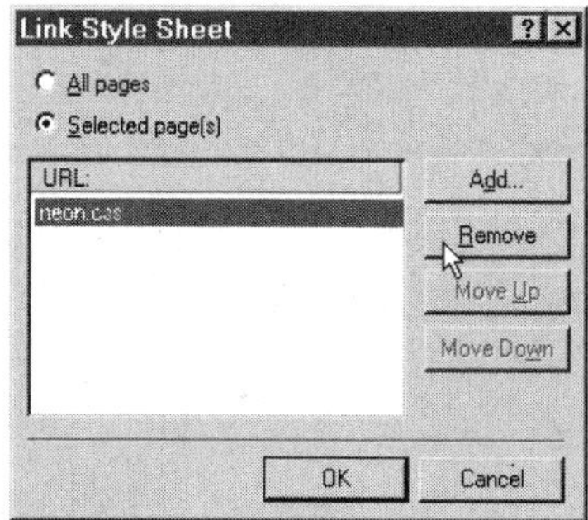

Figure 13.41 To remove a style sheet link, select it and click *Remove*.

To remove links to external style sheets

1. Make sure you're in page view and open the page that's linked to the external style sheet.
2. Choose Format > Style Sheet Links (**Figure 13.36**).
3. When the Link Style Sheet dialog box appears, choose *All pages* if you want to remove all the Web site's links to the external style sheet. If you want to remove the link only for the current page, choose *Selected page(s)*. Select the style sheet in the *URL* window, and click *Remove* (**Figure 13.41**).
4. Click *OK* and the selected pages will lose the styles previously applied by the external style sheet.

Deleting Styles

Whether you're working with embedded styles or external style sheets, you can get rid of individual custom styles at any time. And if you've customized an HTML tag, such as H1, the same process will return the tag to its standard definition.

To delete custom styles

1. Make sure you're in page view and choose Format > Style or click the Style toolbar if it is active (**Figure 13.5**).
2. When the Style dialog box appears (**Figure 13.42**), select in the *Styles* list the user-defined style you want to delete and click *Delete*. The custom style will be removed from the Styles list (**Figure 13.43**).

✔ Tips

- Despite that word Delete, when it comes to standard HTML tags, this procedure is more like Undo. For example, in step 2 if you delete a custom version of a standard HTML tag, such as H1, it will disappear from the *User-defined styles* list But it will still appear in the *All HTML tags* list—just without the custom style it had previously (**Figure 13.44**).
- When you delete a custom style, it will be removed from the Styles list without any warning, so check the *Preview* area to make sure you've selected the style you really want to delete.

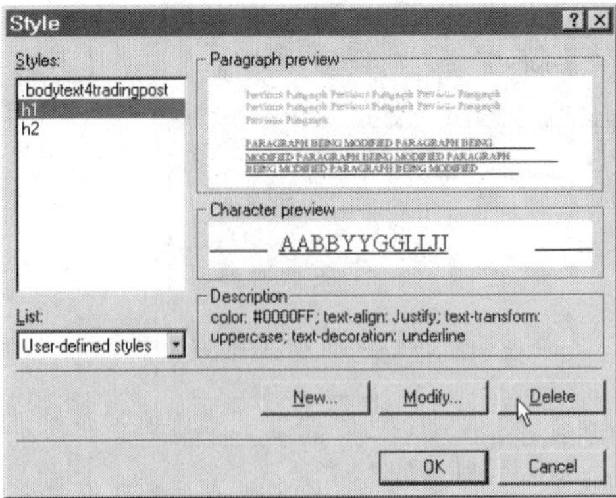

Figure 13.42 Select in the *Styles* list the user-defined style you want to remove and click *Delete*.

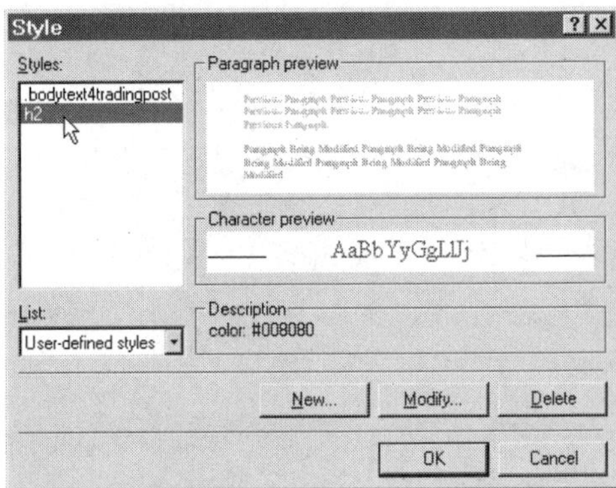

Figure 13.43 Once deleted, the customized *h1* disappears from the *User-defined styles* list.

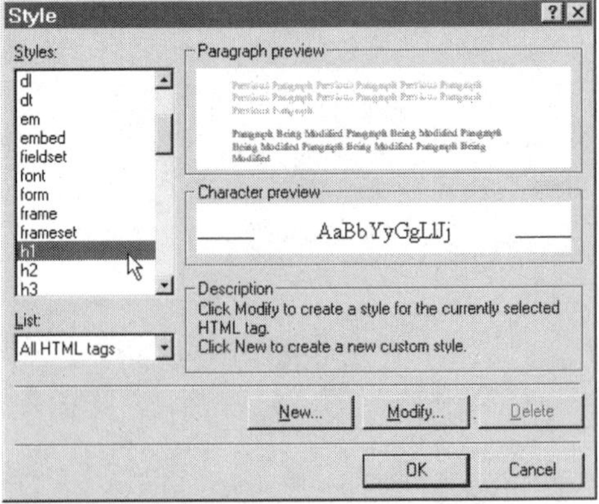

Figure 13.44 Even though you deleted its *custom* style definition, a *generic* h1 tag remains part of your list of *All HTML tags*.

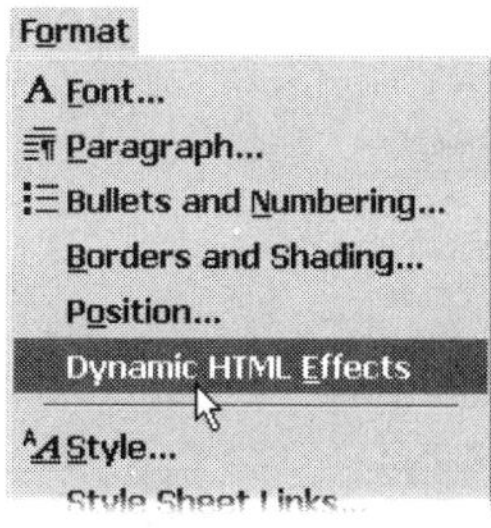

Figure 13.45 To apply DHTML, make sure the DHTML Effects toolbar is visible by choosing Format > Dynamic HTML Effects.

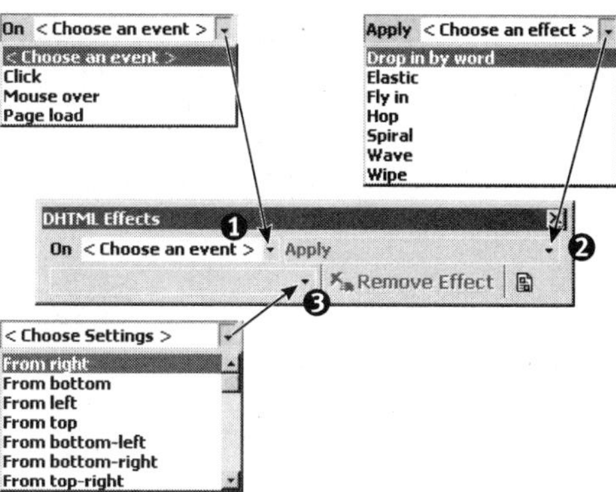

Figure 13.46 The drop-down menu choices in the DHTML Effects toolbar vary depending on which page element you select.

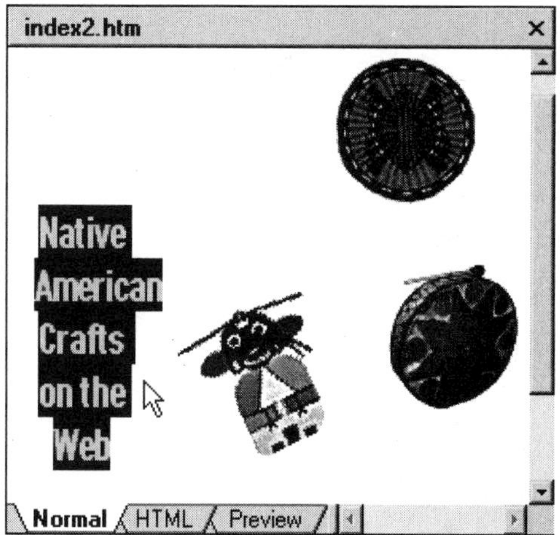

Figure 13.47 To apply an effect, first select a page element.

Using Dynamic HTML Effects

DHTML can be used to zip text around your pages, send graphics spiraling, and trigger events as visitors mouse around your site. The exact DHTML options available vary, depending on which elements you select on a page. In general, there are more DHTML options for text than, for example, there are for graphics. DHTML tags work with version 4 or later Microsoft Internet Explorer or Netscape Navigator. Earlier browsers will simply show static—but correct—versions of your pages, which means browser compatibility is one less thing to worry about.

To apply dynamic effects

1. Make sure the DHTML Effects toolbar is visible by choosing Format > Dynamic HTML Effects (**Figure 13.45**). The toolbar will appear (**Figure 13.46**), and you can move it to a convenient spot on your screen.
2. Select the page element to which you want to apply DHTML (**Figure 13.47**).
3. Use the toolbar's *On* drop-down menu ❶ to select *when* the effect will be applied.
4. Use the toolbar's *Apply* drop-down menu ❷ to select *which* effect will be applied.
5. Depending on your choice in step 4, use the <*Choose Settings*> drop-down menu ❸ to further define the effect.

(continued)

6. If you want, select another page element and apply DHTML effects to it by repeating steps 3–5.
7. Once you're done setting the effects, click the *Preview* tab in FrontPage's main window to see how the effects look (**Figure 13.48**).

✔ Tip

- If you need to adjust the effect, click the *Normal* tab in FrontPage's main window, then click the toolbar and use the toolbar drop-down menus to change the settings. When you want to check the effect, be sure to click the *Preview* tab again.

To remove a dynamic effect

1. Select the page element whose effect you want to cancel.
2. Click on the DHTML Effects toolbar, then click *Remove Effect* (**Figure 13.49**). The effect will be canceled.

Figure 13.48 Use the *Preview* tab to see the final effect. In this example, *Drop in by word* was applied to the headline and *Fly in* to the graphic.

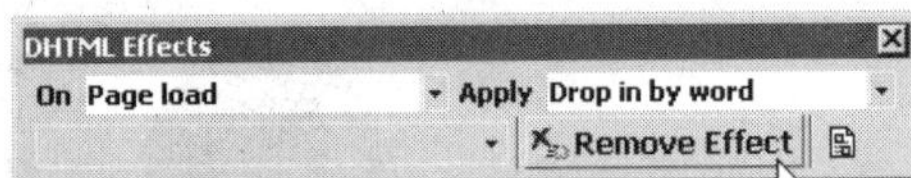

Figure 13.49 To cancel an effect, select the page element and click *Remove Effect* in the DHTML Effects toolbar.

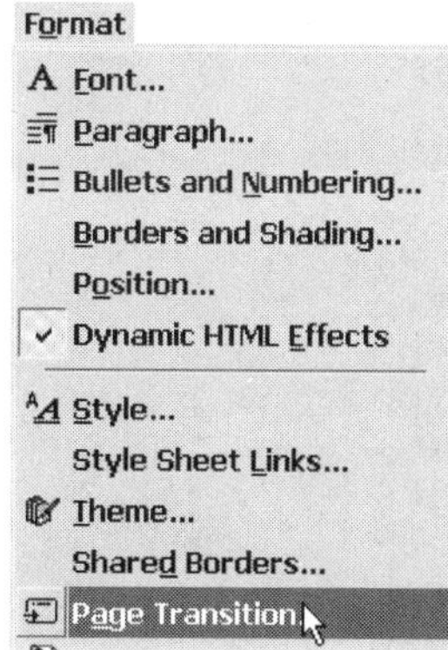

Figure 13.50 To add page transitions, choose Format > Page Transition.

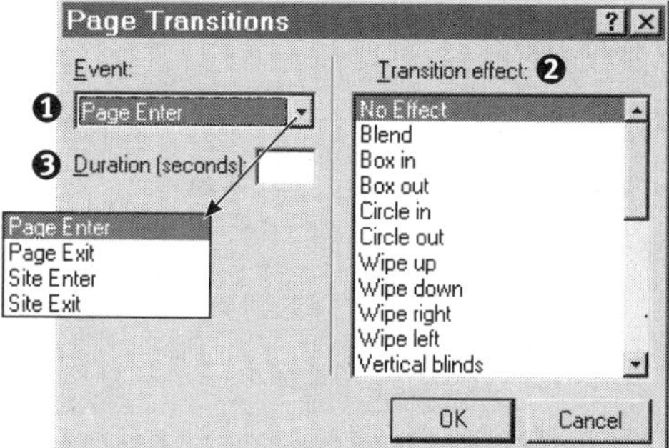

Figure 13.51 Use the Page Transitions dialog box to select an *Event, a Transition effect*, and a *Duration*.

Using Page Transitions

This particular DHTML feature lets you create video-like transitions when a site visitor enters or leaves a page or your site. FrontPage includes more than 20 transition effects. While they are very cool, use page transitions only if you're creating a corporate intranet where you know for certain that *everyone* is using the Windows version of the Internet Explorer 4 or 5 browsers. Page transitions don't work with other browsers, so be careful not to exclude those users.

To add page transitions

1. Make sure you're in page view and the *Normal* tab is selected. Click anywhere in the page and choose Format > Page Transition (**Figure 13.50**).
2. When the Page Transitions dialog box appears (**Figure 13.51**), use the *Event* drop-down menu ❶ to select *when* the effect will be applied.
3. Use the *Transition effect* scrolling menu box ❷ to select *which* effect will be applied.
4. Enter a number in the *Duration (seconds)* text box ❸ to set *how long* the transition will take to complete.
5. Once you've made your selections, click *OK*. Click the *Preview* tab in FrontPage's main window to see how the transition looks.

To remove page transitions

1. Make sure you're in page view and the *Normal* tab is selected. Click anywhere in the page and choose Format > Page Transition (**Figure 13.50**).
2. When the Page Transitions dialog box appears (**Figure 13.51**), use the *Transition effect* scrolling menu box ❷ to select *No Effect*, which is the first item in the list.
3. Click *OK* and the transition will be removed.

PART IV

MANAGING AND PUBLISHING WEB SITES

MANAGING WEB SITE WORKFLOW

Like most publishing, Web publishing is usually a team sport. Writers create stories, editors proof copy and add headlines, artists produce graphics and illustrations, and designers lay it all out. Keeping track of who's doing what on a Web site can be a challenge. Sometimes even if you're doing it all yourself, it's easy to forget key tasks. FrontPage's tasks and reports views can be a big help in managing the workflow on the typical Web site with a zillion and one details.

You can use most of FrontPage's workflow features no matter how you're set up. Others, such as the system of checking Web files in and out (explained on page 313), will work only if your Web server has the FrontPage Server Extensions installed. For more on the extensions, see pages 319 and 344.

Creating Tasks

Essentially you have two choices in using FrontPage to create tasks: a close-focus, from-the-ground-up approach or a broader, top-down approach. Each has its place.

In the close-focus method, you would begin by linking specific files to a specific task, such as "create home page image maps." This works well when you already have a firm sense of exactly what work needs to be done. This is the process explained in *To link files to a task* on the next page, *To link files to a review* on page 303, *To assign a file* on page 308, and *To start a task* on page 318.

This files-based approach, however, may not be the best in every circumstance. Sometimes you may find it more helpful to begin by broadly defining the tasks and not associating them with any particular files. Only later would you create detailed tasks linked to specific files. In those cases, the broader, top-down approach works better, especially if you want to leave it to others to figure out the actual steps needed to accomplish the broader task. This more general approach is explained in *To create a task not linked to a file* on page 297, *To assign a task* on page 306, and *To mark a task completed* on page 317.

Figure 14.1 To link a file to a task, right-click the file and choose *Add Task*.

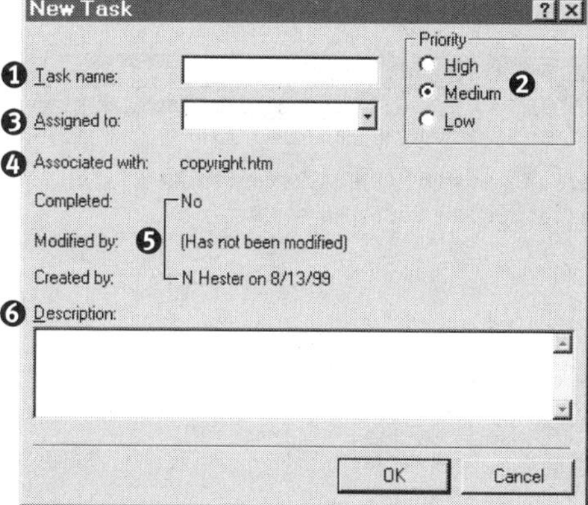

Figure 14.2 Use the New Task dialog box to create and assign tasks.

To link files to a task

1. Switch to page or folders view, or make sure the Folders List is visible.
2. Right-click the file you want linked to a task and choose *Add Task* from the shortcut menu (**Figure 14.1**).
3. When the New Task dialog box appears (**Figure 14.2**), you'll notice that the file you selected is listed next to *Associated with* ❹.
4. Type a short description of the task or give it a name in the *Task name* text box ❶.
5. Use the radio buttons to give the task a *Priority* ❷, though you can do that later if you prefer.
6. Type a name into the *Assigned to* text box or use the drop-down menu ❸ to pick from a list of names. For details, see *To create a names master list* on page 305.
7. FrontPage will automatically supply the information in the middle of the dialog box ❺, so skip down to the *Description* area ❻ if you want to add any details about the task.

(continued)

8. When you've finished (**Figure 14.3**), click *OK*. Repeat steps 2–7 to link other files with tasks if you wish.

9. Switch to the tasks view by clicking the Tasks icon in the Views pane and the new task will appear in the Tasks list (**Figure 14.4**).

✔ Tips

- To launch the files you've linked to a particular task, see *To start a task* on page 318.
- If you want to link certain files to a category instead of a task, see *To categorize files* on page 301.
- You don't have to assign a task when you create it. Instead you can do it any time. See *To assign a task* on page 306.

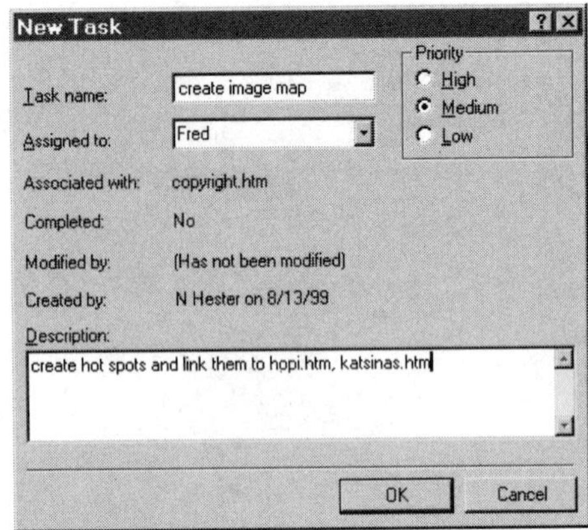

Figure 14.3 Once you've filled in the New Task dialog box, click *OK*.

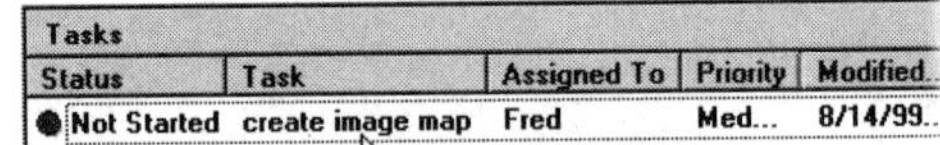

Figure 14.4 Switch to the tasks view to see a list of tasks for building your Web site.

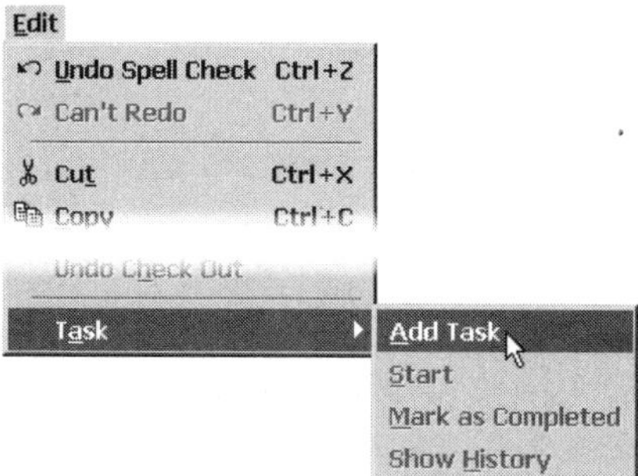

Figure 14.5 To create a task not linked to a particular file, choose Edit > Task > Add Task.

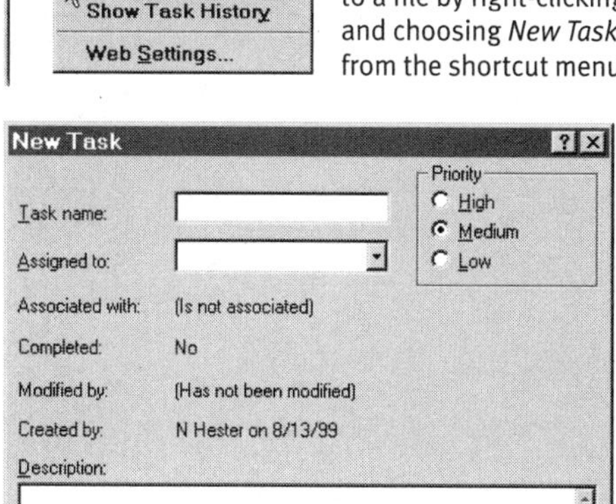

Figure 14.6 You also can create a task *not* linked to a file by right-clicking and choosing *New Task* from the shortcut menu.

Figure 14.7 When the New Task dialog box appears, give it a name, priority, and description.

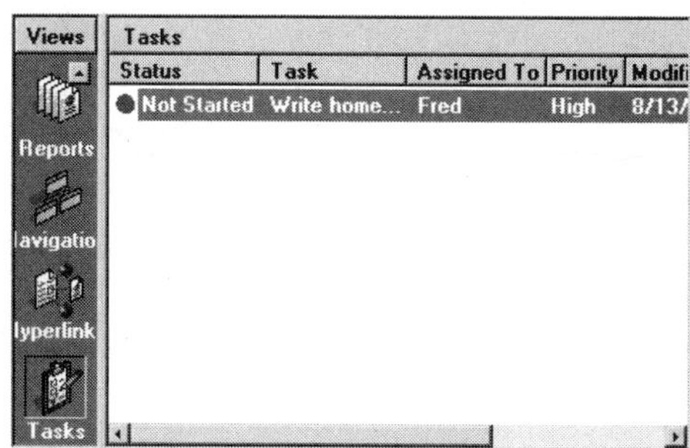

Figure 14.8 After you've created a new task, switch to the tasks view to see it in the Tasks list.

To create a task not linked to a file

1. In any view, choose Edit > Task > Add Task (**Figure 14.5**). Or switch to the tasks view, right-click in the main window, and choose *New Task* from the shortcut menu (**Figure 14.6**).
2. When the New Task dialog box appears (**Figure 14.7**), describe the task or give it a shorthand name in the *Task name* text box.
3. Use the radio buttons to give the task a *Priority*.
4. Type a name into the *Assigned to* text box or use the drop-down menu to pick from a list of names. For details, see *To create a names master list* on page 305.
5. FrontPage will automatically provide the information in the middle of the dialog box, so skip down to the *Description* area if you want to add any details about the task.
6. When you've finished, click *OK*. Repeat steps 1–5 to add more tasks if you wish.
7. Switch to the tasks view by clicking the Tasks icon in the Views pane and the new task will appear in the Tasks list (**Figure 14.8**).

✔ Tips

- Unlike in **Figure 14.2**, you'll notice that in step 2 (**Figure 14.7**) the *Associated with* line says *(Is not associated)*. That tells you that the task you're creating or editing is a freestanding one that's not linked with any file.
- You don't have to assign a task when you create it. Instead you can do it any time. See *To assign a task* on page 306.

Organizing Files

FrontPage helps you organize your Web files with several labeling options. By labeling files by category, for example, you could create a Redesign category for all the files related to the upcoming redesign of your Web site. You can use whatever categories make sense: organizational categories, such as Production; product categories, such as New Widgets. The categories do not appear on the Web site itself, just in FrontPage's reports view.

FrontPage also includes another labeling choice, which it calls *review status* for marking files that should be checked before they're published. By building your own master list of review procedures or mileposts, you can use the reports view to quickly see whether files and pages have been checked over by others on your Web site team. Before you begin labeling files by category or review status, it will speed your work if you first create a master list for each.

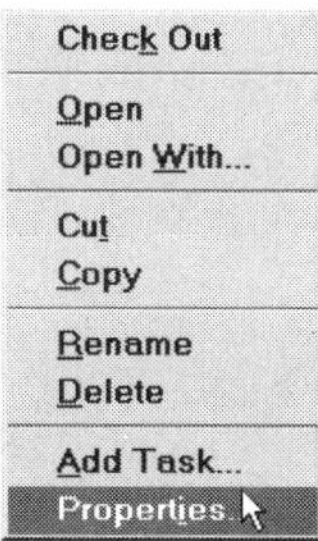

Figure 14.9 To reach any master list for a file, right-click the file and choose *Properties* from the shortcut menu.

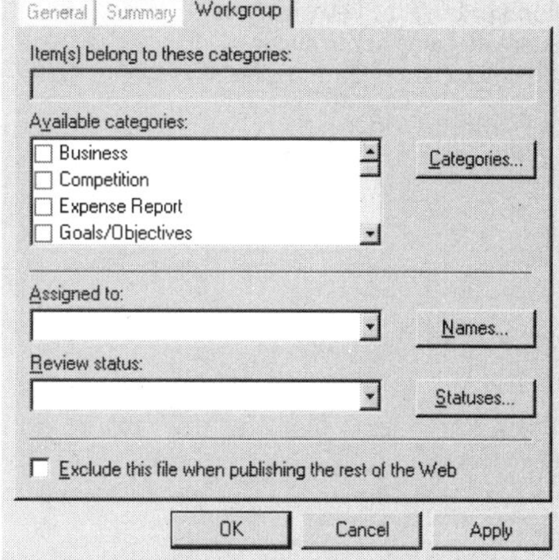

Figure 14.10 Use the buttons in the *Workgroup* tab to create master lists.

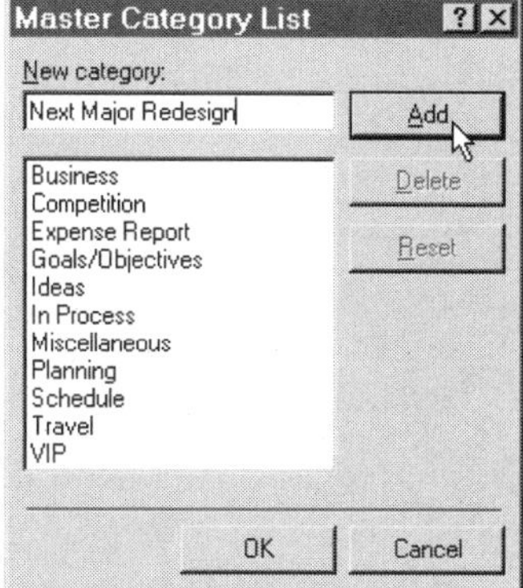

Figure 14.11 Use the Master Category List dialog box to add or delete file categories.

To create a categories master list

1. Right-click any file in the Folder List or in the main window (except in page view) and choose *Properties* from the shortcut menu (**Figure 14.9**).
2. Click the *Workgroup* tab in the dialog box that appears (**Figure 14.10**).
3. Click the *Categories* button to reach the Master Category List dialog box (**Figure 14.11**).
4. Type a category into the *New category* text box and click *Add*. The name will be added to the dialog box's existing list.
5. Repeat step 4 until you've added all the categories you want to the list.
6. Click *OK* and the categories will be added to the *Available categories* scrolling text box under the *Workgroup* tab. To label files by category, see *To categorize files* on page 301.

✔ Tips

- To remove a category from the master list, select one in the dialog box's list, and click *Delete* (**Figure 14.11**). The category will be removed.
- If you change your mind while changing categories in the master list, click *Reset* and the list will return to how it was before you opened it.

To create a review procedure master list

1. Right-click any file in the Folder List or in the main window (except in page view) and choose *Properties* from the shortcut menu (**Figure 14.9**).
2. Click the *Workgroup* tab in the dialog box that appears (**Figure 14.10**).
3. Click the *Statuses* button to reach the Review Status Master List dialog box (**Figure 14.12**).
4. Type a category into the *New review status* text box and click *Add*. The new review procedure will be added to the dialog box's existing list.
5. Repeat step 4 until you've added all the review procedures you want to the list. Click *OK* and they will be available in any of FrontPage's review status drop-down menus. For details, see *To link files to a review* on page 303.

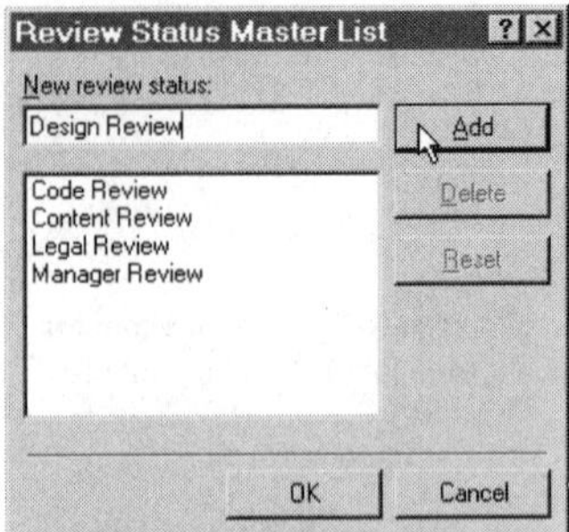

Figure 14.12 Use the Review Status Master List dialog box to add or delete review procedures for files.

✔ Tips

- To remove a review procedure from the master list, select one in the dialog box's list, and click *Delete* (**Figure 14.12**). The review procedure will be removed.
- If you change your mind while adding or deleting review procedures, click *Reset* and the list will return to how it was before you opened it.

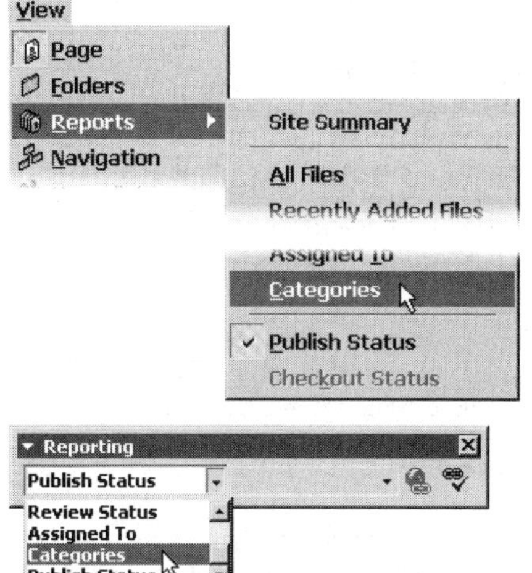

Figure 14.13 To categorize files, choose View > Reports > Categories (top) or *Categories* in the Reporting toolbar (bottom).

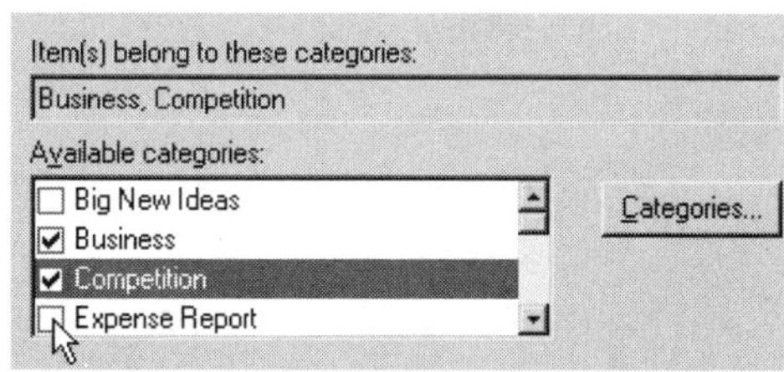

Figure 14.14 Check the categories you want applied to a file within the *Available categories* scrolling text box.

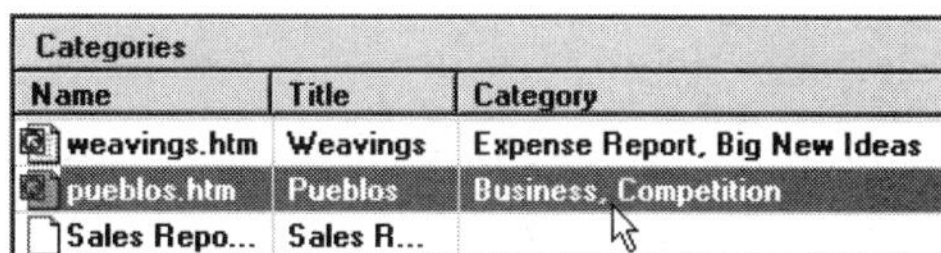

Categories

Name	Title	Category
weavings.htm	Weavings	Expense Report, Big New Ideas
pueblos.htm	Pueblos	Business, Competition
Sales Repo...	Sales R...	

Figure 14.15 Multiple categories can be applied to a single file.

To categorize files

1. Choose View > Reports > Categories or choose *Categories* if the Reporting toolbar is active (**Figure 14.13**).
2. When the Categories report appears, right-click the file you want categorized and choose *Properties* from the shortcut menu.
3. Click the *Workgroup* tab in the dialog box that appears (**Figure 14.10**), then check off the category boxes within the *Available categories* scrolling text box that you want applied to the file (**Figure 14.14**). As you check boxes, the category will be added to the *Item(s) belong to these categories* text box.
4. Click *OK* and the chosen categories will be applied to the file (**Figure 14.15**).

✔ Tip

- You can apply *multiple* categories to a *single* file.

To simultaneously categorize multiple files

1. Choose View > Reports > Categories or choose *Categories* if the Reporting toolbar is active (**Figure 14.13**).
2. When the Categories report appears, press Ctrl as you select multiple files by clicking each in the list.
3. Right-click the selected files and choose *Properties* from the shortcut menu (**Figure 14.16**)
4. Click the *Workgroup* tab in the dialog box that appears (**Figure 14.10**), then check off the category boxes within the *Available categories* scrolling text box that you want applied to the selected files (**Figure 14.14**).
5. Click *OK* and the categories will be applied to all the selected files (**Figure 14.17**).

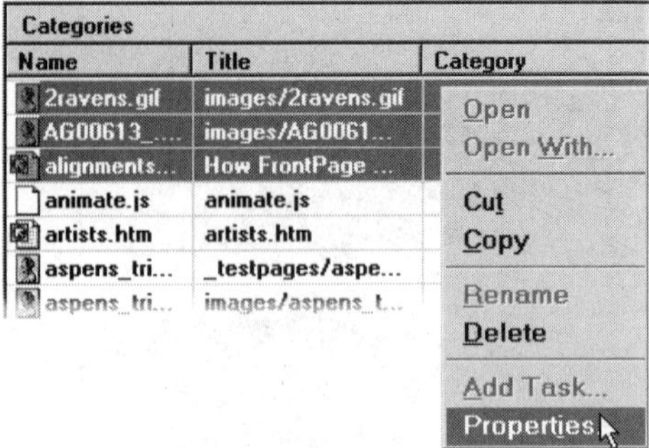

Figure 14.16 To categorize multiple files, right-click the selected files and choose *Properties* from the shortcut menu.

Categories

Name	Title	Category
2ravens.gif	images/2raven...	Business, Competition
AG00613_....	images/AG006...	Business, Competition
alignments...	How FrontPage...	Business, Competition

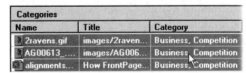

Figure 14.17 Multiple files can have the same categories applied to them simultaneously.

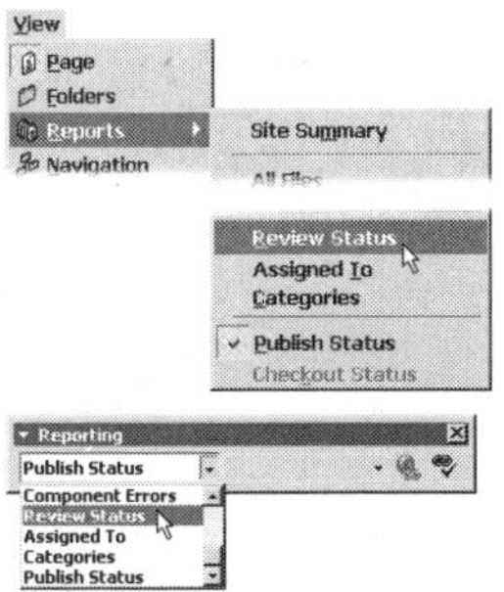

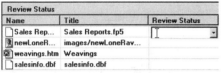

Figure 14.18 To link files to a review procedure, choose View > Reports > Review Status (top) or choose *Review Status* in the Reporting toolbar (bottom).

Review Status

Name	Title	Review Status
Sales Rep...	Sales Reports.fp5	
newLoneR...	images/newLoneRav...	
weavings.htm	Weavings	
salesinfo.dbf	salesinfo.dbf	

Figure 14.19 Click in the *Review Status* column of any file you want linked to a review, and a drop-down menu, with the first line blank, will appear.

Review Status

Name	Title	Review Status
Sales Rep...	Sales Reports.fp5	
newLoneR...	images/newLoneRav...	Code Review
weavings.htm	Weavings	Content Review
salesinfo.dbf	salesinfo.dbf	Design Review
pueblos.htm	Pueblos	Final Signoff
order.htm	order.htm	Legal Review
		Manager Review
		QA Review

Figure 14.20 Use the drop-down menu to link a review procedure to a file or type a new procedure into the text box.

Review Status

Name	Title	Review Status
Sales Rep...	Sales Reports.fp5	Final Signoff
newLoneR...	images/newLoneRav...	
weavings.htm	Weavings	
salesinfo.dbf	salesinfo.dbf	

Figure 14.21 Once a file's linked to a review procedure, the procedure will be listed in the Review Status report.

Review Status

Name	Title	Review Status
Sales Rep...	Sales Reports.fp5	Final Signoff
newLoneR...	images/newLoneRav...	Design Review
weavings.htm	Weavings	Content Review
pueblos.htm	Pueblos	Content Review
salesinfo.dbf	salesinfo.dbf	Code Review

Figure 14.22 By creating a series of review procedures, you can quickly see the progress of work.

To link files to a review

1. Choose View > Reports > Review Status or choose *Review Status* if the Reporting toolbar is active (**Figure 14.18**).
2. When the Review Status report appears, click in the *Review Status* column of any file you want linked to a review, and a drop-down menu, with the first line blank, will appear for the item (**Figure 14.19**).
3. Use the drop-down menu to link an existing review procedure to the file or type a new procedure into the text box (**Figure 14.20**).
4. Release the cursor and press Enter to link the file and the review step (**Figure 14.21**). Repeat until you've linked reviews to all the files you need (**Figure 14.22**).

✔ Tips

- Once a file has been reviewed, use the Review Status drop-down menu in step 3 to select the next necessary review. Or press ←Backspace to clear the menu if all the necessary reviews of the file have been completed.
- Speed up the process by creating a master list of review procedures ahead of time. See page 300 for details.
- A file can only have one review status linked to it at a time, which makes sense if you think of the file as needing to clear a sequence of review hurdles: first this, then that, then the final OK.

To simultaneously link multiple files to a review

1. Choose View > Reports > Review Status or choose *Review Status* if the Reporting toolbar is active (**Figure 14.18**).
2. When the Review Status report appears, press Ctrl as you select multiple files by clicking each in the list.
3. Right-click the selected files and choose *Properties* from the shortcut menu.
4. Click the *Workgroup* tab in the dialog box that appears and type a name into the *Review status* text box or use the drop-down menu (**Figure 14.23**).
5. Click *OK* and the review status procedure will be assigned to all the selected files.

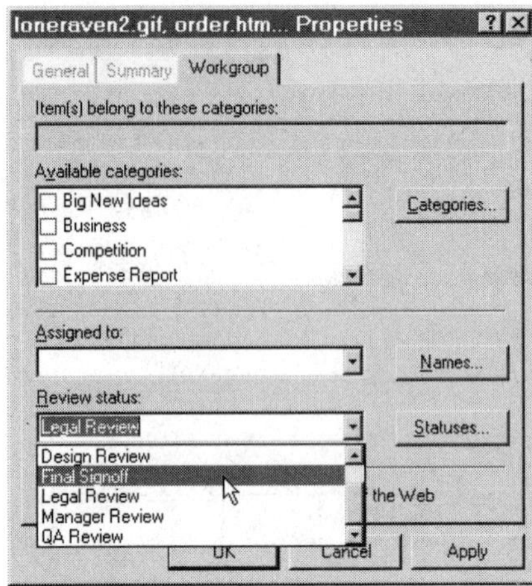

Figure 14.23 Use the *Review status* drop-down menu to apply a procedure to multiple files.

Figure 14.24 The Usernames Master List dialog box lets you add or delete the names of people working on your site.

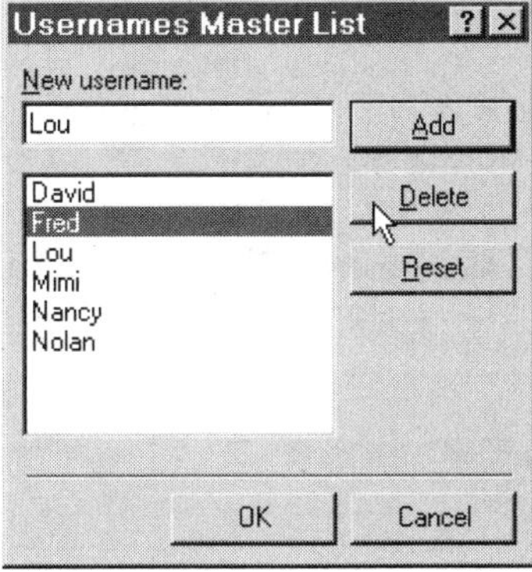

Figure 14.25 To remove a name from the master list, select it and click *Delete*.

Assigning Tasks

FrontPage lets you assign tasks to a specific person or workgroup. It also lets you assign particular files to a person or workgroup, for example, assigning all the image files to the art department. While it's common to assign a task as you create it, you also can assign it—or reassign it—later.

While FrontPage lets you create names for assignments one at a time, sometimes it's faster to go ahead and create a master list of people involved in a project. That way, any time you click an assignment drop-down menu, every name you need will appear.

To create a names master list

1. Right-click any file in the main window or in the Folder List and choose *Properties* from the shortcut menu (**Figure 14.9**).
2. Click the *Workgroup* tab in the dialog box that appears (**Figure 14.10**).
3. Click the *Names* button to reach the Usernames Master List dialog box (**Figure 14.24**).
4. Type a name into the *New username* text box and click *Add*. The name will be added to the dialog box's existing list.
5. Repeat step 4 until you've added all the names you want to the list. Click *OK* and the added names will be available in any of FrontPage's name drop-down menus.

✔ Tips

- To remove a name from the master list, click a name in the dialog box, then click *Delete* (**Figure 14.25**). The name will be removed from the name drop-down menus.
- If you change your mind while changing names in the master list, click *Reset* and the list will return to how it was before you opened it.

To assign a task

1. Switch to the tasks view and click in the *Assigned To* column of the task you want to assign. A drop-down menu, with the first line blank, will appear for the item (**Figure 14.26**).
2. Use the drop-down menu to assign a name or type a new name into the text box.
3. Release the cursor and press Enter to apply the assignment (**Figure 14.27**).

✔ Tip

- If you're in tasks view, it's faster to double-click the task and make your assignment changes in the Task Details dialog box (**Figure 14.28**).

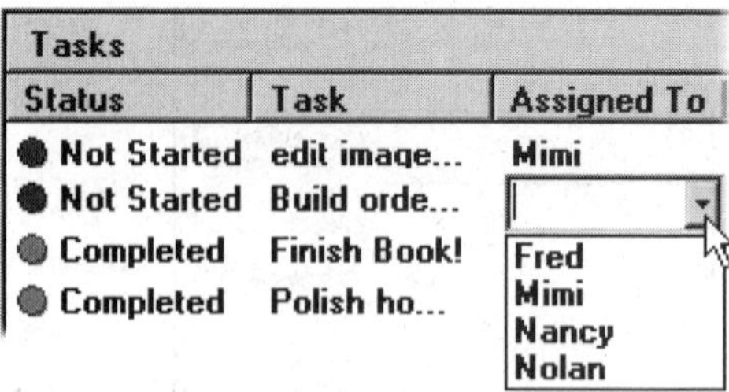

Figure 14.26 To assign a task, click in the *Assigned To* column and a drop-down menu will appear.

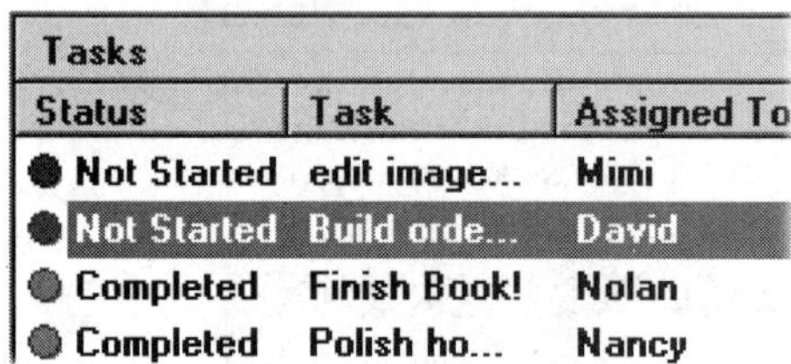

Figure 14.27 Choose a name from the drop-down menu and press Enter to assign a task.

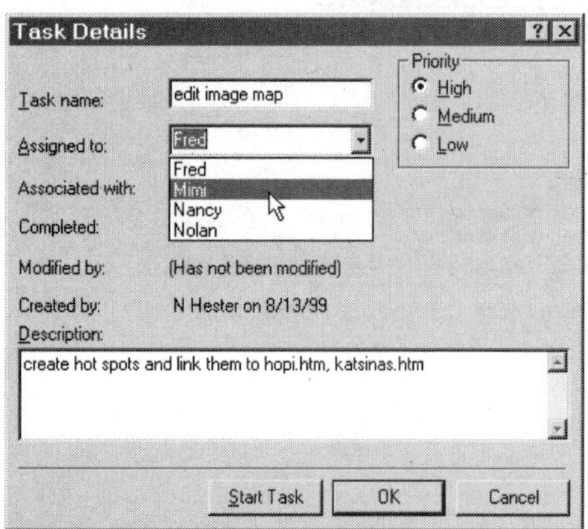

Figure 14.28 If you're in tasks view and want to change an assignment, double-click a task to jump straight to the Task Details dialog box.

ASSIGNING TASKS

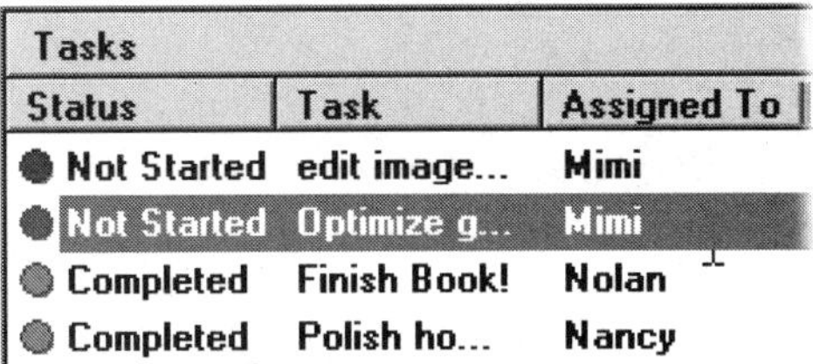

Status	Task	Assigned To
Not Started	edit image...	Mimi
Not Started	Optimize g...	Mimi
Completed	Finish Book!	Nolan
Completed	Polish ho...	Nancy

Figure 14.29 To reassign a task, click in the *Assigned To* column of the task you want to reassign.

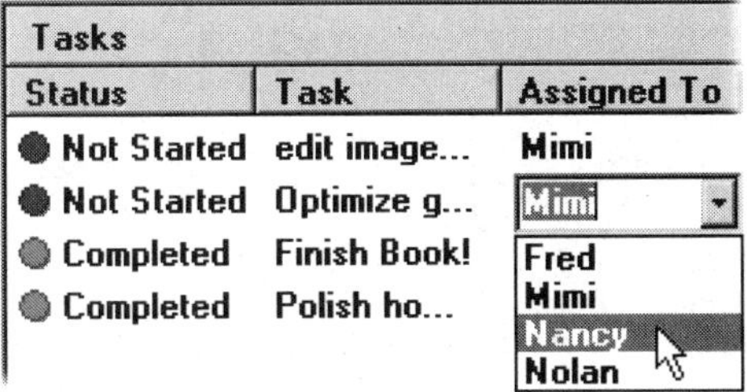

Status	Task	Assigned To
Not Started	edit image...	Mimi
Not Started	Optimize g...	Mimi
Completed	Finish Book!	Fred
Completed	Polish ho...	Mimi
		Nancy
		Nolan

Figure 14.30 Use the drop-down menu to assign another name to the task or type a new name into the text box.

Tasks

Status	Task	Assigned To
Not Started	edit image...	Mimi
Not Started	Optimize g...	Nancy
Completed	Finish Book!	Nolan
Completed	Polish ho...	Nancy

Figure 14.31 Press Enter to apply a reassignment in the Tasks list.

To reassign a task

1. Switch to the tasks view and click in the *Assigned To* column of the task you want to reassign (**Figure 14.29**). A drop-down menu will appear, listing everyone who has been assigned tasks so far.
2. Use the drop-down menu to assign another name to the task or type a new name into the text box (**Figure 14.30**).
3. Release the cursor and press Enter to apply the reassignment (**Figure 14.31**).

✔ Tip

- If you're in tasks view, it's faster to just double-click the task and make the reassignment in the Task Details dialog box (**Figure 14.28**).

To assign a file

1. Choose View > Reports > Assigned To or choose *Assigned To* if the Reporting toolbar is active (**Figure 14.32**).
2. When the Assigned To list appears, click in the *Assigned To* column of any file you want assigned, and a drop-down menu, with the first line blank, will appear for the item (**Figure 14.33**).
3. Use the drop-down menu to assign a name or type a new name into the text box.
4. Release the cursor and press Enter to apply the file assignment (**Figure 14.34**). Repeat until you've assigned all the files you need.

✔ Tip

- By creating a master list of names, you can speed up the assignment process. See page 305 for details.

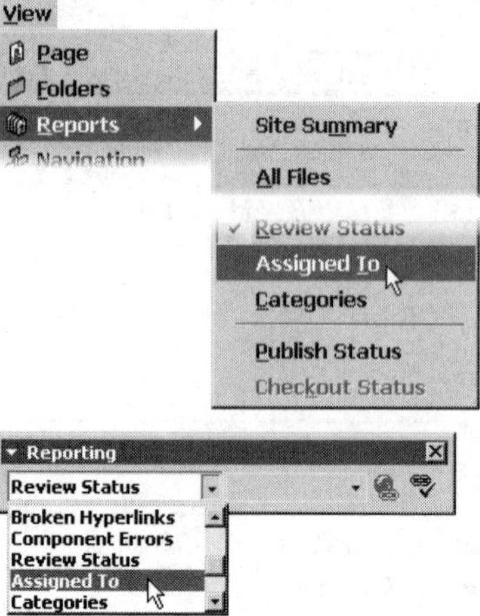

Figure 14.32 To assign a file, choose View > Reports > Assigned To (top) or choose *Assigned To* in the Reporting toolbar (bottom).

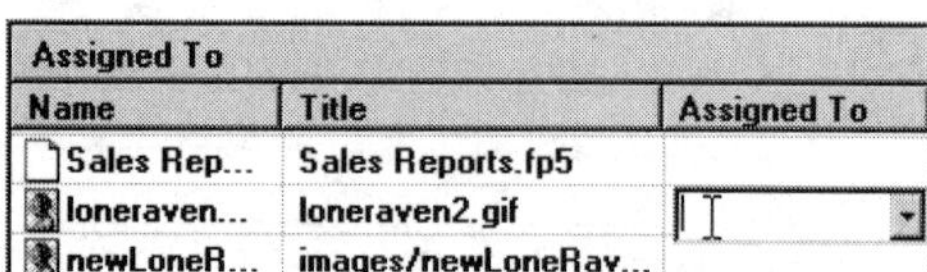

Figure 14.33 Click in the *Assigned To* column and use the drop-down menu to assign a name or type a new name into the text box.

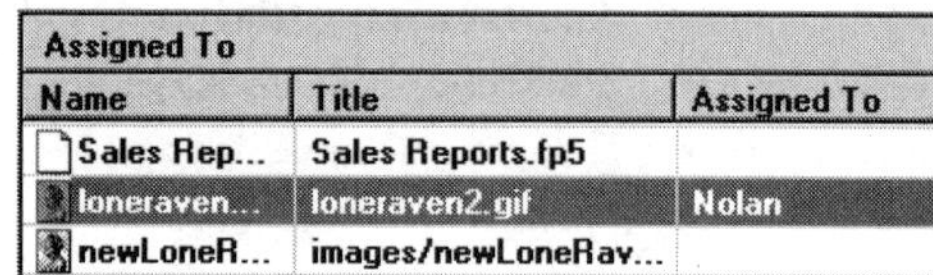

Figure 14.34 Press Enter to apply the assignment to the file.

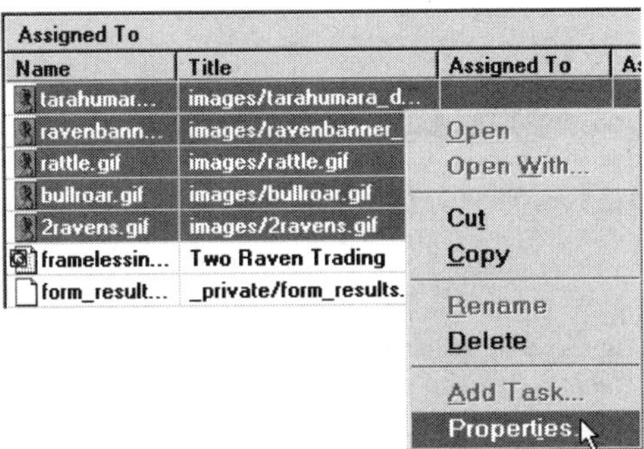

Figure 14.35 To simultaneously assign multiple files, right-click the selected files and choose *Properties* from the shortcut menu.

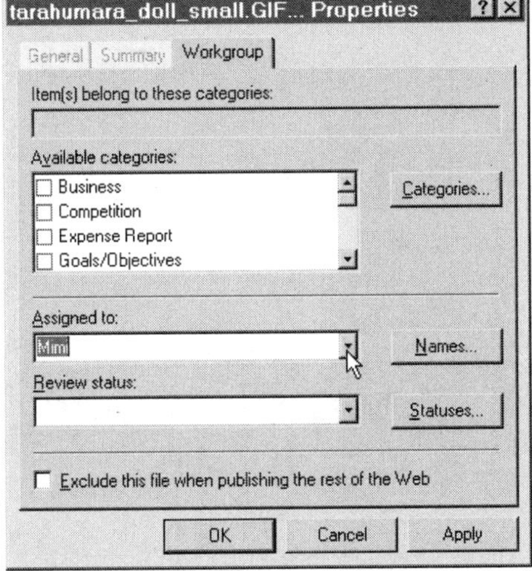

Figure 14.36 Use the *Assigned to* text box or drop-down menu to apply a name to multiple files.

Assigned To

Name	Title	Assigned To
tarahumar...	images/tarahumara_d...	Mimi
ravenbann...	images/ravenbanner_...	Mimi
rattle.gif	images/rattle.gif	Mimi
bullroar.gif	images/bullroar.gif	Mimi
2ravens.gif	images/2ravens.gif	Mimi
framelessin...	Two Raven Trading	

Figure 14.37 By simultaneously assigning multiple files, you can quickly tag who's responsible for what.

To simultaneously assign multiple files

1. Choose View > Reports > Assigned To or choose *Assigned To* if the Reporting toolbar is active (**Figure 14.32**).
2. When the Assigned To list appears, press Ctrl as you select multiple files by clicking them in the Assigned To list.
3. Right-click the selected files and choose *Properties* from the shortcut menu (**Figure 14.35**).
4. Click the *Workgroup* tab in the dialog box that appears and type a name into the *Assigned to* text box or use the drop-down menu (**Figure 14.36**).
5. Click *OK* and the name will be assigned to all the selected files (**Figure 14.37**).

Editing Tasks

As noted earlier, FrontPage lets you change many aspects of a task after you've created it. You can make multiple changes within the Task Details dialog box or change individual aspects directly within the Tasks list.

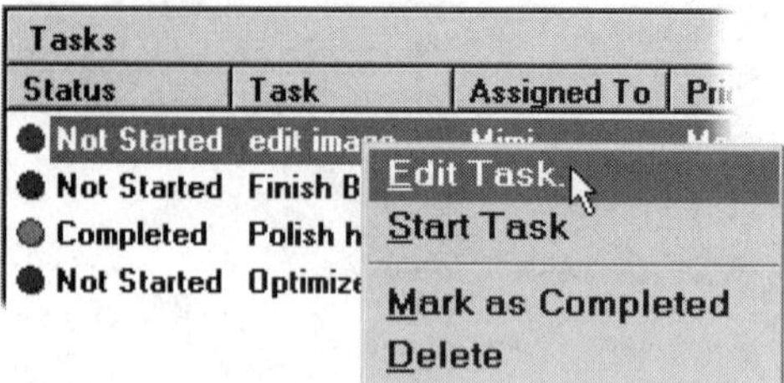

Figure 14.38 To edit a task, right-click it and choose *Edit Task* from the shortcut menu.

To make multiple changes to a task

1. Switch to tasks view, right-click the task you want to change, and choose *Edit Task* from the shortcut menu (**Figure 14.38**).
2. When the Task Details dialog box appears (**Figure 14.28**), use the *Task name* text box to rename the task.
3. Use the radio buttons to give the task a new *Priority*.
4. Type a new name into the *Assigned to* text box or use the drop-down menu to pick from the other names listed.
5. Use the *Description* area to change any details about the task.
6. Click *OK* and the changes will be applied to the task.

✔ Tip

- To reach the Task Details dialog box (**Figure 14.28**), you also can just double-click the task in the Tasks List.

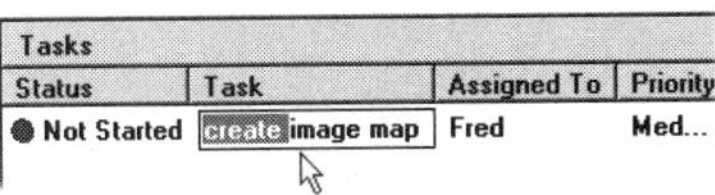

Figure 14.39 To change a task's name, click the item and when it becomes highlighted, type in a new name.

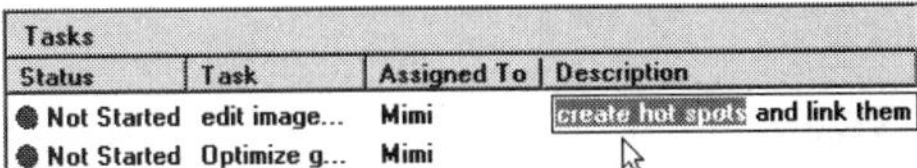

Figure 14.40 To change a task's description, click the item and when it becomes highlighted, type in a new description.

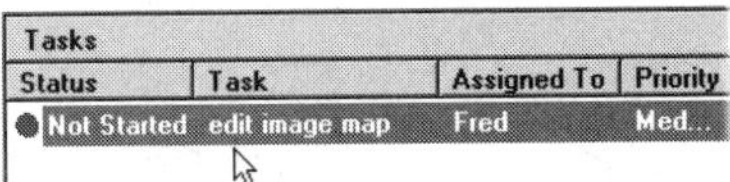

Figure 14.41 Press Enter to apply the change.

To change a task's name or description

1. Switch to the tasks view and click the task name or description you want to change.
2. When the item becomes highlighted, type in a new name (**Figure 14.39**) or description (**Figure 14.40**).
3. Press Enter and the change will be applied (**Figure 14.41**).

✔ Tip

- If a task is listed in the *Status* column as *Completed*, you cannot change its name. However, you can change its description.

To change a task's priority

1. Switch to the tasks view and click *once* in the *Priority* column on the task you want to change.
2. When the task becomes highlighted, click the item's priority once more. A drop-down menu will appear for the item.
3. Use the drop-down menu to change the item's priority (**Figure 14.42**). Press [Enter] and the new priority will be applied.

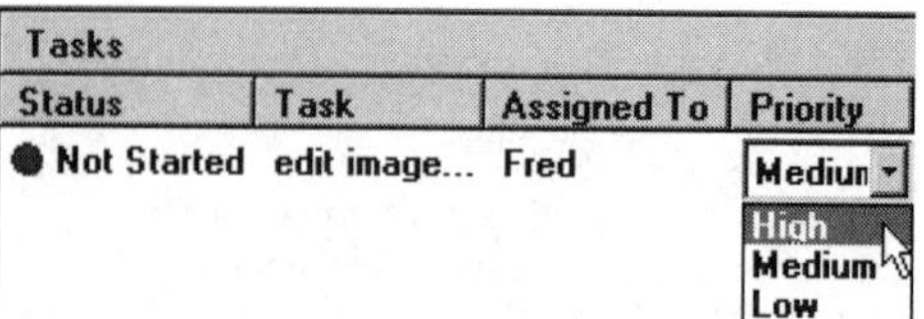

Figure 14.42 To change a task's priority, use the *Priority* column's drop-down menu.

To sort tasks

1. Switch to tasks view by clicking the Tasks icon in the Views pane (**Figure 14.43**).
2. Click any column label to sort the Tasks list by that column's value (**Figure 14.44**).

✔ Tip

- To reverse the sort order of any column, click the column label a second time (**Figure 14.45**).

Figure 14.43 To sort tasks, switch to the tasks view.

Tasks

Status	Task	Assigned To
Not Started	Build order page	David
Not Started	edit image map	Mimi
Not Started	proof all copy	Nancy
Not Started	update catalo...	Lou
Completed	import fall images	Lou
Completed	shrink logo	Mimi

Tasks

Status	Task	Assigned To
Not Started	Build order page	David
Completed	import fall images	Lou
Not Started	update catalo...	Lou
Completed	shrink logo	Mimi
Not Started	edit image map	Mimi
Not Started	proof all copy	Nancy

Figure 14.44 Click the column labels to sort the Tasks list by, for example, *Status* (top) or *Assigned To* (bottom).

Tasks

Status	Task	Assigned To
Completed	import fall images	Lou
Completed	shrink logo	Mimi
Not Started	Build order page	David
Not Started	edit image map	Mimi
Not Started	proof all copy	Nancy
Not Started	update catalo...	Lou

Figure 14.45 To reverse the sort order of any column, click the column label a second time.

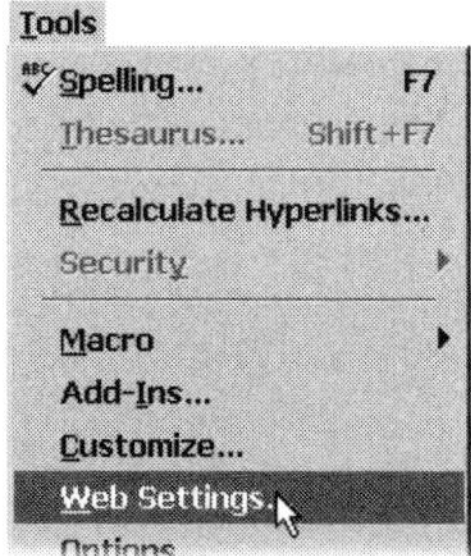

Figure 14.46 To activate the checkout system, choose Tools > Web Settings.

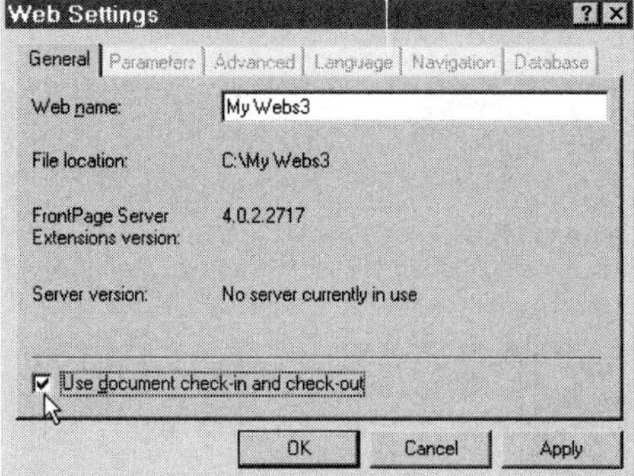

Figure 14.47 Click the Web Settings dialog box's *General* tab and check *Use document check-in and check-out.*

Using the Checkout System

FrontPage's checkout system offers a handy way to coordinate all the work being done on different files for your Web site. While a file is checked out, it cannot be changed by anyone else—a process known as source control. Others can read the last version of the file but cannot make any changes until the file is checked back in. When a file is checked back in, FrontPage saves any changes made to the file.

To activate the checkout system

1. Choose Tools > Web Settings (**Figure 14.46**).
2. When the Web Settings dialog box appears, click the *General* tab and check *Use document check-in and check-out* (**Figure 14.47**).
3. Click *OK* and source control will be applied to the Web site.

To check out a file

1. While in folders or reports view (or with the Folder List visible), right-click the file you want to use, and choose *Check Out* from the shortcut menu (**Figure 14.48**).
2. A red checkmark will be placed next to the file, preventing anyone else from making changes to the file (**Figure 14.49**).

✔ Tips

- If you try to check out a file that's already been checked out, a dialog box will give you the choice of opening the file in read-only status or canceling your request (**Figure 14.50**).
- When you check out a file, FrontPage does not open the file. It just keeps others from working on it. You'll still need to double-click the file to actually open and work on it. And don't forget to check it back in or no one else will be able to change the file.

Figure 14.48 To check out a file, right-click it and choose *Check Out* from the shortcut menu.

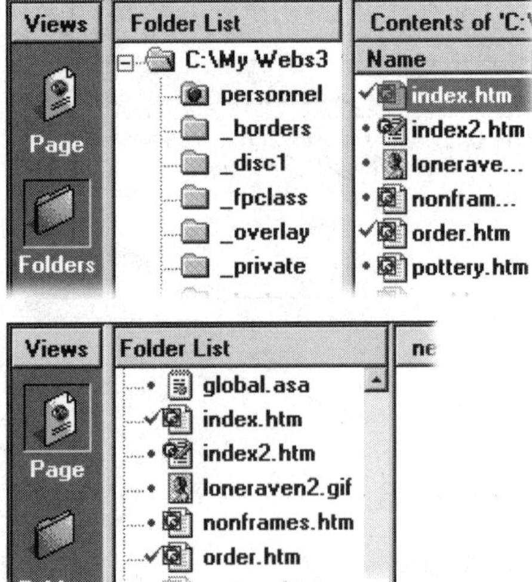

Figure 14.49 Files in use are marked by a checkmark in the folders view (top) and page view (bottom).

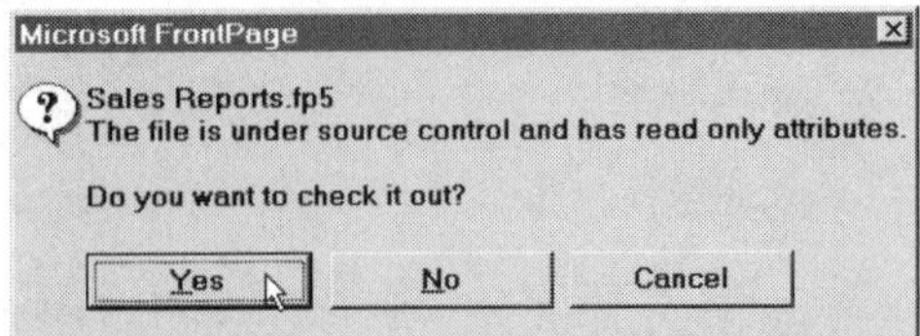

Figure 14.50 If you try to open a file that's in use, an alert box lets you choose to see it in read-only mode or cancel your request.

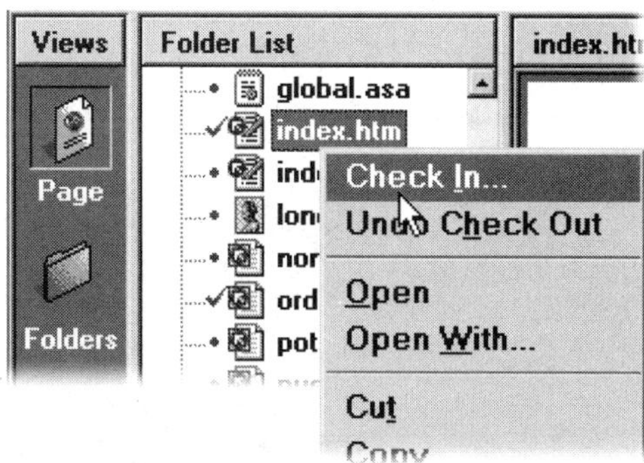

Figure 14.51 Right-click on the file you want to check back in and choose *Check In* from the shortcut menu.

Figure 14.52 Once a file's checked back in, the check-mark alongside it disappears.

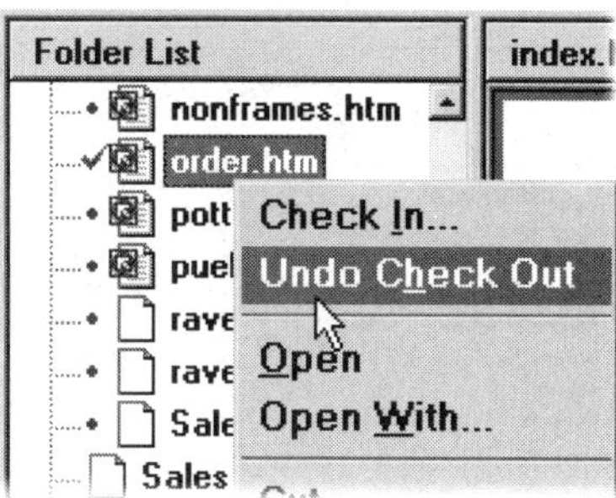

Figure 14.53 If you check out a file and want to check it back in without making any changes, right-click the file and choose *Undo Check Out*.

To check in a file

1. Make sure to first save your changes to the file you've checked out (Ctrl S).
2. While in folders or reports view (or with the Folder List visible), right-click on the file you want to check back in and choose *Check In* from the shortcut menu (**Figure 14.51**). The file will now be available for others to check out and change, as denoted by the disappearance of the red check mark (**Figure 14.52**).

✔ Tip

- Suppose you check out a file, make some changes, and then decide you don't want to make those changes after all. To check the file back in *without* saving those changes, right-click a file you've checked out and choose *Undo Check Out* from the shortcut menu (**Figure 14.53**). The file will be checked back in without being changed.

To see a list of checked out files

1. To quickly see which files are checked out and by whom, choose View > Reports > Checkout Status or choose *Checkout Status* if the Reporting toolbar is active (**Figure 14.54**).
2. When the Checkout Status report appears, files *you* have checked out will be marked by a checkmark, while those checked out by others will be marked with a lock (**Figure 14.55**). The report also includes a Locked Date, which shows when files were checked out.

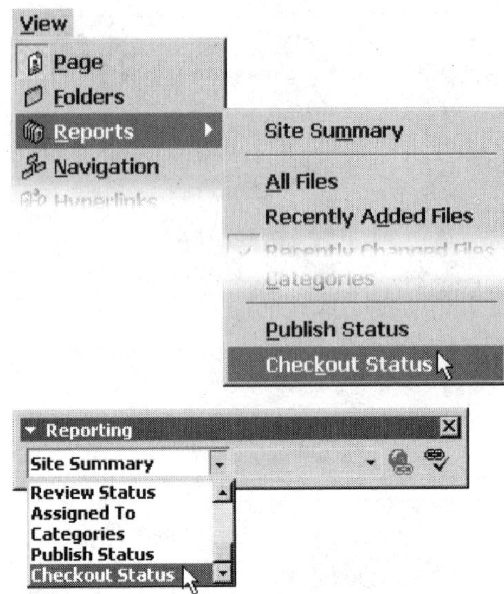

Figure 14.54 To see which files are checked out, choose View > Reports > Checkout Status (top) or choose *Checkout Status* in the Reporting toolbar (bottom).

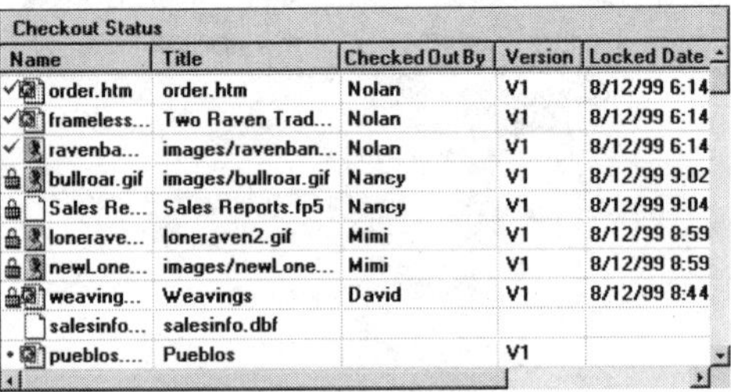

Checkout Status

Name	Title	Checked Out By	Version	Locked Date
order.htm	order.htm	Nolan	V1	8/12/99 6:14
frameless...	Two Raven Trad...	Nolan	V1	8/12/99 6:14
ravenba...	images/ravenban...	Nolan	V1	8/12/99 6:14
bullroar.gif	images/bullroar.gif	Nancy	V1	8/12/99 9:02
Sales Re...	Sales Reports.fp5	Nancy	V1	8/12/99 9:04
lonerave...	loneraven2.gif	Mimi	V1	8/12/99 8:59
newLone...	images/newLone...	Mimi	V1	8/12/99 8:59
weaving...	Weavings	David	V1	8/12/99 8:44
salesinfo...	salesinfo.dbf			
pueblos....	Pueblos		V1	

Figure 14.55 In the Checkout Status report, files you're using show a checkmark. Files in use by others show a lock.

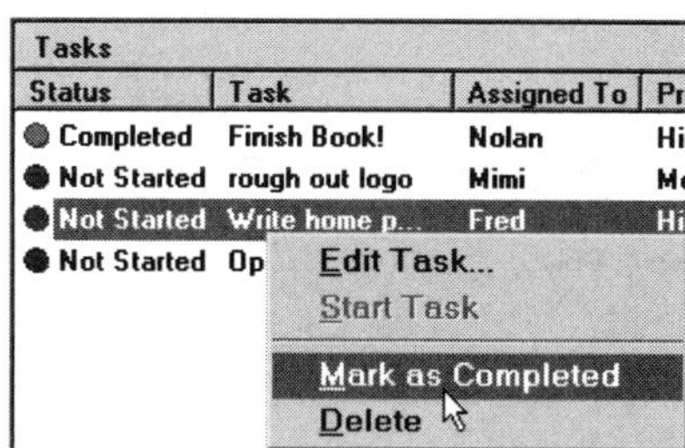

Figure 14.56 Once a task is finished, switch to tasks view, right-click the task, and choose *Mark as Completed*.

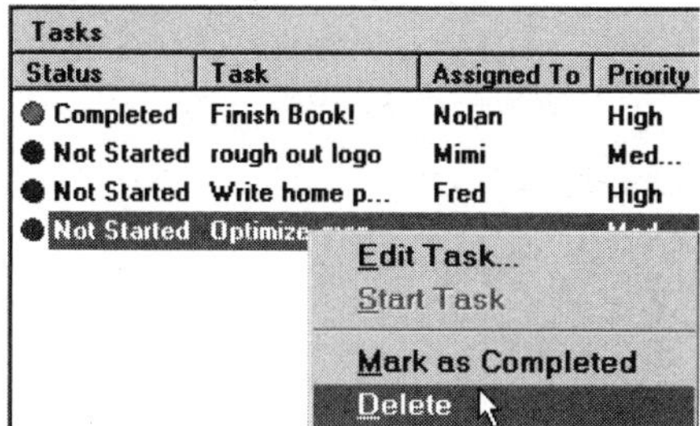

Figure 14.57 To delete a task, right-click the task, and choose *Delete*.

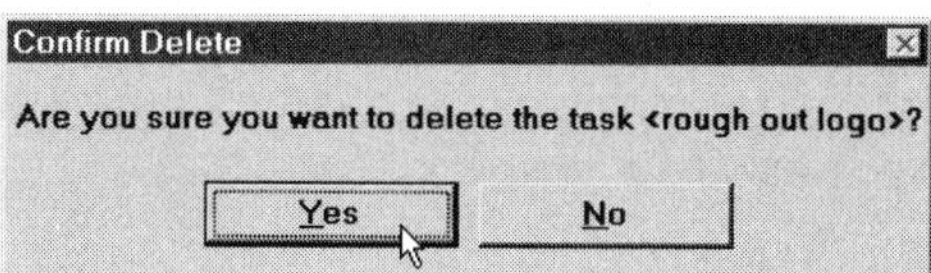

Figure 14.58 When you try to delete a task, an alert dialog box will ask you to confirm your decision.

Completing Tasks

It's fine to assign, sort, and categorize tasks, but at some point you want to get them done. For general tasks not associated with any file, you can mark the task completed or delete it. For tasks with files linked to them, FrontPage offers another choice—Start Task—which launches the files tied to the task, even if they use another application. Once a file's ready to be published, see *To change a page's publishing status* on page 323.

To mark a task completed

- While in tasks view, right-click a task that's been finished and choose *Mark as Completed* from the shortcut menu (**Figure 14.56**). The task's status will change to *Completed* and the task's bullet will turn green.

To delete a task

1. While in tasks view, right-click the task you want to delete and choose *Delete* from the shortcut menu (**Figure 14.57**).
2. When the Confirm Delete dialog box appears, click *Yes* (**Figure 14.58**). The task will be deleted, although any *files* associated with it will remain on your Web site.

To start a task

- While in tasks view, right-click a task whose linked files you want to work on and choose *Start Task* from the shortcut menu (**Figure 14.59**). The files associated with the task will open and, if they use another application, that program also will be launched.

✔ Tip

- You also can start a task by double-clicking it and, when the Task Details dialog box appears, clicking the *Start Task* button (**Figure 14.60**).

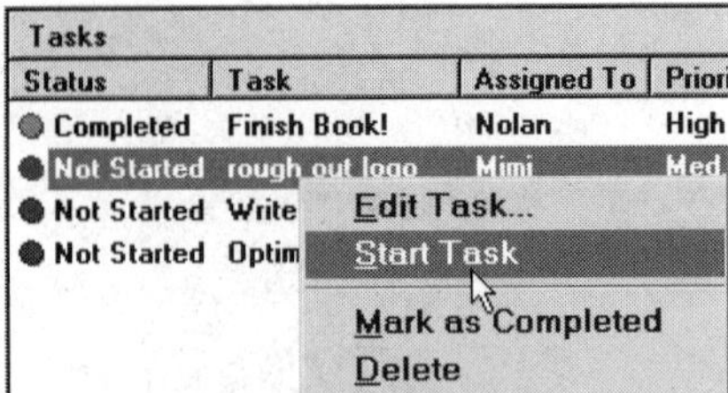

Figure 14.59 If files are linked to a task, right-click the task, choose *Start Task*, and the files will open.

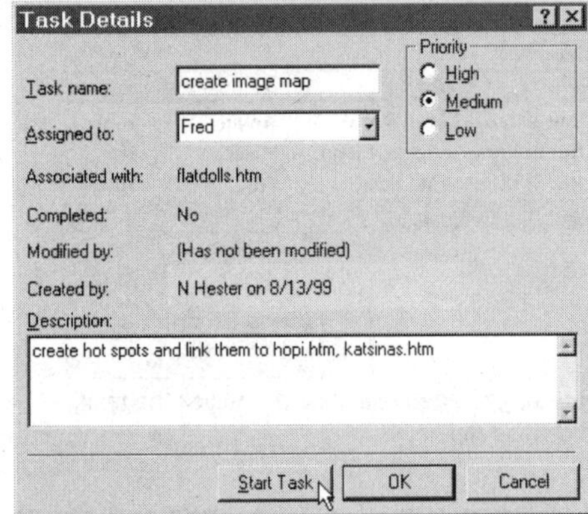

Figure 14.60 You also can open a file linked to a task, by double-clicking it and clicking *Start Task* in the Task Details dialog box.

CHECKING AND PUBLISHING WEB SITES 15

Two crucial steps remain before you actually copy your local files over to a Web server. First, use FrontPage to analyze if any pages have problems, such as broken hyperlinks or slow-to-download files. Second, look at every page with a Web browser to check its appearance and links.

When you're ready to publish, you'll need to have an Internet Service Provider (ISP) or Web Presence Provider (WPP) lined up to host your site, unless you're copying the files to an inhouse intranet. Your ISP's Web server does not need the FrontPage Server Extensions for your Web site's essential features to work properly. However, some of FrontPage's advanced bells and whistles will not be available unless the extensions are installed on the server. The difference is like buying a basic car or one loaded with options: They both get you where you're going, but that CD player sure is nice.

The FrontPage features that require the extensions to work include most of the custom form handlers and many of the components found in the Insert menu. The extensions, which act as translators between your Web site and the Web server are on your FrontPage installation disc. They also can be downloaded for free from `www.microsoft.com/frontpage/`

Checking Your Site

FrontPage's reporting tools make it much easier and faster to get your site ready to publish. Instead of depending on your Web browser to find every problem, FrontPage provides a site summary of possible problems. The reports feature also lets you mark any pages on the site that you do not want published yet, avoiding the all-too-common problem of accidentally publishing pages prematurely. By the way, you'll find it easier to check your site using the Reporting toolbar (**Figure 15.1**). Activate it by choosing View > Toolbars > Reporting.

To check and fix your site

1. Choose View > Reports > Site Summary (**Figure 15.2**). Or if the Reporting toolbar is activated, choose *Site Summary* from the drop-down menu (**Figure 15.1**).
2. When the Site Summary appears in FrontPage's main window, it will list general site information and any problems (**Figure 15.3**).
3. If the summary lists problems, such as *Broken hyperlinks*, double-click that line in the report to see a list of the problem pages.
4. To fix an individual page in the list, double-click it and the appropriate dialog box will appear, allowing you to fix the problem (**Figure 15.4**).
5. Repeat steps 2–4 until you've fixed all the problems.

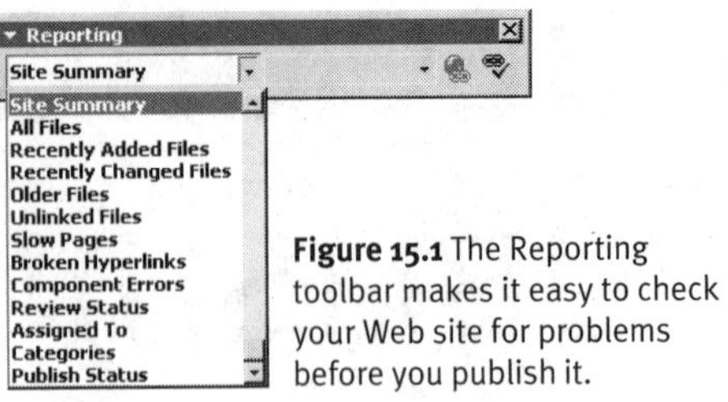

Figure 15.1 The Reporting toolbar makes it easy to check your Web site for problems before you publish it.

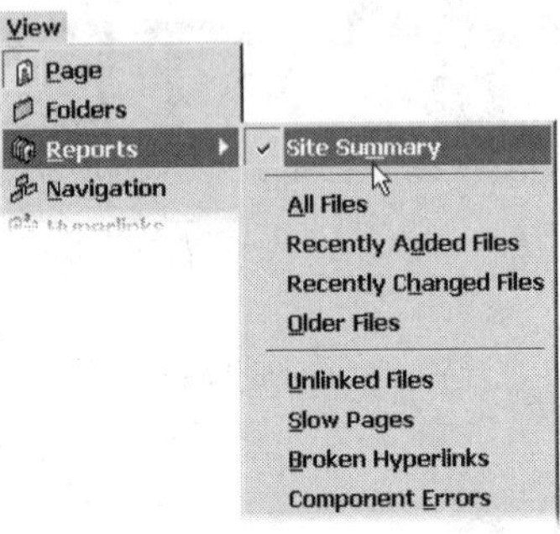

Figure 15.2 To check your entire site, choose View > Reports > Site Summary.

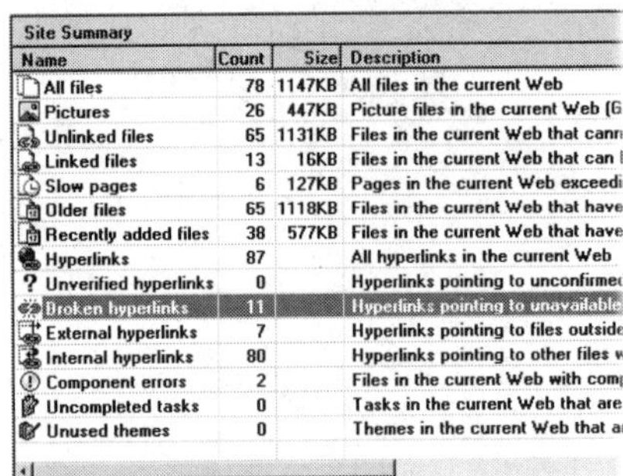

Figure 15.3 The Site Summary report provides a detailed overview of your site's problems. Double-click any line for details.

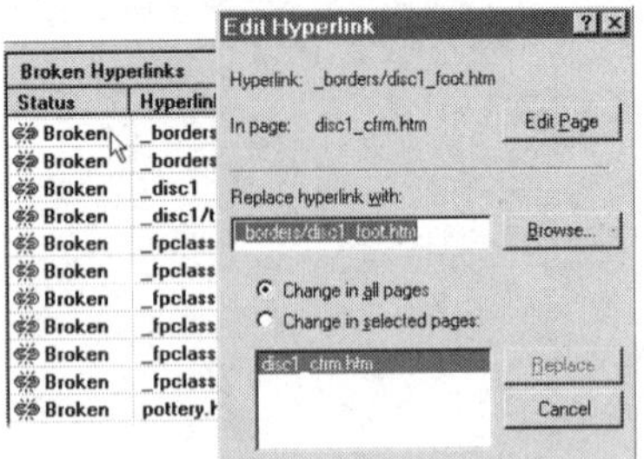

Figure 15.4 Double-click a listing in the Broken Hyperlinks report and the Edit Hyperlink dialog box will appear, enabling you to fix the link.

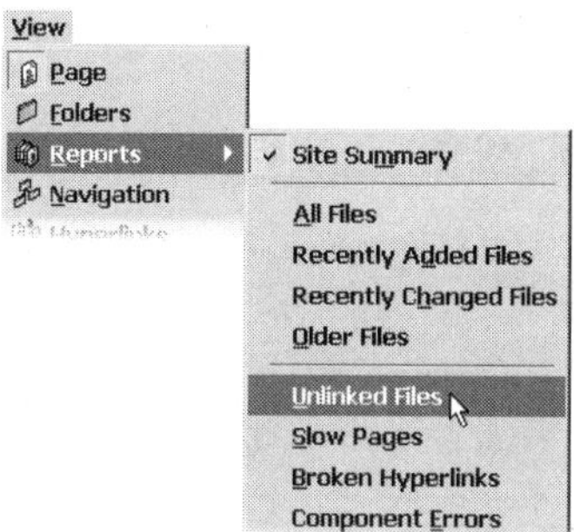

Figure 15.5 To examine a particular problem, choose View > Reports and choose an item from the submenu.

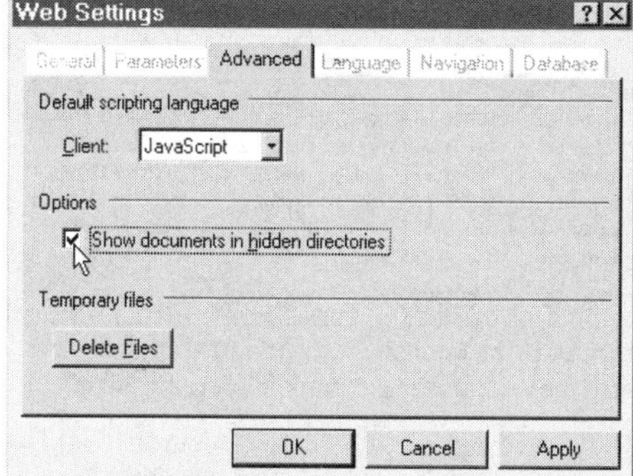

Figure 15.6 To see hidden folders, check *Show documents in hidden directories* under the *Advanced* tab.

✔ Tips

- To return to the Site Summary after you've double-clicked to an individual problem report, click the Reporting toolbar and use the drop-down menu to select Site Summary.
- If you want to check for a particular problem, such as broken links, choose View > Reports and pick the relevant command in the menu starting at *Unlinked Files* (**Figure 15.5**). Or select a choice from the Reporting toolbar's drop-down menu (**Figure 15.1**).
- By default, any files placed inside hidden folders (those preceded by an underscore, such as the _private folder) will not appear in the Site Summary or problem reports. To have those files show up in reports, click Tools > Web Settings, then click the *Advanced* tab, and check *Show documents in hidden directories* (**Figure 15.6**).

Marking pages to publish

Running a quick check of the publishing status of your site's pages gives you a chance to mark pages that are not yet ready for public viewing. It also enables you to switch pages you previously marked *Don't Publish* to *Publish* if you have finished working on them. Running the review doesn't do anything to actually prepare the pages for publication. It's just meant to help keep you from accidentally publishing pages prematurely by highlighting which pages are set to be published.

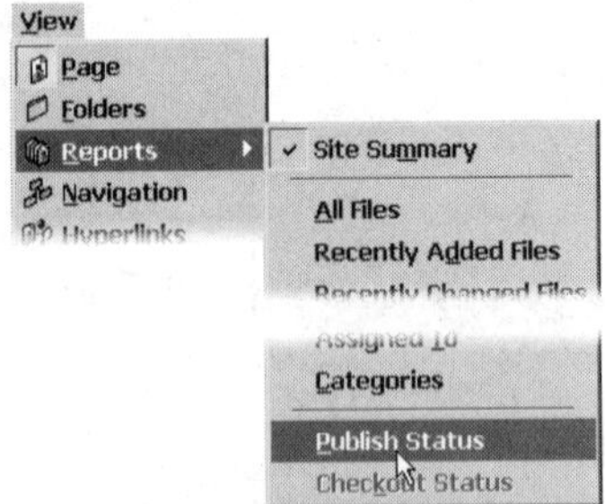

Figure 15.7 To check which pages will be published, choose View > Reports > Publish Status.

To check the publishing status of pages

1. Choose View > Reports > Publish Status (**Figure 15.7**). Or if the Reporting toolbar is activated, choose *Publish Status* from the drop-down menu (**Figure 15.1**).
2. FrontPage's main window will switch to the reports view and show the publishing status of all your site's files (**Figure 15.8**). If you spot pages whose status you want to switch, see *To change a page's publishing status*, on the next page.

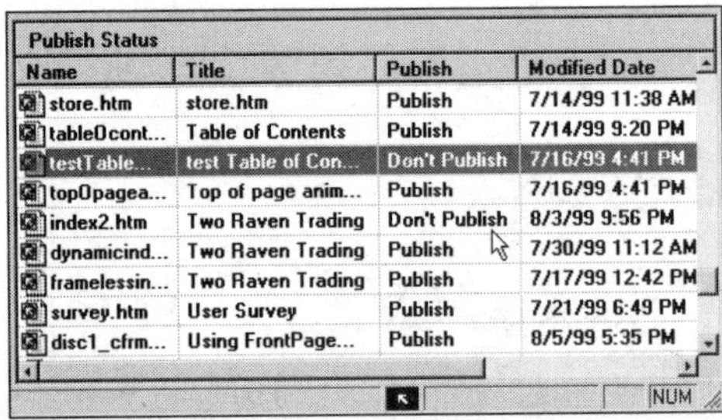

Publish Status

Name	Title	Publish	Modified Date
store.htm	store.htm	Publish	7/14/99 11:38 AM
tableOcont...	Table of Contents	Publish	7/14/99 9:20 PM
testTable...	test Table of Con...	Don't Publish	7/16/99 4:41 PM
topOpagea...	Top of page anim...	Publish	7/16/99 4:41 PM
index2.htm	Two Raven Trading	Don't Publish	8/3/99 9:56 PM
dynamicind...	Two Raven Trading	Publish	7/30/99 11:12 AM
framelessin...	Two Raven Trading	Publish	7/17/99 12:42 PM
survey.htm	User Survey	Publish	7/21/99 6:49 PM
disc1_cfrm...	Using FrontPage...	Publish	8/5/99 5:35 PM

Figure 15.8 The Publish Status report shows which Web pages are and aren't marked for publishing.

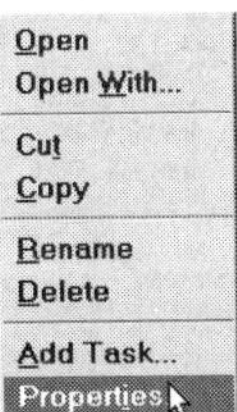

Figure 15.9 To change a page's publishing status, right-click it and choose *Properties* from the shortcut menu.

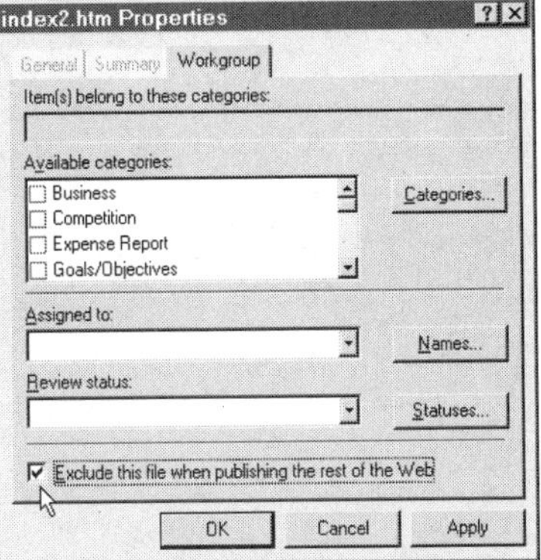

Figure 15.10 Check *Exclude this file when publishing the rest of the Web* to keep a page from being published.

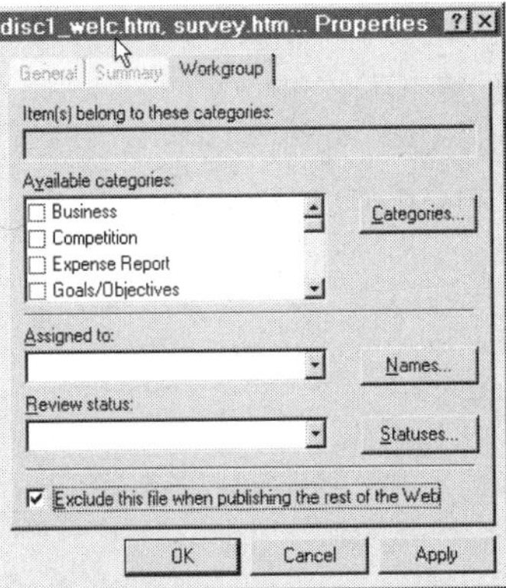

Figure 15.11 If you right-click multiple files and choose *Page Properties* from the shortcut menu, all their names will be listed in the dialog box's title bar.

To change a page's publishing status

1. While in folder or reports view, right-click the page whose publishing status you want to change and choose *Properties* from the shortcut menu (**Figure 15.9**).
2. When the page's properties dialog box appears, click the *Workgroup* tab (**Figure 15.10**).
3. At the bottom of the dialog box check *Exclude this file when publishing the rest of the Web* to turn publishing off. Uncheck the box to turn publishing on.

✔ Tips

- To change more than one page at a time, press Ctrl as you click pages in the Reports list or Folder List. When you then right-click the selected pages and choose *Properties* from the shortcut menu, the names of all the pages will appear in the properties dialog box's title bar (**Figure 15.11**).
- You also can change a page's publishing status from page view. Just right-click the page, choose *Page Properties* from the shortcut menu, and when the Page Properties dialog box appears, click the *Workgroup* tab, and follow step 3 above.

Hiding pages from browsers

Some pages, such as your external style sheets, need to be on your Web server, but you may not want them visible to users. FrontPage creates a private folder for every Web site, which Web browsers won't detect. By placing files and subfolders inside the private folder, you can post files without having the world see them. The underscore at the beginning of the folder name is what hides the folder. You can create additional hidden folders if you like by putting an underscore at the beginning of the new folder's name, such as _Inhouse.

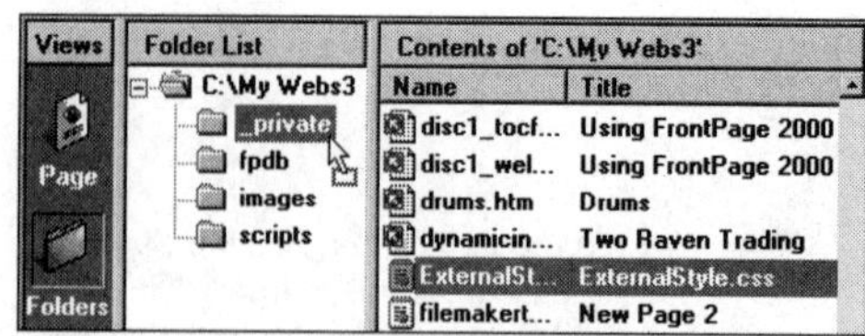

Figure 15.12 To hide pages from browsers, drag them into the _private folder in the Folder List.

To hide pages

1. Switch to folders view and activate the Folder List.
2. Click the file(s) you want hidden and drag it to the _private folder in the Folder List (**Figure 15.12**). The file will be hidden from Web browsers, yet accessible for your Web server.

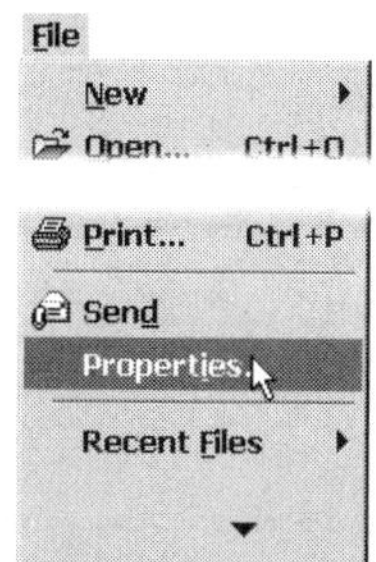

Figure 15.13 To add meta tags to a page, first choose File > Properties.

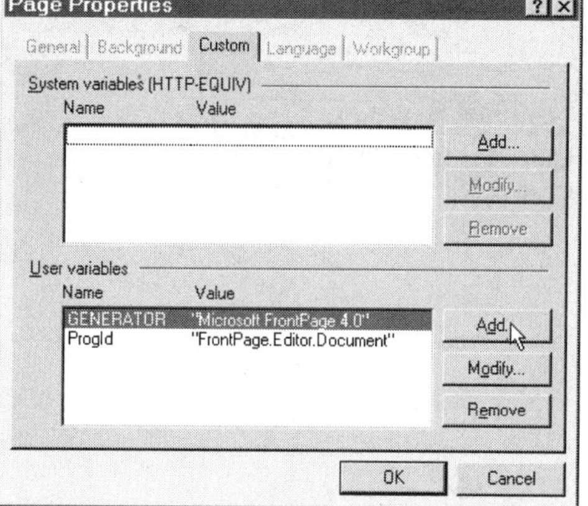

Figure 15.14 Click *Add* under the *Custom* tab to create a new meta tag.

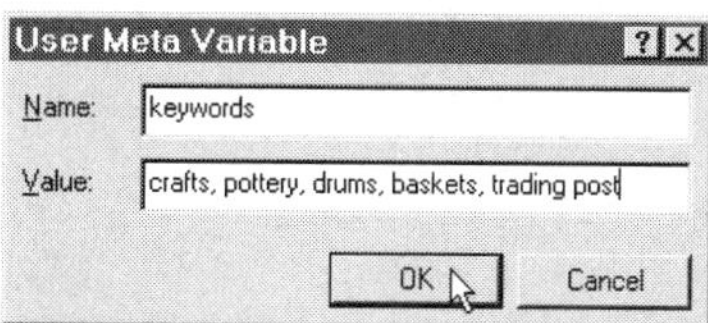

Figure 15.15 Use the User Meta Variable dialog box to add keywords to your meta tags.

Adding Meta Tags for Search Engines

Meta tags are bits of HTML coding, which among many uses, help search engines, such as Yahoo!, Alta Vista, and Excite, create directories to the World Wide Web. FrontPage makes it easy to add meta tags to attract the attention of search engines or keep them out of your site. Adding keyword meta tags makes it easier for search engines to categorize your site. The robot meta tags used on page 327 keep the same engines from indexing your site or following all its links, something you may want to do for an experimental site or one intended just for friends and family. The robot tag won't block every search engine but it will keep out the vast majority.

To help search engines index your site

1. With your Web site open, choose File > Properties (**Figure 15.13**).
2. When the Page Properties dialog box appears, click the *Custom* tab, then click *Add* in the *User variables* section (**Figure 15.14**).
3. When the User Meta Variable dialog box appears, type *keywords* into the *Name* text box, then type the actual keywords that summarize your site's topics—each separated by a comma—into the *Value* text box (**Figure 15.15**).

(continued)

4. Click *OK* to close the User Meta Variable dialog box and the keywords will be listed in the Page Properties dialog box (**Figure 15.16**).
5. If you want to change the keywords, select that line in the *User variables* list and click *Modify*. To delete the keywords entirely, click *Remove*.
6. Once you're satisfied with the keyword changes, click *OK*. The keywords will be added to your site's meta tags.

✔ Tips

- If you want to inspect the normally invisible meta tag keywords, click the *HTML* tab and you'll find the keywords in the section above `<title>` (**Figure 15.17**).
- Always use multiple keywords to create broad *and* narrow descriptions of your site. For example, my site includes the keywords *books* and *web authoring*, but also *FrontPage 2000*. That way people using a search engine will pick up your site in a general category search but also find it when looking for a particular product or service.

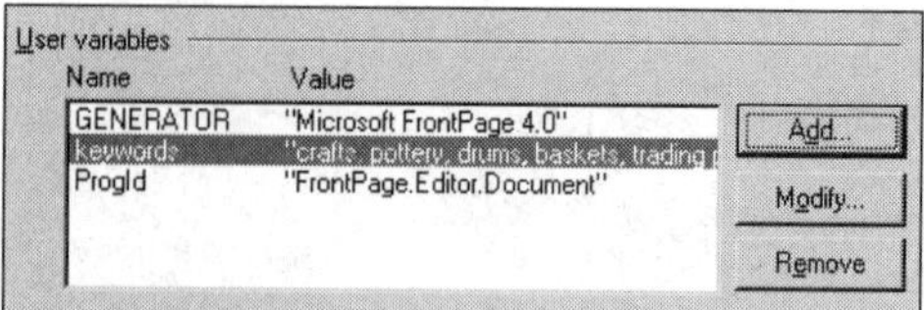

Figure 15.16 New meta tags are added to the Page Properties dialog box.

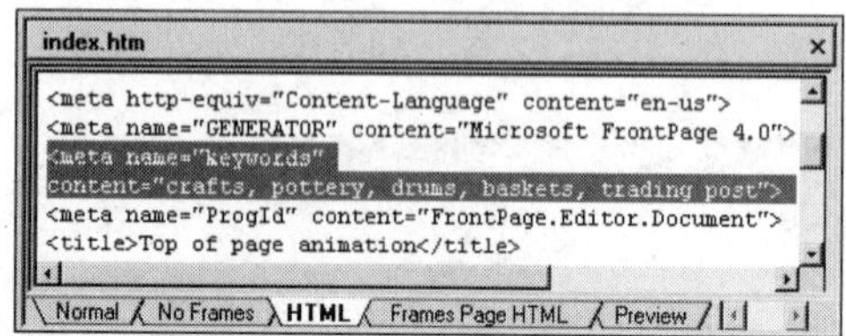

Figure 15.17 To see the normally invisible meta tag keywords, click the *HTML* tab.

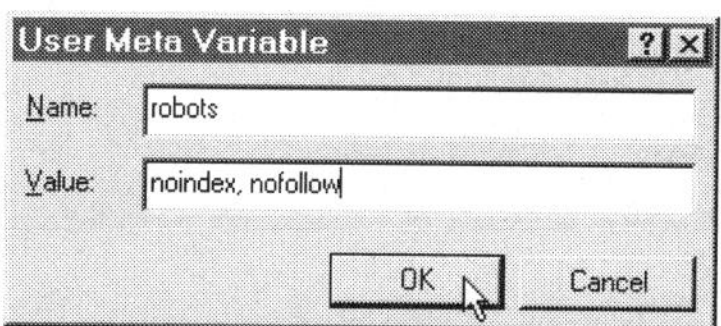

Figure 15.18 To block search engines from indexing your site, type *robots* into the *Name* text box, and *noindex, nofollow* into the *Value* text box.

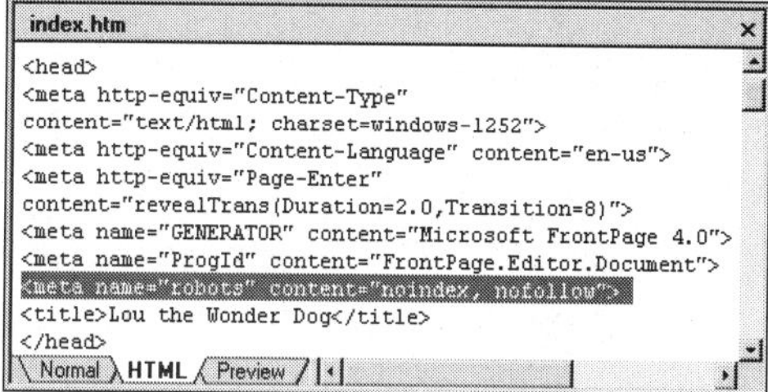

Figure 15.19 Click the *HTML* tab to see the robot-blocking meta tags.

To keep out search engines

1. With your Web site open, choose File > Properties (**Figure 15.13**).
2. When the Page Properties dialog box appears, click the *Custom* tab, then click *Add* in the *User variables* section (**Figure 15.14**).
3. When the User Meta Variable dialog box appears, type *robots* into the *Name* text box, then type *noindex, nofollow* into the *Value* text box (**Figure 15.18**).
4. Click *OK* to close the User Meta Variable dialog box and return to the Page Properties dialog box. Click *OK* and the meta tags will be added to your site's HTML coding (**Figure 15.19**).

Publishing to the Web

After you've fixed your Web pages and marked which ones should be published, you should preview them in several Web browsers. Use Internet Explorer *and* Netscape Navigator (in several versions of both) to check each page's appearance and links, since each browser interprets HTML code a bit differently. Make a point of also checking your pages on a Macintosh, particularly since PC-created images can look a bit washed out on Mac monitors, which run a tad brighter than PC monitors. Depending on how the pages look and behave, you may need to readjust some of your pages to avoid cross-platform problems. For details on which Web technologies work with various browsers, see *Setting Web Browser Compatibility* on page 343.

Once you've fixed any problems found in the browsers, you're finally ready to copy your Web site files from your local hard drive to the Web server you'll be using. Before you start, you'll need to know the server address that you'll be copying your files to, plus a user name and password to gain access to the server. Check with the Web server's administrator if you need help.

By the way, if you want to find a Web Presence Provider that uses FrontPage Server Extensions on its Web servers, the publishing process includes a step for locating one.

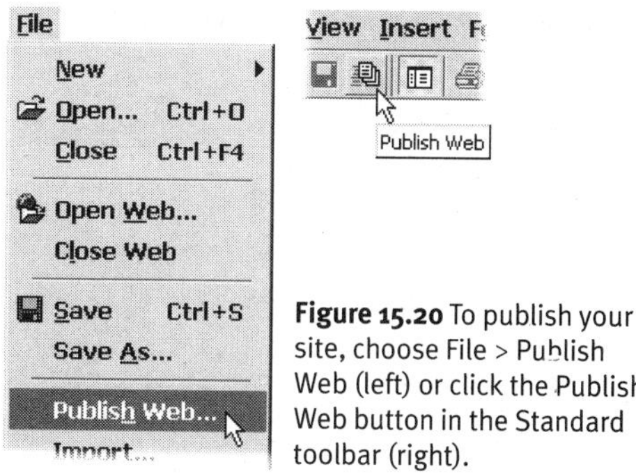

Figure 15.20 To publish your site, choose File > Publish Web (left) or click the Publish Web button in the Standard toolbar (right).

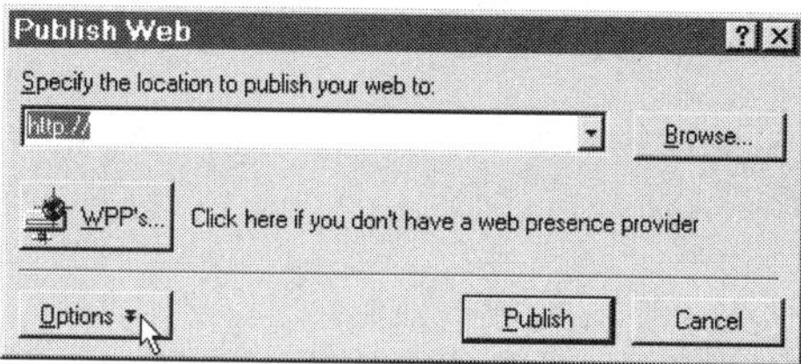

Figure 15.21 To reach all the publishing settings, click *Options* in the Publish Web dialog box.

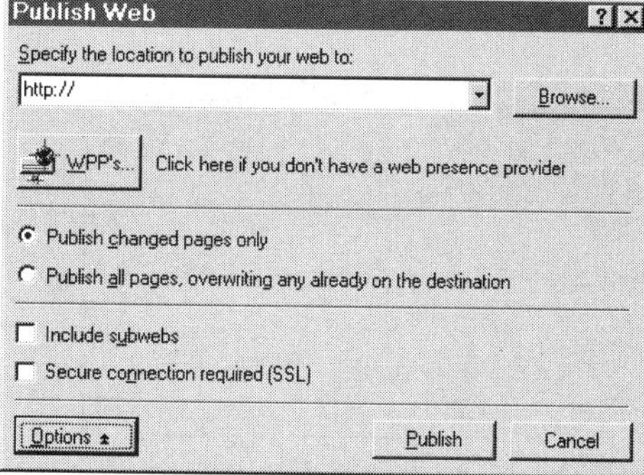

Figure 15.22 Use the expanded Publish Web dialog box to control which pages are published.

To publish your site

1. Open the Web site you want published, then choose File > Publish Web or click the Publish Web button in the Standard toolbar (**Figure 15.20**).
2. When the Publish Web dialog box appears, click *Options* (**Figure 15.21**). An expanded set of choices will appear across the bottom of the Publish Web dialog box (**Figure 15.22**).
3. Choose whether you want to *Publish changed pages only* or whether you want to *Publish all pages, overwriting any already on the destination.* For details, see *Publish Web options* on page 332.
4. Check *Include subwebs* if you want to also publish any subwebs within your Web site.
5. Check *Secure connection required (SSL)* if your Web server supports the Secure Sockets Layer. For details, see *Publish Web options* on page 332.
6. Now that you've set all the options, type into the *Specify the location to publish your web to* text box the location of your Web server. If you've published the site before, click the drop-down menu's arrow and select it there. (Use *Browse* only if you're using http to connect to your Web server. For details, see *Publish Web options* on page 332.)
7. Click *Publish* and FrontPage will use your default Internet access connection to connect to your Web server.

(continued)

8. Type in the user name and password the Web server administrator assigned you when the Enter Network Password dialog box appears (**Figure 15.23**).

9. There will be a brief pause as FrontPage compiles a list of the pages that need to be uploaded to the Web server (**Figure 15.24**). After another pause (the length will depend on how many new pages you're uploading and your connection speed), FrontPage will begin copying your Web pages to the Web server (**Figure 15.25**).

10. Once FrontPage completes the transfer, an alert dialog box will give you the choice of clicking the hyperlink to see the now-published site or clicking *Done* to return to FrontPage's main window (**Figure 15.26**).

11. Once you're done uploading your site to the server, disconnect from the Internet if you're using a dial-up connection.

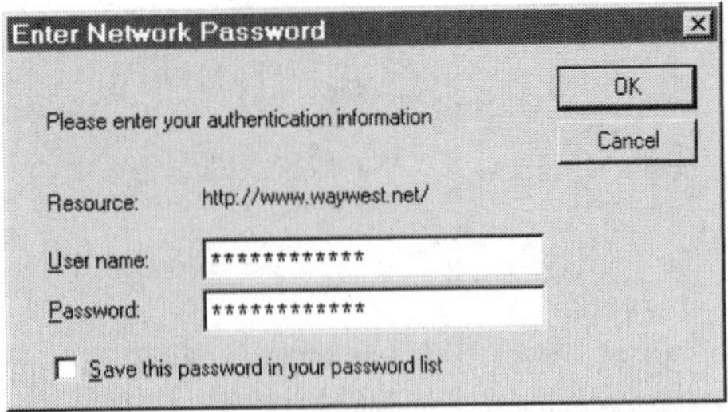

Figure 15.23 When the Enter Network Password dialog box appears, enter the *User name* and *Password* assigned to you by the server's administrator.

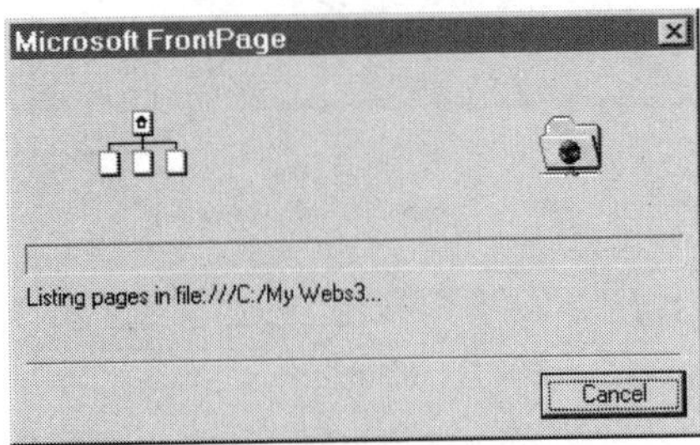

Figure 15.24 Once FrontPage connects to the server, it will list the pages that will be uploaded.

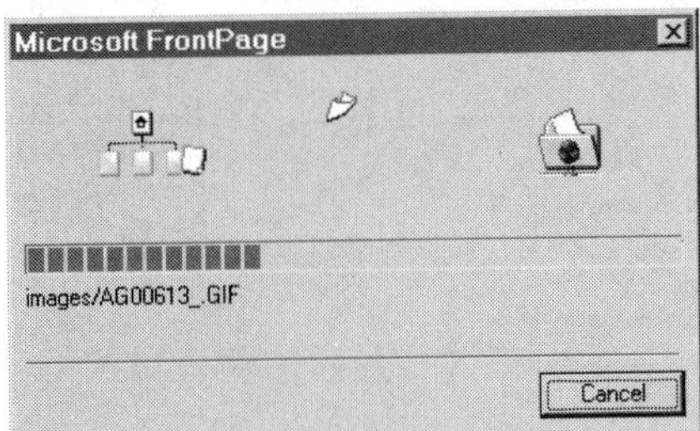

Figure 15.25 After another pause, FrontPage will begin copying your Web pages to the Web server.

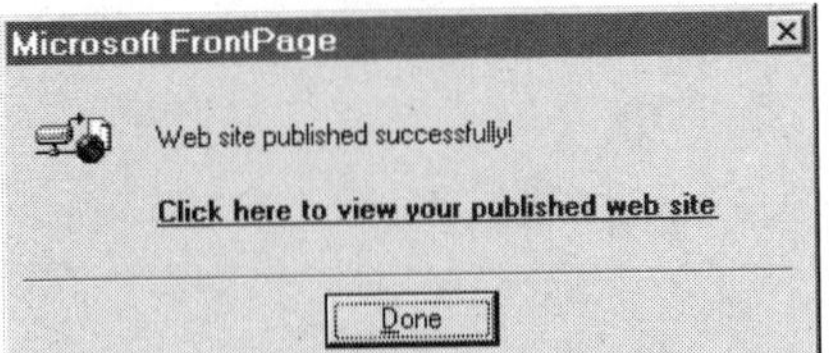

Figure 15.26 Once FrontPage completes the transfer, you can choose to see the now-published site or return to FrontPage's main window.

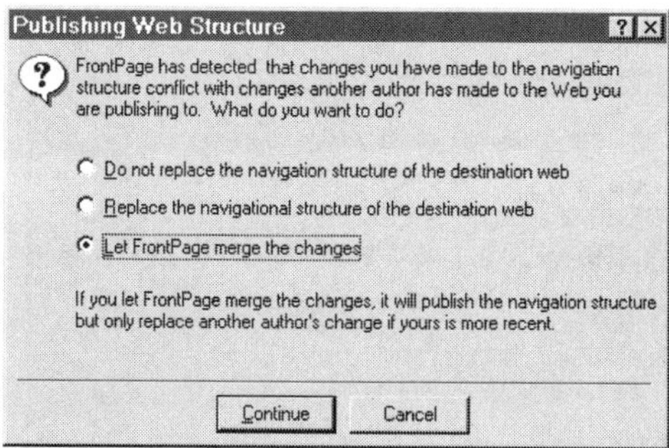

Figure 15.27 When you update a site, FrontPage will alert you if the update will change the site's navigation structure.

✔ Tips

- Depending on how your Internet connection's configured, you may need to connect to your Web server before clicking the Publish button in the Publish Web dialog box.
- After the first time you publish your Web site and assuming your Web Publish dialog box settings remain the same, you can just click the Publish Web button whenever you need to update your site on the Web server. FrontPage calls this one-button publishing (right, **Figure 15.20**).
- If you choose to overwrite pages already on the Web site, FrontPage will alert you if that will change the site's navigation structure (**Figure 15.27**). You'll have the choice of leaving the structure as is, replacing it with your changes, or merging both versions by using only the newest pages.
- FrontPage helps you avoid posting pages that won't work on your Web server. If your server doesn't have FrontPage Server Extensions, a dialog box will alert you if any of your pages require the extensions.

Publish Web options

To reach the Publish Web dialog box (**Figure 15.28**), choose File > Publish Web.

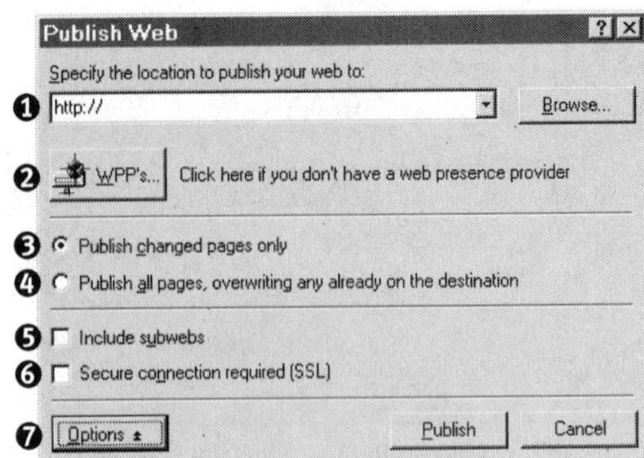

Figure 15.28 Use the expanded Publish Web dialog box to control which pages are published.

❶ **Specify the location to publish your web to:** By default, the text box is set to *http://* but you can use that only if your Web server contains FrontPage Server Extensions. If your server doesn't have the extensions, type in `ftp://` plus the rest of the pathname for your Web server. (For example: `ftp://ftp.mycompany.com`.) If you've already published to the site, use the text box's drop-down menu to find the location. If you're using http, you also can navigate to the location by clicking *Browse*.

❷ **WPP's:** If you do not already have a Web Presence Provider—or want to find one that offers FrontPage Server extensions, clicking this button will take you to Microsoft's Web site where you'll find an extensive list of links to providers that use the extensions.

❸ **Publish changed pages only:** If you're regularly updating your site, this probably will be your most common setting.

❹ **Publish all pages, overwriting any already on the destination:** Use this the first time you publish your site or if you've been adding incrementally to your site for some time and, so, may have no-longer-used files on your site. Choose this also if you've substantially revised your site and want to make sure that no outdated pages remain on the site.

❺ **Include subwebs:** It's sometimes convenient when publishing larger Web sites to create subwebs—smaller webs within the main web for natural subdivisions such as sales or personnel. Whether you include or exclude subwebs in a posting will depend on whether each subdivision is responsible for publishing its own subweb's materials.

❻ **Secure connection required (SSL):** Most larger ISPs offer SSL connections, which add a level of encryption protection for transmitting corporate or financial data. Check with your Web service to find out if SSL is available for your server. It never hurts to err on the side of extra security.

❼ **Options:** Click to show or hide the dialog box's publishing options.

PART V

APPENDIX & INDEX

Installing & Configuring FrontPage

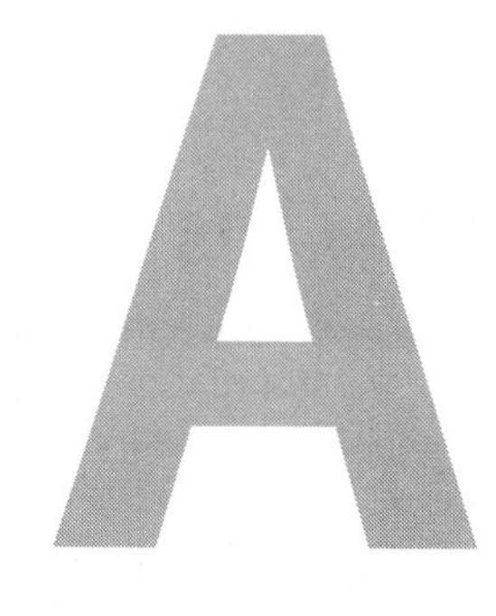

It's tempting to install FrontPage and immediately start building your Web site. But take a minute to configure how FrontPage handles HTML codes, and you'll be assured that your Web site will be compatible with the Web browsers people use when they visit your site. FrontPage 2000 will work with Windows 95, Windows 98 or later, and Windows NT 4.0 or later.

What you'll need before starting

- A PC equipped with the equivalent of an Intel Pentium or Celeron chip. (AMD's K6-series chips are fine.)
- At least 32 MB of RAM (memory).
- At least 36 MB of free space on your hard drive (more to install some of the clip art included on the CD).
- A 28Kbps or faster modem. With 56Kbps modem prices falling every day, just get one and save yourself a lot of frustration. Office networks typically have much faster, hardwired Internet connections, so you'll have plenty of speed there.
- A color monitor capable of displaying at least 256 colors.
- A CD-ROM drive for installing FrontPage.

Installing FrontPage

In step 5 on the next page FrontPage offers you two installation choices: *Install Now* (the standard configuration) or *Customize*. If you need to save hard drive space or want to install FrontPage somewhere other than your C drive, choose *Customize* and see *To install a custom version of FrontPage* on page 338.

To install the standard version of FrontPage

1. Turn off all programs, including any anti-virus program you have running in the background.
2. Put FrontPage's Disc 1 into your CD-ROM drive. Once the CD launches, it'll take a moment for the installation to begin (**Figure A.1**).
3. When the Customer Information screen appears (**Figure A.2**), enter your name and other information. Most importantly enter the *CD Key* number, which you'll find on the back of the CD's jewel case (labeled *Product Key*). When you're done, click *Next.*
4. When the License and Support Information screen appears (**Figure A.3**), choose *I accept the terms in the License Agreement* and click *Next.*

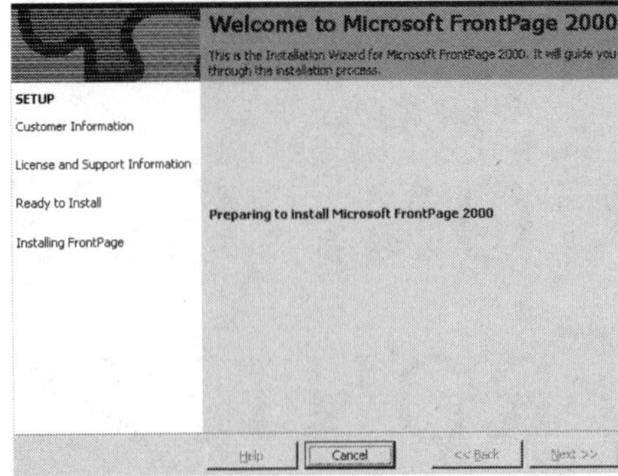

Figure A.1 Once FrontPage's Disc 1 launches, it'll take a few moments before you can begin the installation.

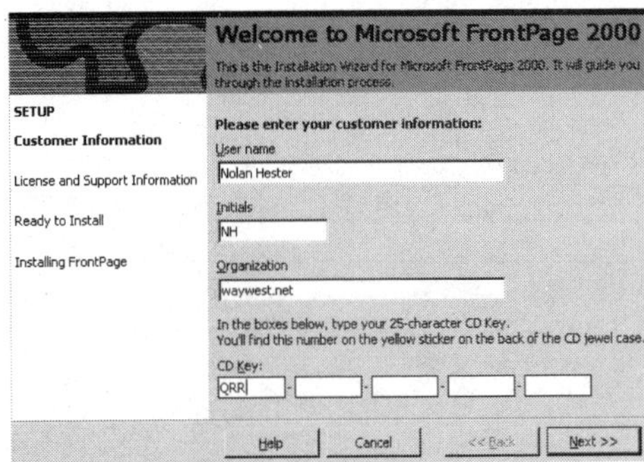

Figure A.2 When the Customer Information screen appears, you'll need to enter the *CD Key* number found on the back of the CD's jewel case.

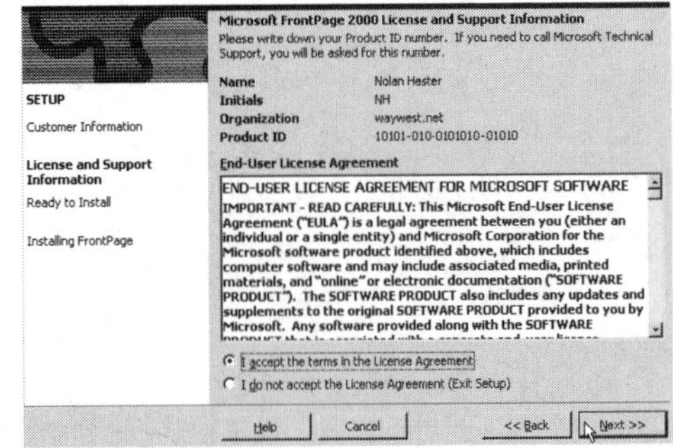

Figure A.3 Choose *I accept the terms in the License Agreement* and click *Next*.

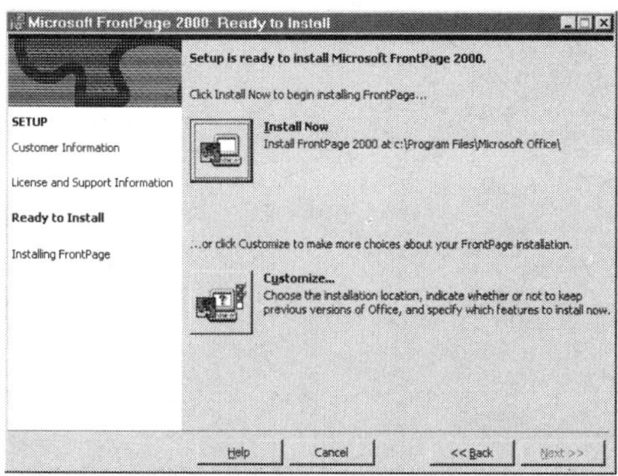

Figure A.4 Choose *Install Now* for FrontPage's standard configuration or *Customize* to control where and which parts of the program are installed.

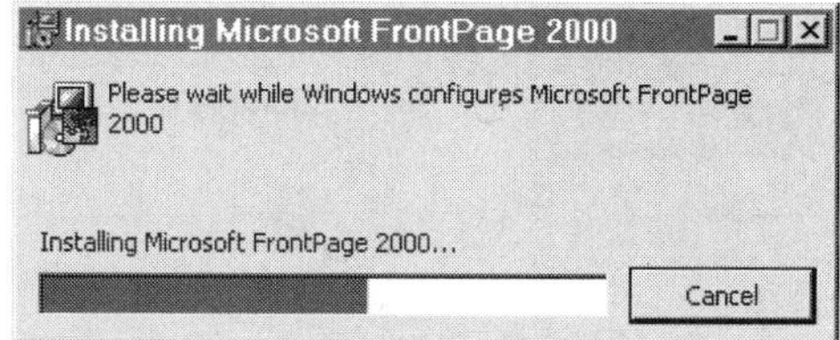

Figure A.5 Once the installation begins, a progress bar appears.

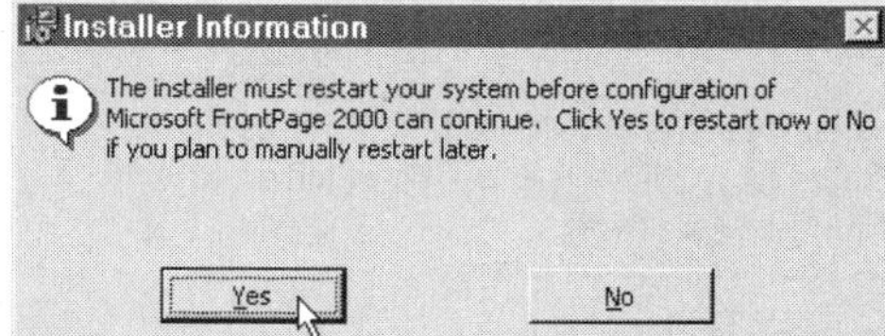

Figure A.6 When the installer asks you to restart your computer, click *Yes*.

5. The Ready to Install screen offers two choices: *Install Now* or *Customize* (**Figure A.4**). Choose *Install Now* and the standard version of FrontPage will be installed (**Figure A.5**).

6. When the installer asks you to restart your computer, click *Yes* (**Figure A.6**). What's next? See *To register FrontPage* on page 341.

✔ Tips

- If you're upgrading from FrontPage 98, you don't need to do anything differently. The installer will detect the earlier version and leave it in place. However, your original Start menu shortcut to FrontPage 98 will be replaced by a FrontPage 2000 shortcut. If you want to keep using the FrontPage 98 program on the computer, you'll need to create a new shortcut to FrontPage 98.
- If you upgrade from FrontPage 98, you can continue using the Microsoft Personal Web Server that came with it. However, the program's not needed to run FrontPage 2000 and some people have found FrontPage 2000's Web Publishing feature easier to use.
- Disc 2 contains Microsoft's Image Composer v1.5. Whether you want to install the graphics program is up to you, but it's not covered in this book.

To install a custom version of FrontPage

1. Follow steps 1–4 in *To install the standard version of FrontPage* on page 336. When the Ready to Install screen appears (**Figure A.4**), click *Customize.*
2. When the Installation Location screen appears (**Figure A.7**), click *Browse* to navigate to where you want FrontPage installed and click *Next.*
3. When the Selecting Features screen appears (**Figure A.8**), you'll need to decide which parts of FrontPage to install—and which to leave out. To reach any subitems, click on the + to expand items in the list. To collapse the list, click the –.
4. Click the drop-down menu of any item to select your installation option for that item (**Figure A.9**). For details on your choices, see **Table A.1**.
5. Once you've made all your choices, click *Install Now.* FrontPage will install your choices (**Figure A.5**).
6. When the installer asks you to restart your computer, click *Yes* (**Figure A.6**). What's next? See *To register FrontPage* on page 341.

Table A.1

Custom Installation Choices		
ICON	TEXT	EXPLANATION
	Run from My Computer	Installs item & default subitems
	Run all from My Computer	Installs item & all subitems
	Run from CD	Runs item if CD in player
	Run all from CD	Runs item & all subitems if CD in player
X	Not Available	Will not be installed
	Installed on First Use	If item ever used, asks for CD & installs

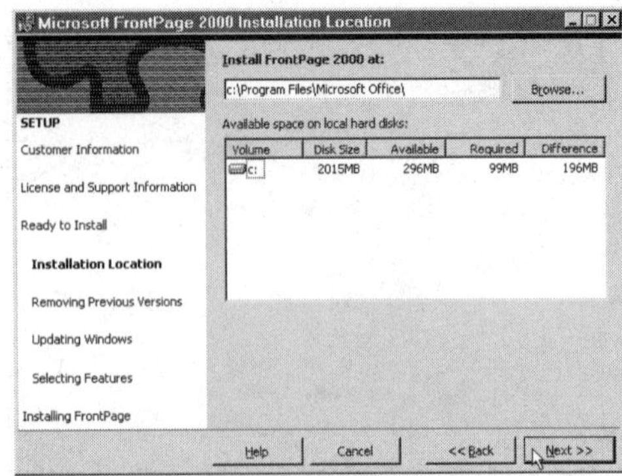

Figure A.7 When the Installation Location screen appears, click *Browse* to navigate to where you want FrontPage installed.

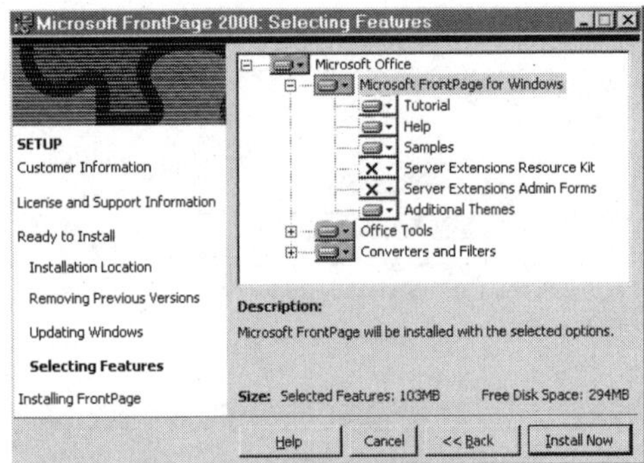

Figure A.8 When the Selecting Features screen appears, you'll need to decide which parts of FrontPage to install.

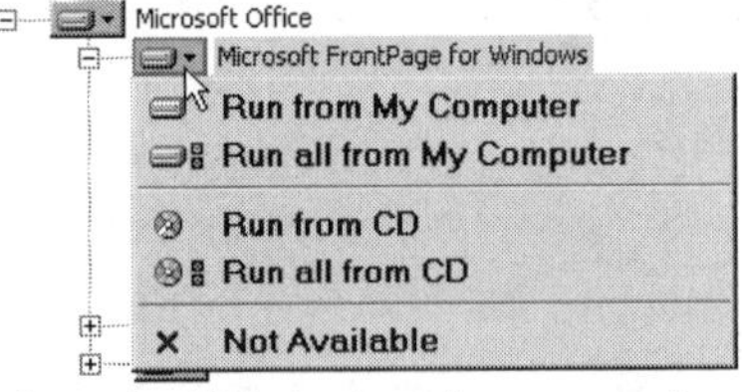

Figure A.9 Click the drop-down menu of any item to select an installation option for that item.

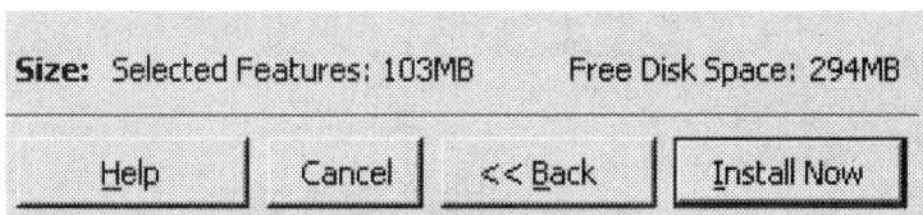

Figure A.10 Use the *Size* and *Free Disk Space* figures to gauge if you'll have enough hard drive space for all your *Selected Features*.

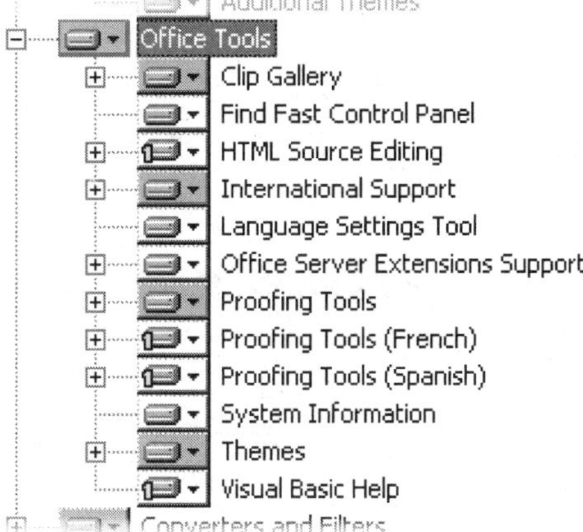

Figure A.11 Click any item to expand it and see which subitems will be installed.

✔ Tips

- It can seem a bit confusing but the + and – in step 3 simply expand or collapse your *view* and have nothing to do with which items will or won't be installed. You've got to use each item's drop-down menu (as described in step 4) to set which items are installed. Awkward? You betcha.
- As you select items to install in step 4, use the *Size* and *Free Disk Space* figures at the bottom of the Selecting Features screen to gauge if you'll have enough hard drive space for all your choices (**Figure A.10**).
- The default installation does not install all the subitems under each item. Click to expand an item if you want to see which subitems will be installed. (**Figure A.11**).
- If you change your mind on what items you need, you can go back and install or remove items later on. For details, see *To repair, update, or remove FrontPage* on the next page.

To repair, update, or remove FrontPage

1. Turn off all programs, including any anti-virus program you have running in the background.
2. Put FrontPage's Disc 1 into your CD-ROM drive. Once the CD launches, the Maintenance Mode screen will appear (**Figure A.12**).
3. Click *Repair FrontPage* if you want to reinstall FrontPage's default installation, click *Add or Remove Features* to do exactly that, and click *Remove FrontPage* to uninstall the program.
4. If you choose *Add or Remove Features* in step 3, the Update Features screen will appear (**Figure A.13**). For details on adding or removing FrontPage features, see steps 3–4 of *To install a custom version of FrontPage* on page 338.
5. Continue clicking *Next* until you're done, then click *OK* to exit the installation (**Figure A.14**). Be sure to restart your computer before continuing.

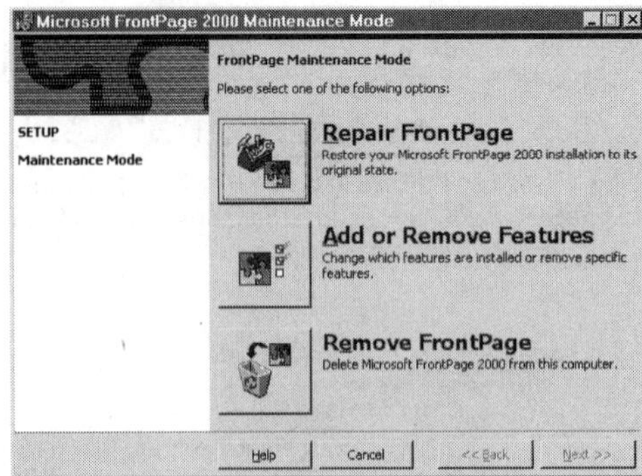

Figure A.12 To repair, update, or remove FrontPage, reinsert Disc 1 into your CD drive and make your choice.

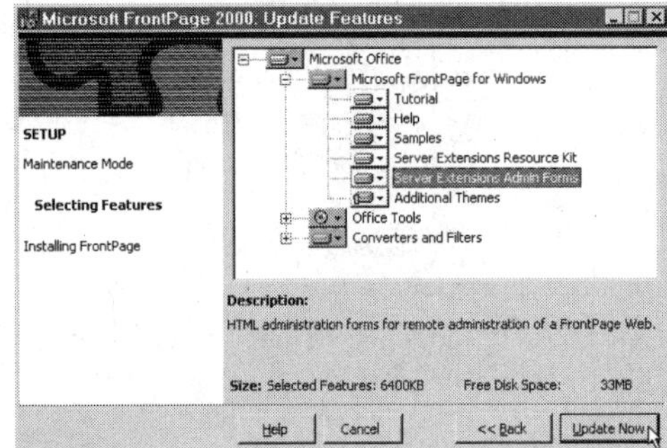

Figure A.13 Use the Update Features screen to add or remove items.

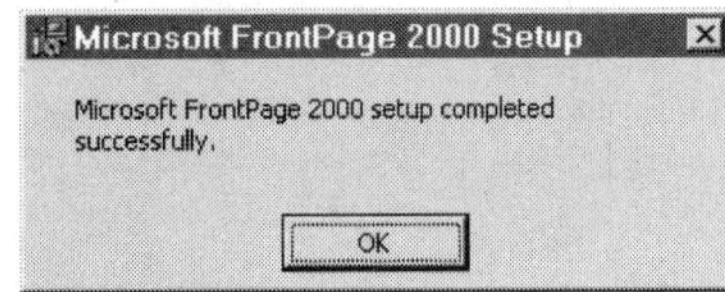

Figure A.14 The installer will alert you once it's finished updating FrontPage.

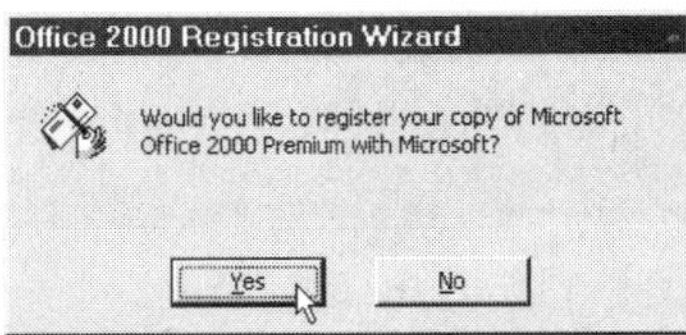

Figure A.15 When FrontPage asks whether you want to register, click *Yes*.

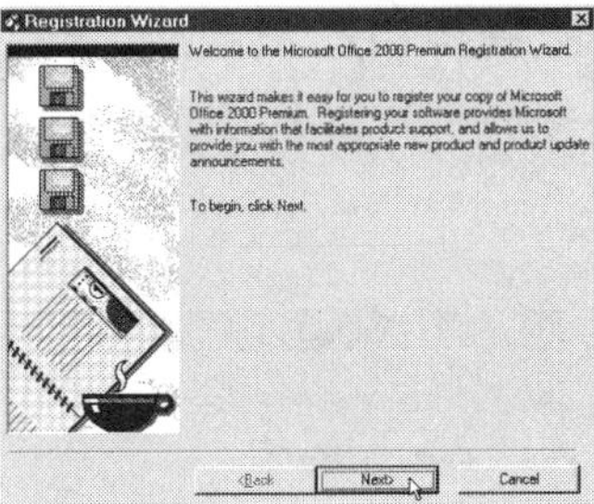

Figure A.16 When the Registration Wizard appears, click *Next*.

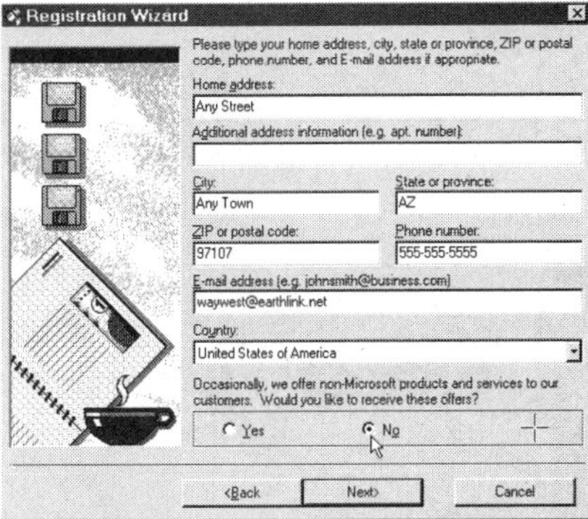

Figure A.17 To avoid junk mail, choose *No*.

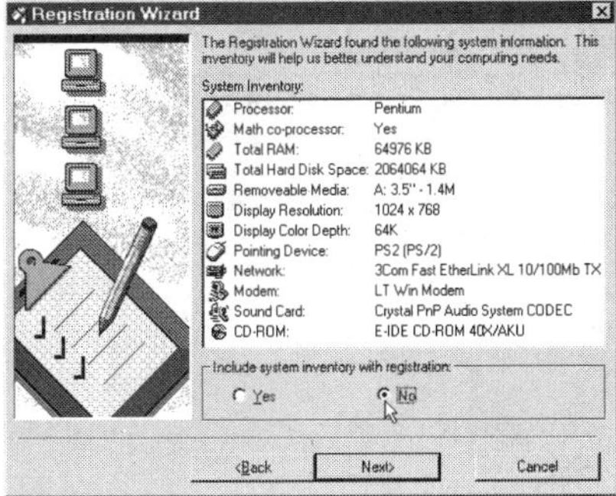

Figure A.18 The Registration Wizard collects information about your computer. If you want to share data, click *Yes*.

To register FrontPage

1. The first time you start up FrontPage, you'll be asked whether you want to register the program (**Figure A.15**). Click *Yes*.
2. When the Registration Wizard appears, click *Next* (**Figure A.16**).
3. A series of screens will step you through the registration process. Most of the screens ask for basic information. Pay attention, however, to two screens. One will *by default* sign you up for junk mail unless you click *No* (**Figure A.17**). Unless your mailbox is lonely, you might want to check *No*. The other registration screen to watch will, again by default, send information on your computer system to Microsoft as part of the registration process (**Figure A.18**). Microsoft says the system information can be helpful if they need to offer you technical support. The information's not required to register, so it's up to you whether to preserve your privacy by clicking *No*.

(continued)

4. After you finish entering your information, click *Connect* and the Registration Wizard will use your default Internet setup to dial a local telephone number and connect you to the Microsoft Network (**Figure A.19**).
5. Once the registration information is transmitted, click *OK* and you're done (**Figure A.20**).
6. The next time you launch FrontPage, your registration number and name will appear in the program's opening screen (**Figure A.21**). Now you're ready to set the defaults for how FrontPage will code your pages, which controls how they'll appear in various Web browsers. See *Setting Web Browser Compatibility* on the next page.

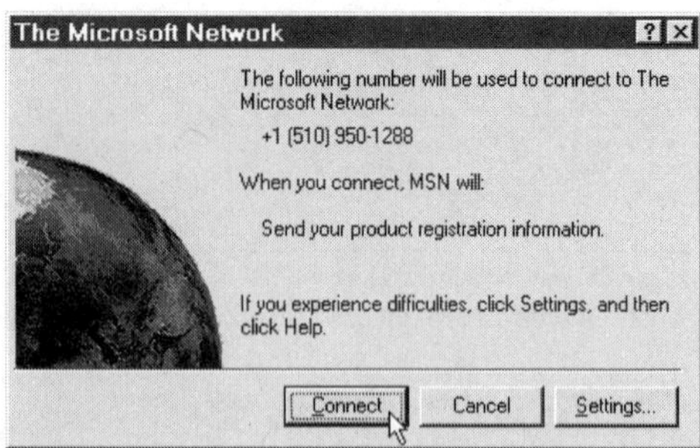

Figure A.19 Click *Connect* to transmit FrontPage's registration information to Microsoft via the Microsoft Network.

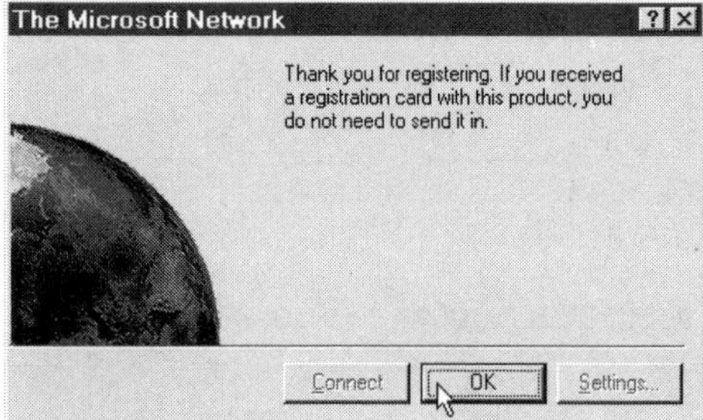

Figure A.20 When you finally finish registering, click *OK*.

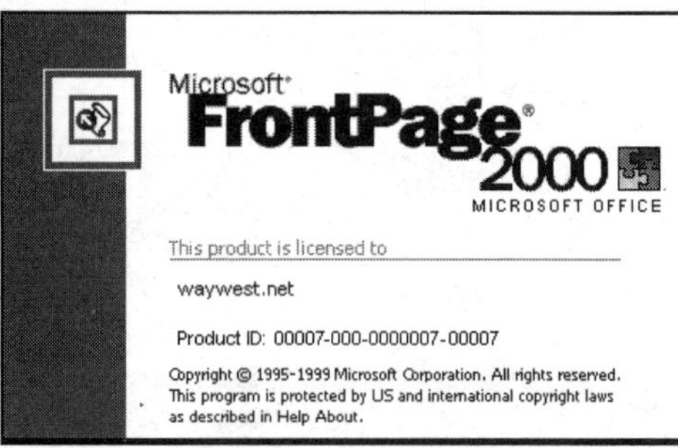

Figure A.21 Once you've registered, your registration number and name will appear in FrontPage's opening screen.

Setting Web Browser Compatibility

If every Web browser rendered HTML the same way, creating Web pages would so simple. In that perfect world, you wouldn't need to remember how different HTML tags look in Internet Explorer vs. Netscape Navigator or which tags work in old or new browsers. Until that day comes, FrontPage offers a decent compromise. You decide which browsers you want to code for and FrontPage automatically generates the proper HTML. Sure, you still have to decide whether to code for the broadest group of browsers—and forego CSS and DHTML—or use the new tags and risk excluding some folks. But at least you won't have to worry about which tags work with which browsers.

To set browser compatibility

1. Choose Tools > Page Options (**Figure A.22**).
2. When the Page Options dialog box appears, click the *Compatibility* tab (**Figure A.23**).
3. Use the *Browsers* drop-down menu ❶ to choose which Web browsers you'll be coding for. Your choice will check or uncheck boxes in the *Technologies* section ❹, indicating which technologies you'll be able to use with that choice.
4. Use the *Browser versions* drop-down menu ❷ to choose which versions you'll be coding for. Your choice will check or uncheck boxes in the *Technologies* section ❹, indicating which technologies you'll be able to use with that choice.
5. Check or uncheck *Enabled with Microsoft FrontPage Server Extensions* ❸. Again, your choice will affect the items turned on or off in the *Technologies* section ❹. For more on FrontPage Server Extensions, see page 319.
6. Once you're done making your choices, click *OK* and FrontPage will base its HTML code on those choices. If you change your mind, you can change the settings any time, though only pages coded after that point will reflect your changes.

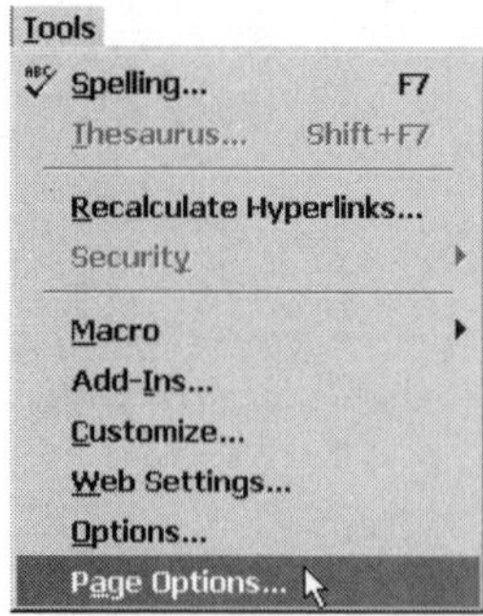

Figure A.22 To set browser compatibility and how FrontPage handles HTML code, choose Tools > Page Options.

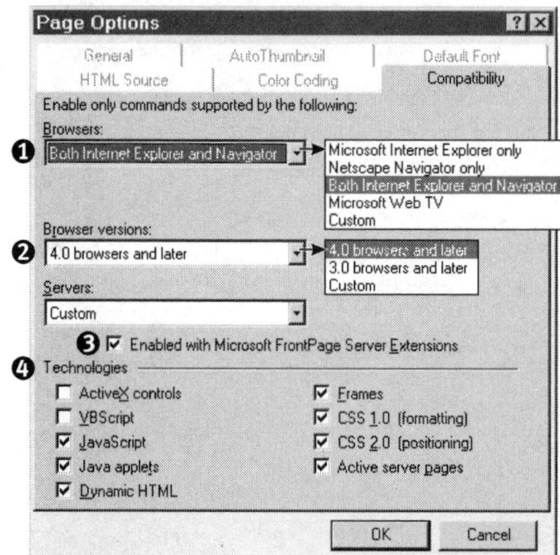

Figure A.23 Use the *Compatibility* tab to set which browsers you want to code for, and FrontPage will automatically generate the proper HTML.

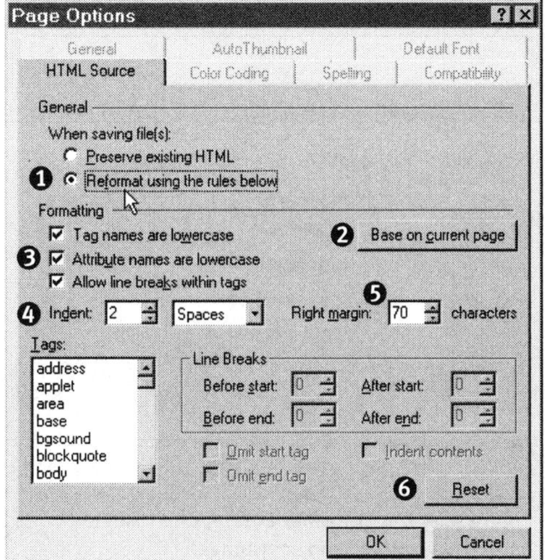

Figure A.24 Use the *HTML Source* tab to set how you want the HTML to appear when you switch to FrontPage's *HTML* view.

Setting HTML Coding Preferences

You don't need to mess with this unless you intend to tweak FrontPage's HTML coding directly. However, if you plan on jumping into your code now and then, these settings let you wrap the code the way you want and color tags just how you want them.

To set HTML code preferences

1. If you have a Web page with the HTML already set just how you want it, open it in FrontPage (Ctrl O). Otherwise, skip to step 2.
2. Choose Tools > Page Options (**Figure A.22**).
3. When the Page Options dialog box appears, click the *HTML Source* tab (**Figure A.24**).
4. In the *General* section, choose *Reformat using the rules below* ❶.
5. If you opened a page in step 1, click *Base on current page* ❷ in the *Formatting* section. Otherwise, check any or all of the three *Formatting* boxes ❸ to set how you want the HTML to appear. Use the text boxes and arrows for *Indent* ❹ and *Right margin* ❺ to set how you want those items to appear in HTML.
6. Now, click the *Color Coding* tab within the Page Options dialog box to set the colors used in your HTML.

(continued)

7. When the *Color Coding* tab appears (**Figure A.25**), use the drop-down menus to change any of the default colors. For details on using the color drop-down menus, see step 4 on page 130.
8. Once you're done setting the *HTML Source* and *Color Coding* tabs, click *OK*. The changes will be applied to your HTML coding.

✔ Tip

- If you change your mind setting items in the *HTML Source* tab, click *Reset* ❻ to return to the original settings.

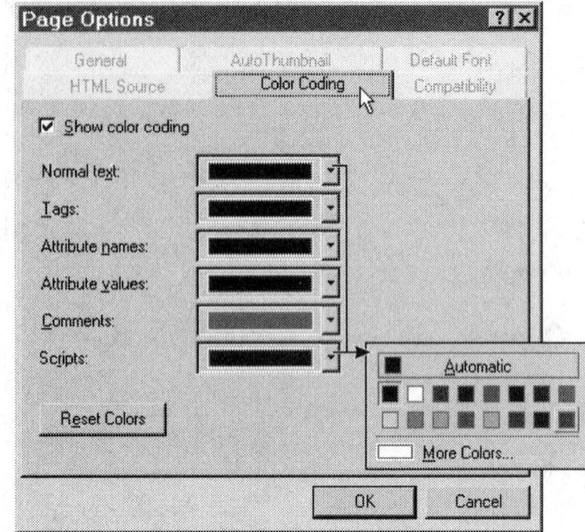

Figure A.25 Use the *Color Coding* tab to set the colors used in your HTML and script tags.

INDEX

C

D

E

F

G

H

I

Q

R

S

T

U

V

W

X

Y

Z